TALES OF
A FINANCIAL
FRONTIERSMAN

David Bertram Gill, November 2011. Photograph by Paragon Lig

David Bertram Gill

TALES OF
A FINANCIAL
FRONTIERSMAN

SIXTY YEARS: 1952–2011

PRIVATELY PUBLISHED IN MARYLAND
ON THE EASTERN SHORE OF CHESAPEAKE BAY
2012

DEDICATION

Writing an autobiography is a rewarding task. Essential to this process is having one person upon whom one can rely on to tell it as it is (or was). In my case that person was Lena, my wife of almost 43 years, to whom I dedicate this book. Without her, I would never have finished it. Nor would it have been as factually accurate and interesting.

My children, Chris, Sarah and Melissa as well as their spouses also encouraged me to persist, and the whole family put on a show and tell of some chapters of the memoir for one of my birthdays.

So, from the bottom of my heart, thank you
Lena, Chris, Sarah and Melissa.

The cover photograph shows a Grumman Goose Amphibian taking off.

Contents

Foreword

by Dean LeBaron

As if sitting in leather wing-backed chairs, enjoying a fireside chat with David Gill in a British officers' club, let us raise our glasses in a toast: "Here's to the frontiersman who endured and forged ahead; who guided his team in shaping a global financial landscape that would lead to stability and integrity in securities markets in emerging countries. Well done!"

In writing Tales of a Financial Frontiersman, I don't think David intended it to be an all-encompassing, comprehensive and authoritative treatment of the many experiences that arose during his tenure at IFC and elsewhere. It is often direct in the way of conversation, candid, and even a bit emotional at times. That is the beauty for those of us who shared some of those moments, brought back to us by his retelling ... selective in part but full of zest and fire.

A quote from Tales provides a capsule view: "This is about the re-engineering of the financial world, about the people involved and about my own perspective and role in all of this. Most of it was unimaginable at the time, much of it unexpected and all of it a struggle against the many supporters of the status quo in many countries and markets. Political will is the most important starting point and it was clear there wasn't much of that. They wanted the benefits of the end results, even if they didn't understand the importance of equity in the broader societal sense."

I had already started venturing into emerging markets when David and I met in Washington, DC, just before he was to retire as head of IFC's Capital Markets Department. One thing led to another, and we understood that our association could develop into a synergy between the constituencies of Batterymarch clients and David's global financial network. Despite coming from a political background, David was not political … he unselfishly opened his address book, sharing his contact list of diplomats, ministers of finance, chairmen of banks, and heads of securities commissions.

In our three years together, we worked on about six funds, most of which did quite well as we were in the right place at the right time, and often early. Commonwealth Equity Fund, under the sponsorship of the Commonwealth Secretariat, was largely David's design and execution … and was accomplished despite laborious requirements imposed by the many parties at the table. At the other extreme, Soviet Companies Fund was intended to offer Western investment in Soviet military technology companies. But the forces of history—and the sheer magnitude of the undertaking—intervened and we had to walk away. In between, we worked very collaboratively on Equity Fund of Brazil, the first South American fund for U.S. investors, and its successor, Equity Fund of Latin America. And the Farm Fund, developed for institutional investors to invest in a new asset class. A bit after David's time, but with confidence from our success in Latin America, we launched Equity Fund of China.

David and I became good friends. We brought different talents to the emerging markets table and, not unexpectedly, encountered a few rough patches as we each held strong convictions about the way to accomplish the best end result. With his steadfast adherence to precise, correct process, David knows if you start with the best and most experienced people, extract details of operation and administration to satisfy many at high levels of government operations, and work in a climate of full disclosure, that a conclusion will be reached which meets the demands of the highest quality. I, on the other hand, often started at the end objective. I was dedicated to bringing the profit potential of new markets to Batterymarch clients as quickly and cheaply as possible. Like a novelist sensing an ending before calculating a beginning, I would have an intuition on where we wished to end in things like target rates of return, diversification and information sources. And I would work backward to produce the process that was likely to get us to the conclusion at the

8

fastest rate and minimum cost. But we complemented each other in our unilateral dedication to clients and achieved a result, not surprisingly, in the middle. The result was often seen by clients as better than either of us working alone.

I also recognized, then and now, that I could not have had the luxury of my approach if David had not established the rules of the game many years earlier. The essential story is that David was dedicated to applying traditional Western processes and standards to new markets, making it feel like familiar ground for investors while, not insignificantly, facing the physical challenges of just getting and working there.

As David describes, we at Batterymarch had the advantage of using our own two jets in parts of the world where schedules were infrequent and unreliable. The planes were the tools that enabled us to visit those places. They were work machines, not luxury travel. My point was that if there was frequent commercial service, other investment managers would have beaten us to the market. We were the second private plane in China, for example, and ran regularly a monthly service to Moscow. Today much can be done with video conferencing and occasional meetings like the World Economic Forum in Davos … but not then. After long hours of travel together—including usually sleeping on the plane between city visits—I grew to respect David's old-school adherence to form and a lot of it stuck with me after he left Batterymarch. And so it shall stick with you as you read his detailed account of life on the frontier between the old and the new worlds.

David Gill is a class act who was able to balance on the divide between one global financial system and another. Through the latter half of the twentieth century, David possessed the wit and presence to lead the rest of us into the next. The detail he brings to Tales will take you to those times with him living through uncertainties and making a new structure for the twenty-first century. The rumbles you hear today in the corridors of traditional institutions started as a breeze through the frontier trees when David first heard them.

Well done!

Introduction

Financial frontiersman? What does that mean? Frontiersman brings to mind the early New England settlers moving into the Wild West. Well, many would call financial markets, in particular stock markets, a form of Wild West. Generally, the farther away they are from home the more such markets are associated with "Wild West" qualities. In that sense I certainly have been a financial frontiersman for most of my career. Contrary to what most people expect, that was especially true for the years I spent as an international bureaucrat.

Of course, I was only following a course charted by many more accomplished others well before my time. Amongst the more famous, Adam Smith comes to mind. Although investors like stability and certainty, the truth is neither stability nor certainty exists in financial markets, and on the rare occasions they do, no money is made. The most exciting part of my professional life has been to be a participant and front row witness in the unimaginable makeover of our financial system since the Second World War. Not only when I was a young inexperienced investment banker did my bosses consider my ideas and schemes "wild," the same happened when I had an opportunity to put the lessons of those early years into practice as an international bureaucrat. It turned out that the conventional ideas missed the point of the massive changes that were underway in which the "frontier" went from irrelevant periphery to critical mainstream. In the words of Dean Acheson, I was lucky enough to be "present at the creation" and have the opportunity to see the experiments and initiatives I undertook at the International Finance Corporation come to fruition. The Third World frontier became emerging markets and, as emerging markets such as South Korea have become more sophisticated, a new term has been developed for new emerging markets: "Frontier Markets."

Sixty years? That's a bit of an exaggeration. I only worked full time for thirty-nine years, but since retiring in 1991, I have continued to be active as a board member, advisor and/or consultant to a variety of public and private financial entities. So I have been involved for sixty years.

Over the years, all three of our children and several friends have asked me what I did when I went to work. It seems I never did a very good job of explaining. So this is my attempt to make up for that—and also how I got to the starting point. The best I managed for the kids was to say I was a financial engineer. They understood engineers built things and fixed things. That's what I did in financial markets.

But I'm getting ahead of my story. This is about the re-engineering of the financial world, about the people involved and about my own perspective and role in all of this. Most of it was unimaginable at the time, much of it unexpected and all of it a struggle against the many supporters of the status quo in many countries and markets. I have divided my story into four parts.

PART I deals with my experience in investment banking from 1952 to 1971. For most of that period I was with Nesbitt, Thomson and Company Limited, in Toronto, Montreal and, finally, New York (1952 to 1969). "NT" as it was called, was one of the leading Canadian investment firms. I pulled off a few "coups" in NT as a deal maker and became executive vice president. Later, I was president of NT's U.S. companies. Getting NT accepted by the New York Stock Exchange in 1968 as the first foreign firm to be a member had its good and bad results. Then in 1970 I switched to Schroder Rockefeller Corporation in New York. Schroder Rockefeller was the U.S. venture capital arm of the Schroder Group, a leading U.K. merchant bank. For me, Schroders was an eye opener to the wider world and the "big league." My arranging its first private bond placement for the U.S. subsidiary of a European company was a challenge. So was getting them into the airline business in the Bahamas as a venture capitalist alongside Commonwealth Development Corporation, which was to play a major role in my retirement life.

Introduction

PART II covers my public sector years (1971—1988) as an international bureaucrat with the International Finance Corporation (IFC), the younger sister of the World Bank. I was very fortunate to be asked to establish the Group's Capital Markets Department ("CMD") in IFC. The task involved helping build financial market infrastructures in some 60 developing countries and establishing over 90 private financial companies in them. It was a unique and rewarding experience. So was just working with more than 50 very bright young men and women from some 20 countries who were on my team over those 17 years. There was so much going on that it is hard to single out anything special. But advising the still very socialist Yugoslav government in the 1970s on how to "decentralize" its banking system was a memorable experience, as was helping build Brazil's securities commission a few years later. Guiding the formation of the first emerging markets investment funds—"country funds"—in the 1980s was something in which I take great pride. One of our Wall Street admirers claimed we had started a new "cottage industry." But that was not entirely true. The first country fund was established in Scotland in the 1890s to buy U.S. railway bonds, which were the fad at the time. Looking back now, I can't think of any job that could have been more interesting: it was worth the personal financial sacrifice. The chart—"Summary of Activities"—lists what CMD did, where, and starting when, and puts it all on one page.

PART III describes my next 16 years back in business, after a fashion. More or less full time with Batterymarch Financial Management (1988 - 1991) in Boston two or three days a week, getting the firm and its clients into "emerging markets." And finally my golden years as a real "pensioner." Since 1992 I have been active as an independent director of, or advisor to, some 40 assorted banks, securities firms, investment funds, asset management companies and development institutions. This latter activity continues. I continue to do this work but on a reduced scale. Some highlights of this period included helping the Inter-American Investment Corporation start the first regional venture capital fund for Latin America and, at the other extreme of size and locale, helping the U.K. government's Crown Agents and the Commonwealth Development Corporation start the first "country fund" for an African country. It was equally fascinating to produce the "action program" for establishing Russia's new securities market in 1993 and to be on the board of a Russian company through the 1998 debt crisis.

PART IV. In case anyone is interested in what may have started me on my 60 years in finance, this is an account of my "formative years."

I have tried of course to be as factually accurate as I can but, in the end, my comments on individuals and specific situations are just my recollections and reactions, as best I remember them. The only factual information I have still is my old "Flying Log Book" that records every flight I made during my period in the navy. Hopefully though, what follows will be entertaining if not educational. If nothing else, writing it has been an interesting journey through time that kept me out of other mischief. But notwithstanding I am still "working," the writing has to come to an end. I started this as "Fifty-Five Years…" Then, as time passed and I still hadn't finished, I decided to go for "Sixty…" as I'm still involved and may be able to continue until 2013 when my last remaining board membership will end at the time that the investment management company I serve is due to be wound up. I have been very fortunate serving on these boards as all have done well for the investors.

Acknowledgments

I wish to thank my family, Lena, Sarah, Melissa and Chris, our many friends and my business colleagues, whose names you will read later on, all of whom have played a part in shaping my life, making it interesting, at least to me, and contributing to this story. The occasion of my 80th birthday stands out in my memory because of the wonderful lunch that IFC put on for me at my favorite restaurant in Washington. Attending were some 30 people, all current or retired colleagues. That was followed by a fine dinner hosted by Rudi van der Bijl and Antoine van Agtmael, both old IFC colleagues and good friends. Sadly, Rudi died of cancer last year. I was devastated. But I think of Rudi often because the "chart" of all my activities with "CMD" that he made for me is on the wall of my den. Rudi was the first person I met at IFC and remained one of my best friends. Antoine also spent more time editing my Introduction than I spent writing it and encouraged me to turn my writings into a real book. When I told him that I was writing a book, he said he would edit the whole thing if I went ahead with it. In the end, Antoine did go through the whole book. I'm very much indebted to him for his sage advice and for the many hours he spent doing this. In that connection, another person I wish to thank is Dean LeBaron—about whom you will read more later—who actually made the publishing of this book possible. And thanks also to Dean for re-introducing me to Marilyn Pitchford, another old friend and colleague from Batterymarch days, who also volunteered for the task of editing and formatting, helping to improve, I am hopeful, the reading of my story.

Most importantly, my gratitude goes to my wife, Lena, who not only put up with me and my comings and goings, but also encouraged me to write this and played the key role in editing it. That was a true labor of love that I can never repay.

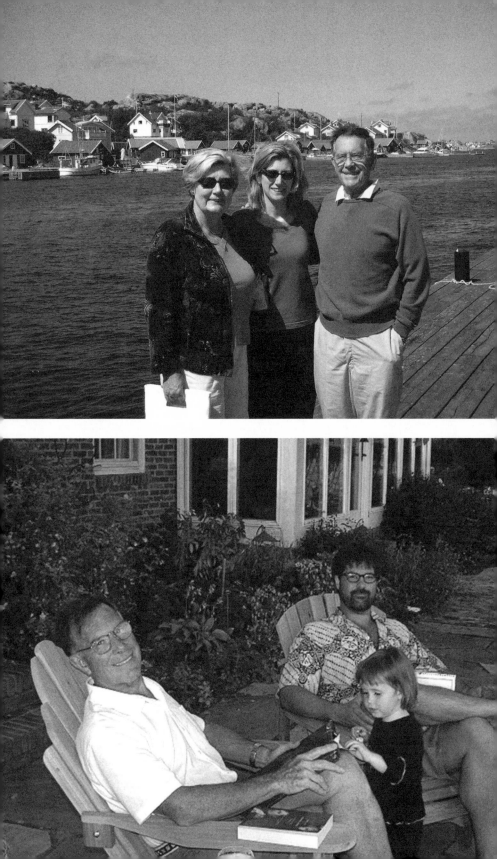

Lena and daughter Sarah
...nt of a little fishing village
... Island of Tjörn, Sweden
... summer of 2009.

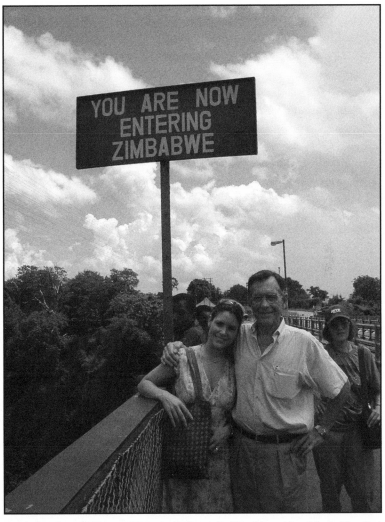

With daughter Melissa at Victoria Falls on the Zambian side of the bridge that
crosses into Zimbabwe, in 2006.

... son Christopher and granddaughter
...lotte (the second of our four grandchildren)
... "Point," Lena's and my home on the
...rn Shore near Easton, Maryland, on the
...ion of my 79th birthday in 2006.

PART I

THE
BUSINESS WORLD
1952–1971

CHAPTER I

Nesbitt, Thomson and Company Limited ... Mainly Learning: 1952–1956

Notwithstanding the Korean War and the consequent increase in defense-related manufacturing, the early 1950s were recession years in Canada. This had contributed to my longer than expected hiatus at graduate school and in the navy. Then, through the university placement center, there came a call offering an interview with one of Canada's leading investment firms. Before going further, here are a few words to explain what Canadian investment firms did.

They were called "Investment Dealers," rather than "Investment Banks," as is the term in the U.S., or Merchant Banks, as is the U.K. term for them. Canadian commercial banks had convinced the regulators that the term "Bank" implied safety of assets: they took deposits and made only short-term loans to local governments or businesses. Thus the word "bank" could not be used by entities that were not Bank of Canada (our central bank) or licensed commercial banks. What Canadian Investment Dealers did were to underwrite and distribute new issues of securities, act as dealers in the secondary market for securities and as brokers for securities listed on stock exchanges. Some, including my firm for a while, also provided investment management services for a fee. That is, roughly, what their U.S. and U.K. counterparts do. Work-

ing for a firm like Nesbitt, Thomson was just right for me. Sun Life would have been fine, but, as an "institutional investor"—the term used to describe corporate or government entities whose business included investing for their own account or on behalf of their clients—their involvement in the financial sector as a whole was more limited and investing activities were somewhat secondary to their insurance business. Unlike the case today when all of them seem to be owned by commercial banks, then all Investment Dealers were required to be independent entities, with all the equity in them owned by employees of the firm.

I reported for my interview at the Toronto office, full of apprehension, dressed in my best (only) suit. The two people I saw were Ian Crookston who was head of the Ontario region and Ross Oborne, manager of the Toronto office. Nesbitt, Thomson ("NT" from now on) was a Montreal based firm. Ian was a very distinguished fellow of English background. He had been with the firm for many years and was, at the time, an older man (to me) of about 40. He was the only one of that age group who had not been in the services. It was never discussed. Ross was different. A down to earth Canadian, he had been a non flying officer in the RCAF. To my surprise, I was hired on the spot, subject only to the usual reference checks. I was told that I would join the Municipal Department. There I would learn how to win underwriting contracts from towns, school districts and other municipal government entities and then convince the Sales Department of our firm to sell them. "Winning" the issue involved, first, doing the research to establish (at least in my eyes) the town's creditworthiness and then bidding for the issue at an auction. The auction was open to all investment dealers and commercial banks that wanted to bid for them: proper democratic process for taxpayer supported government entities. However there were exceptions to this auction process, especially in the case of small towns, as I shall get to soon. I was also told that after six months, if I passed the licensing examination given by the industry association—the Investment Dealers' Association of Canada (IDA)—I could also build my own investor clientele and earn commissions. After another year working on Municipal issues it would then be determined what future I had, if any. My starting salary was $250 a month. I did not realize then that the operative words

were that I could build my own investor clientele and earn commissions. But I did realize that $250 was barely a living wage even in 1952. After all, the navy paid me $350 a month plus substantial benefits. So the thought of earning commissions was appealing, though at the time I really didn't know what that entailed.

As everyone knows, learning is a never-ending process. What I mean about learning in this chapter is learning how to survive and prosper in an investment firm. I learned most of, but not all, the lessons. Had I stayed in the Commerce course at U of T, or gone to a business school, I might have learned faster. Fortunately, most of my peers were as ignorant of business as was I. In those days in Canada few people in business had even BA degrees. In fact, in the hallowed banking business, a university degree was far from essential. I think all of the presidents of our major banks had started out with high school diplomas as clerks in branches of their banks. Later on—around 1955—I found one Harvard MBA who worked for the Canadian Imperial Bank of Commerce: Gordon Leonard. He claimed he was the first and still only MBA in a Canadian bank at the time. A few years after that, I met the only PhD in a Canadian bank. Bob MacIntosh was head of the economics department of the Bank of Nova Scotia. I think BNS then was the only bank with an economics department. So learning was very much a matter of on the job training.

What I learned first was the history and mission of NT. A Mr. Thomson, from Halifax, and a Mr. Nesbitt, from Hamilton, had founded it in 1912. They had also founded a company called Power Corporation of Canada. The latter was a holding company whose objective was to promote, finance and control hydroelectric plants, which was the high tech sector in Canada in those days. They, and a few chosen investors, put up the common stock equity that would provide about 20% of the funds needed for each new plant. Finding the other 80% of the money was why they formed NT. Its job was to sell bond issues and non-voting preferred stock issues in the new enterprises. In those early days, NT salesmen would go literally door-to-door with a brief case of bond and preferred stock certificates and sell them to local residents. Their sales pitch was the new power plant would bring prosperity to the area and

better lighting and heating for the households. So, by buying these securities, the investors would earn a safe return on their savings while
also improving the community. It worked very well. By the 1940s, Power
Corporation controlled most of the power companies in Canada. At the
same time, NT had become a powerhouse of finance—ranking between
first and third each year in the volume of new issues underwritten. By
1952, the second generation Mr. Thomson had gravitated to running
Power Corporation, while still having a major stake in NT. Similarly, the
second generation Mr. Nesbitt had taken over NT, but retained a large
stake in Power Corporation. It follows that NT was Power Corporation's main underwriter of securities issued by Power Corporation and
its affiliates. Peter Thomson was less serious a businessman than Deane
Nesbitt. Deane's father would have been very proud of him. He was a
great man in most ways, and a charmer, if also an autocrat.

By the 1950s, NT was beginning to follow the trend of its competitors in building up an investor clientele—that is, like Merrill, Lynch,
building up a clientele of investors who wanted regular brokerage services and investment advice. But this was really just a means to ensure a
ready market for their new stock and bond issues. In those days, there
were three types of investment firms. The so-called "full service" ones
that were underwriters, dealers and brokers; those that specialized in
underwriting and depended on others to find the investors; and, finally,
those who specialized only in trading securities—the stock brokers the
specialist underwriters used. The brokers tended to have large branch
networks and lots of "customers' men." That was the term the brokers
used to indicate that their salesmen were really working in the interests
of their investor customers. The underwriting firms were more direct.
The salesmen were called salesmen, because that was what they were,
even if their pitch was they were helping investors build portfolios designed to meet their individual needs—pretending to be investment advisors.

In 1952, NT had some twenty offices, from Victoria in the West to
St. Johns, Newfoundland in the East—a 3,500 mile stretch. We had then
about 600 employees, of whom about 400 would have been salesmen.
We also had offices in London and New York, as Canadian securities

were popular in those markets. I suppose we were an "emerging market" at the time. Our capital was only about $3 million Canadian. It is interesting to compare the situation in the financial markets then with the situation now. Not only are all the firms bigger in numbers of employees and capital by multiples of hundreds, but most are owned by bank or insurance holding companies. Also, then, there were very few mutual funds and most savers had their money in bank deposits. Now, there is more money in mutual funds than in banks.

It is interesting also to remember the relationship between the Canadian and U.S. securities firms. While we sold our securities to U.S. investors, U.S. investment banks also saw Canada as a big market for theirs. This produced problems that grew quickly during the late 1950s and the1960s. In the mid 1960s, corporate governance in Canada was primitive. There were no requirements for listed companies to have audit committees, and consolidated financial statements were the exception. Likewise, trading on insider information was not unusual. It was frowned upon, but it was not exactly illegal. There was more speculation than investing, and "buyer beware" should have been the motto of the stock exchanges. Canadian firms did not have research departments that analyzed securities. We had "statistics departments" that compiled data for the underwriting department, and sometimes put out sales pieces on our new issues and how they would fit into an investor's portfolio. As Canadian investment firms were seeing increased and more professional competition from U.S. firms dealing in Canadian securities with all the major Canadian investors, we realized that we had to improve our standards. We saw our clients beginning to expect better financial reporting by companies, better analysis by brokers, and more ethical trading in the markets. So, if we did not improve, we were going to lose our biggest clients. Consequently it was the Canadian investment firms that were encouraging the Canadian securities commissions (each province had its own securities commission; there was not a national one.) to tighten up—not the other way around.

It was as these storm clouds were growing for the Canadian investment firms that I started "learning" at NT. I was one of about three that started that year. I remember only one: Cliff Bird, a short ex RCAF tail

Nesbitt, Thomson ... Mainly Learning

gunner in Lancasters (four-engine heavy bombers). We started in the municipal department together. It was real on the job training and a theoretically simple task. We were to travel around Ontario, find small towns that had financial needs and convince the treasurer that we could raise the money on better terms for them than they would get going through the auction process. I forget the logic of that argument but we often succeeded—and our case was just that we were a big firm that knew how to do it. Then we wrote up the prospectus. This involved a bit of serious research into the town's financial records. But it was all really "cookie cruncher" work. The real problem was when the town treasurer was smart enough to call for competitive bids. Then we had to make serious judgments about credit quality, interest yields for similar issuers in the market and what would "sell." In those days, there were no credit rating agencies in Canada. Besides, these were very small "deals"—between $100,000 and a million. Naturally, getting larger deals for bond issues by the big cities was the territory of the experienced professionals in the firm who specialized in government financing. Still there was a lot of competition even for these small issues. Assuming we won the issue then came the marketing. Most of the buyers were local insurance companies, trust companies (these entities were unique to Canada at the time: they were licensed to handle estates of individuals and foundations and also acted as trustees for bond issues), banks and individual investors. Pension funds were not important then. This diverse and competitive market for these small bond issues was in large part a result of the way the Canadian financial market was structured at the time.

In those days, the Canadian financial system was segregated into the "four pillars"—banks, insurance companies, trust companies and investment dealers. All were independent corporations and cross shareholdings were not allowed, The Bank of Canada and Ministry of Finance dictating the rules. Banks were limited strictly to the banking business—clearing houses for transactions, deposit taking and working capital loans—no long term lending for project finance and certainly no activities in competition with the other three pillars. They could, however, invest their surplus funds in short-term bonds and money market

26

instruments. Insurance companies sold insurance and invested their cash in securities and mortgages. Trust companies could take savings deposits and act as trustees for estates and for securities issues. They could invest their funds from deposit taking in mortgages, and on behalf of the estates they administered they could invest in securities and any other classes of assets approved by the regulatory agency. I recall there was such an agency overseeing approved investments for both insurance companies and trust companies. One of our jobs was to submit the prospectus of each of our new issues for this agency's approval. As best I recall the facts, first mortgage municipal and corporate bonds were automatically approved, as were residential first mortgage loans. The only other automatic approval was for stocks listed on stock exchanges.

I learned all of this while taking my licensing exam and "on the job" in the municipal department. The license, as with similar licenses now, were to ensure one was knowledgeable about the regulations and financial practices to be entrusted with taking securities orders from individuals. Consequently, we also learned how the stock exchange worked and the rudiments of sound investing strategies. Modern diversification strategy was still a science of the future, but we were taught how to build a "model portfolio"—so much cash, so much in bonds, and ten or so stocks in different industries.

Once licensed, I found that I was expected also to be a salesman. You didn't need a license to source municipal bonds so it was a good training ground. So, less and less time was allowed for those small municipal bond financings as we were directed to find investors. For a full service firm particularly, that was where the money was. New salesmen could then learn to get individual investors to buy new corporate bond and stock issues from which the firm made its largest profit margins. I remember we were given lists of what were obviously investing "clients" who had been lost by the firm and told to seek them out and try and do some business with them. We were also expected to compile mailing lists and devise and send promotional letters to prospective customers. It was amazing to me how this kind of promotional thing worked. I actually found clients and became their—that is, from their point of view —"customers' man." I met a lot of interesting people that way. I like to think I did more good than harm to their pocket books but, looking back, NT, at least in Toronto, operated a bit like a bucket shop. We were encouraged to sell our new issues and turn over our clients' portfolios as much as possible to generate commissions. The bad part was the pressure to sell our own issues. While, in the past, utility company bonds and preferred stocks were fairly safe investments, NT went into the mining financing frenzy, along with most of our competitors. This went on throughout the 1950s. It was gold mines, copper mines, uranium mines and oil and gas discoveries. All it seemed to take was a geologist's report that sample drillings had located a commercial ore body or oil field, and a promoter with exploration rights. A company would be formed and the underwriters fought to get the deal to sell stocks, or even bonds, to raise the money to go forward. Some spoilsports pointed out that, in the previous 50 years in the U.S. and Canada, only one in a hundred such financings actually resulted in a company that earned a profit. It was all rather like the dotcom frenzy of more recent years.

I worked hard to move away from the "retail" business, as it was called, and to break into what was called the "institutional" side of sales. In that, my earlier training at university and a bit of common sense helped me. By 1954 I had learned how U.S. firms operated. Merrill Lynch was my role model. There was a concept called "institutional research" where one actually produced a documented argument as to why your clients should buy a specific security. I suppose it was an extension of the prospectus document that justified a new issue of securities but, at the time, as new issues were the main business of NT, it had not occurred to anyone that our "statistics department" could make cases for existing securities and, if well done, it might actually produce more business from the large institutional investors. My simple mind told me that, if Merrill Lynch spent a lot of time and money doing it, it must work. So that was what I started trying to do. My first such efforts were to do with stock exchange listed common stocks. This was because buying and selling them through the stock exchanges generated a lot of commission business on a day-to-day basis, so one wasn't under such pressure to sell the new issues.

During this period, along with two Toronto friends—Don Wright, a lawyer, and Gordon Lennard, who I will mention again later—we formed a little company called "Findapart." It wasn't exactly a "frontier" operation. We specialized in apartment leases —offering our services to both owners and renters. But it was the first in Toronto. We did it because we were all working for large organizations and felt a little startup of our own would be fun. What we didn't realize was it was very limited. In retrospect we should have gone into real property. But probably we didn't have the spare cash for that as all three of us had young families at the time.

My great opportunity in NT came as a result of a stock underwriting we had done for a company Ian Crookston had promoted as a personal private equity deal. He and some friends had established in Canada a company called Superior Propane. It was a copy of a very successful U.S. company, Suburban Propane. Its business was distributing propane to households in the rural areas or suburbs that were not on the main oil or gas lines. It was certainly not "high tech" venture capital. It was just the usual thing that happened in Canada. The Americans developed successfully a new industry. We watched it for some ten years and were finally convinced it would work in Canada too. So we copied it. In this case, after just a few years as a private company, Ian and his friends decided to take it public though an IPO (initial public offering). It was a great success with our "retail" clientele and it went to a reasonable premium over the issue price when it was listed on the Toronto Stock Exchange. But Canadian institutional investors, being conservative as usual, would not buy. After a few more years, Ian and some of his friends wanted to cash in their stock. He realized that, without some institutional buyers, their attempts to sell large amounts would, most likely, cause the stock to collapse. So he asked me if I could write one of my research reports on Superior Propane that would convince the institutions to buy. With the help of one assistant, a very fine young fellow called Jim Stewart, we put together what the market thought was the most thorough report on any Canadian company seen to that date … my first real success as a financial frontiersman. We were fortunate in that Superior Propane, as it was called, was the only player in the propane business in Canada in what was obviously a growth business

—and it was very well run. Thus, it was not hard to make a compelling case that the stock was a bargain. The end result was that Ian and his friends sold their stock, through NT's team of Jim and David, to a dozen or so assorted insurance and trust companies. Everyone was pleased then. However, having almost half of the stock in the hands of institutional investors resulted in another very different problem. More on that later.

Another frontier plan had to do with bonds. Bonds—government as well as corporate—were an important part of the market for investors. I developed a research scheme to promote bond trading. I called it "riding the yield cycle." Bond prices fluctuated as interest rates rose and fell. My thesis could not have been more simple, even if my NT seniors were skeptical. When rates were low and about to rise, investors should sell their short-term bonds and buy long-term bonds of the same quality. A one percent change in interest rates had a much larger effect on the price of a long-term bond than on a short-term bond. Then, when rates were about to rise, the investor should reverse—sell the long-term bonds and buy short-term issues. The point was large investors could not be out of the market so they could not just sell their portfolios if they thought prices were going to drop. Consequently, this strategy, when it worked, just increased their income without increasing the credit risk of invested funds. The arithmetic was simple. When interests rates were high, one sold a Government of Canada 5% bond maturing in three years at, say, $99 and bought a 5% 20 year maturity "Canada" at, say, $90. The interest coupon was the same, but there was an extra $9.00 per $100 par value that could be invested also, increasing the yield to maturity by about 10%. Then, when rates were rising, one sold the 20-year bond (maybe a year later when it was a nineteen-year maturity) at, say, 99 and bought back a 5% two-year maturity at 99. Of course, the trick was timing but, in those days, it was not too hard to anticipate Bank of Canada monetary policy changes. At least I got it more or less right for about six times in a row. Then I had the sense to give it up with my reputation intact. Fortunately, in our small financial world, the Financial Post, Canada's equivalent of Barron's, discovered me—a new (to them) financial frontiersman. This resulted in my writing articles for them on this. Basically, all my articles said was that, for the following reasons, monetary policy is going to change. Therefore, now is the time to switch. Not only did they pay me to write these articles, but also they brought me a lot of business. Another bright idea I had around this time was a simple strategy using "Warrants"—instruments that gave the owners the right to buy the underlying stock at a fixed price for five or ten years. These warrants were usually issued with new bond issues of speculative companies as an added incentive to buyers—they had a fixed interest rate and a promise of getting their money back at maturity, but also a "free" shot at a profit if the issuing company's stock appreciated sufficiently. My gambit was to get investors who already held the stock to sell it and buy the same number of warrants, putting the cash they took out into good quality bonds. The idea was they had almost the same profit potential while eliminating the potential loss if the stock dropped. It wasn't rocket science—just a new way to produce more commissions. Both schemes helped me to get into the institutional side of NT.

Because of all of this, it was not too hard for someone with the right background and some knowledge of how matters were in other countries to get one's bosses to give such success a little cautious backing. So, in 1955 I think, I became the first "institutional salesman" in NT's Toronto office. But I also found out that I still had a great deal to learn. To my dismay, my bosses hired two seasoned securities men—Ivor Murray and Nelson Lane—to actually lead this new group of three. Both had been on the "buy side"—working for a bank and an insurance company respectively—as managers of their previous employers' securities portfolios. Obviously, this was a very good idea for NT because they knew far more than I about how institutional investors worked and they had the inside contacts. That said, I felt rather betrayed, not knowing any better. But, after getting to know them and learning a lot from them over the next six months or so, I got on with it. In those days, one didn't change jobs much so it never occurred to me to take that step.

Thinking back, what I remember now is the cynicism of our management. On the one hand, they, and especially Deane Nesbitt, were elegant, well educated, sophisticated, church going people. They prided themselves on the high quality of our business, specializing as we did in underwriting debt securities. The object of our business with investors, they said, was "preserving capital," not making a higher return on capital. NT had only recently—in the 1930s—become a stock exchange member. On the other hand, we were encouraged by line management to "push" our new issues. Some of those issues, even to junior people like me, did not seem like "investment grade" securities designed to preserve the capital of the buyers. Perhaps the senior members of management didn't know what was going on in the branches. But they must have known that some of the mining stocks we underwrote were not like the utility bonds of old. I suppose an element of greed colored their judgment. I, too, was guilty. While I was sometimes queasy about some of the issues, I needed the money and we were usually paid double commissions. My, and our, only defense was that everyone else was doing it, even our most esteemed competitors, Wood, Gundy & Company and A.E. Ames, with whom we traded places each year for the first, second or third positions in the new issue volume league tables. Canada was still in the robber baron phase in its financial markets.

Naturally, there was more to life in those years than just NT. There was a family life and there was a naval life. In 1952, Bill McDougall introduced me to a charming girl, Ann Gostling, who was graduating in archeology that year from St. Hilda's, the women's Anglican college at University of Toronto. Things progressed and we married in 1953. We moved into an apartment on Eglington Avenue. Ann continued to work at the Royal Ontario Museum. During that time and for several years later we socialized mainly with her friends and their husbands. I have fond memories of Jane and Don Wright, and Beth and Gordon Lennard, as well as Susie and Paul Opler and George and Kittie Fells. Don and Gordon were both Canadian. George was an English immigrant and Paul was from Hungary. He became very successful and was CEO of Canada's largest construction company. Sadly, he died of a heart attack in his late 50s. Ann's parents came from Winnipeg, but moved to Toronto in the 1930s. Her father, "the General," became a good mentor. He had been in the reserve army during the war and was commanding officer of an infantry regiment, The Toronto Scottish. He told me of the amusing discussions he and his brother had about the merits of their respective regiments—his brother was the commanding officer of another Canadian reserve Scottish regiment. They were both born in England. Both were at Dieppe. His brother was killed there. The General's most amusing story involved getting used to being demobilized as a Brigadier general in late 1945. His most difficult adjustment was realizing that no one was opening doors for him any more. Remembering that, opening doors for ladies was the hard part. In the Canadian Army, most of the clerks and drivers were female, so they opened doors for him.

We had many Hungarian, Czech, Greek and other nationalities as immigrants in those days. Most had to start as farm workers for a year. The most colorful were Ian Vorres and Peter Munk. Ian came from a wealthy Greek family and was the best known "young man about town" in Toronto. He went to Trinity College at U of T, became a writer and, eventually, went back to Greece to run the family business. We were close friends for years. I had an interesting offer once from his father when he was visiting. Times were turbulent as ever in Greece. He wanted me to assume legal ownership of the family yacht and have it registered somewhere other than in Greece. As he said, I could use it any time I wanted. He just wanted to get as many of his assets as he could out of Greece. Being a very proper, law abiding citizen, I declined the offer. Several years later, Ian told me his father had lent the yacht to some friends who had rented it to some others. Some time later a Greek coast guard patrol boat tried to apprehend the yacht at sea. The new occupants killed the crew of three, blew up the boat and escaped. They were suspected of being in the process of smuggling arms to somewhere in the Middle East. Just as well I wasn't the owner of record. We visited Ian often in Athens. One of the results of the political turbulence was that the family turned their home into a national museum. They had, at the time, the best private collection of Greek art and artifacts. As they couldn't get it out of the country, they donated it to the State, but the arrangement was the Vorres family could live there so long as there were living descendants. Ian never married, but he adopted the principle caretaker of the family property and his family so they could continue to live there after his death and continue the Vorres name.

Nesbitt, Thomson . . . Mainly Learning

Peter Munk is now famous as the CEO and largest shareholder of Barrick Gold Mines, one of the largest gold mining companies in the world. Prior to that, besides marrying the daughter of NT's other senior director in Toronto, he had been involved in several other less successful promotions, one of which was, in partnership with his brother-in-law, promoting a phonograph manufacturing company whose main claim to fame was that the cabinet was modern Scandinavian in design. They were very successful in Canada —to the point where they received a government grant to set up a plant to export to the U.S. Needless to say, NT underwrote a bond issue to finance it—with a government guarantee. The risk was that, as it was not difficult to put a Scandinavian cabinet around a radio set, American competitors could do the same but would benefit from economies of scale—one of those other theories I had learned along the line. That is what happened. A few years later, the debt bankrupted the company. Our bondholders were bailed out by the guarantee. Peter moved on to other things, tourist resort hotels in Egypt and Fiji, before finally striking it rich in gold.

Another refugee from Czechoslovakia that we met in that period was Michael Koerner. We met at the swimming pool of the Royal Canadian Yacht Club. Michael and his wife Sonja were playing Chess, which we also played. So we watched and eventually chatted. That began a friendship that continues to this day. Michael had just finished his Harvard MBA and was working for Abitibi, one of Canada's leading pulp and paper producers, at its head office in Toronto. It turned out that we had both just recently purchased Star boats. At the time Stars were the most popular class of racing yachts. They are the smallest class to be defined as "yachts" rather than sailboats because they had fixed keels. I remember I named mine "Altair," after the star of that name. In any event, we raced against each other for several years, both of us in quite old boats. Later on, we bought a newer Star together. Stars were a very competitive international racing class. Even the then Soviet Union had a Star fleet. I still have the "International Star Class Yacht Racing Association 1963 Log" to prove it. Owners, except us, would get new suits of sails every two years or so and a new boat every three or four years. We never did well. On the other hand, I prided myself in never coming in last in a race. In fact, once I won a race. But that was because the weather was so bad all but the two oldest boats gave up. It was a fun experience because, until then, I had never bothered about getting the course chart before starting as I always had lots of other Stars to follow. So, suddenly, there weren't any ahead. Fortunately, some of the yachts in the (bigger) racing class that had started their race ahead of us were still in sight. So I figured they would have the same course and just followed them. I came in first and the only Star older than mine in our fleet came in second.

Also around Toronto in those days were many young Englishmen who came to work for a few years before returning to family businesses or other established connections. One worked with me at NT. That was Henry Healy Hutchinson, an ex Guards Officer who actually stayed on in Canada. Others included Oliver Fox Pitt who went on to form his own securities firm in London, and Tim Renton, who became a senior official in the Conservative Party. Peter Stormond Darling was the most interesting. He worked for one of the first investment management firms in Canada, but went back to Warburgs. Of that group—and including all of us Canadians then—he was the most successful. He retired as chairman of Mercury Asset Management, then one of the U.K.'s largest and most successful investment management firms. It was reported in the 1980s that he had the largest salary paid in England at the time. Evelyn Rothschild was also about for a while. I suppose my friends and business colleagues looked upon me as one of these immigrants because I had an English accent then and had been away for 12 years—half my life. The good thing about Canada, and the U.S., is that if you tried to fit in, you were accepted. That was very different from the situation in Canada in my father's day.

This brings me to a less happy part of my family life then. In 1954 my father returned to Canada to have another attempt at a new business. Mother stayed in England. Dad stayed with us for three months. After that—and one month should have been the time to say this—I told my father that he could not stay with us any longer. This was not a pleasant part of my life so I shall not dwell on it.

In the meantime, I continued on in the naval reserve. But instead of almost full time as a recruiter, I reverted to the normal "weekend warrior" status. In my case, this involved one day each weekend at Downsview Airport north of Toronto getting our new reserve squadron organized. Downsview was a commercial field used by several aircraft companies, the RCAF Reserve and our new VC 920 Squadron. I think "C" stood for Composite, meaning it was supposed to have more than one function and thus had several types of aircraft. In our case, we had Avengers for our ASW training and North American Harvards as training aircraft for new pilots. The Harvard had been the standard U.S. Navy advanced trainer for many years. It was a simple two seat single 350 horsepower propeller aircraft that was, supposedly, easy to fly.

The decision to have reserve squadrons was made in 1952, but it was not until 1 May 1954 that my Log Book records my first flight in a VC 920 Avenger. Even this was with my old pal and pilot from 1947, Charlie Bourque. Charlie had stayed in the navy and was on loan to VC 920 as an instructor. Prior to that, all of my weekend flying was in Harvards, just going for the ride. The first was on 9 August 1953. The pilot was LCDR Dick Bunyard, the first commanding officer of 920. Dick had been a Swordfish pilot during the war and had served in the "Ark Royal" when it was chasing the Bismarck. He immigrated to Canada and worked for Eaton's, Toronto's largest department store. Most of our pilots were ex Royal Navy types who had immigrated, as were most of our Observers. I was the only one with recent flying experience. Hence the need for the Harvards for the pilots. I was appointed "Senior Observer," which meant I was in charge of bringing them up to speed. It was the usual work: radio, radar, wind finding and sonobuoy exercises, and dead reckoning navigation. One forgets that from Toronto in central Canada, over 1,000 miles from the nearest sea, we could actually fly for two hours over Lake Ontario entirely out of sight of land. That was because, as was our usual practice, our operational flying altitude was 2,000 feet.

I did not spend my usual summer at Dartmouth or on our Carrier in 1952 as it was my first year at work. I did, however, take off two weeks in July of 1953. I flew with VS 881 out of Dartmouth in Avengers. I was glad to be back for a while. By then, the RCN had its third carrier, HMCS Bonaventure, another ship of the same class as Warrior and Magnificent. The big difference I noticed in the two days in her was the officer accommodation: single cabins, each with its own bathroom … quite a difference from Maggie, where 12 of us were jammed into one bunk room. But maybe it was my seniority then. I never got around to checking.

The good part of having Harvards for our pilots to learn to fly again was that I also got a bit of pilot training. That proved the point that my eye problem was real. I could never land the things: I was always 100 feet too high or 100 feet too low. On the other hand, I turned out to be very good at aerobatics. I could do rolls, loops, Immelmens and spins. The only think I never tried was an inverted loop. Still, by popular acclaim, so to speak, I was voted the best at aerobatics in the Squadron. Our pilots were very generous with their time in teaching me and in the credit they gave me. You can imagine how it pleased me. The original reason for Canada's government deciding to strengthen these reserve units was the Korean War, which was now over. Still, the defense budget continued to include our reserve squadrons. I think it was partly the usual political reason—once a community had such units, the local members of parliament were loathed to see them go. The other reason was the cold war. We had our NATO assignments.

Thinking back to those weekends, I remember five events. Three were sad, one was funny and one was down right annoying. The first two sad ones involved fatal accidents. One summer, the RN sent an aerobatics squadron to Toronto to participate in an air show. I forget exactly what we did, other than fly in formation and have some fun with the visiting pilots. They were a crazy bunch who did things that would be absolutely prohibited these days. For example, I remember once watching the air show from the grandstand by the lakeshore. Four Seafuries raced by in tight formation 100 yards out, but below the height of where I was sitting in the audience. We could see the top sides of their wings perfectly. The sad part was two of their Mosquitoes (twin-engine attack bombers in the RN—but an aircraft famous in WWII as "pathfinders" in Bomber Command) collided. Fortunately, it was at the end of their run when they were turning back, so they crashed in the lake, killing only the pilots. But it could have been a real disaster had it happened over the city.

The second sad one was a serious disaster for the Toronto area. There was an area about 30 miles North of Toronto called "Holland Marsh." It was, as it sounds, a very low-lying area about ten miles by 50 miles, which had been turned into a thriving market gardening farming area. It got its name from the fact that it had been developed mainly by Dutch immigrants. There had been totally unexpected heavy rainfall for several weeks. This eventually put the whole area under water. While there were no fatalities, it involved a tremendous rescue effort to pick up survivors from housetops and treetops. VC 920 participated by spotting people needing rescue and directing in boats and helicopters.

The third was when one of our pilots crashed and killed himself. He was alone, fortunately, qualifying in Avengers. Like most single-engine military aircraft, they had only one pilot cockpit, so once the pilot was considered competent in the Harvards, and checked out on the ground in simulators for the Avenger or whatever aircraft he was learning to fly, he was on his own for his first "solo." As best I recall it, this poor fellow had quite a few hours in the Avenger and was close to being qualified to take up a crew. We never did find a reason for his crash. There was nothing to indicate an engine failure or other mechanical problem. He did not send out a "mayday" —the distress signal. He just seemed to have flown straight into the ground at an angle of about 45%. It was in open country and there were no witnesses. Our guess was that he was trying some unauthorized aerobatics. I was on the court of enquiry. We determined it was pilot error. I suppose the good thing was, in the six years that VC 920 was operating, that was our only serious accident … this despite training many of our own pilots and also doing some carrier flying. Deck landings are difficult, but not dangerous unless you don't have enough practice. That was the real risk our pilots and crews took in carrier flying: not enough practice.

The funny experience was something that happened to our shortest pilot. Avengers are big aircraft, built for big American (and Canadian) pilots. This fellow, Colin Mason was an Englishman born in Hong Kong. The English in those days were on average several inches shorter than we were and this fellow was short even by English standards. In any event, when he was piloting Avengers, he had to have his seat jacked

38

up to the highest position and wooden blocks on his rudder bars (the foot pedals used to steer left or right—I should say port or starboard). One day he was turning in to make the standard carrier type landing that we always practiced. Just as he was leveling out over the end of the runway and getting ready to cut his throttle to hit the spot where the landing wires would be, his seat collapsed to the low position. The result was he could not see out of the cockpit. This was especially disconcerting because, unlike air force or commercial landings where you line up on the runway from some distance out, the carrier technique is a tight turn just before the beginning of the runway. This means simultaneously making sure you are lined up and at the right speed and altitude: three things to do at once compared to two. As he couldn't see out, he was, to say the least both surprised and disoriented at that crucial last second. The inevitable result was a very hard landing that broke the undercarriage. Happily, he was not injured physically. But he was hurt by a lot of kidding afterwards. Colin went on to bigger things. He is now a "Q.C."—a Queen's Counselor, an honorary distinction given to very senior lawyers in Canada and other Commonwealth countries where the Queen is titular head of state.

Other than those events, the rest of the time we just did the usual flying things. As Senior Observer, though, I was in charge of a special training program to produce Observer's Mates, the radio and radar third man in an ASW crew. (I could never understand why the RCN never changed that designation when it had dropped most other RN practices and terminology.) This was quite unique—training reservists to do this. But it seemed to work and I rather enjoyed it.

Another rather interesting aspect of the naval reserve and the Toronto "Garrison" was that we had a number of interesting visitors. I enjoyed especially the annual visit to York of course members of the old Imperial Staff College. This was the War College for senior officers of the British Commonwealth military services. Each year the course would visit Canadian military establishments. York's officers always held a reception for them. They were an interesting group, always predominately Indian and Pakistani general officers, with a small sprinkling from other countries and other services. The most important and, thus, interesting visit of all was when the Queen and Prince Charles came to Toronto in the Royal Yacht, Britannia, to celebrate the opening of the St. Lawrence Seaway. The Seaway was a great engineering achievement, opening up the Great Lakes to ocean shipping as far west as Chicago. It meant a great deal to the Canadian economy. There were also political issues as it could not be built without U.S. support, and there were some opponents. In any event, it was completed and Britannia was docked near York. We did not get to invite (we were advised not to try) her Majesty or Prince Philip, but we did have a reception for the officers of the ship and Lord Louis Mountbatten happened to drop by. We all felt very honored. In return, some of us were invited to visit the ship. It was quite impressive. Her hull was as highly polished as those of our Star boats when they were in top racing condition. I knew from personal experience it took a lot of work.

August 1955 marked the end of my naval flying career. The way it happened was the annoying experience alluded to earlier. VC 920 had gone to Dartmouth for our two weeks' summer training. While there, we learned that the RCN had made some major decisions about which we had not heard before. The first was to purchase the USN's latest ASW aircraft, the Grumman Tracker. This was a large (for carrier aircraft then—especially for our small carrier) twin-engine aircraft with a crew of four. The second decision, which must have been in the making for some time, was to switch to the USN's crewing practice. That is, or was, two pilots and two Observer's Mates—no Observer. What annoyed the Observer community was that this had never been discussed with the senior Observers. Whether it was a good decision or a bad decision at the time was not the point. The point was we did not think it had been thought through. The proof of the pudding, as they say, was in the eating. What happened next was that Observers were told they could choose between applying for pilot training, or transferring to sea duty. To do the former meant passing the eyesight tests, amongst other things. Curiously, by the time all of this happened, the standards had been lowered to the point where I actually did pass. Of course, from my own experience trying to land Harvards, I was not convinced of the wisdom of the new standards, but that was another matter. More importantly, it would take a lot of time, and I didn't think I had the time as I had my business career to advance. So, I gave up flying. However, I still enjoyed the naval reserve—some of my best friends in those days were those I had met at HMCS York. Some of them had even joined NT, including Hugh Franks and Cavan Atkinson. (Years later, the U.S. Navy changed the system and introduced what they called "Radio Intercept Officers"—in other words, Observers. That was ironic to us old hands.)

So I transferred to the "stone frigates" version of sea duty. The last entry in my Log Book indicated that my last flight was on 3 August 1955 in Avenger number 364. The pilot was Lt. Washington and the Observer's Mate was P.O. Gallager. We were doing a night navigation exercise. Actually, I did have one more flight, 12 years later, from Patricia Bay, the west coast RCAF and RCN air station north of Victoria, in another Avenger. My old friend Charlie Bourque was commanding officer of the VC squadron there. This did not get an entry in my Log Book because, by then, I had resigned from the naval reserve and was just a civilian. So I even had to sign a waiver absolving the RCN of any damage to me that might result. I always thought it was a fitting end to my flying with the RCN. Charlie and I had been the first Canadian crew back in 1946. Now Charlie had taken me for my last flight in a naval aircraft 21 years later. Sadly, Charlie died in 1988. As is obvious, the navy has always been close to my heart. But my financial career was becoming much more important. It was also becoming quite exciting. That's the subject of the following chapters.

Les Grands Ballets Canadiens

4848, BOUL. ST-LAURENT, MONTRÉAL — TÉL. 849-8024

August 15th, 1966

Mr. David B. Gill, Executive Secretary,
Nesbitt Thomson and Company Limited,
155 St. James Street West,
Montreal.

Dear Mr. Gill:

As Mr. George Vilim requested today, I am sending you herewith some material on our company which will give you an idea of our work both artistically and administratively.

I very much hope to have the opportunity to meet with you and Mr. Vilim in the near future in order to explain to you the many things that are not in these papers but which, I hope, will interest you.

Yours sincerely,

Uriel Luft
General Manager

UL:CdeR
enclosures

A letter to me at Nesbitt Thomson from Les Grands Ballets Canadiens (1966).
I was being recruited to join the ballet company's board and be the chief money raiser.

CHAPTER II

Nesbitt, Thomson and Company Limited ... Mainly Doing: 1957–1969

I t was not that I had stopped learning. Rather, it was a matter of being pushed into the deep end of the pool. In my earlier efforts to do something new, I was more or less on my own. But now I was able to persuade NT to enter several new markets—not new frontiers for the New York and London markets, but certainly for NT. As I moved into 1957 and beyond, that I was also more involved with NT management gave me the opportunity. This also meant I became involved in the inevitable internal politics. Looking back, they were fun and exciting years in the main. I made a lot of new friends in the firm, and also quite a few enemies. What follows is my attempt to recount the interesting parts as best I remember them.

A starting point is to describe the key personalities in and outside the firm that I remember best.

Until about 1957 I really did not know Deane Nesbitt. He was the God in the distance. I knew he had been a fighter pilot during the Battle of Britain in 1940, and had continued to fly fighters in Europe until the end of the war. Like most men of his generation, he had joined a military reserve unit while in University. In his case it was the Royal Canadian

Nesbitt, Thomson . . . Mainly Doing

Air Force's City of Montreal Squadron, as he had gone to McGill before joining the family firm. But I had heard none of this first hand. Later, when I got to know him better, he rarely talked about it. When he did it was usually a funny story. He joked once about being rather annoyed during the Battle of Britain, when a younger pilot said in his presence only "old men" like him—he was 30rather than young guys, should be the risking their necks as the old guys had already lived their lives. He said he had been shot down three times, but never mentioned any of his victories. He hinted at them once though. This was when commenting about not liking hunting or fishing, which was quite unusual for Canadians. His comment was related to avoiding invitations for those hunting and shooting weekends that were important business/social events then. On the third invitation by anyone who persisted, he would say: "No thanks. I gave up shooting animals when I gave up shooting people." None who got this response tried again. I don't think he ended up as a Wing Commander with several medals just for getting shot down. Deane was an imposing figure, full of charm, but an autocrat of the old order. He has a place in Canadian history as a true leader in the financial world as both a visionary and a risk taker. He built on what his father had started. We developed a love/hate relationship as I grew in the firm. He also taught me the joys of a good martini. Two "doubles" for lunch was not unusual.

Ian Crookston was a different type. Tall, elegant and serious are words that come to mind to describe him. As was the case with many Torontonians, his family had moved from Scotland to Toronto when he was a child. He ran all the Ontario operations and, after Peter Thomson had to sell his stock in NT (there was a legal/tax reason that I will explain later), Ian became the second largest shareholder. Unlike Deane, Ian had never been in the Services although they were about the same age. I never inquired and he never explained. But that was not unusual in those days (the 1950s). We all knew who had served overseas and who had not, but it was never discussed in those terms. Ian was a great salesman. His specialties were Ontario based underwriting accounts and the London market for Canadian securities. He was my first mentor in developing my business with institutions and a great supporter. When

44

his London clients visited, I was usually brought into the discussions and joined them for dinner. Later, when I became executive vice president (chief operating officer), our relationship became a little more complicated. Until then, Deane and Ian had tended to be of equal importance and influence in the firm although Deane, as chairman and CEO, was clearly in charge when the chips were down. But it was interesting how they competed with each other when it came to the interests of their respective underwriting accounts and what were considered their respective geographical spheres of influence. For Deane it was Quebec and East. For Ian it was Ontario and West. The U.S. and Europe were fair game for both. This may sound rather complicated and it was. This will become clearer as my story progresses.

Tom Kierans was another memorable character. He was our first serious analyst in our new research department. He succeeded me in 1969 as chief operating officer. Tom was young, short but sturdy and with a voice that more than made up for his small stature. He was one of the original "Chicago boys"—University of Chicago—and knew it. I was his mentor for a long time as I was a big supporter of research and it was clear he was by far the best we had. He soon became director of research. An amusing story was about the time Ivor Murray, then his boss as the first director of research, invited Tom and his new bride to dinner at his house in a Montreal suburb. This was to meet me for the first time when I had just become EVP. Unfortunately, it was winter, dark and snowing, and Tom had never been to the suburb that was his destination. The end result was they got lost and were an hour late. Ivor and I thought it was a great joke, but Tom felt his career in NT was over. How could the smartest person in the firm ever get over being so stupid! He was forgiven immediately but teased by Ivor and me for years about it.

Bob Learn was another important power as head salesman—first just for Ontario, finally for the whole firm. Bob was ex Canadian army and had gone through France and Germany. Like Deane, he didn't talk about it much beyond telling funny accounts of "snafus" during battles. There will be more about one of Bob's war stories a few pages on.

Then there were the people outside the firm that were either or both important to our business or just interesting personalities. Of these, first was Peter Thomson, son of a founder of the company. As Chairman and CEO of Power Corporation of Canada ("Power"), he was our single most important client. But the dominating personality in Power for NT and for me personally was Maurice Strong, who took over as CEO of Power in the early 1960s. Maurice was the "Horatio Alger" of Canada. He had left school at 14 and worked for the Hudson Bay Company in an Arctic outpost. After a stint in the oil industry where he became the CFO of a small producing company in Alberta, he took his wife and five kids to Africa for two years for the YMCA. After that, it was back to his oil company, Apex Petroleum. As CEO, he sold it to Power Corporation and moved over, first as chief operating officer. After making a lot more money, he moved to public service as President of the Canadian International Development Agency ("CIDA")—Canada's World Bank. This was followed by his appointment as Assistant Secretary General for Environment at the UN. Our business relationship was excellent but it never became personal.

Paul Paine, who took over later as COO of Power, became one of my dearest friends until he died in 1990. We first met in Vancouver in about 1967. He was a lawyer and acted for one of our client companies, an affiliate of Power. Paul had also been a pre war reservist, in the Canadian Navy. He spent five years on Atlantic convoy duty. He said except for the odd few seconds of terror, it was one of the most dull, uncomfortable and tiresome duties of the war. One crossing in rough weather on a small ship in peacetime was enough for me. Besides being an excellent corporate lawyer, Paul was an astute businessman and very good company. He was one of the most articulate and well-read people I knew. One fond memory was a time when we recounted our schoolboy experiments with gunpowder. Paul's was much more dramatic than mine but, having done it in peacetime, the risk he took unwittingly was less. He had found an old saluting cannon, loaded it with powder, shoved a rock in the sharp end and lit the fuse. To his surprise it worked. Unfortunately, he hadn't given much thought to where the cannon was pointed. The result was two holes in the front and back walls of a neighbor's garage. Sadly, Paul and I drifted apart as the years passed and we moved to New York and then to Washington. By then, Paul was Chairman and

CEO of most of Power's financial affiliates. I shall never forget Betty Ann, his wife, calling to tell me Paul had been taken ill suddenly and had died.

There are a host of others, some more and some less influential or interesting than the above, both in NT and outside. I will talk about some of them later when they play their respective roles in the events I remember.

I forget in which year but around this time (1964) I was allowed to become a shareholder of NT. Shortly after that I was elected to the board. NT and all other Canadian investment firms, at that time, were really just small private companies. Then, NT had a net worth of probably about $3 million—not much for a company with some 600 employees and total assets of around $200 million, including our trading inventories of government bonds. Deane Nesbitt owned more than 50% of the stock and Peter Thomson had probably 25%. The rest was owned by the older more senior officers and employees, probably about 20 in total. My initial allocation of stock was 200 shares, at about $25 a share. It was just a nominal amount although $5,000 was a lot of money to me then. The rules governing buying and selling was that the price was 90% of net book value and Deane was the "banker"—the buyer and seller of last resort—as, at the time, Canadian law did not permit companies to buy back their own stock into treasury. Buying was a privilege and was only possible when someone was selling. Selling only occurred when someone left the firm. So there was a waiting list of buyers. Usually, Deane would accumulate the stock of people leaving for a period and then distribute it later to his approved list at the price he paid. As NT was a consistent moneymaker in my day, this meant he subsidized the price buyers paid to some extent, which was very decent of him, but typical of his attitude towards his employees.

I cannot recall exactly when my climb in the internal pecking order started, although my work on Superior Propane must have been a key factor. Nor can I remember exactly when some of the other key events happened. Consequently, it makes sense to start with an explanation of how the firm operated in the late 1960s and my role in the structure as it evolved. The head office in Montreal consisted of the underwriting department, the sales department, the trading department, the research department and administration. Administration covered the treasury function, personnel, compliance with the regulators and stock exchanges and all the day-to-day nuts and bolts activities to keep the machinery of some 23 offices across the country and in New York and London functioning.

For all practical purposes, Deane ran the underwriting department, although it did have a vice president underwriting—John McConnell, and then Desmond Stoker after John retired. NT, as with all of our competitors, underwrote new issues of everything from federal government bonds to common stocks of new companies. The difference between then and now is that, then, investment firms took real financial commitments when they underwrote a new issue. That is, we bought it before we had firm buying orders for all of the issue. Now, with the "book building" system, underwriters take very little risk as new issues are pre-sold. But lots of pricing mistakes were made. That was when the pressure was on the sales department.

Bob Learn, as vice president sales, had two functions. First, managing the "salesmen" in the branch offices and, second, syndicating—distributing—a portion of new issues that NT managed to other investment dealers and brokers in our underwriting and sales groups and negotiating our participations in issues managed by other firms. Bob was a tough professional salesman who had come up the hard way as a sales trainee in Toronto. His sales management function was, primarily, to sell the firm's new issues. As indicated earlier, this was not always easy, as about one in five were either over priced or quite speculative, or both. The difficulty, especially for the retail salesmen, was to make a case to their customers that the new issue was good value and had a place in their portfolios. To the extent that the firm took a real financial commitment when underwriting, there was a serious reason for ensuring good value for investors. One could only lose money for investors in our new issues a few times before they moved their accounts to other firms. So, if they were over priced, NT became an involuntary shareholder in its own issues. Sometimes there would be a run of poorly priced issues. Then, the salesmen tended to become more "customers' men" in the old sense

48

of the term and make sure that they were invested fully in listed stocks and high quality bonds. The more experienced the salesman, the more he avoided the risky issues. Bob's job was to "encourage" the experienced salesmen with special commission arrangements and, well, bully the junior ones into trying harder. Junior salesmen looked after smaller "retail" (individual) customers and senior salesmen dealt with the "wholesale" (institutional) customers and wealthy individuals. A good sales manager realized there was not much point in bullying the people covering sophisticated investors, so there had to be a fine balance. Another incentive with the difficult issues was to give the salesmen a larger than normal allocation of the good issues. Being able to offer a customer a quick profit in an IPO that was already at a premium was the best way to overcome the problem of the losses they took in the poor ones. These days there are regulations limiting that approach but it was routine then. In any event, their job then as now was, first, to sell the firm's underwriting commitments and, second, between underwritings, to generate commissions through trading their customers' accounts. Our "customers' men" were supposed to do this by professing to be money managers helping investors build solid diversified portfolios suited to their investment objectives. At the end of the day, in that period, it came down still to a lot of account churning. That was another problem for the VP Sales. He encouraged churning to keep commission revenues flowing but he had to control it to avoid complaints to securities commissions. Nothing has changed. But today, salesmen are called "account executives" or "investment advisers."

As is the case with most good salesmen, Bob Learn was an extrovert who could get along with anyone. He had a host of good stories. Late one evening, at a company sales meeting, he told a great story about his time as an infantry lieutenant in France. When out on a reconnaissance in a Bren Gun Carrier (a lightly armored personnel carrier) alone with his driver they suddenly come across a herd of over 100 Germans running towards them. Bob's reaction was to go into reverse at full speed to escape. After a few minutes, realizing they weren't being shot at, he slowed for a closer look and discovered they weren't carrying guns, but were just trying to surrender.

Nesbitt, Thomson . . . Mainly Doing

In those days, another key factor in bringing in the day-to-day revenues was having an active and successful trading department. NT had two people who were key operators in this area. One ran the traditional stock exchange trading through our membership in all five of the Canadian stock exchanges. The other was George Mulligan who ran the bond trading desks. He was a jovial Irish Canadian: short, chubby and very good. His greatest pleasure came from the occasions when he bought a block of bonds from the Montreal trading desk of one of our competitors and sold them immediately at a good profit to the same firm's Toronto trading desk. Amongst the stock exchanges, the Montreal Stock Exchange took precedence because that was head office territory, but the Toronto Stock Exchange was where most of the activity took place. Initially, the membership and floor trading was under a separate vice president, but it was largely an administrative function as there were no capital risks involved—unless mistakes were made in placing orders. The more important trading department handled all the unlisted securities and did what trading departments still do. That is, make markets in bonds and stocks. The only difference was, as with the difference in approach to underwriting in those days, we took much larger positions relative to the firm's capital than is done now. (That is after the similar excesses by the likes of Lehman Brothers recently.) Most were in government and corporate bonds, especially those we underwrote. Making a market in our own issues was a service that investors expected. Still, we did try to make a profit trading our own positions for our own account. The difference between then and now was that then investment firms took these risks with their employees' money, not the publics' as is the case now when most investment firms are listed companies.

We did not have a serious research department until the very late 1950s. Growing competition from U.S. firms was what started the trend in all the Canadian firms. As I mentioned earlier, previously we had a "statistical department" which really only just compiled numbers for the underwriting department's new issue prospectuses. Around 1959, Deane brought aboard Gerry Sutton. I remember well that he was the first person I heard using government economic data as a basis for picking promising industries that might have promising companies whose stocks we could recommend. He hired some competent people and re-trained what we had. Tom Kierans was the first, and the best, of the new breed. Gerry was conscious that, to retain morale in his department, there had to be a bonus system as all the other "producers" in the firm received either commissions or bonuses. His first idea, which he sold to Deane, was a bonus based on the number of research reports written. Hearing this, I recommended that it be changed to reports that had investment recommendations that were proven correct by the market over the next year. This was agreed, but Gerry was a little chagrined that it was I who made this rather obvious point. After that, we worked quite well together. He would make his recommendations and I would take his research people around to our institutional clients. That way, we were helping each other and producing a better "product" for our clients. Reading these days about research analysts on Wall Street only giving "buy" recommendations and being rewarded for promoting their companies' new issue businesses, I am surprised about how objective we were in those days. As I will talk about later, we made lots of "sell" recommendations, even for the stocks of our own underwriting accounts—but not before talking to the respective firm's CFO about it.

This leads to the reorganization of the sales and trading operations that led to my first important management promotion. Generally, one moved from junior to senior positions in the firm by winning the commission generating races or getting new underwriting business. However, as research became more important in developing the wholesale business, technical skills began to be recognized. That was how I got into the institutional sales side of the business in Toronto.

Thanks to luck, improving skills, good performance and, most importantly, that both Deane and Ian agreed, I found myself in charge of a new department—the Institutional Trading Department ("ITD"). This brought together all of the traders and institutional salesmen. It was agreed ITD would be based in Toronto. The logic was easy—Toronto was a much larger financial center than Montreal. Notwithstanding the logic, internal politics made implementation of the new setup difficult. Previously, in all the branch offices—Toronto and Montreal included—the branch manager or senior salesmen had serviced the institutional accounts. Now they were all moved to ITD. Consequently, some of the Toronto and Montreal salesmen not recruited by ITD lost out. As there were also institutional accounts in the areas of most of the other branch offices and especially the provincial capitals, they lost those accounts, as they were all to be serviced directly from Toronto. So, along with the pluses for my crowd and the firm (the institutional buyers much preferred professional coverage from "head office"), I made a new list of enemies in the form of some 20 branch managers who saw their most prestigious business go to the sharpies in Toronto.

A benefit for the firm and our clients was in the combination of trading and sales operations. Previously, our traders had looked upon the salesmen as just other customers. They got no better service than our competitors' trading desks. Consequently, our customers had been paying two markups—the traders' and the salesmen's. Obviously, this was no way to handle highly competitive institutional accounts, many of which could deal directly with the trading desks of the U.S. firms. So in combining the two groups we established one overall profit pool. As one team, we encouraged our clients to deal directly with the traders if they wished or with the sales people—whatever made them most comfortable. We were the first major firm in Canada to do this and have both the traders and the salesmen all sitting around one huge trading desk— just like Salomon Brothers in New York, the worlds best bond-trading firm in those days. In those early days we just had telephones and a Reuters/stock exchange ticker for news—no PCs. and Internet connections. But we ended up with a great team and a much bigger profit pool than before. I remember our pool started at 20% of the profits we generated, paid as salaries and bonuses as compared to one third for the other ("retail") sales producers. I suppose we considered this as reasonably fair as our accounts, and the trading profits, were in a sense "house business." But I do recall becoming very angry when Ross Oborne, our vice president administration, wanted to cut it to 19% the following year. I think we compromised at 19.5%. But I couldn't complain too much, we all earned between $50,000 and $70,000 —the latter being my take in 1959, I think. While it was not much compared to the millions made by traders and institutional salespeople today, it was a lot in Canada then.

My "empire" comprised some 25 salesmen and ten traders in Toronto, Montreal, New York, Boston and London. As the institutions could make or break a new issue, I also had a lot of influence over the pricing of underwritings. Equally important in terms of our profitability, I had full control over our trading exposures —what we called our "inventory"—of government and corporate bonds, as well as the small amounts of stocks that were not listed that we might hold. I think our total positions would never have exceeded $400 million, of which 90% would have been short-term governments. The Bank of Canada (BoC), our central bank, had only just started promoting a money market. It encouraged "authorized dealers" to make markets in the then new short term treasury bills by providing Bank of Canada lines of credit to us through arrangements with the commercial banks. This was why our inventories doubled from the $200 million range quite quickly. But it was all small change by today's standards when investment banks would hold billions rather than millions. But it was quite a bit considering NT's total capital of about $3 million at the time. In those days, while the stock exchanges and the BoC did have some limits as to how much we could borrow to finance our customers' business (margin accounts, etc.) and our inventories, they were very lax compared to U.S. regulations. In fact we required no margin at all for short term government bonds.

In any event, the BoC moved us into the 20th century alongside the U.S. and the U.K. Until then (and I don't remember the year), the short-term (up to 180 days) treasury bills ("TBs") had been sold by the Bank of Canada only to the commercial banks. They were required to hold them as part of their liquidity reserves. These instruments were used in this limited way to influence the money supply and interest rates. The new scheme was to encourage other investors to buy them as liquidity instruments and to use the leading investment dealers as the marketing agents, encouraged by generous lines of credit ... and still no margin requirements. The immediate result was that we could participate in the weekly treasury bill auctions for the first time in competition with the commercial banks and, thanks to our last resort credit lines with the BoC, make an interest rate profit just carrying the TBs as inventory. Of course we were pushed to find buyers amongst the insurance companies and large corporations who had previously just kept their spare cash in bank accounts. Over time, the BoC caused the carrying profit to disappear as further inducement to find real investors.

At the same time, the BoC encouraged us to develop a commercial paper market. That is, to get private companies with large cash positions to lend to other companies. This was for short periods—up to one year. It was curious that the central bank had to start this in Canada—it had been going on for centuries in the U.K. and the U.S. and other countries. But Canadians were always slow and conservative. Also, the banks preferred the old regime as they paid zero on deposits and charged the prime rate on business loans to even their AAA rated company credits. The BoC's other agenda item was to create more competition in the banking market. At the time, Canada had five commercial banks, probably the smallest number relative to wealth in any country outside the communist world. Needless to say, asking the investment firms to promote TBs and commercial paper markets was easier said than done. Both we and the companies that began to participate got lots of threats from the banks. We were warned we would lose our lines of credit and the big companies were warned that their loans might be called. Finally, however, we all were read the riot act by the BoC and started playing the game.

An amusing experience for me was transacting NT's first commercial paper deal. Curiously, it was between two major oil companies. (No one thought that direct competitors would cooperate in financing each other's short-term cash requirements.) It was a one million dollar, one-year deal which, at the accepted commission rate at the time, meant a $10,000 profit for NT just acting as an agent and thus taking no risk. So, it was not only our largest "agency" or brokerage deal for the firm ever, but also the largest single commission we had ever earned without any risk. Then came the crisis. Our office manager—Ross Oborne's "man" in Toronto—said we couldn't do it. "Why!" I said in a state of complete shock. "Well," said he, "our brokerage contracts were only designed for six digit transactions and a million required seven." We finally renegotiated the deal as two $500,000 transactions. You cannot imagine the fuss. While we eventually got the brokerage contract system changed, I made another enemy. Fortunately, my two oil company treasurer friends thought it was a great joke. But, in our administration bureaucracy, that probably made it worse.

We had a good crowd of guys—no girls then, although later in New York we had several. Initially, on the sales side I remember Ivor Murray and Nelson Lane and George "Sandy" Watt in Toronto. In Montreal there was Lamont (Monty) Gordon and George Vilim, who also covered Europe. In London the main character, and a special friend, was Matthew Page Wood. Our head trader in Toronto was George Mulligan, assisted by Bob Kay. Over the next few years we added John McIlhenny and Duncan Smith in Toronto, and Ivor Murray went to New York. There, we added Joe Wilson, Hugh Shaw (my old friend from University of Toronto days who came from our good competitor, A.E. Ames) and Ted Delahay, a real money market expert from one of our competitors in Montreal who had worked in New York for many years. Then Duncan Smith went to London and we hired a team of U.S. equity experts for New York. This was Monty's idea and it worked quite well. They were three real characters, including our very first female professional. Frank Veneroso was the leader. He was another character. Duncan's and Monty's moves were part of greater schemes that I will cover later.

One of the delights was that we were all good friends. We trusted each other and worked well together. It is with the warmest of feelings that I look back to those early days (1958 to 1967 or thereabouts) and those good people. In many respects, it was the best period of my business life in that we became a recognized force in the market and we had a good time together. Before writing about our "war stories," I can't help but reflect on some of those people I worked with. It's hard to know where to start—and even harder to convince myself that I'm attaching the right stories to the right people. It is sad to think I have lost touch with almost all of them, but it has been over 40 years since I resigned.

I should start with Matthew Page Wood, who died a few years ago. Mathew was very English. He was Public School educated, but, like so many Englishmen in those days, did not attend university but went straight into business with a London stock broker after the war. He served as an officer in a Guards' tank regiment that landed in Normandy a few days after D-Day. I recall once, going to Normandy with him in the late 1950s, visiting the spot were his first tank was shot out from under him. Finally, he was invalided out in 1947 after having been wounded in Palestine when the British were trying to keep the peace between the Palestinians and the Jews during Partition. He joined a London brokerage firm immediately after being "demobilized" (no thought of going to University first). He must have been about 30 when he joined NT in London in about 1955 as "number two" to a delightful Hungarian pre-war escapee who was in his sixties. Mathew, I suppose, saw joining a "colonial" firm with a chance of running the London office after a few years as a better career path than being a junior partner amongst many in a large London firm. I first met him when he came to Toronto to meet me when the London office became part of ITD. It was rumored that he knew everyone that was anyone in "the city" and certainly was well regarded by Deane and Ian. In any event, I suppose we were both a bit apprehensive. My first impression was that this medium height, slightly chubby, longish dark haired fellow who looked about 50 was very much the outgoing "man of the world" type, and a bit jaded. But he was great fun and hit it off immediately with our crowd in ITD and with our personal friends. When it came time for his boss in London to retire, I had no hesitation about putting him in charge.

Ivor Murray was rather the opposite—smallish, quiet, studious. He was from Nova Scotia and part way through university when he joined up. He volunteered for overseas duty, but ended up in Newfoundland which, as a British colony then, was "overseas" under Canadian rule, but not quite what he had in mind. Perhaps a year older than I, he had gone back to university and then into the insurance business. He was an excellent technician and a reliable man in every respect. He went on to be director of research and then resigned for an interesting new job setting up Canada's first Central Depository about the time I resigned in 1969.

John McIlhenny, "Pilot" as we called him, because he had started as a navigation officer in the Royal Navy and that's what they were called.

He was great fun and one of my naval friends at "York," although he came to NT through Ross Oborne and so started in administration. Born in Ireland, he immigrated to Canada in the 1950s and worked for a bank in their investment department. As an ex RNVR officer, he was welcomed in the RCN Reserve at York during the Korean War period. At the end of WW II he had commanded a flotilla of three motor torpedo boats. He never admitted to seeing any action but had a hilarious story of just after VE Day. He was ordered to take his boats up the Seine to Paris to "wave the flag" as the first Royal Navy visit after the war. In living memory no RN ships had ever visited Paris so why now? Anyhow, the first thing he noticed was that all the other shipping (nothing bigger than the usual Seine barges) gave his three boats a wide birth as they passed. Somehow the French knew they were fueled by high-octane aviation fuel and had a propensity to explode. The next was a rather wild party given the officers by the French navy the night before the official reception. This resulted in his returning to his ship at dawn, a little the worse for wear. This was bad timing because that morning he, a Sub Lieutenant (Ensign in the USN), his crews lined behind him, was to be inspected by the French minister of defense, an admiral, the British Ambassador and his senior naval attaché, an RN Captain. This meant he had to go through the military "drill" and give the sequence of orders to "Present Arms" as the final act in the ceremonial display of respect to the dignitaries. In his haze he completely forgot the six preliminary orders he should have given before giving the final one. Much to his relief, he said, seeing the steely eyes of the Admiral boring through him as if trying to make him and his men just disappear, he heard the single bangs and slaps of his men going through all six motions in perfect unison. Obviously, a much more perfect drill performance than anyone had reason to expect even when sober and wide awake. But, as I had mentioned in an earlier chapter, it's the Petty Officers that really run the show. Neither the Admiral nor the Ambassador said a word about it at the lunch following the ceremonies.

John ended up running our money market department, before resigning a year after I did to start his own firm. John was a great professional and also a good squash player. He, Sandy Watt, Hugh Franks, my good friend Michael Koerner, and I all belonged to the Badminton and Racquet Club and played together a lot. I played all three games—badminton, squash and tennis—but all consistently poorly. I had a good serve but if my opponent was able to return it, I was lost. That was because of my eyesight problem that I first mentioned when I talked about failing the eyesight test to become a pilot. That reminds me of something I was told many years later that rather chagrined me. It was about what happened to Al Bice, one of 803 Squadron's fighter pilots that I had known quite well in 1947 and 1948. In those days pilots had to go to a civilian doctor in Halifax for annual eyesight tests. (I don't recall the navy worrying about observers' eyesight!) When it was Al's turn he drove over to Halifax in civilian clothes and went to see this new specialist. At the end of the tests, he is reported to have said to Al: "Mr. Bice, your eyes are very bad. You need glasses right away. I hope you don't drive like this." Al must have got glasses because he continued to fly in Seafires, then Seafuries and then Banshees (the RCN's first jet fighter). In fact, he ended up some 20 years later as chief of staff of the Canadian Armed Forces. Not bad for a half blind ex RCAF trainee fighter pilot. But that is off the subject.

Lamont (Monty) Gordon, our top equity specialist in ITD, was another character. He was a University of Western Ontario graduate from an Ontario farming family. He was a handsome sophisticated fellow. He had joined the firm in Montreal and came up the same way I did. He had even been in the UNTD and trained as an Observer during the summers. His wedding present from us was being moved to Boston to open an office there to serve the big mutual fund managers and insurance companies based in the area. We gave him this present when he returned from his honeymoon. I don't think his bride appreciated it that much. But he was a superb equity man and the institutional buyers loved him. So, putting him where most of them were based made sense. However, Monty concluded, after about a year, that the Boston institutions wanted to hear from the man in New York, at the market center. He was always very persuasive so he was transferred with our blessings. Only later did he let the other shoe drop when he said he wanted to hire a team of four U.S. equity research people who specialized in taking their recommendations directly to the buyers. This, of course, was why he wanted to move to New York, where most of the important companies were. Monty had two other great interests. One was setting up small companies as a venture capitalist and the other was bob sledding. I'll go into the former later.

The bobsledding story started when he just happened to be in Switzerland at the time of the winter Olympics in whichever year in the 1950s. He noticed that there was no Canadian team entered in the bob-sledding race. So, Monty being Monty, he rounded up some Canadian friends as a volunteer crew and borrowed a sled from the U.K. team. In their first run in the competition, they didn't do too well. On the other hand, not one of them had ever ridden on a bobsled before. Monty cap-tained the Canadian team for many years, doing progressively better. He finally gave up after a nasty crash and a long stay in hospital. As he still wanted do race competitively, he went for something easier: Formula One car racing.

Sandy Watt was a dower Scotsman with a great sense of humor when you got to know him. He had that large angular body and lantern jaw that many Scots had. Sandy was his nickname for George for the obvi-ous reason that he had sandy-colored hair. He too was a 1950s immi-grant who came to NT from another investment firm. Like many of us, he had seen the tail end of the War. He had been a Lancaster (four-en-gine bomber) pilot, towing gliders. Sandy was a very astute dealmaker. He became my second in command of ITD and replaced me as its head when I was promoted to COO. One of the things I remember was his relentless campaign to make me move off the trading desk into a private office. To him, this was more fitting for my rank as a director of the firm and head of what we all thought was its most important unit. I resisted this because I liked being in the action and seeing what was going on. Also, I felt that if being on the trading desk was good enough for Bill Salomon, it was good enough for me. At the time, Bill Salomon was CEO of Salomon Brothers, then the best bond trading house in New York. But when I came back from holidays the next summer, I found Sandy had organized a spacious private office for me. What could I do but still insist on the right to a seat on the trading desk when I wanted it? Previously, my office had been the men's toilet on our floor. Sometimes I wondered about that. But Sandy was right in a way. More and more, I became involved with structuring new corporate bond and stock issues, which had little to do with trading as such.

Also about this time I began to have some influence in organizational matters. My most important "success" in that regard was convincing the board—which meant Deane and Ian—to bring in McKinsey and Company to do a complete strategic and organizational review of the firm. But more about this later. Now is the time to recount some of the operational activities I remember.

The one that probably got the most attention was the first private placement of U.S. dollar denominated Trans Canada Pipe Line ("TCP") bonds after the initial IPO of its stock and debt funding. This was because I out-maneuvered Lehman Brothers, who considered themselves the senior partner in the financing. TCP was the longest gas pipeline built to date and the biggest private financing for a Canadian company. The TCP story is a subject for a book in itself. In fact two books were written about it. One was by a prominent Canadian author and the other by Deane who was one of the key players on the Canadian side. His book was published privately and I still have a copy. The story started in the early 1950s with competing U.S. and western Canadian oil company groups attempting to obtain licenses to export western Canadian natural gas to Winnipeg and then into the U.S. and/or on to Eastern Canada. Both the Federal and Alberta governments resisted these efforts for various reasons. The main one was exporting a Canadian resource that might be needed later in Canada. After some four years, the competing groups were reduced to one—a partnership between the Murchison family from Dallas who controlled Canadian Delhi Oil, a major gas supplier, and International Utilities, another U.S. controlled company with Canadian subsidiaries owning considerable gas reserves in Alberta. The U.S. group, through their lead investment bank, Lehman Brothers, then approached both Wood Gundy and NT for help. The first meeting and the start of a successful strategy was held in Ottawa in 1954, with all players present. Deane played a major role in getting the various federal and provincial government approvals. There was also the need to tie down a twenty years' supply of gas at the western producer company end and buyers at the eastern end—mainly Toronto and Montreal. The Americans had all the sales contracts they needed in the U.S. The key for approval was assuring the Albertan and Canadian authorities that enough gas was going to remain in Canada. Until then, the eastern Canadian gas distribution utilities depended mainly on gas produced from coal or from natural gas from the U.S. These new contracts were the "collateral" for the huge amount of debt financing needed, as first mortgages on the approximately 2,000 mile long and maybe 200 yard wide strip of land through which the pipe ran was not worth anything unless gas was flowing.

In any event, after several years of negotiations and many crises—including bringing in other partners, some Canadian government funding, a steel crises stopping the supply of pipe, and parliamentary debates on sovereignty and subsidies—the initial public offering was made. This was for about $100 million of common stock at $8 a share and $100 million of subordinated debt. This was all a great success and the stock went immediately to the high teens. As a sign of the different times, notwithstanding this having been the largest IPO in Canada ever and thus widely scrutinized, the issue was rationed carefully. All of us "salesmen" (this happened in 1957 when I was still a junior) got allotments which we could place with our accounts. We were also given a list of "special accounts"—individuals who were being given favored treatment by senior management to whom we were not to allocate any of our stock. Nowadays, such treatment could have been considered akin to payoffs. Then, it was perfectly normal practice.

The important event for me was the second private placement of first mortgage bonds that was organized a year later when I was beginning to cover institutional accounts. The issue was for US $100 million. It was therefore quite natural that Lehman was the manager and that Wood Gundy and NT would just get small percentages of the deal. Deane told us that the terms were 20 years maturity and an interest rate of whatever it was. This was based on the fact that Lehman had an order for $50 million from a major U.S. insurance company and that was what they were willing to pay. Being interested in research generally and interest rate trends in particular, I did a little market study and concluded that the bonds could be sold for one half of one percent less interest. This I reported to Deane. He, already feeling aggrieved by our treatment by Lehman, arranged a meeting for us with TCP's VP Finance to make this case. Deane suggested he could get a better deal if they would switch the management. This was eventually agreed to by TCP's board. It was a major deal for them—dumping "their" U.S. investment bank in favor of these upstart Canadians. But we were successful and saved TCP $500,000 a year for 20 years. NT also got a lot of very favorable attention. I got to know TCP's VP Finance very well and he became one of our major money market accounts. Throughout this saga, Sandy, as our number one bond man, and John, as our money market expert, were key supporters. I might have been instrumental in getting the deal, but it was largely Sandy who sold it. To fast forward a bit, I recall, at the request of our research department, going to see TCP's VP Finance to tell him we were planning producing a major research piece on pipeline companies. One of the conclusions was that, at that point, TCP's stock was seriously overpriced. We just wanted him to know that we felt it was better for the company were the stock to come down a bit for a while rather than continue its current climb and then collapse. He agreed completely with our analysis and our conclusions. The stock sagged a bit after our report came out, but our relationship with TCP was not weakened. How different things seem to be now. Investment bankers rarely issue "sell" recommendations.

This brings to mind another TCP related story. The Mur-chisons provided most of the equity finance for Quebec Natural Gas—the Montreal distribution company for TCP's gas. NT played its historic role and sold the company's bonds and preferred stock as IPOs. About a year later, QNG was in deep financial trouble as sales had not grown as quickly as expected. We had to come up with a reorganization plan. This included turning the preferred stock into common stock, and giving the common stock holders some Warrants to compensate for the substantial dilution they would take. Perhaps because of my not-yet-forgotten coup of a year before with TCP's bond issue, I was dispatched to Dallas to explain what we planned to Delhi Oil Company's EVP—

the Murchisons' "number two." Delhi Oil owned Canadian Delhi, which was, in turn, the largest shareholder in both TCP and QNG. It was my first experience meeting a seriously wealthy Texan. I was told to call from my hotel at 10.00 AM for an appointment. His secretary said to go around to his house at noon. They would send a car for me. I showed up at the door of this huge mansion, sweltering in the 90 degree August temperature. The butler told me he was at the pool and led me out. After a very friendly greeting by the man himself in his bathing suit, I was told to get changed before we started our discussion. So, a few minutes later, a very nervous 32-year-old marched forth with my papers in one hand and a towel in the other. He was in the pool with his wife. He told me to leave the "damn papers" on the table and jump in and just tell him the story. So I did. I had barely started before he said "let's have a drink," whistled for his butler, and called for three gin and tonics. I think he had heard "Brits"—Brits, Canadians, what's the difference—liked that in the summer and Texans are nothing if not hospitable. Anyway, we stood up to our necks in the water with our glasses to hand while I tried to explain as tactfully as possible that we saw no way around their equity being diluted by about 90%. Anything less would have resulted in some political turmoil with the Quebec government and their likely nationalizing QNG. As best I recall it, he rather shrugged and just said "time for lunch if you can stay." After lunch and fond farewells as befits a good host and hostess on the departure of a guest, I was driven back to my hotel. It took me a day or so to get over it. I had been simply too overwhelmed by the whole experience. I think it was the first time I had been in a swimming pool that was not part of a hotel or a club. The idea of a business meeting in one was mind boggling. I wasn't even sure how I was going to describe the meeting to Deane and the others. But it must have been all right; because they went along with our proposal and, a few years later, QNG was making money—but not as much for the Murchisons as they had hoped.

Another important event was a Canadian $50 million public debt issue for Rio Algom Limited, a subsidiary of the British mining giant, Rio Tinto Zinc, ("RTZ"). This was to finance the purchase of Faraday Mines, a uranium producer, on which more later. On this occasion we also faced down our U.S. partner who threatened to block the sale of the bonds in the U.S. unless they were named lead underwriter. Usually, some half of Canadian bond issues were sold to U.S. institutions as "private placements." This meant the issue did not have to be registered with the SEC, which was an expensive and time consuming exercise. Our partners thought we would have to accept their terms. This was because, then, it was to be the largest corporate bond issue sold only in Canada. They thought it would be impossible. They were wrong. As always, personal relationships were important.

A brief history is needed. In the mid 1950s, NT, along with most other Canadian firms, sold convertible bonds issued by uranium mining companies. Except for the fact that they were described as government-guaranteed, these convertible bonds were really just disguised equity issues on startup ventures. The "guarantee" was simply a government contract given to the company to buy sufficient refined product at a fixed price to pay to dig the mine and build the refinery, plus a profit. This was fine so long as the company's cost estimates to build and produce were correct. But clever legal wording gave a gullible public a sense that they couldn't lose. Consequently, as with previous mining booms, "everyone and his dog" produced ore samples and feasibility studies to justify financing their projects. And, just like the "dotcom" companies of more recent date, underwriters sold them and investors gobbled them up. Of about a dozen that NT financed, only one, Gunnar Mines, actually survived on its own. After the collapse of the others, an enterprising American, who was described as an ex used car dealer from Brooklyn, came to the rescue and bought up many of them at fire sale prices. This new company, Faraday Mines, that NT also financed, sold out to the U.K.'s RTZ. With the economies of scale, a dozen small mines in the same area didn't need a dozen refineries, so they became reasonably profitable with the existing government contracts. RTZ was one of Ian Crookston's clients. RTZ's "merchant banker" was Kleinwort Benson and the senior partner in charge of the account was Sir Mark Turner, a very charming upper class Englishman. Thanks to Ian, I remember fondly a delightful evening of drinks, dinner, bridge and drinks with Mark, his wife, Ian and me at their London house.

When RTZ decided to buy Faraday, they planned merging it with Algoma Steel in order to use the combined assets to raise the $50 million purchase price. Mark Turner naturally recommended his good friends at NT to the RTZ people to do the underwriting. This was in 1959. Because it was Ian's deal, and because it was in Ontario, Ian managed to short cut the Montreal underwriting department on setting the strategy and structure. I suppose we had some clerical assistance with the prospectus, but it was our deal. That meant it was up to me to figure out the technical details. Fortunately, by then I had enough good friends on the buying side to test out what were, at the time, some rather radical ideas. The end result was, instead of a complex first mortgage bond, we did a "negative pledge" debenture. That meant it gave the buyers the senior debt position because the company pledged not to issue any debt senior to ours. I don't remember why no one had thought of it before. It was really the idea of the chief investment officer of Manufacturers Life, John Beauregard, whose advice I sought. He enjoyed trying new things and had enough money to make them work. I forget how we explained the logic of combing a uranium company with a steel producer. I certainly can't think of it now. But that was the least of our problems. RTZ, also active in the U.S., wanted to bring in its U.S. investment bankers. In turn, they wanted to lead the deal. There were always fights over whose name is at the top of the list (the newspaper advertisement, known as "the tombstone," announcing the deal and listing the underwriters), but this was particularly vicious. Fortunately, Mark took our side, as did the Faraday people. Even more fortunately, the RTZ senior people in London trusted Mark's judgment more than the Americans'. That was how we got trapped into the choice of giving in or selling the whole issue in Canada. Those tough Americans—I really do forget the name of the firm—threatened to write a formal complaint to the SEC and recommend ending the previous practice of using the private placement "out" for all future Canadian deals. We—my team: Sandy and Ivor who was by then in New York—decided we were not going to be bullied and that we could sell it ourselves, all in Canada. Ian and Deane backed us.

We were very fortunate in that RTZ had found a first rate new CEO for Rio Algom. His name was Bob Winters. I forget whether he had an industrial or financial background, but he had a fine technical grasp of what he was doing plus a wonderful personality. I remember that after our last "road show"—in those days we took groups of institutional buyers and salesmen from the other investment firms in our "selling group" to the mines, the smelters and the steel mills. The final event was a grand reception and dinner at the Toronto Club. We must have had over 100 senior investment officers there. Bob spoke to almost every one of them personally and treated even the youngest and most junior like an old friend. I was very impressed. Bob went on into government and became Canada's Minister of Industry. Sadly, he died before the age of 60—of a heart attack while playing tennis at the Badminton & Racquet Club.

Our real problem was pricing the issue. I think we ended up at an interest rate of 4.5%. The trouble was that the investment management industry was just getting started in Canada around then. As the issue was a subject of much discussion in the market because of the circumstances, some of the professional managers made quite a production about the appropriate rate. Naturally enough, they were trying to get the highest interest rate for their clients while we were doing our best for RTZ, Bob Winters and Mark Turner. We ended up pricing it at about 25 basis points (0.25%) below what the buyers said they wanted, but still selling it all and having a decently small price premium in the after market. We took a huge underwriting risk. While we had commitments from institutions and our selling group for half the issue, had the market in general turned against us, we could have lost a lot of money, plus some reputation. Of course, that was where our large retail sales force was very helpful.

An interesting end to this story is what happened to the man from Brooklyn—Samuel Hirschorn. Besides buying uranium mines, he bought paintings—wholesale! He would go into an art gallery—in Toronto or Montreal or New York—look around and, quite often, say to the owner: "I like it. I'll take it." The happy owner would say "which one." The answer was "all of them." Finally, he decided to donate them to the people of Canada, where he had made most of his millions. His proposal was to build a gallery in Ottawa to house his collection, estimated to be worth about $400 million then. His only condition was that it was to be called the Hirschorn Gallery. The powers that be in Ottawa in charge of that kind of thing said public galleries cannot be named after living people. That is how the Smithsonian came to have the Hirschorn Gallery … it was more interested in the collection than the name. I only met him once. That was on a road show, when we were taking a group of institutional investors to visit some of his new uranium companies. All I can remember was that he was short, chubby and prematurely bald. He was the exact opposite of Bob Winters in appearance and personality. But he had a heart of gold, as well as a pot of uranium.

A Superior Propane saga was the first of several problem events to occur during my tenure as head of ITD. It occurred in 1957 or '58. The first word of a "problem" came from John Yarnell, a good client of our money market group who was V.P Finance of Gulf Canada, a wholly owned subsidiary of Gulf Oil. John asked me to drop by, which I did, just thinking it was something to do with our routine business. So, it was a bit of a shock when he told me that they were about to make a public bid (at a reasonable premium over the current market) for a controlling interest in Superior Propane, but wanted to let NT know first. He showed me the press release that they were going to wire to the Toronto Stock Exchange once we concluded our conversation. This was about half an hour before the market close on a Friday afternoon, which was all very proper. I don't remember what we actually said then, but I imagine it was probably just a cordial exchange of immediate thoughts of the next steps. But I think I asked him why Gulf would want it. I think his answer was something to do with vertical integration. The next conversation was back in our office with Ian Crookston, who had yet to see the TSE announcement. He was furious as he looked upon Superior Propane as his "baby"—not an unreasonable attitude for the founder of a successful company.

The subsequent discussions between those of us directly involved—Ian, Jim Stewart (the author of our research report), Monty and me—was a little more focused. We noted that Gulf's formal bid documentation had lots of questionable detail. The most important item was that it was only for about 60% of the stock, which would leave the minority shareholders in a very vulnerable position. It also said we could not declare any dividends during the bid period without invalidating their price. It was clear they were confident that the shareholders would jump at the price and thus their offer would be over subscribed. Ian wanted to fight the bid. The rest of us—supported by Deane—felt that fighting it was not in the best interests of our investors. But we were prepared to try for better terms. The first thing the company did, at Ian's suggestion, was to declare immediately a special dividend that had the effect of increasing their cost by about five percent. The next were company press releases saying the stock was worth much more. Our best move, though, was to get TSE support that they should bid for 100% of the stock so there would not be a disadvantaged minority who would see the price drop substantially from the takeover bid level. The end result was that Gulf did bid for 100% —at their original price.

The last act in this saga, which turned out to be a mistake, was Ian calling a meeting of the institutional shareholders, of which about 90% had bought the stock a year or so earlier on our recommendation. Ian's pitch was just that the stock was worth more. The investors, who had doubled their money in the year, just didn't buy his case. Monty, Jim and I found it hard not to agree with them. The problem was Ian was the typical high level relations man. The technical stuff, even the obvious, was beyond him. The end result was that Gulf got 100% of the company and its investors, Ian included, made a lot of money. Whether Gulf ever made a decent return on their money is a question only they can answer. After the rather public fight we put up, the Toronto Stock Exchange established guidelines for takeover bids that required all shareholders to be bought out at the same price if control was being sought. In the meantime, we all looked a little foolish for antagonizing our investors. Certainly, we got them a few dollars more through the special dividend, but not enough to compensate for all of the pressure we put on them. We had done some good for the quality of the market by getting the takeover rules changed, but that also made as many corporate enemies as friends.

Another fight where I was a fringe player concerned the takeover by the Province of British Columbia of B.C. Electric ("BCE"), the main hydroelectric power company in that province. On this occasion, I was helping Deane as Power Corporation had founded the company and Power was still a substantial shareholder. And, needless to say, NT wanted to continue to make money selling new preferred stocks and bonds for BCE. It was, of course, basically a political issue. The BC government at the time was out for votes and taking over a company controlled by "Easterners" and promising lower electricity rates was good for votes. For some time, rumors had come and gone, which had a depressing effect on BCE's stock. It was off some 50% from its "high" when the bid was finally made at a "generous" 30% premium over the then lower market. Of course, Power and NT made the point that even the previous high price—which was well above the takeover bid—seriously undervalued the company's real worth. My best—or worst—memory of this fight was a meeting with the Provincial Treasurer. This was pure coincidence in that, weeks before, I had made an appointment with him for a Monday morning at 9.00 AM to talk about our money market business. I had arrived in Victoria the night before. I heard on the news that night that the government had just announced its bid. I phoned Deane, but he was away for the weekend somewhere. Not having any better plan, I showed up at 9.00 on the dot for my meeting. I think the Treasurer was as embarrassed as was I. We chatted a bit about the money market then got into the bid. I muttered something about the pricing being a bit unfair—which it was, especially as it was really an expropriation rather than just a bid. But the comment he finally made has stayed with me, and it reflects the regional differences and tensions in Canada that remain still. It was: "You people from Canada don't understand our problems." I had always thought British Columbia was part of Canada even if it was on the other side of the Rocky Mountains.

There were also several other deals in that early period where I had a secondary role. One was the takeover of Canadian Oil Companies Limited ("COL"), an affiliate of Power Corporation, by Shell Oil of Canada. This happened about a month after we received one of the firm's largest ever brokerage orders from a U.S. institution. Our research department had just published a brilliant report on Canada's oil industry. It recommended, amongst other things, the sale of COL. The market, rightly, assumed we must have talked to the management and got

Nesbitt, Thomson ... Mainly Doing

their OK, as we had done with our report on pipeline companies. I happened to be making my annual call on Shell Oil of Canada and, as the report was hot off the press, and I knew they were a large holder of COL, I convinced them to sell. You can imagine the repercussions when they heard about the takeover bid at about 50% more than their selling price. We were lucky they did not file a formal complaint with the SEC, or sue us. There was no way they would believe that we, as investment bankers for both COL and Power, did not know what was going on. I certainly did not. But it became clear to all when Ian Crookston got Shell to appoint NT as their agent for the bid that Ian knew. After that, it was a fight between Deane, on behalf of Power, and Ian, for Shell. But money talks and Deane got over it. No one remembered the brokerage commission I had earned, but a lot of COL shareholders remembered my role in "touting" our research recommendation. I only wished my role had been even smaller. As it was, I had had a good relationship with COL's VP Finance before the bid, both through selling their commercial paper and also because I came up with an idea that produced quite a bit—some $20 million—as I recall it, of new equity that they needed but did not think they could get at the price I arranged. Actually, it was a simple arbitrage deal. They had warrants outstanding that were about to expire and the market had fallen below the exercise price. But the difference was small so we simply agreed to buy the warrants at the few pennies anxious holders were willing to take, exercising them, and then billing COL for the difference, plus a 2% commission. The net price to COL was only about 5% below the exercise price. Had they had to do a new stock issue, they would have been lucky to get the money at 15% below. Unfortunately, the Shell people, after they paid their advisory fee to us, didn't do any more business with NT. I guess they felt that Ian— a friend of the bosses in London—had got his reward and they felt Deane, who had fought hard in the background for Power Corporation, had to be punished. Watching Deane and Ian involved in verbal combat was interesting, but getting caught in the middle was painful.

For whatever reason, I also rather enjoyed the internal administrative schemes in which I became involved, or actively promoted. In retrospect, one of the main reasons I got into this side was because one of

70

my best personal friends—then and now—was Michael Koerner. Michael came from a Czech family that immigrated to Vancouver in the 1930s. We met at the Royal Canadian Yacht Club one day when he and his wife Sonja were playing chess at the swimming pool. My former wife and I also played. That led to talking and, eventually, to Michael and me being partners in a Star Class racing boat. We participated in the RCYC Star Class races almost every Saturday and many Wednesday evenings for years. Michael and I never had any business dealings and never once even had lunch together during the business week. But we would often talk about business in general. As an engineer and an MBA, he knew a lot more about the "nuts and bolts" than I did as someone with only a BA in political science and economics. He was an early venture capitalist and we used to talk about his companies. Once, he showed me around one of his factories that was in the plastic extrusion business. He introduced me, at the time, to such erudite concepts as cost accounting and profit center accounting. More importantly, he made it clear that Canadian investment firms were a generation behind U.S. firms in management technology. He also gave me the idea of having a strategic review of the firm done by McKinsey. This led me to learning about how U.S. firms operated and to seeing Merrill Lynch as a form of model for NT. I was fascinated by his experiences and ideas, and grateful for what he taught me in our many casual conversations. Michael's main hobby, though, was 14th century harpsichord music. I have a disc that he gave me of some he composed in that style himself. Knowing of Geoffrey Payzant's similar interests, I introduced them and they became good friends.

Continuing a bit on the personal side, I would begin a transition to Montreal that would take some months. During this period I stayed at my favorite Montreal hotel, the Ritz, Monday through Thursday. The best part of that is, most evenings I had my pre dinner martini, followed by Dover Sole for dinner at the Ritz's "Maritime Bar." It had a fine ambience as well as a competent barman and an excellent chef. It is such a shame that, when the Ritz was reconstructed about five years ago, they replaced the Maritime Bar with a very mundane bistro.

Talking Deane and Ian into hiring McKinsey and, later, agreeing to

71

reorganizing our accounting systems around the profit center and product costing concepts was not easy. We were the first Canadian investment firm to do this and it made for efficiency, but also a lot of tension. These efforts started in about 1960 and culminated in 1967 when I was made executive vice president (COO). This involved my moving to Montreal and, naturally, upsetting Ian as he saw this as my giving my full allegiance to Deane. This was understandable as Ian had been a strong supporter and I had often supported him in his differences with Deane. But I saw myself, naively, as just trying to bring the firm into the 20th century by following and implementing McKinsey's recommendations. These were fairly straightforward—an organizational chart and job descriptions, plus an ownership structure where the higher your rank, the more stock you should have. It also included a profit center accounting system and a management information system. A comment made 20 years later about my work then really touched me. It was by Tom Kierans, who had succeeded me as COO in 1968, He had gone on to be CEO of another major Canadian investment firm—McLoed, Young, Wier. He said NT still had the reputation of having the best management information system in Canada, and it hadn't changed since my day. So, at least in Canada, I was certainly a financial frontiersman. It wasn't hard—at least the idea of copying what U.S. firms were doing wasn't. Implementing the plan was another matter.

Perhaps I should have stopped there and just been a dutiful COO to Deane—who had agreed to everything I proposed. Unfortunately I felt there was more to do to make NT stronger and more profitable. Perhaps I was a bit terrified by the fact that I had just borrowed some $200,000 in order to move up to the 5% ownership level. Five percent was the level that had to be disclosed to the securities commissions and stock exchanges those days so that the investing public knew who was in charge. Naturally, under the new McKinsey/Gill rules, as executive vice president, I had to be one of them. We actually issued additional stock so all of those in the senior positions could buy up to their appropriate levels. Much to my surprise, borrowing 95% of the amount I needed was easy. In fact, as my good friend from the Bank of Nova Scotia, Bob MacIntosh, called to offer whatever financing I needed, I didn't even think of asking any other bank. I was amazed and embarrassed to get a call from my branch manager at the Royal Bank of Canada, where I had a personal account, that he felt very concerned that I hadn't asked him for the money as "The Royal" was NT's "house ban." Thinking about it now, it told you something about banking practices—or the strategic objectives of Canadian banks. Would a bank normally lend that kind of money to an individual to buy stock in a small private company—unless they wanted to take it over? That, of course, is exactly what happened, but not for another 20 years. In the meantime, I had about $50,000 equity in an approximately $300,000 investment in an illiquid stock. Because of my father's influence and his experience, I was not really that much of a gambler. But it was part of the deal as I saw it. That is probably why I forged ahead with some other internal "improvements" that were not entirely popular and probably contributed to my eventual downfall.

The easy one—in theory—was restructuring the firm from one that was controlled by the regional mandarins to one controlled by the functional experts. We established vice presidents for each of equity, long-term bonds and money markets who controlled all activities in their respective functional areas throughout the firm. This left the branch office managers with only administrative and relationship responsibilities. Of course, it offended some of them, and most were now directors of the firm. One was Joe Wilson, manager of our New York office, who was not happy about losing total control. But New York provided a good example of the benefits of profit center accounting. Joe often noted the profit margin of his NYSE stock trading operation. But he had ignored the capital requirements and thus was upset to find that, when a cost of capital was applied, it was losing money. That most companies in all industries go through cycles of changing from regional to functional control and back again every five or ten years was not something I realized then. Nor did I realize the level of resentment it would cause. But Deane and Ian backed me, so it happened. It was really just extending the ITD approach to the whole firm.

The most depressing and stressful administrative responsibility was presiding over a ten-percent staff cut when Canada, and NT, were going through a major recession in about 1967. More by luck than judgment I had, a year before, given Deane a little two page strategy paper—part of my responsibilities, I thought. Basically, it made two points. First, the trend in the industry was for bigger, full-service firms: the alternative was to be a small boutique. NT was neither and had to choose. Second, our profit margin on revenue was about 0.5% so we could not survive a serious business downturn operating the way we were. I don't think Deane paid any attention. The key point was the second one. The new profit center accounting system showed we were too dependent on our retail branch network that depended on high volume brokerage business. Further, while the salesmen's remuneration was mainly commissions, the fixed cost ratio was still high. Thus, a serious market downturn and a commensurate drop in volume would produce losses quickly. I calculated that it would only take about a 10% decline in volume to put us in the red. It happened about a year later. Fortunately, my staff cut-back program was quickly accepted. Even more fortunately, we were able to work it all out down to the last individual to be dropped without any breaches of security. We announced it on a Friday night and it was completed on Monday. Very painful, but at least it was quick.

I had another rather stressful experience in my first year as COO. This one was on the operational side. Shortly after I moved to Montreal, Deane agreed to buy as principal Canadian Pacific Railways' $50 million of Trans Canada Pipe Lines stock. That is, he committed the firm to buy it at a discount of about 5% below the Toronto Stock Exchange closing price that day. Then, we had to sell it. For a firm with only about $5 million capital at the time, this was a huge risk. Under NYSE rules then—and Toronto rules now—we would have had to have "free capital"—working capital to meet various levels of margin requirements for customer accounts, securities on our books, etc.—of one-third of the $50 million before we would have been allowed to make the purchase even if we had advance orders from buyers. Again, that was the kind of thing Deane did. He told only Bob Learn as VP Sales and me what he intended to do. We had to be geared up to get all our producers to make the sales calls. It was a great relief to get it all sold in a day. Fortunately, the market was on our side.

In those early days, I instituted another change I had learned from watching Merrill Lynch. That was setting up a management training program by hiring bright young business school graduates and giving them a year's training with experience in each of our major departments. We hired about a dozen over the next two years. The ones I remember the most were Jaime Clarke, who we sent to London on the money market side, David Lake, who became a first class research type, and Laurence Bloomberg, who stayed on the equity side. Jaime is still in London and still a good friend. He moved from investment banking to property and now, in his retirement, is an even more serious sailor and Commodore of a prestigious yacht club in Cowes and London. (I'm reminded of the times, years later, when I would crew for Jamie in Saturday races on my way home from visits to Asia after a Friday overnight flight to London, a train to Southampton and a ferry to Cowes.) Laurence had his own investment firm in Toronto and was one of the major players. At around that period, we also sought out good young people with special qualifications. One was Jim Meekison, from Vancouver. Jim was one of the few Canadian Harvard MBAs at the time and we didn't have one. I think it was Sandy Watt who found him, working for what was then W.E. Hutton, a good New York firm in the middle league. Sandy persuaded him to come back to Canada to join our corporate finance department. He was a breath of fresh air for NT. Sadly, though, he left a few years after I did. Happily for him, he made a lot of money as a venture capitalist at the beginning of the cable TV era. Another was Brian Aune, also from Vancouver. He had, in his 20s, made a reputation as an excellent CPA. He was Tom Kierans' discovery. I heard later that he was surprised to find he was hired after a fifteen-minute interview with me. I guess no one had thought to tell him that he had already been "interviewed" by quite a few of our people. We must have had good judgment. After some five years he became Deane's "number two" after Tom Kierans, who succeeded me, resigned. Brian then became CEO when Deane died.

During this period, I attended a number of management courses arranged by the U.S. Investment Bankers' Association. They helped me a great deal with many of the administrative issues I had to address in much the same way my involvement with the U.S. Securities Analysts' Association helped me with that side. I only remember one such meeting, but that was for a quite different reason. We received word of the Cuban missile crisis during it. I recall taking a call from Sandy Watt and our trading people asking for instructions. Both the stock and bond markets had dropped. More importantly to us, our bond trading portfolio had taken a big "hit." The question was, should we do nothing, buy more, or sell. We decided to buy more—as we were talking government bonds there was no issue about free capital—just the risk/reward calculation. We decided if there was all out war we would probably all be killed so it didn't matter what we did with our portfolio. But, if the crisis went away, doubling up would make us a lot of money. It was a pretty easy decision. Of course, none of us realized how close we were to the other outcome.

The U.S. Securities Analysts' Association was a good learning experience for me, as well as a source of clients as their meetings were attended by institutional investors and economists as well as by analysts from securities firms. However, seeing how it was so dominated by the U.S. firms, I felt that we Canadians should have our own. I spent a fair amount of time lobbying the CEOs or COOs of other Canadian firms to back the idea and put up some seed capital by way of appointing some of their analysts as the first fee paying members of the Canadian Securities Analysts' Association. Of course, we affiliated ourselves with the U.S. organization. I became one of the founding directors although I was not an analyst. This was around the time that U.S. analysts decided to establish professional qualifications. That was how the now well known Chartered Financial Analysts (CFA) qualification requirement began. Probably the most useful thing we did, though, was to publicize the importance of higher (U.S.) standards of research and put pressure on Canadian stock exchange listed companies to provide the needed detail in their financial reports. For example, at the time, there was no legal requirement for consolidated financial statements in Canada. This came to a head with a drive to get the press interested. This worked, and the following story tells the tale.

Dominion Stores and Loblaws, two Toronto Stock Exchange listed

76

companies, could not have been more similar at the time. Both were in the food supermarket chain business, both had about the same levels of reported sales, profits and assets. There were only two important distinguishing factors. First, Loblaws was closely controlled by a single family while Dominion Stores' stock was mainly in the hands of the public. Second, the stock market price-earnings ratio given to Loblaws' stock was only about half that of Dominion Stores' price-earnings ratio. Why was there such a wide pricing discrepancy? The answer was that the family controlling Loblaws and their managers had a reputation for secrecy whereas Dominion Stores' reporting was of the highest quality. Key points were that Loblaws did not provide consolidated financial statements while Dominion Stores did. Loblaws did not disclose its ownership in some of its subsidiaries, let alone provide financial information on them. Dominion Stores disclosed everything.

Also in Canada then, corporate governance was weak. However, with the growing number of U.S. investment firms in the Canadian securities markets, pressure from Canadian members of the financial community grew to force better disclosure. The Canadian Financial Analysts' Society took the lead in drawing attention to the problem. The Loblaws—Dominion Stores comparison was the perfect case. After about a year's pressure—both discrete with Loblaws' owners and management and through press articles making comparisons with Dominion Stores—Loblaws finally changed its ways and produced financial information as good as Dominion Stores'. The result, as expected, was that Loblaws' stock's price-earnings ratio increased to the level of Dominion Stores', practically doubling its market value. The lesson is that shareholders of listed companies with devious reporting practices pay dearly through low valuations of their stocks. We, in the CSAS, were pretty pleased about this. Consolidated financial reports became the standard after that.

Around that time, Bill McDougall had suggested to Ian Church, then Chairman of Church Shoes, that he should talk to me about raising money to build their proposed new factory in Canada. Ian was an old friend of Bill's and he had introduced us some years previously. In those days, companies expanding abroad stuck to prudent financing rules.

They raised long term fixed rate debt in the local currency to finance 50% or so of the plant costs. This matched both the life of the plant with the term of the debt and the currency of the expected revenues with the currency of the debt that had to be serviced. That is quite a contrast to what happens these days. In any event I was very pleased NT was given the opportunity to finance an English household-name company. I turned the deal over to one of our young and bright team members, John Moore. John was then on the bond trading desk and I thought this, as a private placement, would be a good experience for him. Unfortunately, it turned out Church Shoes only needed $500,000. But John went to work and raised the money through a first mortgage bond issue that was purchased by a Toronto insurance company. As always, the problem with a small issue is that the absolute dollar cost of doing the deal was about the same as the cost of a large deal. Unfortunately, though, the fee structure was conventionally a percentage and it was hard to ask more than 1.0%. That was $5,000, which barely covered our costs. Still, it was good experience for John and a good lesson for us. We had hoped that this loss leader would give us other opportunities to work with Ian Church's company and that the deal could leader to bigger ones with U.K. companies. But that didn't happen. For me, though, it served me well with my next similar, but much larger, private placement for the local subsidiary of a well known foreign company. That occurred when I joined Schroders.

Probably what consumed most of my time in that early period as COO was a major crisis with one of our underwriting accounts. It was a major problem for me and was partially of my own making. It was a long drawn out saga ending with the restructuring of Laurentide Financial Corporation ("LFC"). Laurentide was a Vancouver based sales finance and leasing company that had been started by two young Hungarian immigrants fresh from the University of British Columbia. It had just become a new affiliate of Power Corporation—one of the last deals organized by Peter Thomson. It was a successful company growing rapidly and recently listed on the TSE. Maurice Strong, then president of Power, wanted me to be on the board as NT would be in the market for LFC bond issues frequently. He felt that there should be

78

some independent directors. Then, there were just the two owners and two from Power on the board. Maurice and I agreed Ivor Murray should also be on the board as, being then our man in New York, he was the direct line to the U.S. institutional buyers of LFC's debt and to their U.S. banks. Deane was less enthusiastic as he considered it a bit speculative. But, as this was my first experience as a director of another company listed on a major stock exchange, his quiet warning escaped me. That was a serious mistake at the time, but I like to think I was vindicated eventually.

My future was at stake here because I was already losing supporters within the firm as a result of the impact of the reorganization along functional lines and the profit center accounting system. The two owners of LFC before Power entered the picture, Peter Paul Saunders and Andrew Saxton, started out with no money and one small transaction—the financing of a second hand car for $1,500. They borrowed the money from a bank as a personal loan and, according to them, learned the first lesson in consumer finance the hard way. They were so engrossed in establishing their company and doing their first lending that they forgot to get the chattel mortgage document on the car. So, instead of having some useful collateral, they had just made an unsecured consumer loan. Fortunately, the borrower was equally ignorant—and honest—and eventually paid all his interest and principal. In any event, five years later they had a public company with a net worth of about $50 million (a lot of money in those days.) with one of Canada's most important companies as their major shareholder.

For the next few years, Laurentide continued to produce good results and the board was content with its half page of financial highlights produced by management for each quarterly meeting. LFC expanded into the U.S., U.K., France and the Caribbean markets. Everything was fine until Canada suffered a financial crisis in 1967 following rapidly escalating interest rates and a collapse of another medium sized finance company, mainly because of fraud. High interest rates and the consequent economic slowdown resulted, for LFC, in a decline in revenues, increasing interest costs and increasing losses from the portfolio. Its stock and bonds declined in the markets, and its bank lenders became nervous.

The board started asking questions. The banks threatened to cancel their lines of credit unless there was a special audit. The auditors, in doing this, became more diligent. This audit, when presented to the board, showed the fine record of increasing profits was much helped by management's internal accounting practices which "front ended" much of the revenue from new business, but amortized the expenses related to it over the life of the loans. This practice had been acceptable to the auditors. The problem with that approach was that, while during periods of increasing business profits accelerated, in a recession, losses accelerated. Management made two mistakes. First, they assumed that they could expand the loan portfolio indefinitely, thereby producing ever-higher rates of profit growth. Second they did not disclose these accounting practices to the directors or to the banks—helped by the fact that the auditors did not feel the need to explain the accounting practices in the Notes to the audited statements and that the directors did not ask the pertinent questions. Ironically, even if we (the non-LFC directors) had asked and been told, probably we would not have objected. It is said that ignorance of the law is no excuse. Fortunately, in those days, that saying did not say ignorance of accounting practices is no excuse. So we directors escaped serious blame even if we did look pretty stupid in hindsight. The Enron scandal sounds faintly similar—the only difference is that in those days we didn't know better.

The first day of reckoning came when the auditors insisted that revenue and expense recognition policies had to be changed and the previous years' financial figures restated. For the then current year, LFC was also required to increase provisions against the loan portfolio because of the impact of the recession on collections. Added to these changes was the effect of higher borrowing costs. Needless to say LFC also had been booking income on a front-loaded cash basis, rather than the more appropriate accrual basis. Also, it was a fixed interest rate portfolio, albeit the average term was short—less than two years—but most of the borrowing was floating rate call loans. The only good news was that there was not a hint of fraud and practically all of the other Canadian sales finance companies were in the same embarrassing leaking boat. The result for LFC was substantial losses and an almost complete wipe out of the company's net worth. As both the bank loans and collateralized debt—a form of first mortgage bonds—had covenants requiring minimum ratios of net worth to debt, the banks tried to call their loans and the institutions threatened to declare "technical defaults" on the bond issues they held. It was a sign of the times that the banks and the institutions, as one of their covenants in their loan agreements, required that the average term of the company's debt be no more than two years to reflect the average term of the loan portfolio and the fact that short term loans were less expensive than long term loans. In the process of digging ourselves out of this mess, we found the lenders now insisted on average borrowing terms of no less than two years. It was a complete reversal—but a sensible one. The problem was getting the money to achieve the bail-out.

Power Corporation and Nesbitt, Thomson behaved responsibly. The first step was to fire the two founders and require them to sell their multiple-vote controlling stock to Power, placing it in full control. For better or worse, I was the one to recommend these steps. I recall still the look of complete shock on the face of my good friend Paul Paine, who was LFC's outside counsel at the time. "How could we do this? They— Peter Paul and Andrew—were no more to blame than anyone else!" My response was simply that, if Power expected NT to raise the money to save the company, it could only be done if we had new management that the banks and the bond buyers would trust as "new brooms." Put simply, we had to find a new CEO who had both a good track record in the same business and a level of personal maturity that none of the others in the company had. It was a hard decision for me too, because I quite liked both Peter Paul and Andrew and did agree that we were all to blame for not doing a thorough job. The important thing was, if Power stood by Laurentide, Ivor and I were confident we could bail them out. Peter Paul and Andrew agreed to this because they recognized that, without Power Corporation's support, the company would be bankrupt and their stock would be worthless. We were very fortunate in finding a new chief executive—"Gig" Gigline—who had been the COO of a major U.S. sales finance company. In the hiring process, he visited me at home. We hit it off immediately although, as a Californian in his sixties, we didn't have much in common at the time. With new management approved by it, Power Corporation committed to a substantial new equity investment, and NT committed to underwrite a convertible subordinated debenture issue. Once we had our new CEO, things went fairly quickly. In one day, I flew from Halifax (where I had had a prior commitment with our branch people) in the morning to Montreal. There, we hammered out the basic deal with Power. That afternoon, John Yarnell (previously Gulf Canada) and Tony Hampsen, the two Power people on the board, and I flew to Vancouver to make the final settlement with the two founders. The meeting that evening in Peter Paul's elegant new home in West Vancouver was quite an experience. They had agreed to sell out. The question was price. Peter Thomson and Maurice had given John and Tony full authority. So I just listened. The end result was they received $2 million for their shares. That was a lot of money forty-five years ago for an otherwise worthless company. They were pretty good negotiators, I thought.

These steps were part of a deal with the banks we worked out to get them to continue their support. Another part of the agreement with the banks was to allow them to place a senior credit officer in LFC's head office with access to anything he wanted. LFC also had to provide a new audit six months after the financing package was signed. One of my many unhappy memories of this saga was attending the annual shareholders' meeting, which occurred about three months after we had sold the convertible issue. The directors had to sit at the head table with the new management. Not surprisingly, well, not to us on the board, one of the resolutions involved suspending all dividend payments. I will never forget the look of dismay from an elderly gentleman who raised his hand, stood up and asked: "Does that mean you are not paying dividends on the preferred stock any more?" And heard the one word answer from the new CEO: "Yes."

Then came the second day of reckoning: the auditors produced their second report. More chastened, they demanded another major addition to provisions, resulting in another major loss for that year. Possibly because the banks had their own watchdog in Laurentide, who had not given any sign that there were still problems, it was hard for the banks to blame others. Consequently, we managed to survive that crisis too. But I learned a lot about the different ethics of U.S. banks and insurance companies in this period.

My first visit to one of our important U.S. institutional customers, which happened a year or so before the LFC debacle gives part of the flavor. He was the chief investment officer of the then U.S. Steel Corporation pension fund. After the opening pleasantries, he asked his question. "Mr. Gill, does your firm work by Wall Street rules or real estate rules?" I had not the slightest idea what he meant. He explained. "Wall Street rules mean a handshake, or even an agreement on the phone, is a commitment. Real estate rules meant that you do not have a deal until cash and contracts had been exchanged." How things have changed! In any event, the second LFC crisis led to two quite different experiences with U.S. institutions. The bad one was with the banks. Of the key banks, the Canadian banks and Morgan Guarantee stuck to the initial agreement. What was then First National City Bank (now Citibank) wanted to renegotiate. As a major player, it was impossible to ignore them. I pointed out that they were reneging when none of the others were. Their key man was very offended. But, we had to give in. The good experience was with the Equitable Life. Just before the crisis they had agreed to the key terms of a private placement of $25 million collateralized notes. The yield was fixed at 8.25% for 20 years, with the standard sinking fund and other covenants. Naturally, until the net worth was replaced, the deal was dead. Then, when the banks wanted to change some of the other covenants, Equitable wanted the same changes. By the time all this was settled, the whole interest rate structure of the market had worsened, and LFC's "going rate" had dropped another notch or two. But, the Equitable's position was they had agreed to the key terms and therefore those terms would not be changed. Had they worked on real estate rules, they could have asked for 10% rather than 8.25%!

In the end, a smaller Laurentide became again a profitable company. Of course, all the shareholders suffered financially for a while. Also, Power Corporation had its reputation tarnished, as did the auditors, NT and all the directors personally. The founders had their reputations destroyed. I survived in NT. Interestingly, my shares in the company recovered to the point where I actually had a profit. Even in those days, all directors of publicly listed Canadian companies also had to be shareholders. I have always been surprised that so few other countries have this requirement in their company laws. All involved recognized that these developments were in everyone's best interests. One of the many outcomes of this experience in Canada was a series of major changes to our company laws, which were Provincial laws. The key one was that all publicly listed companies had to have audit committees of their boards where a majority of the members were "independent" as opposed to management or representatives of controlling shareholders. This subject will come up again later when I get to my time with the World Bank–IFC.

Two other ideas I had after I had got through the LFC crisis was that NT should become a member of the New York Stock Exchange ("NYSE") and also—as a separate exercise—a member of an exclusive London financial "club." I shall write about the latter first.

Actually, the London scheme was far from being an idea of mine. Rather, it was the brainchild of John "Pilot" McIllhenny, who ran the money market department, and Duncan Smith, one of the bright young recruits in his money market department. Duncan, who was a thorough researcher, had noticed that the London "Discount Houses"—the group of 12 firms specially licensed by the Bank of England to deal in U.K. short term government debt—had a guaranteed profit in that the U.K. Treasury Bill rates always exceeded the Bank of England discount rate available only to this privileged group. At the time, the London market was more specialized than the U.S. or Canadian markets. In London, only the twelve Bank of England-approved Discount Houses could deal in short term government debt. Duncan, who had joined us two years previously, had been sent to London to head our small money market unit there—hence his interest. The main idea initially was to promote the new market for Eurodollar Certificates of Deposit—negotiable short-term deposits issued by banks. NT was in fact second only to FNCB (now Citibank) in doing this before it became big business for all the major U.S. firms. But this experience led to Duncan's proposal that we

84

should try to get into the London Discount House club. In any event, Duncan sold the idea to John, who sold it to me. I sold it to Deane and the rest. It took a long time, but Duncan, through careful courting of the man in charge in the Bank of England, eventually got us approved to operate in that market. Not as a fully fledged thirteenth member, but rather through the usual "old boy" arrangement under which the Bank of England "arranged" for the London clearing banks to give us lines of credit against treasury bills at the same rates provided to the "twelve." It was an intriguing experience, especially as Duncan was a Canadian from the west, from a Ukrainian immigrant family, who attended the University of Saskatchewan and thus was quite unknown in the markets. (Behind his back, in NT, he was called the "Dukabour." I forget exactly what that meant, but I think it was what members of a religious sect that had emigrated from the Ukraine were called.) It all rather proved that you didn't have to be an English "public school boy" with inside connections to get things changed in the "City" anymore. Our subsidiary, Nesbitt, Thomson Limited, did quite well in that business. Duncan proved the trust the Bank of England showed him—and NT. I had a call one day from Duncan saying the rumors about a Sterling devaluation were almost certainly true: we should hedge NT's capital in London. I agreed and asked what else we should do. He said nothing. Were we to short more Sterling than our own exposure, it would be breaking trust with our Brit friends. So we didn't. Ethical standards in the financial world were different in those days. There is more about Duncan later.

Joining the New York Stock Exchange was a lot harder. Our profit center accounting system had a lot to do with the idea of doing it. I found out two things. First, while we were doing a lot of NYSE business for our Canadian clients, it was costing us as we had to give up 60% of the commissions to the U.S. member firms through whom we worked. The arithmetic was such that we could recoup the then $500,000 cost to buy a seat in less than three years at our current level of business. The second was Joe Wilson's U.S. stock trading scheme was costing us money. So, why not just join the NYSE? This was easier said than done because, in those days, only U.S.-owned companies could be members. (One Canadian firm, Timmins, was a member from a hundred years back and had been "grandfathered" from this relatively new (about 1940) rule to keep out undesirables.)

I spent months lobbying both the NYSE administration and the SEC to get this rule changed, or an exception made to it. The breakthrough finally came as a result of a meeting at the SEC. My contact there, Irvin Pollack, was then director of the division that was responsible for market operations and registered "broker dealers." He was an absolutely wonderful person. There will be much more about Irv later when I write about my IFC incarnation. (By then, he had become the first staff member of the SEC to become an SEC Commissioner.) I was struck by one thing he just happened to mention when he was deciding whether or not to stick his neck out for us. We were talking about ethics in the business and discussing the SEC rules concerning owning and trading securities. He commented quite casually that he had his own rules for his personal investing. They were simple. He just did not invest in anything that was subject to SEC regulation. But that is another story. He invited the VP Administration of the NYSE—Bob Bishop—and me to attend a meeting with him. He gave a very simple message to Bob. "Change the rule or make an exception. If you don't, the SEC will make a formal recommendation that you do." I forget whether it was a change or an exception but a week later we received the official word that, were we able to buy a seat, we would be able to qualify for membership. Then the really hard work started. The system required the "seat" to be owned by an individual. So we hired a man who agreed to be an employee and enter into the complex arrangement whereby we lent him the $600,000 (the price had gone up over the year it took) to buy the seat. Then, we had to set up a wholly owned U.S. corporation that would be the nominal member firm of the NYSE that employed our "member"—the man who owned the seat who we had financed. At the time companies could not buy seats

Then, all of our people who actually wanted to place orders through our "member" and all our management group had to pass NYSE qualifying exams. Of course, we had to take the same kind of exams in Canada, but they were easier and involved only Canadian laws and regulations. The NYSE exams covered U.S. and State laws. The exams

1957–1969

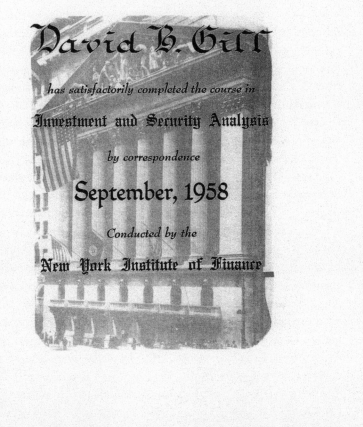

New York Institute of Finance

Successor to

New York Stock Exchange Institute

This is to Certify that

David B. Gill

has satisfactorily completed the course in

Investment and Security Analysis

by correspondence

September, 1958

Conducted by the

New York Institute of Finance

Robert Clunett 3rd
MEMBER, BOARD OF ADVISORS

Albert P. Squier
DIRECTOR

*Completion of the New York Institute of Finance, Investment and
Security Analysts course. September 1958.*

themselves were for three categories. First and easiest was the "brokers" or salesman's exam for the people who actually did the business with clients. Second, there was the office manager exam for the immediate supervisors. Finally, there was the "Affiliate Member" exam for the senior people. This meant Deane and Ian, as well as all our vice presidents had to take it. We all went to "school" for several months. Fortunately, everyone passed. But there was a lot of tension over this, with some of my colleagues claiming I had never told them about exams. As to my relationship with Deane, this must have been one of the last straws as, besides all the work and money, it meant we had to operate at a higher standard of ethics under stricter rules. While Deane and Ian and all of my colleagues were honest people, the standards in Canada were definitely lower than U.S. standards. They did not like the foreign-imposed discipline it required. It was good for our business overall, and certainly it enhanced our "bottom line," but that was another matter.

One thing I was pleased to have been associated with was supporting equal opportunities for women in the company. Ida Ludwick was an example. She started out as the secretary to our money market specialist (Ted Delahay) in our New York office. As our business expanded, she began to be an active assistant to Ted and learned the business. She was so good we started giving her accounts of her own to cover. This resulted in my first experience of gender discrimination. I, as the senior boss, was called by the treasurer of a big New York company that did a lot of money market business with us. He said he would not work with a woman and threatened to cut us off if we didn't put a man on their account. Ted and I talked it over and decided we would tell him we couldn't do that. Happily, and much to our surprise, he calmed down and continued to do business with us. I think, finally, he understood that she was just as good as any of the men he dealt with in other firms. My most vivid memory of her was the day, when I happened to be in New York, when the Six-Day war had just started. Knowing her background, I commiserated with her about it. Her comment was just to say how furious it was that she could not get back to Israel to join her army reserve unit. She added: "This will be the first war I have missed." She had real spirit, which she had already proven. Ida was a quiet, demure woman, despite her spirit. She was married to a delightful man, also in the financial business. Both she and he had suffered through the deaths of their previous spouses and both each brought up, alone, a young son. When they married, they went through the formal adoption process, which gave both kids the same last name and listed them as the parents in their passports. She had amusing stories to tell about going through immigration in several countries and having to explain how she and her husband could have two boys with only a three-month age difference.

By the time I left, of nine professionals in New York, four were women. The women were all paid on exactly the same basis as the men.

Beyond doubt, the most colorful person we had in New York or anywhere else was Frank Veneroso, an American with a BA in philosophy from Harvard. He always wore a three piece navy blue suit and white running shoes to the office—the latter, I guess, to go with his ponytail. But I will talk more about Frank later as he was bigger than life in NT and in my future life with the International Finance Corporation. It was Monty Gordon who brought him and his team of three others into the firm. Monty felt we could break into the U.S. institutional market as equity specialists—combining research with sales. This was the old ITD approach. So he hired away from another U.S. firm this "team" of four who did this, specializing in just a few industry groups. This was a relatively new approach for Wall Street and quite unknown in Canada—except for NT. But Monty was one our stars, so I backed him. It was a bit of a culture shock—two men and two women, and all of them dressed "smart casual" as is now in fashion again. Still, to see these four, three in sneakers, shirts and slacks, and Frank with his suit and ponytail, was quite something.

It is said about war that for 99% of the time it is sheer boredom, and for one percent, sheer terror. It is a bit like that in business to some extent. Most of the time is repetitive deal doing, meetings, planning and plotting, but all routine. I could sum up my 17 years with NT as seventeen years of "flogging" Canadian stocks and bonds to unwitting investors. But there were a lot of highlights—some rewarding and uplifting, and some best forgotten. One of the things rather forgotten is exactly how I managed to get myself from COO in head office to President of the U.S. subsidiaries. As hinted in several places earlier, I suppose I made more enemies than friends in the firm by pushing too many changes too quickly and not getting rid of more of the obvious competition in the firm soon enough. I was not much of a politician and, as Deane said once, to my everlasting annoyance, I was quite naive. Being all of about 40 at the time I was very offended. But he was right, even if it took me another 20 years to realize it. In any event, in 1968 I was asked to go to New York to run the small empire I had built there. Ian became President, until then one of Deane's titles.

In New York, I was a very small fish in a very large pond. Thus none of the deals in which I was involved were of much consequence. But I had a good team and we did some good things. One was the largest NYSE transaction of the year. One of our equity research team masterminded a takeover of another listed company for one of his clients. However, the tensions continued to grow and, as I was the senior person in the U.S. for the firm, I became increasingly concerned about the rather cavalier attitude towards the rules that my friends in Montreal and Toronto were showing. So I resigned in 1969.

On the personal side, I spent the work weeks of my first three months in New York living at the Sherry Netherlands Hotel, my old favorite there since my first visit in 1945. Looking back, the Sherry, the Ritz in Montreal and the Maurice in Paris were all in the same excellent league. Now, more recent experience in London leads me to include the Stafford as an equally fine place.

As over 40 years have passed, probably I have remembered more of the good than the bad. I hope my recollections of NT are reasonably accurate. But they are certainly not a complete history. I'm sure many of my old colleagues will have quite different recollections of many of the events I have described.

Before closing this chapter and moving on to the next phase of my life, I shall mention a few of the other events and activities that occurred in my other life. First, our son Christopher was born on 19 September 1959. Second, because my former wife, Ann, had had a series of serious illnesses, including several hospital stays, I finally resigned from the RCN Reserve in 1960. By then, I was "First Lieutenant" of HMCS

York, our Toronto reserve station. My next job would have been Training Commander, which should have meant my "brass hat," which is how we described Commanders and above. Looking back, I rather regret giving up that chance. But, once I had moved to Montreal, it would have been impossible anyway. It had been rather fun changing from being a "flyboy" to a "fish head." I had taken several two-week summer cruises since 1955 in Destroyers and Corvettes, so I learned a bit about ship handling and running ships' crews. I was also pleased to be taken seriously by the "fish heads" at York. My first job at York was the unpleasant task of being "officer personnel officer" which meant, then, firing from the Reserve some 600 officers who were still on the list, but never seen. That was no way to make friends. In fact, I very nearly lost my oldest and best friend, Bill MacDougall. Bill had gone off to London in 1953. I knew he spent some time with the Royal Navy Reserve and I just assumed he had switched services when it happened in 1960. "It" was his name was on a long list of the next batch to go, and I didn't notice. He didn't get the form letter warning him. Consequently, he was retired just two months before he would have become a Lieutenant Commander. He didn't mention his annoyance about that to me until some 20 years later.

I still have fond memories of my reserve time at "York." Naval shore stations were still called "stone frigates" but, in all other respects, they were run like ships. The job of the First Lieutenant—"Jimmy the One" or "One O," as they were called—was organizing and running the crew and maintaining discipline. This was not always so easy for "weekend warriors." I reported to the Commander, who reported to the Captain. In small ships, there was no Commander, but we had some 500 on the Active List so we were considered a big ship. I remember that, in practice, the most difficult job was making sure there was a duty officer "aboard" over the weekends. (Our regular service complement looked after the weekdays.) My good friend Hugh Franks was in charge of the Roster. We had a simple arrangement. If he could not get "volunteers," he had the duty. As a bachelor then, it wasn't that bad for him. Basically, if the junior officers didn't volunteer enough or failed to show up without due warning and a good excuse they risked being dismissed from the service. The fun part was after our Wednesday night "drills." We officers repaired to the Wardroom for a few drinks. After that, we would usually go to someone's house for some more. Often it was at Cavan Atkinson's, whose wife Peggy had a great reputation for providing smoked beef sandwiches. She was remarkably cheerful and gracious about this. Thursday mornings often came around very quickly. My last day in the Reserve was rather like the first, in that I was considerably embarrassed. On this occasion, my last duty was leading the "Toronto Garrison"—all the army, air force and naval units on 11 November Sunday. It was our Veterans' Day tribute. We marched down University Avenue, one of Toronto's main streets. The Lieutenant Governor of Ontario (the Queen's representative) and all the other military and civilian dignitaries assembled in front of the Cenotaph. As the navy was the senior service, we led the parade. As I was the First Lieutenant, I was out in front as "Parade Marshall," or some such exotic title. I only had to do three things. The first was to give the command to start and the last was the command to stop, both of which I managed to do. The trouble was with the second duty, which was to give the order—"Garrison, Eyes Right"—as we reached the saluting stand which, naturally, was on our right. For reasons I cannot understand, I said, "eyes left." Fortunately, all the units did the right thing. That wasn't too hard as each unit had its individual commander. What flashed through my mind as I did this was my first day in the Navy, arriving late for duty with a dozen others and being reprimanded by a Chief Petty Officer, which was pretty frightening then. No one said a word afterwards. Probably no one but my own Captain even noticed.

Besides many photographs of my time in the navy I have a document that I treasure. That is my formal "commission"—a piece of paper; they used to be on parchment but no longer, not even 52 years ago.

In Montreal I had two interesting non-business activities. One was thanks to George Vilim, who saw a great opportunity to escape himself from what he got me into. That was replacing him as board member and chief fundraiser for Les Grands Ballets Canadiens. This was the local ballet company, run by a charming Russian woman. The board was mainly French Canadian. It used to be said in those days that Mon-

Commission Warrant . . . David Bertram Gill hereby appointed Lieutenant-Commander in Her Majesty's Canadian Fleet, by Elizabeth the Second, 15 January 1955, in what would have been the end of the third year of Her Majesty's Reign. (With a thousand ships in World War II, many Canadians were affronted by calling it "Her Majesty's" Canadian Fleet.)

Elizabeth the Second,

by the Grace of God of the United Kingdom, Canada and Her other Realms
and Territories Queen, Head of the Commonwealth, Defender of the Faith.

To Mr. David Bertram Gill
hereby appointed Lieutenant=Commander
in Her Majesty's Canadian Fleet

We, reposing special Trust and Confidence in your Loyalty, Courage and In=
tegrity, do by these Presents Constitute and Appoint you a Lieutenant=Commander,
Royal Canadian Navy (Reserve), Willing and Requiring you from time to time to
repair on board and to take upon you the Charge and Command of Lieutenant=Com=
mander in any Ship or Establishment to which you may hereafter at any time be duly
appointed, or the Charge and Command of any other Rank to which you may be pro=
moted or appointed, strictly Charging and Commanding all the Officers and company
of the said Ship or Establishment subordinate to you to conduct themselves jointly and
severally in their respective employments with all due Respect and Obedience unto you
and you likewise to observe and execute the Queen's Regulations and Orders for the
Royal Canadian Navy and such Orders and Instructions as you shall from time to
time receive from Naval Headquarters or from your Superior Officers. Hereof nor
you nor any of you may fail as you will answer the contrary at your Peril. And for so
doing this shall be your Commission.

Given by Command of His Excellency the Governor General of Canada
This Thirty=first day March 1956 in the Fifth year
of Her Majesty's Reign.

With Seniority
Of 15th January 1955

Ralph Campriey
Minister of National Defence

treal was 50% English, 50% French and 50% Jewish. The funds came from the box office—about 25%, the Quebec government—about 25%, the English community—about 25%, the Jewish community—about 15% and from the French community—about 10%. This did not make fundraising easy. We were always on the edge of not being able to pay our dancers. Once, after getting an emergency loan from the Bank of Nova Scotia, I rather lost my "cool" as they say, and told the board that the French members simply had to do more. That was not well received but, as I said, I'm no politician. I still have fond memories of watching our dancers perform. I really believed that I was doing something good for some really talented and dedicated people.

The other activity was with the Metropolitan Montreal YMCA. Maurice Strong recruited me to reorganize their financial and administrative systems. It was an interesting task because the Montreal "Y" was a unique organization. It had about a dozen physical locations offering the usual services. It also ran a fully certified university called Sir George Williams College—now known as Concordia University. It had started out as a night school for mature students around the turn of the century. When I was involved it had several thousand students and offered several types of advanced degrees. As a member of the board of the "Y," I was also a member of the board of governors of the university. So, one year, dressed in very distinctive garb, I sat through a full day's graduation ceremony. Sadly, some Canadian extremists, following the anti-Vietnam War rioters, destroyed the university's computer center. It was really tragic because many students had master's degree and PhD theses wiped out. No one was caught and so no one was punished. The innocent just suffered.

I forget whether this was before or after—or during—the "Quebec libre" disturbances helped on by General de Gaulle who actually said "vivre la Quebec libre" at a public meeting somewhere. It certainly gave encouragement to the crazies to do even worse things. We lived in Westmount—the English Canadian enclave that was just a 45-minute walk from the office. Pierre Trudeau, our Prime Minister at the time, did very much the right thing. After a period of escalating violence, including bombings and the kidnapping of an English diplomat in Montreal, he declared martial law. The troops he called out to protect us in West-mount were from a French Canadian regiment. It was a very smart move. On my route to and from the office, I passed a soldier every 100 yards or so. It was both comforting and eerie to be walking past these very young looking French Canadians in full battle equipment including loaded rifles or machine guns. The closest we came to harm was much at a distance. A bomb at the U.S. Consulate that happened to be close by blew-out some of our windows. Some friends, though, had a very lucky escape. Bill Turner, who had succeeded Maurice Strong as President of Power Corporation and thus an obvious target, had a pipe bomb inserted in a drainage pipe of his house. Fortunately, one of the "gang" had a conscience and warned the police 30 minutes before it was timed to go off. The police disarmed it in time so this woman probably saved the lives of the eight or so children that were in the Turner's house and the one next to it. It was an interesting coincidence that I had first met Trudeau at a "fundraiser" at Bill Turner's house when Trudeau was first running for Parliament. I remember him as a quiet but engaging man. He seemed to me very short to be a modern politician. I met him again a few years later when he was Prime Minister. This was at Peter New-man's house in Ottawa. At the time Peter was Ottawa correspondent for Canada's leading news magazine and already a highly regarded author of several biographies of distinguished Canadians. I forget the event, but Trudeau showed up for an hour. He hadn't changed much. One would never have guessed he was our P.M. He just mingled with the other guests and chatted quietly with most of us, one on one.

One very pleasant interlude was a holiday trip to the south of France in 1967. Three Gills, Mathew and Bets Ann Page Wood and a mutual English friend, Donald Pierce, drove from London. It was my first time on an air freighter carrying the two cars and us from Dover to Etaples, then on to Paris where we had lunch in the bar at the Ritz—chicken sandwiches and champagne. Our first nights were at a five star hotel in the Loire Valley. I forget where we stayed in the south. But I do remember I was the "paymaster" for the trip. As it was before the days of credit cards I paid the bills with wads of Francs. In those days we were relatively well off and life in France was much cheaper than now, so we had the best of everything. This reminds me of another trip with the Page Woods. This was to the Moet e Chandon estate near Epernay. I don't remember how it was arranged, as the weekend was really for wine merchants who were promoting their champagne. It was an elegant affair—waiters in "white tie," serving '59 for lunch and '55 for dinner. What was touching was the story told by the widow of the owner. During the German occupation starting in 1940, the 200 staff bricked half the wine cellar to save it from the Germans. They were suspicious, but no one broke the secret despite the fact that the Germans took off the proprietor and executed him.

So, except for taking a two-week Berlitz "French Total Immersion" course, that about sums up my experience of French Canada, working at NT's head office and visiting France. Unhappily, as everyone knows, languages were never my strong point. I had some 600 words of French learned at high school when I went to Montreal. Despite much effort my vocabulary did not increase and neither did my ability to string the words together to make intelligible sentences. But that did not prevent me from making some good French speaking friends in Montreal and later. One of my oldest friends from my Montreal days is Pierre Desjardin, an old Montrealer and sailing buddy. After retiring for the second time, he took up painting and has become quite successful at it. He even manages to compete quite well with Jane, his wife, who has been painting for some 40 years. Likewise, Paul Vien, who became NT's manager for Quebec, was a wonderful fellow. We kept in touch for years after we both resigned from NT. Also, I kept in touch with Charlie Bourque, my first pilot in 825 Squadron. On one of my NT branch office visits in about 1968, I recall spending a night with him and Pat, his wife. Charlie, at the time, was Commanding Officer of the RCN shore based squadron at "Patricia Bay," just north of Victoria, B.C. We had a pleasant evening reminiscing about "the good old days" when we had both been 20 year olds as the first Canadian Navy "crew" in our first squadron, back in 1946. He took me for a ride in one of their "Avengers." It was almost 15 years since I had flown in a military aircraft. It was also my last flight in one. I missed the military "jet age" entirely. Charlie died in 1988.

A sad part of these last years at NT was the collapse of my marriage to Ann, before I moved to New York. A happier part of that ending was my marriage to Lena to whom my good friend Bill MacDougall's wife, Ann Marie, who is also Swedish, had introduced me.

I had resigned from NT after seventeen years with a three-month settlement check, plus the proceeds from the sale of my NT stock. It was a mater of principle. I had no other job in sight. It was a foolish thing to do, but it worked out well in the end.

Lena in our motorboat near our home, with her nephew Erik who was visiting from Sweden

CHAPTER III

Schroders ... A New World: 1970–1971

My decision to resign from Nesbitt, Thomson was a hard one. On the one hand, I had lots of good friends there and 17 years was 17 years. On the other hand, I was rather side tracked and I was unhappy with the way the firm was run, with Deane Nesbitt and Ian Crookston constantly feuding as to who was in charge. The deciding factor, though, was my concern that their disregard for U.S. regulations made me very uncomfortable. I was the one the U.S. SEC would come to first. In any event, there I was in late 1969, voluntarily unemployed, and with lots of obligations. Looking back, I'm not sure that was the best way to change a career, but it gave me some personal satisfaction. Lena and I had quite a laugh about it. Here I was depending on her salary from the Swedish Tourist Office in New York for our survival.

I had several choices of what to do. I could return to Canada and work for a Canadian firm, or stay in New York and work for an American Firm. I had got to know the then president of Merrill Lynch, who was also an expatriate Canadian. This was mainly while trying to learn to emulate the things they did well. To my embarrassment on one of those occasions, I must have gone too far. He interrupted me and said: "Do you mean Nesbitt is for sale? We might be interested." I had to retract quickly as Deane would never have sold out and, at that time, neither would I have agreed. But Merrill was a big firm, and there might have been an opportunity there had I asked. But I didn't. Another possibility was trying to start my own firm. The idea of a consortium had a lot of appeal. Getting as partners a securities firm or bank from each of several countries, each of which wanted to be active in the U.S. securities markets but was too small to do it successfully on its own, should have been possible. I knew a bit about this from my NT experience. While our London and New York offices were good outposts to have for marketing Canadian securities, we were really too small to break into the U.S. market in U.S. securities. We did quite well in London with our "Discount House" but, in the end, we were really in the Eurodollar certificate of deposit (CD) business, competing with the American firms. Likewise, in the U.S., while our team of equity research people did well, our capital limitations combined with U.S. regulations on free capital limited our expansion. This was one of the problems with being a part of a Canadian firm. To my NT colleagues, expanding in Winnipeg, say, was easier to "sell" internally than expanding in New York.

What concerned me about the consortium possibility was that I did not have the personal resources to do it. While I had some friends who were determined to do something like that—my old friend Bill Mac-Dougall and two of the old English crowd from Toronto—I chickened out. In retrospect, this was probably a mistake. The two Englishmen did quite well. Oliver Fox-Pitt and his partner ran their show for some 30 years before selling out quite recently. Likewise, John McIlhenny and Duncan Smith started their own money market company a year after I left NT. That also became quite successful.

One of the first things I did after resigning was to talk over my possibilities with a few friends. Maurice Strong immediately offered me a job with the Canadian International Development Agency, of which he was then president, until I found something more rewarding. I didn't take him up on the offer, but I appreciated very much the show of support. He had resigned from Power Corporation to go into public service. Considering my circumstances then and what happened later (see the next chapter), it was rather ironic that I turned down that generous offer.

Finally, I opted for the easy way out and scouted around the U.S. market. I had sought advice from Bob Heim, an American I had known when he was with Empire Trust and doing business with Power Corporation. At the time he was President of Schroder Rockefeller & Company ("SRC"), the U.S. venture capital arm of Schroders Inc. which was the U.S. holding company of Schroders Limited. Schroders Limited was the top company of J. Henry Schroder Wagg, a major U.K. merchant bank. While I knew a fair amount about the discount houses and the London brokers, I had never had much to do with the merchant banks except for Kleinwort Benson (Rio Algom) and Warburgs. But I certainly knew Schroder's excellent reputation, so it did not take much persuading by Bob Heim to get me to go to London to learn about the firm and see if there was a "fit" for me. Bob was interested in my joining, as he wanted to expand its operations to include securities activities. While Schroders had a special arrangement in the U.S. that allowed it to do commercial banking there (in those days, because of the Glass-Steagall Act, the two functions were segregated in the U.S.), it could not be a broker or an underwriter. But it could do private placements. The latter was what he wanted me to do. In the process, he told me a lot about the background of SRC and the Rockefeller connection. I had not been aware that SRC had been part of the group that initially financed Polaroid and AMD. At the time, SRC had capital of about US $10 million, twice NT's. Schroders Limited, of course, had consolidated capital in the hundreds of millions. To put this in perspective, Morgan Stanley's capital was only about $10 million in the mid-1960s.

The result was an absolutely fascinating three days in London going through the whole operation. At the time, Gordon Richardson was chairman and CEO. He was a very elegant and smart English gentleman of the old school, who went on to be governor of the Bank of England. He was rewarded for his services to the country when Queen Elizabeth elevated him with the title of "Lord Richardson." The others I met and liked there were David Airlie (The Earl of Airlie) who was the very low-key head of investment management. I also met their head of corporate finance, who invited me for a very pleasant family evening at his home in Kensington. Last, but certainly not least, was Jim Wolfensohn who seemed to be the international go-getter. Jim and his wife reciprocated the hospitality I had shown Jim in Montreal. Back then, at the suggestion of Maurice Strong, Jim had called for an appointment as the then international man for Darling and Company, an Australian brokerage outfit. I had invited him home, sight unseen, the night before the meeting I had arranged. What struck me most about all of those Schroders people then was that they were very professional, impeccably polite and sociable, and quite open about their business.

Two things struck me about their offices in London. First, there was always a group of about six or eight of us for lunch each day. The food was excellent and the service of the three or four waiters was superb. But what was surprising to me was that the choices of drinks with lunch were beer or water. No wine. In those days, my experience with the Discount Houses was that even if there were no outside guests, wine was always on offer. (On the other hand, the Discount Houses ended their business day at lunchtime whereas the merchant banks worked through to normal business closing.) The other surprise was seeing in the hallway near the dining room area a door with a sign that read "Directors Only." It was not until the first time I was ushered in before lunch that I realized it was the bathroom. It was just the English form of segregation between the upper classes and the others. Of course, there were no female directors in those days so that was not a problem. I wonder what they do now?

Schroders was quite an empire. Their businesses in the U.K. included commercial banking, carried out under the name J. Henry Schroder Wagg, corporate finance; money management, insurance and venture capital, all handled by subsidiaries. Most of these, in turn, operated in France, Germany, Italy, Switzerland, Brazil and Argentina, Hong Kong, Singapore, South Africa, and the "Dominions"—Australia, Canada and New Zealand. It is strange to think now, in 2011, that it was only a few decades ago that these countries finally became fully independent, even if the Queen of England is still their titular head of government.

Schroders was a listed company on the London Stock Exchange, but the last surviving male member of the family, Bruno Schroder, owned about 30%. A sister, married to George Mallickrodt, also owned a significant amount. Bruno and George were both active in the firm and, like the others, were quiet; low key fellows. Now only an ex president of the U.S. subsidiaries of a Canadian company, which could itself have been a small subsidiary of Schroders, I felt very much the small fish in the large pond. As Gordon Richardson put it quite pleasantly and rather casually, "So, you want a job with us." Until then, I hadn't quite thought of it that way. But in a millisecond, I realized I did. That was when I found out it was not that easy to move to a new job. In the background, I think Maurice had encouraged both Bob Heim and Gordon Richardson to take me seriously, as he knew the Schroders people. I learned that, despite their charm, they were serious business people. I still had to prove to them that I could earn my keep, especially as we were entering one of those world recessions. Apparently I did convince them because a week after returning to New York, I was offered a position as a vice president at SRC, with the understanding that I would become a director after six months if I proved myself. Notwithstanding that I had never got around to applying to any U.S. companies, I accepted immediately. That was a decision I never regretted.

The Schroders New York crowd was not that different, at the higher levels, than their London crowd. Most were bankers as that was the main activity in the U.S.—venture capital was just a sideline. I noticed immediately that they were all Harvard, Yale or Princeton graduates. All of them were excellent professionals with whom I was proud to work. I think I only saw Avery Rockefeller once. Apparently, he only came to the office three or four times a year for a few hours. (He eventually parted company completely; thus, a little later, the name was changed to Schroder Capital Corporation.) Jack Howell, who was CEO of Schroders Inc. and also CEO of the commercial banking subsidiary, was a wonderful fellow: tall, handsome, distinguished, in his sixties, and a joy to be with. Apparently, it was Jack who decided on their new offices into which they moved shortly after I joined. It was a new building, One State Street, at the foot of Broadway, where they were the prime tenants. What struck me was that Jack had chosen some of the lower floors when he could well have selected the usual top floors and had his own office in the "penthouse." He said he rather preferred the view from the sixth floor. Not only could he still see over the harbor, including the Statue of Liberty, but he could also see real people in the streets below. I had never thought of that. However, to fit in with the New World, I suppose, Schroders new offices did not have any doors marked "Directors Only."

At the "working level" were a group of fine analyst types. Brad Warner stands out. A "Yalie," he had been in the U.S. Navy during the Cuban missile crisis, chasing Russian cargo ships carrying missiles. I think he welcomed me as an "outsider" with investment banking experience as, while he was being encouraged to do private placements, he had no experience—and neither had his immediate bosses. Consequently, until then he had concentrated on venture capital investments; that is, startups, as opposed to the less imaginative deals that private equity funds do, and did. Brad and I did some very interesting investment banking type deals together. The first was one for Laurentide Financial Corporation, still a Power Corporation subsidiary. Despite the fact that Deane and the others wanted me off the board to be replaced by one of their own, Paul Paine (then chairman) and Gig Gigline (the CEO) refused to drop me. The greater crisis was, when asked by LFC, I arranged for them two more private placements of bonds with Equitable Life. It seems both the Laurentide and the Equitable people preferred dealing with me rather than NT. This did not please Deane and the others at NT and they tried again to get me off the LFC board. That did not work, but they got their revenge later. Paul had asked me to go on the board of Montreal Trust, another Power affiliate of which he was chairman. I was turned down. I suspect my old colleagues had got to Paul Desmarais, the then-chairman of Power and its largest shareholder.

A very pleasant thing happened with the Equitable around that time. I was invited to the retirement party of the vice president in charge of private placements. While I had known him by then for perhaps three years, we really had no personal relationship. I assumed I was just one of dozens of people who tried to sell him "deals." Further, as the LFC deals were all small—in the $25 million range as opposed to the $100 million or more he was used to. I also assumed I must have been one of the least important. It was a very gracious black tie dinner at the "21 Club" attended by his bosses and colleagues, plus about six or eight outsiders like me. I was very flattered to be included with this small group of "heavy hitters."

My only other business connection with Canada during this period was a hearing before the Province of Ontario Utilities Commission. An old friend from Toronto, Don Wright, was counsel to Union Gas, which was being subjected to an unfriendly takeover bid by Consumers Gas. Both were Toronto based gas distribution companies, competing in the Toronto market and both with slightly overlapping business in other parts of Ontario. Bob asked me to be a "professional witness" to support Union's case to remain independent. In those days the "public interest," as decided by the Commission, was deemed to be just as important as shareholder profits. I guess I was still considered to be a bit of an expert on valuations of securities. The case I was asked to make was limited to the fairness of the price from the view of Union Gas shareholders. It was my first such experience so it was interesting. But we lost and Consumers Gas was allowed to gobble up Union Gas. The latter's shareholders could not have been too unhappy as almost all accepted the bid.

Another deal Brad and I did was the first private placement in the U.S. of the U.S. subsidiary of a Swiss company, Brown Boveri ("BB"). It came to us through the Schroder network, but that did not mean there was not competition. The company's U.S. bankers raised a big fuss, but the Schroder people, by then, had confidence in us. So we were appointed to do the deal. One reason, of course, was that BB's bankers were only prepared to lend Swiss currency whereas BB wanted their U.S. assets to be financed in U.S. currency to eliminate the foreign exchange risk. That was a prudent policy still ignored by many companies, many of whom eventually paid the price. It was, to say the least, a complex transaction. While the parent was willing to guarantee the lender to its subsidiary, Brown Bovari had never done a U.S. bond deal before. In 1971, while BB was a well-known name in industrial and financial circles, it had no Wall Street track record. The tangible assets of the U.S. subsidiary were marginal for any kind of financing. To add to the complications, the plant was located in Virginia and the deal had to be a lease transaction, rather than a mortgage on the plant and equipment. This was to benefit from a State of Virginia tax incentive program.

The end result was, first, we had to get BB to set up a special purpose U.S. subsidiary. The next step was to prove, under U.S. accounting standards, that BB was credit worthy and, thus, that their guarantee had value. The problem here was that BB had never produced consolidated financial statements. The head office people said it would set a bad precedent and, in any event, even if they wanted to do it, they could not get it done with an acceptable auditor within the time period because they had over 80 subsidiaries in some 30 countries. Considering these problems, we decided our best prospect as a lender was the Prudential Life, in Newark. Fortunately, their VP Finance, Ray Charles, was an independent minded person who also liked a challenge. He had only recently agreed to do their first private placement in Mexico. Consequently, he was not averse to trying something new and different with one of Switzerland's leading companies. He assigned the deal to the person on his team who had worked on his Mexican deals, Jay Tata, who eventually came to work with us at IFC. That was quite a coincidence.

The compromise we worked out with BB and Ray was that, if we could produce a credible "combined" financial statement that BB would sign, the Prudential would accept it. This was where Schroders was truly great. Within days, through the Schroder network, we obtained the local audited financial statements of about 40 of their subsidiaries, which added up to over 95% of their total assets, liabilities, revenues and profits. It was actually easy, if you knew how to go about it. First, in many countries such as India, the BB subsidiary was a listed company, only about 60% owned by BB. So it had to file audited financial statements. In other countries, including the U.K., all companies had to file audited financial statements with their respective regulatory authorities—the Board of Trade in the U.K., in those days—listed or not. For a very small fee you could obtain a copy. So, to make the long story short, we went to Zurich one day with our "combined" financial statement. BB's treasurer was astounded. At first he accused us of some kind of industrial espionage. Then he admitted that they had no such figures in their head office, so we could not have stolen them. Finally, after reviewing them for a week with the treasurers of his subsidiaries, he agreed they were correct and signed them. The end result was Schroders made a name for itself in having completed the first U.S. private placement for the U.S. subsidiary of a foreign company that did not have audited consolidated financial statements. It was a long struggle, but well worth it both in terms of prestige and profits. Then again, no one would think of Switzerland as a frontier country.

Brad and I tried to do another private placement brought to us by Schroders. This was to finance the leasing subsidiary of PepsiCo. This was not a happy experience. We had pretty well got it done when there was a change of top management at Pepsi. The new CEO just decided he didn't want to do the deal. That left us high and dry. A lot of time and money spent, all for nothing. But that was, and is, the nature of the corporate finance business.

Probably the most fun deal was the restructuring of a little airline in the Bahamas called Out Island Airways ("OIA"). On this, Marion Gilliam helped me. He was a very charming young man from Kentucky who had one of the most elegant apartments I had ever seen. It was on the East River, with a magnificent view. OIA had been started by two retired Pan American Airways captains and ran an inter island service. What made me fall for it was that they had two Grumman Goose aircraft. This was the same aircraft I had first flown in Trinidad 25 years earlier. I shall always recall my first flight in one of them as they showed me around the islands. It was a typical lovely day and the view was magnificent. On a whim, thinking of my navy days, I asked for a map so I could do a bit of navigating. The pilot didn't have a map, which shocked me a bit. He just said you didn't need one. They didn't fly at night. The weather was always good, and you could see all the islands once you got over 5,000 feet, so why would you need a map? He had a point, I suppose. Their "workhorse" aircraft were de Havilland Twin Otters, made in Canada. These were 20-seat short take off and landing planes very suitable for the landing fields in the out islands.

The financial backers of the two Pan Am pilots were recently retired U.S. executives who were old friends of Gordon Richardson and served as board members of OIA. As always, the connections counted. One was Sherlock D. Hackley III, who had run the Henry Kaiser aircraft factories in WWII. Sherlock was famous for being in the co-pilot's seat of the "Spruce Goose" when Howard Hughes piloted it on its first and only flight in WWII. Few people are around now who would remember the Spruce Goose. It was a six-engine seaplane built in 1944 by Howard Hughes as a troop transport supposedly capable of moving several hundred troops across the Pacific. It was built of spruce to save weight—as was the RAF's famous "Mosquito" twin-engine fighter that saw service during the war. (There was a great WWII film called "The Dam Busters" which featured the Mosquito along with a few well know actors of the day.) But by the time the Spruce Goose was tested the war was over and only the one was built. The other board member was George Woods, an ex CEO of First Boston who went on to be President of the World Bank, of whom I shall say more later. In any event, they decided that OIA could only make money if it could fly to the U.S. To do that, for reasons I don't recall, it had to be a British controlled company to qualify for a license from the U.S. FAA. So Sherlock and George asked their friend Gordon for help. He turned to his New York people who turned it over to me. The rest was relatively easy. We got a U.K. development agency (Commonwealth Development Finance Corporation), the Royal Bank of Canada's Bahamian subsidiary and Schroders to take, between them, a controlling stake. This was my very first real venture capital deal (I don't count the rather speculative underwritings I was involved with in NT) as these were all knowledgeable investors. It was SRC's policy at the time that the dealmaker could also take a stake on the same terms. So I did.

Then the real fun started. As everyone who has anything to do with venture capital knows, the easy part is to make the investment. The hard part is to be able to "add value" and make sure the company succeeds to the point where you can sell at a profit. I was on the board representing Schroders and "adding value." This consisted of going to Nassau for monthly board meetings. At that stage, I think I was just adding to the costs, although I did negotiate another lease deal for them (with Westinghouse, which was in the aircraft leasing business then) to acquire the two twin-engine jets (DC 9s) we needed for the Nassau—Miami—Freeport routes. I learned something about Pan Am then. On my monthly flights, I was often "bumped" from first class. After a few such experiences and complaints I discovered it was to make way for

Pan Am VPs. This was annoying as we had a reciprocal arrangement with Pan Am, paying about half the normal fare while Pan Am's people paid nothing. I'm sure this arrogance and disregard for income was just an early small example of how some of Pan Am's later financial difficulties led to its collapse.

In the meantime, it was a great deal of fun to be back in the flying business. There were a few amusing experiences, some of which I saw first hand and some I only heard of later. At first hand I watched the loading of one of the Twin Otters at a strip on one of the out islands. We took aboard 22 for the 19 seats. As the pilot said, "Who's going to argue with a couple of guys twice your size?" On the same flight, an elderly lady insisted on taking with her into the cabin her prized possession. She was afraid it would be stolen if she left it at home or if it was put in with the luggage. It was a toilet seat. At that particular airport, the ground staff was a lady whose chief jobs were to sell tickets and to clear the runway of the assorted goats, chicken and children running around before the plane landed. The co-pilot was the ticket collector and baggage handler. The other experience I had was of a different nature. After landing for a board meeting, I was called immediately to volunteer to deliver blood. One of our pilots had had a serious car accident. As I had the right type of blood, I rushed off to the hospital and did my duty. But, for days afterwards, I worried about the rusty icebox in which the—I was certain—secondhand needles were stored. Obviously, I lived to tell the tale. But OIA never had an accident and never injured a passenger during its ten-year life. But there was one close call. That was one I did not see, fortunately. It was a Grumman Goose flight with ten passengers. As it was coming in to land on an airfield, only one wheel went down. This made a crash landing, on land or at sea, almost inevitable. But the ingenious co-pilot saved the day. He crawled out to the little loading bay in the nose where the anchor was stowed. He then proceeded to use the anchor line to lasso, or whatever it is called, the lowered wheel and haul it back up. They made a safe, if slightly bumpy, sea landing.

In 1970, the Bahamas were moving towards independence and, while this did not affect our application for a license to fly to the U.S., it did

Out Island Airways—OIA—is now Bahamas Air (important during my time at Schroders). About to board, Lena (and daughter Sarah in a baby carrier) with friends Michael and Sonja Koerner, 1971.

mean unexpected competition. Previously, there had just been a rather defunct government airline and the usual air taxi services. The Squires Group of Hong Kong—famous for running Cathay Pacific—had operated there for a few years, but suddenly pulled out. "Suddenly" was the word for it. One day they were there, the next day everything movable and every one of the expatriates had disappeared. They had been flown off during the night. They obviously knew more about the new government than we did. In any event, every few months a new airline suddenly appeared on the out island routes. Finally, by remarkable coincidence, an airline run by a relative of the new Prime Minister appeared along with a U.S. operating license. Fortunately, the government realized there was not room for all of these airlines and bought us out, turning OIA and the family firm into Air Bahamas, the new "flag carrier." We were paid off with 7% debentures issued by Air Bahamas and guaranteed by the government. It was a relief. We didn't make any money but, in theory, we broke even on our capital, plus interest. The "in theory" part comes later.

My routine business with SRC was reviewing new deals and attending investment committee meetings. I was amazed at how many came our way because of the "network." One interesting one that never got very far was a negotiation for a takeover of Revlon by another Schroder client. I was surprised how open Revlon's top people were with their information despite it not being a stock exchange listed company. Besides the obvious financial information, we had no trouble at all getting five years of their auditor's management letters—the report of the auditors discussing the strengths and weaknesses of the company's internal accounting and control systems, including their recommendations for improvements. This, still in 1970, was at a time when few Canadian companies ever asked their auditors to prepare such letters. But things changed at Revlon so that was another lost deal.

I remember making quite a few calls on new companies that were seeking additional seed capital and companies already in the SRC portfolio. One company wanted to set up a new affiliate to make the special jet engines that provide electric power for large aircraft—the one you see in the tail if you look closely enough. Another was, I think, one of the first to use a new technique to make large caliber pipes (for oil or gas transmission). One of our existing investments was what is now called Hudson General. Then, it specialized in leasing equipment for aircraft servicing. I was asked to be Schroder's nominee to the board, but I felt there was a conflict of interest with Laurentide on whose board I still served, so I declined.

One day in January 1971, Bob Heim asked me into his office and closed his door—something he rarely did. I was obviously very curious. I knew Jack Howell was retiring and that Jim Wolfensohn was replacing him as CEO of Schroders Inc. and I knew there were rumors that Bob was retiring because he was in his late sixties. But, as still a new boy in Schroders, I could not see what any of this had to do with me. I was right. He wanted to talk about something entirely different. What he said was that Gordon Richardson had had a call from Bob McNamara, then the President of the World Bank, asking if they could talk to me about a special job with the International Finance Corporation. IFC was the private sector sister institution of the World Bank of which Mc-Namara was also President.

It was a complete surprise. I knew "the Bank" and had attended a few of their famous annual meetings as a "Special Guest" representing Nesbitt, Thomson because Deane Nesbitt wasn't interested. I had even met a few of IFC's top people at those meetings and once spent an hour with their previous executive vice president. But I had never had any business dealings with them. So I had no idea how this came about. Neither did Bob Heim. He just said I should go and have the interview, but he hoped I wouldn't be tempted to leave Schroders. I agreed. That was not a hard decision in those days. The Bank was a much revered institution so being asked by the world famous Bob McNamara, ex Secretary of Defense and ex President of Ford, to come and talk was very flattering. The next week I received a call from Jim Kearns, the executive assistant to Bill Gaud, the then Executive Vice President of IFC to set up a meeting. A date was set up for the next week. I had not met Bill Gaud before as he had only recently been appointed. I did a little home-work and learned that Gaud had been an important player in the Kennedy administration (I think as head of USAID) and was very much a McNamara man.

1970–1971

On the appointed day I met first with Bill Gaud, who explained the job. It was to be Director of a new department in IFC, which would be responsible for both the Bank's and IFC's work promoting the establishment of domestic capital markets in developing countries. It would provide advice to governments on the infrastructure required and then help the private sector establish the needed financial institutions. IFC would be a sponsoring shareholder in these. The new unit would be called the Capital Markets Department ("CMD"). It would be started with four professional staff, who I would choose, and some support people. But, besides a formal annual budgeting process, he said there would be no real limit on how much advisory and technical assistance work could be financed, nor would there be any real limits on what we could invest when setting up new financial companies. The job was to meet the demand. Much to my surprise, he said no one in the Bank or IFC knew anything about financial markets or how they operated; thus, if I took the job I would have a completely free hand. This did not sound a bit like what I knew about government bureaucracies. But apparently that was the way McNamara operated: if someone came sponsored by people he trusted, he delegated fully. Bill didn't ask me many questions or test my supposed qualifications for the job. In fact, as I recall it, the closest he came to that side was to explain the remuneration system and that joining would entail a substantial financial sacrifice.

After that I spent some time separately with Lazlo von Hoffman, his VP, Moeen Qureshi, his economic advisor, and Dick Richardson, IFC's Chief Counsel. At the end of the day I went home, being escorted back to the entrance by Jim Kearns. He also surprised me by saying rather out of the blue that, unfortunately, the job did not come with a car and driver. I think I managed to hide my surprise at hearing this: asking about a car and driver hadn't occurred to me.

I was fascinated by the proposal—and surprised that I had been approached as my knowledge of developing countries was close to zero, except for my OIA experience. My first reaction was that it sounded much more interesting than "flogging stocks and bonds," which I had been doing for 18 years then—even if Schroders, with its venture capital activities, offered a much broader scope. But I knew little of Washington

113

and next to nothing about international bureaucracies. Lena and I talked about it but, as we were going on holiday to the Bahamas with our new baby daughter, Sarah, and our friends the Koerners, we decided to forget about it for the time being. Consequently, it was with even greater surprise that the next week, while in the Bahamas, I received a call from my office saying Bill Gaud had called and could I call him back as soon as possible? I assumed this was for another interview. But, no, it was to ask if I would take the job. Could I let him know in the next few weeks? I said: "But do I not have to see Mr. McNamara first?" He said: "No, that's not necessary. You were well recommended and he left it to me." I wasn't used to that kind of delegation but I supposed that was the difference between really big organizations and the likes of Schroders and NT, not that Schroders was exactly small. But, after I joined IFC, I did find out from Jim that the reason I had been interviewed was because McNamara had sought the advice of two confidants—Maurice Strong, who he knew through CIDA and the UN, and George Woods, who had been his predecessor as president of the World Bank. Both had recommended me.

The next week back in New York was a difficult one. I wanted to do it. George Woods urged me to take it. Lena was supportive. Bob Heim said it sounded great, but so was Schroders—how about a two-year leave of absence? An obvious drawback was that it involved a significant loss of income. But the challenge made it seem well worthwhile. So I told Bob I was resigning and thanked him for the offer of the two-year leave, which I declined. Still, I was sorry to leave Schroders. While I had not been there long, I had grown to respect both the organization and the people I met there. I had also enjoyed doing the deals.

PART II

THE WORLD BANK
GROUP / INTERNATIONAL
FINANCE CORPORATION:
1971–1988

CHAPTER IV

IFC ...
Finding My Way
in Washington:
1971–1972

The last chapter dealt with how we came to move to Washington in April 1971. This one will cover finding my way within IFC and in the developing countries ("LDCs"), as they were called then, or emerging markets, as they are now called. During my 17 years with IFC I was to visit some 60 LDCs. Some, such as the Maldives, I visited only once. To others, such as Korea and Brazil, I traveled several times a year. I did not keep any records of my activities so my only factual basis for what follows is the one page summary of our activities in each country that my Capital Markets Department colleagues gave me as a retirement gift. That is something that you see framed on a wall in my study. It still brings back memories. As I have been writing this, more and more of those memories have come back. This wonderful reminder of my IFC days was prepared by Rudi van der Bijl, about whom there will be much more. This was the period when I really became a financial frontiersman.

Prior to joining IFC my only working experience in developing countries was with Out Island Airways in the Bahamas during my Schroder days, my visit to Rio for the IMF/World Bank meeting in 1967 and going to Havana and Kingston Jamaica during my navy days. Except for OIA

117

they were really just tourist experiences. So, meeting and working with ministers of finance, central bank governors and leading business people in these countries was fascinating. Learning something about the different issues in the countries and the different agendas of different groups within them took time. But in my two-day or two-week visits, I could never know more than a fraction of what made a country tick. But by the 1980s I began to feel I knew what I was doing, more or less, at least concerning the financial sectors. Hopefully, you will get the sense that the on the job training led to some constructive results. So here is my story.

The Beginning in Washington

The early mission of the World Bank was to finance economic development and to promote domestic capital markets. The objective was to wean these developing countries away from dependence on foreign loans. IFC's mandate was to finance local private companies through loans and equity investments and to promote foreign private investment in such companies.

The Bank's financing mandate was achieved principally by lending to governments to finance "projects" that would contribute to development and that could pay their way financially. Initially, "projects" were Government owned power stations, water works, bridges, government owned industrial and mining companies: strictly bricks and mortar stuff. The capital market development mandate was to be achieved through advising governments on developing domestic financial markets in order to increase domestic savings and improve the efficiency of allocation of those savings. To support implementing these policies—both advice and lending—Development Finance Corporations ("DFCs") were promoted by the Bank and formed in each country. These financial institutions were usually government-controlled but with some private ownership. IFC was an equity investor in, and a lender to, most of those that were not 100% government owned. Both foreign and local financial institutions were sought as investors in them. DFCs were wholesaling vehicles that could finance projects and companies too small for the Bank or IFC to finance individually. As these DFCs were local entities they were specifically mandated also to promote their domestic capital markets. The theory was that the DFCs, with the domestic government and Bank backing, were well positioned to both attract foreign capital and to promote development of the domestic capital market. They also had an incentive to do the latter. A strong domestic capital market would make it easier for them to sell their own bond and stock issues and to raise money for their own investee companies. It was to be a virtuous circle. The Bank wanted to increase its lending. DFCs were vehicles through which they could lend to borrowers they could not otherwise reach, but both the DFCs and their own borrowing clients required collateral—equity—to support their loans. The DFCs, with IFC help, could raise additional equity though a domestic capital market that they developed, as well as from foreign sources.

The problem was the theory was not working so well in practice. The Bank's lending ability was growing at a faster rate than was the development of local capital markets. Consequently, lending was being constrained in part by a shortage of both local and foreign equity. Robert McNamara, as both the Bank's president and IFC's president concluded that one reason for this was that the DFCs were not delivering on the capital market side. Largely this was because most, if not all, of their efforts were directed to their lending business. Until 1970, McNamara had relied on the Bank's DFC Department—the largest unit in the Bank at the time and the only one with a global mandate—to use its leverage with the DFCs they financed to take this seriously. The DFC Department failed here for largely the same reasons the local DFCs failed: their primary interest was increasing their own loan volume. The constraints on lending were addressed usually by simply getting the legal limits on the equity collateral requirements reduced. While this made the loans to the DFCs riskier this didn't bother the lenders too much as the loans were mostly government guaranteed and had at least the moral support of the World Bank.

Much the same was happening with IFC at the time. Starting in the mid 1970s, there was pressure to increase volume. Initially, IFC's loans could be seen as both economically and financially rewarding. Originally, opening up a new industry, or tapping a previously undeveloped natural resource were the main, if not only, justifications for doing a deal. A "project" had to be either a new company or the expansion of an existing one, where the money was to be spent on acquiring new physical plant and equipment. The company had to be at least 50% owned by private investors, preferably mainly local. Later on, more emphasis was placed on ensuring that these new companies were also examples of sound financial management and strong governance.

As with all investing institutions, IFC also had to have an "exit plan" so it could eventually sell out and reinvest the proceeds. The desired exit was to local investors through the local stock market. The DFCs were supposed to be making this possible. But that was not happening. One result was that IFC's exits were mainly to foreign multinational companies rather than local investors. This didn't bother IFC management much as, primarily, the deal volume was the measure of their performance. Selling to domestic investors, especially through a stock exchange, was at the bottom of the priority list. At least that was the case until McNamara changed the rules to comply with the original intent.

That was where the Capital Markets Department ("CMD") was to come in. As a new specialized unit, based in IFC but also working for the Bank, we were to address this problem. McNamara identified it as our first and only priority. CMD was to advise governments on establishing sound capital markets, provide technical assistance to help establish stock exchanges and securities commissions, etc. It was also to sponsor and set up pace-setting financial institutions to operate in these new markets and encourage others to establish similar companies to follow our good examples. Initially, CMD could invest only in the first investment company, or the first mortgage bank in the country. But by the late 1970s, IFC's—and CMD's—investment guidelines became less stringent as the focus began shifting from pace-setting and quality to volume. Eventually, we would invest in the second—and even the fourth—investment bank or leasing company, etc. and lend to commercial banks. But, as the "white knights," especially in our developmental role, we had more enemies in the Bank and IFC than friends. Not only and equity investments had to be for new private sector entities that was the DFC management group under fire for having failed in one of their missions, but CMD was, in their eyes, a group of outsiderseven worse, "Wall Street stock brokers"—who were parachuted in to solve the problem and thus embarrass them.

Learning the ropes in IFC was similar to one's experiences when moving to any new organization. Except the proportion of the working day spent by IFC and Bank staff on internal politics probably exceeds that spent in most other entities. I was to discover this only gradually as the scope of our work increased. Actually, the first consultant I had in IFC warned me about this early on. Of course, I wasn't listening to this ancient academic, as I thought Professor Sydney Robbins to be when I first met him. He said: "David, I've worked half my life in government and half in academia and I go to church regularly. All are hugely bureaucratic and all are consumed by constant infighting. For a long time I thought the church had the record for the proportion of time spent on turf wars and the like. Then I came to the Bank and discovered quickly that it had the record! Be careful." I should have paid more attention to his warning. Failing to do so was going to cost me dearly.

But at the start the people I met could not have been more helpful and open. In fact, one even warned me of the political pitfalls. A long time professional said, with a chuckle: "I'll give you an example of how seriously we take our turf fights. Before I came to the Bank, had I seen someone about to step on a banana peel, my immediate reaction would have been to warn him. Now, my first impulse would be to ask myself which would be best for my career: to warn him or let him slip on it and maybe break a leg."

It was interesting to read again the terms of reference established for CMD. It was impressive how good the Bank and IFC people were at conceptualizing what should be done. Now, forty years later, I can still not think of any way in which the initial intent could have been better expressed. That they were overly ambitious in the light of the resources then made available, and that the Bank staff would decide later that the work was too important to be entrusted to IFC, could not have been recognized then. Nor could the shift in priorities from quality to quantity have been foreseen. Looking back to that time, I suspect the key people in management then would have argued strenuously against a shift to quantity at the expense of quality. In any event, following, word for word, is what was published in the Bank's Organization Manual on 1 September 1971.

Capital Markets Department

The Capital Markets Department is the focal point in the World Bank Group for work on the development of capital markets in the less developed countries. It works in close coordination and cooperation with other Bank Group departments, particularly the Area Departments, Economics Departments, and the Development Finance Companies Department.

The primary task of the Capital Markets Department is assisting in the establishment and operation of sound institutions to channel private savings into productive private investments. It will also concern itself with the institutional and policy framework, which affects such institutions. The area of responsibility of the Capital Markets Department does not include development finance companies or central banks.

THE PRINCIPAL RESPONSIBILITIES
OF THE DEPARTMENT ARE:

- *To identify possibilities of developing new, or improving existing capital markets in particular countries, and with the agreement of the bank Area Department concerned, to stimulate interest and activity within member countries in this enterprise;*

- *To assist at the request of member country governments, their agencies, or private groups in member countries, in defining specific problems and needs in the capital markets and in preparing specific requests for Bank Group assistance in the development of specialized capital market institutions, regulations, laws and programs for the country, in order to stimulate private savings and channel them to investors;*

122

- *To investigate and appraise requests from member countries government and private sources for Bank Group technical or financial assistance for capital market development and to assist Bank Group departments in negotiating loans to and investments in capital market institutions;*

- *To supervise World bank Group's capital market projects;*

- *To develop arrangements through which experts may be identified and made available to member countries to assist them in improving their capital markets and to supervise the work of such experts;*

- *To recommend new or revise World Bank Group policies which will improve or stimulate the growth of capital markets in member countries.*

It reflected the basic point. That is, to quote a well-known economist, Ragnar Nurkse, "capital is made at home." He wrote this in 1953 without any particular reference to LDCs. Eighty percent to 90% of capital expenditures, even in the poorest of LDCs, were, and still are, financed from domestic savings. Thus, to the extent that the domestic financial markets can be made more effective—increasing domestic savings and allocating them more efficiently—the need for foreign capital can be reduced even more.

My first working day at IFC involved filling out forms, being shown where my office was and how to use the phone system. Jim Kearns, the executive assistant to Bill Gaud, IFC's Executive Vice President, was my guide. He also explained IFC's organizational structure. At the time IFC had about ten staff directors. Five of these were responsible for investment operations in the five geographical regions. The others headed "support" departments—financial, legal, engineering, etc. There was also one vice president, Lazlo von Hoffman, who acted as deputy to the executive vice president. This briefing was followed by my first long chat with Bill Gaud. Others followed over several weeks. Between times I also had talks with Moeen Qureshi, IFC's Economic Advisor who had come to IFC from the IMF. Consequently, he knew more about financial markets than any of the other senior people in IFC and thus had been looking after capital markets activities as a side function. He was thorough and perceptive in the advice he gave me on the state of affairs with the countries where IFC was already involved with capital markets work. These were South Korea, Taiwan and Venezuela.

Much of the discussion with Jim Kearns was pretty mundane For example, learning to find one's way around the Bank physically was serious business. The office arrangement brought to mind the term "rabbit warren." In the main office complex alone, housing about 3,000 bank people and about 200 IFC types, there were four buildings, taking up an entire city block between 18th and 19th and "G" and "H" Streets. Each building had its own elevators and office numbering system. For the first year I found it easier to go down the nearest elevator, go outside and walk around the buildings to get to the right one. I needed then to navigate the labyrinth of corridors inside. It is one of the few buildings in the world in which you can be walking along the 11th floor and, without using stairs or elevators, suddenly find yourself on the 12th floor. Jim was also very instructive on which parts of the administrative system would be important for my survival and, most importantly, who to get to know. As I recall, there were about six separate units that dealt with such matters as staff recruiting, office facilities, pay and benefits, etc. Each seemed to be a separate empire with its own set of rules. This was another labyrinth of sorts to be navigated with care.

Despite these minor problems, I learned quickly that the Bank and IFC were very special institutions. First, 99% of the people were exceptionally bright. Second, there were some 90 different nationalities represented on the staffs. Third, there were never to my knowledge any issues related to culture, race or religion even if some of the national groups tended to favor their own. Coming from Canada, I knew something about tribal battles so this was a bit of a surprise. Happily, it didn't take long before I just did not notice that we were a pretty mixed crowd. By the time I retired, CMD had 30 professionals from 17 countries.

But to get to substantive matters, my first hours with Bill Gaud were educational, encouraging and inspiring. Bill was a long time Washingtonian insider. He was aristocratic in appearance and manner, but could out-talk a longshoreman in his own language any time. At least with me, he was always friendly, helpful and open, inspiring confidence and loyalty. He explained the way to get things done at the higher levels. His first point was the importance of getting to know the members of our board of directors (known as Executive Directors (or "EDs")), their "Alternates" and their staffs. His second was the importance of understanding the politics of dealing with Bank staff considering my duties to both entities. At the time, with the exception of the one executive VP in the Bank (Burke Knapp about whom there will be much more later) and the one vice president in IFC (Lazlo von Hoffman), all senior managers in the Bank and IFC were called Directors. This was a bit confusing as EDs were also sometimes referred to as directors.

The EDs were the full time representatives of the some 120 countries who were the Bank's and IFC's shareholders then. (There are some 200 now.) The Bank and IFC were separate, shareholder-owned corporations but legally without national domiciles. As a result they could not be taken to court, which probably was the reason for that arrangement. The only conditions for becoming a shareholder of IFC were that the country had to be a shareholder of the Bank and be able to afford to contribute the nominal amount of cash capital required to subscribe for shares. At that time, IFC's paid in capital was about US $1 billion. Shareholdings in both the Bank and IFC were based on a formula that gave the most weight to GNP. The wealthiest countries were expected to each hold about 9%. The smallest only needed to have a nominal percentage. One would think even the smallest nation could afford the minimum dollar amount required by IFC—probably about $100,000 then. But it did turn out to be an embarrassment for at least one of the new small countries that wanted to join in my day. While there was some prestige value for countries—especially newly independent ones—to be seen as Bank and IFC shareholders, the real reason for joining was more practical. Only shareholder countries could obtain a loan from the Bank or an investment by IFC in one of its domestic companies.

IFC . . . Finding My Way in Washington

Some socialist countries had become shareholders of the Bank but chose not to be shareholders of IFC because of its private sector mandate. Neither the old USSR nor China was a shareholder of IFC at the time. Yugoslavia was the first—by many years—of the old "East Bloc" to sign on. Taiwan was an early shareholder as the "Republic of China," but was pushed out by China in 1971 when China joined the UN, the Bank and IFC. More about that later.

This brings me to the Bank's and IFC's governance. There were about 20 directors then representing shareholder countries. Each wore two "hats"—irst, as "Executive Directors" of the Bank and, second, as "Directors" of IFC. This was, and probably still is, a bit confusing considering heads of departments in the Bank and IFC were also called directors. The largest wealthiest countries with the largest shareholdings —now including Saudi Arabia, Russia and China—have one director each. These are the main "donor countries" as they provided most of the Bank's and IFC's funds. The middle-sized wealthier countries would lead groupings of four or five smaller countries and provide the "ED" for their group. Some of the small countries are in regional groups with one ED for as many as 25 countries. Each ED would have an "Alternate Director" (from another country if he represented a group) and a couple of "advisors," who did the legwork, usually from other countries in the group. The Bank and IFC paid all their expenses, including salaries. Being an ED was a plum assignment for the many professional bureaucrats from the ministries of finance or other government entities in the countries from which they came. The total cost of financing these two permanently sitting boards was around $20 million a year in my day. I imagine it is a multiple of that amount now.

One rather curious and, in some respects, contradictory aspect of Bank and IFC membership was that the cost (relative to a country's GDP) of being a Bank shareholder was small compared to joining IFC while funding available from the Bank was many multiples of what IFC could provide. This reminds me of a rather amusing case of one country "signing up" for IFC. This country—"no names no pack drill"—was very poor and very small and had just recently become independent. It had applied to the UN, where membership was free, and the Bank, where, because only a small percentage of the shares had to be "paid up," the cash amount was very small. A keen IFC investment officer in the region had identified a company there that needed money and met IFC's criteria. IFC's PR people were especially pleased to have a new shareholder sign up within weeks of becoming eligible and then be able to make the first investment there. It would make everyone look good before IFC's board. Then came the shock. The proposal had to be withdrawn. It turned out the country didn't have the $100,000 cash needed to become a shareholder. After much head scratching, a solution was found. By working backwards. Once IFC's several hundred thousand dollar loan was made, the company would have ample U.S. dollars in its central bank account and the country was a significant shareholder in it. Consequently, the company could lend the dollars to the government. It wasn't hard to get a friendly bank to make a bridge loan to cover this. It was a great story and, as much as it may surprise you, it is true although the numbers may be a little off.

The two boards met at least once a week in the early years as every loan and investment had to be presented formally for approval. The dynamics were such that almost all proposals were approved unanimously. But sometimes one of the EDs—or Director if it was an IFC deal— would vote against a project to make a political point while knowing full well that the project would be approved anyway as it only needed a simple majority in favor. Some three-quarters of the EDs represented beneficiary countries. Usually, they were reluctant to vote against one of the other beneficiary country's loans or investments as to do so could invite reprisal. Even the large countries would think twice about voting against a proposal benefiting a protégé country of another donor country. That was politics.

These comments on the boards may sound somewhat cynical, but I did feel that what might be considered "back scratching" occurred from time to time. Still, it happened probably less often than is the case in most countries' legislative bodies. Again, "that's politics." One only has to think how the U.S. Senate operates to see an example of a worse system. Our boards were comprised of people who reported to bureaucrats who reported to politicians. Still, there were outstanding exceptions amongst the individual members—men and women—who said exactly what they thought about a project and, more importantly, knew what they were talking about. Claude Isbister was one such person. Here, I may sound biased as he was a fellow Canadian. But he had been a distinguished civil servant for some 30 years before serving two five-year terms. Canada's group consisted of most of the English-speaking Caribbean countries and Ireland. Claude was fortunate in that Canada had no axes to grind with the Bank or IFC and was generally supportive of all developmental activities. Consequently, he was left a completely free hand by the Canadian government. Claude had the respect of both his fellow board members and the professional staff. Many others were equally bright, well informed and hard working, but most of them were on shorter leashes.

Bank and IFC staffs had, and have, two main duties in reporting to the boards. One was to produce well-crafted documents for the board that would receive more praise than questions. The other was to demonstrate that the project was financially sound and would have an appropriate developmental impact. It may look as if I have the two tasks in the wrong order. However, as one wag in the Bank said: "The perfect project is one that is well received and approved by the board, but for which management never has to disburse the money." Disbursing the money tended to be another bureaucratic hassle as conditions of disbursement had to be met and documented, or waived. Then, if the "project" actually came to life, periodic appraisal reports had to be written and, god forbid, if things didn't go as promised, there was the risk of accountability. And, salary increases and promotions came from the number of board project reports presented. What happened later was of little consequence as staff tended to be rotated as often as military personnel in their world.

As Bill Gaud counseled me, whenever I had a project up for approval by the board, I would offer to see each ED/country director or one of his advisors to discuss it before the meeting. This would achieve two objectives. First, you pleased the EDs by making the offer. Second, if they did have questions, you could answer them in advance. The result was, usually, quick approval of the project with no questions and occasionally some praise. Sometimes, notwithstanding the briefings, there would be a few questions, but usually they were easily answered, as we knew them in advance. My fellow department directors either didn't get this advice or didn't follow it: They rarely offered to talk to board members but often were faced with hard and unexpected questions at meetings. The reality was that, while both staff and EDs wanted the money to flow, staff was paid to prepare impressive reports. EDs' staffs were paid to read them and prove they had by coming up with questions.

In following Bill's advice, I learned that the most helpful director from a practical point of view was the U.S. ED. They (I dealt with some six during my 17 years in IFC) and their staff along with their colleagues in the U.S. Treasury were, 99% of the time, both interested in what CMD was doing and supportive. During my first few months, several people in the Treasury and USAID even called on me separately to offer help and to be friendly in general to a new arrival in Washington. Two of them were especially helpful and kind.

Stanley Grande, then with USAID, was one. Stanley is still a character and remains a friend. He was an infantryman in Italy in WWII, a staff person in the Johnson White House, and then the senior AID official posted to Rio and later to Buenos Aires before returning to Washington. Amongst his many hilarious stories was one where I felt a personal interest. While he was stationed in Rio around 1960, the U.S. naval attaché there had heard the Brazilians wanted to buy an aircraft carrier. Being a good naval type and knowing the U.S. Navy had plenty of them to spare, he got Navy approval to offer them one for $5 million—a bargain considering its size and that it was in full operating order. But the U.S. State Department vetoed the sale on the grounds that the U.S. should not be encouraging an arms race between Brazil and Argentina. When the Brits got to hear about the U.S. proposal, being more pragmatic, they offered to give the Brazilians one for nothing. The only condition was that they had to collect it in the U.K. and outfit it there. The Brazilian Navy thought it was a bargain and signed on. Two years and over $10 million spent in the U.K. later, they had it fixed, crewed and ready for sea. Unfortunately, they could not scrape up enough for fuel for several more months, so its departure was delayed. Finally, they got it to Rio. Naturally, their first cruise was to Buenos Aires to show it off to the Argentines. Unfortunately, it went aground on a sand bank as it was entering B.A.'s harbor. More unfortunately, after a week showing their new trophy to the locals, they went aground on the same sandbank on the way out of the harbor. I loved this story because the carrier in question was good old HMCS Warrior. This was Canada's first carrier in which I served for two years. The RCN returned it to the Brits in 1948 in exchange for a slightly newer model, HMCS Magnificent, in which I also served one summer.

Stanley, besides explaining to me how USAID functioned, gave instructions to all the AID offices in Latin America—his turf then—to look after me whenever I visited their countries. This was a huge help in my early days in Venezuela and Brazil.

John Lange was the other. He was then director of the department in the Treasury that had oversight over international financial institutions. John had been in the U.S. Navy and then the IMF after he got his doctorate in economics. He had served in several Latin American countries as the IMF representative and thus had a lot of useful on-the-ground experience that he passed on. John explained the workings of the Treasury and how best to deal with our largest shareholder. His advice was similar to Bill Gaud's—get to know the U.S. Executive Director and his staff. He added to the list the Treasury people in his and other parts of the Treasury and provided the right introductions. John also introduced the Gill family to the joys of sailing on Chesapeake Bay.

After making sure I understood the importance of getting to know the EDs and the Treasury people, Bill Gaud explained the importance of "coordination" with the Bank and the IMF as a means of at least minimizing future turf war troubles as CMD's activity expanded.

The IMF had its own department that promoted financial markets, but it specialized in banking, so that would not become a problem. More importantly, if properly dealt with, the IMF department could be very helpful in providing insights about the countries and introductions in them. As CMD worked for the Bank as well as IFC, the Bank covered half our expense budget. Thus, my main concern should be to make sure I maintained good relationships with the Bank's many economists

130

and its country directors. Bill told me that few people in the Bank would understand what I was doing, and would care even less—at least in the early days when we couldn't do much anyway. But he also said if I didn't keep them informed, they could become major obstacles.

I discovered there were two major potential minefields that were hard to avoid. First, our advisory work led to many "one-on-ones" with ministers of finance and central bank governors who often followed our suggestions. Sometimes I discovered they were contrary to what the Bank was proposing. Worse than that, they sometimes came to us for advice the Bank thought it should have been providing. The second was with the Bank's DFC Department. Bill Diamond, the DFC Department's director, was always friendly and helpful but, while I didn't realize it at the time, in practice he could not help seeing me as an interloper on his turf. He had grown accustomed to having the final, if not only, say on financial matters. When President McNamara presented me as the expert in the Capital Markets area, this was never fully accepted by the DFC Department and was, in fact, resented. The terms "not invented here" and "not in my back yard" come to mind.

As I found out, "coordinating" with 3,000 people was easier said than done when there are only a few of you to do it. Something Claude Isbister said at a board meeting brought this home to me. I forget the IFC transaction at the time that sparked it, but his comment was: "The difference between IFC and Bank project proposals is that, with the former, you count the words per dollar to be invested and with the latter it's the dollars per word." To put that in his context, he was thinking of the average 100-page Bank project proposal to the board recommending a $200 million loan as compared to IFC's 100 pages to justify investing $2 million. As for CMD projects, our proposal reports had to be pre-approved by several Bank departments as well as at least three other IFC units. To put the same thought slightly differently, even when the CMD staff was up to 30—approximately the number when I retired—we never got beyond three countries per staff member while the bank averaged about 40 staff per country.

I had to learn the hard way about the jealousy aspects of turf fights, but it took me some time to realize this. As an example, a few months after I joined IFC, I reminded Bill that I still had not met Bob McNa-mara. He was, after all, the one who had recommended me to Bill. Com-ing from the private sector, I just assumed that the CEO would want to meet personally with all his senior operating people. Bill arranged a lunch for the three of us a week later. Held in Bob's private dining room, it was just a very pleasant low-key get together. We didn't talk "shop"— I don't think the words "Bank" or "IFC" were even mentioned. It was just about local political events and some gossip about the current ac-tivities of mutual friends—in my case only Maurice Strong and George Woods. He could not have been a more charming host. I was very grate-ful. I thought it was only Ruby, my secretary, and Lena who knew about it. It was over a year later during a heated—for reasons I can't remem-ber—discussion with one of the IFC regional department directors that I discovered otherwise. He was upset about some deal of ours in his re-gion. He suddenly blurted out that he knew I was getting special treat-ment from McNamara. I asked him why on earth he thought that. He said: "Well you had lunch with McNamara and no other director has ever been invited to lunch by him—even as part of a group. Obviously, you are getting special attention." Apparently, word had got out and it had caused all sorts of resentments.

Keeping our EDs and staff colleagues in the Bank, IMF and IFC in-formed led, among other things, to us developing a one-page "Summary of Activities" a few years later. It was also in the McNamara tradition of reporting to him on one page. This, in turn, led to the Chart showing all our activities from 1971 until I retired in 1988. A chart summarizing 17 years work in over 60 countries leaves a lot to the imagination.

There may have been jealousies and occasional turf fights, but the Bank and IFC also had many well-informed and dedicated people who came to our little group for help and advice on specific issues related to their countries. Needless to say, it was mainly the Bank directors and vice presidents who were friendly and helpful. They were above the turf wars of the economists and loan officers struggling for recognition. But that is all jumping ahead in time.

Bill Gaud said the best way to defend myself against the Bank's econ-omists, if and when the need arose, was to have my own cadre of economists of sufficient reputation that the Bank—and the IMF—would respect them. That was good advice. My budget allowed me to hire consultants for professional support so I should take on a few eminent economists. Bill's first recommendation was a brilliant and well-known Harvard professor, Edward Shaw, who was one of the first to write about how an efficient financial system could speed economic development. I went to Cambridge (Massachusetts) to meet him and discuss my plans. I recall being very impressed with him both as an academic and as a fine human being. Another was Professor Ray Goldsmith of Columbia who wrote the first important book on financial institutions in developing countries. Both offered me wise counsel over the years, not just as paid consultants—there were many academics offering these services—but as people with a serious interest in doing what they could to further the cause of development. The third was Professor Neil McKinnon, who also published an excellent book on finance and development that took Ed Shaw's ideas a stage further. Both had been at Stanford when they were writing on this subject.

From my perspective, the best and most practical academic advice came from an academic I mentioned earlier in a different context, Professor Sydney Robbins, then at the Columbia University's business school. Sid had been the first economist hired by the SEC. That was just after WWII during which he had served with the U.S. Army. He had also been a consultant to USAID for its first financial market development exercises in Korea and Thailand in the early 1960s. Even more than a decade after his time in Thailand, he was still well remembered there as the "father" of their securities market. I well remember when, during my third or fourth visit to Thailand, we were asked to prepare a "blueprint for financial market development." My advice to the Thai officials was that we should start with the "Robbins Report" that he had written over ten years previously. In fact, had the Thais followed his recommendations, they would not have needed advice from IFC.

Sid was also great fun to be with. He always had hilarious stories to tell and enjoyed a good martini, many of which we had together. He also was a connoisseur of fine wine and had an excellent cellar at his home in Westchester County. I discovered that some of his "treasures" were then valued in the hundreds of dollars per bottle, which was a lot of money 40 years ago. Some years later, we hoisted Sid by his own (wine) petard, as the saying goes. By the early 1980s, Korea had developed its own wine industry—it produced some quite decent reds. On an occasion when several of us were in Seoul we organized a wine tasting for Sid. We told him that of the six glasses arranged on the table, five were French and one was Korean. Would he pick the best French and the Korean? He was wrong on the Korean—he selected that as the best French. But that was a very small "one up." Sid did more for financial market development in LDCs than any other single person before or since.

I could talk a lot about the many other people I met in other parts of IFC and the Bank whom I grew to know and respect but it would be a long list. So I shall mention just a few now. They were impressive types.

The first was Burke Knapp, the Bank's Executive Vice President. In those days, "grade creep" had not set in. IFC had one vice president and the Bank had about six, as compared to about six in IFC and 20 or so in the Bank now. Burke, an American, was the senior staff person. The Presidents were all political "appointees"—elected by the board but proposed by the U.S. as the largest shareholder. For our European shareholders, the quid pro quo was that the president of the IMF was always a European. These "deals," of course, flowed from the original Bretton Woods agreement when the winning side of World War II established the UN, the IMF and the World Bank.

Burke had no particular reason to be interested in IFC, let alone the newly formed CMD. But he believed in the concept that the only way that poor countries could be weaned away from financial subsidies from the rich countries was through developing their own domestic savings and market oriented financial infrastructures. He supported us in our occasional squabbles with the Bank only when he thought we were right and it was in the best interests of the Bank and IFC. That he tried to get IFC to take the lead responsibility for housing-finance activities rather than the Bank was an example of this. We in CDM had started encouraging the establishment of savings and loan banks and mortgage banks in 1972, at the suggestion of USAID, which was very active in establishing them in Latin America. As a small activity then, no one in the Bank or IFC cared. A little later, as a result of a subsequent major effort by the UN to promote housing finance, the Bank decided to give it some priority. But Burke decided that, as it was more a private sector and a financial markets activity, IFC, through CMD, should take the lead. I was pleased as he had vindicated our efforts, but IFC management was not. So Burke ended up taking the function back for the Bank. I never understood why IFC turned down this opportunity—housing finance became a major program for the Bank and was very popular with its shareholders. It could have done the same for IFC, which in all other respects was eager to find ways to increase its activities and enhance its image. I suspected part of the reason was that it was a turf issue with IFC's regional group who feared, rightly, that they would not be getting much of the glory. Despite, or because of all of that, Burke and I rather hit it off as individuals. There were times when I felt he was the only person in senior management other than Bill Gaud who actively supported CMD's role.

Ronnie Brockus, the Bank's General Counsel at the time, was another supporter. Ronnie was a Dutchman who had been around since the birth of the Bank at Bretton Woods. When I think of it, his was more moral support than anything. IFC's lawyers were very professional, but I sensed their main interest was what they saw as the core business and thus the regional departments. But the fact that they knew that Ronnie had sought me out and supported what we did made an impression. Ronnie—like Burke Knapp and Bill Gaud—was a gentleman of the old school.

Another interesting personality was IFC's Representative in Tokyo, a retired ministry of finance official—Mr. Nishihara: he was always called Mr. Nishihara. To this day I have no idea what his first name was. He spoke excellent, if slightly accented, English and was tall by Japanese standards, slim and distinguished. It was clear that he came from a very privileged background. I remember my first visit to Tokyo in 1971, on the way to Seoul. He had me picked up at the airport, collected me at my hotel, and took me to an elegant Japanese restaurant that specialized in French food. I forget what we talked about—some "shop" I suppose

—but I do remember one story he told me. It was about his first visit to the U.S. after World War II. He was the senior "MoF" man on a "road show" to sell the first Japanese government bond issue to U.S. institutional investors. He recalled that it was a fascinating and somewhat traumatic experience. It could not have been an easy time for him. Actually, it is more what he did not say that impressed me. Few remember it now but Japan was one of the first beneficiary countries outside of Europe financed by the World Bank. It is amazing how quickly it became one of its most important lenders to the Bank and a major IFC shareholder.

I think we both wondered what the other had done during the war—he was older than I, but not much—but we never talked about it. He was a true statesman in the best sense of the term. But, more importantly to me, he was a very straightforward and strong supporter of CMD's role. He served on the board of two of the financial companies I was involved with in Korea. Notwithstanding the tensions between the two countries stemming from the Japanese occupation before and during the war, he got on very well with the Koreans. The Koreans I knew in those companies looked upon him as a friend, not just the IFC representative. He took his IFC work very seriously even though it was a retirement job for him. As to how seriously, an amusing story circulating inside IFC at one point makes the point. Apparently, he was to meet IFC's senior VP and a department director in the lobby of the Imperial Hotel at 9.00 AM one morning to proceed to a meeting he had arranged. The VP showed up a few minutes early. Mr. Nishihara arrived at exactly 9.00. At 9.04 the IFC director had still not shown up. Mr. Nishihara looked at his watch and said to the VP: "Mr. … is not a serious man. We leave now."

As an indication of how important Japan had become as a supporter of IFC—and how well regarded Mr. Nishihara was—IFC agreed to a special arrangement with the Ministry of Finance. CMD would have a man from Nomura Securities seconded to us for a two-year period and treat him as a regular staff member. He—and Nomura—would learn more about developing countries. They would deliver one of their best securities market professionals to help us in that area of our activities. Also, Nomura would "top off" his salary. (While it is felt in the U.S. government that Bank and IFC salaries were too high, they were much lower than in comparable positions in the private sector—even in Japan.) Our first Nomura man was Shuzo Nagata. He more than lived up to his billing, as you will read later.

Staffing Up

My first real task in IFC was to find staff. Fortunately, the Bank system worked well. I had all kinds of internal applicants. My first two "hires" were interesting people and both became friends despite their very different backgrounds and interests.

The first was my secretary, Ruby Tung Yep. Ruby was a Chinese Australian. She was petite, attractive with sharp features and a sharp tongue. She spoke with a strong Australian accent that sounded strange coming from a very Chinese looking person. Ruby was very bright and a serious "workaholic." We used to call her the human computer. In those early days before there were personal computers, I used to dictate to her for hours at a time. She would be there the next morning with near perfect drafts. Ruby was so good that she was in constant demand around IFC and the Bank to do overtime assignments. A lot of the professionals had found that Ruby produced more results per dollar than their own people did. This was a source of contention with other secretaries who also wanted to earn overtime pay. I recall one who went so far as to make a formal complaint about her boss because he shunned her in favor of Ruby. But it was great for Ruby because she liked the money. Despite being lot of fun when you got to know her, work was her life. She invested her money in jewelry and property. Lena learned about the sharp tongue quite soon. The first time she came to my office a few weeks after I had joined she found Ruby on guard at my door. Lena said: "Hello. I'm Mrs. Gill." Ruby said: "I thought so" and sat there just looking at her. But we both grew to like Ruby and enjoy her company. It was a sad day for all of CMD when she decided to retire and go back to Australia.

My first "professional" was Rudi van der Bijl, a Dutchman, born in Venezuela. Besides his perfect Dutch and English, he spoke Spanish,

IFC . . . Finding My Way in Washington

French and German without a trace of an accent, I was told—there was no way I could tell—plus several other languages. Rudi had joined the Bank about a year previously when he was just over 30. This allowed him to escape starting as a trainee in the Bank's "young professional" program—the entry route for professional staff who were under 30 and did not have several years of professional experience elsewhere. The qualifications for that program then included an advanced degree, several languages, and a very high I.Q. A few years' work experience helped. About one in 500 applicants were accepted. In the Bank "work" usually meant academic or public service. In IFC it meant in private business. Rudi had worked for a "think tank" for only a few years. But he must have made quite an impression on the Bank's recruiters as he went directly into the capital markets division of the Treasurer's Department. His wife, France (Fanfan to her friends), was, of course, French, and worked for the EEC office in Washington. That made them the ideal international bureaucrat couple. Rudi was one of the most honest and direct people I have known. Sometimes his comments at internal meetings were seen as critical as he had developed a reputation as always "seeing the cup half empty." His trouble was that his judgments proved correct 99 times out of 100, which made him many enemies. Consequently, despite my recommendations, he was never promoted to a management level. But I grew to trust him more and more and he was truly my right hand for all of my 17 years in IFC. The proof of the pudding as to his strengths was that none of the managers reporting to me had any defensive feelings about his role as my right-hand man. Rather, they all grew to adopt him too as their own sounding board. It was a great loss to IFC when he finally retired after 30 years. Besides his professional knowledge, he knew all the best restaurants in every city we ever visited! Fortunately for those organizations, he spent his next two years at the IDB and then went to work at the Bank for Cesare Calari, a CMD alumnus who became VP Financial Markets, as an almost full time consultant. (The Bank and IFC, being extraterritorial, pay no attention to matters such as age discrimination: retirement age is, or was, 65 and there are no exceptions granted.) Sadly, two years after he retired from his "final" almost full time job with Cesare, he died of cancer. He will be remembered and missed by everyone in those organizations so long as there are still people in them who worked with him.

By the end of the first year, we were up to four professionals. The other two were Daniel Adams and John Lowe, both Americans with Master's degrees from Harvard, who had joined the Bank through the young professional program. Both moved on to other parts of IFC after a couple of years in CMD. As with the military, a prerequisite for promotion is rotation through other units. Dan became an IFC vice president before retiring early to take up ranching in New Mexico. John stayed in IFC until his very premature death. The fifth professional to join was Ernest Kepper, an old Nesbitt, Thomson colleague who I had hired from the University of Western Ontario. Ernie left IFC shortly after I did to work for the World Bank in Indonesia, Saudi Arabia, Kenya and Japan, successively. Tokyo was his last assignment. When he retired he stayed on in Tokyo and built a successful consulting business. As I think of it, Ernie became an almost professional "resident representative." Before he went to Indonesia he had spent periods of three months to two years in Argentina, Brazil, Egypt and Venezuela. Ernie's move to the Bank was one of those political things. I had sent him to Jakarta to manage a program to reorganize the 12 Indonesian state banks that was carried out by a team of 12 retired Canadian bankers and provided with the support of the Bank of Canada. Unfortunately, IFC would not agree to allow him to stay for a second two years so, as the Bank was very keen on the program, they asked him to join the Bank and stay on in Jakarta, which he did.

Our second secretary (I think "staff assistant" is the term now) was Ingrid Menken, an absolutely sweet, innocent 19-year-old from Montreal. Ingrid had taken a secretarial course there and was then recruited by the Bank. She came from a family of German refugees and this was her very first time away from them. I realized she was very bright, diligent and charming, but I did not give much thought to her. So it was a bit of a surprise when, about a year later, Dan Adams and John Lowe came to me and said they had persuaded her to go to university. It was very touching. Both of them, and Rudi, had realized she had a lot of talent but was just too young, shy and inexperienced to realize she could

139

make more of her life. With their encouragement—and an offer of financial support from them that she didn't need because she won scholarships—she went off to university and eventually earned a master's degree.

Later on, three more recruits who made great contributions to CMD joined. The first was Antoine van Agtmael, our second Dutchman. Antoine is one of the most hard-working and intelligent of all the professionals with whom I have worked—in IFC and elsewhere. After the Netherlands School of Economics and a master's at Yale, he worked for Bankers Trust in New York which posted him in Thailand as head of TISCO, its local investment bank. When they wanted him to move back to head office, he decided to make a major career change and make developing markets his future. That was when he applied to IFC. I knew in a matter of minutes that he was right for CMD. We shared some interesting times together in Kenya and Jordan although I missed his somewhat harrowing experience in Nairobi when he and his CMD colleague, Woonki Sung, got caught in a failed coup against the Moi regime in Kenya. To keep out of the way of intermittent gunfire, they holed-up in their downtown hotel for an extra few days. Antoine moved on to the Bank's Treasury department for a few years and then came back to IFC as my deputy for a few more. After that, in 1987, he left to form his own investment management company, specializing in advising institutional investors on emerging markets. His firm, Emerging Markets Management (now Ashmore EMM), has become the world leader in the field. He was much missed and we never lost touch, as you will see in later chapters.

A third Dutchman, Michael Barth, came to CMD after graduate school at SAIS (Johns Hopkins School for Advanced International Studies) in Bologna and working at Citibank. We were together on projects in Korea and Thailand. Antoine, Michael, and Woonki worked on getting our first "country fund" up and running. That was The Korea Fund. In the initial stages, Antoine and I worked closely with the Koreans and Scudder to put the deal together. I spoke with Pedro Pablo Kuczynski of First Boston in New York (a former chief economist for the IFC), but he balked at underwriting $10 million to become a lead manager. On the spot, I committed to taking at least a similar amount as a lead manager, which mollified him, and then immediately called Antoine, asking him to put together a paper over the weekend to be presented to the Investment Committee of IFC to get their approval. Fortunately, the Committee agreed. I remember we were much derided on Wall Street at the time for trying to promote The Korea Fund. This was the second time I had had close connections with three very impressive people from this same small country. (The first time was in my Royal Navy days: see Chapter II.)

Our next recruit was Jay Tata, an American of Indian background. Jay just applied to join IFC and CMD one day in 1989. He had no connections at the time in the Bank or IFC. He had been at Prudential Life as a financial analyst for some years and had just been promoted to vice president. I remember Antoine and I questioned him on why he was prepared to take a substantial drop in both income and rank. His response was persuasive. He said he was not concerned about money and had no doubt he would earn early promotion. As time was to prove, the short, thin Gandhi-ish Jay had a steel backbone. His interest in emerging markets and IFC had been sparked when the "Pru" invested in a deal in Mexico as its first developing country investment. Ray Charles, who had been the Pru's chief investment officer at the time and Jay's mentor, retired. Our indirect connection, which Jay did not mention until he was signed on, was that we had met when I was at Schroders doing the Brown Boveri deal with the Pru. One of Jay's claims to fame with CMD was the "BLADEX" bond issue. Together we overcame the crisis that started when Merrill Lynch backed out as co-underwriter. That racy incident is covered later. Jay followed me to Batterymarch and, when I retired, went back to IFC and then, eventually, to Darby International. We are still frequently in touch.

Shuzo Nagata, "Shu," as we called him, was another wonderful guy. He had been with Nomura for some 20 years, serving in the U.S. and Australia as well as Japan. Consequently, his English was good and he understood our Western ways. He was short and very Japanese in appearance, but he had a great sense of humor and fitted in perfectly. Because he was rather foisted on us, however, we tended to give him assignments to countries that my colleagues tried to avoid. Liberia was one of them. Shu had been trapped in a hotel in Beirut for ten days at the beginning of the civil war, so he was used to that type of situation. Shu's wife was also a special person. Besides being a good Japanese housewife, she was an accomplished violinist, and also somewhat westernized. I remember a department party she attended without Shu, who was away. Lena had called her especially to make sure she would come. Apparently, it was a rather difficult conversation as this would be the first time she had attended a social function without her husband. The end result was she was pleased, and Shu was pleased when he heard about it. It was a sad day when Shu's two-year term ended and he had to go back to Nomura. We kept in touch until he finally retired as president of one of its main subsidiaries.

I was fortunate to have a great crowd working with me in CMD over the 17 years. My first deputy was P.M. Mathew, an Indian from Kerala, who came from the World Bank. P.M. was a wonderful professional and a loyal supporter of CMD. He retired and went home to India. Another of my deputies was Richard Frank, who also came from and went on to the World Bank and even became acting president of the Bank for a brief period. He resigned to become CEO of Darby Overseas International. He was succeeded by Will Kaffenberger who later worked at Emerging Markets Partnership. Many others worked with me over the years and I remain good friends with a number of them. Among those I recall fondly are Francisco Ravecca, Ernie Kepper, Teresa Barger, Michael Phair, Brad Warner, Donald Peck, Cesare Calari and Peter Wall. Also with CMD were Augustin ("Toti") Que, Farida Khambata, Bob Graffam, Gerard de la Fortelle, Prom Malhotra, Nabil Faltas, Woonki Sung, Dan Adams, Vinod Busjeet, Antonio Guerreiro, Julio Lastres, Thomas Bentley, Faustino Garza, Sami Haddad, Julius Makoni, Kumiko Yoshinari, Vijay Advani, Lawrence Clarke, Chung Min Pang, Tei Mante, Felix Chee and last, but not least, was Boris ... a Yugoslav from the then-communist Slovenia. I recall, at a reception we gave at home once for my guys, Boris got a bit carried away during some political discussion and said: "I'm a card carrying member of the Communist Party and proud of it." Another staff member for a short period was Ali Allawi—an Iraqi who had an MIT engineering degree and a Harvard MBA. He eventually went back to Iraq and was Minister of Trade and Defense.

CMD's most colorful character was actually a consultant—Frank Veneroso, who I mentioned in the chapter on Schroders. I wanted him to join the staff but he wanted to keep his independence: for practical purposes he was full time. A Harvard BA in philosophy, he initially knew nothing of finance but was remarkably bright and a quick learner. In a time of suit and ties, Frank wore a bow tie with white sneakers and a ponytail. I have already mentioned some of the other consultants we had. In addition to those helping with our "policy," there were many who worked with us in the field. Hans Horch and Terry Reilly deserve special mention. We were also lucky to receive the help of some senior retired people from U.S. and Canadian financial firms. John Dinnick and George McDonald, successively CEOs of a Canadian Investment firm, come to mind. Also, I remember fondly Ingrid Kennelly, my secretary for my last ten or so years. I inherited Ingrid from Burke Knapp when he retired.

I was very touched by the wonderful 80th birthday lunch that those who were then members of IFC's Capital Markets Department gave for me. The little present they gave me was a bottle of my favorite gin. This was followed by an elegant dinner at my favorite restaurant near IFC arranged by Antoine and Rudi. They also invited Lena and Sarah, being the only one of the kids in Washington at the time. Their parting presents included a wonderful book of letters each had written for me reminiscing about times past and a very impressive framed chart summarizing everything CMD did during my 17 years. Rudi prepared this. It is a Bob McNamara-type presentation—Bob, following Winston Churchill's lead, liked proposals to him to be presented on one page. (For somewhat better visual clarity, the chart reproduced herein is on two pages—144-145.) How Rudi got it all together really amazed me. It remains one of my prized mementos. But talking about my 80th birthday is jumping years ahead of the story.

INTERNATIONAL FINANCE CORPORATION
CAPITAL MARKETS DEPARTMENT
SUMMARY OF ACTIVITIES, FY71-MID 1988
Activities and Impact of Efforts Exceeding Eight Manweeks[a]

| | Year of Initial Contact | Type of Activity | | | | | | Impact | | | | | |
		Financial System Study	Securities Market Study	Policy Advice	Technical IFC	Assistance Other	Institution Building[b] IFC	Legislation	Regulations Supervision	Accounting	Interest Rates	Fiscal Incentives/ Taxation	Continuing Activity
Argentina	1976	✓	✓	✓	✓	✓	3	✓	✓	–	–	✓	✓
Bahrain	1982	–	✓	–	✓	–	–	✓	✓	–	–	–	–
Bangladesh	1977	✓	✓	✓	✓	–	1	✓	✓	–	–	–	✓
Barbados	1983	–	✓	✓	✓	–	1	✓	✓	✓	–	–	✓
Bolivia	1975	✓	✓	✓	✓	✓	1	–	✓	✓	✓	–	✓
Botswana	1987	–	✓	–	–	–	1	–	–	–	–	–	✓
Brazil	1971	–	✓	✓	✓	✓	6	✓	✓	–	–	✓	✓
Cameroon	1978	–	✓	✓	–	–	–	–	–	–	–	–	✓
Chile	1974	–	✓	✓	✓	✓	2	✓	✓	–	–	✓	✓
China	1983	✓	✓	✓	✓	–	–	–	✓	–	–	–	✓
Colombia	1972	✓	✓	✓	–	–	4	✓	✓	–	–	✓	✓
Costa Rica	1977	✓	–	✓	–	–	–	–	–	–	–	–	–
Cyprus	1980	–	–	✓	✓	✓	1	✓	✓	–	–	✓	✓
Dominican Republic	1977	–	–	–	–	–	2	–	–	–	–	–	✓
Ecuador	1976	–	✓	✓	✓	✓	2	✓	✓	–	–	✓	✓
Egypt	1976	✓	✓	✓	✓	✓	1	✓	✓	–	✓	✓	✓
Fiji	1984	–	–	✓	✓	–	1	–	–	–	–	–	✓
Guinea	1985	–	–	–	–	–	1	–	–	–	–	–	–
Hungary	1984	✓	✓	–	✓	–	1	–	✓	–	–	–	✓
India	1977	✓	✓	✓	✓	✓	6	✓	✓	–	–	–	✓
Indonesia	1971	✓	✓	✓	✓	✓	3	✓	✓	✓	–	✓	✓
Iran	1971	✓	✓	✓	–	–	–	–	–	–	–	–	–
Ivory Coast	1976	–	✓	✓	✓	–	2	–	–	–	–	–	✓
Jamaica	1981	✓	✓	✓	–	–	–	–	–	–	–	–	✓
Jordan	1977	✓	✓	✓	✓	✓	2	✓	✓	✓	✓	✓	✓
Kenya	1976	✓	✓	✓	✓	✓	5	–	✓	–	–	–	✓
Korea	1971	✓	✓	✓	✓	✓	6	✓	✓	✓	–	✓	✓
Kuwait	1984	✓	✓	✓	–	–	–	–	✓	–	–	–	–
Lebanon	1973	✓	✓	✓	–	–	1	✓	✓	–	–	–	✓
Malawi	1984	–	–	–	–	–	1	–	–	–	–	✓	✓
Malaysia	1984	–	✓	✓	✓	–	2	–	✓	–	–	–	✓
Mauritius	1984	–	–	–	✓	–	–	–	–	–	–	–	✓
Mexico	1977	✓	✓	✓	✓	–	1	✓	✓	–	–	✓	✓
Morocco	1975	–	✓	✓	✓	–	–	–	–	–	–	–	✓
Nepal	1984	–	✓	✓	✓	–	–	✓	–	–	–	–	✓
Nigeria	1978	–	✓	✓	✓	–	–	–	✓	–	–	–	✓

	Year of Initial Contact	Financial System Study	Securities Market Study	Policy Advice	Technical Assistance IFC	Assistance Other	Institution^b Building IFC	Legislation	Regulations Supervision	Accounting	Interest Rates	Fiscal Incentives/ Taxation	Continuing Activity
								—————————Impact—————————					
Oman	1983	–	✓	✓	✓	–	–	✓	✓	–	–	–	✓
Papua New Guinea	1984	–	✓	✓	✓	–	–	–	–	–	–	–	✓
Pakistan	1982	–	✓	✓	✓	–	2	✓	✓	✓	–	✓	✓
Panama	1975	✓	–	✓	–	–	1	✓	✓	–	–	–	✓
Peru	1980	✓	✓	✓	✓	–	1	✓	✓	–	–	–	✓
Philippines	1972	✓	✓	✓	✓	–	4	✓	✓	–	✓	✓	✓
Portugal	1979	✓	✓	✓	✓	–	1	✓	✓	–	–	✓	✓
Saudi Arabia	1979	–	✓	✓	✓	✓	–	✓	✓	–	–	–	✓
Senegal	1978	✓	–	–	✓	–	1	–	–	–	–	–	✓
Somalia	1984	✓	–	–	✓	–	–	–	✓	–	✓	–	✓
Spain	1977	–	–	–	–	–	1	–	–	–	–	–	✓
Sri Lanka	1977	–	✓	✓	✓	✓	4	–	–	–	–	–	✓
Sudan	1976	–	–	–	✓	–	–	–	–	–	–	–	–
Swaziland	1984	✓	✓	–	✓	–	1	–	✓	–	–	–	✓
Taiwan, China	1971	–	✓	✓	✓	✓	–	✓	✓	–	–	✓	–
Thailand	1972	✓	✓	✓	✓	✓	5	✓	✓	✓	–	✓	✓
Trinidad & Tobago	1978	–	–	–	✓	–	1	✓	✓	–	–	–	✓
Tunisia	1974	✓	✓	✓	–	–	1	–	–	–	–	–	–
Turkey	1982	✓	✓	✓	✓	✓	3	✓	✓	✓	✓	✓	✓
U.A.E.	1982	–	✓	✓	✓	–	–	✓	✓	✓	–	✓	✓
Uruguay	1978	✓	–	✓	✓	–	1	–	✓	–	–	–	✓
Venezuela	1971	✓	✓	✓	✓	✓	2	✓	✓	–	✓	✓	✓
Yemen	1978	–	–	–	✓	–	–	✓	–	–	✓	–	–
Yugoslavia	1974	✓	–	✓	✓	–	–	–	–	✓	–	–	–
Zambia	1974	–	✓	✓	✓	–	–	–	–	–	–	–	✓
Zimbabwe	1982	–	–	✓	–	–	1	✓	✓	–	–	✓	✓
International Underwritings	1984	–	–	✓	–	–	11	–	–	–	–	–	✓
Fund Investments	1986	–	–	✓	–	–	3	–	–	–	–	–	✓
TOTALS		31	45	50	47	18	89	32	39	10	8	21	53

^a CMD assistance has been sought by a total of 75 countries. In addition to the 61 countries indicated in the Table, a lesser time has been spent on each of the following countries: Afghanistan, Algeria, Bahamas, Botswana, El Salvador, Ghana, Guatemala, Haiti, Liberia, Maldives, Mauritania, Paraguay, Rwanda and Western Samoa.

^b The numbers which appear under the column headed "Institution Building - IFC" refer to the numbers of companies or underwritings to which IFC committed to participate. Some were cancelled or subsequently sold. International Underwriting and Fund Investments are originally counted by country nature, except IFC's two international equities and its Asean regional venture capital fund.

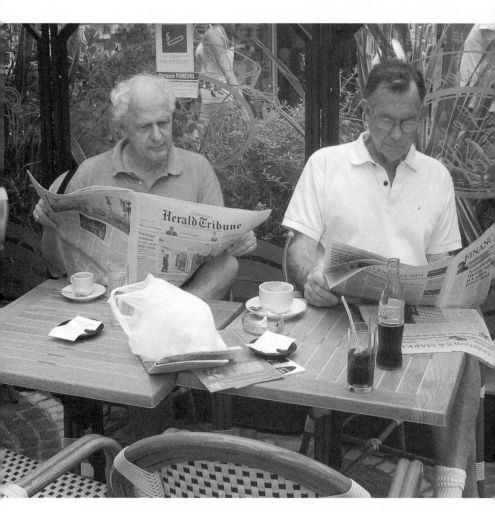

Rudi van der Bijl, the first person I met at IFC and my right-hand man for 17 years, we remained good friends with Rudi and his wife France ("Fanfan" to friends) until his death in 2010. This was taken in Ste. Maxime, France, where they had a summer place. We still remain in contact with Fanfan.

CHAPTER V

IFC ...
Working My Way
Around the World:
1972–1988

INTO ACTION

While I was learning, being introduced around and hiring my own staff, I was also expected to do useful things. It only took about three weeks before Bill Gaud asked me to go to Venezuela for my first assignment. It was the first of seven developing countries I was to visit in 1971. But before getting into the "nitty gritty" of my life in the field, so to speak, I should begin with some comments on the framework of CMD's work.

D**uring** *First, was the advisory work on financial infrastructure.* my 17 years, we were asked to provide advice and organize technical assistance for some 50 countries on how they should strengthen their financial markets. It was evident that there were several key prerequisites for an efficient market beyond having a market economy. The basics were sound contract laws, sufficient savers to invest and private companies to issue securities.

When it came to the actual task of helping a country strengthen its markets, the first step was an understanding on the part of government that the capital market—the market for long-term debt and equity—was

147

as important as the money market. Most developing countries of any size had a money market. (I remember in my investment banking days reading a book called The Bombay Money Market that was published around 1960.)

As recently as thirty years ago, most economists and many bankers tended to take the view that money was money and it doesn't matter much whether companies were financed with debt or equity. Further, they tended to overlook the fact that short-term floating rate loans usually provided by banks were a riskier form of finance than long-term fixed interest rate debt. Unfortunately, the borrowers—including financial institutions—also took that view. I recall once, when I was proposing a long-term bond issue for one of IFC's investee companies to replace its bank loan, one of IFC's vice presidents said: "Why on earth would we recommend that? The interest rate will be higher." That type of thinking is why we keep having debt crises.

It is curious that the popular governmental solutions to debt crises are to provide more debt. In our advisory work we always tried to convince our client governments that, if they wanted a strong capital market, they had to give the capital market, and especially the equity market, the same priority in their thinking that they gave the banking institutions and the money market. We always recommended placing the president of the proposed new securities commission on the same level in the hierarchy as the central bank governor. In most countries, commercial bankers were looked upon as first class citizens while the investment banker and stockbroker were considered second class. It followed that stocks and bonds were not favored investments. (Perhaps recent financial fiascos will change that attitude finally—at least in democratic countries.)

The second step was for governments to recognize the importance of having the legal, fiscal and regulatory frameworks in order. The integrity of the legal system is of paramount importance in any country, not only in terms of human rights and the democratic process but also in making it possible for a market economy to operate. For the financial market the next layer of laws are almost as important. The need for basic contract and company laws is only the beginning. Most of the countries in which we worked had these, albeit they were often inadequate. Many company acts did not contemplate the elementary requirements of corporate governance or even the limited liability concept. Even fewer differentiated between private family-owned companies and "public" companies with many minority shareholders. Of course, the issues related to company ownership and investor protection could have been dealt with in a securities act, but these were even more rare.

Assuming these key prerequisites were addressed adequately, the next issue for market development would be the status of the special laws required to make possible the several sub-categories of financial businesses. For a savings and loan bank or a mortgage bank to be able to function, there would have to be a mortgage law. For leasing companies, there would have to be a chattel mortgage law. Finally, for there to be a viable securities market, a securities act would be needed to establish the basic regulatory structure to supervise the issuance of securities, the ongoing governance of companies open to the public and fair practices in the secondary markets to protect investors. Banking acts, insurance acts and tax laws can all hinder, which was usually the case, or encourage the development of capital markets. Further, we found it pointless to even try to get a country to change its financial market policies if there was not the political will at all levels to support market reform. So, at least in theory, CMD's efforts to help improve the financial system were mainly exercises in agreeing on what was practical. Laws and regulations are fine, but if there is not the willingness or the ability to enforce them they are useless.

Assuming such matters were addressed adequately, tax policy was the next issue because of its key role in encouraging or discouraging the flow of savings into securities. In most countries, the tax laws tended to encourage savers to place their money in government bonds or bank deposits by making them tax free. But there was usually a tax on dividend income and capital gains. Instead, we attempted to encourage savings to flow into stock exchange-listed equities and corporate bonds in order to stimulate the private sector and entrepreneurship. Ideally, tax policies should encourage both savings and investment and be neutral as regards the financial instruments involved. But that would be in the ideal world. In the developing world, I believed that it was important to try and get the bias in favor of government and bank debt instruments reversed in favor of equity. Our logic was simple. If the country wanted to encourage savers to invest in common stocks of local companies, why not give them a tax incentive—or at least remove the tax disincentive—to do so? After all, stocks were more risky and less liquid than bank deposits and government bonds. So, our task was to make the tax code more equity investor friendly. Unfortunately, IFC's largest shareholder, the U.S., did, in those years, tax dividend income and capital gains at quite high rates—not a good example.

The same logic applied to proposing lower corporate tax rates on companies that open their equity to the public and listed their stocks on the local stock exchange. Owners of private companies, especially in LDCs, always benefit from lack of outside scrutiny so why not reward those that are prepared to accept the higher standards of governance expected by a securities commission? Many LDCs followed this approach. And many of them were surprised that the U.S. did not practice itself what it preached then. The U.S. remains one of the few countries in the world that taxes corporate dividends twice. We spent more time on this subject in Korea than in any other country. While I would like to think the steps they took in making the tax regime more equity-investor friendly were based on our advice, the fact was the Ministry of Finance and Bank of Korea people knew very well what they needed to do. Our job was really just to argue their case with some of the skeptics in government who could only be won over if there was support for the changes from the likes of the Bank or the IMF.

Another important fiscal policy issue was how tax and related laws encouraged or, in most cases, actually discouraged the establishment of fully funded pension funds and "collective investment vehicles" such as mutual funds. The "related laws" I am referring to here are those that make it impractical for other reasons to actually establish pension funds or mutual funds or "IRAs." All such vehicles require some type of fiscal agents with defined powers and responsibilities. "Trust" laws are the starting points. Then there are the laws or other practices that help or hinder foreign portfolio investment. Curiously, in the 1970s, many de-

veloping countries established legal and tax regimes to encourage foreign direct investment whereby foreigners could control, and own, up
to 100% of local companies, while those same countries banned foreign
portfolio investment. For inexplicable reasons, there was a feeling that
the latter would involve some kind of "control" of companies that was
even worse than the 100% control resulting from direct ownership.
There was also a—more rational—fear of "hot money" flowing in and
out of their markets as foreigners bought and sold. In order to promote
foreign portfolio investment —one of the explicit goals of IFC—while
addressing some of these issues led CMD to encourage "country funds,"
about which more later.

Our work helping to establish and restructure securities commissions
and stock exchanges was a major component of our advisory work. Most
countries had them—or at least a stock exchange. Some, like the Cairo
and Buenos Aires Stock Exchanges, had even been around for over a
hundred years. I remain proud of our involvement in creating the "International Organization of Securities Commissions" ("IOSCO") in
1983. From its original three members—Argentina, Peru and
Venezuela—plus the United States, it grew to include all the major countries in the Americas. Then the rest of the "emerging markets" were invited to join and finally all the OECD countries. Even OECD countries
that did not have securities commissions joined. There are now about
100 member countries. Some of the new members were represented
first by their stock exchanges (U.K. and Germany) or ministries of finance (France and Japan). Later, they all established separate independent commissions. We were the driving force in getting the original four
to open up. In recognition of this I was invited to be the first non-secu-
rities commission person to be on the IOSCO executive committee—
and I remained on it until I retired from IFC. CMD was especially
honored by the first chairmen of the newly established U.K. and French
commissions—Sir Kenneth Berrill and Yves Laporte, respectively—who
both visited us in Washington several times to seek our advice on setting
up their commissions. I remember one IOSCO meeting in Paris hosted
by Yves. Michael Phair organized it for us and we gave a dinner for the
fifteen chairmen who attended. The evening was actually hosted by

Michael's charming wife Margot, an Anglo Argentine who had lived in Paris and thus knew better than us how to do such things elegantly.

During these years we had developed quite a routine for those entrusted with that job of helping the organizers of these new securities commissions. We arranged visits to and training courses at the U.S. SEC, which were funded by U.S. AID. Subsequently, the SEC organized annual conferences at their headquarters for senior staff members of commissions from developing countries. These conferences were usually followed by a week in New York with Wall Street firms, also funded by AID. As the Canadian securities markets were less sophisticated than Wall Street and as the Canadian regulatory system had a slightly different model than the U.S., we also took them to Toronto or Montreal. In Canada, the provinces had jurisdiction over securities markets so it was the Ontario Securities Commission or the Quebec Securities Commission that we visited. One important lesson they all learned was another difference between the commissions in the two countries. The U.S. objective was strictly enforcing the laws and regulations to protect investors. In Canada, besides ensuring fair play, the task was also market promotion. This was helpful in our work with our client countries because the real job in developing the market was promoting the concept of investing in securities. "Shareholder democracy" was a popular expression. Giving a broader range of citizens the chance to share in the profits from industrial development had a political appeal in countries where a few families usually reaped all the financial benefits. Of course, sharing the profits also meant sharing losses, but that was the next government's problem. With these two objectives in mind, we always encouraged the authorities to call their enabling legislation a "capital markets law" rather than a securities law and to have the first part dwell on the "Capital Markets Commission's" responsibilities for growing the market. Policing it was a second—but equally important—responsibility as investors had to feel they would be treated fairly. Most of them followed this recipe but only Egypt and Turkey used that term.

When our visitors had completed their tours, we typically organized a lunch for them at IFC with the Chairman of the SEC to which we also invited the President of the NASD (Gordon Macklin for most of those years), Irving Pollack, the SEC Commissioner most concerned with international matters, David Silver, President of the Investment Companies Institute (the mutual fund industry trade association), and the president of a local investment bank, George Ferris. We must have had twenty or so of these lunches over the years, usually with about three quarters of these local experts attending at any one time. They were great opportunities for our visitors to test ideas they had picked up with people who had done it all and seen it all. Both sides always seemed to enjoy the exchanges. I think our foreign guests were impressed and pleased that they were given the chance to talk with what were seen as the leaders of the infrastructure side of the investment business. Many were struck by how friendly and open they were, especially those coming from the more formal countries, such as South Korea. Our Washington friends also seemed to enjoy meeting our visitors. At least they kept coming back.

Building Financial Institutions

After doing what we could to help improve the financial infrastructure, the logical next step was to help establish the appropriate financial companies to operate in the markets. We worked in every financial sub sector—banking, leasing, housing-finance, securities firms, insurance, venture capital, investment companies and related management companies. As access to foreign capital was another objective, we also promoted what came to be called "country funds" to encourage foreign portfolio equity investment. And, finally, we participated in initial public offerings" ("IPOs") of stocks and bonds in local markets.

Initially, IFC management was keen on investing in securities firms as they were clearly central to the domestic capital markets. Consequently, our first investments were in these types of companies—in Venezuela, Korea and Taiwan. Gradually, we at CMD convinced management and the Board that the other sub sectors were also important for capital market development. It turned out that leasing—originally strongly opposed by IFC management—became one of the largest components of our own "portfolio" of investments, and the most profitable.

Between 1977 and 1988 we set up leasing companies in Bangladesh,

153

Botswana, Brazil, Colombia, Dominican Republic, Ecuador, Fiji, India (four of them), Indonesia, Ivory Coast, Jordan, Kenya, Korea, Malawi, Pakistan, Peru, the Philippines, Portugal, Senegal, Swaziland, Tunisia, Turkey and Zimbabwe. IFC made a very good return on investment in almost all of these companies. But that they played a very important developmental role in financing small businesses was of even greater importance because of our development mandate. Leasing became one of the three pillars in IFC's strategy for promoting this important part of every country's economy.

From 1980 till my retirement in 1988 we invested in venture capital companies, investment management companies and country funds in and for Argentina, Brazil, China, India, Kenya, Korea, Mexico, Spain, and a regional one for the "ASEAN" region and its affiliates in three of the four ASEAN countries. Unfortunately, we could not invest in the Singapore affiliate as Singapore had "graduated" from WB programs.

Following are my recollections of our experiences promoting these companies—89 in total in my time. First are the stories of the three "regional" deals we did.

The South East Asia Venture Investment Company

SEAVIC came into being because of Peter Brooke. By 1982 when we started working on it, Peter had spun off an affiliate of T.A. Associates, one of the first U.S. venture capital companies. It was—and is still—called Advent International. His idea was that Advent would put together a network of management companies in other countries to establish a global management group. He anticipated, correctly, that many of the companies in which Advent would invest in the U.S. would eventually expand internationally and form foreign affiliates. Likewise, more middle-sized Japanese and European companies would be coming to the U.S. With a global network and a global portfolio of growth companies, he saw great opportunities to develop an additional competitive edge. Advent would be able to provide for its investee companies contacts, business intelligence and capital in the other countries where they might do business. Likewise, his network management partners in Europe and Japan would be able to use Advent's facilities and expertise for their companies. By 1984, Advent had already opened in Hong Kong, so it was only a step further to consider Singapore, and then its neighboring countries.

Obviously IFC, with its contacts and knowledge of all these countries, could help in this process. Consequently, it was not hard to convince him and his partners that an ASEAN regional fund could be successful and also expand his network concept. Fortunately, one of Peter's Advent partners, Tony Haight, had already helped several of their U.S. investee companies set up affiliates in Mexico. Thus they were already partially in the LDC world. Further, Advent's network partner in Holland, Orange Nassau, had interests in the region—typical of Dutch companies—and so were another source of expertise and contacts. The more difficult question was whether we could get investors to provide the capital. Our starting point was that it would be easier to get U.S. and European investors to go along with a regional program than one for a single country new to them. The Asian "Tigers" were well known and in favor, but the countries individually were considered too small for individual foreign funds. We thought it would be possible to raise money locally for the individual funds in each of these countries. The local money would give comfort as to the viability of the program to the potential U.S. and European investors Advent was targeting.

CMD's experience with Advent developing this program was great. First Peter and his team were all easy and fun to work with. On our side, it was Michael Barth, Augustin ("Toti") Que and me. (Toti was an interesting character: a Filipino of Chinese ancestry, he had a PhD from the Wharton School and a sharp tongue which he had no hesitation using to correct his bosses.) We all got along very well, both professionally and personally. Once we had agreed on the general strategy, the next step was to find local partners in Singapore, Malaysia and Thailand. We decided that programs for Indonesia and the Philippines would be started later. As it was, for Advent, starting in three new countries for the first time was quite an undertaking as they would have to establish and staff separate management companies in each of the countries.

While they would second some staff to the proposed regional headquarters in Singapore, they would have to find good local people, which would not be easy.

It took about a year to do it but, in the end, together we lined up three excellent local partners. In Singapore, it was the Development Bank of Singapore ("DBS"), at that time the main DFC. I really don't remember the people involved at DBS, but I do remember it was through them that Advent found Tan Keng Boon who became their key man in the region. In Malaysia, Arab Malaysian Merchant Bank, the leading private merchant bank, became their partner. Curiously, IFC had not done anything in Malaysia in the previous five years or so. Encouraged by the regional department, I had been there a few times to see the government people and the local DFC, but they were not much interested in what CMD had to offer either. So, thanks to SEAVIC, IFC finally had some opportunities to do business there. We were a little more helpful in Thailand, as we knew all the players. In the end, Advent chose Bangkok Bank, the leading commercial bank. In the process of all of this, Peter became very impressed with Toti Que. He asked me if we would release him to join Advent to head up their regional team as they wanted someone from the region, and it was hard to find anyone with any knowledge of the business who also could claim experience in each of the countries. After much soul searching, we agreed. We in CMD had nothing against it, although we would miss him. The problem was the appearance of a conflict of interest: the perception that he was making a job for himself and possibly using IFC as a lever. We did all the appropriate things to establish full disclosure and get the necessary legal and management approvals, so the transfer went smoothly. Toti started with a six-month training period with Advent in Boston.

In the meantime, the next step was raising the money. Of course, this was preceded by the painful task of producing the documentation—a "private placement memorandum" (PPM) as the main selling document, backed up by draft management contracts and shareholders' agreements, etc. This was all complex as there were four management companies and four investment companies (funds), each with its own set of contracts and each involving different issues as to structure, domicile

156

and tax status. It was in November 1983 that IFC's board approved investments of $1 million in each of the regional, Malaysian and Thai funds. We couldn't invest in the Singapore fund as Singapore was no longer considered an LDC. This, along with similar investment commitments from each of the local partners for their respective local funds, set the stage for trying to raise $25 million for the regional fund. It sounds like a small amount today but it was considered a huge amount then for such an exotic scheme. Advent really did all the work. Almost all the money came from institutions that were already investing in other Advent funds. These were some foundations, the Bank of Boston and Orange Nassau. Interestingly, there were also a few multinationals. They invested to gain a "window" on what was going on in the region with an eye to what they might do in those countries. They gave me my first insights as to how the CEOs of such multinationals operated.

As an aside, and thinking of some of the rather bizarre things one reads about the life of such people in recent years, I will recount a "happening" at a reception Advent organized after the first advisory committee meeting held in Singapore. This committee had about ten members representing the investors. There were some ten Advent people and another ten or so people from the Singaporean, Malaysian and Thai affiliates. Advent had also invited a dozen or so local dignitaries. So, plus spouses, there were perhaps 70 people there, standing around an elegant room in one of Singapore's best hotels. I arrived a little late when the room was already crowded so I did not see it immediately. But, then I did! In the center of the room was a single chair. Sitting in it, holding court with people who obviously believed her husband was the most important person there, was the wife of one of the CEOs present. The story I heard afterwards was that she felt her CEO husband was king of all he surveyed so she acted accordingly, as best she understood the role of a queen.

It turned out that making sound investments was not that easy. So, Advent did something quite unique. It established a production facility in Singapore where foreign companies could produce, on an experimental basis, gadgets that they needed and which they might produce from a local affiliate. The idea was that if they found that the costs and the quality were satisfactory from the small runs this factory produced, they would set up a local company and Advent would invest in it. As I recall it, this worked quite well. It was Tony Haight's idea and he moved to Singapore to implement it. I guess the scheme was a result of his Mexican exposure. As, after I retired, IFC invested in two "follow-on" SEAVIC funds, and as eventually the Philippine and Indonesian funds were established, I assume the investment results were better than those from our earlier experiments. Sadly, though, things did not work out between Toti and Advent. They parted company after only a year. Perhaps there was a lesson there for all of us—and one that Peter taught me. That is, in choosing venture capital people, one should avoid the following. First—or worst—commercial bankers. Second, investment or merchant bankers. Third, other types of financial "experts." The best prospects were people who had actually started a small business, turned it into a successful big business—and sold out. That was Tony Haight's background.

Perhaps I have written too much about SEAVIC and venture capital. On the other hand SEAVIC was the most complex and most professionally organized "first of its kind" that CMD had initiated until that time. Several years later, though, we had two other successes that were also firsts of their kind. Interestingly in the context of the steps along the path of financial institutional development I outlined earlier, these two were portfolio investment funds. At the end of the day, though, as a group, IFC lost money in the venture capital funds—not much (3% or so on capital, but before costs)—but a far cry from the 20% plus profit one expected to make in venture capital. It was a fascinating learning experience though. I like to think that the financial cost to IFC was more than counterbalanced by the developmental benefit to the countries. On the positive side, it gave us experience to start what might be called our "fourth pillar"—encouraging the flow of foreign portfolio equity into emerging markets. It is long forgotten but it was Henry Kissinger, then U.S. Secretary of State, who first, quite publicly, proposed that IFC should establish a global emerging markets fund.

Emerging Markets Growth Fund ("EMGF")

EMGF provides the second case study example and is our most gratifying country fund success story. It was not a country fund as such, but the first attempt to do a "global" emerging markets fund, as we felt that many investors would prefer a diversified emerging markets fund to a series of individual country funds. Before getting into how EMGF started, I should explain it developed from a research project that Antoine van Agtmael started—compiling the "Emerging Markets Data Base"—whose purpose was to demonstrate that investing in stocks listed in emerging markets was a good strategy. So, helped by Peter Wall, Antoine compiled an S&P 500-type index, starting with 1976, for the stocks in emerging markets that foreigners could buy, and included regional indices and a global index. It proved our point quite successfully when IFC (mainly Teresa Barger) sold it to Standard & Poor's. By 1998 when this was done, it was no longer "developmental" for IFC as it had become a source of income.

EMGF was to become the first and most successful of the many such funds that tried to emulate it later. But its birth was long and painful. It took some two years and on several occasions it looked as if all our efforts would be in vain. Antoine and, later, Michael Barth worked with me on this. I think Antoine originated the idea of a global fund in 1981. Before joining IFC, he had run an investment bank in Thailand. After going through a boom and bust in the Thai stock market, he became convinced not only that there was plenty of potential in investing in companies in developing countries but also that there was a lot of volatility in individual markets. In a farewell speech in Bangkok to the American Chamber of Commerce, he put forward the idea of a diversified, multi-country investment fund.

We all recognized that most investors knew little about developing countries and believed that the risks of investing in these markets were very high. Moreover, there were no return data and the Capital International (later Morgan Stanley Capital International or "MSCI") index only covered developed markets. Antoine hired Vihang Errunza, a professor at McGill University, to construct the first index for the "Third

159

World" based on 1976–1980 data for just six countries. Although the markets were still very small with a total market capitalization of the fifteen leading markets of only $83 billion, the returns for those years turned out to be very attractive.

With these data in hand, Antoine presented the idea of a "Third World Equity Fund" together with the research data to a group of major institutional investors at a Salomon Brothers conference in September 1981 organized by Peter Gottsegen and Marty Siegel. The Mexico Fund had just been launched by Merrill Lynch (see below for CMD's involvement) and Salomon Brothers was keen on getting involved in the area. In attendance were people like Barbara Morrow of TIAA-CREF, Francis Finlay, then with Morgan Guaranty Trust, and others. The idea was well received but there was much skepticism about the name "Third World." After obsessively thinking about this for a full weekend, Antoine wrote a short memo to me and Rudi, proposing a new name, "emerging markets." We immediately agreed and called our new data base the "Emerging Markets Data Base" from then on. Following Antoine's departure from CMD, I asked Farida Khambata to take over the management of the EMDB. Also helping Farida was Vihang Errunza who, having previously worked with Antoine on this, we borrowed for another six months. Some of the smaller markets, particularly those which were war prone, were going through a rough patch. Another colleague working with Farida, Bob Shakotko, said, partly in jest, that if the more robust markets were called "emerging markets,"maybe these smaller war prone markets should be called "submerged markets." Farida then suggested a better name—"frontier markets"—which was then adopted by the EMDB. Later, of course, it would become more widely accepted.

One amusing aside relates to our discussion as to what we would call the new fund. The first proposal, "Third World Investment Trust," was followed by silence for a few minutes while we each thought about this. It was Rudi van der Bijl who finally said something like "good concept, but poor words." We all realized immediately what he was driving at. So it came to be "Emerging Markets Growth Fund." Antoine, Rudi and I each thought we had come up with the name first but Antoine had the best claim. Unfortunately, as Antoine went off to the World Bank's

Treasury department shortly afterwards, he was not much involved in EMGF's actual promotion. As I will get to later, in 1987 he started his own emerging markets fund.

The initial work of putting together a proposal for such a diversified fund was a far cry from actually realizing it in reality. That would take several years. The next step was to get some initial partners. We saw this as more complicated than individual country funds, so we decided we needed to build a "club"—a small group of prestigious investors who could help us establish a structure and policies that would then make it easier, with the club's support, to attract other investors. We were fortunate that Bill Ryrie, IFC's then EVP, saw the prospects early on and gave the scheme his enthusiastic backing. This led to my being able to bring up the idea at three key meetings Bill held over the next several months. These were with the CEOs of Deutsche Bank, Banque Paribas and the Aga Khan. These meetings were annual affairs when Bill and IFC senior management gave the visitors a presentation on what IFC's plans were for the coming year. These were carefully scripted. I was allowed to include EMGF as one of the few specific projects to be highlighted. Both bankers reacted in almost the same words—"can we join you as sponsors?" It was a little different with "His Highness" as I was told not to bring it up in favor of some other project in Africa. This was because his CFO, Bill Robinson, was known to be opposed as we had already approached him. But, at the meeting, the Aga Khan inadvertently gave me an opening so I did tell him about it. He joined the club on the spot. Bill Robinson, who was present, was not amused. I was sorry about Bill Robinson's attitude because he was a good guy. Bill was Australian and had all the best characteristics of "Aussies:" absolutely straightforward, very blunt, but very smart and excellent company. We had always got along well together and, happily, he bore no grudges.

So by then we had three partners each committed in principle to investing $5 million, making our total, with IFC's $10 million, $25 million. We only needed another $25 million to reach our minimum requirement of $50 million. That became the hard part. Helped very much by Antoine, who knew Tim Prince and Henry Ouma much better than I, we tried the UN Pension Fund which they ran. Henry reactively positively and joined the club. We also got the support of the Abu Dhabi Investment Authority. At that point, with some $35 million spoken for, we decided it was time to pick a manager. The first choice of the group was to have Antoine manage it by leading an "in house" management team. This was very flattering for Antoine and IFC. The problem was that IFC's charter did not allow it to be an active manager of any business. So finally it was agreed that we would follow the conventional route and have an outside manager, but that Antoine would be on the Fund's board as the IFC nominee. We decided to hold a "beauty contest" and invited our partners to join us on a recruiting team. Our only taker was Henry Ouma. The others felt it was IFC's job, not theirs, to select a manager.

We considered about ten and interviewed four. We had several criteria, of which the most important were dedication to the mission, knowledge of the markets, methodology and, lastly, fees. Capital Group scored highest in each category. More importantly, what impressed us was that both Bob Egelston, their Chairman, and David Fisher, then in charge of international and research, came to meet us personally. They said they had a lot of international investing experience but none in emerging markets. They were interested in managing the fund for two reasons. First, they agreed with our case that stocks in the LDCs were undervalued and offered the dual advantages for global investors of reducing risk and increasing returns. Second, they felt that getting to know emerging markets would help with their own stock selection process for all their funds. They believed that a truly global perspective would make their analysis of European, Japanese and U.S. companies within the same industries more realistic. Many business sectors had major companies that were located in LDCs, so following Korean electronics companies and Brazilian steel companies, for example, was important for a global perspective. What struck us the most, though, was that they were candid in explaining their lack of knowledge of our markets, as well as their interest in them. This was made clear in their fee proposal, which was 0.9% and declining with increases in total assets. They said, and we agreed, that they could not make money on a $50 million fund with that fee as they would have to hire a dozen or so additional staff, but they

162

wanted the opportunity as they expected to benefit over time. Considering that managers were charging 1.25% to 1.50% for quite simple mandates, we could not but be impressed. The other firms we interviewed gave us the impression that they were making just a routine marketing pitch. The only exception was Templeton, who was not interested in any foreign market at the time.

So it was really no contest. Capital Group was given the mandate. It was unanimous. For me, of the dozen or so managers with whom I have had some involvement over the years, Capital Group remains the most impressive. While not as large and well known as Fidelity, Vanguard or Templeton, and several others associated with investment banks, such as Merrill Lynch Asset Management, their performance record and management style were second to none. Professionalism with Capital Group was everything. In 1985, when we first met, they listed their strengths as consistent methodology, teamwork and staff continuity. The enthusiasm and the personal involvement of Bob and David continued at a level higher than we experienced with other managers. The results— over ten years later, a fund with some 20 times the total assets of its nearest competitor and a performance track record to match—speak for themselves. Its shareholders have included some 300 of the world's best known pension funds, foundations and insurance companies. At the time we gave them the mandate, our hope was that the Fund might reach Henry Kissinger's 1976 target of $500 million within five years. Actually, they had passed a billion by then and passed $20 billion by the tenth year.

But appointing Capital Group had an unexpected immediate, but temporary, downside. Of the other managers we considered, one was the administrative manager of the UN Pension Fund ("UNPF"). They felt we had not given them a fair hearing. The end result was that the UNPF withdrew from the club. That was a blow. Over the next several months, a few more institutions came in as investors, and others walked away. One of those was Batterymarch Financial Management, a Boston money manager with about $20 billion of equity assets then, whose clients were mainly U.S. and foreign pension funds and foundations. Their claims to fame were fully automated investment and administrative systems. These were quite unique at the time. Batterymarch was owned by Dean LeBaron, who was considered a bit of a maverick, but who had a "blue chip" institutional following. The reason they gave for pulling out was that they had lost patience with the lengthy process. Of course, it could also have been because we had selected Capital Group to manage it and it is never easy for managers to explain to their clients paying fees to other managers. There will be much more about Battery-march later. Around that time IBM's pension fund came in. Also for a while we had the backing of the World Bank's pension fund, but they backed out over a bureaucratic technicality. They wanted us to report to the board that they were considering it. I felt they should do that, as we did not report the names of any of our investors. I was probably wrong on that one as they refused to do so and did back out. We also tried hard to get one or more Japanese investors. Antoine and I even traveled to Tokyo, where Capital Group had many contacts, to give presentations to various investors, but our efforts were to no avail. However PGGM, a major Dutch pension fund became an early investor, establishing a trend that has led to Dutch institutional investors having among the highest allocations to emerging markets.

By then we were becoming concerned that momentum was slipping away and that there might be other defections. Getting past $40 million seemed harder as each month passed. Finally, I took the bull by the horns. I went to Bill Ryrie and said: "Look, we all agree this can be a very successful deal, but confidence is slipping. If we—IFC can go to $20 million, that guarantees the $50 million. If we show confidence, I'm pretty sure we can get some more. Let's go back to the board and get approval for an additional $10 million." Bill could well have said "no" as 20% was IFC's limit to its equity position in any one financing. Thankfully, he still had confidence and agreed to go ahead despite the embarrassment he and IFC would face having to explain this to our board. Fortunately, IFC's board gave us 100% support. And it worked. In the end, thanks to Capital Group, we got $5 million from the ARCO pension fund and also $2 million from the Rockefeller Family.

So, as the saying goes, "all's well that ends well." We were finally able to go ahead with the $50 million, with IFC having to put up only about

$12 million rather than $20 million. It turned out to be one of IFC's best investments with about a 30% annualized rate of return over the ten or so years it held the investment.

"Banco Latinoamericano de Exportaciones, S.A."

BLADEX was our first and only regional banking experience. It was a "greenfield" investment in Latin America's first regional export finance bank, to be incorporated in Panama. While we were not supposed to get involved with banks at the time, this was an exception for several reasons. First, it was the brainchild of a World Bank vice president, Nicky Barletta, who had gone home to Panama to become minister of finance—and was later elected President of Panama—who had convinced Moeen Qureshi, then IFC's only vice president, that it was a worthy idea. Second, it was to finance "non traditional" exports—that is, local agricultural and small scale manufactured items between the smaller countries. The local banks were too small and unsophisticated to do much of this and the large international banks were unwilling to finance these small deals. Third, a dozen of our member countries in Latin America had been lobbied by Nicky to lobby IFC to support it. But except for Nicky in his role as minister of finance, there was no Panamanian involvement until Panama joined the list of promoting countries. Ironically, as it was to finance working capital for exports, it was much more a traditional commercial bank than were most of the large international banks at the time. That is it only made short term loans whereas the latter were moving more towards longer term lending. Structuring BLADEX was as much a political issue as it was a business one. In the end, 23 Latin American country government entities participated as Class A shareholders, and some 100 local private commercial banks and about a dozen major international banks became Class B and Class C shareholders, respectively. International institutions could become Class D shareholders but IFC was the only one. Classes A, B and C shareholders were entitled to three board memberships each, and Class D one. This reinforced the concept that the bank would be majority

IFC . . . Working My Way Around the World

Latin American owned—by the Classes A and B shareholders—and majority private sector controlled—by the Classes B and C shareholders. This later was an IFC condition of investing. So, finally, almost 200 entities contributed the grand total of $10 million as the original paid-in capital in 1977—some two years after we first started working on it. The governments formally approved its status as an official international financial institution ("IFI") with the same corporate tax and foreign exchange privileges as had the Bank and IFC. It was unique in this as it was the only one I knew of then that had this status while also having a majority of the stock owned by private banks.

Our investment officer on the project was Francisco Ravecca, a Uruguayan who had gone to Stanford and then NYU business school before becoming an entrepreneur and then a banker before joining IFC. "Pancho," as he was called, was a typical Latin American of the old school—charming, good looking, fun to be with but very dedicated and hard working. He did most of the money-raising, as he knew most of the players. The hard part was not the money as such but getting the right amounts from the right entities. The larger countries and the larger local banks were supportive but, as their needs for this type of financing were less, many of them favored token investments rather than an amount appropriate to their GDPs. Conversely, many of the smaller countries wanted more than their share. The issue was really not so much the money as the entitlement to board representation and, thus, influence. The first CEO was Arthur Giraldi, an experienced trade finance executive from Bank of America. Art did a great job of setting up the initial systems for the bank and negotiating a sensible structure of lending policies and limits with the shareholders. This latter was another political exercise as the "A" and "B" shareholders were the beneficiaries while the "C" shareholders (the international banks) and IFC were the suppliers of financing to the bank. Fortunately, the shareholding balance we had worked out resulted in very businesslike decisions in these initial key areas.

We had a small internal crisis over this. As it was a regional Latin American deal, IFC's regional vice president, Kurt Eckrich, lobbied to be in charge. Moeen Qureshi agreed. But Pancho Ravecca objected to this arrangement and told Moeen that he was not prepared to be the investment officer unless it was a Capital Markets' deal as no one in the regional department knew anything about banking or trade finance or been involved in a regional transaction, whereas CMD did and had also done other regional deals. Moeen conceded.

BLADEX was a remarkable success. It really came through during the debt crisis of the 1980s when, for a long period, BLADEX was almost the only supplier of working capital loans for exports within the region. One of IFC's other successes with BLADEX during this period of the 1980s was underwriting the first bond issue for a Latin American entity. This was a $50 million five-year Note issue launched in June 1985. Goldman Sachs was our co-manager and the other underwriters were a group of mainly Japanese and European banks. Merrill, Lynch had originally agreed to be the co-manager, but they backed out at the last minute, fearing we could not pull it off. They had a point in being worried. Not only was BLADEX still a small Panamanian company by their standards, but also it was the first time IFC had ever originated a bond issue. What they overlooked was that a few of us had had some experience with Eurodollar bond issues in our previous lives. Our key player was Jay Tata, who had joined IFC the year before from Prudential Insurance. Jay also knew well Lew Weston, a great supporter of CMD's efforts, who had been a Goldman Sachs partner. Gordon Macklin had put me in touch with Lew when I had asked Gordon for help in finding retired Wall Street people who might be interested in working with us as advisors. As the Goldman Sachs' partner in charge of syndications he had a great deal of credibility in the financial community. Lew had been of great help to us in advising governments on securities markets over the previous few years. He was such a warm hearted generous, but modest type that people could not help but like and trust him. That was how it came about that Goldman replaced Merrill as co-manager. We were able to follow up this issue with another one for $30 million the next year. This one had warrants to buy convertible preferred stock as we felt then that it would be useful to open up the possibility of raising equity capital for the future. IFC agreed to have the bank's Articles of Association changed to allow the preferred stock to be converted into

Class D stock. We had the preferred and the warrants listed on the London Stock Exchange to enhance their liquidity, but none of the buyers of the Notes ever exercised their warrants, so that attempt to increase the capital failed.

But the ultimate "coup" IFC had with BLADEX happened after I had retired. In about 1990, when its balance sheet totaled around a billion dollars, they needed additional capital to continue expanding and to comply with conventional bank equity ratios under the Bank for International Settlement ("BIS") guidelines. It turned out to be impossible to get the four different groups of shareholders together to agree on a rights issue. Consequently BLADEX management tried to get the Inter-American Development Bank ("IDB") to buy subordinated debt that could be counted as capital. IDB had difficulty with that as they only lent to governments or to entities guaranteed by governments. While BLADEX had governments as shareholders, there were no guarantees. Several BLADEX board members who knew me from the past (Roberto Bornhausen, the CEO of Unibanco in Brazil, Pancho Ravecca, by then CEO of Banco Surinvest, a regional bank based in Uruguay, and Geraldo Hess, IFC's nominee) asked me if I could help convince IDB. As I knew BLADEX well, and as I had always encouraged equity financing over debt financing, I suggested a stock issue—an IPO on the NYSE. IFC and the BLADEX board were skeptical. We had hoped that Goldman would take the role of lead manager but, much to Lew's dismay and mine, they declined. Their view was that it was simply too small a deal to be worth their time. It was Art Geraldi's successor as CEO of BLADEX, Jose Castaneda, who suggested we approach Oppenheimer & Co. As they were at the time not in the first league of Wall Street players, it was a reasonably sized deal for Oppenheimer and also one that would give them considerable prestige. They underwrote a $100 million offering. It came out at $22 a share and eventually the shares reached about $40. Prior to problems related to its high Argentine exposure it had a net worth at the time of about $600 million and loans outstanding of about $5 billion. IFC sold its stock a year or so later, for an IRR of about 30%. That was not bad for an investment in a start-up bank almost half owned by 23 governments.

Working around the world

Back to finding my pioneering ways, following are two stories that give a flavor of traveling in those days when at least we travelled first class and stayed in five star hotels—if any.

Lena and I had an interesting time getting to Kenya in September 1976 for the IMF/WB Annual Meetings. The fun started in Beirut— after visiting Lena's brother Johan in Addis Ababa on the way—as an even more exciting experience but not at all related to my tasks. We thought we had a direct flight from Beirut to Nairobi. But it turned out to be via Jeddah where we had to overnight. The IFC travel office is usually quite efficient about tickets and visas, but not on this occasion. So, in Beirut, I had to go to the Saudi Embassy/Consulate to get visas. I arrived to find the usual disorderly crowd in the Consul's office and thus could just get to his office door. There was no receptionist so I just waved my red UN "laissez-passer" over my head. Somehow he noticed it and beckoned me forward. Without a word, he looked at me, grabbed our passports, opened them and stamped them, all while still talking away. Imagine trying that these days! The next event was the flight to Jeddah. It was uneventful, except for the fact that all the other passengers were Arabs dressed in a variety of Arab garb. We arrived quite late but had no trouble getting to our hotel—still remember both the ride and the hotel. The taxi driver was a wild man. He was probably doing 100 km/h in the town and totally ignoring all the red stoplights. Fortunately there wasn't much traffic. "The Pilot Hotel" had a big neon sign proclaiming its name in English so one couldn't miss it. It was a memorable night. A very polite English-speaking receptionist checked us in quickly and told us when they would call us in the early morning and make sure we got a taxi. It was a bit of an unpleasant surprise to find our room hadn't been touched since the last guest had left, whenever that was. An unmade bed and dirty towels. After the luxuries of Beirut this was a rude awakening.

My only other bad hotel experience in LDCs was in Istanbul. That was my or, rather, Rudi's and my fault. We had missed our flight from Athens to Cairo because we had overstayed our time on a beach near the Athens airport and thus had to go via Istanbul. Unfortunately it was high tourist season so we ended up in a very shoddy hotel. At least the beds were made, but I'm not so sure about how many times the sheets had been used since the last cleaning.

Moving on to serious matters, meeting key government officials and business people in my "customer countries" and understanding how to operate in this new environment was an ongoing learning experience. An important lesson I learned was an obvious one: while each country was unique in many respects, their problems were remarkably similar. Finding my way in each new country became easier as the years passed, but there was always something new to learn. It is interesting that the last two of the 60 developing countries I was to visit—Kuwait and Malaysia in 1984—could have been so similar but so different. Both were small and under-developed in most senses of the term, but one was rich and one was poor. In one, Kuwait, the senior people tended to be secretive and distant, while in the other, Malaysia, they were open and friendly. At least that was the case then. Now, Malaysia has become almost a wealthy country while Kuwait has not changed much economically.

First impressions count a lot so I shall comment on each of the countries I visited in a general way to give a feel for the receptions received and then describe our work. In the remainder of 1971, besides Venezuela, I visited Korea, Brazil, Taiwan, Iran and Indonesia, more or less in that order. In 1972, I went to Colombia, the Philippines and Thailand—and visited most of the 1971 countries at least once more. And so on as the years passed. I will concentrate more on our operational tasks in these and the other countries where we worked later.

Venezuela

This was my very first IFC mission. I arrived at Caracas airport late at night. It was hot, humid and much more "Latin" than I recalled Rio to be when I went there in 1967. The hour-long drive to the city was not inspiring either. But I was rather pleased with the small, old colonial style hotel where I stayed, the Avilla. But Caracas was not a destination of choice. Being close to the equator, it was hot, humid and unattractive.

As it was in a valley, it also suffered from smog. While the wealth of the wealthy was very conspicuous, the tragedy of the poor was equally so. My marching orders had been to respond to the government request to IFC for advice on revamping the securities market. This included revamping the legislation and their securities commission as well as help in establishing some new types of financial institutions to operate in what was hoped would become a more efficient market. As a country, Venezuela suffered from both too much natural wealth and from being tropical. As the Venezuelan who was the Alternate Director on IFC's board at the time told me: "We Venezuelans suffer from two things. First, our brains have been baked because of where we are. Second, we are so wealthy we don't have to work so we never spend much time even learning how to think." It was both an honest and an accurate statement. One clear example was the state of the financial market. While it looked reasonable on paper, it didn't work in practice.

On my first day, I reported as ordered to the Minister of Finance who gave me the usual enthusiastic and gracious welcome. Then, he turned me over to his Vice Minister, Carlos Emmanuelli, the man in charge of the program. Except for the pleasure of being with Carlos, who was a jovial, casual fellow who, like most Venezuelans, took nothing very seriously, my only memory of that first trip was my required visit to the U.S. Embassy's consular section. In theory, Bank and IFC personnel were only supposed to travel as United Nations' staff, with the appropriate "laissez-passer." As I had not had time to obtain this in Washington, my instruction from IFC's personnel people was to go first to the U.S. Embassy and have my "green card" canceled and replaced by a "G-IV" visa. This was the visa issued to UN personnel resident in the U.S. I was rather reluctant to give up the "green card," but it was prestigious to have the red laissez-passer. The color indicated your rank and red was the highest classification.

During the next several years, Rudi, Sid Robbins and Frank Veneroso and I did a lot there. Frank had resigned from Nesbitt, Thomson shortly after I did but did not want to take on a full time job. As I had wanted him to work for me at IFC, I was happy to have him back as a free-lance consultant. Frank, being intellectually brilliant, read all the books on the subject (there weren't many then) and took to this work very seriously. I had rather forgotten until now that, when I was first interviewing him for Nesbitt, Thomson, he had said he had a BA from Harvard in philosophy, and only got interested in the securities markets when he found his family, as a result of bad advice from brokers, had lost a lot of money. So he read up on the subject and went into the business to recoup the family fortune. I was confident he could make the adjustment to my new world.

By 1976 we had helped the government bring its securities market laws and regulations up to date, helped establish a real securities commission and established two financial companies. The first was supposed to be an investment bank. We couldn't find any foreign companies to participate in the latter, which was supposed to be a market maker in local securities. They were not very successful. But that was Venezuela. A change of government in the early 1980s resulted in a change of financial policies and things went back to pretty well where they were when we started. I believe IFC "reinvented the wheel" there twice more in the 1990s.

One lasting memory involves Carlos and Frank. They, along with Sid, had been working on a major piece of financial market legislation. Carlos was to make a television address announcing it. Early in the evening in question, Lena got a call at home from Carlos. The conversation went as follows. Carlos: "Where is Frank? I need him right away; he took my copy of my speech and walked off with it. I'm on in an hour!" Lena: "Carlos! I'm in Washington and you and Frank are in Caracas. How would I know where Frank is?" Carlos: "Oh." Another lasting memory was of Carlos' car and driver. The car was an old but, for Caracas, impressive black Buick. His driver was a short taciturn tough guy who always carried a revolver. When driving through traffic in the city he would always blast away on his very loud siren to clear the way. No one ever paid attention. I suppose that was democracy in action in Venezuela. Once I asked him why he always had the gun on the seat beside him: "Were we, my colleagues and I, in danger?" His answer was: "No. It's the car I have to protect."

As to the types of firms that would actually operate in the "improved" market, there were two major gaps then. First, there were no real investment banks that could offer a professional level of service as underwriters of securities, dealers and providers of advisory services to issuers and investors. Second, there were no mechanisms to provide the markets with any liquidity. As indicated earlier, we were carried away with the enthusiasm of the challenge and rather overlooked the fact that Venezuela was a small country with a very closed economy. But there were half a dozen or so fairly good listed companies. With the enthusiastic support of the government, we set about filling those two gaps, notwithstanding.

Valinvenca. The first task then was establishing an investment bank, which was called Valinvenca, with the help of the local DFC. They put us in touch with the Vollmers Group, a leading local conglomerate. One of their subsidiaries, Finalven, which was in the auto financing business, became our main local shareholder. I remember well the many meetings Rudi and I had with Arturo Sosa, their main financial man. As I recall it, he was one of the very few sound-thinking businessmen I met in Caracas. We were also very fortunate in attracting Morgan Guaranty Trust (now JPMorgan) as our technical partner. At least we thought we were fortunate. While they provided tremendous prestige and lots of money, they did not in those days know much about investment banking. Their incentive for joining the venture was enhancing their broader interests in Venezuela. But that was fair. They also seconded one of their best securities people, Guido Conill, as the first CEO.

The best part of the saga was that during this very early period in CMD's life we could concentrate our resources on this, our first active client country. Frank Veneroso, Sid Robbins and Hans Horch all played their parts in educating the government in what had to be done to have a working securities market and an investment bank that could actually do something useful. We had a hilarious time doing this and working with our good friend Carlos Emmanuelli and his Ministry of Finance colleagues. Unfortunately we had not yet learned that good intentions were not enough. While all kinds of regulations were changed to the good, the first warning sign came when the central bank refused to accept the fact that investment banks did not—or should not—need the same amount of capital as commercial banks and "financieras," the local version of non-bank finance houses. They insisted that Valinvenca have the same minimum starting capital —$20 million. This was at least ten times more than was needed. I tried to explain that our successful Korean investment bank had started with $3 million in a much larger market. I also pointed out that Nesbitt, Thomson, my old Canadian firm, had only about $5 million capital when I had resigned three years previously. Then, with over 600 employees, it did quite well in an even larger market. Unfortunately, the Vollmer Group, being Venezuelan, had more money than they knew what to do with and Morgan Guarantee, being commercial bankers and having a different agenda, weren't overly concerned. So we went ahead. In retrospect, it was a pity that we had not been harder-nosed about this and the other business arrangements.

While it was partially due to IFC, some of the business arrangements were somewhat bizarre. I recall vividly that this was the beginning of an ongoing struggle with IFC's legal department. The lawyer on our case was an American who had joined IFC from USAID. I had met him through Stanley Grande when he was stationed in Brazil. But that didn't help. The trouble started in preparing the bylaws and shareholder agreement. Fortunately, I had been spared this responsibility in Korea with Korea Investment Finance Corporation ("KIFC"), discussed later, as the lawyers working on that shareholder agreement, knew better than to second-guess Goldman Sachs and Nomura. So this was really my first experience with such negotiations. I had taken what seemed to me the usual approach by establishing what I thought were routine ground rules with him. That was, he should look after all the standard IFC boilerplate and the strictly Ven-ezela/IFC policy issues. I would welcome any advice and suggestions he had as a U.S. lawyer—but he was to deal with Rudi or me on any business points he wanted to make before talking to the other shareholders about them. I thought that was clear and that he had agreed. To my surprise, a few weeks later, I received a call from Guido Canill saying that our lawyer had put in a new clause to the agreement that he found strange. He didn't say he wouldn't accept it; he just wanted to know why it had been added. To my horror, I found that what he had added without telling Rudi or me first was a clause saying in effect: "Valinvenca could only sell listed securities short on an 'up-tick'." This was straight out of NYSE regulations. He obviously thought he was making a great contribution to market development. But he hadn't noticed that selling short was not legal in Venezuela and that the local stock exchange had no rules that contemplated "up-ticks"— that was a rather technical matter only used in the U.S. and simply could not have been understood, let alone implemented, in Venezuela. But more important to me was that such detail did not go in shareholder agreements or bylaws, but rather in operating manuals. I called him in and pointed out that, first, he had broken our agreement by doing this without discussing it with us first and, second, it made us look less than professional. He was very, very upset. Eventually, the legal department backed down on this, but it was clear that our general counsel had marked me as a troublemaker.

The end of the story is that after some five years, Valinvenca was still only doing commercial paper business. We sold out with a small profit.

Sofimeca. The next operation was a firm that was to provide liquidity to the debt market, called Sofimeca. Unfortunately, as this exercise started only a few months after Valinvenca was launched, and several years before our similar successful KSFC venture in Korea, we still did not understand fully what we were doing. In theory, it was a great idea and the company could have played a very useful role if the bond market was as active as we had assumed it would be. In Venezuela then, as in all developing countries, stockbrokers acted only as agents. As small partnerships, they had no capital and thus could not even finance brokerage transactions between the trade date and settlement, let alone make markets or finance margin accounts for investors. So, with our great story, and dreams of glory, we convinced all the local bankers and financieras to participate in a firm that would fill this gap. Again, Frank and Sid helped sell the story. Rudi, cleverly, escaped the role of investment officer. Pancho Ravecca replaced him. I also convinced an old friend from Toronto, John Dinnick, who had recently retired as CEO of another leading Canadian investment firm. John was a great addition to the team because he knew all about market making and the securities financing business and was able to educate our team as well as the locals.

They all respected John. He was, as they say, "larger than life"—an ex Olympic skier, an ex WWII RCAF pilot, a top flight financial man and absolutely full of life.

With all this support, it was not hard to get the company established. But, not surprisingly, there were no foreign takers as a shareholder—even Morgan Guarantee felt they had done their share for the country. The one benefit of that was that it allowed us to get a real professional to be the first CEO. I recruited Bob Kay, who had been the top corporate bond trader on my team at NT, to take a six-month sabbatical to do this. Unfortunately, again, we had missed the point that, notwithstanding the large capitalization of the market, the more important reason there was no liquidity was that there was no activity. We had yet to understand that Venezuelans, like the citizens of most LDCs, simply were not ready to risk their savings in shares of other peoples' companies and that the family owners of companies did not want minority shareholders. Previously, we had played a part in a change to the tax regime that provided listed companies with a lower tax rate and investors in them exemption from dividend and capital gains taxes, but this did not help. While there were the usual half dozen large listed companies, and even some bond issues, the buyers were not interested in trading. Some smaller companies listed to get the tax benefits, but the family investors in them sold only the minimal amount to qualify as listed companies. As we were to learn later, there was not much will behind the reforms so they really had no hope of working in practice. The end result was that Sofimeca, notwithstanding the major support from the ministry of finance, could do nothing because there was nothing to do. Poor Bob Kay had a miserable time. He picked a few stocks that he thought should be liquid and tried to make a market—giving firm bids and offers—but he had no takers on either side at anything like reasonable prices. The same applied to bonds.

When Bob left, the nominee of the chairman of our lead shareholder—Banco Consolidado—took over. As I recall it, he invested in a few stocks and eventually developed a form of banking business. It was an unhappy business for both the local banks and IFC. Our efforts in Sofimeca to move things in the right direction were not well received and, not unfairly, we were seen by the other shareholders as part of the problem. Finally, we sold out to Banco Consolidado for a loss of about 20%. It was one of CMD's largest losses over my 17 years, but it could have been much worse. Some years later Banco Consolidado went under as a result of some scandal that emerged during one of Venezuela's periodic financial crises. But our main mistake was that I had not realized that Venezuelans were too culturally different and too richly endowed with oil for there to be any incentive to change. Several years later, I recall talking to some Colombians about this. They made much the same point. Colombians weren't inherently smarter than Venezuelans—and they too had had their "brains baked" under the tropical sun—they just had to work harder to survive. It was a senior Colombian government official who told me this. He had been to school and university in Canada, so he knew I would understand.

Republic of Korea

My first trip to Asia was to South Korea in 1971. This was immediately after my first trip to Venezuela. Two things struck me when I first arrived. The first was that the Korean War had not been forgotten. The highway from the airport to the center of Seoul was six lanes wide. It was, in fact, an emergency air force landing strip. The second was how markedly poor Seoul was as a city in stark contrast to Tokyo, where I had just spent a couple of days. Once out of the city center—maybe three blocks square —Seoul was a village. Not exactly thatched huts, but almost. But then the per capita GDP was only about $200.

The purpose of the visit was to look into IFC's investment in what was to be Korea's first investment bank, which was being promoted by the government. By the time I arrived Moeen Qureshi had already established the framework—a joint venture with the Korean DFC as the local shareholder and Goldman Sachs, Nomura Securities and Bankers Trust as the "technical partners." Moeen had done an excellent job setting it up with such fine partners. It was called Korea Investment Finance Corporation ("KIFC").

Getting to know Korea and the Koreans was a great experience. The people were very, very tough, but friendly when you got to know them.

They worked hard and played hard. Being taken out to dinner by them, which happened almost every night, was quite an experience—fun but grueling. But, during working hours, they were hard bargainers and deadly serious. They had agreed quickly to accept our "high tech" management tools because they saw they were actually useful. I discovered later that many countries and companies went along with Bank or IFC "conditions" without any understanding of what they meant or much intention of living with them once they had got the money. But that was not the Korean way. The government people and KIFC management followed through and lived up to all of their commitments. The only problem I had with my many Koreans friends was their formality. An amusing example of that was exemplified one evening in Washington with Mr. B.J. Lee, KIFC's first president. I thought I knew him well enough by then to ask a question as it was about the sixth dinner Lena and I had had with him over the years. "Mr. Lee, you have known Lena and me for five years now and we think we should use our first names. But we still don't know yours and we would like to call you by your first name. What should we call you as a long time friend?" With a perfectly serious expression, he said: "Call me Mr. Lee." We settled for "BJ."

Korea's financial market development program had been started in the early 1960s by USAID. Sid Robbins had done all the work for them. In 1970, IFC had been asked by the government to help establish a securities commission, revamp the stock exchange and establish a first "investment bank." IFC was also to organize the necessary additional advice as to the requisite laws and regulations to provide the legal framework. Moeen Qureshi had already started the program. He had brought in Hans Horch to do the technical work on the Securities Commission and stock exchange legislation. Hans was a remarkable person who I got to know and like tremendously. After a year driving tanks for the German army in Russia, he became, as he said, a "guest of the Soviets" for two years in a prisoner of war camp. After his release and after graduate studies in law and economics, his first job was with the Rockefeller Foundation. They sent him finally to Brazil to start their investment fund business there. It was the Rockefeller connection that got him to IFC for this specific assignment. I have many fond memories of Hans; some of these will appear later.

178

Predating IFC's involvement, the World Bank had established a Development Finance Company in 1968 called, not surprisingly, Korea Development Finance Corporation ("KDFC"). As it was a government/private sector joint venture, IFC had become a shareholder and had a very close relationship with the management. Consequently, KDFC was to be the Korean sponsoring shareholder of KIFC—this new investment banking enterprise. The standard IFC formula for starting new companies was applied. IFC would be a founding shareholder with a 20% equity interest. KDFC would be the domestic partner with some 50%. The foreign technical partners recruited by Moeen—Goldman Sachs, Bankers Trust and Nomura Securities—would have about 10% each. This was not exactly a routine investment for them, but they had the foresight to see that the Korean government and Korean companies would be great sources of other business opportunities in the future. All three were to provide staff support as well as money. It was the former that would be the key to the necessary "technology transfer" and thus, ultimately, a successful business. KDFC was mandated to provide local management. This they could do because of the support in building their own professional management they had received over the years from the Bank's DFC Department. KDFC was used to establishing and nurturing new companies.

At the time, Korea had only a small stock exchange and a few part time brokers. The idea was to set up this first investment bank to perform securities underwriting, market making and distribution functions. It was to operate to international professional standards and thus lead the way for other investment banking firms to be established once a more professional securities market was developed. The local brokers had two business lines: trading in government bonds and the few listed stocks and selling a form of corporate commercial paper (three-month loans). This latter was essentially a "black market" business as the investors were anonymous and paid no taxes. A primary objective of the government was to legitimize this business by having the new investment banks underwrite corporate bonds that would be registered with the new securities commission. Companies were encouraged to list their stocks. Those that did were given a lower corporate tax rate then those

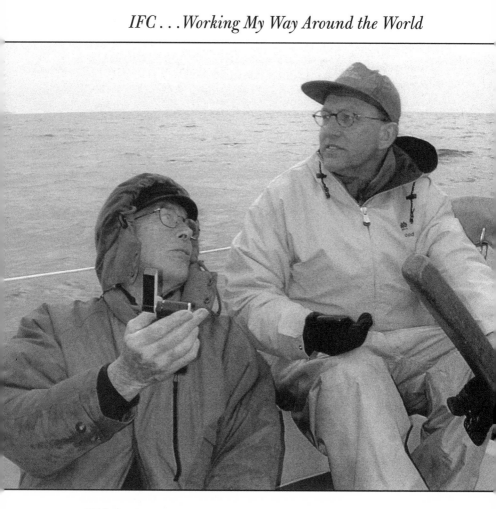

With Antoine van Agtmael on our old sailboat "Windrush" in about 2006. Antoine is a good friend and, happily, he and his wife Emily now have a weekend retreat just 15 minutes from our place.

that did not. Savers were encouraged to buy securities. Dividends and capital gains from listed stocks were not taxable.

The man behind all of this was South Korea's visionary Minister of Finance, Nam Duck Woo. He was always the leading initiator and active supporter of steps to improve the financial system, even when he became Prime Minister. I got to know him very well over the years as this was but the first of many projects IFC had in Korea. He understood then, better than most people in the Bank did, let alone in LDCs, that an efficient and strong financial market was essential to build a strong and competitive economy. It is interesting to look back on this. Korea's GDP grew from about $200 per capita in 1971 to some $10,000 only 20 years later. One of the most embarrassing experiences in my business life was being taken to task publicly by Nam Duck Woo when he was Deputy Prime Minister. At an Asia Society reception in New York, in front of a dozen people, he stated he was very unhappy with IFC and concluded by saying: "Mr. Gill, you have lost face in Korea." This was a result of Bob McNamara changing some details of the terms of a deal we had agreed to with him. It involved an investment in a company that was to play a key role in supporting some important structural changes to the market infrastructure. Minister Nam was the sponsor of the legislation involved and felt IFC had let him down. It was unusual for McNamara to micro manage such details after IFC's board had approved a deal. I never understood why he did this.

Korea Investment Finance Corporation ("KIFC"). KIFC turned out to be one of IFC's great successes. Not only did it achieve the developmental objectives set for it, but IFC also made an internal rate of return (IRR) of around 40% when it started selling its holdings some five years later, in the late 1970s. KIFC became known as the most profitable and most prestigious investment firm in Korea. As we used to say: "It was not the biggest, but it was the best." By the late 1970s, Korea had some dozen similar enterprises. Most, like KIFC, had foreign investment/merchant banks as significant shareholders.

My main contribution, helped by Rudi van der Bijl as our investment officer on the project, was to make sure that KIFC started out with strong internal accounting and control systems and a good management information system. We installed profit center accounting as well as a requirement that the outside auditors provided a "management letter." To my surprise, this project was the first where IFC required such "governance" standards as a condition of their investment. As they were fairly routine for the better Wall Street firms, our U.S. technical partners supported me in insisting on these requirements despite the skepticism of some of my IFC colleagues.

One of the people I got to know through this exercise was Henry "Joe" Fowler, then a Goldman Sachs partner and previously a U.S. Secretary of the Treasury. He was a fine gentleman of the old school and he took KIFC and Goldman's role in it very seriously. I remember him as grandfatherly and very modest. He pitched-in with the younger fellows—Korean, Japanese and American—to help make KIFC into the type of company we had promised the Korean government that we would deliver. I recall fondly that, over the next decade, he always made time during the IMF/World bank Annual Meetings to attend a lunch we held for KIFC shareholders and management.

Presenting the proposal to IFC's board was a bit of an anti-climax. While I suffered a bit from stage fright, as it was my first such experience, I had done my homework with those members who agreed to talk to me beforehand. Consequently, I knew we would have an easy time. More importantly, IFC's procedures required the Investment Officer—Rudi van der Bijl—to make the verbal presentation and answer questions on the written proposal. My job was just to sit at his side and respond to questions concerning policy.

Korea Securities Finance Corporation ("KSFC"). KSFC was my next venture in Korea. KSFC's function was to provide financing to securities companies. That is, make "brokers' loans" as they are called in the U.S. This venture flowed from our ongoing advisory work with the government. Nam Duck Woo, who by then was Deputy Prime Minister, was still in charge personally and saw the need for some form of market liquidity mechanism. Fortunately, we had by then learned from our Venezuelan experience and were able to advise him to follow the more conventional Western approach of just providing working capital financing for investment banks and brokers. He and we realized the commercial banks were too stodgy to follow the conventional system and make short-term loans against securities as collateral. Consequently, KDFC would have to be a specialized entity that could raise its own money by selling commercial paper and bond issues. We also saw this as a great opportunity to push implementation of some additional infrastructure reforms. Nam Duck Woo was fully behind this.

One of the weaknesses of Korea's financial market then—in the late 1970s—was poor accounting and auditing standards. Another weakness directly related to this was poor to non-existent financial analysis of the companies that offered bonds and stocks in the market. It was clear that KSFC's financial success would depend on its creditworthiness. This in turn would depend on its ability to monitor the financial health of both its investment bank and broker customers and the securities they pledged as collateral for their loans from KSFC. To make sure this was possible it was imperative to improve the country's accounting and auditing standards. At the time the Korea Stock Exchange ("KSE") required listed companies to publish audited financial statements, but there were no standards. From the small audit firms of the day companies could buy a signature for $500. Then, for an additional $500, they could get the auditors also to check that the asset column actually did add up correctly and equal the liability and equity column. It followed that that fee scale did not produce high quality auditors. So we agreed on a "package." The Ministry of Finance would establish an audit department that would be responsible for licensing auditors, establishing audit standards and setting minimum fees for audit services. These auditors would be the only ones acceptable to the KSE as auditors for listed companies and for audits of financial institutions dealing with the public. KSFC would establish criteria for analyzing both securities firms (to establish credit limits as borrowers from KSFC) and for companies issuing securities (to establish the quality of their stocks and bonds which would be the collateral provided by the securities firms). KSFC would have a research department that would cover both the securities companies and the listed companies, but the securities firms would be expected to provide their own analysis of each of the securities they were pledging as collateral. This program would provide the basis for the development not only of high quality auditors (the fees set by the MoF for audits of listed companies started at $10,000, a lot of money in Korea then, making the auditing profession a worthwhile career), but also the beginning of a securities analysis profession. The incentive for the securities firms to do good research work was that the interest rate on loans to them would be a function of the quality of the collateral and their own credit ratings. The loans themselves would be for working capital to finance securities underwriting and investors' margin loans provided by their brokers.

We agreed KSFC itself would be owned by all the financial institutions with something over 60% of the stock, plus the MoF and IFC as "influential" but minority shareholders. A government lending agency would provide a substantial low interest rate loan and the central bank would provide conventional line-of-last-resort facilities. The latter would encourage banks to be lenders to KSFC. IFC would also make a term loan as an additional factor to encourage other lenders to favor KSFC. Over the years, KSFC was a great success. I like to think it made a major contribution to the quality of the market, both in terms of increased liquidity and in establishing much higher auditing and securities analysis standards. On the latter, as I will cover in detail later, Scudder (a U.S. investment manager) vindicated this claim when they were doing their due diligence for establishing the Korea Fund—the first "country fund" IFC sponsored—and listing it on the NYSE. Our only problem with KSFC was selling our shareholding. The Koreans were not pleased that, after some five years, we wanted to sell—not because we were displeased with our returns or with the company, but only because we were not needed and IFC was supposed to revolve its portfolio. But they saw it as something that might be misunderstood as a vote of lack of confidence. Consequently, and because it was not really open to foreign investors, they were reluctant to give us a bid for our shares. Finally, though, they did.

Korea Development Leasing Company ("KDLC"). KDLC was next and our first leasing company venture. Our local partner was again KDFC. Our foreign partner was Orient Leasing, a Japanese company that was then the largest leasing company in the world. The first step was assisting the Ministry of Finance with the legal, regulatory and tax infrastructure. Our good friend Nam Duck Woo was 100% supportive, so this was not difficult, albeit it was time consuming. The most difficult aspect was convincing IFC management it was a good "developmental" project. Till then, somehow, leasing was not considered by IFC management to be part of the capital markets so first we had to make the conceptual argument for it. Then, the implementation in Korea was also a task.

A key to efficient financing of leasing companies was to establish a trustee arrangement that could assure lenders that all of the lease receivables were held in a pool as collateral for all senior debt, be they bank loans or bonds. As leasing is a banking-type business, the funding structure is usually 10% to 20% equity, an equal percentage of subordinated debt and the balance secured debt. The secured lenders had, thus, the comfort of a 20% to 40% "cushion" against default problems. As the collateral was both the title to the leased assets, which would all be vehicles or equipment with ready resale markets, plus the lease contracts of the lessees, collateralized loans to leasing companies were considered good risks. The problem then in Korea was, despite the government having set up the necessary legal, accounting and tax rules to make it possible for banks to act as trustees of pools of collateral to make collateralized loans possible, none of the Korean banks would agree to be trustees. I remember being told by the Ministry of Finance man looking after this that he had arranged an appointment for us with the CEO and other senior people of Korea Commercial Bank. He said this government-controlled bank's CEO had been told to do what we wanted. But when we met, the CEO denied any agreement and professed complete ignorance of the matter. In the end, after another round with the MoF, they capitulated and set up an excellent system for KDLC. What proved the point on the importance of this arrangement happened a year later, when KDLC was still a very young company. We arranged what would be the first syndicated loan for a private Korean company without a government guarantee. It was for $15 million and had a five-year term. The key was that the lenders, led by Standard and Chartered Bank in London, understood the collateral trust arrangement and were comfortable with a leasing company where Orient Leasing and IFC were the sponsors. I remember the final negotiations in London very well. On the way there from Seoul I began to feel considerable pain in my left foot. By the time of the meeting the next day I could hardly get my shoe on as my foot had swollen so much. On the way home I had to cut off the top of that shoe. Fortunately, my friendly family GP, referred by the Bank's health department, diagnosed the problem as gout. I was terrified: I had heard drinking too much red wine and eating too many offals caused gout. I loved both. But he said that was an old wives' tale and prescribed the right medicine. The problem went away after about two months and, happily, it has not returned, so far.

Later, KIFC became our technical partner in a securities firm in Egypt and the leasing company played the same role in our first leasing company in Bangladesh. It was very rewarding to see that these two Korean companies could, after only some ten years in business, take on IFC's "technical partner" role in other developing countries.

As will be gathered from the above, my experiences in Korea were very rewarding to me. We have a lasting memory of those days on the wall over our living room fireplace. It is the original oil painting of a floral scene done by one of Korea's leading painters used by KIFC for their Christmas cards.

Thailand

My first visit to Thailand was on my way back from my first trip to Korea. The Thai Minster of Finance had asked that I go there as soon as possible to meet the head of their newly established securities commission/stock exchange, the Securities Exchange of Thailand ("SET"). As I discovered, the chairman of the local DFC—the Industrial Finance Corporation of Thailand ("IFCT")—had set up all of this. I will never forget this visit.

I arrived at Bangkok airport from Seoul at around midnight and was nearly forced to spend the night in the international arrival area because I had failed to get a cholera shot. Fortunately, I had a telex (there were no faxes or emails in those days) with me from the Minister inviting me to a meeting the next morning. Consequently, the immigration officials relented—so long as I would get a shot before leaving the airport. For that, I was taken to the adjoining Thai Air Force base and left to wait in the hospital for a medical officer. It was a repeat of a "rusty needle" experience in the Bahamas a year previously. But what could I do? So, around 3.00 AM, they deposited me at my hotel. At 7.30 I met with the Governor of the Bank of Thailand, his deputy governor, Sukri Kaewcharoen, the SET president, and our IFCT friend. While the time and circumstances were not great for me, I did understand immediately why so many people had told me that the Thais were special people. They could not have been more gentle, polite and gracious. It was agreed IFC would advise them and that I would be back. Over the next 15 years I was there two or three times a year. During those years I got to know Sukri and his family well and we have had many good times together in Thailand and in the U.S. On that occasion, though, it was back to the airport at about 10.00 AM for the SAS direct flight to Copenhagen and then home.

At the request of successive ministers of finance and central bank governors, we organized several technical assistance programs for the SET. Of great help to us in this work was Sid Robbins again. Sid had prepared a securities market development plan for the Thai government in the mid-1960s as a USAID project. Consequently, it was easy for us to develop a program for them; it was Sid's plan. That it required a new crowd in the government and IFC sponsorship to get it finally endorsed was a pity as much time was lost. The experience was my first example of the difficulty of understanding when a government was really serious about making changes. At that time, though, the central bank had a very able governor—Dr. Snoh Unakul. I had been impressed that he showed up to meet me at 7.30 on the morning of my first visit. He took financial development very seriously and had the clout to get things done.

Dr. Snoh knew that one of Thailand's problems was weak accounting and financial control systems in government departments as well as in businesses. Consequently, we became involved in helping several ministries as well as the SET develop better accounting systems. Thailand, in this respect much like Korea and Indonesia, had not had the benefit of a financial infrastructure based on sound accounting practices. One

187

of the good things the old British Empire did for its colonies was to provide Scottish accountants, both for Government and business. The other 19th century "Empires" did not encourage that kind of technology transfer and didn't pay much attention to the art of accounting in the first place. This accounting exercise was one where we had the full support of the Bank. That reminded me of a very pleasant evening in Bangkok with the Bank's chief accountant when we were working on this. A French ballet company was visiting and we went to one of their performances. What was typical of Thailand in those days was that, unannounced, the King and Queen came. During the intermission we joined a small crowd who were looking at the royal Rolls Royce. It was bright yellow in color and parked at the front door. Parked behind it were six bright red Mercedes that belonged to the members of their entourage. There were no police or guards of any kind. The small crowd just, very respectfully, walked around the Rolls, peaking through the windows.

Another, but very different, experience was related to our helping IFCT establish the first mutual fund management company in Thailand. This was one of Sukri's initiatives after he had left the SET to become CEO of IFCT. The original shareholders were IFCT, IFC, several local financial institutions and Nomura. For the first few years everything went swimmingly. The market kept rising and money flowed in. Then came a serious stock market collapse. Unfortunately, Mutual Fund Company ("MFC"), as the company was called, had also speculated in the market with its own capital. The collapse made MFC and many other financial institutions technically bankrupt. The government panicked and organized a bailout. This was in the form of a government fund that was authorized to buy stocks from these financial institutions at their cost. MFC dithered and it looked as if they might miss the deadline to get the necessary approvals. It was Sid Robbins who saved the day. He just happened to be there for us and was invited to attend a management meeting at MFC. The CEO was concerned about losing face if he had to apply. Sid, with the weight of IFC behind him, said: "You will lose even more than face if MFC collapses and you are fired, which is what IFC will insist on." They saw the point but complained it was too late to get the formal letters written requesting the bailout. These requests then had to be countersigned by three different government offices. Sid apparently just said: "Get them written right now and give them to me and I will look after it." They did and he did—by going himself to each of the three offices and demanding that the signatures be provided then and there. No Thai could say "no" to Sid.

Taiwan

Then came Taiwan, also in 1971. Rudi and I spent three weeks there, looking into the mechanics of starting an investment bank with the local DFC as a sponsor. This was another follow-on from one of Moeen's exercises. The government earlier had asked IFC to make recommendations on its securities market regulations. Hans Horch had been there doing that the previous year. Lazlo von Hoffman, IFC's only vice president at the time, took this project very seriously and clearly did not trust Rudi and me, as newcomers, to do a good job of it on our own. So we were accompanies by two IFC lawyers. I recall he insisted we spend three weeks there on the theory that we could not learn enough about local conditions in any less time.

Looking back, meeting, as we did, all of the senior members of government who, until 1948, had run Mainland China, was a special experience. When they fled the Communists, they took with them all the machinery of hundreds of manufacturing plants, along with most of the art treasures of China. This was a truly gigantic logistics achievement. The then minister of economy was the man who had masterminded the whole exercise. He was a small, bald, quiet, obviously elder man who spoke excellent English. It was hard to imagine him managing that task. On the other hand, his group of mainlanders achieved many miracles in turning Taiwan into the economic powerhouse it became. While they maintained tight political control, they left business to the indigenous Taiwanese. Consequently, the latter—at least the middle and upper classes—were quite content. They made a lot of money by local standards and lived well even by our standards. It was also fascinating to hear how their million man army, which came across with their leaders, was used to build the physical infrastructure—the highways, bridges,

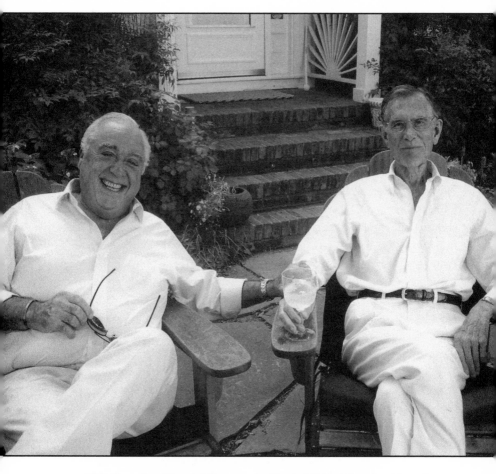

With Francisco (Pancho) Ravecca, in March 2011, at Lena's and my home on the Eastern Shore near Easton, Maryland. Pancho is also one of my oldest and best friends despite Pancho and his wife Rosie living 6,000 miles away in Uruguay, where Pancho has become a rancher.

dams, power stations and schools. Previously Taiwan had been a subsistence rural economy where the locals had little education and no experience in government or business. This transformation was carried out in remarkably few years. But Taipei was still not much of a city in those days. There was one four star hotel and a lot of Chinese restaurants. The most imposing buildings were the new national art gallery and the palace. Rudi and I stayed at a smaller hotel near the airport that had a tennis court. Tennis was about the only entertainment available and three weeks in Taiwan was a long time.

After we had made our rounds with the government people, we were introduced to the business community. The DFC chairman was our guide. First came the bankers, and then the brokers. I was surprised at the low commission rates the local brokers charged for stock transactions. Consequently, when asked to talk to the brokers to explain our ideas for modernizing their capital markets, commission rates was one of the matters I raised. I commented that they would need at least 2% commissions if they were to provide high quality service to investors. Here, I was thinking of decent research and sensible advice on building balanced portfolios. Their reaction was: "If we charge more than 1%, we will lose all the speculators." It just had not occurred to me that speculating was what the Chinese felt, then, was the sole purpose of a stock exchange. I had thought that, as the Canadian markets were less sophisticated than the NYSE, I as a Canadian would have some receptive listeners. The fact was the Chinese had been trading for many centuries longer than had we. But they were very polite about my pontifications.

The actual work of putting together the new "investment bank" — explaining what we needed the local sponsors and the government people to do—was complicated. But they were quick learners and anxious to get IFC's support. Likewise, with Hans Horch, two lawyers and Rudi, the report writing required was easy. Towards the end of our stay, the senior officials we knew organized a dinner for us—French food for a change. What was surprising was that there was also an abundance of excellent French wine. Foreign wine was one of many items that were not allowed to be imported. But I suppose when it's a dinner hosted by three cabinet ministers and the governor of the central bank, the rules can be broken. We, of course, had to reciprocate. Fortunately, I could seek advice from our lawyers, both of whom had been there before. They arranged the wine from the local bootleggers. I wondered if they were the same ones used by our government friends.

There were two other memorable events. The first was a weekend tour of the island hosted by our DFC counterparts. I had never realized how large it was, or how mountainous it was in the North. I can still visualize some huge gorges, crossed by incredible bridges. These, our hosts told us, were the pride of the army—and their construction had cost many lives. The second was leaving for a weekend in Hong Kong organized by Rudi. While I had never been to Hong Kong before and thoroughly enjoyed the break, what was really very touching was what happened when we passed through immigration on the way back to Taipei. It happened to be the very day that Taiwan had been thrown out of the United Nations when Mainland China claimed their seat. No one had said anything about the news during the day. But the young female immigration officer who took our UN "laissez-passer" smiled sweetly at us and said in quite good English: "This passport is no good anymore. We don't need United Nations." How right she was—as proved by how well Taiwan did without the IMF, the Bank and IFC. But it was a sad day for us as it also meant that all our work was for nothing. As Taiwan was out of the UN, it also had to relinquish its shareholdings in the Bank and IFC, losing its eligibility for our investment support.

I returned to Taipei in 1990. The city had changed as much as Seoul. It had become another large elegant city, rivaling Hong Kong.

Brazil

As a result of what I thought was a sign of good will and cooperation, Bill Diamond sought my advice on a financial project in Brazil. Previously, Bill had been discussing it with Moeen. This led in 1972 to my first IFC visit to Rio since my visit for the IMF/World Bank annual meeting in 1967 during my Nesbitt, Thomson days. The Bank decided to turn the project over to IFC as CMD was now officially in charge of such exercises. As we got into it, though, I suspected the Bank people

192

were just smart enough to want to get rid of it. It was a line of credit to be made available to Brazilian investment banks. Previously they had just acted as brokers for new issues.

Brazil is a beautiful country and Rio is spectacular. The people could not be more charming. Importantly, the ones in the central bank and the ministries with whom we dealt were also bright and very reliable. At the time of my first few visits, the government people were being forced to move to their new capital, Brasilia. At the time, Brasilia was rather like Canberra, which was called, with justification, "seven suburbs in search of a city." Brasilia had no charm and was also in the wilderness, almost two hours by air from Rio or Sao Paulo. The President of Brazil of the day had decided the capital should not continue to be in Rio but, rather, be in the geographical center of the country. Obviously, that was good politics. But it was not a desirable place to live. Consequently, whenever I asked for a meeting with one of my opposite numbers in Brasilia, I would suggest the Copacabana Hotel in Rio, my favorite watering hole and by far the best hotel in Latin America. They were always quick to agree. The end result was many, many business meetings held over lunch by the hotel pool. Brazilians were also a casual, fun loving crowd.

As to the "project," as soon as I read the documentation, I realized that no investment bank would use the proposed line of credit. This was because the Brazilian regulations at the time required the issue price of a new securities issue to be fixed some 60 days before they could actually sell the issue. In New York and Toronto, you fixed the price the day you signed the underwriting commitment. Further, you didn't sign until the day you could start selling the new securities, which meant not until you had received reasonably firm commitments from serious buyers. So why would a Brazilian investment bank, in a much more volatile and illiquid market, make such a commitment two months in advance? I tried to convince Moeen that the money would never be used even if the consortium of Brazilian banks that had agreed to it might actually sign the contract. Moeen, who felt we were obligated to the Bank to support the deal, was adamant that we should go ahead. So, Rudi, as the Investment Officer, again produced the required report to the board. This was one that I did not volunteer to discuss with board members.

Fortunately, Moeen, who had felt my lack of confidence in it, decided to replace me at the table. The proposal was approved, but Claude Isbister, the director representing Canada, made a statement. He said pretty well what I had told Moeen. Afterwards, Moeen expressed indignation that Claude did not support the deal. Many years later, I discovered that Moeen had confided in others that he thought this was a Canadian conspiracy as a result of my expressing my concerns about the deal to Claude. But I had never mentioned it to Claude. He had just understood from his own experiences in finance that it was an impractical proposition. Five years later, the IFC commitment was canceled, as there had not been a single drawing on it. I wondered why the Brazilian banks had agreed to the deal, as they had to pay a commitment fee and knew as well as I did that they would never use the money. The answer, I learned later, was that it gave the individual banks some excellent public relations in their market. The Bank and IFC were highly regarded, so a line of credit from IFC was similar to a bond issuer getting a AAA credit rating from S&P. That was obvious in retrospect but, at the time, I was just a simple guy from Toronto.

Later, and notwithstanding I had stepped on some toes in Brasilia, we were asked by the Bank of Brazil to help them establish a securities commission. They agreed that it should be modeled on the U.S. SEC and that the commissioners should be from the private sector. I remember participating at the central bank in its interview of the prime candidate for chairman. That was Roberto Teixeira da Costa, a well-regarded investment banker. Some of my fondest memories of Brazil were the many discussions we had with Roberto and the other commissioners when they were in the organizational stage. I can still remember Roberto's job interview given by the central bank deputy governor in charge of the exercise. Quite differently from most countries, until then the central bank had been responsible for supervision of the market. I can't remember the man's name but he was bright, personable, good looking and about 40. He was a typical laid back Brazilian who, despite appearances, took his work seriously. The interview was at his home in Brasilia. In fact, it was in the kitchen. I remember this because I remember commenting beforehand on the rather odd calendar on the wall. It

194

covered about two years and seemed to be counting the days to the end
of the period. He explained that all the bureaucrats there had such cal-
endars. They gave you the number of days left until you could move
back to Rio. All of them had been forced to go to Brasilia for a three year
"hitch" when the central bank finally gave up and followed the rest of
the federal government departments to Brasilia. Apparently, the central
bank had resisted the pressure the longest. Besides him, there were two
other officials present. Roberto, I recall, was dressed in a blazer and gray
slacks. It was the first time I had met him and he gave the impression
that he was interviewing them. That was fair enough as he was the CEO
of a leading investment bank and didn't need or want the job. They all
knew each other so it was a pretty friendly discussion—mainly in English for my benefit. They told him they wanted him to run the securities
commission as a private sector type operation—one of my suggestions—
rather than as a government department. He would be fully responsible
for choosing staff and organizing it. That was it. Roberto signed up. My
work with him and his colleagues continued for several years.

The first step was finding the right commissioners. The structure
rather followed the U.S. practice, but giving the commissioners more
the role of a board of directors. His approach, which I supported, was
to get people with expertise in different aspects of the market. One was
a chief financial officer of a major company. That was Geraldo Hess.
Another was a successful stockbroker. The third was a securities lawyer.
Last but not least was Francisco Gross, a banker. Roberto, Francisco
and Geraldo were the ones who really ran things. We had discussions
on the commission's policies for the market, its structure and the functions that should be allocated to its operating departments. They
worked out a detailed plan and I arranged to have it reviewed by the
SEC through the good offices of Irving Pollack. About that time I received a subtle warning from the SEC. Apparently, for some ten years
previously, the SEC had received literally dozens of Brazilian "trainees"
from the central bank and from securities firms, all funded by AID. They
left the impression that they were in the U.S. primarily for shopping expeditions. Fortunately, I was able to assure them that this crowd was serious. I accompanied them on their tours to the SEC and then to the

Ontario Securities Commission. Finally, we had our usual lunch with the SEC Chairman and the usual crowd of suspects from my list.

Roberto and company went on to do a first rate job with their commission for the first five years. Then, they all went back to private business. I kept up with Roberto, Geraldo and Francisco for the next ten years or so. Thereafter, these successful business people were succeeded by the more usual bureaucratic types. The chairmen—and I knew the next three—were all first rate. But below them one could see the decline in quality. The first serious blow came after only a few years and was an obvious sign of things to come. The commission had charged a major Brazilian company's CEO with insider trading. His reaction was: "Your rules don't apply to me. This company is 80% government owned and I am appointed by the minister." The commission appealed and lost. Still, the evidence shows that Brazil has done pretty well in developing a strong market, at least compared to other Latin American countries.

Indonesia

My involvement with Indonesia started with a call in May 1971 from the embassy with an invitation to lunch. A deputation of some ten people from the Ministry of Finance and Bank Indonesia, the central bank, entertained me for an excellent Chinese meal in Washington's best Chinese restaurant, during which they told me what they needed from IFC. It started with rebuilding what had been the Batavia Stock Exchange. I was skeptical because I knew there were no public companies there and, with a GDP per capita of less than $100 at the time, hardly any local investors. Still, they insisted I go there soon. As Indonesia was a large and important country for IFC and the Bank, I went shortly thereafter, in late 1971.

The first occasion was the usual short visit to meet with the Minister of Finance, Ali Wardana, and the central bank governor to talk about what they wanted and what IFC could do to help. They pointed out that the Dutch had left them with no trained people to run the country, let alone build a domestic financial system. So they wanted IFC help to bring their financial markets into the 20th century. I was very relieved that they had got beyond just asking for help with their stock market.

Ali Wardana was a Harvard trained economist—a beneficiary of an excellent USAID/ Harvard program to train talented people to run governments in countries that had just become independent. Consequently, he understood completely the basic problems they had. But it was the first time I had been to a country where the local people had received no technical training of any sort. Under the Dutch, all managerial jobs were in the hands of Dutch expatriates. Worse, education beyond elementary school level for the indigenous people was almost non-existent. It was the first time I experienced, at first hand, the consequences to a country of not having even trained bookkeepers. There were no reliable financial statements and no means of establishing financial controls. Without reliable basic data, how could a country have a banking system, let alone a capital market? That the key people in government were well trained, largely thanks to Harvard and USAID, was fine. But the trouble was it was only the top few hundred in a country of 100 million then that had this advantage. Of the rest, few had even a high school education. Consequently, Indonesia was to become a major commitment for us.

My second visit to Indonesia was an eye opener. Previously, I had met only the top people. Now, we were involved at several levels in the government on how to develop a market system. These middle level managers had learned the objective of having a capital market, and that was fine. The problem was they still wanted to start with a stock market. Fortunately, with leadership from Ali Wardana, they accepted the logic of a "critical path" plan we prepared for them to get where they wanted to go from where they were. This started with training bookkeepers and accountants. I recall mentioning at one point that Zambia, which I had recently visited, had some 200 qualified CPAs whereas Indonesia, with 20 times the population, had only one at the time. Sadly, the reason was that during the aftermath of their war for independence from the Dutch, they had expelled all the foreign accountants along with many other technically qualified foreigners they should have encouraged to stay.

Ernest Kepper, my fellow Canadian who had followed me from Nesbitt, Thomson, and I started work on our plan. Our counterpart, guide and confidant was a Bank Indonesia deputy governor called Sulwan.

He had been part of the group that had come to Washington to meet me. Sulwan was a delightful person. He had been on the fringes of the Harvard program so, besides speaking excellent English, he understood the basics of finance. Our proposal was that they should concentrate first on improving the banking system. After that, they could expand the term of financing by encouraging mortgage finance and leasing. Only after they had made progress in those areas should they start working on the infrastructure for a capital market. This did not please them at all. Some still yearned to have the old stock exchange opened again. Intellectually they could accept that the banking system had to be improved, and that there was a need for a banking law, etc. But, at the practical level, it was hard for them to accept that their corrupt and inefficient state run banking system had to be fixed first and that without reliable bookkeeping and financial control systems not even that could be done.

For the first time, I realized that IFC's client countries all tended to look upon stock exchanges as an important symbol of nationhood in much the way that, in the 1950s and '60s, having a national airline was felt to be proof of their independence. In any event, in this initial planning phase, we finally came to an agreement with Ali Wardana that IFC's "master plan" was the way to go. IFC would look after the basics of the banking system. We would also help them to get other governmental agencies to finance programs for those other components of the financial system—including the stock exchange. On the face of it, our program worked quite well. The U.K. helped with leasing, the Dutch government with mortgage finance, and the U.S. with the securities market.

In the meantime, Ernest Kepper and I thought we had got the Canadian International Development Agency ("CIDA") to finance our work with the five government-owned banks. As I knew Gerry Bowie, the then Governor of the Bank of Canada, I went to Ottawa to get his personal help. We felt we needed some twelve experienced bankers and accountants each specializing in a different aspect of banking, to spend at least two years in Indonesia, working directly with the banks. They would establish accounting and management information systems, as well as basic policies and procedures for credit analysis and asset and

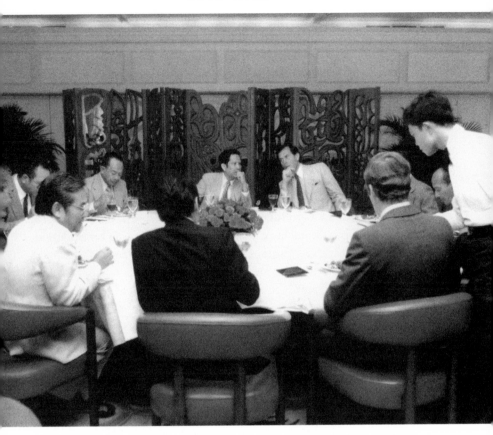

Lunch in Bank Indonesia in 1974. (BI had the best restaurant in the country.)

liability management. The idea was to get the five major Canadian banks to second people who were just about to retire. Gerry thought it was a great thing to do for Indonesia and that the banks would have no trouble finding qualified people who would enjoy the challenge. He called the CEOs of the five banks to ensure that they would cooperate. The Canadian banks agreed to deliver twelve experts. IFC agreed to second Ernie and Edmond de Gaiffier, a "young professional" from Belgium then with IFC, to go to Indonesia for two years to administer the program. Then came an unexpected problem: while CIDA had agreed in principle, they couldn't seem to get around to actually allocating the approximately $4 million required. Weeks dragged into months. Finally, Ali Wardana and the Governor of Bank Indonesia lost patience and said they would pay for it themselves. This was embarrassing for Ernie and me. But we were very impressed as it was unprecedented that a poor country's government attached such priority to what was considered by most bureaucrats in the Bank and IFC at the time as a rather exotic exercise.

My fondest memory of Indonesia from those days was a weekend in the country during my second visit. A group of the Bank Indonesia deputy governors and some of the Ministry of Finance people took me to a Pertamina (the national oil company) rest house in the hills about a hundred miles from Jakarta. It was a beautiful old colonial villa nestled almost on the top of a mountain. Below was a vista of miles of jungle with no other buildings in sight. There were about 15 in their party. I was the only guest. What I remember most was a few of them, late on the second evening, telling me about the revolution and their own parts in driving out the Dutch. I recall vividly their description of some of the battles in which they had participated. They had only spears and swords at first, they said. They only got rifles when they actually bested individual Dutch soldiers. Twenty years later, they were quite relaxed about it all. In fact, they quite appreciated the help they got from the Dutch and cooperated with them well. I suppose it was much like the relationships between the Koreans and the Japanese. The ugly part was in the past and largely forgotten or forgiven. I also remember staying at Sulwan's house and meeting his family. He and I played tennis at the Bank

200

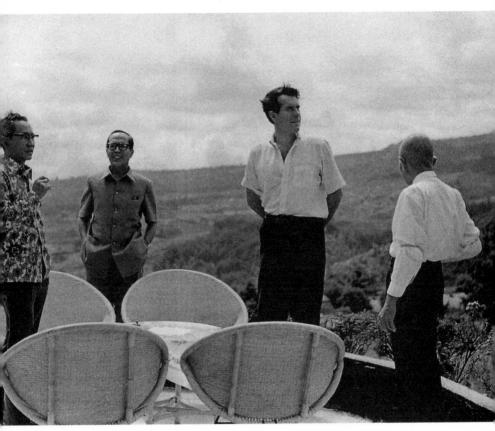

*left to right: Santoso (from the Ministry of Finance); Sulwan (Bank Indonesia);
"me"; Oey (Ministry of Finance). Taken in the hills about
100 miles from Jakarta, in 1975.*

Indonesia sports club. In one game a colleague of his who was half my size and who seemed twice my age soundly defeated me.

Those were, for me, the good days in IFC and in Indonesia. Unfortunately, as we all know, Indonesia changed over the years and much effort on our part and theirs was wasted as new politicians replaced the technocrats. But, regrettably, IFC also did not follow through as it might have. Towards the end of the two years, the Indonesians asked if IFC would continue the program for another two years. They offered to pay all the costs, including the salaries and allowances for the two IFC staff on secondment. Sadly, IFC would not go along with this. It was never clear to me why this was the case as Indonesia was an important country for IFC. However, the Bank recognized the value of the work and took over the project. It was fortunate that our "coordination" with the Bank worked well on this occasion. The Bank's regional director for SE Asia, Bernie Bell, had taken a personal interest as he saw the potential benefits. I had spent a lot of time over the year talking to him about it and he spent time with our team in Jakarta when he visited. That relationship worked well and made it easy for Ernie and Edmond to decide to accept a transfer to the Bank's staff so they could continue with it.

One of our efforts had been to find an actual investment project to keep IFC management happy. One was found by Augustin ("Toti") Que. Toti was the brilliant and colorful young investment officer from the Philippines I have mentioned before. Toti though was an entrepreneur at heart. He tried to establish an "industrial insurance" company in Indonesia. This was a 19th century Scottish scheme. The idea was working-class people would make something like 50 cent equivalent premium payments weekly in cash to agents who came around to their homes or work places. It seemed like a good idea for poor countries. Somehow, though, it gave many of us the feeling that it could be exploited, so we gave it up fairly quickly when we had difficulty finding a suitable partner to run it.

Bank Indonesia realized that IFC's management liked investment projects much more than these advisory exercises. Consequently, the governor suggested we might want to invest in one of the new merchant banks that he wanted to start. We declined to do this, as we were skeptical about the viability of securities market-type firms then. So we suggested a mortgage bank as something that could make an important contribution fairly quickly. He agreed to this. As the Indonesian legal system was based on Dutch law, we decided we should seek help from Holland on establishing an appropriate mortgage law and helping found a mortgage bank. So, P.T. Papan was eventually established with a Dutch mortgage bank as our technical partner. I don't remember much about it but I gather it is still operating. Rudi van der Bijl masterminded this first investment project.

Jay Tata, with his insurance experience from working for the Prudential in Newark, produced our first successful insurance company venture anywhere—not just in Indonesia. Canada's Manufacturers Life ("Manulife") was the technical partner and a local bank became the local partner. It specialized in "group life" policies—that is insurance plans sponsored by employers who made the premium payments on behalf of their employees. The benefits were that employees had their lives insured at lower rates than if they bought coverage individually themselves—if they could buy insurance at all. But we had the usual problems getting IFC management to go along with this first insurance venture. There were some residual suspicions after Toti's efforts even though CMD actually dropped it, not IFC management. But, fortunately, Manulife had considerable political clout through Canada's finance ministry, which helped. The company turned out to be a great success for its first several years.

Iran

Sherif Hussein, IFC's regional director for the Middle East at the time (1971), insisted that financial markets work in Iran should be given a high priority. So, accompanied by Sherif, off I went to Tehran. This was my first experience working with Sherif. Later, he led me to Egypt so I need say no more about what a fine person Sherif was.

Tehran, despite it being in Asia, was a mixture of Mediterranean type charm and elegance—in the northern suburbs—and typical North African poverty in the rest of the town. But the food was good and the wine quite passable. The officials we met were helpful and polite. I had one rather amusing experience towards the end of my first week. Sherif had taken me to the home of the Minister of Finance. During our conversation he asked how I was enjoying his country and was there anything he could do for me. I took this opportunity to explain that Lena was still in New York with our three-month-old daughter, and I had not been able to make phone contact. This was obviously embarrassing for him to hear. Even though everyone knew their phone system was a mess, no one was supposed to talk about it. I guess I should have been more diplomatic. In any event, we were in the process of moving to DC and Lena was stuck with the problem. So I said it would be very kind of them if they could help me get through despite it being past 11.00 PM in New York. He immediately summoned an aide and bellowed his orders. This fellow bowed and scurried off. A minute later he returned with a small black suitcase, opened it on the coffee table and produced a strange looking phone. As he was a well-trained English-speaking aide, he insisted on placing the call himself. Besides, as it was obviously some kind of military communications linkup, I couldn't have done it anyway. I heard him say: "May I speak to Mrs. Gill please." There was a pause and then he said: "Oh, well, when she returns please tell her Mr. Gill called." He just turned to me and said: "The servant said she was out to dinner." I was a bit embarrassed and the Minister was highly amused.

My Iranian venture was short-lived. All they wanted was an investment bank. Bill Gaud killed the idea at birth. I never understood why. But the revolution there a few years later made me wonder if Bill still had his U.S. government connections. The sponsor was to be the local DFC, run by a delightful Iranian, Gassam Karigou. I remember being invited to his home for lunch one Friday (the equivalent of Sunday in Iran and most Muslim countries). I rang the doorbell and minutes later it was opened by a very attractive blonde wearing a bikini. It was his Swedish wife.

The Philippines

What made the Philippines especially pleasant was the charm and graciousness of the people, plus the fact that most spoke English as a result of it having been a form of U.S. protectorate since the Spanish-American War. The government of the day was anxious to improve the quality of their markets. Naturally, they were patterned on the U.S. system. The problem was in the implementation. As in most developing countries, the senior people were well informed and the ones we dealt with knew what had to be done. The trouble was in the middle and lower levels. There were just not enough trained people—proportionately many more than in Indonesia or Thailand, but still not enough. Dan Adams, our investment officer on the exercise, did all of our studies and we made our recommendations. They agreed to everything. But, except for the financial companies we helped to form (a venture capital company and a leasing company), nothing much happened. Perhaps their SEC and the two stock exchanges became a little more efficient but, as the current state of affairs indicates, the quality of financial disclosure and actual enforcement of best practice regulations still leaves a lot to be desired. Presumably, corruption also played a role.

Still, I have very fond memories of many people I met there during my first visit in 1972 and subsequently. Cesar Virata was a first rate minister of finance—and the guiding light behind our activities there over some ten years. He still had time to try to move things even when he was Prime Minister. On my second visit I had met a delightful Filipino investment banker—"Ting" Rojas. I had heard from others the story of Ting and his wife. In WWII both had been forced to watch the Japanese decapitate their mothers and fathers for hiding American flyers who had been shot down. They did not actually meet until after the war when he was at Harvard and she was at Wellesley. Both were on U.S. scholarships awarded to children of parents who had made such sacrifices during the war.

The Marcos's were an interesting couple in very different ways. Undoubtedly, their way of running the country had a lot to do with the problems we saw and the greater problems that became more evident much later. During my time there, I once came to Mrs. Marcos' attention. She too was interested in housing finance and, when she had heard we were promoting it, she wanted to meet me. This was just before an IMF/World Bank annual meeting that was to be held in Manila. I received an invitation to breakfast delivered the night before to my hotel.

IFC . . . Working My Way Around the World

I was instructed to be at the front lobby at 7.00 AM. At the appointed time, one of her aides took me to a waiting car for the ride to the palace. I was shown into her reception room and there was this very attractive middle-aged lady, beautifully quaffed and attired in an elegant royal blue dress. I didn't notice her shoes—that became a topical subject in the press much later. She was warm and gracious but, after the formalities, she was also all business. During our breakfast she quizzed me thoroughly on what the Bank and IFC were doing about housing for the poor. She then invited me on a tour of some of her housing projects. This seemed to be quite impromptu. We set forth in a minivan with four of her female aides and drove out of the city towards the airport. We passed an area where they had built large barriers beside the road and it was clear their purpose was to hide the shacks housing the poor that lived there. Our destination was just past this barrier. It was a new development of single-family houses for lower income people. As we stopped and got out I noticed a few people staring and then pointing at us. Soon a crowd of 50 or so, mostly women, surrounded us, laughing and clapping in that typical Philippine fashion. It could all have been staged but, if so, it was very cleverly done. I couldn't believe it would have been worth the effort to impress one lowly bureaucrat. So I was impressed.

During the IMF/WB annual meeting, I met Imelda again. This was while boarding the Presidential yacht for a trip to Corregidor. There were about 100 of us in total. Imelda saw me with Lena in the receiving line and turned immediately to her husband to introduce me. I was billed as the IFC person who was supporting low-income housing. Ferdinand was very gracious and expressed appreciation. This took a while and stopped the line. Behind us was IFC's then Executive Vice President. He was evidently annoyed to find we were receiving this special attention. The tour of Corregidor was an emotional experience. We watched a film showing the Japanese invasion and the surrender of the American and Philippine troops which became a little embarrassing for us bureaucrats. President Marcos, standing in front of us, was very explicit in talking about the atrocities the Japanese committed after the surrender. Sitting in the front row of the little theatre were several Japan-

206

ese who, because of their rank in the Japanese government, were invited on the cruise.

Our most successful endeavor in the Philippines was helping a company called "Piso Leasing." This was a rather fun experience as everything we did in the Philippines had its lighter side. To start, "piso" means "penny" in English. We didn't like the name, but our Philippine partners, led by Ting Rojas' investment bank, insisted on it. We did not have a foreign partner because they didn't feel they needed one. Because of the U.S. connection, leasing was fairly well known there, but Piso Leasing was the first independent leasing company—the rest were departments of commercial banks. Roland Young, who was one of Ting's partners, managed it. He did an excellent job. Interestingly, trying to develop leasing that would benefit the poor, they leased, amongst other such low-cost machines, sewing machines. Some years later, when the company had become important, they changed the name to a respectable sounding "All Asia Capital and Leasing" and branched out into merchant banking. I understand they were increasingly successful until the 1980s Asian crisis. Apparently, moving into venture capital brought them down in the end. We also tried venture capital. This was not a success.

Another interesting Filipino woman I met was Senator Helena Benites. Besides being one of very few female Senators, she was president of the Women's University. On one occasion she had Lena and me home for dinner to meet some friends. While there one of her friends told a story about faith healing. A guest staying at her home was an Italian woman who had a brain tumor. This, she told us, had been removed the day before. She saw the faith healer moving his hand over her skull. She felt nothing but the tumor was gone.

Colombia

Because of its history and the contrast with Venezuela, I enjoyed my visits to Colombia starting in 1972. Also, it helped that we achieved a great deal there of relatively lasting value, despite the country's problems. I recall querying someone in the ministry of finance as to why it was easier to get things done there than it was in Venezuela. The immediate response was: "We don't have oil so we have to work." My first visit was with Rudi van der Bijl. Bogota was relatively peaceful, but not a city to wander around at night. But most Colombians made the most of things and tried to improve their lives despite the civil strife.

Our task started out as the usual one of advising the government on strengthening their capital markets. The Government's emphasis was on the Bogota Stock Exchange. It had been around for many years, but there was not much activity. Fortunately, it turned out that there was another important convergence of interests between the government and IFC. The former, helped by USAID, had started developing a rudimentary savings and loan association system. Not only was this an important way of encouraging domestic savings, but home ownership was also seen as something that could help build political stability in the country. In the Capital Markets Department, we had put housing finance institutions high on our priority list for countries with poorly developed markets. It could help extend the term of debt financing in countries where long term was otherwise two years or less—as in Korea. We had been encouraged along these lines by USAID also for the reasons mentioned. But it was only after a major selling job that we finally got IFC management agreement to let us try and establish a savings bank in Colombia. There were philosophical questions raised by IFC's economists as to whether this type of entity was actually a "capital markets" institution. Commercial banks certainly were not considered so and involvement in financing them was taboo at the time. This was how and when the turf issue with the Bank started that I had mentioned earlier.

In the end we persevered. "Davivienda" became our first housing finance company and the first savings bank in Colombia. We put together a group consisting of a local commercial bank and a local insurance company as the main investors and IFC took its usual 20% equity interest. Government support was in the form of legislation we proposed to make it feasible. This meant some major changes to the banking regulations and the tax regime. Davivienda became a very successful company and led to the establishment of many more similar ones under the same enabling legislation. Jorge Mejie Zalazar, the CEO of Banco de Bogota, our local sponsor and the leading commercial bank, provided the management staff. Had it not been for this, it could not have been as successful as it was financially and in financing middle-income housing. This was the first time our counterpart had been a commercial bank rather than a DFC. The reason was there was not a national DFC but rather a group of local ones in different cities, but not one in Bogota. Further, we needed a national institution as sponsor, and it was only the banks that had national networks. Much later we did do a deal with a regional DFC—in Cali—Corporation Financiera del Valle. They were excellent people and consequently I agreed we should go along with them without a foreign partner. Our investment officer on this, in 1986, was Michael Phair, a Canadian who had joined us as an investment officer from Toronto Dominion Bank. He had been stationed in both Panama and Mexico City for some years, so he spoke Spanish well and understood the culture. I believe the company is still doing well financially despite the tragic problems of the country. Colombians are serious hard working people. But I suspect that most of their business is unrelated to the securities market. Sadly though, in 2000, the Colombian government changed the tax regime and all the local savings and loan banks, including Davivienda, ran into severe difficulties.

On the lighter side, I still have visions of Frank Veneroso there. He was doing a study on agricultural finance for the Bank then. He was reported to have been seen in the jungle close to the Brazilian border, riding on a mule and wearing his usual navy blue pin-striped three-piece suit and a "boater." He was heard to be muttering something about: "Only the crazy people in the World Bank would dream up an idea to start cattle ranching in a jungle by offering a loan program that would give each farmer just enough to buy half a cow."

Chile

Chile was one of the two (the other was Korea) most rewarding countries in which we worked. More importantly, most of the changes we helped bring about during the 17 years I was involved have remained in place and were improved upon later. Chile was also very interesting because we were asked to start our work there within months of the change of government in 1974. Because of the politics—Chile's new government was not well accepted by many of IFC's shareholders—our work for the first few years was done under the auspices of the Organization of American States ("OAS") rather than by IFC directly. Our Bank colleagues didn't want to have anything to do with the new regime for obvious reasons. This made it much easier for us as we didn't have to spend an inordinate amount of time "coordinating."

Rudi's and my rather incognito first arrival in Santiago was entertaining. The airport, not surprisingly, was rather austere, as was our immediate reception. I remember getting off the plane and going through a long immigration process. But that was not much worse than entering the U.S. in Miami at the time. Then came customs. I only had my usual hand baggage so I was first in line. But there was no one to interview us. I waited ten minutes or so. The line grew longer behind me. The only Chilean "official" in sight was a young soldier with a machine gun that seemed bigger than he was. He was just standing at the exit looking as bewildered as we looked frustrated. Finally, it having been a long overnight flight, I thought "to hell with it!" I picked up my bags and just marched past him. I ignored him and he ignored me. I confess I wondered a bit about what would happen when I tried to leave the country without a customs stamp in my passport, but I decided that was next week's problem. Our handler, who was waiting outside, took us to the dismal center of what is still a rather dismal capital city. Santiago is almost in the center of the long, thin country. Unfortunately, it is about 50 miles inland, in a valley in the Andes. So it did not have the busy activity of a seaport but it did have the disadvantage of being prone to smog. A curious thing about the Hotel Carrera was that the top floor bar was separated from the main dining room by an indoor swimming pool. It was so cunningly decorated that, if you were not completely alert after your drink(s) at the bar, you could easily walk right into the pool on the way to the dining room.

Because it was just a few months after the revolution (or coup, if ones thinks of it that way), the government officials we met were all military people. They wanted a market economy again. They knew that meant private banks and stock exchanges—and most of them remembered them from the not too distant past—but being professional military peo-

210

ple, they didn't really understand what that meant in practice. As most of the professionals in those fields had fled the country and not yet returned, they had no one to ask for advice—except us. On that first trip we only decided on a general plan of action, including the agreement to send Hans Horch to flesh out the plan and make recommendations. What I remember most was the day they took us to the main port city—Valparaiso—which is about 80 miles northwest of Santiago. Two admirals hosted us. There was no clear reason for the trip that we could fathom, other than to show us another part of the country. We had lunch at the local hotel, which was a rather attractive beach resort. There was a large crowd of "tourists" also having lunch in the large dining room overlooking the ocean. They were all young men in their late twenties and early thirties with brush cuts speaking English with American accents. Interesting.

Our activities in Chile moved along quite well for the next ten years. The exciting times came with the "debt crisis" of the1980s. By then, the local technocrats were in charge—the "Chicago boys" who had fled Chile during the previous regime and now returned. One could wonder how they got into such a mess but, at the time, the wealthy countries wanted to lend and the Chileans became overconfident and financed expansion almost entirely with borrowings rather than with equity finance. It was really the old story as to what happens often when the brightest economists are in charge. Few of them have any concept of the need for adequate equity financing to support the debt. The end result was that the country and its companies were all very over-indebted. Thus, when the crisis hit the region and the foreign banks refused to continue lending, the system collapsed. The Chilean government's first actions were to take over the financial institutions and companies and assume their debt. The good thing was that they were fast learners. We had Frank Veneroso write a paper advising them on how to handle the aftermath of the collapse. He called it "Re-writing the Nation's Balance Sheet." Basically, it said a country is like a company. When a company can't pay its debts, what you do is try to negotiate with the lenders and bondholders a conversion of some of its debt into equity. As Frank pointed out in his report, most of the companies were reasonably well-

run enterprises that did, or soon could, show a reasonable level of profits from operations. Consequently, allowing them to collapse made no sense as it would only cause more unemployment and make it even harder for the economy to be revived. So, what Chile should do was offer to exchange government debt for the equity in the companies that were taken over by the government. Then, rewrite the rules so the country could start again with a rational financial market with financial institutions and industrial companies each having a prudent level of equity to support the remaining debt. They loved it. It was really just common sense but, by then, the local "Chicago Boys" had learned their lessons. We did a lot of rule rewriting with them in those days. One of the most important involved setting up a system for requiring fully funded pension plans. Another was establishing the broadest and most flexible debt conversion regime in any of the countries that were suffering during the crisis.

One of the first people in the government to support our program was an old friend from Washington, Rolf Luders, the then finance minister. Rolf had fled the country along with most of the Western-trained economists and joined the OAS. After the revolution Rolf returned to become the chief financial officer of one of the new private conglomerates. When that group was bankrupted and was taken over by the government, he became minister of finance. Sadly for him, a year later his CFO past came back to haunt him. After untangling the financial mess in his old company, the authorities alleged that he had acted improperly and jailed him. After that happened, the finance minister who was in power longest and was our most effective client was Hernán Büchi. He was the best of the Chicago Boys. He was in his late 20s and it was reputed that he bought his first suit after he became minister. But he still looked like a hippie. Thinking back, I don't recall seeing him in a suit—he always wore slacks, a sports jacket and loafers. What impressed me the most was that after he agreed with us on a specific reform, he would actually get it implemented. So, despite appearances, he was a tough, efficient administrator. Of course, it was easier when you could operate by decree rather have to deal with legislators. Whatever one thinks of other actions of that military dictatorship, they turned an economic dis-

aster with a non-functioning financial system into the most stable economy in South America. Even today, we can still learn lessons that could be used in the U.S.

Until then, banks had only swapped their non-performing loans to individual companies for shares in the same companies. That is, conventional corporate restructurings on a company by company basis. Loans to governments were only being restructured as new loans to the same governments—"Brady bonds," etc. We promoted the idea of a "Chile Fund," based on equity acquired in the process of converting debt into equity. The government agreed it was a logical next step in "restructuring the national balance sheet." Jay Tata and Teresa Barger worked on this one. We worked this out with Midland Bank and Hernan Büchi. The delight of working with him is that, despite being a professional economist with no business experience, he was both a quick learner and very decisive. As I remember it, Jay and I called on him to explain the proposal. The secondary market for Chilean debt was valuing it at about 60 cents on the dollar. Midland was prepared to swap $50 million par value of bonds for $30 million of Chilean listed stocks. They would buy them in the market, but they could also buy stock the government held if the fund wanted them as part of a rational, balanced portfolio. The investment decisions would be made by a separate management company to be run by Sergio Undurraga, the investment manager of a major insurance company. IFC would be a 20% shareholder of the management company, as would Midland. The staff would control it with 60%. Midland would agree to a five year "lock in" during which they agreed not to sell their shares in the fund, so long as the manager could buy and sell securities in the market. It took about 45 minutes for Hernan to agree. He just instructed his staff to do it. Five years later the $30 million portfolio was worth close to $100 million. Everyone was happy.

Lebanon

Lebanon was the first truly Middle Eastern country I visited. In 1973 Beirut was beautiful, exotic and elegant. It used to be called the Paris of the Middle East. Luxurious looking buildings, fine restaurants, chic

women, etc, I can't think of many cities that could compete with it in the U.S. or in Europe. The countryside was beautiful: it also used to be called the playground of the Middle East. One could ski in the mountains in the morning and swim in the sea in the afternoon. How things have changed since then, beginning with the start of its civil war in 1975.

It is hard to remember exactly why the government wanted IFC's advice. In fact it was probably really just Sherif again, making sure his customer countries were looked after. There is not much anyone can teach a Lebanese banker—except rudimentary corporate governance, but that was never a subject of interest. The then Minister of Finance said they needed to strengthen their capital market. However, rather like Indonesia, they did not have many companies that could issue securities. Unlike Indonesia, though, they did have lots of people with money—plus many others from the neighboring countries who kept their money in Lebanese banks. The problem was those with the money were smart enough to have most of it invested in Europe or the U.S. and to deal directly with the bankers where they had their accounts.

We concluded the only thing we could do that might be useful was to try and promote a housing finance company. Rudi van der Bijl took over this deal, which we did with a Lebanese partner and two U.K. insurance companies. It was called the Bank of the Near East ("BNE"). Our Lebanese chairman, quite reasonably, decided he really didn't want to go into mortgage lending during a civil war—he made that clear in 1976. After that, his business was foreign currency trading. Fortunately, he was quite good at it. The problem was he seemed to making commissions personally on many of the transactions. I recall complaining about this to one of the London shareholders. The CEO of that institution felt it was not something that should concern us. Rudi and I decided we should sell. Fortunately, the other shareholders were glad to be rid of us. It was sad, really. I felt abandoning ship during a civil war was not what we should have been doing. On the other hand, while all the Lebanese I knew were charming, honorable people, their views of business ethics were quite different from ours.

In any event, BNE was established and started operating. Rudi and I continued to visit Beirut for the next few years and had several inter-

esting experiences. I had not heard machine guns firing or seen rockets flashing across the sky for a long time. I remember sitting by the swimming pool of the St. George Hotel having lunch one day, seeing this going on in the distance. The St. George was a grand hotel in the old style. Sadly, it was destroyed early on in the war. During later visits we stayed at "Summerland," a beach resort hotel half way between the city and the airport. One day, again lunching by the pool, I heard the sound of jets nearby and got up to see what was going on. The Israeli Air Force was attacking a Palestinian camp about two miles away. It was fascinating to watch their dive bombing runs. I hadn't seen anything like it since the Battle of Britain. But I was the only one of the hundred odd people there who was bothering to look. It is amazing how used to warfare people can become. We IFC people gave up going to Beirut soon after Summerland was destroyed.

By then BNE's offices had been damaged and getting about the city was becoming dangerous. I remember we had to change cars and drivers before crossing from the Muslim side to the Christian side. We invested in 1975 and finally sold out for about a 6% IRR in about 1980. Soon after we invested, BNE hired a new general manager—Roy Karaoglan—a Lebanese who had worked for the United Nations Development Program ("UNDP"), and who was an excellent administrator as well as a very honest person. He turned out to be the only person we could really trust to keep us informed as to what was happening in the bank. Roy and his wife, Aida, stuck it out in Beirut through the first eight years of the civil war. After several years as a banker in London, Roy joined IFC. This was after I had retired.

In 1979, we were asked back again to study the feasibility of a discount house. Antoine, who had then just joined us, was the investment officer, but we came to the conclusion it would not work. I recall how on this visit Antoine and I went sailing near our beloved Summerland Hotel but had to return to the beach when an unmarked helicopter with machine guns sticking out the sides hovered ominously just above us. We were later severely scolded by Aida Karaoglan at one of her fabulous dinners; she pointed out that the crews loved to use little boats as target practice.

What happened to Lebanon and its people was a tragedy. Some five percent of the population was killed and most of what had been a beautiful, vibrant city was laid waste by the time the war ended. But one of the interesting aspects of Lebanon was that the local banks continued to prosper during the war.

One other interesting thing happened to me when visiting Beirut. Our chairman's wife took me to Damascus one day. I think it must have been just before the civil war started. We went there in their chauffeur driven Cadillac. The countryside was not that interesting, but our experience at the border was. I guess it was the usual way wealthy Lebanese behaved when they had to deal with Syrian "peasants." The Lebanese border guards had waved us through. At the Syrian checkpoint, rather than join the long line like everyone else, my hostess just told the driver to park the car and take our passports directly to the guard. This he did, pointing at the car. When the driver got back, the guard waved aside the others and beckoned us through. I assume money changed hands. What I was shown of Damascus itself was not that interesting to me, but it certainly has a fascinating history and a most impressive mosque. There were some attractive suburbs and the usual bazaar. Of course, we drove into this mass of small stalls and multitudes of people, scaring several walkers in our way. I was glad to get back to Beirut. That said, I was very grateful to have been taken there.

Yugoslavia

My introduction to Yugoslavia started with a visit from the Bank's economist for the country. Dieter Hartwich was a gentle and polite German who went on to become a senior official of the European Investment Bank in Luxembourg. Dieter told me that the Minister of Finance wanted to bring some flexibility into their banking system. His idea was to start by allowing regional banks to be a bit competitive. Dieter thought IFC in the form of CMD could help. So, would I go there with him to talk to the Minister and the Governor of the central bank, whom he thought was supportive? This was in 1974 when Tito was very much in control and the country was still seen as a bastion of communism. I was fascinated by the idea. Yugoslavia had been a long time shareholder

216

of the Bank but had only recently become an IFC shareholder. There was a message there.

On my first visit I was accompanied by an experienced Bank loan officer—I don't recall his name, but he was a sensible fellow. He taught me a lot about the system and introduced me to the key people. He also escorted me around the country and told me of his experiences. One of them made it clear that one should not get too close personally to any of the citizens. A Bank colleague of his who was an engineer working on some dam project got to know a Yugoslav female engineer on the job. They became quite close. She took him home to meet her parents. Then she disappeared. He sought out her father, who was reluctant to be seen with him. Eventually he learned that the woman had been punished for fraternizing and had been sent to another part of the country.

The Minister of Finance was a large healthy looking youngish man whose favorite English expression was "no problem." On my first meeting with him my Bank handler brought him what I discovered was his favorite present from visiting foreigners. It was a selection of coloring pencils. You couldn't get such things in Yugoslavia then. I suppose that was just one of the things school kids learned to live without—if they ever knew such things existed. He was very open with us about their financial system. He said it was very inefficient and very high cost to borrowers. To me, it was surprising to hear a communist official admitting such things. Later, the Governor of the central bank said much the same thing. So it was clear that they were quite serious about opening up their system even in those early years. I don't recall the details, but I did have discussions with the CEOs of all of the large regional banks and some of the local banks. Again, I am not completely clear on my reactions at the time, but I think I had two impressions. First, they had been told to support the new Party line of opening up the financial system. Second, they had no idea what that meant. My bank colleague and I traveled around the country—from the sophisticated north—Slovenia—to the primitive south—Montenegro. It was incredibly interesting. We visited local government officials, managements of "enterprises" and farm families. Never had I eaten and drank so well in a so-called poor country. I suppose it was staged to some extent. But the people we met could not have been more welcoming. Thinking of what has happened since, I could not have imagined such a major collapse, not only of the communist system—which I guess we were witnessing—but of what otherwise seemed a cohesive nation state. This was over a period of almost three years.

Towards the end, we had to respond to the Minister of Finance's request that we provide lines of credit to a group of banks, each concentrating on different regions of the country, to "on lend" to small businesses. Brad Warner was our investment officer for this. We proposed the approach that we found successful in Kenya—lines of credit but with business advisory services attached. Unfortunately, but unsurprisingly, their analyses of their creditor companies were based strictly on Soviet-style statistics and there were no references to assessments of management competence. They were all government-owned anyway, so I suppose it did not matter. Of course, in the Soviet-style socialist countries, meeting physical production targets was all that mattered for the plant bosses to be rewarded. As one cynic said, if the target was a million shoes a year, it didn't matter if they were all left-foot shoes or all right-foot shoes. It followed that they had refused to accept the idea that they should have business advisory services. So, our recommendation was to drop it. IFC management, as this was also a highly politicized program, decided to do it anyway, but through the IFC regional department. In the process the advisory service was dropped and the loans were made directly to the banks for "on lending"—that is, for the banks' accounts—to the small businesses. This way the risks of these small business loans being for IFC's account and risk directly were removed. On the other hand, the developmental impact was much diminished too. That the banks eventually disintegrated with the decline of the country was another story.

There was, of course, a lighter side. A weekend in Dubrovnik was great fun. Not that anything special happened there in terms of our business activities. But it was a historic, beautiful town, especially for those interested in things nautical. Then, in every town, we would have dinner in local restaurants. Always, in the best communist tradition, we would sit at communal tables of a dozen or so people. The food was always excellent and very ample. So was the "Slivovitz," the local vodka drink. Everyone always ended up singing and we few foreigners just became part of the evening's group. I often wondered what it would have been like had we been in Russia then in the same kind of restaurants. (From what I have learned since, it would have been much less fun, with poorer food, but maybe better vodka, and certainly less talking and laughter.)

The end result of some three visits to Yugoslavia was a fine report that my Bank guide and I wrote about what they should do, but it was ignored by both the Yugoslav government and Dieter's bosses in the Bank. Sadly, once again, the objective of the management of the Bank and of the loan officers was to lend money. Details as to the efficient use of the money were not that important.

Tunisia

Tunisia was still very French in flavor. My only real memory was how attractive Tunis appeared, with its picturesque houses on a steep slope, all with white walls and light blue doors and window frames. It reminded me of arriving in Lisbon from the sea when I was in "Warrior." Probably the most interesting part of that trip was just being in the regional Air Moroc flight. It stopped off in Algiers to let off a local football team in full uniform. Whether they were Moroccan or Algerian I had had no idea. I also had no recollection of why we went there although some ten years later we helped set up a leasing company with a French bank. We did some advisory work for the ministry of finance in about 1974 which is probably what led to the leasing company. But as Tunisia is a French speaking country it was a job I was happy to delegate to Rudi.

Zambia

In 1974 I made my first visit to a Southern African country. To display my ignorance of the "Tropics," I assumed I would see jungles as I had in parts of Brazil. No such luck. There may have been jungles somewhere, but not near Lusaka, the capital, or Livingstone, the second city. One forgets that just because a country is in the tropical zone, it is only tropical if it is close to sea level. Most of Zambia's lowlands are in fact at least 3,000 feet above sea level. That makes quite a difference to the temperature, especially during the winter and at night.

The Zambian government wanted us to establish a savings bank in which IFC and a government entity would be the major shareholders. The ministry of finance people intended contributing government bonds as their capital contribution. Unfortunately, they wanted to value the bonds at about twice their market worth so that deal fell through. We did however help them do a local distribution of stock in the Bata Shoe Company subsidiary there. Most interesting to me was visiting Victoria Falls. I arrived in a taxi just past sunset and was told by a soldier on duty that tourists could not go to the viewing point after sunset. But he took pity on me, placed his rifle against a tree, and walked me along a path to the edge of the river. It was a great view and it was very considerate of him. I don't think things are as relaxed around there now.

Morocco

Think of Humphrey Bogart in "Casablanca." It was my first port of call in North Africa, albeit I had seen the coast of Morocco in my Navy days. On arrival at the airport at Casablanca, I had another taxi experience. Rudi was supposed to have been there to meet me. He wasn't so, after waiting a while, I took a taxi into town. A few minutes into the ride I just happened to see a cab racing past in the other direction with Rudi in the back. My first reaction was to tell my driver to reverse course. But I thought "too complicated, let him learn a lesson." I regretted that a few minutes later when, in the middle of nowhere, my driver pulled off the road and stopped behind a parked car. He then turned to look at me and asked, in his broken but quite passable English, if I would change cars and let his "friend" drive me the rest of the way. Rather indignantly I refused. He just shrugged his shoulders and went on the way. It never occurred to me that I might have been kidnapped or robbed. We were all pretty innocent about such things in those days. In any event, Rudi and I did whatever business we had in Rabat. All I recall is that the ministry of finance people we met seemed quite disinterested in financial market development despite their masters having asked us to go and had arranged the meetings. But they were gracious hosts to visitors to their country and took us to an elegant restaurant for lunch. It was my first experience of eating with my fingers. Rudi and I finally went off to Marrakech for the weekend. Purely coincidentally, our Rabat meetings were on a Thursday and our next were to be the following Monday in Tunis. Marrakech was a beautiful place. I remember the streets in town were lined with orange trees in full bloom and one street had a wonderful view of the mountains in the distance. We stayed in a very elegant French colonial palace of a hotel. It's hard to describe but the hotel, the environs and the other guests made me think what it must have been like there in the 1930s and '40s: it was a time warp.

Bolivia

Bolivia will never be a tourist destination, but nevertheless I found my way there in 1975. I think it had something to do with USAID. Arriving in La Paz was an experience in itself. Being at quite an altitude, it was almost in the clouds. The city had two sides: the typical Latin American modern business district and upper class suburb and then the rest—the rest being the equally typical slum shacks occupied by the very short and dark "peons." It was the first time I had seen a truly indigenous group. What struck me about them otherwise were the strange hats they all wore that looked rather like old "bowler hats" as found in "the city" in London years ago.

Anxious to do a deal in a small poor country to please IFC's board, we broke most of our rules there—and later paid the price. IFC was very keen to do more in the smaller and poorer Latin American countries at the time, so Bolivia was near the top of the list. We had been asked to do our usual advisory work on improving the capital markets in 1975 and spent a fair amount of time on that. But IFC also wanted an investment project. When I went there later with Rudi to see what could be done the only thing that looked reasonably safe was housing finance. By this time, 1977, IFC no longer bothered about only setting up the first company of its kind. We could even invest in an existing entity if we could make a developmental case. After searching around for a while we found a commercial bank that also had done some mortgage lending.

Here was our opportunity. We could make an investment in it if it promised to do more mortgage lending. As the principal shareholders and the CEO—an ex-governor of the central bank—were keen to have IFC involvement, they agreed to this readily.

We already knew the weaknesses of their financial system through our advisory work. Consequently, we knew where to look for "skeletons" when we did our appraisal of the bank to establish a reasonable valuation. Auditing standards, accounting and management information systems, were the concerns. In reviewing the loan portfolio we found that many of the mortgages were one or more years in arrears on interest and principal payments but no loss provisions had been made. When asked why, the answer from both the management and the external auditors—a local affiliate of one of the "big five"—was "the market values are four times or more the amount of the mortgages." This led to asking why, if this was so, they hadn't been able to either get at least their interest payments. We then discovered that the bank had few fully documented mortgage contracts as collateral for their loans. That of course was why the loans were in arrears—the borrowers knew full well that the bank could not claim title and therefore could not foreclose. We should have stopped then, but we went ahead anyway as they agreed to clean up their act. As protection, however, we insisted on a "put" to the largest shareholder. We also got them to establish sensible provision policies and establish a strong management information system, including monthly reports broken down by product and by branch office. We thought we could rely on the CEO because of his background. As part of our advisory work, we also determined we would make an extra effort at following up the bank's performance including reviewing their monthly reports. This was even more intensive than CMD's already rigorous "preventative supervision" program for all our equity investments. As it was a small investment, the cost of doing this exceeded any possible dividend return we might have made, but that was part of the cost of a development exercise. I sent Gerard de la Fortelle and Pancho Ravecca to advise on the operations of de Banco Hipotecario Nacional (National Housing Bank).

The problems started about a year after we invested. The first was a fraud in the bank's branch in Santa Cruz, the second largest city. The manager was in cahoots with the treasurer of his biggest client. They fled to Brazil with about US $250,000, or about five percent of the bank's net worth. The bad part was that it was we, in Washington, who discovered it—not management in La Paz. That there was something suspicious was obvious from the monthly report: the branch's footings suddenly jumped by $250,000 to about $750,000. Of course, by then it was too late. This, plus several other problems with management over the next six months or so led us to recommend to the chairman and principal shareholder that he get a new CEO. This caused a political crisis: we had accused Bolivia's most respected banker of incompetence. Bolivia's Executive Director on IFC's board even lodged a complaint with our President. That kind of thing rarely happened so I was faced with much explaining to do as such complaints go to the full board. Fortunately, our case was solid and thus professionalism won out over politics. Besides, McNamara was very supportive of staff. We exercised our "put" and ended up with about a 3% return. A year later we were vindicated in Bolivia too as the CEO of the bank was finally replaced.

Panama

I had been there before, in 1946 and 1947, passing through the canal during my Navy days in "Warrior" and thus remembered Panama City, vaguely, when I returned for IFC in 1975. Nothing much had changed. Other than the hot steamy climate the only thing of note I remember was an incident some years later—perhaps about 1980—when I happened to see the wife of the Prime Minister waiting patiently in a line in front of a bank teller. In 1975 her husband, Nicolás Ardito Barletta, was finance minister and much responsible for my first visit. As to our activities there, I have told already the BLADEX story.

Argentina

The famous sentence, "Don't cry for me, Argentina," could well be rephrased as "Don't cry for Argentina." This may sound cynical, but in most respects Argentina is very similar to Canada in terms of resources, population and level of education. The main difference is that Canada has about ten times the GDP per capita now. Tragically, the GDP per capita of each country was roughly the same 50 years ago. Buenos Aires was called, and still is, the Paris of South America. After the years of Peronist socialism, a new government asked for our help in 1976 and off I went. They were revising their securities market laws and wanted our advice. While they had all of the trappings of a modern Western market, including a 100-year-old stock exchange and a securities commission, 30 years of socialism and corruption had destroyed the ethics of the market. Unfortunately, there was no will to change and, consequently, our efforts produced very little results. The local stockbrokers wanted to establish their own bank, supposedly to provide liquidity to the market. I sent Gerard de la Fortelle and Pancho Ravecca to evaluate the proposal for the creation of the Banco de Valores, an investment bank that would be owned by all of the stockbrokers. Gerard and Pancho recommended against the proposal based on the evident conflict of interest—in reality, it was directed more to enhancing the stockbrokers' own profits. We could see no real role for IFC in this. However, I did enjoy working with their SEC people. Juan Etchebarne, the chairman at the time, was as a delightful person: urbane, handsome and very dedicated to his job. Few now remember that IOSCO, the International Organization of Securities Commissions, was founded originally by Argentina, Peru and Venezuela as the "Annual Conference of Securities Commissions of Latin America."

One memorable Argentine SEC experience actually occurred in Washington at an IOSCO meeting hosted by the U.S. SEC. We were all gathered at the SEC for the formal annual meeting. It just so happened that the day before the British had started their attack on the Argentine troops that had invaded the Falklands. On the platform at the meeting was the U.S. SEC chairman, as host of the meeting, Gustavo Petricioli, president of the Mexican commission who had hosted the previous annual meeting, and Juan Etchebarne, as Argentina was to host the next one. The SEC chairman had made his welcoming speech. The next speaker was Juan Etchebarne who was supposed to welcome us to Argentina. Instead, he made an impassioned attack on the British and said he was returning that day to fight for his country. He then left. Especially as Geoffrey Knight, the very gentlemanly and likeable President of the London Stock Exchange was there representing the U.K.—the U.K. did not have a securities commission then—there was an embarrassed silence. Then, Gustavo Petricioli called out to me, at the back of the room and asked if I would fill in for Juan. I did so, but I have no recollection of why he asked me or what I said.

The sequel to this experience happened about a year later. An Argentine associate who had a connection to the President of Argentina asked if there was any way I could send a message to "No. 10" saying that the President would like a reconciliation with the British. He knew that a friend of mine, Alan Walters, was an advisor to Mrs. Thatcher. I agreed to pass on the message. The answer finally came back to me. It was, if the Argentines were willing to allow British Airways to resume their London-B.A. service that would be seen as a sign of goodwill. I passed it on. Some six months later, I read in *The Washington Post* that British Airways was to start flying to B.A. again the next month.

The government also asked us to do a line of credit to banks, as we had done in Kenya. Fortunately, this collapsed. But we did commit to a less than successful venture capital company.

Lena and I had an amusing experience driving in a taxi from the airport to B.A. We got into conversation with the driver, who spoke quite good English. He regaled us with all the horror stories stemming from the mess his country was in. We asked him who or what he thought was to blame. He said: "The Italians: too many of them here." Eventually we asked him where his roots were. He said: "Italy."

Ecuador

Quito had a very attractive Spanish colonial part of town. However, the attractiveness of architecture and the setting was rather spoiled by the central bank building. That tended to be a characteristic of many in poor countries—a large modern central bank building dominating the rest of the city's buildings. The thing I remember most was landing at the airport. The approach down the valley was climaxed by passing between two rows of tall buildings that seemed only a few yards away on both sides.

We did a fair amount of advisory work for the securities commission. The chairman was a very bright and tough lady who was a cousin of the President. She left no doubt as to where she stood on any issue. One interesting experience was on the occasion of an IOSCO annual meeting a few years later. Ecuador had joined IOSCO at our suggestion and she had gone to the previous year's annual meeting. She lobbied hard to be able to host the next year's meeting. As she was the first female commission chairman, Ecuador was accepted readily. The highlight of the meeting in Quito was the formal opening ceremony. This she organized in a reception room at the ministry of finance. As we trooped in and sat down we were rather surprised to see that armed soldiers ringed the room—one about every ten feet. Finally, on to the dais marched the members of the board of governors of Ecuador's securities commission. They were all in army officer's uniform and all seemed to be at least generals. There were about seven of them, all short and stocky and all looking very serious. She made her welcoming speech in English and then introduced her commissioners, one by one. They turned out to include the minister of finance, the governor of the central bank, and a Supreme Court judge. She concluded by saying: "These people before you have reduced our fine country to the deplorable state in which you find it." Judging from the absolutely blank expressions on all their faces, I assumed none understood English. I wondered what they thought when they found out what she had said. Of course, her cousin was the President, which presumably gave her some protection. He died in an explained plane crash a year or so later.

Maldives

It was also in 1976 that I first went to these exotic islands about a thousand miles south of Sri Lanka. There are some 200 of them, supporting a population of less than 200,000 then. The airport is on one island and the capital, Malé, is on another about a ten-minute boat ride away. Some of the other islands have hotels, but most are just fishing villages. The main sources of income are from tourists and issuing stamps. The latter was a brilliant idea. Probably 99% of them are sold to stamp collectors—the faces range from local scenery to Mickey Mouse and Donald Duck. But the local Monetary Authority (the central bank) has nothing much to do. There is no local currency and their gold reserves are stored in the second floor of a building whose first floor is the Malé jail.

You may ask why I went. The answer is Prom Malhotra had discovered that the Maldives was the only country that was an IFC shareholder and that did not have a local commercial bank or an investment from IFC. So IFC management was glad to approve this boondoggle to see if we could dream up some kind of local financial institution. We failed. Interestingly, the Maldives now has a stock exchange with four listed stocks. But their total market capitalization is only about $100 million.

Sudan

Sudan was a culture shock in 1976—and of course still is. Khartoum was the first city I had visited with Rudi where he didn't know any restaurants. The local government people were very pleasant to us and, for reasons that were not clear, seemed determined to have a stock market despite there being no securities. I recall our handler, a central bank deputy governor, made a real effort to show us the sights. He was particularly keen on taking us to the spot where General Gordon had been killed.

Khartoum was a desolate looking city—hot, dry and dusty with few paved streets. Our hotel was a half star with a swimming pool that did not attract us despite the sun and the temperature. I was reminded of my brother-in-law Johan's and an American friend's great achievement when they were both posted there. They formed the Upper Nile Yacht Club. It was small and exclusive. There were two members and two boats—local dhows that they rented. Johan's friend, Alan Bergstrom, at the time U.S. Consul, became a good friend later when back in DC. He had had a harrowing time there after Johan left. The U.S. Ambassador was assassinated. Alan was arrested by the Army and came close to being executed. Obviously, things had changed a lot since that revolution. Our hosts could not have been more gracious. On our last day they gave us a fine farewell dinner. Even cocktails and wine were served despite it being a strict Islamic society. This was evident as the drinks were served from little airline bottles. It is striking how a country's interests can change.

Egypt

In 1976, just a few months after the Soviets withdrew from Egypt, Sherif Hussein, my IFC colleague, told me his new government wanted to move quickly to revitalize its markets. This was well received in IFC so Rudi and I went to Cairo for a week. I had not realized that the old Cairo Stock Exchange had been the third largest "in Europe," as the government people put it, in the pre-WWII period. Looking back, it was one of my more bizarre trips. Cairo was full of Western carpetbaggers, looking for opportunities so the few hotels were full. Consequently, we were put up in a private apartment. I remember Rudi and me, sitting on our beds after dinner wearing our overcoats and drinking brandy to keep warm. There was no heating and it was a very cold winter. Actually it was in April. I thought it was supposed to be warm by then.

As expected, the finance ministry people took a keen interest in what we were doing. But there were the usual problems of visionary plans at the highest levels but no one to implement them. This was hardly unusual after a decade or so of socialist government. Most of the ministry of finance and central bank people simply didn't have the training or experience to understand what was needed to make an efficient market.

Cairo had had a thriving stock market up until the 1950s. Those who were still around who had been involved wanted it back. In fact, the chairman of the stock exchange—who had been chairman when Nasser took over—told us the fascinating story of what happened immediately afterwards. The Members got together and concluded that they had no choice but to shut it down and liquidate their firms. All the companies listed had been nationalized so the activity had dropped to zero. Their first step was to tell the new minister of finance their plans. He asked them to hold off for a few days while he thought about it. Much to their surprise, when he called them in again, he asked them not to close down. They said they couldn't afford to keep things going. He responded saying he had talked to the governor of the central bank about it and they had a proposition for them. The compensation to shareholders of the listed companies that had been nationalized had been government bonds. These would be listed on the stock exchange and holders could trade them. The ministry would pay sufficient listing fees to ensure that the stock exchange could pay a minimum staff to keep the doors open. The central bank would cause enough trading for the commissions to be sufficient to make it worthwhile for the brokers to stay in business. It was never clear to the members why the new government wanted to hedge its bets that way, but it was an offer they couldn't refuse. So, all through the socialist period, the Cairo Stock Exchange and its members continued to work away, but at an even more leisurely pace. My recollection, from working with Terry Reilly on the Capital Markets Law under an AID project, was that the brokers said they were paid a salary by the government for many years.

This meeting with the Cairo Stock Exchange ("CSE") had been arranged by the "capital markets committee"—the group of government people who were designated as our counterparts. It came about at a meeting in the ministry of finance building. This was during, I think, our second visit. We were discussing the infrastructure changes that would have to be made. We had been going through our usual routine— "first things first: How is the accounting system? The banking system? Is there a money market? When are you going to privatize companies? All these things need attention before it makes any sense to think about a stock exchange that would handle stock transactions again." Missing our point, one of them said: "But we already have a stock exchange: it's been operating for a hundred years!" While telling us about it they commented that it was a fine old classic marble building with Grecian columns. One of us asked the obvious question. "Oh. That's interesting, where is it?" There was a silence as they looked at each other. Finally, they admitted that none of them remembered where this distinguished building was. By the end of our meeting they had found out. It was just a couple of hundred yards from the ministry building where we were. So some of them walked us round to see it. It was a very gracious building with "Cairo Stock Exchange" in English, French and Arabic on equally elegant plaques by the front door.

The minister of finance of the day had appointed a central bank deputy, Fouad Hussein, as his point man for capital markets. Fouad became the first chairman of the "Capital Markets Authority," the name we had coined for new securities commission type entities. Later, he became minister of finance. It was when he was in that latter job that I had my most memorable experience in Egypt. In those days, it was not safe for Westerners to eat in any other than the main hotel restaurants in Cairo. Fouad had arranged a lunch at the Cairo Automobile Club attended by a dozen or so of the local VIPs. I was the guest of honor. When we entered, my heart sank. I could tell right away that this was not a place where I should eat a meal. But what could I do? I could not risk insulting him so I did my duty—and paid the price. It took about a month to get over the case of typhoid I caught there. I remember complaining to one of the physicians who treated me in DC that I had had a booster shot just before I had left for Cairo. So how could this happen? His sobering response was that had I not had the booster I would have probably died. Nevertheless, over the years, Fouad and I became great friends and had many great times together. One of Lena's favorite necklaces is a simple one that Fouad gave her.

There was another great experience that Rudi and I shared on our first visit. Fouad called us one morning to say we had been asked to explain what we were doing, to their equivalent of the chairman of the senate finance committee. He lived in Alexandria and we should be ready to drive there immediately. "Immediately" turned out to be four hours later so we missed lunch. After a three-hour drive, we were taken directly to the senator's office. The questions started immediately. 10.00 PM had passed and we were hot, tired, thirsty and hungry. Sometime after 11.00 he finally said: "Well, it's getting late. Can I take you to dinner?" We were relieved and grateful, but after hours in his rather grubby office and our dining experiences in Cairo, we weren't expecting much. Then came the surprise. We entered what could have been an elegant nightclub in Paris. It was absolutely full: people were drinking, eating and dancing—and this in a city that had been a Soviet stronghold only months before. During a truly delicious meal, I commented to our host that I thought their (Egyptian) wine was excellent. He looked at me rather coldly and said: "Mr. Gill, I'm glad you enjoyed it. After all, it should be fairly decent: we have been practicing making wine for 5,000 years." This fine evening was capped the next day—Friday, their weekend day—when he took us with his family to their beach place. It wasn't exactly Saint-Tropez, but close enough. He and his wife were gracious hosts yet again. When we were finally driven back to Cairo and deposited at our hotel, we found two cases of the wine I had praised were with our bags.

During all my visits over the years, I found the Egyptians I met to be good professionals and fun to be with. They made it clear that they preferred Westerners to their previous foreign guests. One of our handlers told us a story making this clear. He said he had been the Egyptian air force liaison officer to the Soviet air force people at one of their air bases during the seven-day war with Israel. On the first mission they, the Egyptians, flew, they lost three of their 15 MIGs. The Soviet squadron commander, he said, was quite insulting about it and said they couldn't afford to risk their planes any further so his Soviet pilots would fly all future missions. Then the remaining 12 aircraft went off on the next one. None returned. Our handler sounded rather pleased with his story.

Unfortunately, despite the efforts of several ministers of finance, it took until well after my time before they made real progress in developing their financial system. But we tried. As a result of our extensive advisory role, we were asked to establish an investment bank. This was about three years after the end of their two decades of socialism. We should have known better, even if Egypt had had a large and thriving stock exchange up to the 1950s. The good news was having Korea Investment Finance Corporation (see later) as our technical partner. The bad news was everything else. We had devoted a great deal of time doing a survey of the so-called listed companies that had been privatized the year before by the new government. We even arranged for a corporate finance professional from McLeod, Young, Weir, our Toronto investment banking friends, to spend six months preparing research reports on the 20 leading companies. This was thanks to Tom Kierans who by then was CEO of McLeod. This was another warning experience that we ignored, foolishly. Not only were the audits meaningless, but the managements just would not cooperate. So, after those six months, we knew little more about the issuing side of the securities market than we had before we started—except that one could not rely on any financial statements. As to the "buy side" of the market, we did not need a six-month study to know there were very few investors likely to buy these securities anyway. But the authorities were determined to go ahead and three of the leading local banks joined us as shareholders. On our side, enthusiasm overcame common sense and, besides, a deal in Egypt in those early days made us look good before our board. Fouad Hussein, who had just retired as minister of finance, became the full time chairman. As he had been the leading supporter in the government for capital market development, we thought he was a good choice even though he had no business experience. He was supported by one of the rising stars in KIFC who was seconded for a year to be CEO. Mr. Oh, who really was very good and a typically determined Korean, had a rough time. After three months he started sending cries for help. There was just no business to be done and Fouad was not being helpful. In fact it seemed that all the Egyptians involved were doing was spending money on acquiring the trappings of high office. We pulled Mr. Oh out after six months and bullied the local banks into buying us out after about a year. Mr. Oh ended up as CEO of Korea's leading financial firm. Fortunately, he forgave us for the ordeal we had put him through. Our Korean friends were very good that way. They knew we had done them more good than harm.

Kenya

This was the first Southern African country where we had a substantive involvement. It started in about 1976. By developing country standards their financial system was in good shape. We established what was a new program for IFC: to make long-term project finance loans to small companies. IFC could not afford the administrative costs of making loans directly to companies below about $2 million at that time. The cost of supervising the ones on the books was probably about $50,000 a year. These costs made it clear that any investment of less than $2 million was going to be a loss maker for IFC regardless of its inherent profitability. IFC's strategy used then, and still now, was a dual strategy—several very large deals would subsidize a few small ones. Another approach could have been to streamline the investment and supervision processes. Our board would not approve that back then, as they wanted to approve each investment. Thanks to a suggestion from one of the Bank's economists, we came up with "agency credit lines." That was using banks as agents to make project loans to small businesses for our account. I think we coined the acronym "SMSEs," meaning small and medium sized enterprises. So these lines of credit became known as SMSE lines. Later, the Bank changed the term to "SMEs."

The first of these agency lines was with the Kenya Commercial Bank ("KCB"), which was government owned. Promodh Malhotra, an Indian who had been with Citibank before he joined IFC as one of our investment officers, handled it. Prom was a bright, independent minded fellow who was a born dealmaker. Our plan was to offer KCB $2 million that they could, for IFC's account and IFC's risk, lend to local companies as project loans with five- to ten-year fixed interest rates to finance expansion. We had three main conditions. First, KCB would agree to establish a "Business Advisory Service;" second, KCB would provide the necessary working capital needed to finance the additional business expected; and third, they would ensure that the borrowing companies met our credit criteria. This latter included some additional equity from the company's own resources to provide adequate collateral for our loan. We also established an upper limit of $200,000 for our loans, as we wanted to have a minimum of ten such borrowers to ensure some diversification.

As we, the CMD people involved, were mainly equity investors, we were very conscious that the key to success of this program would be the quality of management of the borrowing companies. Even in developed countries, small companies tended to be one-man shows where the owner had limited skills in preparing business plans, maintaining proper financial controls and, as his business expanded, developing—and delegating to—a management team. A venture capital company making an investment in such a company would only do so if it had confidence that the owner was prepared to address these issues and that it, the venture capitalist, had the ability to follow up and provide manage-out our having to bear the high cost involved. That was where the business advisory service came in. It was obvious that commercial banks making only short-term working capital loans secured by inventory had no ability to assess five-year project loans, let alone such matters as marketing, financial management and cash flow forecasting. The only way this could be done was for the bank to establish a special unit with new people and to give this unit the necessary authority to approve loans and then oversee the companies. This of course would be costly.

Prom came up with the solution. The Commonwealth Secretariat ("CS"), based in London, served as a United Nations equivalent for the ex British dominions and colonies. At the time, some 60 countries—from wealthy ones such as Canada and Australia to the small and poor ones such as Kenya—were members. The CS had a technical assistance arm, much like the UN Development Program. Prom had heard of this and convinced me that they would finance this advisory unit. So, I sent Prom to London to find out. Much to my surprise he came back with an agreement that they would finance two experts in this work to work with KCB for a period of four years. All KCB would have to pay was their office expenses in Nairobi. Fortunately, Philip Ndegwa, the CEO of KCB, was a farsighted Kenyan. He agreed without hesitation. The two men the Secretariat sent were Indian bankers who had done similar work for an Indian long-term lending agency. Prom met them and felt they could do the job. So it was all agreed.

When we had finally negotiated all of the details with KCB and were preparing our report recommending the transaction to our board, we had to face up to the fact that this was the first time IFC had ever given another financial institution the authority to make transactions on IFC's behalf. We had had a lot of trouble with IFC's lawyers over this. They were convinced our board would never agree to delegate their authority to make loans to a Kenyan bank as they still insisted on approving each of IFC's transactions. However, following my usual custom, I had already consulted the key board members and they were on our side. Giving up a little authority under controlled conditions to execute a new scheme that would meet their latest priority was justified. There were other arcane issues, such as how we would file the records of all these

234

ment help when needed. Obviously, the whole point of our making these small loans through an agent bank was to make sure this happened with small transactions, which we eventually overcame. At our board presentation on this, Prom's introduction added that this was an entirely new scheme. As we were dependent on KCB, with whom we had done no previous business, and on the CS's people running the advisory service, we had to assume that we would lose 50% of our money. But we thought it was worth it as an experiment to meet the new objective of financing small businesses. We were applauded for this, much to the chagrin of all the naysayers in IFC. What was even more gratifying was that, some seven years later, we were able to report back to the board that our twelve loans had all been paid off in full. It was really quite surprising. There had been a few times over the period when some of the borrowers were late with interest payments, and one almost went into default. But, all the businesses KCB had selected had expanded and done so profitably. This probably would not have been the case if the Commonwealth Secretariat had not extended the term of its two advisers for a further two years and if KCB, after the six years, had not agreed to take over funding the advisory service. So, in the end, while the return on our loans at the going interest rate was not spectacular, this was widely recognized as a development success.

I remember visiting KCB about a year after the program started. That was when I got to know Philip Ndegwa. He was a very attractive man. Well educated, a good banker and very friendly. I recall that he invited me to dinner with his family at home once, where I met his Scottish wife and his two teenage sons. It was a delightful evening. Another memory of that evening was being driven to his home in his car. The driver was listening to the radio quite intently. I focused on what was being said just in time to hear the President of Kenya making a broadcast address to university students. Apparently, they were threatening to go on strike over an increase in fees. He was imploring them to understand the problems and restrain from more violence. I had not realized until then that there had been some rioting earlier that day. I left the next day and thought no more about it. But two weeks later when Antoine van Agtmael and Woonki Sung were in the country, matters got out of hand.

They were confined to their hotel for several days until the riots ended.

In Kenya, we invested also in an existing merchant bank, Diamond Trust. This was an Aga Khan company. The Ismaili management was smart and sophisticated (and, many years later, became involved in a big scandal). As I recall it, we had very lengthy negotiations as to our entry price which would be through a rights issue for new stock. The key existing investors would agree to transfer their rights to us. We had just started being encouraged to go into existing companies rather than only sponsor firsts-of-its-kind in order help speed up IFC's own investment program. Also, we were encouraged to do more in Africa. I had nothing against either of those worthy objectives. But I did feel that our entry prices should reflect going market rates. In this case, I had picked a return of 23% on net worth as the basis of our purchase price. The management was very unhappy about this because it was well below the going price of the stock, which was listed on the Kenyan Stock Exchange. Of course, that price was easily manipulated so it meant nothing to us. Further, we had to protect the interests of the UN Pension Fund which had agreed to invest alongside us, but as a passive investor. That said, the Aga Khan crowd hated the idea of a rights issue where they perceived IFC was to make quick profit at their expense. "That's not being developmental," they said.

Over the next ten years we did quite a lot more in Kenya, including investing in a leasing company in partnership with the Aga Khan who was very active with the large Ismaili community there. Sadly, though, crime worsened over the period, so it became increasingly depressing. On the other hand, our companies did reasonably well.

Years later, when Philip had became governor of the central bank, he asked me to help him in his task of revamping their securities markets. His particular concern was that Kenya had a number of private financing companies which he felt were run by people who did not have the necessary skills, but that is another story.

Ethiopia

Lena and I went to Addis on the way to Kenya in 1976 as Lena's brother, Johan, was there. A historic place, of course: 5,000 years of his-

236

tory and a claim to matching Jerusalem as an early Christian site. But it is a barren, arid country. Its only charm is its people who seem remarkably friendly and peaceful, despite their bad press over Eritrea. Still, Lalibela is a town to be seen, with its 12 churches dug into the ground rather than towering above it. It was the most poverty stricken town one can imagine. Unpaved streets, no street lights. And the houses not only have no running water or power, but the ground floors are essentially just shelters for their goats and sheep. The hotel where we stayed professed to be a Hilton but I doubt if it was listed in any Hilton brochures. Water for the sinks, showers and toilets was delivered twice a day in buckets. Lunch and dinner—for the two days—looked exactly the same: road kill. Getting to Lalibela by plane was an interesting experience. The plane stopped at an intermediary airport. As it landed the pilot warned the passengers to pull down their window blinds and keep them down. I was tempted to peek but didn't. Afterwards, Johan told us this was fortunate. One of his Embassy colleagues had done it a few years back. He was caught and spent a night in jail before the Embassy got him released. Apparently the town was a military garrison.

11th Century underground church in Lalibela, Ethiopia, which Lena and I visited in 1976 as a side trip between Lebanon and Kenya. Taken from above, this picture shows the church in the form of a cross. One had to take a staircase carved downwards into the mountain to get to the entrance of the church.

Mexico

I first met Gustavo Petricioli, then the chairman of Mexico's securities commission, in 1976 in Buenos Aires. We were attending the Third Annual Conference of the "Inter-American Conference of Securities Commissions and Like Entities" hosted that year by the Argentine securities commission. (IOSCO is now almost as well known as its banking counterpart, the Bank for International Settlements.) Gustavo told me that the Bank's regional vice president for Latin America had suggested to him that he should seek our help in revitalizing Mexico's securities market. I must have satisfied him because I was invited to visit him in Mexico City the next year. Gustavo and I developed a great relationship over the years, but I don't think we accomplished much for him. More than anything, it was a matter of our both being ahead of our time. Mexico then was very inward looking, largely as a result of its historic distrust of the United States. In the financial market, it meant no foreigners were allowed to own securities firms. The inevitable result was a market dominated by the major commercial banks. As with the Argentine decision makers, the key players liked things the way they were. Still, we spent a lot of time trying. This, of course, was a mistake in that we were ignoring our own rule of only spending time in countries where there was a serious will to do something. As best I recall it, the reason we tried was because the Bank wanted us to. Also, as the Mexicans we dealt with were charming and good company, it wasn't hard.

One person I enjoyed particularly was Roberto Hernandez. At the time he was president of Acciones y Valores, a brokerage firm, and chairman of the Mexico Stock Exchange. He went on to become the largest shareholder in Mexico's largest bank—Banamex —and very wealthy. But Gustavo was the most interesting. I forget which President had been his early mentor but he told me some fascinating stories about how things worked in the Mexican system. He had ridden the rising tide with his mentor but, at some point, failed him. His punishment was to be removed from some prestigious job and become appointed "commissioner of football." No one much played football in Mexico in those days. Gustavo must have done some of the right things because he became minister of finance and, later as a retirement job, ambassador to the U.S. But Gustavo always took things lightly. My last time with him was lunch together in Washington in about 1990 in my Batterymarch days. At around 2.30 he looked at his watch and said: "Well, I'd better get back. I'm hosting a lunch for our political attaché who is going home. I'm due to toast him at 2.30." This wasn't a reflection on how good our relationship was or indifference to his attaché. Rather, it was just that lunch is anytime between 2.00 and 5.00 in Mexico so it is hard for Mexicans, even in the U.S., to take such details as U.S. lunch time habits too seriously.

In the early 1980s, and after much effort, we convinced the Mexican authorities that they should allow the establishment of what would have been our first "country fund." I will write more about this later. For now, I shall just relate what went wrong. After about two years' effort in getting the local regulations changed and putting together a group of investment banks to participate in the management company and underwrite the IPO, the Mexicans changed the rules. Initially, Gustavo was a great supporter of the idea but, when he became minister of finance, he had to be above the fray. True to our mandate, we had required an independent private management company be formed to run it. The shareholders were to be a few Mexican brokerage companies, Merrill Lynch and Deutsche Bank as the foreign providers of expertise, and IFC. At the last moment, after IFC's board had approved our investing in it and IFC's role as an underwriter of the IPO, the Mexicans insisted that the largest shareholder (who would really control the company) would be a government-controlled brokerage firm. I told them IFC would have to pull out—after I had discussed it with Merrill and DB who agreed to stay on. For a time this caused a lot of ill feeling both in Mexico and with IFC's management. But the fact was that IFC should not only refrain from investing in government-controlled companies, but having such a company manage a fund listed on the NYSE would put investors at risk. However, the Fund became the first NYSE-listed country fund and led ultimately to many more country funds. Its IPO was a success and investors who stayed with it did well even though the Mexican market would go through major ups and downs.

India

In 1977 I went to India for the first time with Promodh Malhotra. This was somewhat contrary to our procedures in that the government had not expressed much interest, but India was an important country, so worthy of an exception. Besides, Prom was a great salesman and he thought he could work miracles in his homeland. Actually, he did. Our first call and our best contact was with H.T. Parekh, the chairman of the leading Indian DFC in which IFC was a shareholder. I shall never forget that first meeting. It displayed the impressive entrepreneurship and level of influence DFCs had even in countries like India where new ideas and private enterprise were not especially welcome at the time.

We started discussing with H.T., as we called him, what IFC could do in the financial sector considering that, except for this DFC and the some small brokerage partnerships, all financial institutions were 100% government owned. Prom said: "How about a housing bank to help lower and middle class people buy their own homes?" This had not been rehearsed with me, but it was an excellent initiative on Prom's part. We explained what we had done in Colombia. H.T. was convinced in short order. He brought in his general manager to hear about the idea and get his reaction. Inside an hour, we had agreed that he would sponsor it and get governmental approval. Amazingly, considering the complexities of the Indian bureaucracy, but as a testament to H.T.'s influence and prestige, the Housing Development Finance Corporation ("HDFC") was established as India's first private sector financial institution. HDFC went on to become a highly successful financial institution run by H.T.'s nephew, Deepak Parekh, and a major player in India. When its stock became listed, it ended up as the largest holding in the portfolios of most foreign funds investing in India, and it later spun-off a large successful bank.

Over the years, Prom went on to promote and get established a string of leasing companies in most of India's major cities. So, despite an inauspicious beginning, we became quite active there. One area in which we at first failed miserably though was in trying to modernize India's securities market. I cannot recall how we became involved, but I guess

240

it must have been that Prom persuaded the minister of finance to make a formal request. As everything did in India, it took a long time before we saw results of a major study of the mechanics of the securities market but it ultimately led to the establishment of the National Securities Market; the ending of the dominance of the Bombay stock exchange and a small group of brokers; the elimination of a trading system that resembled an options market more than a stock market; and the "de-materialization" of physical share certificates. Farida Khambata and Teresa Barger were the investment officers most actively involved in this.

I found India otherwise a very disconcerting country. The government and business leaders I met were very smart and courteous. But the level of poverty at that time, especially in Bombay, was truly appalling. At least on the surface, and as far as I could see during my limited exposure to both countries, it was worse than in Egypt. In Cairo, walking the streets was a reasonably pleasant experience. In Bombay, even in the most upscale part of the city, one was constantly besieged by a crowd of child beggars. One could not but be very moved by how ravaged and thin they looked.

Spain

It was hard to see why Spain was on IFC's LDC list. But I recall the argument of Spain's elegant and charming ED, making his case that several regions were under-developed. He wanted us to sponsor—in 1977—a venture capital company that was being sponsored by a French venture capital group. This was how I met Dominique Oger, who was seconded from the French company to run it.

Jordan

Jordan was the second Arab country to ask for CMD assistance. What struck me the most about Amman—it was the only part of Jordan I saw during my dozen or so visits—was that, despite its small size and remoteness from Europe, it was a surprisingly sophisticated and friendly Arab capital. Still, it was a small town as compared to Beirut and Cairo. All the senior government people, most of whom were originally Palestinian, were very professional.

I had several interesting experiences. On my first flight on Royal Jordanian Airlines, I saw and talked to the only female flight crew member I ever saw in the Arab world. She was a "Third Officer" or Engineer—at the time aircraft controls were less automated than they are now so a third man, or woman, in the cockpit of multi-engine aircraft was needed. Another was jogging one snowy morning. It was April and there were a couple of inches on the ground, which was quite unusual. Through the snow I suddenly saw a very short young soldier pointing a very large machine gun at me. I stopped, and probably looked as nervous as he did. Then I realized I had been running towards the Soviet embassy building. So I just crossed the street and walked by him, slowly. He smiled as I passed and I waved. Another event was during one evening when I was having drinks with some of my Jordanian friends in the lobby of the Amman Intercontinental Hotel. Suddenly, there was machine gun fire and the zing of bullets passing close by. Everyone dove under the tables. The Jordanians, I discovered afterwards, thought it was an attack by extremists. It turned out to be one of the cooks shooting at one of the waiters who he thought was trying to steal his girlfriend. Fortunately, his rage got the better of his aiming and he only succeeded in putting a lot of bullet holes in the walls and the large plate glass front door. A few policemen showed up minutes later and everything went back to normal.

Jordan's efforts to establish a securities commission began in 1977. As with Brazil, it was a central bank initiative. Said Nabulsi was the governor. He was of medium height, a slim fellow who often gave the impression of being shy. But this did not hide his intellect. His approach was much like that of the Thai central bank. Because of the small size of the market, it was to be a combined securities commission and stock exchange. They named it the Amman Financial Market ("AFM"). For a small country, Jordan had a reasonably diverse set of banking and insurance companies and a fair number of quite large, for Jordan, publicly traded stocks. The brokers, not surprisingly, were part-timers whose main activities were as money traders and insurance agents. The person in charge of the AFM was Hashem Sabbagh. He had been in the insurance business previously. He and I spent a lot of time together over the years. He was a dedicated, hard working fellow, and a lot of fun to be with. We arranged for him to go through our, by then, standard training program in Washington and Toronto. I often wonder what became of him.

What was especially interesting to me was to learn from the listed company CEOs and CFOs what they expected to gain from a more efficient and better-regulated market. The short answer was more capital from foreign sources. That made Jordan very different from the other Arab countries, all of which banned foreign portfolio investment. More importantly, the reforms to their market did in fact lead to foreign portfolio investment in the 1980s. In some respects, this was surprising as it took investment managers much the same amount of time to research this small country as it did for larger countries, such as Brazil, that offered many more investment opportunities. There were only a handful of companies big enough for even a token investment. I suppose they were attracted by the seriousness of the Jordanians and that it had become a dependable market for foreigners. That it was then the only country in the region where investing made possible sense also helped. Investment funds investing globally needed geographic diversification.

Said Nabulsi wanted us to help start a merchant bank. He made sure all the necessary rules were put in place so the company could function. The local stock market was already quite active and the financial information on the listed companies was fairly good. Consequently, the prospects for a merchant bank seemed reasonable. The merchant banking affiliate of the then Midland Bank in London, Samuel Montagu, became our technical partner and Petra Bank was our lead local partner. We called it Jordan Securities Company ("JSC"). For the first three months we arranged for another ex McLeod, Young, Weir man to help them. George McDonald, who succeeded John Dinnick as CEO and had just retired himself, loved the idea of spending some time in Amman helping the local staff. Sending George and his wife was easy for us as a Canadian government program covered his expenses and he had no desire for the type of fee our scales would have allowed. One of my mistakes was going on the board of JSC. Fortunately, our investment officer, Sami Haddad, a very fine Lebanese, got us out of trouble before it was too late. He warned me that the Arabic version of the board meeting minutes was consistently quite different from the English version we were sent. They were telling us what we wanted to hear, but were actually doing what they wanted to do.

We suspected that a lot of the business was less than sound. Shortly after Antoine joined the CMD, he and Sami were on a due diligence visit when Antoine smelled that something was wrong. He pretended great interest in their computer system and had them print out all kinds of reports. Then—to JSC's dismay—they took the reports back to the hotel and analyzed the data. That's how we found that JSC had violated their investment guidelines by financing trucks for Iraq in a deal Ahmed Chalabi (the primary owner of Petra Bank) had brought to them. Apparently, JSC financed the leasing of a large fleet of trucks to what turned out to be a "front" Jordanian company financed by Petra bank. The trucks were last seen crossing the border to Iraq. JSC was never paid and would have gone bankrupt had not the central bank bailed them out. In any event, after about two years, we told Said Nabulsi that we wanted out. He arranged for some of the locals to accommodate us and give us a modest profit. I was amused that the Samuel Montagu people made a point of saying they were staying in because of the importance to them of the country relationship. They wanted us to know that they took such matters much more seriously than IFC, which obviously should have taken it more seriously than they did. For better or worse, we got the last laugh as they finally retreated about a year later.

At the time, Petra Bank was considered the most innovative private bank in Jordan. Of course it was not in the same league as Arab Bank, which was the largest private bank in the region and also based in Jordan. But Arab Bank wasn't interested—they must have known more than we did. In any event, Petra Bank was run, and largely owned, by Ahmed Chalabi, an expatriate Iraqi who has gained fame recently because of his role in the run up to, and the aftermath of, the Iraq War. At the time, we were especially taken by him as one of his uncles (it seemed strange at the time as Ahmed was the older of the two) worked for us. This was Ali Allawi, then a 26-year-old genius with degrees from both MIT and Harvard, and two years working experience with an oil firm, who could absorb technical financial data better than anyone I knew. Ali and Ahmed had a great joint story. Prior to the revolution in Iraq, Ahmed's family had been the wealthiest Iraqi family and Ali's was number two. After the revolution the order was reversed. Ali's family had been clever enough to move themselves and their money to London. Ahmed, who was the older of the two, was a very interesting and amusing fellow. But his business practices were a little different from ours. He appointed one of his men as the CEO. That was where the trouble started. Other than brokerage operation and short-term loans—including the one for the disappearing trucks—JSC didn't do much that I remember.

Our other venture in Jordan was another leasing company. Again, Petra Bank was our local partner. By coincidence, while we were doing our initial homework on the leasing industry, Rudi and I had visited U.S. Leasing International in San Francisco. I knew of them as a leading U.S. independent leasing company from my Laurentide days (see Chapter II). I don't recall his name, but the CEO and principal shareholder was a very engaging 40-something who commuted to work on a motorbike. We thought they would be interested in a venture in Jordan and they were. Sadly, once U.S. Leasing and IFC paid in their money, neither Chalabi nor the CEO he had brought in from Petra Bank would discuss anything about what they were doing. U.S. Leasing finally decided they were not going to risk their reputation that way and told us they wanted out. So we both sold our stock to Chalabi's group for a small profit.

Dominican Republic

This was one of my one-day, one-visit stops. I recall it only as the first of the old Spanish Caribbean islands and thus my receiving a very gracious reception. Santo Domingo reminded me of Quito. At least the architecture did. But it was a seaport which made it much more interesting to me. We were establishing a leasing company there. But I had retired by the time it started up.

Sri Lanka

This was my last port of call in 1977. Colombo was not exactly a modern city but an improvement over Bombay and Dhaka. Again with Prom, we were doing one of our bank SME lines of credit. Later we also promoted successful leasing and insurance companies. I found the people very friendly and straightforward, which is probably why we did so much so quickly by IFC standards. Small countries next to giant neighbors tend to be that way. My lasting memory shows this. The CEO of the leading bank complained in a joking way that I had devoted only one and a half days to his country, which he said probably reflected a fair priority rating considering the size of the economy.

Our first venture there was a leasing company. Later, Jay Tata organized an insurance company. It was the same group insurance scheme that worked so well in Indonesia with Manufacturers Life: they came along with us. While obviously a smaller deal, it also worked out well. In Sri Lanka we were fortunate in that we already had our leasing company there and our local sponsor in that—Aitken Spence—happened to have an insurance agency. So they had little difficulty in talking the government into granting the necessary approvals.

Nigeria

Nigeria was not a pleasant country to visit, at least not in the late 1970s, when I went there twice. Besides being hot and steamy, it was dirty, dangerous and the food even in hotels was inedible. It was a great shame because Nigerians generally are smart and hard working, and many are well educated and honest. Lagos, except for a few square blocks, was a large slum with open sewers. Considering it was a rich country because of its oil wealth the squalor and poverty was inexcusable. On the other hand, the even oil richer Venezuela had similar problems despite a much better educated populous. Undoubtedly that was, in part, because of the general corruption at all levels and especially the street crime. The corruption is well illustrated by the following story. A reporter interviewing the minister of industry accused him of insisting

246

on being paid 10% bribes on all contracts. The minister's response was: "That's an insult! I never accept less than 20%." One of my CMD colleagues who was Nigerian told me about crime. He had been to Nigeria for his sister's wedding. On the way back—they lived in the North—he had to stay overnight in a Lagos hotel. As he started getting into a taxi for the usual 4.00 AM flight to London, a fellow countryman rushed through the door and asked if he could go with him. He claimed there were no more taxis. My colleague agreed. Halfway, on the open highway, the taxi pulled off the road and stopped. The other passenger, gun in hand, told him to strip and get out. As he stood there stark naked with no money, no passport and no luggage, he said: "You can't do this to a fellow Nigerian!" The response he got was: "You're lucky you are Nigerian. Otherwise I would have just shot you." On my two visits I was picked up at the aircraft door by an armed guard and escorted to the hotel—and returned the same way.

Not withstanding all of that, I shall always remember fondly the Nigerian Securities Commission ("NSC") and George Akami-khor, the then chairman. George was a very charming and bright individual. He came to IFC to visit me several times, often accompanied by Aliede, chairman of the Nigerian Stock Exchange. His task was to persuade me to visit to advise them. I liked them both and, besides arranging the usual visits for them, Lena and I had them to the house several times. What struck me most about them was their professionalism. There was really not much we could teach them. The only problem they had with their respective jobs was dealing with the pervasive corruption of the country. George often asked me to visit Lagos. I always found reasons not to go: IFC would not pay for it as it was clear there was nothing we could add. Finally, the NSC offered to pay my British Airways first class ticket to Lagos so I could be the keynote speaker at a securities market conference being held in Calabar. So I went. It was quite an experience. I was the only foreigner at the conference and I think there was only one other foreigner in Calabar—the local UN representative. But the quality of the conference was absolutely first rate: it could have been a meeting run by the NYSE. The local speakers knew their stuff and it was interesting to hear the brokers lambasting the central bank and ministry of finance people for having financial policies and rules that were detrimental to market development. There were no holds barred!

Calabar itself was an interesting town. It had been an embarkation port for slaves being sent to the Americas. At the docks there was still a very large old fort cum prison from those days. I remember being driven around town in a minibus that had been arranged by the locals to show the men from Lagos the sights. I noticed we were often waved at by schoolchildren (all in smart school uniforms). I assumed they were waving at the only white man but it turned out that what was attracting them were the important men in suits from the big city. One of the sights was the cemetery. What was touching is that all the men gravitated immediately to the grave of a Scottish nun who had been there as a missionary in the late 1700s—she was much revered by the men from Lagos.

Uruguay

Uruguay is a wonderful country to visit but not the best in which to do business. Montevideo is a small scale Rio without the mountains. Punta del Este ("Punta") is one of the world's more charming resorts, often called the Saint Tropez of South America —despite the Miami-like skyline vista as you approach. But the old town has much charm and the yacht club can be compared to the RCYC in Toronto. Sadly, wealthy foreigners, mainly Argentines, have cluttered the old fishing harbor with gleaming 100-foot "stink pots."It makes St. Michaels and Oxford harbors look pretty small. Even Annapolis is less impressive in comparison. The reason IFC became involved could have been considered a conflict of interest as we supported a merchant bank being promoted by a Uruguayan ex staff member, Francisco ("Pancho") Ravecca, who retired from IFC to do exactly that. Pancho's idea was that setting up an investment bank-type of institution, backed by diversified, very strong and well-respected banks, would provide the necessary credentials and recognition to be able to tap into international financial centers during the "lost decade" of the 80's—as Enrique Iglesias, the head of the Inter-American Development Bank, referred to this decade—when it was practically impossible to raise any money from Latin American countries. His thought was that strong shareholder backing should do the trick, and it did, as Surinvest managed to raise the money it sought.

We had been advising the government on their securities market since 1978 and the signs were encouraging. While a small country, it was relatively wealthy and had a well educated work force. It had been known as the Switzerland of South America. This was partially because of its banking system and partially because of its social security system that, at the time, was quite advanced by American standards. By the time we invested in "Surinvest Casa Bancaria" we had still not noticed that the politicians were better at making promises than keeping them. We thought we were investing in a merchant bank that could do leasing, money market operations, market making and financial advisory work. But the government never did get around to making the necessary changes in the regulations to develop leasing and, as with other similar small countries with socialist governments, there was not much going on in the capital markets. But, as an open economy with effectively no corporate taxes then, it was a good location for a regional bank, which was the plan. Pancho had put together a fine group of shareholders: some local individuals and a group of foreign banks that wanted exposure to Uruguay and a tax-free entry to other markets. The banks were Midland Bank, Banco Roberts, the leading Argentine merchant bank and Unibanco, one of the leading Brazilian commercial banks. Since then of course, all the banks' names and owners have changed. The original plan was that Pancho was to be chairman and the chief marketing man and that Midland would second a professional to run the bank on a day-to-day basis, following all of Midland's administrative and credit policies and rules. They hired an Italian banker to take on that job. Unfortunately, as with most expatriates who took such assignments, he moved on to the next job two years later, as did the next three. More and more, Pancho became CEO in practice.

Notwithstanding that Surinvest could not do the business in Uruguay we had expected, it managed to make money over the years, paying its shareholders a dividend of around 20% most years. Pancho was a great salesman and developed a large international correspondent banking business as well as a good trade finance business with Argentine and Uruguayan exporters. But it had become obvious that the only way it could continue to be successful was to become a bank. The Uruguayan central bank, possibly feeling guilty about past broken promises to IFC and the other shareholders, promised to grant a banking license. But it took them another ten years to actually deliver it. I was on the board for the entire time I was in IFC and for the next 11 years. It was quite a ride. The worst period, of course, was during the 1980s debt crisis. Adding to Surinvest's miseries in the period, the central bank established a regime whereby industrial companies could escape their bank borrowing obligations. It survived in part because IFC agreed to convert its senior loan into a subordinated loan with the right to convert it into common stock. As was usually the case with such debt restructuring deals, both sides benefited. IFC eventually converted at what was an attractive price at the time. But for several reasons, including that consortium banks usually do not last more than five years or so, Surinvest ran into more problems in the 1990s. These I will cover in my last chapter.

Portugal

After the dictatorship ended in 1978, the new government sought our advice. I first went there with Antonio Guerreiro. He was our only Portuguese investment officer and one of our best. Eventually he went back to Lisbon and founded his own merchant bank, which became very successful. It was a fascinating experience to see a country that had just escaped a failing regime. I had remembered Lisbon from my visit there with the navy in 1950. Then, it was a clean, vibrant city. By 1979 it was decidedly run down. But I found the people to be exceptionally charming and the new government people very bright and receptive to our ideas. Unlike Chile, though, the new decision makers were not "Chicago boys" so things did not move quite so quickly. The important thing was we did develop strong relationships with the key government people and many in the financial community. They were easy to work with and very generous with their praise for our work with them. These feelings about Portugal were probably biased by a speech made by the governor of the central bank at a dinner he hosted for me during my last visit. He made it clear that he believed CMD had done more for Portugal than had the Bank or the rest of IFC. I think he really meant it.

Our first project experience in Portugal was especially interesting. It was an expansion of the merchant bank that had been established a few years previously by Antonio Guerreiro (another conflict of interest issue that the Bank board accepted). I had mentioned in an earlier chapter how his bank had bought control of the leasing company we had established in Portugal. But this was after we made our investment in his firm and after we had sold out of the leasing company. Antonio was a first rate operator and our investment, once we got over the following hurdle, went very smoothly and produced attractive profits for IFC, which did not sell out until 2001.

The hurdle was that the Bank's DFC in Portugal, in which IFC was an investor through its regional department, complained to our management that investing in Antonio's company would be competitive. I was never sure whether it was the Bank or IFC's regional department that caused the problem. Either way, Bill Diamond, whose investment it was and who was on the DFC's board, created havoc for a while. He claimed that the DFC's shareholder agreement contained a clause that said IFC would not compete with it. We made the case that IFC's charter contemplated competing investments and we had equity investments in as many as three companies in the same business in many countries. Also we said it was expressly understood with all our partners in all our investments that we might go into similar ventures. Further, we said that the two companies were in quite different parts of the financial business. That satisfied IFC and Bank management, but not Bill Diamond. The next thing that happened was IFC received almost identical letters from the DFC's foreign bank shareholders in France, Germany and Switzerland, all claiming unfair competition and breach of the agreements. This stopped us for a while as Bill Ryrie, IFC's then Executive Vice President, caved in to this pressure. Then Tony had the bright idea of going to another French bank that was one of his shareholders and whose president had been on IFC's board. I still remember going to Paris with Tony and making our case to him. He was as outraged as were we. He wrote his own letter to the Bank's president saying that IFC had an obligation to foster competition. So we won, and made a few more enemies. To me it was just another example of the problem Bank

251

economists had understanding the difference between banking—mainly lending for their own account, which was what DFC's did mainly—and mer-chant/investment banking—mainly agency/brokerage transactions in equity and debt for other peoples' accounts. Yes, there was some competition between the two types of "banking," but it was at the margin and it was good for the economy.

Later, after that tug of war, we helped established the first leasing company. With the encouragement of the ministry of finance it was an easy task to find a local bank and team up, yet again, with a French leasing company. It must have filled a need in the economy as several other groups decided to do the same. There were eventually, I think, about five established over the next year. Also, several commercial banks established leasing divisions.

What I recall the most about our activities there were the several technical conferences we had organized, all of which turned a profit for the sponsors. We had used professional conferences before in other countries to get wide support for what we were doing. Portugal was the first where we were able to make them profitable. Our concept was similar to our position on governmental assignments—people who paid for our services, or to attend a conference we organized to promote financial markets, would take it much more seriously than those who received the proverbial free lunch. The one we arranged on leasing finance was so successful that the profit was enough to finance the establishment of a leasing association in Portugal.

Something I will also remember is a discussion I had with the CEO of the French leasing company while we were walking back to our hotel one afternoon. For reasons I can't remember I had commented on the difficult time teenagers had growing up in the world then. His response was it was a lot easier for them now than it had been for teenagers during World War II. He told me of the time he had had trouble with his two teenage sons a few years previously. He said he took them to the cemetery of his village in the South of France and showed them the graves of several resistance fighters who had been killed by the Germans. They were all teenagers. He said he told his sons these were teenagers who really had trouble growing up. I was rather humbled by that.

Saudi Arabia

Saudi Arabia was the first Gulf country to invite me to visit. This was in 1979. Subsequently I was asked to go to Kuwait, the United Arab Emirates and Bahrain. This was another situation where it was decided we should help, as they all were buyers of Bank and IFC debt and were often passive investors in our deals. So their governments were entitled to some reciprocation. CMD was the part of IFC that interested them the most as all except Saudi Arabia had aspirations to become regional financial centers. Mainly what we did was write reports on aspects of their financial markets and how they could get into the international game. Even in those days Saudi Arabia had a very large stock market. But all of the Gulf countries—and Lebanon—prohibited foreigners from buying their listed stocks during that period. However the central bankers, who in each country had the responsibility for their securities markets, seemed more interested in talking about the subject than doing anything.

I asked Frank Veneroso to write the reports on the issues they wanted analyzed. One was looking into an initiative the Bahrain government wanted to explore. This was to establish a global electronic market listing all the world's stocks. The theory was that because of their time zone half way between Europe and Asia, they could operate when the other markets were closed. It didn't work. Another person we sent there—to the UAE and Bahrain—was Matt Ardron. Matt had been the main inventor of the world's first automated stock market system when he worked for the Toronto Stock Exchange. We Canadians were very proud of that and that the TSE system was later used by several other stock exchanges, including Paris. Matt used to wax eloquently on how annoyed the Parisian brokers would have been had they known that their transactions were being executed on an IBM mainframe located in Toronto. General de Gaulle of "Vive le Quebec Libre" fame would have turned in his grave. Nevertheless, neither of these countries bought the system. I suppose the respective governments (who ran the markets) were influenced by their brokers. As with NYSE brokers, none wanted to change from the old ways of floor dealings. (In those days one would never have imagined that the NYSE would end up being owned by for-eigners.)

We also arranged for Ernie Kepper to go to Riyadh as an advisor to the ministry of finance. I believe his Indonesian experience had some-thing to do with that. He and his family were there for some four years. I was never clear what he was doing for them. The Bank, however, was very pleased. He was still on their payroll so he was their man in Riyadh. When I visited (for one day), I remember Ernie's comments on the joys (limited) of living there as an expatriate. Still, it was interesting to see those countries, especially the small ones. I will always remember the beauty of the harbors with their fishing dhows and the sandy beaches nearby. The beaches were the closest I got to their deserts—that was more Ernie Kepper's thing. He used to tell me stories of going on camel excursions with Saudi friends and having barbecues deep in the desert. I suppose one can get used to it. On a more serious note, some of the Gulf countries could have emulated Singapore but none did. I felt the two most important reasons were, first, the cultural differences and, sec-ond, their oil wealth.

Peru

Peru, which I visited first around 1980, was an interesting country only because of its extremes of poverty and wealth, especially as seen in Lima. Certainly though Machu Picchu is a world heritage site.

We made one investment there: the first leasing company in the coun-try. It was a joint venture with Societe Generale's leasing affiliate and Banco Wiese, the leading private bank in Peru. We called it Sogiewiese. It was the first of many such joint ventures with French banks. I had not realized how strongly the French authorities had promoted leasing. They had seen its economic merits long before we had. Rudi, with his strong French connections, was behind this. Each of the French banks had a leasing subsidiary and there were also some independent compa-nies as I had mentioned earlier. The French authorities had gone as far as promoting specialized leasing activities to the point where even per-sonal yacht financing via leases was specifically encouraged. So, once we started promoting leasing and Rudi had zeroed in on the French

254

banks, France's Executive Director encouraged us and gave us introductions to all the key people in the field in Paris. "SG" was glad to join us in Peru. Besides it being a good business in itself, it also gave them an entrée into the country. What I remember especially about this was that it continued to be successful during the 1980s financial crisis in Latin America. SG finally bought us out at a very attractive price in the middle of the crisis.

Zimbabwe

Zimbabwe remains my favorite country in Africa. I will write a bit about recent truly tragic events there in a following chapter. But in 1982, when I first went there, I was impressed both by the charm of the people and of the countryside. Victoria Falls, which I first saw from Zambia, is one of the wonders of the world. A hundred or so miles south is one of Africa's great game parks. Even Harare the capital had a small city charm. In those days one could wander around the main streets during the evenings in complete safety contrary to the general impression in the rest of African towns. That attests also to the charm of the people. Miekles Hotel in Harare was considered one of the best in Africa. Again, in a small land-locked country (now 11 million population) one would not expect to find a sophisticated center city hotel with four excellent restaurants and a quality of service and food as good as most four-star London establishments. That it was the second wealthiest country per capita in Southern Africa says much about the ability and education of the people. What has happened in the last few years is a tragedy.

One of the most interesting leasing companies we had was in Zimbabwe in 1982. It was not the first leasing company there—Zimbabwe had a quite sophisticated financial market—but it gave us the opportunity to meet another IFC target. That was to promote locally controlled companies. UDC, as it was called, started out as the wholly owned Zimbabwean subsidiary of United Dominions Trust ("UDT"), a U.K. financing company that provided a range of asset financing services to small companies and individuals. UDT decided they wanted out of Zimbabwe and offered to sell UDC at ten cents on the one-dollar par value. Jay Tata heard of this somehow and went to work. The first problem was that IFC's charter, quite reasonably, prohibited IFC from buying out existing shareholders. What Jay did was to put together a syndicate of local financial institutions and EDESA, a Swiss entity. This latter, a form of miniature IFC for Africa whose shareholders were a group of U.S. and European banks, was run by Rene Gerber, a delightful, dedicated man. The Swiss also were to provide any ongoing support local management needed. This group agreed to buy out UDC at ten cents on the dollar and to subscribe to a capital increase at one dollar, for a blended price of about 55 cents. IFC would subscribe to a second capital increase at the 55-cent price. As this was for new shares, our problem was solved. Our case to IFC's board was that, as a result of this financial engineering exercise, UDC's ownership had been repatriated with some 70% of the shares in local hands. UDC went on to be a successful leasing company with 100% local management. It also spawned affiliates in Botswana and Malawi, making it the second (KIFC being the first) of our investee companies to help broaden the financial markets of other LDCs further down the developmental ladder.

The now well-known less pleasant aspect of the Zimbabwean authorities came to light when we sold our stake in UDC. The company had, quite legitimately, obtained U.S. dollars to pay us and had them transferred to the central bank. Because of long delays in getting the money out, we sent Jay to remind the governor that, as an IFC shareholder, Zimbabwe was legally obligated to deliver our dollars to our New York Federal Reserve Bank account. His response was to tell Jay that he had 24 hours to get out of the country or he would be jailed, so he took the next flight out. I don't know whether IFC ever got the money.

Turkey

It was not until about 1982 that we were asked to advise the government on financial system reform. We received a telex from the Turkish Ministry of Finance urging IFC to urgently help with a governmental decree (used by the military government of that period) that would establish the first formal Capital Market legislation. The problem was that the decree needed to be ready for approval less than a week later. I hurriedly sent Antoine and Terry Reilly out to Istanbul. By the time of their arrival, they only had the afternoon and night to complete the 50-or-so-page document. They were able to hire a formal UN translator as an English-speaking typist and drafted the law that night. The next morning, they handed it to the Undersecretary of the Ministry of Finance who helped promulgate it later that week.

Turkey had always interested me as a country because of its history, its involvement in NATO, and the reluctance the EU had, and still has, in granting it membership. It's also a very beautiful country populated, at least in the parts I knew, by very charming and hospitable people. Rudi van der Bijl accompanied me on most of my visits. One thing that struck me immediately was the efficiency of the shuttle flight service between Istanbul and Ankara, the capital. It was as frequent and busy as the NY - DC service. The difference was the in-flight service was better and the cabin configuration more comfortable. I suppose, as in other countries where the capital is less interesting than the business center, the locals like to be able to be able to get there and back in one day. That was certainly also the case in Brazil.

Unfortunately, its history was a major stumbling block when it came to financial reform. Its quality of financial reporting and disclosure was, along with Egypt, the lowest of any non-communist country I had visited. One reason was that its parliamentarians had some kind of monopoly on approving company financial statements. Consequently, they were not going to give up this perk to allow the establishment of professional auditing firms. In any event we completed our task as best we could. One result was the formation of a securities commission—the Capital Markets Authority. While our institution building efforts resulted in several new financial entities, including a leasing company, we backed away from forming a real investment bank to set an example for the local small brokerage companies. The main reason, as we explained to the authorities, was their unwillingness to deal with the auditing issue. We did not want to give the impression IFC was endorsing the local listed companies in whose securities such an entity would have to deal. Many years later, things changed for the better, but that was after my time.

During my time, though, two rather amusing events occurred. The first was a visit to IFC by the ex IFC staff member who had persuaded us to work there—Ozul. By then he was minister of finance and his older brother was Prime Minister. He wanted us to launch a country fund for Turkey. He paused after saying this and then said: "I suppose we had better not call it a Turkey Fund."

The other event occurred during a conference that the Capital Markets Authority had organized with our help. I had made the closing presentation and the conference was scheduled to be closed formally by the new minister of finance who had just been sworn in. She was a charming, very Western looking lady who had taught economics. Several years later she became Prime Minister. I stepped down from the podium so the CMA chairman could introduce her. Instead he said she had called to say she would be 15 minutes late as her ceremony had been delayed. So we had a 15-minute break. After about 20 minutes an agitated chairman came to me and said: "David, can you speak again for a few minutes? She's going to be another ten minutes. I'll come up as soon as she arrives." What could I do but agree. I ad-libbed for ten minutes. There was no sign of him. On I went, hoping I was not repeating myself. Finally, after more than half an hour, he showed up with a big grin and took over. The minister then made her remarks. They took about 30 seconds. She said "congratulations, I wish you all success" and then told a story. She said a schoolmate of her young (about ten) son had approached her that morning and asked if he should buy stocks. She told him he should get his mother to sell her jewels and spend the money on stocks. Even the local brokers in the audience were a bit perplexed.

Less entertaining was our experience supporting an investment bank. It—Global Securities—was established shortly before I retired. I used the word "supporting" because it was another investment that was not really justified. It was already in existence as a small brokerage firm. We just helped it become bigger but, unfortunately, better only in the sense that it did become a leader with international investors. Regrettably, as so often happens in developed countries as well as in LDCs, greed brought it down in the end as it started borrowing at short term with floating rates and lending at long term with fixed interest rates.

Pakistan

It was some years before I made my first visit to Pakistan. My immediate reaction to Karachi was that it was quite different from Bombay or Delhi. What sticks in my mind mainly is that the police —and there were lots of them—were all armed with AK47s whereas the Indian police all seemed to be carrying World War I Lee Enfield rifles. My only other recollection was a saga over turf. It involved Farida Khambata, an Indian national who Antoine van Agtmael had persuaded to join us from the Bank's pension investment department, as our investment officer for an investment in a merchant bank there. The local partner was a leading industrial multinational, Packages Ltd., whose chairman and CEO, Syed Babar Ali, was a very senior and distinguished Pakistani who had been a friend and client of IFC for many years. The foreign technical partner was to be American Express. For some reason, possibly because Babar Ali was the regional department's main contact there, the regional department felt it should be their deal. We thought this was cleared up without contention, as it was clearly a CMD deal. Then came complaints from American Express that Farida was not behaving in a professional manner. Naturally, we followed this up. To everyone's embarrassment, it turned out that the Amex person working on the deal had no complaints. The letter had been written at the suggestion of someone in the regional department. The Amex person had been told that such a letter would result in the deal being turned over to the regional department and that would result in the terms for Amex being more favorable than otherwise. When all of this came out Farida was formally vindicated. But the deal collapsed, which turned out to be just as well.

Greece

As with Spain, I found it hard to see why Greece should have been on the list. But it was great to be able to go there as it is a beautiful country. Also, one of my old friends from Toronto lived there. Ian Vorres was from a well-known Greek family that had one of the country's best-regarded art collections. Over the years I had got to know Ian's father

quite well. During one of the military takeovers—I think it was in 1967—
he asked me if I would help them by taking on legal ownership of their
"boat." (I may have recounted this story earlier.) It was a motor cruiser
of about 100 feet. He said I could use it whenever I happened to be in
Greece. Being a very conservative young type, I decided it would have
been a bit dishonest so I declined. A year later Ian confided that they
eventually lent it to a friend who lent it to another friend and it turned
out to be a big mistake. The boat was apprehended on the way back
from goodness knows where by the Greek Coast Guard but not before
the "owners" departed in a speedboat after sinking it. The three crew
members all went down with it. I suppose they were smuggling guns or
drugs or both. Lena's father, an archeologist who had specialized on the
ancient Greek postal system, chided me for not having visited the
Acropolis during any of my three trips to Athens. I did so on my fourth,
stopping by on the way to the airport. My mistake was telling him. I am
still a poor tourist.

My IFC task was to advise on improving their stock market. A memorable experience was that the Deputy Minister of Finance with whom
I was to work suggested we (I was with Lena) stay at the beach and he
would drive me back and forth. I said I thought this would take a lot of
time in their awful traffic. He said: "Not at all, I live nearby and I'll pick
you up at 8.00 tomorrow morning for our 8.45 appointment." He
turned up on a motorbike: it was a fast but terrifying trip. In the end we
did nothing of consequence in Greece. But we were well entertained
when visiting. Amongst other pleasant events was being taken by the
Deputy Minister to a taverna. He put on quite a performance during the
show, dancing on a table top.

Jamaica

I had gone to Jamaica for a conference some time in 1981. Although
I had nothing scheduled with the government, I was asked to call on the
Minister of Finance, Edward Seaga, who later became Prime Minister.
When ushered into his office and introduced, I noticed a television camera was filming away. After the briefest of preliminaries, he said he would
like IFC to provide Jamaican investment banks with the same line of

credit that we had provided in Brazil. I explained why it was not a good idea as it had been a failure in Brazil. He was displeased and made it very clear that I was not welcome back. Interestingly, though, Jamaica then had a very well structured financial system that operated quite efficiently. The infrastructure they had inherited had remained in place.

Ali Allawi came with us (Lena and me) on that trip. The three of us had dinner that night and, sad to say, he rather upset Lena because of his impeccable (Iraqi) manners. When speaking to her, he looked at me rather than her. Apparently it would have been considered rude to look at, let alone speak to, another man's wife.

Kuwait

I don't remember much about my visits. The only one of note was making a presentation in Kuwait at a lunch meeting organized by the ministry of finance. There were about 200 people present and I was to give my talk before lunch. I was led to the podium and introduced by one of the deputy ministers. While he was doing that I noticed that the podium was in front of an impressive hot buffet layout that looked and smelled delicious. I had barely finished the first 30 seconds of my talk when someone walked up and took the microphone away. Several thoughts flashed through my mind. Had I said something insulting? If so, what was it? Had they just decided they wanted to eat right away? What should I do know? The audience was still sitting looking at me. So I just continued. It turned out that the microphone wasn't working. I wish they had thought to tell me as it was not a fun experience standing between that excellent buffet and a stiff-looking audience that I feared was much more interested in eating lunch than listening to me.

Barbados

The Caribbean Financial Services Company, in which we had invested for "developmental" reasons, was another one of those lost causes. There was always pressure to do things in the Caribbean, but few deals to do. So when we were asked by USAID to help them with a project there we agreed. They thought more could be done to start up small businesses in the region. They knew this would involve equity investments—something like venture capital. They also knew there was a lack of financial skills and that financial advisory services were, or should be, in demand. There was also a need for term financing. So we helped establish the company. USAID had agreed to make it a $5 million 3% term loan, which was a fine subsidy intended to encourage others to become shareholders. These other shareholders were supposed to help them provide the services to support this. Besides the request from USAID, IFC's regional department was also being pressed to support this by some of its important clients in Trinidad and Jamaica as well as Barbados. So, here was a chance to do another merchant bank. I knew that Jamaica had quite a good securities market and that Trinidad was coming along. So, maybe we could make it work.

Barbados had been chosen as the base as a "neutral" country in the region. Besides, Courtney Blackman, the governor of the Bank of Barbados, was a brilliant and highly regarded banker. He was also a strong promoter of the idea. I remember Courtney fondly and well. We played tennis once in Mexico City the day after we had both arrived for some conference. Not surprisingly, as he is a champion player, he beat me badly. But, as he used to say to any audience whenever we met for years after that, I really won because he was so exhausted he couldn't get out of his bed for two days. He hadn't been able to take the high altitude, but it didn't seem to bother me. The CEO we hired was an entertaining Barbadian called David da Costa. David had some hilarious stories about the history of his family, who had lived there for four generations. His grandfather used to send his shirts to an English laundry—in England. It was about a seven-week cycle in the sailing ships of the day. His father used to take his family—including eight kids—to Europe each year by ship, first class. Sadly, but not surprisingly, the company never did much beyond short-term loans. Probably the best value from it accrued to Bob Kay, my Canadian friend who had spent a while in Venezuela. I convinced his firm to let him spend a week a month there for the first year to try and train the management.

Other Countries

Then of course, I visited several OECD countries … and Singapore. During my initial contacts with IFC's board members many, representing OECD countries, suggested I should visit their capitals. I should call on their ministries of finance, etc. and get to know the financial institutions in their countries interested in the developing world. This I did in the case of seven of them during my first few years. I have already talked about my several meetings with U.S. and Canadian finance and AID officials in Washington and Ottawa, so there is no need to expand on those. Mr. Nishihara introduced me to his colleagues in the "MoF," as well as the contacts I needed at Nomura and Yamaichi Securities in connection with our work then in Korea and Iran.

I made calls on the government finance people and some banks and securities companies in the U.K., France, Germany and Australia. None of these meetings were exactly memorable in themselves. I was well received by the senior people—the senior civil servants. The curious thing to me then was the rather indifferent reception from the worker-level people. Usually, the assistant secretaries (or deputy ministers, depending on the country) would arrange these meetings. I recall two such, one with CIDA in Ottawa and the other with the Australian equivalent in Canberra. In both cases there were twenty or so present. I made my pitch, followed by questions. It was clear from the response, or lack of it, that they were not interested. I think in both cases it was just that, as they were in the game of giving grants or making loans to governments, capital market development was just not a familiar subject. Further, neither Canada nor Australia had AID programs that provided equity finance to private enterprises, except through their interests in IFC.

The U.S., U.K., France and Japan were the countries most interested in our capital markets work. They were already active in many of our client countries through both government aid programs and their commercial entities, especially their banks. Over the years, we had joint ventures with Lloyds Bank and Midland Bank from the U.K., and with Credit Lyonnais, Societe Generale and Sogelease, an independent leasing company, from France. I learned also at first hand how senior French government people moved back and forth between the public service and business. Several of the French EDs I met in Washington later became chairmen of the major French banks with whom we did business. These connections certainly helped us later on.

The discussions with government people led to some visits to their embassies in our client countries. Mostly, though, it was the U.S. and Canadian embassies that I went to. I found the U.S. Embassy people the most open and helpful. For whatever reason my Canadian cousins, as friendly as they were, tended to look to me for information on the country; I had expected it to be the other way around. The exception was the Canadian Ambassador to Yugoslavia when I was there. Besides being very knowledgeable about the country, he was also very hospitable.

Unfortunately, I missed a very important OECD country in this period. That was Holland. Holland has a very sophisticated financial system, similar to that of the U.K. Of special interest was its strong mortgage banking system and its fully funded private and public pension funds. At least I discovered the former in time to seek their help for Indonesia. What I missed until much later was that the Dutch had their own IFC-type aid agency—FMO—which was similar to the U.K.'s CDC.

I visited Singapore in this period for two reasons. First, it was on the way to Indonesia and, second, because I had heard a lot about Singapore's remarkable transformation from a small, poor island with a few million people and no resources to one that had an impressive financial market and was becoming rich. I had no real contacts there. On our board, Singapore was in a group of Southeast Asian countries and, at the time, did not have their man as ED or Alternate. They were no longer poor enough to be a client country, but not rich enough to be a donor country. I seem to recall that I visited someone in the Development Bank of Singapore through a Bank connection. The country was outstripping both South Korea and Taiwan and thus there were lessons to be learned. One was that already having its basic institutional framework—starting with a solid commercial legal base and a strong accounting profession—it was easier for Singapore to move ahead than it was for Korea and Taiwan, which lacked both. More interesting, though, was what Singapore had done once their Malay-sian connection was broken and once Britain, in the mid-1960s, declared that they were abandoning their ex colony. Caught between two potentially aggressive large neighbors, Malaysia and Indonesia, they had a political/defense problem as well as an economic one. Their response to the economic problem was impressive.

On the financial side, they concluded that, because of their position half-way in time zones between the U.S. West Coast and Europe, they could become a financial center linking both continents. This was helped by another key early decision—to make English the official language rather than Chinese. Their success was what attracted me. Singapore had become a money market center, establishing the Asian Dollar market. Also, they were one of the first "developing countries" to establish a fully funded pension scheme. This was truly impressive in scale—it had some $170 billion of assets at the time. Also, contributors to it could withdraw money to buy apartments. Even in the 1960s the government saw the merits of home ownership as a means of enhancing political stability and increasing individuals' savings. Singapore's founding father and first Prime Minister—Lee Kuan Yew—deserved the credit for this and for Singapore's future prosperity. He was, and still is, a giant of a man. While writing my first draft of this part of my memoirs, I read his memoirs From Third World to First. It was an incredibly impressive and moving story, giving a fascinating insight on what was going on from 1965 to 2000, not just in Singapore and Southeast Asia but throughout the world, from the perspective of a Chinese Singaporean. While it is easier to mold a country that is small in size and population than a large one, it is clear that there were many other Third World countries that, with good leadership, could have been almost as successful as Singapore. Critics say that its economic success was at the expense of some freedoms. That is true, but one gets the impression that most of the citizens feel that these costs were well worth it.

Starting in about 1980, we were asked to do some advisory work in Cyprus for the Ministry of Finance. This involved improving their position as an offshore banking and head office locale for companies operating in other countries. We also formed a little merchant bank called Cyprus International Securities Company ("CISC") which was managed by Andreas Aloneftis, a charming fellow who later became Minister of Defense.

I went also to Malaysia in 1984 or later, but I don't remember much about it, except what Malaysia was to do with Advent, which will be covered in more detail later.

CMD also worked in countries I never got around to visiting, such as Cameroon, Costa Rica, Fiji, Ghana, Guinea, Hungary, Ivory Coast, Nepal and Yemen. Despite the fact that I had not visited Nepal, my colleague, Farida Khambata, tells the story of the time she met the head of the Nepal Stock Exchange in Kathmandu: "He could not believe his luck. He was actually meeting someone who personally knew his hero … the biggest honor of his life was to shake hands with a person who had shaken hands with THE David Gill. The fellow who was to head the Exchange was so in awe of David that I received much reflected glory when I convinced him that not only had I seen but actually spoken to and, even more, had shaken hands with David Gill!" It is with some embarrassment that I include this vignette, but I do so because it reflects the far reaching impact of the dedicated work of all the people in the Capital Markets Department and the reflected glory that I would sometimes receive as its head.

What did I learn?

The first lesson from these first years was that the old adage, "you can lead a horse to water but you can't make it drink," applied very much to the advisory side of our work. There was no point to being proactive and trying to get government officials to seek our services. The usual reasons that a capital market is inefficient, or non-existent, include all or any of the following:

- A command economy;
- Lack of an educated middle class;
- Weak legal framework;

- Poor fiscal and monetary policies;
- Weak corporate governance; and
- A small, poor economy without the "critical mass" for a working market.

Further, even in the cases where the senior government people came to us for help and demonstrated that the technocrats were serious in wanting to improve their market, there were still serious risks. The first was a change in government. The second, and more serious in the long run, was lack of political will at the voter (or influence wielding) level—a function of the level of education, ethical standards and the state of democracy. In most developing countries—and in quite a few countries with an established democratic system—the business community or other vested interests really determine what governments do. As I am neither a professional economist nor a political scientist, I will not claim to know which factors are the most important, or whether there are other factors I should have added. In finding my way around the Bank and our client countries, I just tried to be pragmatic and learn from our successes and failures.

An important factor in those days was that our resources were limited and the potential demand was infinite. Our limited resources reflected several things. First, not many in the Bank in those days believed that the financial system was important. Second, quite reasonably, not many were prepared to put their trust in that small group of newcomers from Wall Street or other suspect financial centers. Third, the Bank and IFC were loan-driven so providing advice to governments was often seen as detraction from the main business. What I found really important was that IFC was having difficulty articulating to its staff, its board and the world at-large the degrees of emphasis that should be placed on its "developmental" role versus its "profit seeking" role. Most believed the former cost money and the latter made money. That was why our resources for advisory and technical assistance were limited. But some, including I (as I found this out in those first years), believed that with a sound infrastructure, a given investment would be more profitable than otherwise. I tried for years to convince the scorekeepers that it was possible to keep IFC's accounts in such a way that money spent on the developmental role was segregated from the costs of doing investment deals. Giving visibility to the costs of development would make it easier to justify it as, compared to investment costs, the amount was small and the benefits clear. But that was a continuous battle that I will talk about more in the next chapter.

What all this led to was the gradual development of a workable methodology for both assessing what we should do when approached for assistance and, if it seemed worthwhile, how to go about providing it. This was a small first step to showing that we were prudent with these limited resources. But the main advantage—and it sprang from those first hard-learned lessons—was that it helped our client countries focus on what was practical as well as what was desirable. This was a variation of another old adage: "Better to teach a person how to fish than to give (or lend) him one as, if he knows how, he won't go hungry when the giver goes away."

The methodology itself was only common sense. There were just a few basic steps. The only hard part was actually taking them. The skills needed were not that great. Experience was the main thing.

The first step was to try and make sure the client country was serious. We discovered that asking for CMD's help did not mean there was sufficient dedication to follow through and do something to improve their market. To this end, we prepared a checklist of questions for them to answer. This required an analysis of their economy and an audit of the current status of their legal and institutional framework. The focus was on the actual and potential issuers and buyers of securities and the financial intermediaries. It was a good six-month job for several professions. We did it ourselves for several client countries at first when we couldn't find people at the working level in them with the interest or understanding to do it. Under these circumstances we should not have been surprised that these countries implemented few of our recommendations. "Not invented here" as the saying goes.

The second step—if they completed the first—was to work with the government to draw up an action plan to get from where they were to where they wanted to be. We learned that if they did not see it as their

In D.C., Lena and I greet the Jordanian Minister of Finance at the World Bank Annual Meeting, in 1986 or 1987.

Signing some contracts in the World Bank / IFC board room about 1980.

plan the implementation of it would still be difficult. We encouraged the government to establish a "Capital Markets Committee" of senior government officials to oversee this process and to take the lead in "selling" the program to the skeptics in government, the vested interests who benefit from the status quo and the public.

The third step was how to implement the plan. That involved assessing the skills available locally and then what outside technical advice they would need to do the work required. Important considerations were how long would it take, how much would it cost and who would pay. If these issues were not faced up to at the beginning, progress would be slow.

The fourth step was implementation of the technical assistance work. This could include preparing new laws and regulations, establishing more market oriented fiscal and monetary policies, structuring the necessary governmental institutions and strengthening the accounting profession. These involved finding and recruiting "experts" and getting one of the aid agencies to finance them. Also, staff of new institutions needed training and this had to be planned.

We quickly learned that it was best to make sure that the legal and regulatory structure was in place before we got involved in what became the final step. That was helping establish the private financial institutions to actually operate in the market. When it came to this type of "institution building," as we called it, we also learned that it made sense to concentrate first on the traditional lending institutions before worrying about securities companies. That is, mortgage banks, savings and loan banks, and leasing companies. These institutions made it possible to "extend the term" of savings and investment. Later, once savers became accustomed to debt instruments with longer terms than the usual call deposits, one could move to encouraging the stock market.

The ultimate aim was to encourage ways to increase the flow of savings into equity instruments. In most under-developed countries—rich or poor—"ownership" of the economy—the business enterprises—was almost always in the hands of governments and or a small group of wealthy families. Most of our more successful client country governments understood that spreading the wealth—shareholder democracy—

271

was good for the economy as well as for social stability. An efficient financial market increased the rate of savings and allocated it more efficiently than could any command economy. But of course there are exceptions. (It's interesting how progress in spreading the wealth in the U.S. has slowed, if not reversed, in recent years. I imagine there will be political consequences in the years to come.)

Another, almost contradictory, lesson was that often it needs the "kick start" of an autocratic, but enlightened, government to make changes that would last. Our experiences in Korea and Chile were good examples of this. It is interesting that in both cases the governments of the day, in different ways, opened the doors for democratically elected governments later. An additional factor that applied in both the Korean and Chilean examples was the extent to which the countries were and are still dependent on exports. The more this is the case, the more the people and their governments are exposed to market forces, thus seeing the need to adopt international standards. Singapore sets the record in this regard, much helped by its strong institutional infrastructure and the sound economic and fiscal policies the government adopted right after the final break with Malaysia in 1965.

Another lesson I learned was the validity of Bill Gaud's advice provided to make sure we were coordinating with the Bank. To this end we had formed a "Capital Markets Coordinating Committee." The core group included Bill Diamond as the director of the Bank's DFC department and the Bank's senior economists for each of the regions. It also included two people from the IMF's Capital Markets group. We had monthly meetings with agendas appropriate to what was going on at the time. We welcomed all and sundry to attend. Agendas and Minutes were circulated to all Bank and IFC—and IMF—department directors and anyone interested. As the Bank had endless meetings, it was not surprising that attendance at our meetings was sparse. But it did serve as a useful way to keep the several hundred people who felt they had the need to know informed.

Eventually, I realized that the basic internal problem we had was that, while some Bank staff understood that an efficient financial market could speed "real" economic development, most did not. The Bank's

Articles were clear in stating that beneficiary countries should be helped to become financially self sufficient and that strong domestic capital markets were crucial to achieving this self sufficiency. But the professional staff's reward system was tied directly to the volume of loans approved by the board. Amusingly, the quest to increase loan approvals led one Bank wag to say: "The best project is a loan approved by the board but never disbursed." The point was that staff got rewarded for the approval rather than the actual impact. After disbursement of the money came the process of monitoring what was done with it. This was time consuming and often frustrating, but there was neither reward for a loan deemed to be successful nor a penalty for one that failed. The same principles applied to IFC staff.

Besides an incentive system that awarded "approvals" rather than "impact," there was the further problem that most of the Bank staff—the loan officers and economists—were academics rather than practitioners or entrepreneurs. Because of the very nature of their immediate tasks, they tended to favor "command" economies rather than market economies. To say that many of them were socialists would be unfair. But many made it clear that they saw little connection between a market-oriented financial system and economic development and no need for such things as stock exchanges which were often viewed as irrelevant and even harmful casinos. Of course, this thinking applied much more to the rank and file than to the senior managers. But there were exceptions. Memorable was a meeting of IFC and Bank senior management to discuss "turf" issues—the division of duties between the Bank and IFC. The IFC side was somewhat stunned to hear one of the Bank's most senior officials say something like: "It's simple; it's public sector activity unless IFC can prove it should be private sector." My thought at the time was that he must also believe in the principle that you are guilty until you can prove you are innocent. Fortunately, Burke Knapp, the Bank's number two at the time, took the opposite view.

In attempting to deal with this built-in bias I learned how to use and take advantage of Bob McNamara's scoring system. This was important because, as indicated, rewards were based on loan or investment projects approved by the board. Because of the technical assistance part of

CMD's mandate, much of our most useful work did not get "scored." Not only was this hard on our professional staff as it affected their remuneration, but it also had a serious impact on the amount of budgetary resources allocated to us. So, we devised a "score card" of our own that fitted into his system. While we did not convert many Bank staff to our belief that good advice and technical support was just as important to development as loans, we did continue to get the board's support. The score card was a one-page summary of everything we had done in each country and when. I was touched on my retirement to be given a plaque showing this for the 75 countries over my 17 years with CMD. Notwithstanding all of this the budget turf wars continued and I never did find out how to win them. In fact, we lost more as each year passed.

During the first few years, it was understood that CMD's expense budget, of which the Bank covered half, would cover all the advisory and technical assistance work carried out. Later, IFC management decided it did not want the implied obligation to the Bank to do this technical assistance work. Consequently, Bank support was cut to 25% of our expense budget. This cut in support happened even before the Bank became interested in doing this type of work itself. While not noticed in the IFC scheme of things, what we were doing was clearly appreciated by our client countries. Bank staff was hearing this from them. When that started, Bank staff decided they should be doing this popular thing themselves. Naturally that led to the Bank questioning the remaining support they were providing to CMD. However, regardless of the motivation behind these budgetary changes, cutting back on our free services was the right thing to do. The best client countries understood this. Still, some of the others complained that, as the Bank provided "free" technical assistance, IFC should too.

We learned to describe CMD's role as policy advice only. We would not charge for that but the client country would have to use their own resources or find other aid agencies to finance the more detailed technical assistance work that followed from it. For example, our review of the current state of the financial system might result in a recommendation that a leasing industry could be a valuable addition as it would help finance small businesses. For this to be possible it would be necessary

In my office at IFC in the late 1980s.

to have a chattel mortgage law and the legal/regulatory infrastructure to implement it. Likewise, the tax regime should not discriminate against financing equipment by leasing arrangements. Solving such problems usually would require help from appropriate experts from countries that had a successful leasing industry. CMD's budget continued for some time to cover helping them decide where to go for such technical assistance help, finding the funding for it and managing the actual program. I believe now IFC seeks outside funding also for the advisory work.

Finally, the most important lesson I learned was that, despite the differences of culture, religion and race, the world really is a global village. I have mentioned this in relation to how well our very mixed group in CMD worked together and with our client countries. For me it was the same whether I was in Zambia, Bolivia, Egypt or Korea. We all had the same needs and motivations and we could all develop trust in each other and enjoy one another's company. One did not understand this living in Toronto, or even New York. Traveling as a tourist, or even as a businessman, one did not see the local people in the same light as one did working with them "on the same side of the desk." That was really the greatest strength of the Bank and IFC—and the other UN type institutions, and some multinational corporations. The staff people were taken into the confidence of the people in the client countries because they knew our job was to help them. They—their countries—were our shareholders, we were their employees. It was a good feeling. I was proud to belong to an organization that had earned such trust. I was doing my best to make sure I continued to deserve it.

Unfortunately, with the passing of years since those days, I have learned that the Bank and IFC were hiring younger and less experienced people. They often had a degree of self-importance and arrogance that annoyed many in the LDCs. Fortunately, this change was slow in coming and I had retired in 1988 before it began to become noticeable. I was 62, the bank's optional early retirement age—though I could have hung on till 65, when one was then obliged to retire. But I thought three final years in the private sector were a good idea. Now, of course, 65 is considered too young for retirement. It's also becoming a fiscal issue as we "golden oldies" now tend to live longer than expected and thus many

defined benefit plans have found they weren't as well funded as the plan-
ners thought. In any event, after all, I had spent 17 years by then in public service and, despite enjoying (almost) every day of it, it was time for
a change. By coincidence, I had met Dean LeBaron, head of Batterymarch Financial Management, at a conference in New York just a few
months before my sixty-second birthday. (See next chapter.)

*With
[S]arah,
(top).
[Me]lissa
[and] Lena
[1]980.*

PART III

BACK
TO BUSINESS:
1988–1991

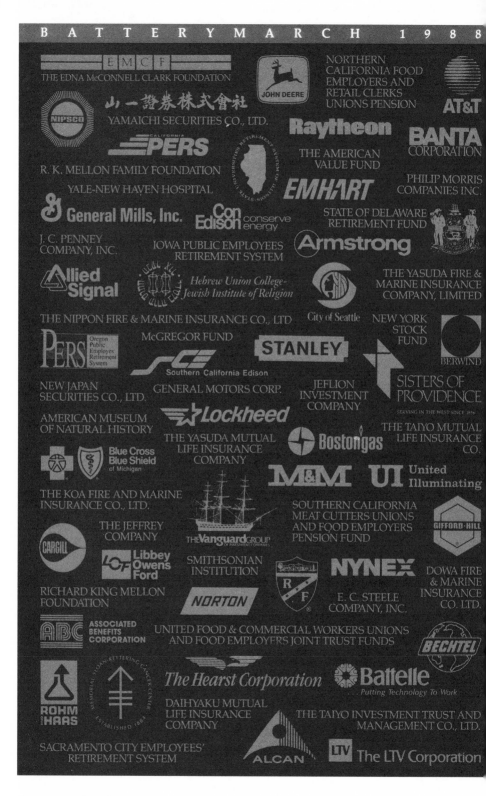

Batterymarch produced very elegant annual reports. The one just out shortly after I joined had on cover the corporate logos of most of its major corporate clients.

CHAPTER VI

Batterymarch
Financial Management . . .
Another New World:
1988-1991

THE BEGINNING

In the last chapter I mentioned meeting Dean LeBaron at a conference in New York. I was impressed with his presentation on the equity markets and consequently invited him to speak at a conference in Buenos Aires that I was organizing on behalf of IFC and the Argentine securities commission. We hit it off well both professionally and personally. I must confess I was also enthralled by the fact that he, besides owning 100% of his company, owned a Gulfstream II ("GII" with "tip tanks" for extended range which we used quite a lot as I will get to later) and a Hawker Siddeley 125 ("Hawker"). He, as a U.S. money manager, was also a financial frontiersman. A short while later he proposed that I join him and become chairman of Batterymarch Investment Systems ("BIS"), an affiliate that would lease Batterymarch's ("BFM") very high tech, automated system to investment management companies in the U.S. and in other countries.

We came to terms quite quickly—an attractive salary and two bonus arrangements. The first was tied to Batterymarch's own results and the second to BIS's. If it became anywhere near as successful as Dean thought, I would make a lot of money from BIS—Dean said millions although in the end it turned out to be thousands. But, just as important to the Gill family, as money was not a primary objective, the agreement included an arrangement under which I would not move to Boston. Rather, I would spend two or three days a week there—or on the road —and Batterymarch would provide me with an office in DC. It was a very satisfactory arrangement. Normally, I would fly up on a Tuesday or Wednesday morning and back on Thursday evening. In those days, it was an easy trip: little more than two hours "door to door" from our house in Georgetown to the Boston Harbor Hotel where I stayed. It was actually quite pleasant—a decent breakfast on good old Eastern Airlines, then a scenic water taxi trip through Boston harbor followed by a two-minute walk to the hotel and a further five minutes to the office. In DC, we established a fine office in the Georgetown Harbor complex, with a view of the river. I could actually sit out on the little veranda when the weather was clement. Ingrid Kennelly, my secretary from IFC, also retired in order to join me. Dean sublet this office from his old Harvard friend, Bob Monks, who ran an institutional investor service. Bob was a great fellow to know. He was one of the first corporate governance activists and remained one for several more years, running the "Lens Fund," which specialized in taking large minority positions in companies with weak managements and turning them around. However, his main claim to fame was being the founding Trustee of the Federal Employees' Retirement System and Administrator of the Office of Pension and Welfare Benefits Administration in charge of the private pension system (ERISA) in the U.S. The Boston Harbor Hotel was quite a comfortable place too. As a regular visitor I was well looked after and always had a room overlooking the harbor.

Theoretically, the Batterymarch Information Systems program—internally subtitled "Batterymarch in a Box"—would allow a new management company to be established without the need to go through the otherwise painful procedure of hiring portfolio managers, strategists and analysts as well as setting up management, trading and administrative systems and buying the related hardware. Similarly, these efficiencies could benefit an established traditional manager. It would be, essentially, Batterymarch's high tech system for administrative economy, low transaction costs and the ability to implement an almost infinite number of strategies and controls. With the BIS system, one could essentially use Batterymarch's own systems to manage, trade and administer client portfolios, establishing the risk and reward parameters for each portfolio to suit client requirements. Then the system would make the necessary buy and sell decisions to keep the portfolios within those parameters. The trading system that was connected executed the orders automatically with brokers who signed contracts to participate in the automated auction system. This system, for Batterymarch too, avoided the need to pay for securities analysis and trading departments. It thus made it possible to offer investment management services to institutional investors at lower than average fees while earning for Dean an above average rate of return. I was a little skeptical about stock selection and portfolio building and balancing systems that were based 100% on ratio analysis from statistical databases. But the fact was Batterymarch had at the time some $20 billion under management from a blue chip list of U.S. pension funds and foundations. The actual investment results over almost 20 years for all its portfolios put Batterymarch in the top quartile of all managers. Likewise, the trading system was producing an average commission rate of less than two cents a share compared to the NYSE institutional average of between ten and 12 cents. Who was I to argue with such success? As it turned out, I had much to learn, as did Dean.

I should state here that what follows is a great deal about Dean. Dean was Batterymarch. Many of his ex partners—and there were quite a few —considered him a control freak. That was why they were ex partners and that is why Dean insisted on owning BFM 100%. Still, Dean was, besides being brilliant, great fun to be with. We got along very well together and had much fun on our many trips. Coming from 17 years in IFC, it was refreshing to be working with, or for, such an intellectually interesting, free-spirited and fun person. It helped that he let me do more or less what I liked. He said when I signed on: "You will have a lot of fun and make much more money for much less work." Of course, all of this related to when I was new and Batterymarch was doing very well. When times became tough a few years later, the stress took its toll on Dean.

Ready to board the GII with Dean LeBaron following a 1989 stopover in Papua New Guinea after marketing calls in Australia trying to sell Batterymarch Investment Systems ... BIS.

Batterymarch Financial Management

My first few months were devoted to learning about Batterymarch and its people. Because of its style, it had a very small staff at that time—about 35 in total—of which eight were portfolio managers. In addition to strategy development, they mainly managed client relations and tried to line up more business. The overall approach to investment management—with much of the management handled by the systems—was different than in the conventional sense. In a separate group were the "techies" who designed and upgraded the systems and kept the machinery running. There must have been about eight of them. The rest were assistant portfolio managers and other administrative personnel. The office was in the Boston Federal Reserve Bank building. It was "open plan" and quite small. Dean commented frequently that it was also very quiet. As most everything was automated, there wasn't much talking—and certainly none of the usual shouting by stock traders. The conventional firm with the same business base would have four or five times the staff and floor space. At that time, my comparison was with Morgan Stanley Asset Management, which had about the same amount under management: Capital Group, Scudder and Templeton, which I also knew well, were all much larger businesses. This high tech approach to running the firm resulted in low costs and thus low management fees. As best I recall, they were about 0.15% for large accounts, compared to at least double that charged by other firms, and were capped at a maximum of one million dollars thus sharing investment efficiency with clients by charging lower management fees. I think the average account size was about $300 million. More than a few benefitted from the cap. In the overall picture, Batterymarch's returns for its investors were pretty good, but a problem arose which I shall get to later.

The firm was structured as a Massachusetts Business Trust. I forget exactly what that meant, other than that it was a limited liability company. That is now common under the laws of several states. Then, it was unique to Massachusetts. One consequence was that we, the senior people including Dean, were all called "Trustees" with no distinctions, in part to remind us that we were fiduciaries to our clients, more than officers responsible to our company. I suppose, to paraphrase George Orwell, Dean's Trusteeship was weightier than ours. That reminds me:

286

Dean, as the 100% owner, thought it amusing to say that all business decisions were made very democratically, "always by a market capitalization weighted vote." While looking into the implications of this structure, I confirmed what I had assumed about my own BIS title. Being called chairman of BIS on a business card looked impressive, but it had no meaning whatsoever. Under Massachusetts' laws, trusts had no boards of directors or officers. There could be one or more legal trustees appointed with the authority and responsibilities provided in the deed of trust. Dean was the legal trustee. The rest of us were just given the title. Dean had set up BIS the same way as BFM—as a Massachusetts Business Trust—with himself as the sole legal trustee. Consequently, I could call myself whatever I wanted so long as I understood I had no legal powers or responsibilities. My only rights were to my remuneration and bonus arrangements and BFM's very generous "benefits." The health and life insurance plans were better that IFC's, as was the pension plan, although I did not discover the latter until I retired three years later. At the time, as I already had IFC's health insurance and pension, these latter were unimportant in the context of a three-year arrangement and the possibility of making seven-figure bonuses if BIS worked out.

BFM produced very elegant annual reports. The one just out shortly after I joined had on its cover the corporate logos of all its major corporate clients—some 50 at the time—so it was rather crowded. I recall it showed a net worth of about $20 million, but no indication of profits. Rumor had it that it was about $20 million for that year and that the business was probably worth about $200 million to an interested buyer. This wealth probably helped explain the other benefit described next.

BFM also had a small associated company called Boston Group Services ("BGS"). This also had a quite small staff. The "services" provided were the two jets, a small amphibian and an elegant old 72-foot motor yacht called "Hathor," after an Egyptian queen of that name. That staff consisted of three pilots, one marine captain and about four assorted mechanics and clerks. As I shall talk about in more detail later, all of these were used for business travel and entertaining. Probably the capital and operating costs exceeded the real benefits by a wide margin even if the costs were tax deductions for Dean under the trust set-up. But, to be fair, Dean had probably donated more to his alma mater, Harvard, over the years than the total value of his "toys." Also, he did love flying and had been a qualified private pilot. That was one of the fun parts of BFM. I can't say I objected to these luxuries as all of us "Trustees" could use them for business and, to some extent, pleasure whenever we chose. Dean's only complaint about our using the jets was that none of us seemed to learn that he had told us we didn't have to ask his permission. We just had to arrange it with the chief pilot who did the scheduling.

Placing a description of the organization in Toronto that ran the Canadian accounts, Batterymarch:Canada ("BC"), after BGS does not seem right. But as I spent much more time with BGS than BC, it seems fair, notwithstanding that I was also labeled a "Trustee" of BC. As with all of Dean's companies, it was a separate entity for a reason. In this case, it was simply that Canadian clients preferred dealing with Canadian entities. It was fortunate that two of Dean's early associates were Canadian —they became the owners of BC, which licensed Batterymarch's portfolio management technology. Tania Zouikin, who was from Montreal and had earned her MBA from the Sloan School at MIT, was in charge. A few years later, BC and the Toronto office were closed, and Tania moved back to Boston and Batterymarch. Tania was a real professional and a tough lady. I recall visiting BC's office in the old Flatiron Building in Toronto on several occasions, but I can't recall why. Her main clients were Alcan in Montreal and the Canadian subsidiaries of General Motors and Ford, which were located near Toronto.

In learning about the mechanics of BFM's business I was surprised to find out how many countries had databases covering the hundreds or thousands of companies whose securities were listed on their stock exchanges. I knew this was so in the U.S. from my period in IFC and learning about Value Line. As I discovered later, even India and Malaysia had them. This came up as BFM also ran an international fund for Vanguard. "International" meant any country outside the U.S. In practice this meant the wealthy European countries and Japan, Australia and Canada mainly. "Global" accounts were ones that could invest both in the U.S. and internationally. That's just the terminology.

The investment management business is a people business and

288

1988–1991

BFM's managers—I mean Trustees—were all characters. The techies lived in a world I still don't understand, so I won't talk about them beyond saying they were all very quiet, likeable, hard-working and eager to please. Goodness knows how much time they spent trying to explain to me how all the machinery worked. As it was, I never did learn how to work the large high-powered PC that came with my office. Fortunately, I received special treatment in the form of my own secretary (Dean was the only other to have one) so I could continue to dictate my letters and "think pieces" as usual. I inherited Jeannie Curhan from Dean. She was a delightful New Yorker of "a certain age" and as good as any of my IFC ladies—except Ruby who was incomparable. Jeannie was also a charmer with a great sense of humor. I was absolutely delighted to hear just recently that she and another Batterymarch Trustee, who joined after my time to run the emerging markets business, were married in 2001. The managers I remember best were Lynne Gage, Marilyn Pitchford, Jack Arena, David Lazenby, Larry Speidell, Rich Gula and Jim Ullman. Lynne was one of the original employees and Dean's right hand man, so to speak, amongst the managers. Marilyn was the administrative and financial chief. Both were smart, charming and reserved ladies. Jack, Larry, Rich and Jim were long-time solid investment professionals. I sometimes wondered how they enjoyed the number-crunching approach that was the Batterymarch way. I had more to do with Jack and David than the others, as they became the emerging markets experts, and Jim became more of a pal as I got into my third year. But Jay Tata, who followed me from IFC, was my real kindred spirit as an old colleague and the only other person who was not a professional investment manager. By the end of my time, Jay and David were the emerging markets team as Jack had retired. David was what I would have called a trainee when I joined. As he happened to speak Portuguese, he became Jack's apprentice. He was one of the most dedicated and hard-working people there. Though he was young, Jack, Jay and I —and the clients—quickly learned to trust and respect him. On the lighter side, when Jay Tata followed me to BFM, we often dined together at a harbor side restaurant called The Sail Lof—also on the harbor and about a five-minute walk from my hotel.

Batterymarch Financial Management

While talking about people I met at and through BFM, Gordon Binns and David Feldman stand out, as did Charley Ellis. They were great friends of Dean as well as having a business relationship. Gordon and David, respectively, ran the General Motors and AT&T pension funds, two of the biggest private ones in the U.S. at the time. Both were clients with well over a billion dollars each entrusted to BFM. Charley Ellis ran a consulting firm specializing in measuring the ratings of investment managers given them by institutional investors. This was basically a market polling business, as best I could understand its methodology. He sold the results to both sides. Gordon and David were always interested in Dean's latest strategy. Consequently, they were always on our trips in the GII to explore new market opportunities. As leaders in the investing community they were great sources of knowledge to me and both were good company. Sadly, Gordon died in 2002. He is greatly missed. But more about all of these people as I get into my many entertaining experiences with them.

During my first few months, besides trying to learn about the "black boxes," I spent a lot of time traveling the country with Dean and the managers, accompanying them on visits to clients. This was just to learn what the business was about. But, apart from visiting cities I had never seen before, it became quite a standard routine. Until then, BFM had had an excellent performance record. Consequently, as the standard presentation on performance compared to the clients' specific targets and limits could only be well received, the responses varied only between very satisfied and satisfied. The main interest was in new investment strategies. Interestingly, the client who always seemed to give Dean the hardest time during presentations was Gordon Binns and his team. This was despite the fact that Gordon always bought into Dean's new ideas.

Now, I shall get into the nuts and bolts of what I did.

Batterymarch Investment Systems

Batterymarch Investment Systems was supposed to be my job. Dean had rigged up the GII as a flying demonstration room cum classroom.

He had fitted in three of his high powered PCs which had the system programs installed in them. The idea was to fly the world to demonstrate the system to likely buyers. Dean visualized them as being banks and insurance companies in Europe, Japan, Australia, Hong Kong, and the U.S. that wanted to establish investment management affiliates. I added the Middle East, Mexico and Brazil to the list.

Usually, our group consisted of Dean, one of the portfolio managers and me. Dean was to be the visionary. The manager was to explain the Batterymarch methodology and the use of databases in the strategy, research and allocation process. I certainly had no specific expertise so I suppose I added a little gloss as an ex World Bank/IFC type who knew already most of the people we were seeing. In his visionary role, Dean would explain how all this came together so that the user could set himself up as almost a one-man-band management company—with BIS and BFM as his backups. Looking back, I'm not sure what I could really add. Dean claimed I could be his alter ego, which was a great idea if I could ever understand the technology. Actually, I did eventually get a rough idea of it and even put together a couple of "think pieces" to explain it that I used at several conferences. For the first year it was quite exciting. I even began to visualize myself as running this large network of management firms from behind the scenes and making huge amounts of money.

I don't recall in exactly what order we went where during those years. I certainly don't remember much about our sales pitches. So, what follows are just the highlights of the trips themselves: the fun parts. The realities will be explained later.

One of the first was to the Middle East. Besides selling BIS, this was also to call on the Abu Dhabi Investment Authority, where Dean and I both had old friends. ADIA had been a Batterymarch client for several years and I knew them as they had invested in EMGF, and Hareb Al Darmaki, who was responsible for all foreign investments, and I were on the EMGF board. There was also to be a presentation to the Islamic Investment Fund in Jeddah. Because of these two events, both Larry Speidell (for ADIA) and Jack Arena (for IIF) came along. I had arranged a meeting with the Saudi Arabia Monetary Authority in Riyadh where

I knew the then Governor. So we spent about three days in Saudi Arabia —one in Riyadh and two in Jeddah—and one in Dubai. But the high-light was Jeddah— jogging in Jeddah to be precise. We had arrived in the GII early in the afternoon. As they, Jack and Larry and two of the three pilots on the trip, were all relatively young, and Dean and I slightly crazy, we all had a ritual of going for a jog on arrival wherever we were going. So, around 4.00 PM, we started out—six of us. We headed to-wards where we were told was the corniche, arriving around 20 minutes later. It was really very attractive—a beautiful boardwalk and a lovely view of the harbor and the Red Sea. There were well kept flower gardens along the route and, every quarter of a mile or so, some excellent large sculptures. Some were Henry Moore's. There were also, at corners of main streets leading to the water, some very strange monuments, if one could call them that. One was based on a twin-engine plane, a DC 3 I think; another on some kind of motor vehicle. Each was elaborately perched on a pedestal type structure. After about half an hour the sun started sinking over the water: it was a beautiful sunset. We couldn't re-sist keeping going as every few hundred yards there was something dif-ferent to see. Along the way, a local fellow—probably in his early twenties—picked us up. He took us for Americans and wanted to prac-tice his English, which was quite good. He told us he was an engineering student and wanted to know all about us. He stuck with us for about an hour but tired before we did. We were overly ambitious or, more likely, none of us macho types wanted to be the first to give up. And that is how we ran into a little trouble.

When we were well into our second hour, we finally came to our senses and decided to start back. It was getting well into dusk—which happened quickly there. But we had no idea where we were and had no map. We concluded that we had gone reasonably straight to the corniche and turned right about 90 degrees to head along it. We felt it had curved slightly to the right so, with four who should have known something of navigation, we concluded that turning in a direction related to the po-sition of the setting sun would get us back. We started finding ourselves in progressively smaller streets as it got darker. The locals were no help as none we ran into spoke English. In fact, as we were running through a souk-like district we attracted a following of young kids who were laughing and pointing at the crazy white men. They of course attracted the local dogs, some of which also followed along, yapping away. By now we were well into our third hour. None of us was prepared to admit defeat so on we went, but even the younger of us were happy to go at a slower pace. Fortunately, eventually, after nearly four hours, we stumbled on our hotel. It was a great and fun experience for the first 90 minutes or so. But the last hour was hell. The good news was that the locals were friendly—or just thought we were too crazy to bother with. After all, wearing shorts we obviously didn't have much of value to steal, and I guess the six of us must have looked fairly strong. I laugh to myself whenever I think of that jog. Over the years I have jogged in many places where joggers were rarely seen, such as downtown Bangkok and Belgrade, when it was still the capital of Yugoslavia, and enjoyed the different experiences. But none was such fun as jogging in Jeddah.

The next trip was to Australia. Besides trying to sell BIS, we had another task. I had talked Dean into participating in the International Organization of Securities Commissions ("IOSCO") annual meeting, which was being held in Melbourne. It was to be my last IOSCO meeting and I was going to miss my role on its executive committee. It wasn't hard to convince Dean to go; it was great publicity for Batterymarch. I had arranged for BFM to be the main event as a "guest speaker" with a difference. We put on a play-type course or demonstration on how to establish an emerging markets country fund with Papua New Guinea ("PNG") as the country example. I had recently published an article in a financial journal on this so we already had a written script. Kathy McGrath, the then director of the SEC's Investment Companies Division, which was the supervisory unit covering investment managers, played a part in our show. Dean met Jay Tata at that event, which led to him joining BFM a couple of months later as a Trustee specializing in emerging markets. The only other more or less memorable event was a dinner I put on to introduce Dean to the chairman of the Australian SEC who I knew from my IOSCO days. It was a very pleasant evening. Also with us were David Ruder, then chairman of the U.S. SEC, and a friend of Dean's who ran the largest local investment bank and who did most of

BFM's stock trading in Australia. But nothing of consequence resulted from our various marketing calls to Australian institutions while we were there.

On the way back from Australia, we stopped off in PNG. That was quite an experience. Dean owned a plantation there on the north shore on what is still called the Bismarck Sea. This was so named because German settlers had founded most plantations on the coast. The area had quite a history. Some of the local hill tribes were known to be cannibals still. During WWII the area had become famous as the Bismarck Sea was part of the straits between PNG and Guadalcanal which were one of the main supply routes for both sides. Several major sea battles were fought in them, during one of which PT-109 of Jack Kennedy fame was sunk. A local story has it that, when it became clear that the Japanese were about to invade the area, the Australian settlers—the next largest group—fled. The Germans, though, stayed. They said they had no need to flee; the Japanese were their allies. But they overlooked the fact that the Japanese who did land might not speak German or English. That turned out to be the case and they were all slaughtered. One can understand that, to the average Japanese soldier, all white men looked the same. At least, that's the story. Another interesting fact that was certainly true as we saw the proof with our own eyes was that, because of the very dry climate, metal did not rust or rot. Consequently, there were many crashed aircraft in the area that were still in the shape they were when they came down. It was quite eerie to see them. The paint was long gone, but the fuselages and engines, bent as they might be, looked as if they had crashed just a few days ago. Likewise, with very clear and deep water, many sunken ships were quite visible. Because the area was so far from civilization, it hadn't been worthwhile for any of the usual junk merchants to source the area for scrap. Dean's plantation itself was a very large rambling place, with rather minimal creature comforts. But the staff did produce excellent meals. It was a unique experience, living surrounded by very primitive locals. This was the life of his resident manager, an old and dissipated looking Australian. But what could one expect. On the subject of jogging, I jogged alone along the beach from Dean's plantation and through several native villages. I was told it was quite safe to do this during daylight, and so it was. Dean said he had had the place for several years so he could have a first-hand experience of the "developing world." He had yet to show a profit from the plantation, and realized he was unlikely ever to.

We also made a trip to Japan. The only thing I remember about that was a stopover at Guam on the way. It was my first visit—and last, I hope—to any of those South Pacific islands, famous from WWII days. It did not remind me at all of the musical "South Pacific." Guam was then a Japanese honeymoon haven. There seemed to be tens of thousands of them. Of course, we did our usual jog. The scenery was uninspiring. The only things of interest were seeing probably twenty Japanese faces for every white or local face, the many shooting galleries, which seemed the popular sport for the young couples, and the Japanese war memorial. Oddly, there didn't seem to be a U.S. war memorial.

Jay and I went on our own in the GII once to try and bring in our French and Dutch friends. The two main Dutch pension funds were PGGM, which served the medical industry, and ABP, the largest, which served the civil servants. Marinus Keijzer at PGGM was a friend from EMGF days. But he stayed loyal to Capital Group. I forget the name of the ABP man. We at least got him to come to Boston. Unfortunately, the Batterymarch system did not impress them—the Dutch are a pretty conservative lot. Being typical Dutchmen, they made that abundantly clear to us. I think we saw about four banks in Paris, plus an affiliate of one of them that Antoine van Agtmael introduced us to. I don't recall its name but, as they had invested in Antoine's fund, we thought they were a good prospect. Two of their people did come to Boston, but that was the end of it.

BIS came to an end after about two years. We were about to set off on a trip to the Gulf countries for a second round of visits. The anchor prospect was SAMA (the Saudi Arabian Monetary Agency) whose Governor was still receptive, so we seemed to have at least one good prospect. While planning for this, I finally realized that the programs that were going to be displayed on the GII's computers were simply displays of what was being planned. The data was pre-loaded, because communications outside of the U.S. were not always reliable and we could not trust that we could get live data feeds by telephone. That was reasonable. But it was also becoming clear that many of the prospects wanted systems that would be unique to them, requiring too much customization and too many changes. This was counter to what we were offering—a generic packaged system. These problems became clear to me during a chat with the chief techie. He happened to mention that he thought it would take some several thousand man-days before BIS would be up and ready for testing under all circumstances. So I asked some questions and got some answers. As I recall it, it went something like this: "What did those man-days mean in actual time to completion?" The answer was: "With the present number of systems people, maybe two or three years." "What did testing mean?" "Seeing if it would work!" "What do you think of the prospects?" "I have no idea; we are just trying to implement Dean's idea." To say the least, I was both surprised and concerned, so I confronted Dean. "Do you realize that what we are trying to sell is a concept, not a system that presently works? How can we, honestly, ask SAMA and others to consider buying it without telling them that we are at least two years away from knowing if it will work for their unique applications?" It did not take him long to realize that telling the whole story would end our efforts, so we canceled our appointments. A while later, Dean told me he had abandoned the whole plan. While he had, probably, spent at least $10 million on developing the system, he realized it would take even more to find out if it was marketable. Obviously, it was a blow to him. I certainly was not pleased. But at least I had avoided the damage my reputation would have suffered had we continued. Nevertheless, I was rather enjoying Batterymarch, so I didn't mind too much continuing doing what I had also been doing on the side. That was promoting BFM's emerging markets funds.

Dean faced another, more serious, blow around this time. It came to light while we were on our previous marketing trip—to Sweden. From the business perspective, this started out badly and ended up badly. But, otherwise, it was an enjoyable trip. We, Dean and his "significant other," Faviana, and Lena and I started out in Stockholm where I was to introduce him to the local bankers and insurance people. We were fortunate in being able to recruit Lars Kalderen, who had recently retired as head of the Swedish National Debt Office, which was a body that had to approve all national debt issues, to make the arrangements. The meetings went well enough, but the elegant reception we held at the Grand Hotel was a disaster. We had sent some 200 invitations and expected about 100. The five of us arrived five minutes early to receive our guests in the hotel's best ballroom. The flowers, the buffet and the waiting staff were all excellent. But only six or so people showed up. We discovered afterwards the reason. First, the invitations had just given the location as the hotel. Second, the hotel had neglected to post the usual notice in the lobby giving directions to the event. Lars, who was mortified by this, told us later that a lot of people had come to the hotel but, finding no notice and not finding any of the staff who knew about the event, just assumed there was a mistake about the day and left. Dean, in his gracious way, just made a joke of it. The next day we flew to Gothenburg, visited SKF and Volvo, and then retired to Lena's family place on Tjörn for the weekend. Tjörn is a beautiful island, as we all know, so Dean and Faviana had a great time seeing West Coast Sweden for the first time.

The second disaster struck in the form of a message from Batterymarch that the latest quarter's performance results were the worst BFM had ever faced. Instead of the usual one to three percentage points above the averages, they were about ten below. As best I remember, it turned out that the reasons were related mainly to two characteristics of the system. First, the stock selection system gave a heavy weighting to price-earnings ratios. This was reasonable enough, but the "earnings" element was in turn based on the previous reported 12 months' running average. Then, as there was no way that the system could allow for current significant changes as "company visits" and discussions with management were just not part of it, sudden changes of fortune were missed entirely. What had happened was that the stocks of defense companies had taken serious hits in the market. I forget the details, but there had been a cutback in defense spending some months previously and the initial but inevitable consequences were just coming to light. Several of the companies had issued earnings warnings and the market had finally figured out that most of them would be lucky to have any profits the next year.

297

Batterymarch Financial Management

So, the prices of their stocks had been falling. Statistically, that meant the price-earnings ratios in the Batterymarch stock selection system made these stocks strong buys. So, automatically, the system sold what appeared to be expensive stocks and piled into these cheap stocks. Second, the system did not have strong controls to assure reasonable diversification between industry groups; this reflected the belief that, to the degree that controls are added for lower risk, prospective returns are also limited. The result was some of the portfolios under management ended up with over 40% in these defense industry stocks. Fortunately, a number of Batterymarch's clients had established diversi- fication limits in their original contract that prevented this over-concentration in their accounts as the system did allow for setting specific limits required by individual clients. So, it was not a complete disaster. Still Dean had a lot of explaining to do. But the end result was a drop of some 30% in assets under management—partially because of the market and partially because some clients jumped ship. I was amazed that more didn't, as the results continued to be below average for several more quarters. It was another lesson learned for me. Professional investors can be very forgiving. I recall one of them telling me that, if performance over three or more past years had been good, and if the manager had not deviated from agreed strategy, they would continue with him for a while. But obviously some took the short-term view.

Equity Fund of Latin America

As mentioned in an earlier chapter, when I was still at IFC, Dean had withdrawn from participating in IFC's Latin American fund that was in the process of being established. As Dean had invested quite a lot of time on that project, he was reluctant, naturally, to abandon the idea completely. So he asked me if I could help him establish BFM's own Latin American fund. Obviously I agreed although I recognized that the IFC/Capital Group combination was very stiff competition to be facing.

Jack Arena and David Lazenby, with their Brazilian experience with Equity Fund of Brazil that BFM started in 1987, shortly before I joined, were a natural management team. We did our homework to establish that the Batterymarch system could be operated in countries such as Mexico, Argentina and Chile. We went off to the countries to establish formal arrangements for the necessary administrative and brokerage services with some of my old contacts. The main ones were Acciones y Valores in Mexico, Banco Bozano Simonsen in Brazil and Banco Roberts in Argentina. In Chile, we teamed up with the Bankers Trust brokerage affiliate there. Brazil and Chile were more complicated to operate in than were Argentina and Mexico as the local laws required a separate local closed-end fund. As Batterymarch had gone through the process in Brazil, there were no surprises. The next step was preparing the private placement memorandum and the marketing material. The real work, though, was getting potential investors to consider what was going to be the first such regional fund. That IFC was marketing their fund at the same time actually helped as the word got out on the street much more effectively than had BFM been alone. Still, as I discovered, Batterymarch's real advantage lay with its list of blue chip investors who had confidence in the firm and its methodology. They were prepared to give Dean's proposal the benefit of the doubt.

A mistake we made was deciding we needed a placement agent. I proposed Salomon Brothers as they had demonstrated their interest in emerging markets, including having previously organized a conference for IFC. We were also approached by Bankers Trust ("BT"), which was trying to establish itself as a marketer of international securities issues. Salomon proposed a fee of 3%, which was high but not unexpected for a complicated and small, by their standards, deal. Bankers Trust proposed 1%. Dean was attracted to the latter but I persuaded him to work with Salomon as, clearly, they were more experienced and professional. Unfortunately, Salomon had a rather complicated approval process of its own which resulted in Dean finally losing patience and deciding on Bankers Trust. I can't blame Salomon for being careful. Their reputation would have been on the line if they failed to market it successfully and, more importantly, if the fund was a failure, their clients would be damaged. In the end, BT could really only claim a half-credit for one investor that was not a Batterymarch client. That was the Delta Airlines pension fund, which took about 5% of the fund. The rest of the investors were

90% Dean's clients—with GM and AT&T pension funds taking over 50% between them. Another 5% came from the then British Telecom pension fund whose manager I knew well.

The fun part of the exercise was the road show courtesy of the Batterymarch flight department. We rounded up the heads of the GM and AT&T pension funds, Gordon Binns (who sadly, died a few years ago) and David Feldman, respectively, and the chair of the State of Oregon pension fund, Carol Hewitt, as well as Allan Hodgson from Alcan. On our team were Dean, Jack Arena, David Lazenby and me. So off we went with both aircraft. Santiago was the first stop. The only memorable events there were the whole crowd, except for Gordon, jogging around Santiago the first day and visiting a winery. For all the obvious reasons, Rio was the most interesting stop. Geoffrey Langlands of Bozano Simonsen was our tour guide. Geoffrey had been marketing Brazilian securities to foreigners since the mid-1960s, so he knew exactly how to organize the show. My only contribution was a very pleasant dinner hosted by Francisco Gros, my old friend from the securities commission who was then president of a major industrial company. On the more serious side, Geoffrey organized some very good company visits. While GM and AT&T had invested in Equity Fund of Brazil, this was their first visit to the country. I think they and all the others with us realized for the first time that Brazil was a serious industrial powerhouse. Two of the companies we visited were clearly "world class" and, through their exports, could prove it.

Argentina was a very different story. The beautiful city of Buenos Aires was still very run down then and the industrial infrastructure was clearly antiquated. But it was clear that the country had immense potential. Fortunately, our friends saw that and, as history proved, our timing for investing there couldn't have been much better. Unfortunately, what would have been a pleasant event—a few days at one of Puchi Rohm's ranches—had to be canceled because Jack Arena became quite ill and had to be "medevaced" out (from Santiago) in the Hawker. I was very embarrassed about canceling because Puchi, who was CEO of Argentina's leading merchant bank, had forsaken going to his otherwise most important gathering of the year—the Inter-American Development

300

Bank annual meeting—in order to be our host. He was very gracious about it though.

The end result of the tour was that all four of our client-investor prospects signed up. But that was just the beginning of the process. The next step was convincing the working people in each of their organizations to go along with it and write up the proposals for their respective investment committees. AT&T was relatively easy because Teri Goodale, who was in charge of their international investing, accompanied us. Alcan was also easy, at least for me, because Tania Zouikin had to look after them, as Alcan was Batterymarch:Canada's client. Carol Hewitt had no issues from her staff, but there was a fuss with the investment committee. Apparently, the rules for such public service bodies were such that committee meetings were held publicly. While usually there was no audience, on this occasion she was faced with major opposition from a politician who showed up. Apparently, he had, somehow, been offended by an action of a Mexican agency over some real estate deal. The result was a deferral of a decision until the next committee meeting and a lot of press publicity. Fortunately, it appeared that publicity was what the fellow wanted, so, once he got it, he dropped his opposition. That left GM. While Gordon Binns was very tough on those of us trying to sell him something and on his staff, the latter did not just let him have his way on deals that he liked. Rather, they were just as tough as he was in doing their due diligence. Actually, Gordon had warned me to be very careful with Susan Ezrati, his new researcher. He said she had just joined the pension fund group and had previously been with GM's production people, analyzing proposals for new production facilities, most recently in Korea. She had a reputation for being both very smart and very thorough. Consequently, I got to know Susan quite well. She was very professional and knowledgeable, but very low key about it all. I also got to know Chuck Tschampion who was in charge of international then. Chuck was also a good sort. That they knew Brazil and were used to Jack Arena was half the battle. But I became the expert on the other three countries.

The Batterymarch team also went to Europe, Australia and Japan. It became apparent that Bankers Trust's 1% placement fee was producing for us what it cost, which was practically nothing by Wall Street standards. No free lunch! BT, while big as a money manager in the U.S. and other countries, had little credibility as marketers. It was quite evident from our meetings in Sydney that BT Australia had a substantial amount of money under management in Australia but no interest in investing in our fund. That was quite reasonable from their point of view. But it made it clear that the investment management side of BT had no confidence in the judgment of the marketing side of BT. I tried towards the end to apply a little pressure to their top securities market man in New York. That some $130 million of the $150 million came from Batterymarch clients who had not even seen a BT person did not bother his conscience in the least. That GM and AT&T resented the arrangement, whereby the 1% placement fee for the entire amount raised was paid by the fund, did not concern him at all, despite their being presumably important customers of BT in other areas. Still, the marketing exercise was a lot of fun.

In many ways, though, the more difficult task was handling the administrative and legal work in the countries and with the investors. Mexico and Argentina were easy. There were not any special rules about foreign portfolio investors. But Chile and Brazil both required us to establish locally-domiciled closed-end funds to be established and through which the regional fund invested. This meant appointing banks as the legal administrators and local sub-advisors to be seen as the local investment managers. It was not difficult but the negotiations regarding fiduciary responsibilities and fees were time consuming—lots of lawyer time and paperwork. That said, it was a crucial part of the work. The contracts with the investors—the shareholder agreements and the management contract—were routine stuff in principle but complicated under the circumstances because a regional fund was fairly new territory for Batterymarch and its clients.

All's well that ends well. Finally, we raised some $150 million. I was rather pleased about the amount because it was slightly more than IFC raised for its fund. Another thing I was pleased about was having British Telecom's pension fund as an investor. I more than earned my keep on that alone. Not too bad for just "helping out."

Commonwealth Equity Fund

In a previous chapter, I described my involvement with the Commonwealth Secretariat in London. They approached me again to help them establish a "Commonwealth Equity Fund" to invest in the developing countries of what used to be the British Empire. (Actually, there are still some 50 "colonies" remaining in that empire, a fact that few people know. Of course a lot of them are small island nations in the South Pacific and the West Indies.) The Secretariat was a form of mini United Nations for these 50-odd countries. CEF was an initiative supported by all Commonwealth heads of government at the Secretariat's last annual meeting. I pointed out that, as I was with Batterymarch, were I to do this it would only be fair to let Batterymarch manage the fund if I were successful in getting it started. As I pointed out, when promoting an investment fund of any sort, one had to start with a proposed manager unless, as was the case with EMGF, it was being promoted by a group of investors. In this case, a political body with no money to invest was sponsoring it. As it became clear to me over the following years, while the Secretariat's people were dedicated and hard-working, these initiatives to establish investment funds were more in the nature of political statements than serious financial commitments. Not one of the "developed" countries that endorsed them ever actually put any of their money where their collective or individual mouths were.

I had this first conversation with Peter Unwin, the then Deputy Secretary-General. He was a fine example of the professional British civil servant. He had been in the Foreign Office and had just finished a term as Ambassador to Hungary. This was to be his last assignment before retiring. Much to my surprise, he said he saw nothing wrong with having a U.S. manager. So, I told Dean what was proposed. I said I would like to do it but that the chances of successfully raising the money for such a fund were pretty remote. As I saw it, the only advantage to Batterymarch would be a lot of publicity in the major Commonwealth countries that could lead to other business. He agreed, mindful of the doors I had opened for him already in the U.K. and Australia when we were promoting Equity Fund of Latin America.

Batterymarch Financial Management

What BFM agreed to do was carry the entire expense of making the case for such a fund, marketing it and then managing it through Batterymarch:Canada, to add a Canadian flavor. This was well received in London but, later, it produced a rather complicated legal issue for BFM's U.S. clients, which was then resolved. We proposed a management fee of 1.375% and the usual arrangement for charging the fund, if successfully launched, a maximum of $500,000 for our start-up costs. This was agreed, with the only condition that we use BZW, the merchant banking arm of Barclays Bank, as a placing agent. Barclays apparently had also made a proposal to manage the fund and the Secretariat felt it owed them something. I was a bit surprised that they agreed, for this Commonwealth endeavor would have a U.S. entity in charge, with a U.K. institution in second place. But even more curious was that a Japanese investment Bank, Nikko Securities, was also brought in as "underwriter" of the issue. Apparently this was because a very high-powered Japanese lady with important diplomatic connections in London was a senior person in Nikko Securities, a leading Japanese brokerage firm, in London. All this was fine with us. These important institutions should make money-raising easier and they were both new connections for Batterymarch. The last "political" details were the domicile and the denomination of the capital. It was agreed it would be domiciled in Bermuda for Commonwealth and tax reasons; the shares would be denominated in U.S. dollars as that was the international investment currency; and it would be listed in Luxembourg, as that was less complicated than a London listing. I was impressed with all this pragmatism. But we did agree with the Secretariat that the fund should have a U.K. chairman of its board of directors. We chose Sir Kenneth Berrill, the recently retired chairman of the U.K. Financial Services Authority, who I knew well from IFC days. We also selected as members of the board Peter Unwin, Michael Caine, the lady from Nikko Securities, an old Australia colleague from IFC, Neil Paterson, who had retired to Sydney, and Bishnodat Persaud, a nominee of the Commonwealth Secretariat. I was also selected.

The next job was actually making the investment case. As far as Dean was concerned, this was my show. I recruited Jay Tata to be the marketer and the portfolio manager. In reality, the only countries of likely interest to investors were India, Malaysia and Pakistan. The others were either too small or too underdeveloped. Sri Lanka, Jamaica, Barbados, Zimbabwe and Kenya were examples of the first group. Bangladesh and Nigeria were examples of the second group. The problem was that the Commonwealth was not a "region" as far as professional investors were concerned. We made the best of it by claiming that the unifying factor was that English was the common language and they all drove on the left side of the road. It was a true and slightly amusing story, but hardly relevant. The important point was that India represented some 50% of the GDP of the target group of countries, and India was a hot market for U.S. investors. What also helped us was that the Indian securities market was closed to foreigners, except for two closed-end funds—one organized by Merrill Lynch and the other by Morgan Stanley—that had been given special concessions. Our friends in GM and AT&T had expressed an interest in large part because it would provide an additional way to invest in India, but we didn't know that at the time. So, the investment case hinged on gaining conditions of entry into these markets that would give us an investment edge. In most of the countries it was the simple matter of actually being able to buy listed securities and then being able to sell them and repatriate the foreign exchange proceeds.

With our game plan organized, and with the help of the Secretariat, Jay and I embarked on visits to the countries to work out the details with the financial officials. This was a fascinating series of expeditions. We started in New Delhi, where Kenneth Berrill, who knew all the senior Ministry of Finance people, joined us. Several had been students of his when at Cambridge. The end result was agreement for a five-year closed-end India fund that would be wholly-owned by CEF. The next stop was Karachi, Pakistan. There was no difficulty in getting the necessary access to their listed stocks, although it was a lengthy process. But Karachi is not a favorite city, so I don't remember much about it. Then we went to Kuala Lumpur, Malaysia, which was a much easier exercise. What we needed was favored treatment of some sort because the Malaysian stock market was already completely open to foreigners. As I recall, it took about 15 minutes with the then Minister of Finance. In exchange for exemption from their 10% tax on profits from stock trans-actions, we agreed that the fund "logo" would be the orchid, Malaysia's national flower. Again, this was the benefit of Commonwealth Secretariat sponsorship. All the heads of government and finance ministers had supported the initiative, so following through was a pretty straightfor-ward matter. We did not stop off in Sri Lanka because Jay and I knew the country pretty well and we knew there were no problems. We had made a few investments there during our IFC days and knew foreign portfolio investors were welcome to participate directly in their stock market. Besides, our ex colleague from IFC and my old friend Brad Warner was, at the time, advisor to the Sri Lanka Securities Commis-sion. So he could brief us on anything new. We asked Brad to join us for our weekend "R & R" in the Maldives. That was one of the delights in having the GII. It was only a few hours from KL, while it would have been a day and two changes of aircraft to fly commercially. We had an excuse for our visit: the Maldives was a Commonwealth country.

The Maldives is one of the world's more interesting—and bizarre—countries. With a population of about 400,000, it is spread over some 1,500 square miles but on about 200 separate small islands. The capital, Malé, which was also the only town, takes up one of them and the airport another. The rest are mainly fishing villages and hotels—one per island. The transportation in Malé was by bicycle and a few old taxis. Out of the capital, it was by boat. Oddly, the inter-island service was run by some Swedes. I had gone there first in about 1980 to see if we could help them establish a financial market. The banking system was com-prised of three branches of Indian and Pakistani banks. Except for some-thing called a Monetary Authority, that was it. And that was the way it had remained in 1990. In practice, tourism was the only industry. Those locals not employed by the tourist business were fishermen or trades-men, plus a few employed in manufacturing, as I will explain later. They had no currency—all cash transactions were in U.S. dollar bills—there were no coins so everything cost multiples of a dollar. The main—if not only—exports were postage stamps and knitwear. The locals had cashed-in on tourists and stamp collectors who wanted or needed local stamps so they designed thousands. There were fish stamps, island

stamps, portrait stamps, and Mickey Mouse and Donald Duck stamps
—all of them sold well. A funny/sad story about Maldives manufacturing
exports was circulating around the Bank at the time. The Minister of
Industry (who probably also had other jobs as well) was in Washington
visiting officials to try and get the quota on locally produced sweaters
increased. The trade official he met told him he had worked miracles
and so was pleased to tell him that he had got the quota increased by
25%. The plaintive response he received was: "But, sir, that means only
five extra sweaters a year!" Woolen sweaters were, and probably still are,
their only manufactured goods; even the stamps were imported. Such
are the problems of very small countries. Anyway, after landing we spent
a very pleasant two days at one of the hotels. The water sports, especially
the scuba diving, were great. The coral reefs and the fish life are amongst
the most beautiful to be found anywhere in the world. The accommodation and food was not bad, but the water from the taps was a light
brown in color. As I recall it, the seven of us—Kenneth, Brad, Jay, our
three pilots and I—were the only guests. But there were no investment
opportunities.

After the Maldives, we flew straight back to Boston. Later, Jay and I
and Dr. Bishakha Mukherjee went on another due diligence trip in the
GII to Jamaica, Barbados and Trinidad to look into investment possibilities. Bishakha was the Secretariat's very able chief economist. An Indian, she had read for her PhD in economics at LSE and was good
company as well as a source of a lot of additional useful contacts and
information. This trip reminded me of my naval days as much as my
visits with IFC. The islands had not got any better over the ensuing
years. The only investment opportunity large enough for the fund was
the Montreal-based electric power holding company that had subsidiaries on all the islands. While several of these subsidiaries had shares
that could be bought, the amounts available were small and there was
no liquidity. That had always been the problem with investing in the
Caribbean islands—as well as in many other small countries. The good
companies were all small and closely-held by the locals or groups of foreigners who had been involved for generations. The new good opportunities were snapped up by those already there. The rest went to the

"IFIs," such as IFC, who usually overpaid or were mainly concerned with just making investments for developmental or other reasons. If there were any exceptions they were the banks that were being changed from subsidiaries of Canadian or U.K. banks into locally-controlled stock exchange listed companies. In most cases the only reason the stocks were listed was that shareholders of listed stocks received tax breaks.

The next trip was our marketing trip—due diligence for GM and AT&T. There were no other customers, as not even our BZW friends wanted to spend the time. From GM there was Chuck Tschampion and from AT&T, David Feldman and Teri Goodale. Dean and Jay came along for the first part of the trip. After nearly a year working on Equity Fund of Latin America, we were all on excellent terms. Our first stop was London. We arrived at Brown's Hotel where I had made reservations only to find they claimed we had no reservations. I forget where we ended up, but Brown's arranged something nearby. It was not a good start to the trip. I was very upset that Brown's staff was so cavalier about this, especially as I had been staying there quite regularly for over 20 years. That was the last time: I switched allegiances to the Stafford.

From London we flew to Harare. Our old Zimbabwean colleague from IFC, Julius Makoni, who was now working there, had arranged the meetings. The first was with the president and principal shareholder of a manufacturing company. He said quite openly that there was no future for investors in Zimbabwe and he intended to leave the country as soon as he found a buyer for his company. The stock market had done well in recent years—while one of the smallest, it was one of the world's best performing because the economy was still strong and the financial infrastructure was quite sound. But the government was becoming increasingly socialist and nationalistic. This was not surprising as Mugabe was a Marxist. But there was the lingering hope that he would not tear down what he had inherited despite some evidence to the contrary. The second meeting was with the governor of the Bank of Zimbabwe. When we arrived, I was ushered into his office immediately and the others were asked to wait. The governor was there with his senior advisor on loan from the Bank of England. They wanted to know what we wanted. The governor said he trusted me because he knew I had been with IFC, but he didn't like the idea of these other foreigners coming to question him. The "Brit" and I tried to explain that they were just passive investors interested in the possibilities in Zimbabwe. They were not interested in controlling any companies, and the Commonwealth Equity Fund, which they were considering, had been endorsed by his own government. They just wanted to ask his views about Zimbabwe's economy. I said: "Think of it as a press conference!" That was a bad idea: he didn't like the press. Anyway, after half an hour of wrangling, he finally invited them in. But Dean had lost patience by then and had just left with the others in tow. Julius, who was with us, was mortified and also slightly frightened. He lived there and knew the Governor's reputation. He also knew what had happened to Jay when he pressed him for money owed IFC. As mentioned in an earlier chapter, he told Jay he had 24 hours to leave the country or face being thrown in jail.

Fortunately, our visit to Kenya was much better. Ernie Kepper, who was then IFC's resident representative in Nairobi, made all the arrangements. We had some good company visits and saw the appropriate government people. The Aga Khan crowd, who had major business interests there, did all the right things, including arranging for us to visit a newsprint company "up country." As the GII needed a longer landing strip than the one nearby, we flew there in two small aircraft. It was quite interesting to see this large timber operation, miles from anywhere. All the managers were Indian. This followed, as an Indian group owned the plant. All the equipment was from a similar plant in India, which was being newly-equipped with more modern stuff. As they explained, it was part of their strategy to use second-hand equipment in plants in "emerging" markets. We spent that night in a game park lodge nearby. That was rather fun—I think it was the first time in a game park for any of us. We slept in very elegant tents with bathrooms attached where the shower water came from canvas buckets hanging from the tent pole. The staff apparently filled them with hot water every afternoon and morning. The next night, back in Nairobi—our last in Kenya—Watti Kepper, Ernie's wife, put on a very fine reception and buffet dinner for us, during which we met even more of the local movers and shakers. So, we departed Africa with a more upbeat attitude, even if Dave Feldman had commented dryly that investing in Africa was hardly a serious business.

We spent the next day in the Seychelles, as the GII could not get us to Kuala Lumpur without a stop. I had wanted to make the stop in Mauritius but the pilots were concerned about having to make two 2,000-mile flights over the Indian Ocean. We stayed at a pleasant beach resort hotel and did the usual tourist things for the half day of daylight. However, I really didn't feel it was a friendly country, albeit a tropical paradise of sorts. On the other hand, I had an embarrassing experience while there that might have colored my view of the place despite it being entirely my fault. I had realized suddenly—with the help of Andy, our chief pilot—that I had forgotten we were losing a day as we were still going east. It was very, very embarrassing to have to phone my friend Malek Merican and cancel our visit to Malaysia. He had made some impressive plans for us. Quite rightly, I was in his bad books for quite some time. It would have been better had we skipped the 1,000 side trip to the Seychelles and gone directly to KL.

Our last stop was Seoul. "Why there?" you ask. South Korea is not in the Commonwealth. Correct, but South Korea is a company of global interest and Dave wanted to go there so that's where we went. You don't argue with prospective investors. My KIFC friends did us proud. Some excellent company visits and also opportunities for shopping. I think everyone was impressed with the showroom of the Samsung household appliance factory. They had an absolutely fully automated kitchen. You could sit at a table and turn on and off stoves, washing machines and open and close doors and windows throughout the house. Chuck, Dave and Teri were less impressed with the traffic in the suburbs: it took us over an hour to cover a couple of miles.

Then it was straight home, with just one fueling stop. Finally, we landed at Westchester Airport to drop off our friends. For some reason, Gordon and Susan, along with Dean, were there to meet us. After the usual pleasantries, Gordon turned to Chuck and said: "Well, what should we do?" Chuck just looked at me and laughed. I guess he knew they had already decided to invest because of India. The rest was just window dressing.

As always, the basic decision was followed by the messy detail of the terms and conditions. The first issue was that neither GM nor AT&T was prepared to buy shares in a fund that was stock-exchange listed. BZW insisted on that, claiming it was the only way they could get investors. The formers' point was that shares of closed-end funds, once listed, tended to trade in the market at a 20% to 50% discount to net asset value. There was no way they could buy a listed stock at $10.00— the proposed offering price and thus also the NAV—and then have to write it down to market on their books the next day. As GM and AT&T were committing to $25 and $20 million, respectively, plus one million each from GM's Canadian and U.K. subsidiaries, we had to find a solution. In the end, it was to structure the fund as a company with unlisted convertible preferred shares, which they would buy, and common shares that would be listed on the London Stock Exchange that BZW's clients would buy. The Barclays Bank pension fund had agreed to $8 million, so BZW was able to tell their prospective investors that the fund already had about $55 million. That should have been a great selling point for them for raising an additional $50 million of common stock. During this period Jay and I had tried IFC, but my friends said that, as we were already boasting about having raised $55 million, they could not make a case that IFC was needed. Oh well!

For three weeks, one of Tania's Canadian colleagues stayed at the Ritz in London to be available to make follow-up presentations to prospects BZW lined up. BZW only found one of the two prospects we had in London. The other was with Commonwealth Development Corporation, which I had approached. I knew them well. John Eccles, the then Chief Executive, and his colleagues received Dean and me graciously and agreed to a $5 million investment. That the managing director of Barclays Bank, Peter Leslie, was also CDC's chairman helped. Unfortunately, it turned out that CDC's charter prohibited them from investing in regional companies. They started work on getting the charter changed, but it took too long—some six years. So Barclays' pension fund looked like the only U.K. investor. BZW had a standard approach to marketing new issues. When I discovered what it was, I became quite concerned. It seemed to be little more than a mass mailing of a prospectus, a contract form and a closing date for signing up a day before the listing. There seemed to be no effort at all to contacting decision makers to plead the case. They said: "That wasn't done." There were a few harsh words. In any event, they proceeded down their critical path. One item on their agenda was to ask the sponsors, the Secretariat and BFM, to send out invitations to a reception celebrating "the launching." This was to be held at Marlborough House, the headquarters of the Secretariat, on the pre-set date of listing. Marlborough House, which had been Queen Victoria's residence, was two palaces down from Buckingham Palace. It would have been a great location for a reception and in itself would have attracted a lot of guests from "the City." They proposed this some ten days into their marketing program, but they had still not found any buyers for the common stock. Consequently, I cautioned the Secretariat that sending invitations before we were sure there were at least a few buyers risked serious embarrassment if the event had to be canceled. About three days before the listing date, BZW informed us that they were withdrawing. They had no buyers.

While I was not completely surprised by this, I had not realized the extent of the problems it would create. I assumed our $55 million would hold and we would just go ahead with a smaller fund. Wrong! Gordon Binns donned his tough guy hat and told me in no uncertain terms that he had been promised a $100 million fund and we had better deliver. This occurred during a meeting in his office, shortly after BZW walked away, that Dean had arranged to confess and see what should be done. Present were Gordon, Chuck and Dave Feldman, plus Dean and me. The worst part of our confession was having to say we were not 100% sure that Barclays' commitment—also for the convertible preferred—would hold. I noticed that Dave Feldman was just watching the show and smiling slightly. In the end, our marching orders were clear: if we wanted to hold GM and AT&T, we had to find more investors. The first step was to go on bended knee to IFC. So I wrote to my old colleagues explaining what had happened. I reminded them that when they turned us down they said it was because, with GM and AT&T, plus BZW, they could not make a case that IFC could add anything. Now, it was clear they were needed. Fortunately, they came through for us. I knew I had the backing of my CMD colleagues—Michael Barth, then Associate Director, and Farida Khambata would make the recommendation. My successor as director, Chuck Sethness was, I was told, sympathetic. But it was up to the investment committee and then IFC's board. Finally, they came in for $7.5 million. Also, Antoine van Agtmael's emerging markets management company came in for a similar amount. That was the sum total result of another three months' effort. That is, besides keeping Barclays. Fortunately, it was enough for Gordon Binns.

Then, all we had to deal with was the tedious task of getting agreement on the documentation from some six groups of lawyers. We had hired Clifford Chance in London to look after BFM and the fund. Jay Tata, with his usual thoroughness, had gone to his contact there, Adam Signy, who was then a relatively junior partner, and offered a simple proposal. "Adam, we want you personally to work on this and we want you to agree to cap your fee at 100,000 pounds." Jay had worked with Adam before on the BLADEX deals and used then the same approach. Adam accepted. He understood completely that Jay and I were all too aware how legal firms, working for Wall Street investment banks or City merchant banks, never worried about legal fees because it was always the investors who ended up paying. We didn't go along with that. So Adam worked hard to make it a simple process. Unfortunately, the lawyers for IFC and the main investors had the other approach. But we finally had our closing—just a signing of contracts and wire transfers: no launching party. The only "public" event noting CEF's birth was an article in the Financial Times. Somewhere in the middle of it there was a comment that read: "... two U.S. financial institutions, that put up about 80% of the money, saved the Commonwealth finance ministers who had promoted the fund from a lot of embarrassment."

So, at this stage, in late 1990, BFM had three emerging markets closed-end country funds up and running. With about $250 million invested, they produced some $3 million fees. Then, BFM had to earn those fees: that was Jack's and David's job. I just had to worry about governance. Dean was not big on such matters as board meetings. That the investors in Equity Fund of Brazil had agreed to the trust structure solved his problem on that one. But we had to have them for Equity Fund of Latin America ("EFLA") and CEF because both had needed to be stock exchange listed. He picked Luxembourg as their laws required only two meetings a year and we could have both fund meetings at the same day in the same place. However, we found to our dismay that the Luxembourg Monetary Authority, which had jurisdiction, had decided recently that they wanted to repair their image. It took a lot of time to go through their new approval process. In retrospect, it would have been easier to have listed the fund on the LSE in London.

By the time CEF was launched, we had already had two board meetings of EFLA. Gordon and Dave were on the board, as was Dean's friend Charley Ellis, as Dean felt his own participation would not be appropriate. I was chairman. On the CEF board we had Kenneth Berrill, Peter Unwin, Neil Paterson, Michael Caine and Bishnodat Persaud as the Commonwealth people, along with Gordon and Dave, and Tania and me from Batterymarch. We had asked the Japanese lady from Nikko to step down, which she did finally. Then, Bill Ryrie from IFC joined a little later, and Bishnodat Persaud resigned. The first board meeting of CEF was in Bermuda and was quite uneventful. Everyone likes Bermuda. The second was in Monterrey, Mexico. Gordon insisted on that, quite properly, as he felt at least one meeting a year should be in a country where we were investing and he had never been to Monterrey. I asked Roberto Hernandez, my old friend from the Mexican stock exchange, to make the arrangements for us. It was a bit tense when we arrived because, except for my first phone call to him making the request and his agreeing, we had heard nothing from Roberto or anyone else in Acciones y Valores, his company. Further, while I didn't know much about the place, I did know it was not a destination of choice. However, Roberto came through quite well. Amongst other things, he gave an excellent dinner for us attended by the Governor of the Bank of Mexico, who I had known for some years and respected immensely, plus the five leading Monterrey industrialists. After dinner we had a 90-minute discussion on what was right and wrong about Mexico. That was a great success. What was not was the schedule of company visits: there weren't any. This was because Roberto assumed meeting the bosses was sufficient. Gordon expressed his displeasure. Dave Feldman was quite happy about it, as he was known to say occasionally: "If you've seen one factory, you've seen them all."

Our first meeting of the two boards in the same place was actually held in Leningrad in early 1991. Why Leningrad? Was it because it was neutral territory? No. It was because Dean was then promoting his Soviet Companies Fund, about which much more later, and he wanted to impress the Soviet officials who would be there. Bill Ryrie was the only board member missing; the USSR was not an IFC shareholder then. The first event, a reception organized by BFM at the local leading hotel, was quite impressive. All the local luminaries showed, not that I would have recognized any. I was told much later that the youngish man who was shepherding the mayor of Leningrad around was named Vladimir Putin. So, one of my claims to fame is that I have shaken hands with the head of state of the world's second most important country. Our meetings were held the next day in the main reception room in the old royal palace. It was one of the most elegantly decorated rooms I have ever seen. I recall being a bit disconcerted while playing my role as chairman of the EFLA board session. While I was doing my chairman stuff, I noticed my colleagues were all looking directly over my head. I didn't think I could have bored them that much in the three or four minutes I took. Afterwards, I found they had been looking at the life-sized portrait of Lenin, which was on the wall directly behind me. As to the substance of the board meetings, we were fortunate that both funds performed quite well while I was around. But that didn't prevent Gordon from keeping Jack, David and Jay, who had joined the management team to run CEF, on their toes with many, many piercing questions.

Farm Fund

My next assignment for Dean was his Farm Fund. One day in the office in Boston he wandered over and started discussing his own investment portfolio. He mentioned that, as his income was 100% tied to the securities market, he kept a lot of his money in other assets in order to have diversification. One such portfolio was farmland. He explained

that there were several firms that specialized in managing farm investments for financial institutions and he had some money with one of
them. He thought it was odd that hardly any foundations or pension
funds invested in farms. All the money seemed to come from insurance
companies and individuals. As an expert in promoting "frontier" funds,
what did I think of Batterymarch promoting a farm fund? Did I think
he could, or should, try and sell it to his pension fund clients? My response was to say I hadn't the slightest idea. I had never even thought
about farmland as an investment class. So he asked me to give it some
thought. Much to my surprise, when I was provided with the data, I
found that it was a very large asset class. This was obvious when one
thought about it. The U.S. has millions of acres of farmland. Even if
most wasn't worth much per acre, it was still worth about $700 billion
in total in 1988. Also, it turned out that there was 40 years of data on
returns on investing in farmland and that these returns, at about 10%
annualized, compared reasonably well with returns from residential, industrial and commercial real estate. I looked up the returns from a paper
I delivered to some economists' conference in 1990 on asset allocation.
The information came from Ibbotson Associates, a well-known data
source.

I also discovered that the two component parts of the farming business were becoming increasingly better understood by the participants.
Being a producer of farm products—grains or animals—is one "business." Being an owner and improver of farmland is another. I found that
while, historically, family farmers have always owned the land they farm,
even if they have had to mortgage it, an increasing number were concentrating on production and willing to rent or lease the land from other
owners. That, apparently, was, and is, what some investors, and especially the insurance companies, were beginning to see as the opportunity. It dawned on me that the insurance companies saw it first as they
were the main ones making long-term mortgage loans to farmers. The
banks, of course, concentrated on the short-term loans and, in any event,
were not normally long-term equity investors—and certainly farm land
is a real long-term investment as it is one of the least liquid assets around.
Another point was that large-scale commercial farming was a recognized

and successful business activity and pension funds were not averse to owning shares in such companies. Thus a farm fund could be considered in the same light. The main differences being only that management was contracted out and that the farm property would be a diversified spread in the case of a farm fund, whereas a commercial farm company would have internal management and assets largely in only one area. Consequently I concluded that a farm fund would make sense and recommended to Dean that he proceed. But I also emphasized it would be a challenge similar to convincing the clients to buy emerging markets funds. My chief concern was that BFM had no expertise to do it. So I suggested he should first buy one of the farmland management companies. This he did, picking the one that was managing his farm portfolio. This was a small company with, I think, only six professionals, based in Hartford. They had all worked previously as the farmland investing group of a large insurance company that decided to get out of the business. They were a very pleasant, low-key and very professional crowd, as one would expect. At the time, their largest client was their previous employer, which had given them a contract to liquidate its farmland portfolio.

Jay was given the job of preparing the placement memorandum and organizing the marketing. I went along for the ride. We had done our own due diligence by being taken around to farms all over the country. That in itself was an interesting experience, going from cotton farms in the Deep South to grain in the Midwest, to cattle in the foothills of the Rocky Mountains. About the only specific occasions I remember well were, first, seeing for the first time real sharecropper poverty—the small huts that they lived in on one of the farms in the South. The other was the first time I had a meal of catfish. This was provided by a wheeler-dealer farm real estate broker who was taking us around various farms in his part of the South. He obviously had done it before. In any event he had delivered to the GII as we were taking off around lunchtime a box lunch. It was a local specialty—fried catfish and shrimps. It was delicious.

The next step was the usual marketing exercise. This was a great disappointment. We found no serious takers during our due diligence trips.

Batterymarch Financial Management

This meant that our initial sales calls had not been well received. By then, we were beginning to realize we were ahead of the market—or the Batterymarch clientele knew something we didn't. In the end, it was only AT&T and Bell South that went along with the idea. They both put up $50 million—not in our fund, but as separate accounts to be managed by BFM under contracts with their own sets of goals and guidelines. But, with a 2% fee, that was revenue of $1 million a year, so it was probably worthwhile for Dean in the end. So yet another financial frontier experience for me.

Equity Fund of China

I had little to do with Dean's China fund, which was well received. But I did have an interesting experience on the fringe. I went to Shanghai with him once during the early stages when he was meeting the local officials. What was more interesting though was my second visit for him. This took place around the end of 1991, after I had retired from Batterymarch. Dean had been asked by the Ministry of Finance people to organize a securities market training lecture for some MoF people in Shanghai. He asked me to go there and perform for him. In the audience were about 20 mid-level managers. My interpreter was a young woman who looked hardly out of her teens, but she was incredible. I talked for about five hours in total, pausing every couple of minutes for her to translate. By the amount of time she took at each turn, I guessed she must have been doing it faithfully. But as to accuracy, how could I know? However, the audience remained attentive and their questions seemed entirely relevant to what I had said, so they must have been satisfied with both of us. Afterwards, I asked her where she had learned English; she was absolutely fluent, with a trace of an American ascent. She said at university in Shanghai. I then asked how long she had had been translating. She said six months. I couldn't believe it.

The next day, a Saturday, she took me to lunch and then on a tour boat down the Yangtze River. The restaurant was large but elegant. The tables were occupied by groups of eight or ten of what looked to me to be the local yuppies. Each had a cell phone conspicuously on display

318

on the table. The boat trip gave me my first insight as to the size and industrial capacity of Shanghai: two hours seeing shipyards and factories packed solid on either side of the river. There were two other interesting things that I saw which also surprised me. First, were the young policemen on the boat—I knew they were police because they had shoulder emblems in English reading "Economic Police." As far as I could tell I was the only white person amongst the 100 or so passengers. So why the English and what's an economic policeman? Second, when we reached, eventually, the open countryside, I noticed small clusters of what I thought were small apartment buildings. When I asked about them, she said: "No, they are farmers' houses—the farmers around here have become quite rich since they could own their own farms." I forget how much Dean raised for his China fund, but he had obviously been very successful in courting Chinese officialdom. Arrangements were made for several young Chinese professionals to intern at Batterymarch for varying periods of time, working on matters related to the China fund and learning about U.S. investment management. Eventually, after my time, Virginie Maisonneuve, a young French woman who had worked for a Scottish money manager and had spent a year at a Chinese university and was fairly fluent, became manager of the China fund.

Soviet Companies Fund

This brings me to my last exploit with Batterymarch. While it was much more interesting to me than farmland, it was not successful for Dean. He must have spent more than $5 million trying to organize his Soviet Companies Fund, which was probably five times more than it cost for him to get into the farmland business. But, after two years' effort, it came to nothing. This was in part because he was more than five years ahead of the market and in part because he started with an urealistic strategy.

Dean's strategy had three components. The first part, the concept, was fine: establishing joint ventures between Soviet military-industrial companies, Western strategic partners and Western institutional investors. The second part involving implementation on the Soviet side was reasonable in theory but less in practice in 1990 when the Soviets were still secretive and had no understanding of Western management. Dean's plan was the Soviet parent military industrial companies were to split-off their commercial businesses as separate subsidiaries and open them to foreign investors. But it would be very difficult for them to transfer such physical assets and the relevant employees in a legal and transparent fashion. The third step—initially contemplated—also was impractical. The foreign investors, the strategic partners of the Soviet companies, were expected to participate in an automated bidding process for their interests in these new companies. The Soviet companies would go along with the idea, based on their own ideas of what their commercial businesses were worth, but why would Western companies bid for such assets without doing their standard due diligence? He believed there would be many bidders for each of the joint ventures Batterymarch would organize. Early on, Dean recognized that this bidding process was unrealistic.

Later, Dean wrote a book about his Soviet and China experiences, called Mao, Marx & the Market, but it didn't go into much detail on these technicalities. It's a fascinating book and well worth reading as it goes into all his experiences with the government people and the companies. Consequently, I will concentrate here on my own experiences on the sidelines dealing with the mechanics.

This all started as a consequence of Dean having been invited to participate in a seminar put on at Harvard for a group from the Soviet Military Industrial Commission (the "Commission"). The Commission ran all military production facilities, including atomic energy and all commercial aircraft and ship manufacturing plants. The theme was turning "Swords into Plowshares"—why and how to switch from producing military equipment to producing commercial and consumer goods. Dean asked me if I would like to go along and, naturally, I said yes. Dean's pitch was they should privatize the companies and establish an investment fund that would bring together Western industrial companies, as strategic partners, and financial institutions, as investors, in these Soviet companies. The investment fund would act as the catalyst, putting everything together. The Soviets were intrigued. Dean invited them to come to his house the next night for dinner and further discussion. They were a very interesting crowd. One mentioned casually that he had been to Boston five years previously. When asked about it he eventually said that it was only Boston harbor—he had been in a submarine. On his side, Dean proposed modestly that he could raise a billion dollars from his clients for the "Soviet Companies Fund" that Batterymarch would run.

The upshot was, after a visit to Moscow, Batterymarch and the Commission came to an agreement. The Commission would sponsor the proposal in Russia and pay Batterymarch's local expenses. BFM would bring the investors and also the prospective strategic partners and cover all the U.S. expenses involved in putting the fund and the individual joint ventures together. Dean's counterpart was Vladimir Koblov, the "First Deputy Chairman" of the Commission. This quaint title meant he was the chief operating officer. The Prime Minister could have been considered the President, with Gorbachev as Chairman. Goodness knows how many people worked for Koblov in the 5,000-odd factories he controlled. But he was a mild, easily approachable grandfatherly type—at least that was the impression he gave me when I met him some months later. As the resident emerging markets fund expert, I was asked to help out. By the time of my first visit a few months after our board meetings for the Latin America and Commonwealth funds, Dean had all the logistics worked out. They were quite impressive. He had hired a couple of young Americans who spoke Russian and had some financial experience, outfitted the office provided us and set up residence in an impressive government house, also provided by the Commission. Vladimir Koblov also provided several "handlers," the chief of which, Vladimir Sidorovich, was in charge of arranging all our meetings.

The office was rather grubby but spacious by Soviet standards then, and very well located in a quiet street off one of the main avenues. Our house was another matter! Even by Western standards it was very comfortable and with a design faintly similar to some of Frank Lloyd Wright's houses. It was situated in a large well-cultivated garden on a quiet street with several similar houses in an area called the Lenin Hills, near Moscow University. On the ground floor were elegant living and dining rooms, plus a billiard room equipped with a large color television set. There were six large bedrooms upstairs. The staff was incredibly good—excellent meals, well-served and quite amazing "upstairs" service. I remember vividly the surprise I felt when I came back at the end of my first day staying there. That morning, without thinking about it, I had left a shirt, my pajamas and some underwear on a chair. When I came back, there they were, all laundered, ironed and starched. Starching the shirt was fine, but starched underpants? This was done every day. In 1990, there were no remotely decent hotels or restaurants in Moscow, so these houses were provided to impress visiting VIPs. It was said Richard Nixon stayed once in "our" house. This only changed in mid-1991 when the Metropol Hotel, located between the Kremlin and the Bolshoi and managed by the Intercontinental, was opened. Strangely, but typical of the Soviets, during the first few months it was in business, if you weren't staying there or could prove you were invited by a guest, you couldn't go in even if you were a foreigner carrying your passport.

During the 14-month period I was involved, I flew to Moscow in the GII some half a dozen times and stayed for periods of a week to ten days. So, having our sponsors make the house available made staying in a very unattractive city at the time bearable. That our dining room was the best restaurant in Moscow, if not the whole of the USSR, accessible to foreigners, also helped. The winter of 1990/91 was especially unpleasant. It wasn't that cold, but it was overcast almost all of the time. Generally, one didn't see the sun after arriving until one left. As I will get to in the next chapter, Moscow has become quite a civilized place now. As to my work there, much was fascinating, some experiences were exciting, and some were worrisome. It was the latter that made me feel towards the end that I had to part company with Batterymarch. But, first I will describe some of the more memorable experiences.

We made a lot of factory visits. The first were to the "hi tech" companies. In those days they were the producers of rockets and space vehicles. Seeing the Proton rocket production line at the Khrunichev plant near Moscow was an awesome experience. There were twelve of these giant rockets on the production line. Tucked away in a corner of the huge building was a spacecraft being serviced. A memorable experience was meeting and chatting with the general managers of the company that built the rockets and of the company that built Mir. In my den is a picture of Mir with a spacecraft docking with it. It is autographed by these two incredible people. They were all impressive looking and clearly tough characters. They had to be both tough and smart to end up running companies comparable in size and efficiency to Boeing and Ford. Their plan to privatize part of their businesses was to produce a global wireless telephone company based on their satellites. It was a great idea, as now proven.

While many of the products built in the Soviet Union were shoddy, that could not be said of those things they considered important, such as rockets and military aircraft. We went to several electronics factories but only saw their consumer goods production lines—the "plowshares" parts. Not only were they of poor quality, most were 1950s vintage in efficiency and style. But we knew these same factories, somewhere else, were producing first class military and space equipment. There was one interesting exception to the shoddiness. This was the Proton Production Company again. Amongst other things, they were producing excellent ski equipment. One of our colleagues managed to buy some ski poles—made of titanium. They cost him fifty cents at the black market exchange rate.

One factory visit was almost frightening. It was a chemical plant in a small industrial town called Ufa in the foothills of the Urals. I remember we flew there in their company plane. It was a two-hour flight in a twin-engine propjet flown by two young characters wearing ski jackets. The company boss was with us and, as I recall, he was one of the "old school" who believed everyone should make toasts with full glasses of vodka. It was a grueling experience. The plant itself looked a hundred years old. The floors were covered in grime and the many pipes in the production process were rusted or covered in rotting asbestos. Fluids were dripping and the odor was overpowering. We feared we were being poisoned, but the workers seemed quite unconcerned. I still have a souvenir of that trip—a ski hat with the emblem of the local town's sports

Above: Before our November 1990 meetings of Directors of Equity Fund of Latin America and Commonwealth Equity Fund—I'm seated on the far side of the table, at the end— we meet with St. Petersburg (Leningrad at the time) Mayor Anatoly Sobchak and his staff at Mariinsky Palace.

Below: Meeting at Mariinsky Palac Petersburg with Mayor Anatoly Sobch (to the Mayor's left) his assistant Vl Putin—the future President of Russi other members of the Mayor's staff.

club. We had a very congenial lunch there with a crowd of the towns-people looking on. They were very friendly and curious. We were probably the first group of crazy Westerners they had ever seen.

The good thing about that small town was that it looked much better than Kharkov, the second city of Ukraine. This was an all 'round bad experience. Fortunately for Dean's plans, we did not have any "investors" with us. So we flew there from Moscow with Aeroflot, rather than in the GII. The first problem was that Moscow's domestic airport was a bit disorganized in those days (now, it's more like London's Terminal 5). There were no monitors showing which flights were leaving from which gates and when. We found our way to our flight only because, just before the advertised departure time, a crowd of people suddenly rushed to a gate. That was our flight, and what a flight it was!—a junky, dirty, old twin-engine jet, absolutely full, including passengers in the many broken seats. Kharkov airport was another thing. It was an old looking Victorian style red brick building that could have been a barracks. From there we drove to the main hotel. From the entrance you could tell immediately the direction to go to the washrooms. Fortunately, we were not staying overnight. I don't recall what we were going to see there, but I do recall the many unpaved streets in the city and its suburbs.

Besides a few trips with Dean and his investors to Moscow, I had two occasions when I stayed there for a week or so as the "resident" for Batterymarch, overseeing his staff in the Moscow office. For this job, Dean had had cards in English and Cyrillic printed for me calling me the "first deputy chairman" of Batterymarch Moscow. He seemed to be impressed with the title. I never used the cards. There were three professionals then, the two men mentioned previously, and a young lady from Tennessee, Kim Malone, a graduate of Princeton and the Harvard Business School, who were working on deals for the fund. Kim was an adventurous type, in her early twenties. About two years previously, she had gone to Moscow on her own to learn Russian at Moscow University. The student quarters were in a 20-story apartment building. Poor Kim said she didn't know anything about the eating arrangements and ended up living on potatoes she boiled on a hot plate in her room for the first week.

Vladimir Lenin looms over the proceedings at the EFLA Directors' meeting at Mariinsky Pala (At first, I didn't realize why my colleagues were looking over my head during my brief opening remarks ... I didn't think I could have bored them quite so quickly.)

*With CEF Directors Neil Paterson and Ken Berrill and my Batterymarch
(and former IFC) colleague Jay Tata.*

1988–1991

Then she found there was a cafeteria for the students in the basement. The Batterymarch office also had three Russian secretaries, all of whom spoke good English and were, we assumed, part-time KGB. We also had Jeff Braemer, a bright young Batterymarch associate from Boston as "major domo."

These experiences in Moscow were both rewarding and worrying. Rewarding because, through Vladimir Sidorovich, we could meet whomever we wished and, consequently, I met a lot of interesting people. We were afforded much the same level of access I had in IFC when visiting developing countries. I will get to the worrying aspect later. Vladimir, in his early 40s and a physicist and specialist in laser technology, had been in charge of the optics industry for the Military Industrial Commission, and had all the "perks" that go with the job. These included an apartment in one of the better buildings, a dacha and a car and driver.

Our task was to learn about the two or three leading companies in each of the industries that Dean thought were good prospects for investment. Vladimir would tell us about the best ones and we would start the process by asking him to arrange first meetings with the head men. The company managers would come to our office or we would go to theirs, as we wished. Such were the contacts of Vladimir and the instructions given by Vladimir Koblov. The latter had shown us once a letter signed by Gorbachev authorizing cooperation with Batterymarch. So there was no doubt all doors were open to us. I remember calling on the deputy ministers of aviation and of atomic energy to get a different overview of their industries. Both were short, grey individuals, not at all as impressive as the company bosses. We were working on some aircraft manufacturing deal—the Soviets were to build the airframes and the Americans were to provide engines and avionics. The most interesting meeting, though, was with the head of the Sukhoi Aviation Company. He was an absolutely delightful man. In appearance and presence, he could have been mistaken for an academician in a top American or European university. He came with his portfolio of diagrams of new aircraft they wanted to build—the civilian ones, not the military ones—as he assumed his company was to be our chosen partner to joint venture with

329

1dimir Sidorovich (L) with EFLA and CEF Directors
·rdon Binns (General Motors) and David Feldman
T&T) in front of the Cathedral of St. Basil the Blessed
Red Square, Moscow, November 1990.

*Touring the labs at Machinostroyenia—a scientific research facility for space
exploration near Moscow—with its capable general manager,
Gerbert Yefremov (white coat).*

Boeing or Airbus. He also brought his daughter along. She was a strik-
ingly beautiful 20-something blonde, who spoke very good English, as
did her father. I asked Vladimir afterwards why he had brought her. He
said she had got entangled with some Russian pop singer and Daddy
was trying to get her away from him. He had heard our group of Westerners included some eligible bachelors.

Our house also gave us the opportunity to entertain our Soviet contacts. With the staff and their access to supplies, we had one of the best
tables in town. So we had some memorable dinner parties. But some-

times the toasting got a bit out of control. I recall one evening when our number one guest was a senior person in the administration of their space program. After an impassioned speech about goodwill between the U.S. and the USSR, he took off his watch and, saying "this watch is an astronaut's watch and has been in space," he gave it to me as a sign of his friendship and gratitude for what we were doing. Flustered, I returned the toast and gave him my watch as a token of our friendship. Lena, who had given the watch to me, was very unhappy to learn about this, especially when one of my colleagues much later happened to mention in passing that one could buy such Soviet watches in the Arbat for $10. I like to think I balanced out that mistake later when I bought a painting by a well-known Georgian artist. I saw it at an exhibit at the Georgian Cultural Center in Moscow. It was priced at one thousand rubles at a time when the official exchange rate was still $2 to the ruble. I gave our junior handler, who was known as a bit of a fixer, US $250 cash and just told him if he could get the painting and cover the costs with that, the rest was for him. He did. I recall I had to sign various documents at the airport when I was leaving with it. It was packed in a strong wooden box frame and must have weighed a hundred pounds. During these prolonged stays, during the evenings when we weren't entertaining or going to the Bolshoi, we watched television. It just so happened that the Gulf War was in the build-up phase and then in the fighting phases when I was there. It was quite an experience to be watching it on CNN while in a Soviet guesthouse.

The worrisome thing was that it was clear to me that we had several major problems with Dean's plan.

First, there was really no practical way at that time that the Soviet companies could break out "commercial" subsidiaries and organize them as Joint Stock Companies. The structures of the companies were extremely complex. Shifting legal ownership of assets would have been nearly impossible then. The accounting was incomprehensible to us— and not very relevant to them. And the labor rules made moving workers around very difficult. In addition, with very few exceptions, the companies did not have the facilities or the worker skills to make competitive commercial goods. And, if that was not enough, it was unclear who ac-

331

Related to our due diligence work on Soviet Companies Fund, we were given access to the premier companies in the Soviet space program. Here, we view one of the satellites at Machinostroyenia.

The Proton rocket production line at Khrunichev, the Soviet Union's principal manufacturer of launch rockets, at its plant near Moscow.

tually owned the assets. One mistake Dean made was working only with the Soviets despite being warned by several of them that, even before the collapse of the USSR, it was actually the Republics in which the plants were situated that owned the assets. I had urged him to establish himself with the Russian Federation especially, but to no avail, as Dean felt it would be a conflict of interest since Batterymarch had the mandate and support of the Soviet Union and not the Russian Federation. In the end, it was only LOMO, the Leningrad optical company and the space industry companies that did succeed in establishing subsidiaries that made joint ventures possible, albeit several years after Dean had given up trying.

Second, the Western multinationals had their own ways of organizing joint ventures and were not likely to be very receptive to ideas that were not invented in-house. Being taken on tours of the USSR at someone else's expense was one thing. Buying into a joint venture designed by a third party was something else.

The same thing could be said for the many institutional investors that went along with Dean on these trips. While some, including AT&T, were early participants in private equity funds in Russia, none did it the Batterymarch way. I think Gordon Binns and Dave Feldman gave Dean the benefit of the doubt at first, as they had benefited from going into his other emerging markets funds. But the Soviet Companies Fund ("SCF") was, to coin a phrase, "a fund too far," especially so early in the game.

It became evident that even Dean's strongest supporters as potential investors in SCF were beginning to see this. Dave Feldman told me at one point that, while AT&T would like to get into business in Russia, they would only do it their way. Gordon Binns finally warned Dean that he had to be careful not to misrepresent himself, or General Motors, to the Soviets. He was becoming concerned, as was I, that the Soviets thought Dean actually had the $1 billion he had promised. Gordon began to realize that they would not have been doing so much for Batterymarch had they not been convinced the money was there. And the very fact that GM and AT&T people came several times with Dean lent credence to that belief. I think Dean had convinced himself that he could pull off all three missions—establish commercial subsidiaries of Soviet companies, get the strategic partners to participate in the joint ventures, and deliver the institutional money to the SCF. I don't believe that there was any deliberate attempt to misrepresent. Dean was very persuasive and had pulled off miracles before.

At about this time Dean asked me to move to Moscow for the next six months to "finalize" things. I declined. That was the beginning of my exit from Batterymarch. But I still felt real friendship for my new Soviet friends, especially Vladimir Sidorovich, and a sense of obligation to help where I could. I remember two very interesting events in Washington in that connection.

The first was a visit to the U.S. that Dean arranged for the company bosses. While they were in DC, Lena and I held a reception for them. I don't recall who came from Moscow, but some 30 Soviets came to our house, along with Dean and several other Batterymarch people. It was a pleasant warm evening and most people moved from the living room to the garden. What made it memorable was a conversation Lena had with one of the company bosses. He had been looking up at our narrow four-floor old Victorian row house when he turned to Lena and asked: "How many families live in this house?" She, slightly taken aback, said: "Why just us: David and me and our two daughters." He looked at her and, with a wistful expression on his face, said: "You know, during my whole adult life I have dreamed of having a two-floor apartment." Such was life for a man in the USSR who ran a manufacturing business with at least 25,000 workers. But still, he had a dacha, his company aircraft and the usual car and driver.

The second was a time in mid-1991 when Vladimir Sidorovich came with a lawyer colleague from their ministry of foreign trade. With Vladimir was his wife, an accomplished concert pianist, about whom I shall write more later. The colleague spoke excellent English and had spent six months with a New York law firm on some exchange program. The reason for their visit was, on behalf of the Military Industrial Commission, to visit Senator Glenn to help them contact a U.S. company that specialized in disposing of out-of-date munitions—the old fashioned non-nuclear type. The Commission wanted to contract this company to do the same for them. They had asked Dean for help and he had arranged an appointment. I was asked to go along. This was held out as just asking for some cooperation in contacting an appropriate private company and encouraging them to take on the assignment of helping the Soviets get rid of a lot of WWII ordinance. Apparently, they had tried the U.S. Embassy in Moscow and were referred to Senator Glenn who, at the time, chaired the Senate committee responsible for oversight of this kind of thing. We showed up at the Senator's office at the appropriate hour, stated our business and waited to be presented. Instead, two young staffers came out to the reception area and asked why we expected the Senator to intercede. The short of it was they were referred back to the Embassy. That was strange, but it became even more so later on.

While they were in DC, the three of them stayed at our house: we considered Vladimir a friend by then and, besides, we found all the Russians good company. On the Sunday, we took them sailing in "Windrush," our sailboat. They really enjoyed this—sailing from Annapolis around to our favorite restaurant, the Riverside Inn, for crabs. The visit was all good clean fun. Then, about two weeks later, I received a call in the office. Ingrid said: "There is a Ms. ... who says she was from the FBI on the phone. Will you talk to her?" Ingrid looked very doubtful, no doubt wondering what I had done. So I talked to the lady. After the introductions she said she would like an appointment to interview me. I asked her what about. She said: "I can't tell you. It's classified and this is not a secure phone." I don't remember whether I was more curious or more concerned. In any event, we set a date. When she—a quite young, average height and appearance dark haired woman—came into my office she did exactly what you see FBI agents do in the movies. She said, "I'm Agent ..." and thrust her large badge and identification card at me. I followed the script and looked at it carefully and then looked up at her face. Then I broke from the script. Spontaneously, I just said: "But that isn't you, you look quite different." She turned a deep shade of red, paused a few seconds, and then said: "Oh, I see what you mean. I've just had a new hairdo. I guess it's much shorter than it is in my photo." After that, she got down to business quite professionally. She

A full-size model of the Mir—"Peace"—space station at Khrunichev. At the time of this picture,
Mir had been in orbit for about five years. (After 15 years in space, a planned "deorbit" and
break-up in earth's atmosphere occurred on 23 March 2001.)

wanted to know why I had those three Soviet citizens staying at our
house, why we took them sailing around Annapolis (and past the Naval
Academy) and why we had a large party for them. I explained all—starting with Batterymarch's activities and the meeting we were supposed
to have had with Senator Glenn. I concluded with the suggestion that
if the FBI was curious about all of this they should talk to the Senator
and to Dean LeBaron, or maybe the CIA should. She just took copious
notes and thanked me for my time. I should have thanked her. I have
been entertaining people with the story ever since. But the only consequence I am aware of is that Dean received an FBI cross-examination

of sorts about a month later. We both thought it was hilarious.

One never knows why security organizations do things the way they do and how seriously to take them. As an old military type, I always give them the benefit of the doubt. Vladimir's wife, Natalya Antonova, several years later when they were visiting us again in DC and well after the fall of the USSR, told us an even more curious story involving, indirectly, the KGB. At the time, she was an Assistant Professor of Music at Moscow University, as well as being one of the USSR's leading pianists. She was told she was being considered for promotion to full professor. While it would have been a great honor, she said it would also have involved joining the Communist Party. She didn't want to do that, but refusing to do so would have resulted in a KGB investigation. She didn't want that either, but how was she going to get out of the situation? After whispered conversations with some well-connected relatives in places that couldn't have been bugged, they came up with a solution. She went to the university authorities and said she just could not accept the promotion because she felt there were several people more deserving than she was. She said her conscience and her regard for the others were such that she could not live with herself if she was promoted when one of them should have been. She told us she never really knew whether they believed her story or not, but the whole matter was dropped. Either they knew what she was up to and were sympathetic, or they were good Communist Party men and really believed in the purity of her heart.

To complete my Russian saga, after about March 1991, Dean convinced his old Harvard friend and trusted personal lawyer, Paul Rugo, to spend six months in Russia. Consequently, I missed both the excitement of being there when the attempted "coup" to overthrow Gorbachev occurred and the difficulties between Dean and the Russians that resulted in Batterymarch pulling out. Dean's position was that his Soviet sponsors were becoming unreasonable. They started demanding payment for services they had agreed to provide, such as the house and cars, but were failing to deliver the Russian joint venture opportunities. I'm sure that was all true, but I suspect the Russians became difficult because Dean was not delivering on his promises. In any event, Dean's position was that Batterymarch withdrew because it was impossible to do business in Russia after the breakup of the USSR. That was also true. As I said at the beginning, Dean was years ahead of his time.

During this period, there were two other events that I remember well for quite different reasons. The first had to do with Dean's approach to marketing. The second was a strange skirmish with IFC.

Dean was always keen that I kept up my connections. He had wanted to bring Hathor, his 72-foot motor yacht, to Washington the September I joined Batterymarch to use to entertain my connections who would be visiting for the IMF/World Bank Annual Meeting. I said it was too close to my retirement to try and make such a splash. We agreed to do it the next year. Consequently, in August 1990, I began sending out invitations to a series of evening dinner cruises on Hathor. Unfortunately, nature intervened to complicate matters. First, there was a storm the week Hathor was en route from Boston so she was a day late arriving. Second, the weather got even worse for the first evening and we had to put on the show at home. But the last evening worked out quite well. Bill Ryrie and his wife Lady Kathleen joined us, as did about a dozen visiting banker friends. The Gills and the Tatas played host. Dean felt it was our show so didn't come. The only ones I remember though were Bill Emmott and Clive Crook, from the Economist. I remember that because they wrote an article about it. Our event that evening won what they called "the Economist's prize for the best private dinner of the week" at that year's Annual Meeting. Also they pointed out that, unlike other events put on by the international banks where the guests would spend just a few minutes before moving on to the next, Batterymarch had a captive audience for the evening.

The other event was related to my being asked to give testimony before a U.S. House of Representatives subcommittee that was concerned with IFC's access to the U.S. capital markets. Goodness knows why they were doing this. IFC had been selling bond issues in the market for some 30 years. I was a "friendly witness"—my choice of position. I was just supposed to be knowledgeable on the subject and was expected to say what I thought. I had to provide a written submission and then a verbal presentation before the Committee in open session. As it was the first time I had done anything like this, I made a serious effort to be thor-

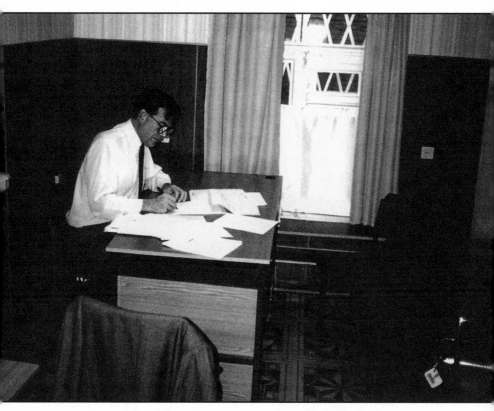

My desk was whatever space was available in our small office in Moscow.

ough. Basically, I was supportive of IFC, saying it was doing good things and deserving of access. Having been told that suggestions were welcome, I suggested that more equity financing by IFC would be beneficial to the developing countries and that some form of partial privatization of IFC should be considered. Much to my surprise, despite my having contacted my friends in IFC to seek factual information to back my supportive position, Bill Ryrie wrote to me to say I should not be appearing as a witness. This was quite curious as I was retired and could do what I chose. More importantly, how could a foreigner who was admitted to the country as a resident alien decline such a request? In the end, the subcommittee heard the witnesses, including me, asked a few questions,

The dacha, Batterymarch's elegant home in Sparrow Hills, Moscow.

Batterymarch's office at Merzlyakovsky Pereulok No. 8 in central Moscow.

and closed the meeting. The audience totaled about a dozen people, some of whom were from IFC and the rest, I assume, were connected to the other witnesses. All much ado about nothing in the end.

Finally, some time in the spring of 1991, I told Dean I wanted out. We agreed I would stay on as a "Senior Advisor" for a while and continue on the boards of the two funds. This was important to me because some of the investors were friends I had encouraged to join and I wanted to keep an eye on things. This I did. And I must admit I had some pleasant times at several board meetings in interesting places. About a year later, with the help of Dave and Gordon, Dean began planning to merge the two funds. He had already merged the Brazil fund into the Latin America fund, which made sense. It was obvious that this was not an idea that appealed to me. I talked to Jay about resigning. He suggested I should stick it out in the interests of our few investors. This I did but, presumably encouraged by Dean, Dave asked me to resign from the EFLA board. This I did. A few months later, when it became very apparent that AT&T and GM had agreed to the merger, I decided it was time to resign voluntarily from the CEF board: I saw no point in hanging around until asked to resign.

It turned out that several of the CEF investors made it clear that they did not see the connection between Latin America and the Commonwealth countries. When Dean asked IFC and Emerging Markets Managers (Antoine van Agtmael's company) to agree to the merger, they demurred and were bought out by GM and AT&T. The latter two had no objections and were quite happy with the terms. IFC had played its developmental role and had no justification or desire to continue in a rather complex new arrangement. Antoine had no desire to continue explaining to his clients why they should continue to pay two fees (his own management fee plus the fund management fee, even with his being much reduced) to be in funds investing in markets where his company could invest for them directly with lower costs. This was the ideal time for me to withdraw. This was my second retirement—at the more usual age of 65.

Much to my surprise, in the process of retiring, when I "signed off" the legal and tax stuff, I found that, besides a payment from the profit

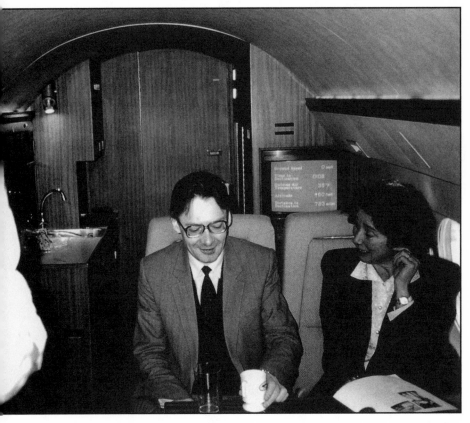

Vladimir Sidorovich with IFC's Farida Khambata en route to Moscow on the GII, February 1992. Over time, Vladimir would become a friend, and we would have occasion to see each other even after the conclusion of work on Soviet Companies Fund.

sharing plan, I also received one from the defined benefit pension plan. I didn't know I was signed up for it. It seemed rather irrelevant to me as a "pensioner" already when I started with BFM, so I had never inquired about pension arrangements. Even more surprising was about a year later when I received another check from the pension fund for about the same amount as the first check. Apparently there had been some miscalculation as to how much was due under the U.S. Labor Department rules. It seems Jim Ullman, who retired about the same time, discovered this.

342

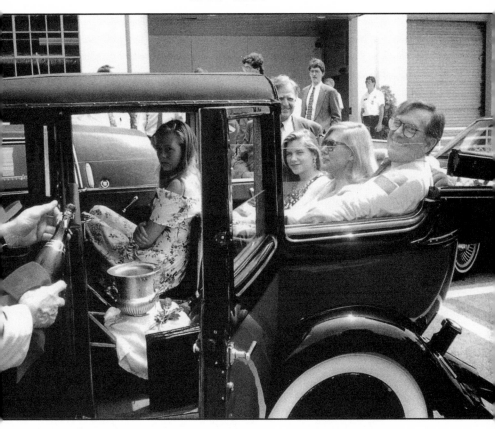

Going out in style, Dean arranged a memorable "farewell" from Batterymarch in 1991. On arrival in Washington in the GII, accompanied by a group of Batterymarch colleagues, I am met by an antique Rolls Royce carrying my dear Melissa and Lena. (A friend of Melissa's sits in the front.)

The actual parting on my retirement as a "Trustee" was quite a performance and showed Dean at his most charming best. It was clear that Dean felt that my departure was a bit of an embarrassment for him even if we had agreed at the start that I would join for only around three years. But he could not have been more gracious about it. On my last morning, he said he wanted to take me out to lunch before I went off to Logan Airport to fly home on the Eastern Airlines shuttle. The two of us got in his car and he drove out through the north of the city. I wondered where we were going until I recognized we were on the route to the small field where he kept his planes. We arrived there to be greeted by Tania, Marilyn, Jeannie, Jay and a few others. We all boarded the GII and had a great lobster lunch on the way to Washington National. Jeannie delivered several elegant going away presents. The one I really treasure is a two-volume, beautifully bound in red leather set of the 56 "Think Pieces" I had produced during my IFC time and while with Batterymarch. When we landed and parked, I thought there would be the final handshakes and waves. But no! Up to the plane drove an antique Rolls Royce with an open passenger compartment of the type from which "Royals" are seen waving. Waving a greeting to me from it were Lena and Melissa (by that time, Sarah was a Navy lawyer in Honolulu). Then there were the final waves as we drove off to Georgetown, champagne glasses in hand.

I was very touched by it all.

On The Side

During my first year with Batterymarch, with Dean's agreement, I handled a few IFC loose ends I had left behind. One was a project to establish a global debt conversion fund. Michael Barth and I promoted this idea as a follow-on from the Chile and Argentina debt conversion funds. Kumiko Yoshinari was our investment officer. We started with the EMGF strategy of forming a core group of sponsors. By the time I retired we had strong indications of support from Deutsche Bank, the Industrial Development Bank of Japan and Morgan Guaranty Trust—now J.P. Morgan—along with IFC, that made us a powerful foursome. I had told Dean I had to continue with this as I owed it to IFC, and Michael and I had just got the backing of DB's then chief executive. He was someone we had known for some time as he had been head of international previously and a supporter of EMGF. But it had really been Christian Strenger and Helmut Mader, president and head of the securities market department, respectively, of Deutsche Bank Capital Corporation in New York who had got the ball rolling. Both had been actively involved as early members of the EMGF sponsoring group and

With CEF Directors Neil Paterson (C) and Bishnodat Persaud (R) during the welcoming dinner before the meetings of Directors of EFLA and CEF in Shekou Industrial Zone in Shenzhen, China, March 1992.

shared our vision that the debt fund could be equally successful. By then EMGF had grown to almost ten times its original size.

I went to several organizing meetings in New York and Frankfurt with Michael and Kumiko. The initial plan was that the three banks would each contribute $50 million market value of their defaulted sovereign loans to LDCs, and IFC would pay in $50 million cash. From this starting point of $200 million, the sponsors would form a special purpose management company to be staffed by people we selected. There was an informal understanding that Michael would take a leave of absence from IFC to run this company. By early 1989, we thought we were on

345

Meeting of CEF Directors in Shekou, China, March 1992.

Steven Fang, assistant to the chairman of China Merchants Holding Company and a former intern at Batterymarch, provides an overview from a scale model of Shekou, March 1992.

Dean LeBaron (standing) and Yuan Geng, chairman of China Merchants and an influential contributor to economic reform in China, during a banquet hosted by China Merchants following the March 1992 meetings of Directors of EFLA and CEF.

epresenting IFC with Hans Horch (second left) at a Financial Times conference—"Doing Business ith Russia"—I would cross paths with Dean (right) at the Hotel Metropol in Moscow, November 1992.

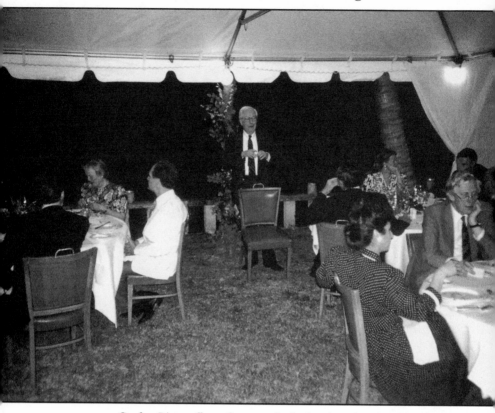

*Gordon Binns offers a few remarks during the welcoming dinner
before the EFLA and CEF Directors' meetings in Bermuda, April 1993.*

the verge of being ready to announce our plans and start approaching
other banks to raise a further $300 million. You can imagine our surprise
when Morgan Guarantee suddenly pulled out of the deal! One of their
senior people just told us that they had made this decision at a recent
meeting of their executive committee. Till then, we thought their commitment was firm. We tried to get several other U.S. banks to replace
them, including Citibank and Bankers Trust, all of whom declined. At
that point, we dropped the idea. This was very sad because, as demonstrated three years later by the performance of the Chile and Argentina
debt conversion funds, a global debt conversion fund would have been
a great success.

Another IFC matter was not exactly a loose end but rather a some-what prestigious (non-cash) bonus resulting from my former IFC role. I had the pleasurable experience of being invited to Venice in late 1988 to attend my last meeting of IOSCO's Executive Committee despite no longer being the IFC representative. Venice is always a pleasant place to visit and this time I went in the usual Batterymarch style in the Hawker. But it was just a one-day meeting, and I was not representing IFC. Rather, I was there at the request of the Chairman of the Brazilian securities commission, who could not go and who insisted I attend as his proxy. At the Brazilian Embassy in DC, I was given a very official piece of paper appointing me. It was rather flattering to be asked to rep-resent the Government of Brazil at an official international meeting. I was also especially pleased to able to earn my keep. IFC, for whatever reason, did not want to send Rudi van der Bijl, who the IOSCO board wanted to succeed me. This was a pity both for Rudi and IFC as Rudi knew more about it than anyone else in IFC. Inexplicably, IFC just dropped out entirely, losing a key connection to the international secu-rities markets.

At this meeting, curiously, the representative of the Quebec Securities Commission, who had elevated himself to the position of Secretary of IOSCO, made a formal proposal. This was to reduce the official lan-guages of IOSCO, into which all documents had to be translated, from four to two. He proposed dropping Spanish and Portuguese and leaving only English and French. (He probably said French and English but no matter!) The Italian and Australian members didn't say anything. Nor did the only Spanish speaker present—the Chairman of the Venezuelan securities commission—whose mind was elsewhere. Consequently, I made a statement. It went something like this. "As the representative of the Brazilian government, I wish to register Brazil's objection to this proposal. Spanish was the first official language, as the founding mem-bers of IOSCO were Argentina, Peru and Venezuela. English was the second. Portuguese became the third official language when Brazil joined. French became the fourth language only when France joined a few years ago. Consequently, the Brazilian chair considers it quite in-appropriate that it be proposed that two of the founding languages be dropped." There was a brief silence and then the Venezuelan member came alive and made a brief but impassioned speech in support of my position. The Australian chair quickly put the matter to rest by saying it was clear the consensus was to make no change to the official languages. I don't think my colleague from Montreal ever forgave me. He well knew I was from Toronto.

Thinking of Rudi in connection with IOSCO, he—IFC—asked me to attend another last meeting. This was a conference in Paris on savings mobilization that was sponsored by Credit Agricole, then France's largest bank. I remember only two things about it. First was a lunch at the bank hosted by Jacques Lyon, CA's very handsome and charming president. For reasons I never found out, but I suspect it was because Rudi had put him up to it, at one point he turned to me with a big smile and said: "David, you are a Canadian and you come to Paris very often. Why don't you speak French?" It was a good question, but it was odd coming from someone who hardly knew me. The second was the trip home. Dean, as usual, had insisted that I fly to Paris in the GII—all by myself. It seemed logical to give Rudi a lift home. On the way, we decided to stop off in Lisbon to see our old colleague and good friend Antonio Guerreiro. We had a delightful dinner in my favorite fish restaurant in Cascais and spent the night at the Flamingo, one of the most attractive beach hotels I know in Europe. It is a few minutes walk from the restaurant and situated on a cliff overlooking the harbor.

My only other extra-curricular involvements during my three years with Batterymarch were through Morgan Stanley, the Thai Fund, and Surinvest in Uruguay. I stayed on the Thai Fund board as IFC's nominee. This was very pleasing to me because it allowed me to continue seeing my Thai friends, Sukri and Snoh. As to Surinvest, I'm not sure whether IFC saw me as their nominee, or just accepted the fact that the management and the other shareholders wanted me to remain. As I shall be writing more about Surinvest in the next chapter, I shall say no more about it now.

Related to the Thai Fund was a less-than-happy incident just about a month after I retired from IFC. A few days before I attended a scheduled meeting of the Malaysia Fund board, IFC told me it was replacing me on that board with Michael Barth. I felt this was quite reasonable: I had already been asked to resign from the EMGF board to make way for Michael. What I did not expect was the way it was done. I arrived at the meeting intending to tell Dick Debs, the retired Morgan Stanley man who was chairman, that I was resigning. Before I could do so, he announced with some embarrassment that he had received a call from IFC telling him I was being replaced. He said that he understood their position but normally a new board member's name was submitted in advance. Thus the other board members would be able to go through the motions of voting to elect the new person who would then stand for election at the next shareholders' meeting. After the somewhat embarrassed silence around the table, Dick said that as IFC had been the sponsor of the fund, they might as well go ahead and agree. Dick made a very gracious speech of thanks for my services at the end of the meeting. Michael told me the next day that he was very upset about what had happened and had expressed his embarrassment about it to his bosses. That was probably why there was no move to have me removed from the Thai Fund board. But it did not prevent a rather surprising call from someone in the IFC Treasury department. It was to demand that I pay over immediately to IFC the last director's fee payment while I was still at IFC. "That's our property" was the curt statement. They seemed to have forgotten that I had always given the money to IFC when I received it each quarter even if I didn't always get around to doing it the same day the check arrived.

It was very gratifying to me that Morgan Stanley—Barton Biggs— asked me to continue to be involved with their funds. They could just as well have taken the view that as I had joined a competing firm and was promoting direct competition in the LDCs, I should resign. But Barton did not do so. Rather, when they launched their first global emerging markets fund—Morgan Stanley Emerging Markets Fund— Barton phoned me and asked me to go on the board. This was very pleasing to me. Then, the next year, I received another call, this time from Warren Olsen, Barton's professional fund President and chief fund administrative officer. He said Barton would like me to go on the board of his latest country fund venture—the Latin America Discovery Fund.

Batterymarch Financial Management

This raised again an early matter I discussed at the time with both Dean and Barton and then discussed again in this connection. Now, I would be on the boards of two funds operating in the same geographical market. Would either of them consider my involvement as a director of fund boards managed by the other as giving the appearance of a conflict of interest? Both agreed that, so long as appropriate disclosures were made, this would not be a problem.

I really enjoyed those three years back in the business world and working for a U.S. company that was also quite international in scope. I had forgotten that BFM also had quite an international group of people. Besides Americans and Canadians, there were at least one from each of Britain, France, India, Nepal, Russia, Switzerland and China. That was quite a mixture considering the professional staff was less than 40 at the end of my time. Anyway, when I turned 65, I felt it was about time to retire, more or less.

CHAPTER VII

Retirement,
After a Fashion:
1991–

Really retiring was not something I had in mind. Perhaps there would be more time with the family and a little more sailing. But keeping in touch with my friends and colleagues around the world and continuing to be involved with the financial markets was also important. Fortunately, my old relationships continued to be supportive so, as you will see, I continued as a financial frontiersman, even if at a slower pace.

I had heard from several older friends that, when one retired, you discovered quickly the difference between real friends and business friends. The latter tend to disappear rapidly when you are seen to be no longer in a position to do much business with them. That did not seem to be the case for me. A number of my old friends in IFC asked me to do advisory and consulting jobs, and serve on a few boards as their nominee. Also, both Batterymarch and Morgan Stanley allowed me to stay on their boards. Not only that but, within a few months, I was contacted by several people and organizations that I had not had much to do with before. To some extent, my "think pieces" must have helped a bit too. They had been widely circulated and they could give people an idea of what I could do for them.

On the subject of my "think pieces," looking through them again—in the two beautiful leather-bound volumes Batterymarch produced as one of my retirement presents—raised two rather disturbing thoughts.

353

Retirement, After a Fashion

The first was how my main themes—separation of functions in the financial markets and governance—ran through so many of them, making them all look too similar in content. The other was how many I had written on the subject of automation in the securities markets. This latter started with my IFC theme of promoting electronic trading markets, as they were known then. It ended with my Batterymarch time when it seems I was suddenly an expert on the subject of automating the investment management process. While three of them were published in financial journals, they didn't seem that profound when I read them again, some almost two decades later. In any event, in the end, it was corporate governance that became my principal stock in trade, with emerging markets, obviously, as the geographical beat.

My retirement business life started with my memberships on three of Morgan Stanley's and two of Batterymarch's emerging markets fund boards, plus Surinvest. Now, I'm down to one, Canada Investment Fund for Africa, after hitting a peak of 23 around 1996.

Coming back to the beginning of my story, how should I go about telling you all what I did when I went to work when I was really retired? To start, as you know, I didn't have an office to go to; unless you call my den at home an office. Many friends who had retired said it was good to have an office, if for nothing else as a place to go. Still, an office meant a secretary, paper work and a lot of unnecessary hassle. I concluded it might be easier to face up to learning how to use the word processor, get an extra telephone, and do it all in the comfort of home. Notwithstanding not going to an office, my dear daughters still continued to ask what I did—especially when I went to work for days or weeks in New York, Boston, Europe, South America and Asia. So, what I shall do is write about each retirement job separately, more or less in chronological order of when they started. This means starting with some of my IFC activities advising on capital markets development work, then more with Batterymarch, and then to the Inter-American Investment Corporation (BLADEX and Advent International) and Crown Agents (a U.K. government agency). After those experiences, I will get around to my initial functions as IFC's nominee on the boards of two Russian companies and three South American investment funds, as Commonwealth Development Corporation's ("CDC") nominee on the boards of two CDC private equity funds and finally my duties for the Commonwealth Secretariat that included being on the board of the Mauritius Fund. The CDC connection became Actis, CDC's management company spin-off that became the manager of the two CDC funds—that is, Commonwealth Africa Investments ("Comafin") and South Asia Regional Fund ("SARF"). CDC remained the major shareholder in both and thus called the shots—including my position on the boards. My remaining activity is chairman of the special purpose company that manages the Canada Investment Fund for Africa—CIFA. It was called CIFAGP, the GP meaning "General Partner." As I was beginning to discover, both managers ("GPs") and investors ("LPs" or Limited Partners) were beginning to prefer the partnership structure over the limited liability company structure.

IFC—Consulting

During the first few years IFC asked me to do a lot of advisory work for them. This was quite interesting in some cases, but it involved a lot of report writing, which was less fun.

Cyprus came first. Doug Gustafson, IFC's regional director for that part of the world, said the Cypriot financial authorities wanted to establish Cyprus as a regional financial center. The local Development Finance Corporation ("DFC"), majority owned by IFC and the Cyprus government, was charged with preparing recommendations for the Ministry of Finance and had asked Doug to recommend an "expert" to help them. He suggested me. They knew me and I knew them from my IFC Capital Markets Department ("CMD") days when we established together the first investment bank in Cyprus. I visited three times in the process of doing this advisory work. It was pleasant to see old acquaintances again. I remember still one very pleasant dinner with the head of the DFC and his predecessor. The latter was then Minister of Defense. We had an interesting discussion on Cyprus' military power, or lack of it, as compared to Turkey, and the threats they faced.

My recommendations were to start by strengthening governance and the financial professions—accounting and legal personnel. All very obvious points and straight from CMD's recipes, but I suspect not much attention was paid to them. What they ended up doing was acting more as a waypoint for money going to and from Russia and India. That is, Cyprus became a tax haven.

Lebanon was next. The task, for IFC's Middle East Department, was to advise the central bank on steps to develop their stock market. This was really enjoyable. Lebanon had always been one of my favorite countries. It was wonderful to be able to return after close to a 20-year absence. The young investment officer who shepherded me around, Michael Ayoub, was a Lebanese who had gone to the American University there and been both bright and lucky enough to win a scholarship to MIT. He was very young at the time for an IFC professional, having only recently gotten his Master's degree, but what he lacked in experience he made up for with enthusiasm, hard work and a lot of local knowledge.

But, sadly, Lebanon then and now remains a tragic country. One supposes that now a majority of the population is Muslim, but split between the two usual warring groups. Still, the Christians, who for years had run the place and prevented a census in order to continue the facade that it was a majority Christian country to keep control, also split. One can only say that it is in better shape than its Muslim neighboring countries are now.

During our visits, besides introducing me to the Minister of Finance, the Governor of the Bank of Lebanon, on whose behalf we were working, and many other luminaries, Michael introduced me to his parents and many of his old friends and their parents. The graciousness and hospitality of the Lebanese always touched me. Michael's crowd was a good example of this: an Old World level of courtesy that one does not see so much these days. This was also his first visit back to Beirut in some years, so our visits to his old friends, whom he had not seen since the middle of the civil war, were especially touching. Two of them were girls in their twenties. As they were single, they lived with their parents so the visits were teas with their families. Both these girls had stayed in Beirut through the war by choice. One had been a journalist and one an ambulance driver. Both were modest about their lives in that period, claiming they were just living their lives as were most Lebanese. But I could see that they and their families had the means to have left had they so chosen. It is hard for a Westerner to understand the Middle Eastern way of thinking: how some could be such brutal extremists while others were kind, gentle and peaceful, but still very patriotic. I still have the feeling that the Muslim/Islam devotees today are much like 16th century Catholics must have been.

Once, Michael took me for a drive and lunch in a small village in the mountains. It was in an excellent old hotel with fine food and service. On another occasion, one Sunday, we drove to Sidon, about 20 miles south of Beirut. What I remember were the truly amazing traffic jams. On the two-lane highway there were often five lanes of traffic, much helped by the two half-shoulders, but much hindered by the series of roadblocks courtesy of the Syrian army. By that time, Beirut itself was just beginning to be rebuilt, but much of the old city and the harbor area was still a wasteland. What had been restored quickly were many excellent restaurants. One couldn't find much better in Paris.

On the business side, the mission was to rebuild the local securities market. It had never been much because the Lebanese economy was always based on trade and tourism. There were all the trappings of a stock exchange, but not many stocks. I was to give strategic advice on how to get more listings and more investors. The main issue was whether they should follow the U.S. or the French system. They chose the French. That was not surprising considering the strong French connection and that the French government agreed to pay for the exercise. While we were there, they also asked me to review the plans for launching a new real estate company to be called Solidaire. This was the dream of the then Prime Minister, who was assassinated last year while PM again, who had made a fortune as a contractor in Saudi Arabia. The business was to finance the reconstruction of the city. Owners of the ruined buildings were to contribute their property in exchange for stock. Then there was to be an "IPO" for some $600 million—a lot of money in those days. It was a truly grand scheme—I saw the drawings and models produced by the French architects who were doing the work—but it seemed overly ambitious, financially, for such a small country. The Solidaire people asked me to be one of their financial advisors, but I declined, as it was clearly a ploy to get IFC support. But the deal was done and the money was raised. I suspect most of the cash came from the Saudis. So, the Beirut stock exchange's market capitalization went from around $50 million to over $700 million, almost overnight. But there were still less than half a dozen stocks. The Lebanese followed the general Gulf countries' principle of allowing only other Arabs as foreigners able to buy their listed stocks. This did not help the price of Solidaire, which went slowly downward for the next several years. They did however, issue warrants that foreigners could buy; they could not exercise the warrants but rather only sell the warrants to Lebanese or other Arabs. Still it was a way to play the local market.

We called on all the local bankers, who were making more money than ever, although it still remained unclear how. It was amazing. The six or so main banks had all survived the ravages of the war, at least financially, but not their offices; they were all in new office buildings. IFC had provided one of its SMSE (for small businesses) loans to a group of them. They were all complaining, as Lebanese do, that the IFC interest rate was too high. IFC's solution was simple: get cheaper money from someone else if you can and we will cancel our loans. The Bank of Lebanon governor was a very charming man, youngish, good looking and very hospitable even by Lebanese standards. He was also one of the smarter central bankers in the region. He and his equally charming wife entertained me at home once. On another occasion when he felt he should but couldn't, he arranged for me to receive an invitation to a very elegant dinner being put on by who I discovered was the "Perle Mesta" of Lebanon. He had arranged for me to be taken to this by another couple who were friends of his. The governor's driver took me in his official new Cadillac to their house to meet them and have drinks first. Their house was a lovely large old place with a beautiful garden, surrounded by a formidable stone wall that had somehow survived the war. It could have been a mansion in Paris. They explained that our hostess entertained a dozen or more people for dinner three or four times a week. She was single, in her sixties, very rich and didn't like to go out. So her dinners were a form of small open-house affairs. But she always also invited strangers to the city who were friends of her friends. Apparently, I qualified. That dinner was quite a lavish affair with some 20 guests. Her house—actually, it was a mansion with about five acres of gardens —was in the hills. There was a magnificent view of the city and the ocean.

From the above, you could not but get the impression that my visits to Beirut consisted of nothing but social activities. That is so and there are two reasons. First, the hospitality of the people was so outstanding that it had to be recognized as well as appreciated. Second, in practice, there was just not that much one can do in the financial market there.

Saudi Arabia. I think the reason I was asked there was that I had been the keynote speaker at a conference in Abu Dhabi in 1988 on the subject of privatization and structural adjustment. As stated before, Riyadh is not my favorite city. To paraphrase an old saying: "first prize is one day in Riyadh; second prize is two days in Riyadh." I won second prize twice. A more enjoyable part of my experience there resulted from my agreeing to call on Advent's representative. He was an American called Rosenberg and he and his family lived in an American enclave. It could have been a suburb of any American big city and seemed to be considered sovereign U.S. territory. Even liquor was consumed openly in the houses, something that, had it occurred in a house anywhere else, would have gotten the people arrested and imprisoned. At the time, Advent was trying to get a contract to invest in Saudi companies the money that was to come from some counter-trade deal with one of the U.S. defense companies. In the course of this he introduced me to the then defense minister, who was one of the royal princes. He also had some role in the financial markets, which was the excuse for the meeting with him. He was a charming urbane fellow. I assume he knew more about military matters than he did about financial markets.

I called on the Governor of the Saudi Arabian Monetary Authority ("SAMA") again, as it ran the local stock market. This was an embarrassing experience. After I introduced myself he said: "You don't remember me, do you?" I was mystified and probably looked it. So he reminded me that we had met at the Abu Dhabi conference. He had been a deputy governor of SAMA when I had been there previously. The Saudis had a fully automated trading system, of which they were rightly very proud. At that time, it had a market capitalization of some $20 billion, making it one of the largest in the emerging markets after South Korea and Taiwan. I also visited the head of the Gulf Cooperative Committee ("GCC") who had actually asked IFC for me to come. He arranged for me to visit the three largest banks (two of which were joint ventures and run by secondees from their U.S. parents). These three were also big in the money management business and, after the European fashion, in stock broking. I was also sent to meet the CEO of one of the listed companies, a conglomerate, as I recall it. As was usual in Saudi, I really didn't pick up any useful insights from any of these people. Probably this was why IFC didn't bother to send one of its own people with me.

Compared to Lebanon, Saudi Arabia is a large country with quite a lot of big companies. But all tend to be either offshoots of the oil industry, contractors or service companies. As seems to be still the case in all the oil rich—and some of the poorer—Arab countries, they don't really produce much of anything besides oil. So they end up with one basic export and use the money to import practically everything they consume, except services. I was interested to find they had a special company, also government run, that was the local, and only, share-registry company. Unlike most other countries in the West, banks could not act as share registrars and no company could keep its own share registry. All of this was quite advanced. It was a pity that their market, as with all the others in the Gulf and the Middle East, except Jordan, could not be accessed by foreign investors unless they were Arabs. In the end, I submitted a short report, but I forget what I recommended. I doubt if anyone paid much attention. As I recall it, the only comment from the main recipients (SAMA and GCC) was that it should have been longer.

Thailand came next. This was an exercise to which Michael Barth, who was then Associate Director of CMD, invited me. The task was to advise the Thais on the development of a long-term bond market. It was fun to go back to Thailand with Michael. While I had been there twice with Morgan Stanley since retiring from IFC, it had been some six years since I was last there doing a developmental job. We saw all our old friends, including Dr. Snoh and Sukri. But there were no really eventful things to record. At the time, everything was going well economically and financially for Thailand so fine tuning their securities market had high priority more for IFC than it did for them. I don't think our efforts had any impact. The only thing I remember was that traffic in Bangkok was even worse. Instead of having to allow half an hour to get from one address to another, it now took 45 minutes or more. Expressways and overhead rail lines were being built, but very slowly.

However, we made our ritual calls on the governor of the Bank of Thailand, the Minister of Finance, some of their underlings and talked learnedly about the need for domestic long-term debt instruments so companies could borrow at fixed rates in baht. Everyone understood and supported the theory that capital investment in such long-term assets as cement plants or factories should be financed by equity or long-term debt—"matching maturities" and "matching currencies" to use the technical terms. But the financial officials of the borrowing companies were quite happy to continue borrowing dollars short-term at floating rates that the foreign banks lavished on them at interest rates far lower than a baht rate would have been. The Thais and the foreign banks didn't learn the lesson until their financial crisis in 1997-1998.

Argentina was another story. This was much more fun for me as it was a follow-on from both an earlier exploit concerning "privatizations" and my involvement with the "country fund" business. Julio Lastres was the CMD manager for South America then. He asked Frank Veneroso and me to help him with a very grand scheme. It was to establish a "national investment fund" whose assets would be the $2 billion-odd value of shares in Argentine companies that had already been privatized but in which the government still owned minority positions. The Minister of Finance had told IFC and others about their desire to sell, as they needed the cash. I was especially pleased that IFC was promoting this because it was a theme of one of my "think pieces"—to establish what I called at the time "National Investment Trusts" that would hold assets set aside for sale by the government where the government would be the initial holder of the shares of the Trust. The idea was the manager

361

of the Trust could sell assets for cash and use it to buy listed securities to build a more diversified portfolio. The government, as controlling shareholder, could sell shares in the Trust to willing buyers, and "cause" the Trust to pay it dividends from sales or out of earnings. The scheme would have two advantages: first, permit privatization in an orderly way probably at better prices than mass sales; and, second, build a major national "country fund" which would strengthen the local equity market. So, here was a first chance to see if it could work in practice. In the end it didn't happen because a U.S. bank offered what the government thought was a better deal. But I was pleased to see that several Eastern European countries did use the same approach in later years more or less successfully—but without my help.

I must have visited Buenos Aires five or six times with Julio and his colleagues over the year we were involved. Julio was one of IFC's better entrepreneurs. He had negotiated a contract that would have provided IFC with a very substantial fee if we could establish this fund or contribute in some other way to achieving attractive prices for their shares. The "or" part turned out to be very important, as you will see. We started by developing the plan. Our plan was exactly as just described. Once we had the plan on paper, and a strategy to implement it, we presented it to the then Minister of Finance, Domingo Cavallo. I recall well our meeting in his office with him and a few of his assistants. We had Dan Adams, who had risen to the rank of Vice President for Latin America, Julio, Frank and me. Much to my pleasure and surprise; he gave us the go-ahead. I suppose on the old theory that no good deed should go unpunished, Dan, after thanking him, changed the subject to Argentina's current problem—the falling foreign exchange reserves caused in part by the fixed exchange rate to the U.S. dollar and the consequent fall in exports. Dan gave the standard WB/IMF line that the dollar-peso link had solved many problems, especially inflation, but it had now caused this bigger problem. Consequently, Argentina should cut the tie. This was ignored then but they did it some years later.

Our next step in the program was to seek out fund managers who might take on the job. Our short list included Capital Group, Templeton, Scudder (because the latter managed a specialized Latin America utilities company fund for IFC) and Morgan Stanley. All had done Latin America funds and there were really no other credible choices. So, Julio and a couple of people from the Argentine Ministry of Finance and I made the rounds in New York. This was rather fun. But, as we knew they were all competent to do the job, our questions really only related to the strategies they would establish to manage the portfolio; how they would go about selling shares of the fund to maximize cash to the Ministry of Finance; and, finally, what fees they would charge. I think we were most impressed with the responses of Scudder and Morgan Stanley ... the former because they clearly had the best understanding of what was needed, and the latter because Barton Biggs offered the lowest fee proposal. Julio thought this was because Barton saw this fund as a great opportunity for Morgan Stanley's corporate finance business and was willing to manage the fund as a loss leader for them. I rather doubted that; I suspected Barton had forgotten that part of the deal was that the management fee had to be shared with others, including IFC, leaving only half for the manager. Capital Group didn't seem interested, for reasons that weren't clear. Templeton, not surprisingly, asked the highest fee. But the real problem with them was that Mark Mobius only participated by phone and the ranking Templeton man—actually, the number two of Franklin Management that had recently taken over Templeton—seemed to be distracted during most of our presentation.

We were all very pleased about having two good proposals to bring back to Cavallo. But, unfortunately, Chemical Bank, who was also a player with its own proposal to sell these bits and pieces, was able to outbid us. While we might have been able to provide more money, it would have taken a few years and we could give no guarantees. Chemical, on the other hand, was able to produce a couple of immediate firm bids for some of the companies. Cavallo, not unreasonably, concluded that some cash in-hand was more important. So we lost the deal. Fortunately, Julio had been smart enough to make an arrangement with Chemical beforehand that, were they to get the deal, IFC would get a fee. Exactly how this came about was not clear to me, but I assume both sides felt they were getting some downside protection.

A pleasurable part of it was that Julio had arranged a very attractive fee arrangement for me whereby I would receive what was in effect a bonus for achieving results. Cavallo's acceptance of our proposal qualified me for the first half of this. Had we actually got our fund idea established, I would have received another bonus payment. I'm not sure how he did this as IFC consultants normally were paid only the paltry daily fee. I didn't ask; I just filled out the forms he gave me.

Mexico. The next year, after Mexico's latest financial collapse, Julio asked me to participate in a similar program there. With some mixed feelings, I decided to decline. The intent here was to find ways to bailout the leading Mexican banks, in which IFC had some investments. From my experience with Advent in Mexico, and my previous knowledge of how the banks were financed and how they operated, I was not very sympathetic to seeing the owners bailed out. I certainly did not want to be part of the process. But, Julio did undertake the job and completed it very successfully for IFC. IFC's share of the bailout money was actually guaranteed, indirectly, by the Mexican government. Normally, IFC is not allowed to accept governmental guarantees. While it would have been an interesting experience, the end result was such that it was just as well that I passed. I would have been a nuisance for both IFC and the Mexicans.

Chile. My next exploit for IFC was in Chile. I was asked by Rudi van der Bijl to participate in a review of the two Chilean debt conversion funds and their management company. The intent was to decide how the management company could find new business once the two funds were liquidated. As I had mentioned in an earlier chapter, these debt conversion funds were amongst my last IFC activities. Four years later, they had each tripled in net asset value, making their investors—mainly Midland Bank—a return on their original loans of 100% or so compared to the 8% they would have earned if the loans had been paid off at maturity. Rudi had me visit Chile about three times to attend the funds' board meetings and to look over the management company. Moneda Asset Management, as it was called, was still run by Sergio Undurraga and Antonio Cruz. They were still the same solid and knowledgeable professionals I remembered from some four years back. They were doing a first class job, but had paid little attention to what they would

do next. My recommendation to Rudi was that they should try to establish two successor funds, one for foreigners, aiming at the usual pension fund market, and a domestic mutual fund. Curiously, despite the growing sophistication of the Chilean market there were no mutual funds of consequence in Chile other than the local pension fund schemes. These had made the whole population aware of the merits of mutual funds. But somehow none of the local managers had thought of following through.

As I have probably made clear already, Chile, in my view, is a rather colorless country and the people we met there in the financial world, while bright, well trained and hard working, tended to be on the quiet side. Consequently, I cannot remember any specific events worth recording beyond the cold business facts. But, at least, Sergio and Antonio, pushed hard by Rudi, did eventually begin to expand their horizons. So, IFC remained as a shareholder and Rudi stayed on their board. Thanks to Rudi again, and to Jay Tata, I was later asked to serve on the board of the fund for foreign investors they established a year or so later. I will get to that in due course.

Poland. Some time after my departure from IFC, the Poles decided to set up a stock exchange and requested assistance from IFC. Although after my time, the following typifies a general understanding of capital markets in many of the emerging economies. Farida Khambata was asked to go to Poland to start the dialogue with the newly established Polish SEC. She met with the gentleman concerned and his entourage: "Initially he was very cordial but as the meeting progressed and as I tried to sketch out a possible regulatory framework, it was clear he was upset. The more I discussed, the angrier he became. For the life of me I did not know what was causing the grief as he did not seem to object to anything in particular. Finally, he could not contain himself and he screamed: 'You do not want us to progress. The U.S. is the world's most free market and all you have been doing is to talk to us about regulations.' The penny finally dropped in that he equated a free market with one that was completely unregulated! Once I understood the concern it was possible to explain that any market needed regulations. Once this was accepted, peace was restored and we got on famously. Towards the end

of the assignment he said he would like to establish a stock exchange and we were discussing where it should be housed. Suddenly he said: 'I have it. We will put it in the Lenin Museum.' In the Museum, I gasped. 'Yes', he responded: 'We will put Lenin's statue in the garden and house the exchange in the Museum!'" And so it was done.

Russia. My last assignment was really the most fun, the most challenging and the most frustrating, but I will be forever grateful to Cesare Calari for asking me to undertake it. This was to help him advise the new Russian Federation government on setting up their securities market. Cesare, at the time, was the CMD Manager for Eastern Europe. This exercise started, I think, in 1992 and, despite the many man-years of effort by IFC and many other organizations, it is still a work in progress. In 2008, 15 years later, the Russian market was still at best immature. But, when one considers where it started—there was no rule of law, let alone contract laws or property laws and no people who understood how it should operate or, indeed, why one was needed—much progress had been made.

Cesare asked me to do this because I was the only person associated with IFC who had had any previous on-the-ground experience there. For all the obvious reasons, bringing Russia into the World Bank/IFC fold had top priority, so no effort or expense was spared. The trouble was every development institution wanted to make their mark doing the same thing. Besides Hans Horch and me—and eventually literally hundreds of other IFC consultants over the next several years—the WB, the IMF, USAID, the German, French, British, Canadian, Japanese and some other national development agencies plus many NGOs including Harvard University were all represented in force. Some of them were doing one or two very useful technical tasks—from improving farming technology to trying to establish savings and loan banks, to building a real central bank. Others, like the WB and the IMF, were trying to redesign the entire financial system. IFC concentrated on the securities market and privatizations. The Russians had just launched their voucher system where every citizen received vouchers entitling them to bid at auctions for small pieces of state enterprises. (Dean LeBaron would have been pleased to discover one of his ideas was being used

even if in a way quite different from his plan.) The IFC teams did a great job in that area, organizing real auctions, not just for shares in companies, but also for such physical things as trucks and tractors so individuals could set up small businesses. This was where the hundreds of consultants were needed around the country.

My job for Cesare was to design a securities market infrastructure, prepare a critical path plan to implement it, and help IFC convince the government to execute the plan. The first two parts were easy. The old CMD had prepared such plans for several countries so the building blocks were there. It was mainly a matter of tailoring a plan to local circumstances. That was easier said than done, because local circumstances changed day by day. On the other hand, as it was a case of starting from scratch, there were very few bad rules or vested interests that had to be countered—except of course the basic vested interest of those who didn't like change. That said, it was fascinating to see how things had changed since my last visit for Batterymarch only two years previously. However, it took about a year and some four visits to finalize IFC's recommendations and submit a written document. Looking through it now I note it was dated 1 April 1993, from hindsight a date that could not have been more appropriate. While much of the infrastructure—the laws, regulations and institutions required—had been in place for years, the political will to live by the basic rule of law was building still, only slowly. From what one reads currently, there is still a long way to go. As you will hear later when I write about the National Registry Company on whose board I served for seven years, I know this from first-hand experience.

Again, it was an opportunity to see a country from the inside. "See" was, and is, the operative word. One saw a lot and heard a lot. But, if you thought you had learned what was going on, you were dreaming. In any event, during the process of doing this job, Cesare and his colleagues took me to meet all of the movers and shakers of the time, the usual government officials, including the crowd looking after the privatization program. The Russians we met were all very bright, very highly educated and quite fluent in English. They knew financial markets were something they had to have, and securities markets were an important part of them. Many had read a lot about them and some had visited Western markets. But, as mentioned earlier, political will is the most important starting point and it was clear there wasn't much of that. But they did want the benefits of the end results, even if they didn't understand the importance of equity in the broader societal sense. .Looking back years later, I think of my fondest, and least fond, memories of those times in Russia. Here are some.

The first was a simple one: staying at a new Russian hotel—the Metropo—for the first time. It was large and elegant, with excellent service but mediocre food. I remember arriving direct from DC one evening at about 7.00 PM local—and 3.00 AM my time. Feeling a little hungry I went to the smaller of the two restaurants and ordered an omelet. The waiter pointed out that omelets were not on the menu. I suggested they could probably produce one anyway. He called over the maître d'. The same conversation was repeated. Then I called for one of the managers. I exclaimed that they must have eggs in the kitchen for breakfast! He agreed. Therefore, as they also had cooks in the kitchen, one of them, surely, could make an omelet. He gave in and I finally got my omelet. It was perfect. This wasn't a matter of bad service; all three were courteous and fast. They were just still used to the Soviet way of doing things.

On the business side, we attended several privatization auctions where the bidders were using vouchers. IFC had done a great job of organizing these, especially outside of Moscow. On one occasion, Claudia Morgenstern, then a CMD associate director, took me to Nizhny Novgorod, the Detroit of Russia, previously called Gorky. Then, in the Soviet days, it was a closed city, as I found when we tried to go there during my Batterymarch days. We called on the mayor and the governor of the Province to explain what we were doing. At least that was what my IFC handlers told me was one objective. The other was for me to get a sense of how the vouchers were handled as a form of money to buy assets. This was important as one of the items on the work program I had prepared was, of course, establishing a mutual fund industry. No securities market should be without one! And they were certainly good vehicles for promoting private savings in securities as every citizen had vouchers and few had cash. The more enterprising of the mutual fund promoters set up voucher funds. You could sell vouchers for cash—a dollar or two worth of rubles if I remember correctly—so it was easy to talk people into exchanging their vouchers for, say, five dollars of so-called par value of the fund shares the management companies were selling. The smarter fund managers ended up with millions of vouchers this way and then used them to buy big stakes in individual companies. I'm sure the managers did better than the investors but, again, that is another story.

I was taken to see the CEO of one of the largest companies in Nizhny to discuss what he thought of the program now that his company was privatized through an auction. Through his interpreter we discovered that the company's workers had all followed orders and turned in their vouchers for stock. At the following shareholders' meeting they followed orders again and voted for all their bosses as directors and managers. What had upset the CEO was that one of the voucher funds had bought up a large amount—some 10%—of the shares outstanding, but the manager of the fund didn't offer to call on him. The CEO said: "When I heard what he had, I sent him a message, telling him to come to my office the next week. He didn't show up! How can you be expected to deal with shareholders like that?" He was a tough, burly character with a ferocious frown and a booming voice. Of course, by our standards, they were both wrong. A new 10% shareholder should want to interview management—preferably before buying the shares. The manager should seek out his new major shareholders, not expect them to seek an appointment with him. Back to reality, I could well see the manager playing the popular game Russian bosses played a lot, then, when they were unhappy with a big shareholder. He would be barred from shareholders' meetings. Or he would find his shares did not appear on the company share registry. Or, if it was in a city like Nizhny where the bosses controlled everything, his plane would not be allowed to land. In the process, people got killed sometimes. But having seen some of the people that did elbow their way into companies like that, I had some sympathy for the old-line bosses.

On the other hand, Nizhny had a very enlightened governor who, at least for a few years, was a strong supporter of IFC's program to establish voucher auctions. To digress a bit, the relationship with the governor ended up as a bit of a scandal. He took off with an IFC lady and the two of them apparently ended up working for a Western company with which they had "connections" and which had benefited from some considerable contracts from the Nizhny government. The lady in question was well known locally as the only foreigner who had brought her dog with her. I remember meeting the dog.

The auctioneers that IFC trained became the builders of the Nizhny stock exchange. IFC called it a stock exchange but it was really a continuous auction house for anything that two people were willing to trade. Seeing it in action was quite an experience. I was rather proud of my IFC connection, seeing dozens of these young college-aged kids who were teaching the Russians the basics of economics and markets at the ground level. And Nizhny then, in 1992, was very much the Wild West of Russia. (Well, Siberia was even wilder, I was told, but I never got there.) There was one hotel and two restaurants in the town. The hotel was a remnant of the Soviet days. The best one could say for it was that it was reasonably clean. The dining room was something else. They had lots of eggs, but not much else besides potatoes. Unfortunately, the eggs were always well done. In fact, they were usually burned black around the edges. Breakfast—burned eggs, sausage, bread and tea—cost less than 50 cents, but it still was not exactly a bargain. But the good news was that the two restaurants were clearly owned by the local business Mafia—lots of very good food, fairly well cooked and lots to drink. In both, the bars were bigger than the dining areas and much more crowded. On my first occasion at one for dinner I did my usual thing and just asked the barman to put the ingredients for my martini on the counter so I could make it myself. In Moscow I had trained a few bartenders on the finer points of making decent martinis and my pupils had seemed to welcome my efforts to teach them. This was not so in Nizhny. Worse, I was soon the center of attention of half a dozen large young men who were clearly not impressed. I beat a hasty retreat.

In Moscow, our counterparts included the Harvard development people who were advising the government. The one who was in charge was Jonathan Hay, a tall gangling young lawyer who always looked as if he had slept in his clothes. They worked for Anatoly Chubais, the man

Yeltsin had put in charge of the privatization program. They both—Chubais and Hay—exuded confidence and reliability. They seemed to get things done and their support clearly helped getting the central bank and ministry of finance people to go along with our ideas. But, as it turned out later, they, including one of the other senior Harvard people, had succumbed to the local "standards." Chubais became famous for several things. First, he organized the "loans for shares" plan which was really a scheme to let the budding "oligarchs" buy the biggest companies in Russia for next to nothing. Another was to boast in 1998 that he had "conned the IMF out of $20 billion." Jonathan Hay and one of his Harvard colleagues were caught in very bad conflict of interest situations where it was believed they used insider information to help associates became very successful speculators in the government bond market. But this was the way Russia was then. A more general example of bad practices was the way the so-called brokerage firms operated. One of their popular practices was buying up the small shareholdings of factory workers at a fraction of their value on behalf of the company bosses. Brokerage commissions of ten percent or more were considered quite reasonable.

It was sad, though, to see the new growing poverty that was the flipside of how the new wealthy were living. It was awful to see the old pensioners in the streets selling their belongings, or just trying to trade them for food. It might have been considered ghoulishly funny to see an old pair of shoes offered, but not so funny when you saw what was obviously a mother's treasured jewelry going the same way. At that time, ten dollars a month was enough to live on for the average older Russian. Fortunately, rent and utilities were practically free. There was serious crime in the streets. According to my IFC friends, I was the only foreigner they knew who had been more than two weeks in Russia who hadn't been mugged at least once. One thing that got on the nerves of many Russians we met was how most of the money being spent by the West in supposedly helping them was actually being paid to the literally thousands of foreign consultants, advisers and staff people employed by the hundreds of different organizations operating in Russia. I suppose the "trickle down theory" applied, as these people were in Russia and they spent a lot of their money there; some even employed Russians.

As a last observation on Russia in that period, I will recount a comment by the chairman of Russia's then equivalent of the U.S. Senate Finance Committee. With three of my handlers from IFC we had called on him to explain our recommendations and seek his support in getting the Duma to pass a few related laws. After we had made our case he looked at us, sighed and said something like: "I'm sure you are sincere, and that what you are suggesting is sound. But what I don't think you realize is that none of us here really understand any of this and that we have more important things that have to be done now. Worse is that every month I receive at least one delegation like yours, anything up to 20 people telling me what I should do. Then they go away, never to be heard of again. On top of that, one group will be telling me to do one thing and often the very next group will be telling me to do the opposite! What do you expect from me?" I sympathized as I remembered meeting a group from the IMF who had prepared a large document as a blueprint for bank deposit insurance. It was a fine concept but in talking to them I discovered that they had no idea of the quality of the Russian banks' assets and thus no idea what the cost of the insurance would be or who would pay. As they said, thinking about that was the job of another group.

My involvement in Russia was to continue, but in a different way, as I shall report later.

FMO and IFU

During this period I also spent some time with both FMO, the Dutch IFC-type entity, and IFU, the Danish equivalent.

I had gotten to know Frank Smit, the COO of FMO, quite well over the years as FMO invested in several of my IFC projects. In my retirement he had asked me to conduct what amounted to some training programs for his investment officers. The subject was venture capital investing. Sven Riskar, who had been an IFC vice president, learned of this so I ended up doing the same thing for IFU as well. I found both organizations and their people to be very easy to deal with, and it was always pleasant to go to Copenhagen and to The Hague.

It must have been a couple of years later when Robert Binyon of CDC, who I will write more about later, asked me to line up a speaker on private equity for the annual get-together of the CEOs of the European "DFIs"—Development Finance Institutions. I suggested Peter Brooke, but Peter couldn't make the date, so Robert asked me to do it. Apparently CDC was in charge of that year's meeting. This was another very pleasant exercise. The meeting itself was held in Helsinki, a city I hadn't visited since 1952 and about which I will write more later. There were more DFIs in Europe than I knew existed. That is not just the British, Dutch, German, French and Danish, but also the Swedish, Norwegian, Swiss, Austrian, Spanish and Italian. They were a great crowd to be with and asked me to join them for their entire agenda. The last evening—it was in June I think—we had a great cruise around Helsinki harbor and a fine dinner at the Helsinki Yacht Club.

Sometime in 1992, Sven Riskar, presumably also remembering my deal-making in those days, asked me to help them sell a large stake they had in a Pakistani cement company called Fauji Cement. It was an interesting experience. I met with Fauji's chairman and several of the key directors, all of whom were retired army generals, as the company was controlled by the army's pension fund. We interviewed several merchant banks about doing a distribution of the $20 million-odd value of the shares IFU wanted to sell. As the company was already listed on the Karachi stock exchange and fairly popular with foreign investors, it was an easy exercise. Initially, I had tried to interest Morgan Stanley in taking it on. For them, it could have been a fairly simple secondary trade. But they declined. I guess they thought it was too small a deal. We ended up with a U.K. merchant bank that one of Sven's colleagues knew. Much to my surprise, these people insisted that it be a very formal secondary, complete with a full prospectus. The result was it took a couple of months to accomplish and cost IFU quite a bit more in transaction costs. Had MS taken it on, they would have treated it as just a brokerage transaction and "crossed" the purchase from Fauji and the sale to a few institutional investors on the Karachi stock exchange. On the other hand, participating in the "due diligence" exercise was interesting, especially meeting the group of retired Pakistan army generals who were involved. Some were the senior management of the company and another was the representative of the army pension fund, the controlling shareholder.

IFC—Directorships and Advisory Boards

I will start with the IFC board memberships.

Banco Roberts. Julio Lastres asked me if I would be interested in serving on the advisory boards of two banks he was involved with. The first was a subsidiary of Banco Roberts in Argentina. I knew them well of course, so I was glad to do it. The real reason was that IFC was promoting a second private equity fund for Argentina that this affiliate of Banco Roberts was to manage. The not-so-hidden agenda was that I would be able to raise new money for them. When I met Enrique Ruete, the then CEO of the Roberts holding company, I made it clear that I was skeptical about being able to deliver what I suspected they wanted. I said if there was to be a second fund, the shareholders of the existing fund, including IFC, should be seen as supportive. This did not seem to be the case. Further if IFC couldn't find new shareholders, it was unreasonable to expect me to be able to do so. I think he thought that I was just being modest. I had had a lot to do with getting Advent's Latin America fund going, so he assumed I could repeat the miracle. In the end, he agreed that the terms of reference for my three-year contract would be to advise the manager of the fund on improving their governance and performance. If I could raise money, too, that would be received gratefully. It was a pleasurable experience over the period. The young Dutchman they had hired to be the actual manager was sound and receptive, and I always enjoyed going to B.A. for meetings. The highlight was attending one of the annual meetings that was held in Punta del Este, my favorite South American watering hole. It came to a rather unfortunate end, however, when the CEO of the management company himself decided, quite arbitrarily, that I was no longer needed. I had to point out to Enrique the reason I had insisted on a written contract was there was nothing I could do to help and that I wasn't going to expose myself to the implicit risks, which was why I wanted the contract.

Banco Liberal. Julio's other project was with Banco Liberal in Rio. Fortunately, this was a much more straightforward matter. IFC was in the process of providing a financing for the bank and Julio wanted someone to keep an eye on things at a level beyond what could be expected from an investment officer. Aldo Floris, the CEO and 85% owner of the bank, was one of the more delightful Brazilians I have met. His story, of which he was very proud, is worth telling. Aldo, the son of an Italian immigrant, went to work at age 14 as a "runner" for a Rio brokerage firm. By the time he was 17 he had figured out that he could not get ahead in business unless he finished his education. So he went to night school and finally got a university degree. By then he had learned on the job, been promoted several times and had made some money. So, when the owner of the firm decided to retire, Aldo bought control. Besides being a very bright businessman, he was good company, gracious and full of Latin charm.

I don't think I contributed much to either IFC's deal with him or his business. The IFC financing was a line of credit for underwritings that reminded me of something similar IFC tried in Brazil in 1971, just as I joined. It made no financial sense but, for Banco Liberal, then just a small brokerage operation by Brazilian standards, it provided some prestige. My contribution to Aldo was to try and help him find a foreign partner for his fund management business. He wanted to develop this as investment management was in its infancy in Brazil then. But, as his main business was in debt instruments, he didn't have much credibility, so my efforts failed. That said, I did open the doors for him in London to Schroders, Morgan Grenville and Mercury Asset Management, then the three largest U.K. investment managers. Later, he found Nations Bank (now Bank of America) himself. They bought him out for some $100 million. Sadly, I heard in 1999, after the 1998 collapse, that he was accused of a massive fraud. I suspected it might have been political but there is no way of knowing. But Aldo was a delightful companion. I remember going sailing once in his 45-foot Swan. He called it "The Happy Hooker."

Retirement, After a Fashion

Moneda Chile Fund. My last IFC Latin America experience was as a board member of the Moneda Chile Fund, which was listed on the Dublin Stock Exchange. The fund was to specialize in small listed companies. This was mainly thanks to Jay Tata. Moneda Management—Sergio and Antonio—naturally, managed it. For some strange reason, IFC did not invest in its own invention. Rather, it only organized the marketing and the IPO, using Jay's securities group and Warburg's as the placement agents. (We had become involved in a lot of "distributions" of shares in companies and funds we had established to the point where we set up a small group under Jay Tata whose function was to find buyers for portions of these issues, mainly as private placements. Often, we would set up a "selling" group with a U.S. investment bank or a U.K. merchant bank to share the work and the fees resulting from a placement.) As both Rudi and Jay were behind this, and as IFC had no money at stake, they had a free hand in nominating directors. They picked Kenneth Berrill to be chairman and me to be chairman of the audit committee. We were joined by Varel Freeman, another ex IFC man, who then represented the fund's largest investor—Chemical bank Capital Corporation—and two fine old Chilean friends of IFC. One had been a senior official at the central bank and the other was Jorge Carey, who had been an IFC lawyer before returning home to practice law.

We had meetings in Santiago in March and in New York in September. As always, Sergio and Antonio did a very professional job in running the fund and in handling the administrative matters. Rudi came to the board meetings for the first three years as he was on the board of Moneda Asset Management for IFC. Unfortunately, IFC then chose to sell out of Moneda, so Rudi couldn't attend any more. This was a pity because Rudi always kept things interesting, either by his somewhat outrageous statements or—and more importantly—by insisting on the occasional meeting outside Santiago. One of these was to an estancia 100 miles south of Santiago, where we held our meeting and spent a night. However, after the first few years, I began to find the meetings and the visits to Santiago rather dull. Consequently, when Chemical Bank sold and was replaced—happily for the fund and Moneda—by Hambrecht & Quist, a San Francisco venture capital company, I began to think of resigning. This feeling was helped along by the fact that they, H&Q, wanted to leverage the fund by having it borrow. While some closed-end funds did this, I felt it was quite inappropriate for a fund investing in small Chilean companies where many of the fund shareholders were individuals. Besides that, there was the problem of local rules, which restricted our ability to do this.

Chile still required all foreign investment funds to have a minimum five-year life. Consequently, were the borrowing to have been made, a new five-year fund would have to be structured. Much time, effort and money was spent on lawyers and on holding shareholders' meetings and petitioning the regulators to get around the problems. As it was clear from the beginning that we would never get regulatory approval, I felt it was an unjustified waste of the other shareholders' money. It was perfectly fine for H&Q, that owned about a third of the stock and would have achieved what they wanted, but not so for the rest. At another level, I felt we had a reputation risk that was not compensated by the small fees paid. Consequently, I resigned, as much as I regretted that it meant fewer occasions to see my good friends, the Berrills. In recent years, I realized resigning was not such a bright idea. I could have taken the view —as did Ken Berrill—that we could still look after the interests of the minority investors. More selfishly, had I stayed on the board, I could have continued, probably to this day, going to Chile—and "Punta"on the way—once a year and to New York or wherever the second meeting was held. (Subsequently, the second board meetings were held in such places as Dublin and Istanbul.) Ken didn't resign until he was 88.

One very pleasant memory I have of this though were the two days the Gills and the Berrills spent at the estancia I mentioned earlier that Rudi introduced us to. It was a very attractive 17th century colonial style ranch building nestled in the foothills of the Andes, run by a very gracious Chilean couple. It had been in the hostess' family for some six generations. Part of the charm of the place was that she brought her guests into the atmosphere it must have had when Chile was still a Spanish colony. The first evening she entertained us with a formal dinner. One had the feeling—from the elegance of the dining room, the candelabras, the old silver, and the waiters in white jackets and gloves behind each chair—that we were back in the Chile of 1800. But that feeling disappeared for a while when we found that, of the six foreign guests that night, five of us had been to Cambridge University.

Global Securities. One IFC board assignment I was especially grateful for initially was Global Securities in Istanbul. This was thanks to Cesare again. As he put it, he always turned to me when he had a difficult investment to handle. As it happened though, Turkey was one of my favorite countries and Istanbul one of my favorite cities. Global Securities billed itself as the best and largest stock brokerage firm in Turkey. It was certainly the largest and had the top share of foreign business, which suggested it was the best. That said, the largest shareholder and its CEO were suffering from the results of too much success. IFC felt he was cutting corners, as did a few of his best customers, including my old friend Antoine van Agtmael whose firm, Emerging Markets Managers, was also a shareholder. Antoine told me that he could understand them trying to maximize their commissions, but continuing to do it with one of his own shareholders and largest customers after he had complained several times was not smart. The Istanbul Stock Exchange had discount rates for major customers of which Antoine had every right to consider himself one.

So, armed with this knowledge, I went off to my first board meeting. All of the Global people were as charming, gracious and hospitable as Turks always are. They were also very professional in the way they told me about the business and how they ran the company. In those respects they were as good as any Wall Street brokerage house. Their problem was they were as greedy and arrogant as any firm on Wall Street. It was really a pity. Global finally came to grief when they started gambling in the local bond market. It was the old story, borrowing short and lending long, and getting caught in a credit crunch. But that happened long after my time. My concern then was that, after a good start to the relationship, their interest in what I had to offer was very limited. They did not want to hear that commission gauging was unethical as well as a dangerous business tactic. In one sense, Morgan Stanley gave me the opportunity to start my retreat.

Warren Olsen, who was president of the 12 Morgan Stanley funds

378

on whose boards I served, called me one day to say their lawyers had decided that my Global directorship made me an "interested person" rather than an independent director on their fund boards. Consequently, I had either to resign from the Global board or from the MS fund boards. That was not a hard choice to make. But I was very surprised about this because I had notified MS in writing over a year previously of my intention to join this board and they had not expressed concern. It turned out that one of their lawyers had noticed that my "C.V." for the upcoming proxy statement listed Global as one of my director-ships—as it had the previous year. Their concern was that as Global was one of the funds' brokers, I was an interested party. I commented that Global received less than one percent of the funds' business so it didn't seem material and asked if they had checked with the SEC. They said they had. This also surprised me. I checked with my SEC contacts and was told that, had MS asked them, they would have made an exception for me on the grounds that this and similar relationships actually en-hanced my expertise as a fund director and all that was needed was dis-closure. I always suspected that what really concerned MS's lawyers was another problem. That was, one of MS's portfolio managers had been a shareholder of Global when it was a private company. That was con-trary to MS's own internal rules and, as MS didn't know their man had not disclosed his interest, they were also guilty of failing to make dis-closure. On the other hand, they had no way of knowing what their staff member was up to. In any event, Global's CEO was very gracious about my resignation. He even wrote IFC to say I had provided a lot of useful advice. That they didn't use it was another matter.

BACA Ukraine. This brings me to my second to last completed (termi-nated might be a better word) board assignment for IFC, Bank Austria Credit Anstalt—Ukraine ("BACAU"). BACAU was, or is but under a different name, a commercial bank based in Kiev. I had Mary Ellen Isk-enderian, Cesare's successor as CMD manager for Eastern Europe, to thank for this very interesting experience. Ukraine did not seem to have improved much in the economic or political sense since my last visit some three years previously. But Kiev was a much more attractive and cleaner city than Kharkov. What appealed to me about this assignment was the Austrian connection. BACA was based in Vienna, which I had never visited before, and I was told most board meetings would be held there. From the beginning, it seemed BACAU had a "Murphy's Law" problem. First, within a month or so of the bank being established as a joint venture between Credit Anstalt (75%), IFC (20%) and a local Ukrainian bank (5%), Credit Anstalt ("CA") was sold to Bank Austria; hence, BACAU was the name when I arrived. That caused the obvious internal confusion in Vienna. Then, the Ukrainian central bank rules started changing, which severely disrupted the start-up. Third, about a year later, a German bank—HVB Bank based in Munich—bought BACA, which caused even more upheaval. To add to the miseries, BACA established operating policies for BACAU that resulted in its missing the most profitable area of activity in the Ukrainian financial market in 2001. This was the local treasury-bill market in which all the other foreign banks were quite active. Consequently, BACAU was the only one that showed a loss that year. On the other hand, doing business in Ukraine was very high risk. Local companies were not reliable and the few large foreign companies could choose their bankers from the surprisingly large number of them. As I recall it, there were three French banks, Citibank and three other foreign banks, as well as the local ones. BACAU had the added disadvantage of being the smallest in capital and thus at a considerable market disadvantage as its loans to individual client companies could be no more than 25% of the bank's net worth, so they were smaller in amount than their competitors' loans. As the cost of administering loans is not related to size, their interest rates had to be higher than competitors' loan rates.

Despite the problems of the bank, I really enjoyed my association with the Austrians, especially with their managing director in Kiev, Rudolf Hodel. He was very straightforward and dedicated, and good company, He was quite mortified with the loss for 2001. It had been the first time in some 20 years running units of CA that he had faced an annual loss. That the main reason was unrealistic head office policies was no consolation for him. The Austrians and, later, the Germans all struck me as very sound and honest bankers. (Writing today one wonders how different the current financial climate would be were those old staid prudential rules still being followed.) I had not realized how farsighted they were about the prospects for Ukraine, albeit they were both mainly following their Austrian and German business customers who were doing business there. Another thing that struck me was that all the Austrian banks' internal reporting was in English. Also interesting was just attending these board meetings in Vienna. There were five BACA people, one Ukrainian (the head of the local bank that owned 5% of BACAU) and myself. The Ukrainian spoke no English and never said a word although he had a very able interpreter. The latter displayed complete fluency as well as a good knowledge of banking when we talked together after the meetings at lunch.

As to IFC, I was impressed to find that they had a very active operation in Kiev. It was not so much investing, but rather their technical assistance program. They had some 200 full-time consultant types—largely financed by the Canadian International Development Agency grants—who were helping Ukrainian small businesses and teaching the merits of corporate governance. I got roped into this exercise and made a speech on the subject to a group of some 50 of their advisors and then wrote a corporate governance piece for their quarterly journal. The whole operation was run by a Ukrainian woman that IFC hired locally. She was a real find. This was very useful work—just the kind of thing that IFC was good at. I have no special memories of Kiev, other than that the local best hotel was still a Soviet type monstrosity with Intourist quality food and service. It even had the old floor ladies at desks by the elevators keeping guard over who came and went. Seeing Vienna, of course, was a treat.

All this came to an end, however, when IFC decided they wanted to cut expenses and have only one person represent them on the boards of their two bank investments in Kiev. They had decided that Irving Kuchinski, another old IFC colleague who had retired some years after I did, should be the one. This was because he was on the board of another HVB Bank/IFC joint venture in Eastern Europe and thus knew the new people better than I. When told, I offered to resign immediately, but my new IFC manager asked me to wait a while why they sorted out the details, as maybe it wouldn't work out. I found this very curious and potentially embarrassing for two reasons. First, HVB had proposed, as soon as they took over, that the bank's capital should be doubled. This was, or should have been seen as, a strong endorsement of the original investment. Also, it was an even stronger indication that they could make the bank successful. I had been a strong supporter of their strategy and the capital increase at two board meetings and had urged IFC to participate. But IFC declined. As HVB Bank took up all the new stock, IFC's share was reduced to 10%, which meant, under the shareholders' agreement, that they were no longer entitled to board representation. The second concern was one never knew how IFC would explain such a change in board nominees: any arms' length observer could conclude that I had been asked to resign because I was not performing. It took me only a day to conclude that I should resign immediately rather than wait for a final decision by IFC. So, I wrote my letter of resignation to Peter Kolle, the very effective chairman of what by then had just become HVB Ukraine and who was in charge of Eastern Europe for HVB Bank. Peter wrote back a very gracious and flattering letter, thanking me for all I had done for the bank. I was very touched. First, I hadn't done all that much and, second, he was a no-nonsense type from whom you would not expect much more than an acknowledgement. It reminded me how easy and effortless it is to be gracious, but how rarely people are. I think the only other sentiment of that sort expressed on my departure from any organization was the one from my IFC Capital Markets Department colleagues when I finally retired as an IFC advisor/consultant. Besides a fantastic going away dinner, they gave me a beautiful copper plaque with some kind words engraved on it. Reading it now gives me again a very warm feeling for those bright and loyal troops. The wording, I suspect, was Rudi's. But that is off the point.

Some six months later, quite accidentally, I heard that IFC had spent a few more months wondering what to do about HVB Ukraine and finally decided to say they wanted to subscribe to the capital increase after all and nominate another person to the board. Apparently, their two offers were not accepted, which must have been an embarrassment for IFC, even if deserved.

Surinvest, again. I wrote about the early part of my Surinvest experience during my IFC time. I had remained on the board during my Battery-march years, but nothing noteworthy happened during those three years—except the 1988 financial crisis in Latin America. But, partially thanks to its stronger shareholders and to Pancho Ravecca's connections in Europe, we sailed through that fairly easily. After that, it was not until 1995 that Surinvest became interesting again.

Pancho, as CEO of Surinvest, proposed establishing an offshore bank and soon thereafter a holding company structure, as there was growing concern about the political situation in Uruguay. The country had always been known to be dominated by socialist politicians, but they had always taken a very hands-off position on the banking system. This seemed to be changing under a new even more leftist government. Consequently, the shareholders decided to take the defensive measures he suggested. This turned out to be a bit of a struggle as some of Surinvest's shareholders were opposed—mainly Banco Roberts as they wanted to handle that part of Surinvest's business. In any event, a Cayman Islands bank license was obtained and shortly thereafter, in 1995, a holding company called Surinvest International Limited ("SIL") was incorporated to own Banco Surinvest and Norinvest Bank as subsidiaries. Norinvest Bank would handle trade finance and other transactions between lenders and borrowers acting through Surinvest when both were non-Uruguayan. While Surinvest's profits were not taxed directly, the transaction taxes were high and expected to increase, so this arrangement was very beneficial. These days, what we were doing is referred to as increasing tax efficiency. Then, it was called "tax avoidance." That was different from "tax evasion." The distinction, of course, is largely a matter of legal positioning. I was always rather amused that a U.S. bank, a Dutch bank and IFC as shareholders, each of whom always claim to follow the spirit of the law, all accepted this.

That we were able to establish a bank in the Cayman Islands that was owned by a holding company owned by a consortium was a tribute to Pancho and IFC. The Cayman monetary authority had just gone through a house cleaning and had stopped licensing banks that were not controlled by one respected shareholder. Consequently, most of the board felt it would be impossible. The Cayman Islands had a mixed reputation then. On the one hand, it was a British colony and its Monetary Authority, that combined the jobs of a central bank and a financial institution regulator, was in practice run by the Bank of England. On the other hand, it was known as a money laundering center. Also, it was one of the better, and safer, Caribbean resort islands. It was one of the few where it was safe to walk around at night. We chose it as our offshore haven as it had a much better reputation than Panama and was less expensive than Bermuda, the next nearest possibility.

Other than the tortuous process of getting the license, the only thing I remember was the final step in that process. I had to sign the first audited financial statement, as I was to be chairman of Norinvest Bank's audit committee. The audit was easy as on the asset side we had cash in a local bank deposit—a one line item—and on the liability side we had capital issued—another one line item. The Notes were two in number: the facts of incorporation and the details of the share ownership. The amusing part is the formal signing took place in the bar of a local restaurant where we were giving a dinner for all those involved.

Looking back on SIL from 2011, one remembers more of the good times than the bad. For me, it was a challenging, rewarding, fun and frustrating experience. For IFC, it was rewarding for the first 15 or so years. It survived two regional financial crises, produced a good financial return and had an excellent reputation internationally as a trade finance bank. It had also been a very satisfactory dividend payer. That it survived the initial roadblocks set up by the Uruguayan government and the 1980s financial crisis was a miracle even with substantial help from IFC. But it must have been very frustrating for IFC since about 1997 when things started going seriously wrong both for the bank and for Pancho Ravecca personally. The declines in profits and in Pancho's support from the board were obviously directly related. That the board members, except for Geraldo Hess, Dan Adams and me, were all CEOs or senior officials of their own shareholder entities did not help. Unlike their predecessors in Surinvest's early years they did not see Pancho as an equal. They were socially and professionally jealous, as he was better known and more respected by many of the more important bankers in Europe and the Americas than they were. Pancho did receive, and deserve, most of the credit for the early successes. But the feeling became "what have you done for me today," to quote an old Wall Street saying. As CEO he had to be held responsible for the later problems and was certainly to blame for many of them. That two of the loans that went bad were to companies in which IFC was a major shareholder was no comfort. He was chairman of the credit committee.

An important underlying problem, though, was that it was a consortium bank that had outlived the objectives of its foreign shareholders—the more recent ones as well as the first three (Unibanco, Banco Roberts, since bought by HSBC, and IFC) that remained. The "local shareholders" were still a group of Pancho's Uruguayan and Argentine friends.

Most consortium banks last only about five years. Then, fights generally commence over ownership. The original objective is always to give a group of like-minded banks a window on a new market—the catch was to offer these banks exposure to a potential market by just getting their feet wet. Eventually, each of the shareholders decided that either it is a good market—in which case they should have their own operation there—or it is not, which means they want to sell out. So, normally, one of the shareholders buys out the others. While Uruguay is an interesting market and while Surinvest was quite unique, I never understood how it continued so long as a consortium bank. One founding shareholder, Midland Bank, did pull out quite early on, but it was replaced by another three: Rabobank and Banco Bice in Chile and Philadelphia International Investment Corporation ("PIIC," owned by what was then Philadelphia National Bank and is now Bank of America). The only logical reason that I could think of was that the board members enjoyed the relationships with their partner banks, and especially with IFC, and found they did get some side business. Certainly, Banco Roberts, Unibanco and Banco Bice benefited substantially from Pancho's introduction to Capital Group. Besides the relationships with Emerging Markets Growth Fund shareholders, their fees as administrators of EMGF would have been around a million dollars annually. Also, Rabobank benefited. They almost literally stole Surinvest's Argentine trade finance unit's staff and took all its business when they set up their own operation in Buenos Aires. The other shareholders all thought the way they did this was questionable, but none were going to make a fuss about it as Surin-vest was too small to be the cause of a rupture of larger relationships.

How Rabobank got the trade finance clients was another issue that worsened relationships between Pancho and the others. He had been becoming more vociferous on the point that SIL's small capital base— about $20 million at the time, divided between Surinvest and Norinvest —made it very difficult to compete for the best export customers in Ar-gentina. His maximum customer exposure was $5 million—25% of net worth. The large international banks had no trouble making trade fi-nance loans of multiples of that so it was easier for the better borrowers to just take money from the big boys. To add to the misery, at the time Argentine trade finance lending was a highly desirable business so the "spreads" were very low. The big banks could both borrow on better terms and also benefit from lower administrative costs per dollar of loans. That is, the transaction cost per loan was the same regardless of the amount of the loan.

I don't remember exactly why or when things started to go wrong. I suppose it was a gradual accumulation of these differences. Differences between the shareholders themselves were clearly one reason. Some wanted SIL to remain 100% in trade finance, as it was the least risky business, while others wanted more diversification. Then, that Pancho was determined to do what he thought best for the bank was seen as Pancho considering it "his" bank and ignoring the others produced an obvious relationship problem. Loan problems and the 1998 financial crisis resulting in falling earnings and losses was another obvious reason for discord. But it was probably Pancho's refusal to go along with the board's proposal to cut staff by 50% to cut costs that was the final and key issue. I will get to that later. In 1995, the board, unanimously, had elected me as chairman of both the audit committee and the remunera-tion committee. But before that there had been some conflict between shareholders about even having an audit committee. Two of them saw no reason for it. It's amazing to think now that as recently as about 1996 there would be opposition to a bank having an audit committee. Even in Uruguay, starting in about 1998, not only did banks have to have audit committees, but also they had to meet monthly and provide the central bank with meeting minutes. But that is digressing from what happened. As I recall it, the board was unanimous in 1996 in feeling that the remuneration of senior management had to be reviewed. Needless to say, Pancho was quite open in opposing this. In any event, this became a mandate of the remuneration committee whose other members were the directors from PIIC, Banco Bice and IFC. This also became a problem for Pancho as, when the differences grew, my efforts to be rational were seen as efforts to support him for purely personal reasons. In any event the first real sign of trouble for Pancho came when the remuneration committee changed its mind on his pension arrangements. This was after the board's agreeing to substantial salary increases for the whole senior management group and starting a "defined contribution" pension system going forward.

All had started well. After the first candidate to advise the remuneration committee turned us down at the last minute, I asked Ced Ritchie, the retired chairman of Bank of Nova Scotia and an old friend, to advise us. The deal was SIL would pay his and his wife's expenses but otherwise it would be pro bono. The end result besides the remuneration package was a proposal to cover past service—Pancho had by then 18 years as CEO. The catch was all but he—because of his years out of Uruguay—were qualified for pensions under the Uruguayan bankers' pension plan. So the issue was whether to ensure Pancho either could qualify—which meant guaranteeing seven years more employment with SIL—or the shareholders providing at least what the other scheme would have provided. It became clear that not everyone wanted Pancho around for another year, let alone seven years. Recognizing then that he would be forced out as CEO, I suggested the most cost effective way of dealing with the past service matter was to keep him employed nominally as chairman but not CEO for the seven years at a salary of less than a third of his then salary. This would qualify him. I had talked about this to him and he had seemed willing to accept the inevitable on this basis. But the rest of the committee didn't like the idea. Eventually, we agreed on an up-front cash payment which might have been more or less the same amount if one considered the then present value of the proposed new salary over seven years.

Retirement, After a Fashion

To my complete surprise, a month or so later, two of the members then opposed what we had agreed. They denied ever agreeing to the proposal. It was one of the strangest business experiences I had ever had. I recall commenting at one point that I could understand people changing their minds on matters, but I did not understand why it was necessary to try and rewrite the record. (The minutes of the board meeting approving the pension arrangements had been signed by all the board members, obviously including the two who had changed their minds.) Matters moved rapidly from debating pension plans for management to a movement to replace Pancho immediately without any settlement. I made no friends when I said at a meeting of the shareholders that I found it very questionable that they, as individuals, each working for banks that provided them with generous pensions, were prepared to throw someone out after 18 years with nothing. But Pancho had antagonized all of the foreign shareholders. Who was right or wrong was no longer relevant. That he would not agree to cut the staff by 50% was the final straw although I think he was right on that. It took his successor appointed to do it some two years to get around to executing the staff cutback, causing a major banking industry strike even then.

I had several discussions with the local shareholders, who still had about 10% of the equity and a subordinated loan of about $1.5 million to SIL, about what to do. They decided that they would support replacing him so long as he was treated fairly and so long as all of them were bought out. They agreed Pancho had lost all support and that the foreign shareholders were justified in wanting him out. But they also felt the foreign shareholders were also to blame for the problems as a result of their own performance. That is, they couldn't agree amongst themselves as to SIL's future direction and none individually seemed to have many good ideas. Consequently, and especially as the locals were individuals with their own money at stake, while the other shareholders were all large banks, they did not want to be at their mercy. This we made known to the rest of the board. At the next meeting the proposal to drop Pancho was approved unanimously. This was followed by a rather bitter negotiation as to what was fair treatment. The foreign shareholders' proposal started with a title but no money of consequence—it

388

might have been six months' salary. We felt this was not fair treatment for 18 years and with no pension. In the end he received roughly five years' salary over 18 months.

A final act to this saga was a letter I received, signed by five of the six foreign directors, presumably in their capacities as shareholder representatives, asking me to provide the evidence that proved the board had approved some of the previous financial arrangements for Pancho. I forget the details but I do remember my response was to have them sent a copy of the relevant board meeting minutes containing resolutions approving them. In accordance with Uruguayan law, the minutes had Surinvest's corporate seal stamped on them, had been notarized and were signed by all of the directors, including five of the six who signed the letter to me. The sixth signature would have been that of the IFC division manager responsible. Geraldo Hess, as IFC's nominee on the board, would not sign it. I was distressed to hear, a couple of years ago, that Geraldo, only in his 50s, died of a heart attack.

Notwithstanding the unhappy ending, I still have several fond memories of Surinvest. As always, it came down to people. Pancho's local partners were great fun. Milton Fornella, who was vice chairman of Banco Surinvest for a while, was a fellow "clarito" (martini) man. Also, the first board of directors included some very fine people. Roberto Bornhausen, then CEO of Unibanco, and Enrique Ruete, CEO of Roberts, were highly competent and charming people with whom I kept in touch for many years. Life goes on.

Advent Latin America. Shortly before I finally departed from Batterymarch, I received a call from Gunther Mueller, Inter-American Investment Corporation's ("IIC's") Managing Director. I had known him only casually as a serious and hard working Mexican, stuck with a rather difficult job. Compared to the World Bank, Inter-American Development Bank ("IDB"), IIC's parent, was a very political organization with even less understanding of equity markets, so that relationship hindered more than it helped. Gunther said he had heard I was retiring from Batterymarch and wondered if I would have time to help IIC promote what would be the first regional private equity fund for Latin America. I was very pleased and agreed. It turned out that Gunther was the only one of IIC's top management that felt it was a practical proposition. Nevertheless, Gunther and I plotted and planned and eventually came up with a proposal that I thought made sense and could be sold to a private equity management firm.

The first step we took was to talk to all the private equity fund managers we knew. This was a rather discouraging exercise as, of the four we saw, only Advent was interested in Latin America. Knowing Peter Brooke and having had him visit Brazil with me in my IFC days certainly helped. After much discussion in Boston and in DC we came to agreement on how to proceed, with Advent as the manager.

The next step was organizing a trip to the key countries for Peter. Gunther arranged the Mexican part for us and I made the arrangements for Argentina, Brazil and Chile. In Mexico City, we met all the usual potentates, including the now well-known (as the world's first or second wealthiest person) Carlos Slim. In the other countries it was mainly my old pals. I also took Peter to Uruguay to meet Pancho Ravecca who at the time was also on the Capital Group advisory board for EMGF. Peter and Pancho hit it off very well and, consequently, after Pancho gathered a very well-respected group of potential shareholders to join the Fund, Peter asked him to be involved. We had decided there would be a "regional fund" and four "country funds"—in Argentina, Brazil, Chile and Mexico. Investors would be able to invest in the regional fund and/or in the individual country funds. Needless to say, the "usual suspects"— including Banco Roberts in Argentina and Banco Bozano Simonsen in Brazil—agreed to organize the country funds and find local investors for them. The regional fund would make its investments through the country funds. That is pretty much the same structure as the South East Asia Venture Investment Company ("SEAVIC") that Advent/IFC set up in 1988. Advent would establish a special purpose Latin American management company in Argentina. As it was difficult to find in the area a well-experienced private equity professional, the CEO position was offered to an Advent officer, Ernest Bachrach, an Argentine who worked for Advent in London. Pancho was to be the non-executive chairman. I was to be the chairman of the regional fund's advisory committee whose other members would be nominees of the investors. As fees were a key issue, the division of the spoils was decided in advance of the marketing. As usual, the fixed fees were to pay for the basic salaries and expenses of the managers. The "carry" was to be divided 50-50 between the professionals doing the work and the management/sponsoring group, Advent and IIC, sharing equally in what was left over after Pancho's 5% and my 2.5% and then whatever percentage any large key investor demanded. I was very surprised at Peter's generous offer to share the carry with Pancho and me—we had not asked for anything. Pancho did most of the preliminary road shows in South America to get the local partners and later throughout several U.S. states, together with Peter, to raise the money. I had been paid a fee by IIC. Pancho, while helping as a result of personal friendship and his firm conviction of the benefits the funds —LAPEF—would bring to Latin American economies, certainly deserved to be well rewarded. But, as you will see later, this was Peter's approach—not that of his colleagues working on the deal—and he only went ahead with it after asking IIC's specific approval of the arrangement. Likewise, I asked IIC for their approval of my fees.

It took Advent about a year to raise the money. IIC had committed $5 million to the regional fund and $2.5 million for each of the four country funds. Pancho and I were only able to help with our friends in FMO and DEG, the Dutch and German IFC lookalikes. Both pledged to invest. But the Dutch turned down Latin America in favor of Advent's Eastern Europe fund. It was a rather funny experience. As I was about to depart to call on FMO, Peter asked me to deliver also the "Placement Memorandum" for this other fund, with which I had no real involvement. Naturally I did so. It turned out that I must have been a better Advent salesman for Eastern Europe than for Latin America. Gunther and Pancho brought in Nafinsa, the Mexican version of IFC. But the rest of the investors were all Advent clients.

Finally, about two years after Gunther first asked for my help, the fund started operating. Sadly, by then, Peter had retired and appointed Doug Brown as CEO. Doug was a brilliant investment manager, which was why Peter chose him. But his style in dealing with investors and other associates was the opposite of Peter's. It took a fair amount of pressure to get the new Advent to live up to Peter's promises to Pancho and me. One suspected that once the money was raised, we were no longer needed and thus paying us fees for our chairman roles and, eventually, our shares of the carry was to be avoided. That it was known we were not very impressed with their man in Argentina who happened to be Doug Brown's protégé made matters worse. The end result was, after about two years, Pancho was rather unceremoniously dumped, much to the annoyance of at least one of the U.S. pension fund investors. But he did receive a fair settlement for his share of the carry. At around the same time it became clear that the local partners were not very welcome either. This had been very embarrassing for Pancho and me as they made it clear that they resented being ignored. So they just stopped coming to the semi-annual investment committee meetings.

By then, I started thinking it was time for me to move on. Fortunately, Advent gave me the perfect opportunity to do so without sacrificing too much of the financial benefits. What happened was I saw, in the third annual report of the management company, that there had been a distribution of the carry as a consequence of a profit being taken on one of the fund's investments. I discovered that, not only had I been the only one entitled who had not been paid, but that I had an income tax liability about which I had not been informed. For reasons I will never understand, Advent at first denied I was entitled to my share of the carry paid out and then denied they had not sent me my copy of the income tax documents that they had sent to the IRS. This meant, legally, I had defaulted on the capital gains tax I should have paid on my share of the "carry." It took harsh words and letters from my lawyer before they finally agreed they had erred and made a settlement. Looking back, though, the experience was very positive. Advent was by far the best, in terms of professionalism and, most of the time, relationships, of the half a dozen private equity management companies I knew at that time. One of my more memorial trips around Latin land was one with Peter and Anne, his wife, when we were introducing him to our friends there. It was not that anything especially exciting occurred—it was just that they were delightful company.

BLADEX. The continuation of the BLADEX story, mentioned earlier in Chapter V, started when I was wandering around IIC. I was approached one day by an IDB investment officer who had heard I was there. He said he was trying to arrange a subordinated loan for BLADEX but was running into trouble with IDB management. The problem was that, while BLADEX was largely owned by governmental entities, it was not 100% government controlled. IDB's charter, like that of the World Bank, allowed them to lend only to governments, or government owned or guaranteed entities. Obviously, BLADEX did not fit because a majority of its stock was owned by private banks. While it was possible that BLADEX could have gotten some governments to guarantee a loan, it would have been complicated. Further, BLADEX needed a subordinated loan, which governments don't like. So, while IDB wanted to help, they couldn't find a way. My suggestion was that what BLADEX really needed was more equity and they should do an IPO on the NYSE.

At the time, Roberto Bornhausen, Geraldo Hess and Pancho Ravecca were all serving on BLADEX's board. I called Pancho, told him what was going on, and suggested my solution. Pancho talked to our two friends and they agreed. This led to my being asked to talk to BLADEX's board and explain. In theory, it was simple. But most of BLADEX's directors were government officials who knew next to nothing about raising equity and, if anything, were suspicious of the U.S. stock market. I pointed out that, because of BLADEX's excellent track record over the past ten years and because the U.S. market for emerging markets equities was strong, they would probably be able to issue stock in the U.S. market and get it listed on the NYSE. Equally important, I explained that the "cost" of raising more equity would be far less than the interest rate cost of a subordinated loan. BLADEX would not have to pay cash dividends if the existing shareholders didn't want them and the dilution in their shares of the profits would be minimal. My conclusion was that it would also be easier to raise equity this way than it would be to find the debt money.

My three friends supported this approach, as did the IDB people. The rest of the BLADEX board was pretty skeptical. They felt they only needed about $25 million but, at the time, the minimum size requirement for NYSE listing was $60 million. They did not understand that the prestige from becoming a NYSE listed company would help them in many other ways and that a larger capital base would make the cost of borrowings lower than otherwise. In any event, finally they asked me to develop a plan and take José Casteñeda, BLADEX's CEO, to New York to sound out some potential underwriters—there was nothing to lose from trying. We talked to Goldman Sachs, Bear Stearns and Oppenheimer Unfortunately, despite help from Lew Weston, the retired Goldman partner I knew, the Goldman people who received us were pretty junior: to them it was a small deal and BLADEX was an unimportant potential client. Bear Stearns and Oppenheimer, both being much smaller firms than GS, were much more helpful. Their respective CEOs received us and both offered quite attractive propositions. I advised them to go with Goldman anyway, despite the higher fees they wanted, as being brought to market by one of the then three leading firms on Wall Street would add immensely to BLADEX's reputation. In the end, they went with Oppenheimer, partially because their fees were lower and partially, I suspected, because they were a little offended by the Goldman people. The IPO turned out to be a great success. It was offered at $22 a share and rose over the next year or so to over $40. Since then, the stock dropped to about $5 and recovered recently to around $18.

Things went rather down hill for me after that. Pancho Ravecca had to resign from the board when he was forced out of Surinvest. Later, we had some internal dispute about fees so I decided to resign too. As with the Moneda Fund, this was when I was on a lot of boards and I didn't need the hassle.

KDIFC. My next story is about my time with Korea Development Investment Finance Corporation ("KDIFC"). It had been one of my early venture capital/private equity projects with IFC back in 1985, but I was not asked by IFC to become involved then. However, in 1993, Michael Barth, then in the World Bank, put Yeo Yun, the CEO, in touch with me. Yeo had been trying to get IFC support for a capital increase, without success. Michael thought I could help KDIFC and that I would wel-

394

come a reason to renew my Korean relationships. He was right on the second point. I failed on the first. But I tried.

I looked up KDIFC recently in IFC's booklet listing all its financial institution investments. Curiously, under the heading "Financial Sector Segment," it indicates its role as providing "access to smaller savers and borrowers." In reality, KDIFC brought together sophisticated institutional risk takers willing to invest in the equity of new or small growth companies. It did little lending, and then only to supplement and lever its equity positions. Yeo was a delightful fellow with great charm and a wonderful sense of humor. He understood the West completely, even to the point of putting his "first name" first on his English business cards. Also, he had first class credentials as a venture capitalist in the classic style. He had been head of the Korean government's "high tech" start up company, having started life as an engineer.

I remember well my planning sessions with him and his management team over the first year. They had several problems. The first was the company structure as a "fund" but with internal management. The second was the general attitude in Korea to financial incentives for managers of any type of company. The end result was that KDIFC was more in the nature of an industrial holding company, with managers paid at levels not related to the risks and rewards of the intended business. Notwithstanding these impediments to their performance, they actually had a very good track record since 1986 when they started investing. On a "cash on cash" basis, they had an internal rate of return on investments sold by 1992 of about 25%.

The problem was, because of KDIFC's structure and the dividend policy established by its shareholders, the company had a diminishing capital base but a rather fixed—and increasingly high—expense ratio. It was a "catch 22" situation. Because of their high expense ratio—about 7% then, they could not attract more money for a capital increase and, because they couldn't increase their capital, they couldn't reduce the expense ratio. Of course, IFC claimed they could have cut their costs. But with a staff of only four professionals, some 20 investee companies and their own corporate structure, this was not really possible unless they were to liquidate most of the investments. That approach might have been fine for IFC, DEG and Credit Agricole, the main foreign shareholders, but it wasn't for the Korean shareholders.

After a three-year struggle, the issue was settled when one of the Korean shareholders bought out all the others and turned KDIFC into an internal equity financing mechanism. In one sense, this was a vindication for Yeo. The buyer had been one of KDIFC's early start-up financings that had turned out to be very successful. Another vindication was that a U.S. private equity management company—Tom Barry's Zephyr Management—asked KDIFC to joint venture with them on a Korea private equity fund. This was closed out some five years later with an IRR of over 40%. Tom asked me to go on the board of that fund, but I declined for some reason. That was a bad mistake. In any event, I enjoyed my trips to Korea over the three years that I was Yeo's advisor. It was fun to see old friends from KIFC—then Hana Bank—KDLC and KSFC. I remember well seeing Mr. Oh again; who was then a very senior man in the Korean financial system. The last time had been when we had to rescue him from the IFC/KIFC disaster in Egypt. Also, it was fascinating to see how Seoul had grown since my last visit in 1988. The city had become not only three times as large, but also very clean and elegant.

Safron. Another rather brief assignment—about three years starting in 1998—was as advisor to a Middle East private equity management company called Safron Advisors. Brad Warner, my old friend from Schroder and IFC days was working for them and persuaded the man in charge, Basil Al-Rahim, to take me on. This time, it was because they felt I knew something about the business but, needless to say, I'm sure they also thought I could help them raise money. From my point of view, it was fun to be involved with people from the Gulf and from Lebanon again. Basil was an Iraqi who had learned the business while working for the Carlyle Group in DC The major investors in his first fund were also on the board of his management company. They were from Saudi Arabia, UAE, Oman and Lebanon. The biggest player was a bin Laden—a very low key charming guy who, whenever introduced would say: "My Father had over 50 sons with his many wives. I don't think I ever met the one you are thinking of." I remember he said this to me while we were sitting in a bar in Paris while he was drinking a Scotch.

I attended some four of their board meetings in London and Paris. At these meetings, Basil suffered a lot of criticism as a consequence of not having sold any of his investments in Turkey and in Egypt that apparently had been made some three years previously. It was a bit unfair but he made the mistake of fighting them. The end result was the shareholders got together and forced the liquidation of both the fund and the company. It was fun while it lasted, as all of the people were good company. Basil subsequently went back to business running a London based merchant banking operation for the Gulf countries. This time, he has quite an elegant advisory board, including an ex U.K. Chancellor of the Exchequer. I was not invited to join, a decision I quite understood. But sadly, I heard from Brad that Basil was killed quite recently in a civilian aircraft crash in Iraq.

Mauritius Fund. A very different experience was my almost twelve-year involvement with Crown Agents and the Mauritius Fund. This started sometime in 1992 when I received a call from an old friend I hadn't seen in over a decade, Henry Dale, who was still running the financial institutional side of Crown Agents("CA"). CA is a very old established U.K. governmental organization whose function is to assist what had been the British colonies but now included any small country seeking its services. What it offered was assistance in negotiating trade contracts, training programs in the U.K. for their people, the hiring of expatriate experts, and managing central bank reserves. For the latter service, they had an investment management arm that specialized in debt instruments. Henry had become involved in promoting what was to be the first emerging markets country fund for an African country. CA, along with CDC, Genesis Asset Management, a London firm that specialized in emerging markets, and Mauritius Commercial Bank ("MCB"), had set up a management company to promote and run it. As they had no expertise in the equity markets, Henry asked William Knight, another old London friend, who had Mauritian connections, to help him on that end. He wanted me to help structure and market the proposed fund and join the board.

This was a very appealing idea for me. A country fund for a small

African country would be quite a challenge. I then learned that Mauritius, while small, had a very well educated, hard working population that produced a higher per capita GDP than any country in Africa except for South Africa. I also remembered we, my part of IFC, had done some advisory work there in 1988. I think it was one of my one- or two-day efforts. Our marketing pitch included calling it the "Singapore" of Africa. That it happened to be in the Indian Ocean 1,000 miles from Africa, with a predominantly Indian population and with strong Chinese and European minority groups, was the basis of this case. I fell in love with the place after just one visit. While little known in the Americas, it was and is a tourist haven for Europeans: friendly people, beautiful beaches, tropical forests, mountains, excellent French, Indian and Chinese cuisines and good hotels. It also has an excellent physical infrastructure of roads, power, telecommunications and services. So, not surprisingly, it had a strong growing economy and thus a good story to tell investors.

By the time I became involved, they (CA and the other sponsors) had set up a local management company, Mauritius Fund Management Company ("MFMC") and prepared a prospectus appropriate for a London Stock Exchange listing. Besides Henry, the main players were Richard Carrs from Genesis, John Heywood, who had been selected by Genesis to be chairman of the fund, my old friend Donald Peck on the CDC side and some people from Warburgs, the placement agent Genesis had chosen. Richard, a Genesis partner, was a prince of a man: gentle, low key, and a very well-rounded professional portfolio manager with a great deal of African experience. John was an engaging upper middle class Englishman who had spent much of his career in Hong Kong and China, mainly in commerce. He took the job of chairman very seriously and tended to try to run the fund after the fashion of a 19th century English industrialist. He was more thorough in his due diligence and attention to strategy and detail than most fund chairmen I knew, notwithstanding that his ideas on corporate governance were also rather 19th century. We clashed a lot on that at the beginning, but we both compromised eventually and soldiered on in reasonable harmony.

The first problem, as always, was finding investors. The Warburgs people produced few and there was a serious risk we would fail to find the minimum $20 million or so needed to make it financially viable. Henry asked me to try my U.S. friends. This was not well received by Warburgs who claimed they had already covered the market. I suggested that Richard Carrs come to the U.S. and visit IFC, the UN Pension Fund and Antoine van Agtmael's company. I was rather surprised when Richard's senior partner called to say he thought it "would not be a good use of Richard's time." However, I prevailed and Richard "sold" all three of them. But, as I understand it, Antoine said at the time: "Richard, I expect you to be running this fund personally, not those other people."

With sufficient money raised, the fund shares were listed, and the board went off to Mauritius for our first meeting. Unfortunately, it was a rather rocky start. John had seen no need for an audit committee. He only gave in when I insisted and pointed out that IFC and other U.S. shareholders expected one. The final compromise was to have an audit committee comprised of all the directors, with John chairing it. At that point I was tempted to resign but, instead, just declared I would not serve on the committee. All rather pointless at the time, but it was a matter of principle with me, as two of the five directors would be considered "insiders." After that, the board meetings were serious business but rather fun. The only odd thing was John's insistence that there should be annual budgets that included revenue budgets. It was the only fund I knew of where the managers were expected to forecast the next year's dividend income and capital gains. So, each year for the next ten years we had one meeting in Mauritius, usually in March, and one in Paris, usually in September. One day in Mauritius was devoted to calls on the Minister of Finance and on the CEOs of our investee companies, and one day to the meeting. Again, a very thorough and professional approach not matched by many of our peer funds. MCB always hosted a lunch, which was always excellent even by Mauritius' high standards. We used to think of the MCB dining room as the best restaurant in town. Our Paris meetings were always remembered mainly for the excellent dinners. John used to foster competition between Robert Heim, chairman of MCB, and Pierre Guy, the bank's GM, in finding the best

Enjoying a brief respite at a beach in Mauritius in 1994, while there for a meeting of directors of the Mauritius Fund.

medium-priced restaurant. They were always very enjoyable events.

Sadly, while Mauritius Fund's performance was fairly good, its final year was not glorious. For whatever reason, the Fund's bylaws established a ten-year life unless shareholders voted in the ninth year to extend its life. Genesis' senior partner went to great lengths to encourage an extension. Fund managers always do this if they can, but the machinations behind the several annual general meetings required to do so were a bit messy. Finally, he did succeed in getting shareholders to agree to turn it into a Mauritius trust vehicle, which gave it another year and the hope for more. But this only happened after IFC, the UN Pension Fund and Antoine were able to sell out just before the last AGM at a 20% discount from net asset value. Their action indicated that, had they stayed in, they would have voted against the new scheme and thus it would have been turned down by shareholders again. One reason they were opposed to an extension was there were no governance arrange-

ments proposed, which automatically raised their suspicions. So, the knowledge that the U.S. investors would accept a deep discount was an incentive for a Mauritius company with inside knowledge to buy them out. For the sellers, as the quoted price in London was a 50% discount, 20% looked good. I always felt that the 50% discount that had prevailed for several years was a reflection on the quality of governance and the London listing. During that period, discounts for SEC-registered funds averaged around 20%. When its legal status changed to the trust form there was no longer a board of directors, so we were all retired.

Morgan Stanley Funds. Now I come back to Morgan Stanley or, more to the point, Morgan Stanley Asset Management, of which Barton Biggs had been the founder and was chairman and, in effect, chief investment officer. "MSAM" as we called it, was a wholly owned subsidiary but it seemed quite independent of the investment banking parent. It had then about $20 billion under management, mainly from U.S. pension funds. Most was in debt investments rather than equity. Now, MSAM manages hundreds of billions, including a family of mutual funds attracting individual investors. By 1991, when I retired from Batterymarch, I had known Barton already for over 15 years. I had the greatest respect for him as a person and as a professional. David Fisher and Mark Mobius were just as good, or even better, managers, but they were both low key and did not have the universal reputation that Barton had in those days. (Since then, Mark has become a serious and well respected pundit on the markets.) I was grateful that he had kept me on the board of his first country fund after I retired from IFC and joined Batterymarch; that he invited me to join two more, despite my being then a competitor of sorts, was very pleasing. Of course, being Morgan Stanley, Barton didn't really feel Batterymarch was much competition, but that is another story that I learned only after I retired from Batterymarch. In any event, I felt we had got along well and that the respect was mutual.

That must have been the case still around 1993 when he reorganized the boards of all his funds and made a few of us directors of all 12 of them. Then, in another reorganization a few years later, he reduced the size of the boards, but kept me on. By then, of course, I was just another old pensioner with very few useful connections for him. People in the know used to say that there were only three qualifications to be on Barton's boards: to have been a U.S. Marine; to have gone to Yale; and to live in Greenwich. I don't think all the others qualified on all three counts, but I didn't qualify on any. This reminds me of a comment one of his MSAM colleagues made about the changes: "Now we have a well diversified board." I thought: "Yes, one is a Canadian, one lives in San Francisco and one in Boston, but we are all white males." I mention this in the context of what Barton felt about shareholder democracy and independent directors. He said once at a board meeting: "Make no mistake about it. Morgan Stanley controls these funds." This was correct. Morgan Stanley, as broker, held title to the holdings of many of its customers—including voting rights—so they probably would have won any shareholder meeting agenda items. I remember him making that point more subtly again on another occasion. Looking through the very professionally prepared board documentation package, I noticed in the middle of the 50-odd pages a new agenda item that was not in the original agenda. This was the election of a new director that we were to approve. The name and job title was there, but nothing else. This was the first we had heard of adding another board member. Barton had never mentioned it. I had never heard of the man before although it turned out he was a very successful German industrialist. Fortunately, Barton withdrew the item the day of the meeting. I don't know why, but I don't think it was because he was embarrassed about having forgotten to tell us that we were expected to vote for him. In reality, Barton's attitude was fair. Through Morgan Stanley "his" investors probably owned the majority of the funds' shares. In those days investment firms that held their customers' shares could vote them as they saw fit—usually to support management.

Now in his 70s, Barton still is, and deservedly so, a highly respected investment strategist and Wall Street guru. That said, as the years passed and as he became more successful, he became rather distant from his boards and from the day-to-day management of the funds. I began to realize, during the two years before I reached the retirement age of 73, that he had advised the boards to put this into the Fund's bylaws in 1997. But that is getting ahead of my story. Until about 1995, the board meetings were substantive, serious events. We met three times a year in New York and once a year in one of the countries or regions where we invested. The audit committee—of which I was a member throughout the period and chairman for three years—met twice a year. Each of these meetings met the highest standards of governance at the time. In fact I recall using the meeting agenda and documentation formats as examples for several other boards I joined subsequently. MSAM could not have been more professional. I recall a situation when, shortly after a new fund had been launched, Barton announced to the board that the stock trading side of MS had been trading for its own account in the newly issued shares. This was against SEC regulations and, by the time it had been discovered and stopped, they had made a profit of some $750,000. He said this profit had been turned over to the new fund and the SEC had been informed, but he advised the board to hire our own lawyers to seek redress. Obviously, it was highly unlikely that the SEC would ever have discovered this and it would have been impossible for the board to have done so. It was a commendable action.

I recall four wonderful due diligence trips to the countries for board meetings.

One trip was to Thailand, Hong Kong/China and Singapore. One was to South Africa. Another was to Brazil. The last was to India. Each was a major logistical exercise involving 30 or so assorted board members, important investors and spouses plus six or more MSAM people. There were some memorable occasions. One was in Johannesburg. It was a dinner in an elegant local restaurant. The guest speaker was the recently retired president, who had just been replaced by Nelson Mandela. He gave a very sincere, moving talk about the transition, but I found it almost embarrassing. We were in a corner of the main dining area, near the bar. People, as they do in bars, were talking loudly and almost drowning him out. None of the South Africans seemed to care that he was there talking about his role in making history.

I will never forget our trip to the world's largest iron mine, in Brazil near the Amazon. We flew from Rio to the nearest airport in a formation of three DH 125s. It reminded me of my navy days in 825 Squadron. We then went in four motorboats down the Amazon to the mine site. On the way, the boat I was in developed a fire in the engine and we had to be rescued by one of the other boats. I had visions of the boat being surrounded by alligators as it sank. As to the mine site, I had never seen such a gigantic hole in the ground, nor such huge bulldozers and trucks. It was the largest open pit mine in the world. We stayed the night in a company camp in the jungle. It was quite an experience—rather similar to an African safari camp. An indication of Barton's opinion of me at that time was indicated by something he said at a dinner in Rio. It was just a group of about 15 of us. I had been asked to give my views on Brazil. Barton started by saying: "Listen to what David says. It's important." Not many people say that kind of thing when the person in question is an old pensioner.

The visit to South East Asia was less interesting to me as I had seen everything and everybody we saw before. There were three things I re-

404

member. The first was a dinner in Singapore. Attending, besides the 15 or so of us, were about five of the local VIPs including the son of the PM who was, I believe, minister of defense at the time. We sat at a very large round table. I was placed to the right of a Singaporean lady whose husband was a publishing magnate. She engaged me in a long and loud discourse on what she thought was wrong with Singapore's version of democracy. This was a very sensitive subject, especially with senior government people present. For a while, there was silence around the table, except for the two of us. I could see my Morgan Stanley friends eyeing me and wondering how I was going to be polite to her while also avoiding a small-scale diplomatic debacle. We all talked about it afterwards. They thought it was hilarious listening to me dodging the verbal hand grenades. The second incident happened as we were crossing a form of municipal border into Shenzhen, the very large and modern city in China just outside Hong Kong. I suppose it was similar to the old USSR; even the locals had to have internal passports to move around. In any event, one of us took photos from the bus of the border post with its uniformed police and soldiers. The bus was stopped and we sat in it for two hours. Apparently photos were not permitted. We found out later that we were only allowed to continue because a large sum of money changed hands. Finally, while we were in the Chinese industrial area over the border from Hong Kong, we visited an electronics factory. In it were hundreds of young girls, all working standing at their machines. In the question period afterwards, one of the wives asked the factory manager why seats weren't provided. The answer: "It would take too much space." This sparked some less than diplomatic comments about workers' rights, etc. The manager's response was: "We offer the best jobs around. If these girls didn't work here, they would be working in the fields for 12 hours a day. When you leave, look at the line outside our employment office." He was right on his last point; there seemed to be thousands lined up.

India was another experience—and the last trip Barton organized. I think it was in 1995. We visited Bombay, Delhi and "the pink city"— Jaipur—and Agra. The trip there was by bus from Delhi. It was quite an adventure: a rickety old bus speeding down a very crowded two-lane road, with trucks, cars and buses seemingly racing each other in each direction. Barton had had the rather bizarre idea of holding our required board meeting in this bus. Fortunately, even he decided it was impractical. But seeing this part of the old, beautiful India made it all very worthwhile. By the end of this trip, it was becoming evident that Barton had had enough of being a tour guide. I can't say I blamed him, but, for my last four years on his boards, it became increasingly obvious that he did not take our meetings as anything other than a necessary chore imposed by the regulators. This was also in part our fault. As "friends of Barton," none of us objected much to the decreasing amount of time devoted to them by MSAM portfolio managers and the fact that Barton himself tended to arrive at the beginning and then wander off after a few minutes, often not to be seen again. That said, the administrative side was always handled impeccably. This was very much to the credit of Warren Olsen and, following Warren's departure, Michael Klein, who were the official "presidents" of the funds in the legal sense but also the MSAM chief administrative officers of the funds. Warren was on the job until about 1996. Michael took over from him and stayed until 2000. By Michael's time, he was actually presiding over the board meetings themselves. I felt Barton's declining interest was a result partially of his growing success and the expansion of the other parts of MSAM's business and partially because of the merger between Morgan Stanley and Dean Witter ("DW"). As one wag on Wall Street put it in a WSJ article, it was a marriage of "white shoes and white socks." For those too young to remember these terms, "white shoes" were what the New York elite used to wear in the summer. "White socks," on the other hand, were what were worn by teenage country girls. Dean Witter was best known as a "wire house" based in Chicago. In any event, it was felt that the DW crowd was taking over. MSAM became MSDWIM. It was clear Barton didn't want anything to do with the DW side. But, increasingly, there were pressures for "synergy" and one suspected that standards were declining as a result. One amusing indicator was that we went from having sit-down lunches after board meetings, to buffet lunches during them, to buffet breakfasts during them, to coffee and donuts. Then, one day, Warren announced with a grin that "Barton has nixed the donuts."

That said, till the end of my time on the boards, we did have an elegant dinner once a year. That was especially the case when Fred Whittemore was on the board. Fred was a retired MS partner who was a Broadway "angel." He always arranged for us to go to a show after the dinner which added much to the enjoyable part of the MSAM experience.

Over this period, my relationship with Barton began to deteriorate. This probably started with the obvious. I was becoming a bit of a troublemaker. Also, I was becoming a bit uncomfortable with the way Barton was running our meetings. While the administrative side was handled very professionally, less and less time was spent on the actual portfolios. As Peter Chase, one of the original "friends of Barton" had said once: "We spend an average of five minutes on each country where we invested." Obviously, just a fraction of a minute was spent on the individual companies. This was to some extent inevitable. At any one time we would have had equity investments in some 15 emerging markets, plus Japan, Australia and New Zealand, Hong Kong and Singapore. Through the three debt funds, we were investing in probably a good half dozen other OECD countries. Consequently, the list of companies could easily have been at least 200. That said, it was a very different approach to that taken by, for example, Capital Group. Just for the record, I'll list the other MS funds (after the first four country funds already mentioned). The equity funds were Asia Pacific, Pakistan, Turkey, Brazil and Russia. The debt funds were all "global" in investing and had pretty well the same policies in practice but there were three separate vehicles: Emerging Markets Debt Fund, Global Opportunity Bond Fund and MS High Yield Fund. I suggested merging these three debt funds as they were indistinguishable in practice and should also have been in performance, but for some reason the latter was not the case.

The first occasion when I caused some serious trouble was when I objected to the fee MS wanted to charge to underwrite a rights issue to expand the capital of one of the funds. My first concern was that expanding the size of closed-end funds, while good for the manager as it meant more fees, was not necessarily good for the shareholders. My starting point was closed-end funds were already beginning to trade at discounts to net asset value and I believed a major—and obvious—reason was that the supply of new shares was outstripping demand. This led to my concern that, besides the fact that the merits of the rights issue were dubious, MS was being appointed lead manager of the underwriting group for a fee of 3.75% of the total amount. I felt they were only entitled to a fee on the amount not subscribed by shareholders and that, in any event, the fee was far too high: 2% would have been reasonable. This was considered very offensive. In the end, the part of the fee going to the other members of the syndicate was reduced, but MS as manager retained its original percentage. I think the only reason that happened was that, behind the scenes—no one supported me during the board meetings—Fred Whittemore agreed with me; he told me this afterwards.

Another incident happened when Barton proposed a rights issue for one of the funds where the rights would be non-transferable to, as he said, "reward the fund's loyal shareholders." I commented that non-transferable rights penalized shareholders that did not have the cash to subscribe. I was the only director to object. I remember having to point out that the draft minutes of the meeting that we received eventually said that the vote had been unanimous and this had to be changed. As it turned out later, those who subscribed were punished rather than rewarded—the net asset value per share dropped from over $12 to under $6 over the next few years, which was something of a record for a debt fund. At the time of my objection, of course, I had no idea that the NAV would drop, let alone by so much. The next little clash occurred close to the end of my term. The agenda had an item asking approval to change the index against which most of the emerging markets equity funds were measured from the IFC index to the Morgan Stanley Capital International index. Both were perfectly fine indices. I had, though, noticed that, in the small print, it was disclosed that MS had increased its ownership in the joint venture company that produced the MSCI indices from 15% to over 50%. I commented to Barton that this seemed a little self-serving of MS. However, I suspected that was a bit of MS-DW "synergy" at work, and not Barton's choice. My last issue, just before my retirement date came around, was to propose that the funds have a "lead independent director." Barton gave the appearance of being noncommittal, but when I suggested this was "best practice," one of his friends said: "no, it's unique practice." That was the end of that. But now I gather it is required practice. But he did establish a nominating committee of the board. I heard, shortly after my departure, in the context of another reorganization, that two of our group of original directors were dropped. I was surprised about one of them and inquired. I was told the reason was he always arrived for meetings late and left early. I remember him as someone who did arrive five or ten minutes late and leave a bit early. But his time at the meetings was many multiples of minutes more than Barton's. One of the members of the committee also tended to be around for only the first five minutes. So there was probably another reason.

I had two other rather strange run-ins with Morgan Stanley around the time of my retirement. Both involved my "deferred compensation account." Barton had rather pressured us a few years back to take our fees in shares of the funds, to be placed in these accounts. The idea was, first, it would look good to investors were we to do that and, second, income tax would be deferred until we started withdrawing cash when we retired as directors and over a five-year period. Some ignored this, but three of us agreed to do it, although I only deferred about a third of my total fees.

The first problem I created was to ask that the arrangement be changed so I could withdraw the money over a ten-year period and, during this period, withdraw any amount I chose each year—from zero to the total amount left. Very graciously, MSAM agreed and the appropriate changes were made and approved by resolutions by each of the fund boards. That involved a lot of legal paperwork for MSAM, and I appreciated it. Then, to my surprise, a year later—close to the end of December—I received a call from MSAM saying I had to take my money out in ten equal installments over the years and the first check was in the mail. While this was not life threatening, it was very annoying, as I had done my tax planning based on not withdrawing any of the money in the early years. So I objected. It turned out that MS's lawyers had made the wrong judgment but, according to Bill Brennan, who does my taxes, this was an obvious error that even MSAM should have known about. I had to give in, but only after I collected from MS all the legal and accounting costs I had to bear to change things.

The second run-in ended up quite embarrassingly for MSAM. Over about a year I had been questioning them about the rate of return figures they were showing in my quarterly statements on my deferred income accounts. I received separate statements for each of the seven funds. For some of them, the rates of return seemed reasonable. But for three of them—the three debt funds—they made no sense at all. To keep it simple, each of these showed the amount of dollars of my director's fees ("contributions") that I had put in, the amount of dollars that had been paid as dividends and reinvested and the remaining value. What I happened to notice was that, for all three that I had contributed to, each was roughly the same total amount as the sum of dividends and the final values were roughly equal. To me that meant the rate of return on those accounts was approximately zero. But MSAM's statements showed annualized rates of return of around 15%. It was all very strange. Common sense should have been enough to make it clear that $100 invested with income reinvested that was still worth only $100 three years later could not be a return of 15%. I still have that correspondence somewhere.

Looking back, the performance of the funds, which is what really counts, wasn't too bad in my day—not that I had any influence on it. But one of the many "consulting" firms that measured such things had reported, sometime around 1998, that they had slightly below average performance and slightly higher expense ratios compared to their peers. I was rather surprised about the performance. Barton's strategic positions usually turned out to be right. I discovered towards the end that the portfolio managers did not have to follow his guidelines, and most didn't. This became very clear to me at the end of 1998, after the Russian financial collapse. At our September meeting he reported that the Global Opportunity Bond Fund had had about half its money in Russian debt and, consequently, its NAV was down some 50%. The other two, the emerging markets debt fund and the high yield fund, were OK. In fact, the high yield fund had moved out of emerging markets debt entirely. How could their strategies be so different? Answer; the three managers went their own way. Barton rather panicked over the Russian crisis. He even insisted we approve changing the name of his Russia fund to take out the word Russia. I had come to this meeting directly from Seoul, where I had been visiting Yeo Yun. I had been impressed by what I saw there so I immediately looked to see what our exposures were to Korea. The Asia Pacific fund had zero in Korea whereas the "global" emerging markets fund had six percent there. Why should the former, which had more reason to invest there than the latter, have nothing when the latter had a high exposure—"overweight," to use the technical term? Same answer: obviously I didn't know what I was talking about. As I recall it, this was the meeting at which Peter Chase had said: "We get about five minutes per country per year."

Maybe I'm being unfair to MSAM and to Barton, as we were his accomplices. It leads to the question of what is an independent director. Legally, those of us on his boards all were independent. But, as he made clear, MSDW, now MS again after another name change, controlled the funds, and we accepted that. We directors were just as responsible as was Barton and MSAM.

Finally, in 1999 I retired having reached the magic age. Barton arranged a very elegant dinner on that occasion for the two Thai directors that he had encouraged to resign at the same time and me. My years with MSAM were a great experience. While the last few paragraphs dwelt on some of the problems, on balance I would do it all again. One always knows better what should have been done after the event. I even did quite well financially from my deferred compensation plans which finally matured a few years ago.

First Newly Independent States Regional Fund is a rather mouthful of a name for this Baring Brothers managed, Luxembourg incorporated and listed closed-end fund that invests mainly in Russia. At the time Barings was one of the highest regarded London merchant banks with a well respected fund management arm. I was very grateful to Cesare Calari again who asked me to join the board as the IFC nominee. I think it was because of the work I had done for him on the Russian Securities Commission project in 1993.

This was—and remains—a rather complicated story, with some similarities to my Morgan Stanley experiences in the 1980s and 1990s. The good news is that, since it was launched in 1994, it has been one of the best performing listed closed-end funds around, with an annualized return to investors through 2004 of some 18%. The bad news is that it has been a perfect example of "Murphy's law"—what could go wrong or be done badly did go wrong and was done badly. So how could it have produced such great results? There were two reasons. First, Russia's securities market performed very well over the period. Second, Mike Calvey, who, as the CEO of Baring Vostok, Baring's private equity management company in Russia, has been managing it since 1997 and has done a first class job.

IFC asked me to go on the board in 1996 when Will Kaffenberger, IFC's vice president for Eastern Europe at the time, decided he wanted off the board. Cesare Calari said at the time: "David, you know we always call on you when we have a problem we don't want to handle." The "always" was a bit of an exaggeration, but it was certainly the case with FNISRF, which I shall now call just "NIS." Will told me there were a couple of difficult issues, one of which would require him to take a position against a U.S. government entity, OPIC (Overseas Private Investment Corporation). As an IFC officer, it was politically hard for him to do this. Once I was on the board, I could follow my conscience on this as an independent director representing the interests of all shareholders and, if I agreed with his position, this could not be faulted, nor could IFC be blamed. The other issue was that Barings were behaving rather badly in their role as manager and, with his ex boss, Bill Ryrie, who had just retired as IFC's CEO, on the board as a Baring's nominee, this was an embarrassment for Will and IFC.

To give a brief background, Baring Brothers had promoted "NIS," starting in 1993. IFC had been persuaded to take a 10% stake. Also, EBRD was expected to take a 10% stake. This was largely because it had a very prestigious initial board, with Arthur Hartman, retired U.S. ambassador to Russia and to France, and number two in the State department, as chairman. Arthur, it turned out, was also a great supporter of the ex Solomon Brothers Russia hands led by Terry English and Mike Calvey who originated the proposal. Also an initial independent director was Dudley Fishburn, retired Editor of the Economist and Conservative Party MP for Chelsea and Kensington. That Bill was involved gave his

IFC friends a lot of comfort initially but, apparently, IFC's board was a bit concerned about the appearance of a conflict of interest as he had only retired a year previously. Probably this diversion of attention resulted in what ended up seeming like a lack of due diligence in the details of the investment. This is where Mr. Murphy got his foot in the door, as you will see.

But first, I should explain the structure of the Fund and the corporate relationships. Terry's and Mike's firm, Sovlink Corporation, was in the business of doing deals in Russia and was the sponsor and the "Investment Advisor." They shared the 2.5% management fee with Baring Asset Management ("BAM"), a subsidiary of Barings. BAM was to manage the Fund overall and especially the "listed" (on the Moscow stock exchange) securities. "Unlisted" securities (private equity) would be subcontracted via Baring Private Equity Partners, the nominal manager to Sovlink. Later, Baring Vostok Capital Partners, a joint venture between Barings and Sovlink, was formed in Moscow to take over the management. Bank of Bermuda (Luxembourg) was the Administrator and Custodian. Warburgs had been hired as the Placement Agent. The U.S. Overseas Private Investment Corporation ("OPIC") had provided a $30 million loan that was to be collateralized through a subsidiary of the Fund set up for the purpose that it would always hold Fund investments worth twice the amount of the loan.

IFC in its enthusiasm decided to be a placing agent, along with Warburgs. Marketing IFC securities deals, such as this, was Jay Tata's job at the time. He was instrumental in recruiting the College Retirement Equity Fund ("CREF") that became another 10% investor, as well as several other well-regarded institutional investors. Raising $160 million for the first "Russia fund" was quite a coup for both Barings and IFC.

The first board meeting I attended was in Bermuda. We stayed in an excellent hotel, dined in fine restaurants, were taken on a boat trip by Bank of Bermuda who, along with Barings, orchestrated a well-organized meeting. Despite the care for our creature comforts—no one does this better than British merchant banks—that was when it started going down hill. Will said that the main issue I had to watch for was the OPIC loan contract. It turned out that, with the agreement of Barings, OPIC had instructed the Fund's lawyers to change their contract to give them all the investments as collateral. I agreed with IFC—and with EBRD and CREF—that this was wrong and contrary to the agreements between the Fund and its shareholders. I also objected to the fact that Barings, without consulting the board, had started paying itself its management fee of 2.5% on the amount of the loan despite the fact that the contract was not yet even signed, let alone money disbursed. Fortunately EBRD and CREF were both represented on the board: Barbara Jacobs for CREF and Kurt Geiger for EBRD. They had both made the same points at the meeting. There was a tremendous row, with Arthur, Dudley, Bill and Terry all supporting Barings in claiming that the new OPIC contract was satisfactory. That the supporters of Barings had all been appointed initially by Barings and thus were conflicted didn't seem to worry them. After several board meetings it was agreed that the OPIC contract had to be changed and that Barings had to return the fees they had charged. It was also upsetting to find that the Fund had been charged some $1 million in legal fees to set up the OPIC contract in the first place. Later, we convinced them that the terms of the loan were so unattractive that we should cancel it. This was done. That fight brought on the next battle, which was replacing the Fund's first legal firm, as it had become painfully apparent that they were working in Barings' interests rather than the Fund's.

This next skirmish had a good side. BAM's portfolio manager had done a good job. The $160 million equity portfolio was then worth some $400 million by mid-1998. But Barings had not proposed paying a dividend out of profits that had been realized. We—Barbara, Kurt and I—pointed out that the prospectus required the fund to pay as dividends all realized capital gains and earned net income. We proposed that these profits, which amounted to over $100 million by then, should be paid out immediately. To our surprise, the BAM people refused to do so, making great claims that they could produce even more profits. We pointed out that they had no choice—their contract with the Fund specifically required it. The response of the portfolio managers was to say that, if they had to pay out realized profits, they would not take profits in the future. It was not until Barbara put on the record what they had said, which would be in the meeting minutes—that they were managing the portfolio to maximize their fees, not to add value for the shareholders who were paying the fees—that they gave in. The other Barings' directors did not support us.

This series of exchanges over two meetings brought into focus another mistake IFC and the other key investors had made during the initial negotiations with the promoters. The management contract stated that BAM would receive a fixed fee of 2.5% of NAV annually, plus a 20% share of the profits of the fund after an 8% "hurdle" rate of return had been earned. The industry practice for funds investing in listed stocks —"portfolio" funds—was a fixed fee of only about 1.5% at the time— less now for large funds. For private equity funds the normal practice was a fixed fee of around 2.5% of the original committed capital, plus a 20% share of the profits after the hurdle. What Barings was actually getting then was the best of both worlds. Their fixed fee at the time was 2.5% on the $400 million market value rather than on the original $160 million paid-in capital. Then they were also getting a share of the profits. There wasn't anything we could do about this until Barings discovered another mistake in the original management contract that they wanted rectified. Of course, this worked against them. I was absolutely amazed that the contract had been so badly written. It was worded in such a way that the share of the profit could only paid once the 8% hurdle was earned twice—making it a 16% hurdle. Obviously, this was unfair. However, by that time, we had had enough. It also happened that, for the previous six months or so, we had been complaining that other operating expenses charged by Barings to the Fund were too high. In addition to their 2.5% fixed fees, the expense ratio on the $400 million resulting from other expenses worked out to about 2%, for a total of about 4.5%. As we pointed out, the average ratio of other expenses for similar funds was less than 1% and the total for similar funds was about 2.5%. So, we three directors said in effect: "OK, we will agree to change the contract to solve your complaint, but only if you agree to 'capping' the fixed fees and expenses at 2.5%." Capping expenses is a fairly normal practice for portfolio funds. The expenses are a responsibility of the manager so, if he lets them get too high, the difference comes out of his fixed fee.

415

Retirement, After a Fashion

Our stand was, to say the least of it, not well received. Bill Ryrie threatened me with complaints to IFC. Arthur Hartman tried to complain to Jim Wolfensohn, the then president of the World Bank. The end result, after months of argument, was a good solution for the Fund's shareholders. It came in several parts. First, it was agreed the fund would, for the future, concentrate on private equity, selling down the listed portfolio but retaining a base capital of about $150 million to be operated under private equity rules. That is, as investments were liquidated, the initial capital committed plus profits would be paid out to shareholders. Second, as there would no longer be an active listed portfolio, BAM would resign as manager in favor of Baring Private Equity Partners. Third, Baring Vostok, run by Mike Calvey, would be the actual "manager" of the fund. Sovlink, because of its initial contract, would remain as an advisor and continue to receive half the fees. Finally, the fee structure was redesigned along traditional private equity lines.

Towards the beginning of this story, Jay Tata had joined BPEP and encouraged John Dare, its chairman, to form an advisory committee. This was established with Gordon Binns, Kenneth Berrill, Michael Caine, Bill Ryrie, Lord Baring and me as the members. It didn't help that my advice to John Dare on how to handle the squabbles with the Fund in this capacity were not entirely to his liking. Still, I think we added some value to BPEP during the semi annual meetings we had. One of them happened to be in August 1998, just after the Russian market collapsed. I recall Gordon and I both made the point that there would be a strong recovery eventually. I don't know whether any of them did anything about it. I know I didn't personally. I already had some money in the Morgan Stanley Russia fund. BPEP wound-up this committee shortly after Jay resigned. It was rather evident that we, the members, felt a lot closer to Jay than we did to the other BPEP people.

Back to the Fund, once our differences of opinion were resolved, Mike Calvey did all the right things—both as an investment manager and as a CEO with a rather active board of directors to handle. We all had the highest regard for him. Writing now, ten years later, the Fund has shown the best performance of any of the listed emerging markets funds over the last five years—something like 18% annualized. Of course, that was helped by returning the $100 million of early profits to shareholders—and so did paying attention to corporate governance. But most important was Mike's professionalism. He was the best private equity manager any of us had known. He built a very strong team, based in Moscow, mainly comprised of Russians. Besides the remaining listed stocks, they actively managed some 20 direct investments located from Siberia in the East to Ukraine in the West and Georgia in the South. Some of the people, moved in as CEOs of the companies, had harrowing stories to tell of the "Wild West" attitude of Russian business people. One of the senior managers of one of our companies was murdered on the job. Now, in 2011, things are a lot more civilized in Russia and doing business there is much more straightforward. Mike says the "oligarchs" have begun to realize that honesty really is the best policy—at least now that they have each made their first billion or so.

During the 1998 financial crisis we had a board meeting in London when Mike made the point that there were tremendous values in the market as many of our investee companies needed more capital. The end result was that I proposed to IFC that they lead a capital increase. They did and the result was a return of about 40% annualized when the new fund was liquidated about five years later.

Now, probably helped by IFC's support when it was needed, even our board meetings were quite civilized and often quite fun, thanks to Mike. He always organized meetings to include interesting Russians and make them interesting events. One was a dinner with Gorbachev. Especially considering there were at least 30 of us there, Gorbachev put on a wonderfully intimate show. He didn't make a speech; he engaged us in conversation. One could see how the man grew to such power. Another occasion was having a former Soviet Cosmonaut and a former American Astronaut for dinner. They had both been the first of their own countrymen to walk in space. It was amazing how similar they both were in appearance and in their personalities. It was a touching experience, listening to the two of them reminisce. It reminded me of the time with Batterymarch when we met the two Soviets who had been the chief "designers" of the space station Mir and the Proton rockets. The latter were, as I mentioned before, two tough Jack Welch-type managers. The

Astronauts were both fun loving ex fighter pilot types.

However, all good things come to an end, and the Fund was finally liquidated a few years ago. Mike put on a wonderful "last dinner" in Moscow for the few remaining directors—Arthur Hartman, Dudley Fishburn and me—after our final board meeting. This was after a reception given by one of Mike's partners in his home outside Moscow: a vast modern house with lots of modern art and a large well groomed garden; lots of vodka, champagne and caviar. An earlier event Mike organized around another board meeting was in the tunnel under Red Square— from the Kremlin to open country about 20 miles east of Moscow—that had been built when the Germans invaded in 1941. It was the escape route for the Politburo members in the event the Germans actually took Moscow.

National Registry Company. My last remaining IFC involvement was with National Registry Company ("NRC"). This company was a direct result of the advisory work that I had done in Russia for Cesare Calari. Because of all the stealing of names from companies' share registries when the oligarchs competed to control them, it was essential if there was to be confidence in the market that share registries be run independently. So, our proposals to the Russian Securities Commission included setting up three separate share registry companies that would be owned by institutions taking no more than a 20% interest each so there would be at least five owners. In theory, they could then be trusted to be honest in handling company registries. All listed companies were required to choose one of these registries and hand over their own share registries to them. The end result was something like what happened in the rest of the world, except that in most other countries the registries tended to be run by commercial banks.

IFC then put on its institution building hat and agreed to sponsor the first independent registry. This was how NRC was born. We concluded a technical partner was essential and picked Bank of New York as the largest provider of that service in the U.S. We also attracted EBRD because of their more direct interest in Russia. Finally, we found two local partners, Lukoil, the largest Russian oil company, and UNEXIM

Bank, one of the leading local financial banks that was controlled by Interros, the holding company of a leading oligarch, Potanin. The deal was BNY, through two affiliates, would take 30% and provide the technology and the management. Lukoil would take 20% and turn over not only the Lukoil registry but also its "in house" registry to Nikoil (it was hoped that the actual Russian word would make it sound at least more like a financial entity than an oil company), which would be their shareholder. UNEXIM Bank would have 20% and provide customers from Interros' associated companies. EBRD and IFC would take 15% each and provide a form of political umbrella as well as customers from amongst the companies in which they invested.

BNY, in its role as technical partner, brought in three of its managers from New York to run the company. Dimitry Schatiloff, one of their registry people, was made president. Dimitry was of Russian parentage and his wife, Helen, was from Ukraine. Dimitry spoke fluent Russian and knew the business well, but he had never before been a CEO, so it took him some time to learn that part of the job. But he was a first rate person and wonderful company. Our initial problem started with BNY's systems people. I can't remember his name but their "lead director"—they were entitled to three, including Dimitry—insisted NRC install an IBM system. This turned out to be great for IBM because NRC became their first customer in Moscow and the contract BNY insisted on signing, which cost NRC $1 million a year, allowed them to install a large mainframe. We were paying for capacity ten times the maximum total volume even the most optimistic forecasters of the Russian market foresaw ten years ahead. In our wildest dreams, we never thought we could get more than 30% of the market. Nikoil was very upset about this, claiming their system, built by their own systems people, was good enough and NRC could have used it for nothing. The BNY people spurned this, saying it lacked sophistication and the technical integrity needed for a system operating in Russia. BNY was probably right on the integrity point, but I suspect this argument was one reason why the Lukoil account was never transferred, and why Nikoil and NRC were never merged as planned and agreed initially. As indicated later we won this battle, finally, and the two BNY people in charge of the systems went back to New

York, leaving Dimitry as the only BNY person still on the NRC payroll.

Cesare asked me to join the board after all of these decisions had been taken. My job was to try and solve the ensuing problems. It was only gradually, during several delightful dinners with Dimitry, that I learned the stories behind the stories. Needless to say, what looked fairly reasonable to IFC and EBRD on paper didn't work out that way in practice. First, the Russian Securities Commission allowed some 300 so-called independent registries to be formed, many of which were really controlled by listed companies. That meant a ridiculous level of competition for companies actually agreeing to give up their registries. But a lot of companies simply stayed with their disguised in-house registries. Lukoil quickly became the first sinner. They refused to transfer their registry and so kept it with Nikoil, which they claimed was now independent. So, not only did NRC lose its largest expected customer, but also one of its own shareholders became a competitor. We thought we had found a solution when I read the documentation for the Lukoil ADR issue for which BNY was the custodian. It said very clearly that NRC was to be the registry. Otherwise, Lukoil would have to inform all the ADR holders in writing of their decision not to have NRC. Neither event happened. So, Will Kaffenberger, Cesare Calari and I went to New York to lodge a formal complaint directly with BNY's CEO, Tom Renyi. In theory, BNY as the custodian had the right to force Lukoil to do something. Much to our surprise and annoyance, Renyi and his colleagues made it clear that Lukoil's ADR business was much more important to BNY than NRC so they weren't going to do anything about it. Unfortunately, IFC wasn't sufficiently interested to make an issue over it either. On the positive side, Interros did do the right thing. It turned over the registry of Norilsk, the world's largest nickel mine, which Interros controlled. Over the years, Norilsk provided NRC with more than 50% of its profits. But neither IFC nor EBRD provided any customers, so we were all sinners except UNEXIM.

My first year on the board of NRC was quite a learning experience. I knew nothing of the intricacies of a registry business beyond that it was operated by an elaborate computer software system. So monitoring it, especially at the board level, meant taking a lot on faith. My fellow board members were a good crowd, though. The BNY types were more technicians than managers—and one, Ken Lopian who joined a little later, was mainly in the business of winning ADR contracts. Our chairman was Mikhail Alekseev, the nominee of UNEXIM. Mikhail had been an official in the Soviet Ministry of Finance, with a PhD in Economics. He spoke perfect English. He ran the meetings as efficiently and correctly as anyone I knew in the West. The Nikoil nominee (and they changed quite often) tended to be what one would expect from the old Soviet system—bland most of the time, but uncompromising on any matter affecting Lukoil. A charming young Belgian was the first EBRD representative. But he moved out of EBRD after a year on the board to go into banking in London. His replacement was Kanako Sekine, a very smart Japanese lady with a lot of charm and a great sense of humor.

In my first few years, my main contribution was developing decent governance practices. It wasn't that the others were against such practices; it was just that they didn't understand them. For example, under Russian law, a company's audit committee was comprised of non-director representatives of the shareholders. There was nothing wrong with that in principle, but our audit committee didn't seem to meet with the auditors, nor did the auditors report to the board on the occasion when the board was supposed to approve the annual financial statements. Then, our first external auditors—the Russian office of one of the better Western firms—didn't seem to understand that audits were supposed to be completed to specified standards and within a time limit. At least the local audit partner and his manager didn't seem to understand despite the former being a Dutchman. I caused them to be replaced. Unfortunately, as it turned out, I also insisted that our cash reserves, some $8 million, should not all be held with UNEXIM, but diversified in at least four banks and in some government paper. This was absolutely correct in theory but a big mistake in practice as you will read later. Fortunately, in those first years, NRC was doing reasonably well for a new company. In 1997 we made a profit and for the first months of 1998 we were doing even better.

The key to our getting business was that serious and knowledgeable investors knew that companies whose registries were with us could not play the games other companies did. Names could not appear magically as new shareholders and real shareholders did not have to fear that their shares would suddenly be recorded as owned by someone else. The flip side of this was that the Russian business "Mafia" types would prevent company managements from transferring their registries to NRC. I suppose that not transferring was better than facing the wrath of the Mafia types: they had been known to use real physical force to make sure shareholders voted the right way at annual meetings. From 1996, when I started on the board, right through 2000, getting into any Russian office, including NRC's, involved showing passports and being cleared by machine gun toting security guards. But I never saw any serious problems or even any street muggings. Still, in NRC's branch offices we heard the story was different. There were several subtle and some less than subtle attempts by local Mafiosi to get us to rig the shareholder lists for annual meetings and in advance of hostile takeovers. Now, though, it seems the preferred method of attack is a lawsuit, so things have improved. But the main thing was we were building a reputation for integrity and it was paying off. Our list of companies whose registries we held was growing despite the fact that our fees were higher than most other registries.

Then came the Russian financial collapse. The first problem we faced was all the banks collapsed and our government paper became worthless. So, NRC's net worth dropped almost overnight from some $9 million to $1 million. That amount reflected mainly goodwill as our total start-up expenditures were mainly in PCs and software programs. Fortunately, Interros stood by us and honored most of the $1.5 million we had with UNEXIM Bank. The other banks just walked away. Whether Interros would have done this had we had the whole $8 million cash with them will never be known. But what is known is that they defaulted on large commitments to EBRD and IFC. It was rumored that UN-EXIM—and all the other Russian banks—transferred to their owners all their assets with any value before going into receivership. This less than ethical behavior kept the oligarchs afloat through the crisis. Interros produced a new bank called Rosbank that became their shareholder in NRC. I suppose it will never be known what really happened to the real financial and hard assets in that period. But one got an indication from an indiscrete statement made by Anatoly Chubais after he had left government to run UES, the main Russian electric utility company. He said quite openly that "they" had tricked the IMF out of $20 billion. Who the "they" were and who got the $20 billion is also unknown, but they weren't old Soviet pensioners.

The second problem was revenue collapsed as share trading dried-up and as our customer companies could not pay their bills. So NRC went from a small profit in 1997 and the first months of 1998 to a gigantic loss. Not only had we lost our cash reserves, but we had also lost the some $50,000 a month interest income on them. As I recall it, in 1998 our operating expenses were over $300,000 a month, of which some $100,000 were contractual leasing costs to IBM and the U.S. software company that provided our systems. Our revenues dropped to practically nothing. We were technically bankrupt. I recall our new auditors wanted to state in our year-end report that NRC was not a "going concern." Fortunately, by May 1999, when they were producing the draft financial statements, our position was improving so they dropped this qualification, which applied to our U.S. GAAP accounts. Strangely, the Russian accounts—the only ones we had to submit to the RSC and the central bank—did not show a loss. I never understood this and found it expedient at the time not to inquire. The main thing was our auditors were quite happy signing off on both statements—one showing a loss and a negative net worth and the other showing a profit and a positive net worth. We had cut some $50,000 a month from our variable expenses, mainly by reducing staff and salaries. EBRD and IFC had made more or less formal commitments to participate in a capital increase. And business was picking up. Also, Dimitry had done a wonderful job of salvaging some of our banking losses by swapping assets. Our auditors didn't help by claiming these antics would produce a tax bill, but we survived. By the end of 1999 we had even managed to replace IBM with our own systems developed in-house. Not only was the "hardware" just our own PCs but also our people, helped by some Russian systems specialists, produced software programs to run the business. This, of course, vindicated Nikoil's initial complaints about IBM. They were quite gracious in only saying "we told you so" very gently once. So, by 2000, our monthly costs were down to about $200,000 a month and our income was approaching that figure.

Then a new tragedy struck. Dimitry died of cancer. It was a truly sad time for all of us. Helen was now a widow, with no children to comfort her. We, both the NRC staff and the directors, all felt we had lost a good friend. To this day it still makes me sad to think of it. The funeral service in the Russian Orthodox Church on East 55th Street in New York was very moving. Besides his many relatives and friends, all of the board members were there along with several people from IFC who had known him. I can still see his body in his coffin; his face had his usual cheerful expression.

Life goes on. We appointed NRC's general counsel as interim president. The search for a new CEO ended up with us appointing a Rosbank nominee. This did not work out well although he, Alexi Goubin, had done a fine job in running the team that built our own systems to free us from IBM. I suppose it was the old story. A man excellent at a technical job—be it lawyering, marketing or IT—does not necessarily make a good CEO. After a year and several bad errors of judgment on his part, we were all losing patience. As the ringleader in getting him out, it was not unreasonable that Mikhail would ask me to be the one to tell him he was to be replaced as CEO but could stay as VP of IT. He did not take it well and chose to resign. It also became my job to explain the change to the other vice presidents. It was an interesting experience for me as a foreigner to be telling a group of Russians how their business was going to be run. In any event, we chose NRC's VP Marketing as the new CEO. Happily, Oleg proved himself. I didn't know it until recently when Helen Schatiloff told me, but he had been Dimitry's choice to succeed him. But illness overtook him so quickly that he did not have a chance to tell us.

2001 and 2002 were both good years for NRC. Its reputation in the market continued to grow, as did profits. The latter, though, were largely thanks to Norilsk, which went through a major shareholding restructuring. Unfortunately, while NRC proved itself during this period, IFC decided it wanted to sell out. In one sense, this was quite reasonable.

IFC had been a shareholder for seven years and its Charter suggests it sell its holdings, preferably to local investors, once its investee companies are in sound shape. Unfortunately, IFC management also muttered about a "reputational risk." That, of course, was always there in the Russian registry business, but it was declining as each year passed. Naturally though, IFC's position upset EBRD and the Russian shareholders because they were all in NRC because of IFC. This was a festering wound, but fortunately, IFC did not make it a major issue. It also followed that none of the other shareholders were prepared to bid for IFC's stock. The solution for IFC came unexpectedly. An Australian company that specializes in the registry and share certificate transfer business worldwide—Computershare—bought a minority interest and, finally, bought out IFC. Shortly after that, my role as the IFC director ended.

In any event, during my period on the board, I would visit Moscow about three times a year for board meetings, During the first few years; Dimitry would take me to dinner alone the night before the meeting to talk about life in general, his life in Moscow, and NRC. These were always pleasant occasions, albeit it meant a long day for me as I would fly there directly from DC with a three-hour stopover in London. I learned a lot from these evenings—not least of which was learning to like and respect Dimitry as both an individual and a professional. It became quite clear that he put his responsibilities to NRC ahead of his responsibility to his employer—BNY. It was during these sessions that I first found that the contracts with IBM and Safeguard were nothing much to do with a practical approach to doing NRC's business in Russia. Rather, as BNY was being paid a vast sum (relative to the size of NRC) to run the company, having all the technical work farmed out to U.S. companies they knew made it possible for them to avoid doing much work themselves. That these contracts ate into profits didn't matter that much to them as the ADR contacts were more important. As it was, as a form of performance bonus, they received the first 5% of net profit anyway. Starting sometime in 1998 after Dimitry died, we, the board members, would have dinner the night before the meeting, hosted by Mikhail. We would discuss what was on our minds about the company and, thus, pretty well cover the whole agenda, plus what was not up for formal discussion. Consequently the meetings usually took only the morning so I was able to take the British Airways late afternoon flight back to London where I would spend the night.

A final observation on my experiences with NRC is to note how Moscow has changed even since 1996. Over the ten years that I visited, the decor of the hotels and restaurants, the quality of the meals and the service—and the prices—all steadily improved, or increased. It was the same with the traffic to the airport. At the beginning, it took about 20 minutes from the Kremlin area. Now, it takes over an hour, even outside of rush hour. Fifteen years ago, the city was dowdy. By 2006, while still not Paris, there are many elegant new and refurbished buildings, and many of the people are dressed quite elegantly. The top quality restaurants, since about 2000, are as good as any you will find in New York, London or Paris. They have prices to match. One, I suppose recognizing their prices are a bit over the top, even offers half portions at only 2/3rds the price. Some are quite fun. One Ukrainian restaurant even has a farmyard in the center complete with a live milkmaid, a cow and chickens running around an authentic looking straw covered dirt floor. On the face of it, Russia is certainly catching up, but Moscow is not Russia.

Commonwealth Development Corporation Directorships

As you will remember, I had had many contacts with CDC over the years and had always enjoyed their people. So I was quite pleased when, in about 1993, my old colleague from IFC, Donald Peck, called me. Donald had joined CDC shortly after I retired from IFC. Our paths had crossed only about once a year after that. He knew I was passing through London and suggested we get together for lunch so he could introduce his new boss, Robert Binyon, who had just joined as CDC's financial markets director. Robert was a kindred spirit. He had spent some 20 years in merchant banking with Morgan Grenville in London and Tokyo and then with a Japanese bank, in London, before deciding to move on to a more wide ranging career in public service. This lunch was at

426

Robert's club, the Travellers. We just had a friendly chat about what was new in CDC and the latest gossip about IFC. It was very pleasant, but I didn't give much thought to it until I heard from Donald again a month or so later. Could we get together with Robert again? I forget where and what we talked about. But it was just another fun discussion about nothing special. If I suspected anything about why this was happening, it was that they were interested in my activities as an independent director of the Morgan Stanley funds. But I liked them both and thoroughly enjoyed our discussions. Finally, Robert asked to meet me separately. After the usual proper English pleasantries, he asked me if I would be interested in going on the board of the Africa private equity fund he was promoting for CDC. This was one of the initiatives they were engaged in with the Commonwealth Secretariat as part of what the latter called the "Commonwealth Private Investment Initiative." He and his colleagues felt I could make a contribution as chairman of the audit committee. Obviously, I was very flattered. It was great to find myself still remembered by those two fine institutions. Equally important to me was that Robert became a true friend despite many differences in our respective backgrounds.

Robert's task was to raise the money. This he did, bringing in government agencies in Singapore, Malaysia, Brunei and South Africa as well as Zimbabwe, Mauritius and Botswana. Between them they invested $38 million alongside CDC's $25 million. Joe Pillay, then Singapore's High Commissioner to the U.K., was to be chairman. As always, the CDC people were very gracious to me. I was invited to Marlborough House, the headquarters of the Commonwealth Secretariat, and then invited to the Commonwealth Secretariat annual meeting in Edinburgh where the formation of the fund was to be formally blessed by Nelson Mandela. This was in 1995. The fund was named Commonwealth Africa Investments, Limited, but we called it "Comafin."

COMAFIN. Of all the funds on whose boards I have served, Comafin has been the most interesting. While with IFC I had been involved in several investments in three Commonwealth African countries, but I had not actually spent much time in any of them. I did not even know that Mozambique had joined the Commonwealth (because of a marital connection of Mandela). CDC set up a wholly owned management company subsidiary (Comafin Management Limited ("CML"), in Harare to run it albeit the actual investing decisions were made in London by regular CDC investment people. With the possible exception of the Chile Fund and the Mauritius Fund, the board spent more time actually doing what directors are supposed to do than for any of the others. My part, the audit committee, was taken seriously not only by me but also by the whole board and the CDC professionals. However, unlike most private equity funds, the board, rather than CDC as the manager, had the final say, at least in the legal sense. (As the passage of time proved, this was not a good idea: it was hard for part time board members to question full time professionals on the technical details, especially when the latter were putting CDC money on the line too.) During the first four years when we were in the investment mode, the board's investment committee rarely questioned CDC's recommendations—neither the deal itself nor the pricing. In practice, CDC was often in a better position as a secured lender to deals where Comafin was an unsecured lender as well as an equity investor. But I will get to that later. Because of the way Comafin was structured, and thus our direct involvement in buy and sell decisions, we got to know the investee companies very well. Equally importantly, we directors got to know each other well.

Comafin had a fascinating board. Joe Pillay, its chairman, is a remarkable person. Before going to London, he had run Singapore's Monetary Authority, its investment company and been chairman of Singapore Airlines. In appearance and demeanor, he reminds one of Gandhi. He also has Gandhi's steel spine, as the few who have crossed him have learned to their cost. On a personal level, he is great company and has a wonderful sense of humor. Pen Kent was a CDC director and had been a deputy governor of the Bank of England. He was a very down-to-earth person, a great bird watcher and a fine companion. Sadly, when he retired from the CDC board, he resigned from Comafin too. Our other three shareholder nominees were from South Africa, Malaysia and Brunei. They were Dato Yakub Abu Bakar, Deputy Finance Minister of Brunei, Azlan Zainol, who was the CEO of the Malaysian Employee

Provident Fund, and Greg White from the Development Bank of Southern Africa ("DBSA")—South Africa's IFC. All but Greg were on the audit committee. CDC had also nominated three other "independent" directors (I was the fourth). They were Sam Jonah, the CEO of Ashanti Goldfields in Ghana, David Phiri, amongst other posts ex Governor of the bank of Zambia and Ambassador to Sweden, and Joe Wanjui, chairman of Stanbic Bank in Kenya. As a group we have all become good friends. Besides working together, we have had many congenial long dinners and evenings, talking about this and that. Notwithstanding that we come from eight countries on five continents, we all found we have much in common besides Comafin.

After two false starts with other CDC people seconded to the job of running CML, Jag Johal, an old CDC hand from India, was put in charge. Jag was one of the best fund administrators I have known over the years. I use the term administrator in the narrow sense: he and his team of two Zimbabwean professionals handled all the "back office" work including reporting to a rather demanding board. This became very apparent when we started asking him for his own analysis, rather than just CDC's status reports on the companies in our portfolio. They were almost as good as Mike Calvey's, despite the fact that Mike had many more years' experience as a manager and also the support of a relatively large well-trained staff in Moscow. Further, while Jag made no investment or divestment decisions, he executed some excellent sales. His position was difficult because, while being a CDC employee and being paid by CDC, his job description said he was to act for Comafin under the direction of the Comafin board. This put him often in the position of having to negotiate across the table from his own employer and paymaster. The board had several disagreements with CDC over the final two years when, as the fund had a ten-year life, we moved into the divestment mode.

This divestment stage started when it began to be apparent that CDC's and Comafin's interests were diverging. First, CDC was a long-term holder while Comafin was not. Second, and more recently, new management in CDC led to changes in strategy which in turn led to CDC changing its attitude towards some of our investments that no longer fitted their strategy. When the U.K. Government decided to privatize CDC, they decided they needed a, shall I say, securities-market-friendly chief executive rather than a business manager type. The then CEO, Roy Reynolds, was an engineer and had been CEO of a major Shell affiliate. So, the CDC board replaced him with Alan Gillespie, who had recently retired as a Goldman Sachs partner and thus fit the new bill perfectly. But he was a deal doer more than a hands-on manager, even of the financial type. Thus he and some of the people he brought in had a different approach to the more down-to-earth types already in CDC. The resultant internal changes and conflicts found their way down to the level of how they managed Comafin and its shareholders. Robert Binyon had brought the shareholders in at least in part on the basis of it being a continuation of a long relationship. By then, CDC had done a lot over the past 50 years for Singapore, Malaysia, Brunei and the African countries particularly. Consequently, they saw their investing in Comafin with CDC as moving from being very junior partners to almost equal partners in a project that would be developmental as well as financially rewarding. Certainly, the three investors from Asia did not see Comafin as a commercial investment. The new CDC didn't seem to see the relationships that way.

By 2002 we had made 18 investments in seven sub-Saharan African countries. Most of my experiences in the process bring back pleasant memories. One of the most interesting was the beer company we bought into in Maputo. We had one of our board meetings there so we could inspect it. I had heard a lot about Mozambique when it was a basket case even by African standards. Lena's brother, Johan, who had lived there then as a Swedish development aid official, told us many horror stories of starvation, civil war and corruption. So I expected the worst notwithstanding that the new government was supposed to be more enlightened. Actually, Maputo wasn't a bad town. But perhaps the local hotel colored my view. It was an old Portuguese colonial style building, right on the Indian Ocean, which had been restored. It was as good as any Orient Express hotel and looked a lot like the Copacabana Hotel in Rio. It was stunningly beautiful. The brewery was another matter. (It reminded me of the decrepit chemical factory I visited with Batterymarch in the foothills of the Urals.) I thought at the time it could never be a successful investment. It would have to be rebuilt but, fortunately, our main partners were two European breweries, Guinness and a French one, plus some locals who had been enticed to buy the stock with money loaned by the company. They were needed for political reasons and probably thought it was a free ride. I thought it was a pay-off. My concern seemed justified a year later when the European partners started fighting. But, much to my surprise, the French partner bought us all out. Comafin made a 17% return on its investment.

North of Mozambique is Tanzania, another less than successful country. As we had two investments there, we visited for a board meeting. Our first investment seemed very promising. It was a telephone system designed for poor countries based on pagers for the subscribers and a network of telephone booths that were connected to the headquarters by a cellular phone type line-of-sight system. When the pager beeped, the subscriber went to the nearest telephone booth. Payment was by a debit card, which they bought from the company with cash up front. I thought it was a great idea and was very impressed with the promoter. She was a very bright and attractive woman from Liberia who had been to Harvard Business School. It was the Harvard connection that got her the financing. Unfortunately, based on her success in Dar es Salaam, she decided to expand the company across Africa. That brought her down, so that investment was a complete write-off. Our other investment there was in an apartment hotel operation for expatriates spending six months or so in Dar. This was quite successful for a few years. Then others copied the concept to the point where it was just breaking even, the last I heard.

We had three investments in Zambia, which we visited for the first time in 2002. Lusaka is not a pleasant town—a bit like Canberra in that it seems more like a collection of suburbs without a real center. I remember walking around for a couple of hours one day. About half a mile from our hotel, I came across what turned out to be the High Court building. It was an impressive and well-guarded structure—especially that day as there was a large demonstration outside. But it was all very peaceful so I felt no qualms about milling around with the demonstrators and

Retirement, After a Fashion

I felt no qualms about milling around with the demonstrators and watching the soldiers who were just watching us. One of our investments was a shopping center called Manda Hill. It looked just like any shopping center in a small U.S. city—lots of smart shops and very clean and attractive public areas. It even had an English type pub in which we had lunch. They provided excellent pub food and first rate service. We made a reasonable profit from Manda Hill, which we happened to own 100%. We also had minority interests in a cellular phone company and a zinc processing operation. The former suffered from competition from a new government company, which can be the kiss of death in a country like Zambia. The second was in an old lead and zinc mining/smelting plant about 100 miles north of Lusaka. It was interesting to see this very large plant in the middle of nowhere. The ore had run out so it had been abandoned long ago. Then a retired British mining engineer decided that the tailings could be processed using a new technique. CDC supported him. I hope he succeeded as it takes some dedication just to live so far from even local civilization in a very barren semi-desert area. It's not at all the lush jungle type area one thinks of as typical of southern Africa.

Our two ventures in Kenya were disasters. The first was a company called African Cargo Handling, which operated at Nairobi airport. CDC had a senior loan and we both had some equity. CDC decided a year after we invested to sell to an airline company. They took advantage of their senior position to get most of their money back at Comafin's expense as we only had equity. The second was a company called "Sulmac," a farming operation that CDC had bought from a major multinational company that wanted out of Kenya. As CDC in those days often managed businesses directly and as agriculture was one of their priority sectors, they obviously thought they had made a good purchase and let Comafin take 29% at their cost. That was about $2.5 million to us. Purely by coincidence, on a flight to Nairobi, I happened to sit beside the CDC man who was managing it. This was shortly before our money was paid over. A year later, CDC told us we had to sell our 29% stake with theirs for a total amount of one dollar. Their case was that they now saw no future for the company, but had been bid $8 million or so

432

more types of aircraft than anyone I knew. After working the land for more than 50 years, they weren't very happy about what was happening. Our guide, the next day, told an even more harrowing story. While he was white, most of his fellow guides were black. Several of them had told tales of the "veterans" in their villages literally breaking the arms of women whose husbands were suspected of voting for the opposition.

I feel so sad about Zimbabwe and its people. It is a beautiful and inherently wealthy country that has been destroyed. They used to export grain; now they have to import it. Tourism was, next to agriculture, the largest source of foreign exchange. Now, there are very few foreign visitors. That reminds me of the last time I stayed at Miekles Hotel in Harare. It is, or was, considered one of the best in Africa, albeit it is a business hotel. It had four restaurants, all with different themes, but all with excellent service and delicious food. They used to be full, but not when I last stayed there some six years ago.

Comafin had one other "regional" investment. That was African Lion Limited, a private equity fund that specializes in start-up mining ventures in Africa. Early stage mining has always been a risky business, as I remember from my Nesbitt, Thomson days. As I recall it, only about one in a hundred ever got to the point where they paid dividends. African Lion had the additional problem for us of a disappearing management. When CDC put us into it (that is an investment in both the closed-end fund and the special purpose management company controlled by an Australian group), there were three professionals running it. Two were based in Johannesburg and one in Melbourne, where the parent management company was based. A year later we were down to the one in Melbourne. I asked if we had a key-man clause. CDC hadn't thought of that.

My Comafin story would not be complete without talking about Onesimo Musi and Fungayi Mungoni, CML's finance director and investment manager, respectively. They were both locally educated and well qualified professionals. One thing that impressed me tremendously about them was turning down the opportunity to be moved to CDC's Johannesburg office. Paul Fletcher, then CDC's top Africa man and now its CEO, asked me about this proposal before he made it to them. At the time, 2001, Zimbabwe was going through what then seemed to be the worst of the Mugabe period. Moving to Jo'burg would also give them the opportunity to join the mainstream of CDC rather than be just local hires of a small affiliate in Harare. To my surprise, they both turned down the offer. First, they were proud, courageous Zimbabweans—and certainly not Mugabe supporters. But second, they did not like the terms nor feel they had much to learn from the Jo'burg team. They preferred to stay and take the risk that CDC might close down the Harare opera-tion. Jag turned down the offer too. Obviously, Joe Pillay and the rest of the board would have been happy for them had they accepted, and we told them so. On the other hand, we were glad that they were prepared to stay with Comafin alone despite the fact that, in only a few years, it would be liquidated. I like to think their dedication was helped also by the fact that they knew they had the complete support of Comafin's board, especially Joe's. Their decision was followed by a rather unfor-tunate crisis.

During 2002 we had our third and fourth bad experience of CDC taking advantage of Comafin. This came to a climax at a board meeting when Paul Fletcher took exception to the rest of us continuing to talk amongst ourselves while he was absent temporarily from the meeting. At the time, CDC had two "management" directors on the Comafin board, but Valentine, the other one, was not present that day. As Paul was probably aware, the other shareholders had already pretty well de-cided to take advantage of their contractual right to cancel the manage-ment contract with CDC, so I can understand his being upset. But what he actually said when he returned and when Joe said we had continued discussing matters was quite strange. He said: "You have no right to continue discussions when I am not present." I could not believe that Paul would make such a meaningless statement. Joe responded equally directly but entirely properly: "Mr. Fletcher, board members have every right to discuss with any other board members anything they wish at any time they wish. It is standard practice and you should know that." I was surprised when, a few weeks later, Paul called me and said: "David, you know far more about these matters than I do. But surely what I said at that meeting was right." I just said he was wrong and that in some

438

countries there were accepted procedures where directors, who were not part of management, scheduled separate meetings without management directors present specifically to discuss what they felt about management, or anything else they had on their minds. What was more surprising to me was that he asked me rather than one of his own lawyers. I was reminded of all this recently when I read in the Financial Times that the U.K. financial regulators had announced the requirement that non-management directors of all listed companies have formal separate meetings on a regular basis.

I'm sure Paul Fletcher's direct public rebuke to Joe contributed to what happened at our next board meeting. We voted formally to cancel the management contract, applying the article in the contract that said a vote of 75% of the non-CDC shareholders could do this. The next step was to be a shareholder meeting—held as a formal written resolution by mail rather than a physical meeting—to ratify this decision. No one was more surprised than I when DBSA, whose director, Greg White, had been the most outspoken supporter of the decision, did not ratify it. This happened around the end of October. I assume CDC, which had $300 million to invest in Africa in 2003, had twisted their arms. The immediate result was that Joe Pillay announced that he was resigning. As he put it: "It seems I have lost the confidence of the board." My immediate reaction was to call Simon Cairns, CDC's non executive chairman, and say: "If Joe resigns it will be a major problem for CDC as Joe is still the most highly regarded financial man in S.E. Asia." I added that, while DBSA's behavior didn't help, the problem started with CDC and Paul's intemperate criticism of Joe. I said he should write Joe and apologize. Sadly, I got the impression that Simon didn't care that much. Fortunately, though, Robert Binyon and Jag did. The end result was that all the directors agreed that we should call a special board meeting and an EGM in Singapore on 5 December 2003, with two special items on the agendas: first, to ask Joe to withdraw his resignation; and, second, to review the management contract proposal again. All the board members wrote Joe asking him to defer his decision and agree to chair this meeting.

For this meeting, I flew to Singapore on Singapore Airlines, which I have always considered the world's best. As the meeting was in Singapore, and Joe had been chairman, it seemed fitting. Curiously, from DC —really from Newark—the first-class fare was then about $9,000 compared to $12,000 on British Airways which, while a first-rate airline, is not quite as good as Singapore. I have written a bit about Singapore already. It's not an exciting city, but I always enjoy going there because I admire the people so much.

Fortunately, the meeting went smoothly. DBSA redeemed itself and, in advance, CDC had agreed to amend the management arrangements and thus address our concerns about it. Our intent was to have control of CML and the initial plan was to demand that CDC sell us 51%. This negotiation became a lengthy process that was not really completed until our next meeting in Jo'burg. But, in any event, at that meeting in March, CDC agreed to expand the CML board from three to five and to elect two Comafin directors, thus, with Jag on our side, giving us effective operating control of it. I like to think I played a useful role here. Joe, typically gracious, took on-board one of my suggestions, which was we should seek control of CML through control of its board, not through ownership. He agreed that it was not necessary for us to try and force CDC to sell Comafin a shareholder position. This might have been a "break" issue for them because Paul had been making a great point with other DFIs that CDC had to have 100% control of its management companies.

In brief, CDC proposed to divide itself into a management company, "Manco" (finally incorporated as Actis), that would claim to be a commercial type private equity manager, and a portfolio investing company, "Investco" (retaining the original name, CDC), that would contract the management of its investments to "Manco." Apparently, the objective was to privatize "Manco" by selling it for a small sum to the current management. In this way, Alan Gillespie and Simon Cairns could claim to have achieved the U.K. government's goal to privatize CDC. Coincidentally, Paul Fletcher would be one of the main beneficiaries of this deal. The concern, as we in Comafin saw it and as Michael Barth (at the time, CEO of FMO) put it so well to a group looking into this for the U.K. Government, the real issue was not the new structure of CDC, but

the mandate given to, and the technical and ethical quality of, the people chosen to run the two new entities. That was a very tactful way of putting it. FMO had invested in many CDC projects over the years and had not had a good experience. More recently, Alan Gillespie and Paul Fletcher had both made comments at meetings with DFIs that had not gone down well. Teresa Barger (then in charge of IFC's investments in funds) and Michael Barth had both told me of this and said individually they were surprised at the pitch made to them. That is, that Actis (Manco) would manage not only Investco's (CDC's) assets but would also expect to manage money for other DFIs and for the private sector investors. It was clear to MFO and IFC that CDC's professionalism had declined since Gillespie and Fletcher had become involved. This was hardly surprising as neither, as good as they may have been in their previous businesses, had had any previous private equity experience. This rather amused me when I heard it because, after Alan Gillespie resigned, there was an ad in the Economist for a CEO of Actis. I called Simon Cairns at the time and suggested an old Advent hand, Nick Callinan, as an excellent candidate. I had started by saying to him: "As we all know there are no qualified people in CDC...." Simon responded by saying it was more important to have someone who knew the CDC client countries and they already had an internal candidate. That said something about the professionalism of CDC's own board at the time. That said, and as I will write about later, Actis became a very successful management company and over the next several years attracted quite a lot of new money to manage. So Simon turned out to be right in the end.

Around that time, Jag retired and was replaced by a new hire—Richard Robinson. Richard was English but living in Johannesburg, a lawyer by training. He was a fine manager but a little too blunt at times. However, as Comafin had by then a private equity remuneration package, he was quite well rewarded for his efforts. By this time the management contract had been transferred to Actis. Their partner in charge, Nkosana Moyo, a brilliant and charming Zimbabwean, had reorganized the bonus "carry" to reflect the fact that the new management's job was to salvage the mess that had been inherited. So the bonus was based on the value the new management added starting from a realistic current value of the portfolio.

Retirement, After a Fashion

The final Comafin board meeting was held in 2006 in Livingstone, Zambia. As Lena had been to Victoria Falls she didn't want to go again, so I took daughters Sarah and Melissa. We had a great time—we went first to Botswana, then to Livingstone. But it was sad to see the end of Comafin. However, as the end involved selling Comafin and its last investment to Actis under an arrangement that there would be a final payment to shareholders when the tag ends were sold, Nkosana asked the independent directors to join the special purpose management company's board to look after shareholders' interests. This involved several more meetings over the final year. The last of the meetings was in Johannesburg, or rather an attractive suburb. It was rather sad—it was just Joe Wanjui, David Phiri and me as directors, and Richard Robinson as CEO. We just rubber stamped the final agreements between investors and management and had a rather nostalgic dinner together.

South Asia Regional Fund ("SARF"). This brings me to my other CDC/Actis involvement—another closed-end private equity fund sponsored by CDC and the Commonwealth Secretariat. Again, it was thanks to Donald Peck, CDC's man in South Asia who would be running SARF, and Robert Binyon that I was asked to join the board and be chairman of the audit committee. I well remember Roy Reynolds, CDC's CEO at the time, saying when we were first introduced: "David, you seem to be the conscience of CDC."

CDC started promoting SARF in 1996. Later, when the core shareholders had been lined up, they—Simon Cairns, Roy Reynolds and Robert Binyon—asked me to go with them to Edinburgh for the launching. "Launching" is the U.K. term for formally announcing the establishment of a fund. This time, it was to take place during the Commonwealth Heads of Government meeting, an event that occurs every two years. The diplomatic term was "in the wings of ..." which means not as part of the official program but as a separate event during the meeting period. We, the interested parties and the various reporters there for the occasion, gathered in a separate room. On the podium sat the Prime Ministers of the U.K., India and Pakistan, plus a few others, including Simon Cairns and the Secretariat's Secretary General ("SG").

1991–

The preliminaries were amusing. The Pakistani PM had not been invited to the podium because, at that time, no money from Pakistan had been committed. But the fellow just marched up and edged himself into a chair next to the Indian PM. One noticed a few glares from the others. The ceremony was quite brief—a short speech of introduction by the SG introducing Tony Blair, who waxed eloquently for a few minutes, followed by a "thank you" from Simon.

It had been a pleasant two days in Edinburgh—my first visit since my Navy days in 1950. CDC hosted a fine dinner in an old hotel that was about an hour into the country. The rest of the time until the following evening, Simon, Roy, Robert and I wandered around together sightseeing. It was very gracious of them to include me considering I was just a "hired hand"—and part time at that.

I have just looked through the private placement memorandum that CDC produced to promote SARF. After recounting the Comafin experience, it noted how well CDC had done over the previous ten years or so in India. Listed in it were some dozen investments with IRRs of between 30% and 50%. Of course, there must have been failures too, but they had no obvious need to report those—all in all, an impressive performance. Likewise, I had rather forgotten that, around the developing world, they had raised over $100 million for other private equity funds they had managed in 12 countries, as well as investing in a dozen funds managed by others. But that was the "old CDC."

We—Simon, Robert and I—visited Toronto to try and get a Canadian investor for SARF and also to attract a chairman for CDC's next fund that would invest in the Caribbean region. On the former, we had, thanks to old friend Ced Ritchie who was the recently retired chairman of Bank of Nova Scotia ("BNS"), almost got BNS to commit $20 million. This would have been a political investment on their part as they had never invested in Asia. But, sadly, the Indians and the Pakistanis tested their nuclear bombs just before the closing with the obvious negative political consequences. That was too much for BNS so they backed out. On the second point with the help of Michael Koerner, we did convince a long-standing acquaintance of mine, Hal Jackman, to take on the task of becoming chairman of the Caribbean fund. That

turned out to be not my best move. Hal had said he had long given up commercial activities—after increasing the already substantial family wealth, he had moved on to be Lt. Governor of Ontario, chairman of the board of governors of the University of Toronto and otherwise devote his life to good works. Simon and I convinced him that CDC was also a "do good" operation. A little over a year later, the "old CDC" had been transformed to the new CDC. One of Alan Gillespie's early decisions was to walk away from the Caribbean fund because it was not sufficiently commercial. Obviously, Hal did too.

SARF had its first board meeting in Bangalore, where Donald Peck had his main office at the time. As Bangalore was the high tech center of India and the Fund expected to make investments there, it was an especially appropriate place to go. I had been there once before in my Batterymarch days and much preferred it to Bombay (now Mumbai) or Delhi. It was cleaner and more fun. Monkeys jumping around in the trees by the streets were much more entertaining than seeing the cows wandering the streets in Agra. As was the case with Comafin, the board was an interesting, very diverse group. Our chairman was a very distinguished and handsome Sri Lankan, Ken Balendra, who had been chairman of John Keells Holdings, the biggest private company in the country. He was then, in his retirement, chairman of the largest government owned bank. From India there were two members. Deepak Parekh, my old friend from HDFC days was asked by CDC to be one of the independent directors. Deepak was also on my audit committee. He is now, after establishing a major new bank that is now India's largest and a leasing company, probably the most important private sector financial man in India. Unfortunately, this has meant he was not able to attend many of our meetings. The other Indian was nominated by the three Indian financial institutions that were shareholders. This latter post rotated yearly. Next comes my old friend from Pakistan, Syed Babar Ali who I had known since my IFC days. Syed, who is my age, was a prominent industrialist and former Minister of Finance of Pakistan. The other directors included C.K. Hyder from Bangladesh, Russell Seal, representing CDC's own board, and Robert Binyon, representing CDC management. Russell was a fine person, a retired CEO of BP and very

444

worldly-wise and experienced. Unfortunately, he too retired from the CDC board and also from SARF's a year later. Finally, Muni Reedy, chairman of the State Bank of Mauritius, and Jean de Fondaumière, CEO of Swan Insurance, were elected to the board as the Mauritian nominees. Robert and Jean were also on the audit committee.

Generally, SARF operated the same way as Comafin in that both were corporations, both had audit committees and CDC managed both. Likewise, CDC was the largest investor with $25 million of $115 million in SARF. Finally, in both cases, the other shareholders were government entities from the region plus Singapore, Malaysia and Brunei. Despite the sponsorship of the Secretariat, the backing of the Commonwealth Heads of Government, and CDC, none of the wealthy Commonwealth countries have supported either of these two funds. The differences between the funds were in the structure and style of management. As Comafin was structured with an investment committee of the board with final investing authority, its board had to be much more "hands on" than SARF's, which had no such direct responsibility. (For clarification, U.K. law makes it clear that directors are responsible, ultimately, for everything that happens, whereas U.S. law puts responsibility with the CEO.) With the benefit of the Comafin experience, CDC recognized that, in private equity funds, the investors and their representatives on the boards normally did not want investment responsibilities—and that was why they hired professional managers and paid fees to them. Consequently, the SARF structure gave management full control of buy and sell decisions; thus there was no investment committee of the board. Of course, the more conventional legal structure was a partnership, with the manager as the general partner responsible for everything and the investors being limited partners and thus responsible for nothing. This partnership approach flowed from U.S. laws affecting pension funds and foundations, the main investors in funds. That is, their incomes were non-taxable only so long as they were not "in the business" of running things. Why CDC decided to structure Comafin as a corporation always surprised me. SARF was different. As they wanted it based in Mauritius because of the favorable tax treaty between India and Mauritius, it had to be a corporation because Mauritian law did not then contemplate partnerships.

Retirement, After a Fashion

The managerial arrangements—as opposed to the corporate structure—were different also because CDC's manager for Africa was based in London, whereas CDC's manager for South Asia was based in Delhi and had private equity and fund management experience. That the individual happened to be Donald Peck, who was already highly regarded and would be personally responsible, also made a difference. At a different level, the administrative management of Comafin, being handled by CML in Harare with dedicated staff, was much more professional in its communications and documentation to directors than was the administration of SARF. The CDC staff in India handled fund administration and had responsibility for the rest of CDC's portfolio there as well. Technically, though, because it was incorporated in Mauritius, SARF had a Mauritius company—International Management (Mauritius) Ltd.—as the legal administrator and investment manager. Legally, CDC Delhi was the "investment adviser" to the Mauritian manager. This was all very complicated, but one assumed that the added administrative costs were more than offset by the potential tax savings. At the time, had SARF been incorporated in India, taxes on profits would have been some 40% as compared to less than 5% in Mauritius under the tax treaty. Naturally, countries that make a business of being "tax havens" make a point of getting something in return—such as these administrative arrangements for which they can charge fees.

These differences in structure and style had two other related consequences. First, because of the London-Harare difference with Comafin, there was a little "we versus them" feeling in CDC. But, with SARF, as the same people in India made all the decisions, there was not this division. The end result was SARF did not have the conflict of interest situations that plagued Comafin. Second, Donald Peck was much more of a free spirit than the London-Harare crowd. Thus while, on balance, he made better decisions faster, he didn't see the need for communication and bonding with board members. This is not to say that Donald kept secrets or was indifferent to his board members or shareholders. It was rather the opposite. The problem was only that the written documentation was often too detailed and rather late. But he made up for this in his very open discussions at board meetings. Donald had

446

a doctorate in history from Oxford. Sometimes, we thought of him as rather the absent-minded professor type. I recall once he completely forgot we were supposed to have an audit committee meeting. But we all loved him.

So, back to events during SARF's life. For many of the reasons mentioned above, there were not so many colorful experiences to write about since it began operating in early 1998. The general plan was to have one meeting a year in Mauritius and one in a country where we invested. As I had been to Mauritius so many times, these trips were no longer much of an adventure for me. But the first SARF meeting was. Donald held it at one of the more attractive beach resort hotels, which would have been great had we not arrived about 12 hours before a major cyclone hit the island. The end result was we were all confined to our rooms (actually individual cottages with a bedroom, living room, etc.) soon after we arrived as the island and the hotel battened down. For dinner—individually in our rooms—the hotel provided each of us with some truly delicious sandwiches and a bottle of excellent French wine. That is everyone but our BP friend who it appears the hotel forgot was there! Russell was quite stoic about it and only mentioned it in passing the next morning. While the storm seemed to do a fair amount of damage to the picturesque thatched roofs and pulled up a few trees, to me it didn't seem much worse than a Chesapeake Bay thunderstorm. I had broken the curfew and left my room to look around a few times. The next day we had our meeting and then a dinner at one of my favorite restaurants on the beach. The food was fine as usual but they had been without electricity all day so there was no ice for my martini. After that experience, Donald decided to hold the meetings in the otherwise quite decent commercial hotel in Port Louis, the capital, on the harbor. I knew it well because Mauritius Fund had been an early investor in it and the associated shopping mall. It was really a quite attractive set-up, but if one was there much more than overnight it could be boring. There was nothing to do and nowhere to go except walk around the harbor. The swimming pool was just a large bathtub located in a corner of the building and exposed to the sun for about an hour a day. So for Donald and Robert, who tended to stay just one night, it was fine. For the others, it was less so.

447

Retirement, After a Fashion

Consequently, after staying there once, on subsequent occasions I simply stayed where I chose to stay. Finally, I selected "Le Cannonier" as my favorite hotel. I had gotten to know the ambience as I walked to it along the beach from the hotels slightly closer to town where I stayed for Mauritius Fund meetings. It had a wonderful setting, on a peninsula to the south of Grande Baie, the little fishing town some 20 miles up the coast from Port Louis. The promontory had been the site of a late 18th century fort, with lots of the buildings still remaining and cannons scattered about. I have always felt it was the best site with the best view of all the eight or so hotels I visited over the years. That said, Donald, who had made several investments in Mauritius for CDC, described it as "down market," which was true. A room and breakfast was about US $100 and it was definitely a family hotel. Most of the clientele were French and Italian, many with very young kids. The last time I was there I saw a really touching sight one evening. Most nights after dinner, the hotel puts on an outdoor floor show. This particular evening, walking by just before it started and looking at the audience sitting around, I saw two little girls who couldn't have been more than three, putting on their own dance show; the poor little dears looked as if they had only just learned how to walk.

Donald and his team made most of their investments in India. That was perfectly natural as the Indian economy dwarfs that of the rest of South Asia. Donald took us to see several of our investee companies based in the cities where we had our meetings. Our first, BPL Communications, in August 1998, was a small investment in terms of our percentage of the company's equity so we did not have any influence but, at $7.4 million, it was a quite large commitment for our fund, We were in good company though as besides some important foreign financial institutions, France Telecom and AT&T were both significant investors. Unfortunately, the Indian promoters ran it as if they were 100% owners. The bursting of the telecom bubble and fighting between the promoters and the other shareholders resulted in our having to write down the valuation considerably. All the foreign shareholders took the local shareholders to court over several serious violations of the investment agreements—one of which involved a major dilution of our ownership.

Another early investment, SIFY Technologies Limited, an Internet service provider, suffered a similar fate, but it was an exciting roller coaster ride. Our $12 million investment was, at the top of that bubble, worth over a billion dollars on paper shortly after it got its NASDAQ listing. Donald had tried to sell even to the point of suggesting to the board that the fund "short" the NASDAQ index. Sadly, and foolishly, the Indian government regulations prohibited an "India fund" from transferring locally purchased stock into the NASDAQ variety, so we could only sell at the local Indian price; but, despite that being much more realistic, there were no buyers. This was typical of the inflexibility of the Indian bureaucracy and the illiquidity of the Indian market at the time. The irony was that Indian government-controlled institutions owned some 20% of SARF's stock, so this decision cost India some $400 million.

Another early investment was in a much more mundane company that produced plastic tubes and the like—Shree Rama Multi Tech was its name. That too has been written down substantially although Donald was clever enough to sell some of our holdings at a good profit when it went public soon after we bought in. Our other six Indian investments were also in "old economy" stocks—a bank, a tractor manufacturer, a cable TV outfit, two manufacturers of household chemicals and a software company. I used to be surprised at the number of brilliant, articulate Indians one meets or hears about who are in the IT business in the U.S., as well as in India. (One of our most recent investments was in a U.S. software company that is owned and run by Indian nationals resident mainly in the U.S.) Then one remembers that, from a country with a population of over a billion, it's not really surprising that there are so many.

We had one meeting in Colombo where we had made two investments. One was SARF's first and it didn't seem to me a good idea at the time. The second worked out quite well. The first was in Aitken Spence & Co, a local conglomerate that I knew well from IFC days. It struck me at the time that it was stretching the rules for private equity. The company had been around for a 100 years, had been listed on the Colombo Stock Exchange for ten or so and was quite successful. All we were doing was buying some additional stock issued during a local underwriting. Our holding was less than 2%, so we had no influence on management. Four years later we sold out at a small loss. The second investment was in South Asia Gateway Terminals Limited, a new container facility. This was a "greenfields" investment and thus quite justified, albeit our share was only about 4%. This company did well and we made a reasonable profit.

In Bangladesh we made one investment, in Grameenphone Limited, a local mobile telecom company whose sponsoring investors are Telenor, the Norwegian state phone company that runs it, and Grameen Bank, a very successful local bank catering to "micro" businesses and small savers. Regrettably, the very able promoter of the company has had his reputation tarnished recently. Nevertheless, this has been an excellent start-up investment where we made an IRR over 30%. Dakha, the capital, is quite a place. It has the teeming population of Bombay and the colorful "jitney" jeep taxis one sees in Manila. But it is not a tourist destination.

Sadly for Syed Babar Ali, while we managed to visit Lahore for a board meeting, we never made an investment there. Lahore was an interesting city—much more attractive than Karachi. Donald took us to dinner at a restaurant in the old town with four floors of small dining rooms and a roof restaurant. It had a beautiful view of the old city, gloriously floodlit in green, red and white searchlights. The food was actually cooked in the street outside and hoisted up the outside of the building, floor by floor. Fortunately, Pakistan was a quiet country in those days.

We had a meeting in Bangkok once. Other than that Robert Binyon lived there in his CDC role as managing director for S.E. Asia, I can't think why. But Syed, still trying to make up for Lahore, hosted a great dinner at "The Fish Restaurant," so named in English without a Thai translation. It is in fact now a giant and very modern fish shop. You go to the counters and order what you see that you like. Then, you either take it home or have it cooked beside your table. The place can seat probably 700 people. It could be in Los Angeles. I first went there in about 1973 with my old friend Sukri. Then it seemed a rather Westernized Thai fish restaurant where you could choose your own fish from

450

Picnicking off Mekong River. Local man (L), Donald and Lucy (seated) Peck, "me" (seated), and Robert Binyon (R), my old friends from Commonwealth Development Corporation.

Lena and I with local kids on the Mekong River in Laos.

Cliff towering over the Mekong River, Laos.

ponds on the grounds rather than from a U.S. supermarket-like fish counter. Then, it might have accommodated 100 at the most. On our other evening there, Robert had us home for dinner with Sukri and his wife, whom we hadn't seen in ten years.

But the best part of our Bangkok meeting was that Robert took Donald Peck, his wife Lucy, and Lena and me to Laos. Luang Prabang, the old capital, was not what I expected. It was not an old French provincial town, but it was not a typical Asian village that one might expect to see in northern Thailand. It was something very much between those two extremes and also between the old and new. Another surprising thing, to me, was we never saw any police or soldiers. At least, we never saw anyone in uniform or carrying weapons. But it was a small Asian town, with thirty or so Temples—or was it 15 that I was taken to twice each? The ex king's palace looked like the typical middle-sized, Westernized suburban house that one sees in many parts of South East Asia. One could, for an extra U.S. dollar equivalent, see his collection of four old Cadillacs and Rolls Royces. The food in the local restaurants, that I had expected to be the best combination of French and Asian, was mediocre. I felt it all came from the same central communist kitchen. We did, however, find a French bistro/deli that provided quite good French type baguettes. (There were lots of tourists so there were French, English, and even Canadian and Swedish style eating places.) But the highlight of our three-day stay was our trip up the Mekong River. For $20, a 4'10" very elderly looking fellow and what might have been his ten-year-old grandson took us for the day in his equally ancient narrow old long boat powered by an ancient outboard engine. It looked like a dugout canoe. It was great fun but rather spooky at times. The river around there was fairly wide, muddy and swift. Every half hour or so, we would see a similar boat with local passengers. Occasionally we ran some rather formidable rapids. I had visions of Humphrey Bogart in the African Queen dragging his boat towards the shore—and then of patrol boats on the Mekong during the Vietnam War. We stopped off in some very primitive Hong villages that seemed to be still in the 18th century. But lunch was quite a contrast. Our guide took us ashore and, after a half-hour hike through the jungle, brought us to a waterfall. We camped on the rocks at the bottom and ate our baguettes and drank our French red wine from quite elegant wine glasses we had borrowed from the shop. It was quite surreal. It made me think of a Bergman film.

There was one unfortunate incident in the SARF saga. After the first ten years, the board agreed to a two-year extension. Missed, however, was extending the management's fixed fee. To address the problem, Actis asked for $785,000 to cover this, pointing out that this was a smaller amount than previously, thus they understood that in the final years with a smaller portfolio shareholders should not have to pay the full fee rate under the original contract. We thought this was reasonable, but were rather put off when they suggested further that the board should be cut from eight to four and board fees reduced from $7,500 to $3,750 a year. I'm sure it was coincidence but these proposed savings just happened to equal in total what Actis was asking for itself. In any event, several directors representing shareholders decided to resign. However, we pointed out that the $7,500 fee was less than half the going rate, thus a reduction was unacceptable; the portfolio may be smaller but our governance responsibilities were exactly the same.

As I write now in 2011, SARF is finally close to closing down—after an extension of two years and running six months beyond the second maturity date. One problem seemed to involve some legal issues concerning the last investment. The latest concern a few regulatory problems relating to the duties of the appointed Liquidator and the procedure for directors' names being taken off the Mauritian Companies Registry.

Comafin II. My final involvement with the Commonwealth Secretariat was initiated by Bishakha Mukherjee, the CS's "Observer" on the Comafin and SARF boards. Thus I suppose it was natural for her/them to turn to me for advice on "Comafin II."

At the Comafin board meeting in April 2000, Ian Goldin as a board member and as CEO of Development Bank of Southern Africa ("DBSA") had announced: "DBSA believes it is time to start preparing for a follow-on fund—Comafin II—subject to only one condition. DBSA is prepared to commit $25 million to it so long as it is not to be managed by CDC, but by a private management company. I don't have to tell you the reason for this condition." Naturally, this statement caused upset in CDC but support from the CS and nods of approval from our directors from Singapore, Malaysia and Brunei.

After the meeting, Bishakha asked me what I felt about the prospects. My fairly positive response led to my being asked to help further the cause. The next step was that Greg White, Ian's successor on the DBSA board, and I worked out a plan to proceed. I had started though by suggesting that perhaps a compromise on the management arrangement might be desirable. My thought was a joint venture between a private company and CDC, using CML as the vehicle. This seemed logical to me as there were no private management companies with much experience in Africa at the time and CDC did, after all, have many people on the ground there. This was not well received. Encouraged by the Secretariat, however, the South East Asian shareholders continued to support DBSA's proposal. Then, Greg While and I produced a summary private placement memorandum that included a proposal that, once we had built a core group of investors—three or four—we would invite them to interview a short list of prospective managers and let this group decide which one to appoint. I had suggested this because it was an approach that worked quite well for EMGF. (See my account of this adventure during my IFC days in an earlier chapter.) This was agreed. The next step was to approach Joe Pillay and ask his views. He was very supportive of a Comafin II and our approach, but warned us that Singapore was very unlikely to participate because the authorities felt they had done their duty for the Secretariat and Africa. He agreed though to make the proper introductions for us.

A few months later, by then May 2001, Greg, Joe, Wanjui, our Co-mafin board member from Kenya, and I visited Singapore, Malaysia and Brunei to present our proposal. This trip brought back many fond memories. I hadn't been to Kuala Lumpur for some ten years. My last visit to Singapore had been with the Morgan Stanley fund boards. Both places were much the same, though. The only striking feature was the new Pertamina office building in KL—the tallest in the world. As expected, we were very well received, but the responses were naturally noncommittal. In Brunei, which I had never visited before, we were graciously received by the Deputy Minister of Finance (the Sultan is also the MoF). Not only was he more positive about participating, but he also took us to dinner at one of his clubs, along with one of his colleagues. The latter, after dinner, took us to see the hotel the Sultan's younger brother had built. He didn't comment about it but we assumed he knew that we knew that it had gotten the younger brother "cut off" from the family money. The hotel was absolutely spectacular. It spread over what seemed to be some two hundred acres of grounds on a beach, with many individual small two- or three-story buildings with guestrooms and/or dining areas, separated by well-groomed gardens and swimming pools. It was beautifully designed and decorated and looked much like a small village. Our guide commented on only one thing— the glass sculpture in a corner in the main lobby. It was of an elephant, about three feet by three feet, sitting on a small table. He said it had cost over $500,000, but it was completely unprotected. It would have taken only a small accidental bump by someone walking by to knock it off and smash it. Apparently the rooms cost only around $300 a night as compared to the $200 plus at the other local hotel, the Sheraton where we were staying, which didn't have even a real dining room. Had it been in a well-known resort area the rates would have started at $1,000.

We spent the next several months trying to get our two best prospects —Brunei and Malaysia—to agree to move to the next stage. We had given them our list of prospective managers. This came down really to only two with any experience in African private equity, and neither of these did any business outside South Africa. I supposed it was hard for our Malaysian and Brunei friends to see DBSA as a world leader and the CS as a financial entity. Almost in desperation, I suggested to the CS that we join-up with IFC as a means of regaining some momentum. IFC had been trying for a year to find investors for their "Privatization Fund for Africa," for which they had obtained their board's approval to commit up to $50 million. They agreed. This was in November 2001. Consequently, I sounded out Teresa Barger the director in charge of IFC's investments in funds to see what she thought of our plan.

My case to her was that IFC had not been able to find money for their fund after getting their board approval a year earlier, thus they needed our help. What we brought, which IFC needed, was $25 million from DBSA and the strong likelihood of money from the S.E. Asian shareholders of Comafin. What IFC brought, that we needed, was some of their money and their prestige. The idea was that both initiatives would be mutually supportive. The Commonwealth financial authorities would be impressed with IFC's sponsorship and its money. The CS would introduce Zephyr Management to our prospective investors in the expectation that they might actually invest in both funds. Our proposal to IFC was that their fund "down load" some of their money to our fund—Comafin II—and treat it as a sub fund. That would mean IFC could consider all the money in Comafin II as money that could be counted as matching funds for their fund. This was important for IFC as they were supposed to invest only 20% of the total raised. In theory, for all of IFC's $50 million to be available, the total raised would have to be $250 million. This was not going to happen. But DBSA's $25 million and a potential $50 million from our friends from Malaysia and Brunei was $75 million more than they had before and from sources they had not been able to tap on their own. She commented that her board approval included appointing Zephyr Management as the manager, so, were we to combine forces, we would have to drop our idea and accept Zephyr. Fortunately, Zephyr had been at the top of our list anyway, so I thought that would work. As it was, I had known Tom Barry for some 20 years during his Rockefeller days and as an initial investor in EMGF. Everything I had heard about him since had been positive and he had certainly done well in Korea in partnership with my old friend Yeo Yun at KDIFC. I was quite confident that I could convince all on my side that we should drop our original idea of having the core group choose the manager.

By a fortunate coincidence, the Secretariat's new Secretary General, Don McKinnon, had a meeting already scheduled with Jim Wolfensohn, then president of the World Bank and IFC, for the upcoming January. Apparently, Jim welcomed the idea as, probably because of his Australian heritage, he had already indicated he wanted ways to collaborate with the Secretariat. The end result was our joint venture with IFC was endorsed enthusiastically at the highest levels.

Retirement, After a Fashion

This all made it look easy at first. For DBSA, Brunei and Malaysia, having IFC support, endorsed directly by the Word Bank's President, gave our friends more political cover as well as additional professional support. The only difficult part was explaining why we had to drop the idea of the core group choosing a manager and accepting Zephyr, an unknown quantity to them. But, as Zephyr was also endorsed by IFC, they accepted the change, despite sniping from CDC. At a Comafin board meeting in London in March, shortly after we had reached this agreement and with several other CDC types present, the CDC people accused Zephyr of incompetence and accused IFC of not having done its due diligence on Zephyr. Both IFC and CDC had invested in a Zephyr-managed fund for Nigeria that had had some difficulties so, in a way, they had a point. But their statements were unpleasant. They reminded us that we had promised our investors a competition for the management contract. It was pretty clear that CDC still hoped they could get our group to go with their new fund. My counter-attack was a spirited defense of Zephyr and IFC. Fortunately, I seemed to win the day. The more difficult task of sorting out the details then started.

The first issue was over the relationship between the two funds. After several rather convoluted meetings in DC and in London, Zephyr—Tom Barry—talked IFC and DBSA out of my proposal that Comafin II be a sub fund of IFC's fund and into a scheme involving two parallel funds, one of which would be called Pan Africa Investment Partners (PAIP) and one called Pan Commonwealth Africa Investment Partners (PCAIP). Both would be managed by Zephyr and treated as one fund with identical strategies—except PAIP's geographical weighting limits would favor North and French Africa by 15%, whereas PCAIP's limit would favor Southern Africa by 15%. To no avail, I pointed out that potential investors would be hard put to see the difference and, for the European investors particularly, PAIP would be favored. It would also lead to investors thinking that there was no need for two funds. That would be a quite rational business judgment, but following through with it would have eliminated the Commonwealth participants' support. I don't think Tom or Teresa really understood that the only reason Brunei and Malaysia would consider investing in a private equity fund in Africa was

458

political. That it was to be managed by a U.S. firm made it that much less attractive for them. In the end, we agreed there would be two funds.

The other issues were the terms and conditions. These were in two categories, and both involved much more haggling than I expected. The first was the funds' policy statements. The second was the terms of the manager's contract. It was not until July 2002—six months later—that they were settled between IFC, DBSA and Zephyr. The Secretariat and I played mainly the role of referees between the IFC and Zephyr. We also saw our role as including saying what we thought our investors could be expected to want. The only difference expected was that there would not be a Comafin type investment committee of the board to approve each investment; this would be left to management. There were many long meetings in DC and in London during which we tried to work things out. From the Secretariat, it was principally Bishakha and me, with Winston Cox, from Barbados, as Under Secretary General sometimes presiding over meetings when Teresa and Tom came to London. It was all much more complicated than was my EMGF saga. From Zephyr, it was always Tom, although towards the end his two principal managers, Mark Jennings and Runa Alam, also participated. Greg White was initially the main player from DBSA. But, in the end it was "TP" Mahloele, as their head of private equity, who was mainly involved. In IFC it was Teresa who made the final decisions, but Anne Chacour as Teresa's investment officer on the project and Ayaan Adam, speaking for IFC's Africa Department, were the main negotiators with Tom.

From a practical point of view, the policies and business terms of a fund cannot vary too far from the norm if buyers are to be found. That is, investors expect a diversified portfolio—15 to 20 separate investments across a range of industries and, in the case of a regional fund, countries. In private equity, they like to see the fund owning sufficient equity in a company to deserve an active role in its management so that it can "add value" as an active investor rather than as a passive one. That is why, for a fund in the $100 to $150 million size range, they are prepared to pay the manager in the range of a 2% fixed fee on the capital committed plus a 20% share of the profits, after a hurdle rate of return, as compared to around 1% fixed and no profit sharing for "passive" managers. Adding value takes time and skill and has to be paid for. IFC and DBSA agreed to such a fee structure for Zephyr. On the other hand, the policies of these funds as finally agreed allowed the manager to make as few as seven investments. This made the fees look high. Investors in private equity funds also tend to expect the legal structure to be that of a partnership rather than a corporation. Mainly because DBSA needed, for its own legal reasons, that the funds be Mauritian corporations, our two funds had to have governance structures somewhere in between. That is, the structure Zephyr proposed and IFC and DBSA accepted is that the "legal" board of directors would consist of two Mauritian residents (a requirement for all Mauritian companies), who would follow the "advice" of an "advisory committee." The latter is what partnerships have normally and their terms of reference specifically exclude any decision-making role for investors. The former is, of course, what funds with a corporate form have and their terms of reference—and most company laws insist on—usually state specifically that the board has ultimate responsibility. This is all perfectly legitimate under Mauritian law for companies that have no Mauritian shareholders. A Mauritian friend told me that the local ministry-of-finance people call such advisory committees "shadow boards."

My reaction to this structure was that it would have been better to have a standard board of directors, as does SARF. That is, the usual seven to nine members, of whom up to seven are shareholder representatives and two Mauritians. A partnership management structure could be likened, in this sense, to a racehorse while a company structure could be described as a workhorse in comparison. My clever remark to them was that what you have now is something that looks like a camel. But, as I also commented: "I'm just an advisor; it's your money."

Especially distressing to me was that after all these matters were settled and private placement memoranda produced, there would then have to be another round of negotiations with the prospective investors. In April 2003 Tom proposed, and IFC and DBSA agreed, that there would be a first closing in June, with about $50 million. This was expected to come from DBSA with their $25 million, FMO (the Dutch IFC equivalent) with $15 million and IFC with $10 million, because of its normal limit of investing no more than 20% of the total—plus any others who were ready by then, such as Brunei. He also proposed that the $50 million be invested in only four deals—including two that were already investments in his other funds. I expressed concern about this. First, launching with only $50 million would look odd with IFC as the sponsor being the smallest participant. I proposed that IFC get approval to invest at least $25 million, as EMGF was an established precedent for IFC having a higher share than 20%. Second, FMO was not yet committed, as their due diligence hadn't been completed. Third, this made the fee structure very much out of line. Zephyr would have been getting $1 million a year to make two new investments. However, I could see why IFC went along: their board approval would expire at the end of June, as it would reach its two-year cut off-date. Still, I could sympathize with Tom. Zephyr had spent a lot of money already promoting the fund and it would not be until the first closing that they would get their costs reimbursed. The problem was, as I saw it, that even if DBSA and FMO went along, the first closing might be the only closing. At the best of times, private equity for Africa was a "hard sell" and this was the worst of times. Further, the terms and structure of the deal were not the easiest to explain. Consequently, once the fund was launched, the pressure to get additional investors would be off as would any feeling of obligation that other Comafin investors had to invest. Certainly, Don McKinnon would feel no need to write more letters to finance ministers pleading for money. Rather, he would be in the happy position of being able to announce "mission accomplished" at his next Finance Ministers' meeting. All he had proposed was a Comafin II, not a Comafin II with a specific minimum amount of money.

In any event, as of October 2003, only IFC, DBSA and FMO had signed up, for a total of $40 million. I was asked initially to go on the advisory board of this but decided it had become too complicated so I declined—much to the relief of all concerned. To the best of my knowledge the Fund did quite well. In its second year, Tom Berry convinced one of the Saudis to invest $100 million in it. It was originally to be called Comafin II, of course. But that became Zephyr Africa. Finally, with the Saudis as the largest investor, it became Kingdom Zephyr Africa.

Retirement, After a Fashion

The Canada Investment Fund for Africa ("CIFA"). Fortunately for me as I was quickly running out of fun things to do, in 2004 the Canadian government announced an Africa initiative involving $500 million that was to include $100 million for private equity investment in Africa. When I heard they were calling for bids from managers to run it, it occurred to me that there was an opportunity to get involved. I knew there were no Canadian equity managers with African experience so the bidders were likely to be Canadians with no real qualifications for the job —Banks—or foreign entities such as CDC. Clearly, with its offices across Africa and its large private equity portfolio in Africa, CDC would be the best qualified foreign bidder.

I concluded that the best way to win the bid was for the most likely (with some related experience and connections in Ottawa) Canadian firm to joint venture with CDC. I remembered that my old friend from Montreal days, Carl Otto, ran a fund that invested in emerging market debt instruments—mainly IFC "B" loans. (When IFC made a loan to a company, it syndicated part of it to other investors. These had IFC protection—the name and any agreements as to availability of foreign exchange to pay the obligations—but the buyers accepted the full commercial credit risks.) In any event, this gave his company, Cordiant Capital, wide experience in emerging markets, if not in private equity, and, with strong government connections, the best chance of winning the bid. I called both Otto and Paul Fletcher to suggest they get together on a proposal. They did and they won the bid. My reward was to be asked to join the board of the special purpose management company they set up to run the Fund—CIFAGP ("GP" meaning general partner). CIFA was structured as a partnership with the usual fee arrangement— 2.5% fixed on the capital plus a 20% share of profits (the "carry") after a basic 8% return to investors.

This bidding process had started just before Actis was spun-off to be the CDC manager when the U.K. government was attempting to "privatize" CDC. But it ended up keeping CDC and its $2 billion portfolio. (It "privatized" Actis by selling 60% of its very small capital to the managers.) So, Paul Fletcher, the CDC CEO, and a small group of the professionals moved over, leaving Richard Laing as CEO of the new CDC.

Fortunately, these internal changes did not cause any problems. The new CDC would invest in CIFA and Actis would inherit the management role to be decided.

At this point Carl retired and was replaced by his number two, David Creighton. David is a fine manager and an all round good man. My opinion of him is colored, probably, by the fact that he is also a serious sailor, having braved most of the world's oceans either cruising or racing. Cleverly (able to use others' boats over the years), only recently has he acquired his own boat in Chester, Nova Scotia, one of my favorite places. By remarkable coincidence, his grandfather, "Dinty" Creighton had been a Nesbitt, Thomson vice president when I joined NT, so I had worked for him. It was odd that, after more than 50 years, I should end up working for Dinty's grandson. For me CIFAGP was also a reason to go back to Montreal. Staying at the Ritz there again reminded me of my having practically lived there for three months in 1967 when I was moving from NT Toronto to NT Montreal. Another remarkable coincidence was, years later arriving in Papeete in Tahiti with Lena once, the hotel manager there asking: "Are you the Mr. Gill who stayed at the Ritz in Montreal for three months?"

As Actis was both much larger and more experienced in emerging markets equity than Cordiant, it demanded a 70% interest in the profit flow and full management and administrative authority of the joint venture. Cordiant went along with this. Since activities started in June 2005, things have gone along smoothly. Of course, the general recession of the last couple of years saw the portfolio move from healthy gains to a 50% decline from the original amount committed of over $212 million. By 2008, the end of the investment period, there were 18 investments across Africa. They included a bank in Rwanda and several small mining companies and oil companies in and around Nigeria. The resource companies had Canadian sponsorship and thus were well known to Cordiant.

Our board meetings were held usually in London in conjunction with Actis' annual investor meetings (AIM) in April and the EMPEA (Emerging Markets Private Equity Association, the industry trade group) meetings in November, giving me opportunities to still visit London once or twice a year. This will continue until 2013, when CIFA is due to be wound up. If it does, that will mean I will have been involved in finance for more than 60 years. In fact, at our last meeting in April we considered the possibility of asking investors to extend its life by a year or two as some of investments were hard hit in the 2008 financial crisis and thus likely to take longer than originally expected to reach full value. So far, writing in August 2011, CIFA has moved along in an orderly fashion, with Actis doing its job of running it efficiently and Cordiant discretely staying in the background. Occasionally, David Creighton has asked me to intercede in a few issues, all of which were easily resolved. The fun part of those meetings so far was that Actis held the pre- or post-meeting dinner in elegant and/or exotic locales. One was literally on the Tower Bridge. I hadn't realized that the bridge design was such that it could accommodate several hundred attendees at dinners or receptions hosted by whoever wanted to pay the going rate. The last, in April 2011, was in a famous building designed by Indigo Jones called the "Banquet Hall" at Whitehall almost directly opposite "Number 10." It accommodated easily the 200 guests invited by Actis, most of whom were nominees of the investors who had interests in CIFA and other Actis funds investing in Africa.

My only regret about CIFA and Actis is that meetings have never—at least so far—been held in any of the countries where it invested. One reason for my regret is that some of the companies sounded very interesting. For example, Mouka Foam in Nigeria produces the foam used in making mattresses, and Sinai Marble is one of Egypt's major exporters. It also has interests in banks in Nigeria and Rwanda. Most of the investments are in South Africa. A slightly embarrassing item came up at our last meeting, thanks to Peter Olds, Actis' new man in Jo'burg, who must have done his homework on taking his new job. In any event he pointed out that the management contract between Actis and the investors stipulated that there would be two meetings a year, one of which would be in a country where the fund invested. As we had never done the latter, it was agreed that we would seek a formal waiver from investors. So our London meetings will continue.

As to the people on the GP board and the CIFA "Investors' Panel" members, there were quite a few. The CIFA contingent was comprised of David and me plus one of his colleagues. Actis had five members, including Peter Schmidt, a South African based in Jo'burg, and Adiba Ighodaro, a Nigerian Actis partner based in London. (Another small world story: I used to know Adiba's father when he was the Commonwealth Secretary General in London.) The investor nominees included Rod Evison of CDC. The others were a South African, a Government of Canada man, a fellow from NY Life and a lady from ADIA that I used to know from my EMGF days—Bodour Al Tamimi.

The meetings tended to be on the formal side because most people lived in London or thereabouts, so there was little in the way of afternoon or after dinner gatherings that was part of the fun of the Comafin and SARF meetings. David stayed at his club and I stayed at the Athenaeum. Looking back and thinking of my other experiences with private equity funds, especially Comafin, I realize I haven't had much to say about CIFA. That was also because CIFA was a seamless private equity fund operation. That said, as chairman of the CIFAGP board and because it was incorporated in the U.K., I did have some specific governance obligations. Consequently, as there was not an audit committee—typically the case with such funds—I made a point of having a meeting with CIFA's external auditors (KPMG) once a year to go over the annual financial statements. I think Anthony Cecil, KPMG's partner in charge, was pleased about this as it gave him and them the opportunity to fulfill their due diligence obligations. But, again, there were never any serious issues. In fact he spoke very highly of Actis' back office operations in India where they handled all of their accounting and control functions for the whole firm and their funds under management. As best I saw, there were few major issues or crises on the operational side—other than the down market. That said, they are a very professional group and I'm very fortunate to still be on the GP board. Unlike Morgan Stanley Asset Management, there is no retirement age and no one has even hinted at the reasonable thought that new blood might be a good idea. Amazing—CDC and its predecessor and follow-on companies have put up with me for over 40 years.

Fading away

All that remains is to say something about how these experiences as a financial frontiersman over all these 60 some years so far have played a role in shaping my life.

The lessons are simple. If you have some skills, are diligent and have lots of luck and are in the right place at the right time, you can have a rewarding and fun life and maybe make a contribution to others. As the book The Outliers put it, 10,000 hours of practice is important in gaining the skills. Another important point is, in making decisions, make sure you have all the facts and that you make every effort possible to verify their accuracy. Remember the Laurentide near-collapse described in an earlier chapter? Because of that traumatic experience I have taken the subject of governance very seriously ever since. In fact, my remaining few retirement jobs, including two as chairman of audit committees, came my way largely because of my (relative) expertise in that field. Clearly, part of the fading-away process is that, as time passes, there are fewer frontiers, financial or otherwise, in the sense of new ideas, countries or other schemes to come up with. I suppose corporate governance was my last frontier, as well as one of my first, although it was hardly a new idea in itself. Rather, it seems a lot of people—and institutions—don't pay much attention although its main components are just common sense and honesty. Think of recent banking scandals in New York, London, Geneva, etc.—not to mention countries such as Greece, Iceland and Ireland.

On the positive side, I think of the many business friends I have made during my financial life who have remained personal friends. In Toronto, there is Hugh Franks. In Montreal, David Creighton. In New York, Brad Warner. Sadly, in those three cities many good friends have died with the passing of 60 years. Cavan Atkinson in Toronto will always be remembered as will Paul Paine in Montreal. In Washington, only Michael Barth and Jay Tata and Teresa Barger are still about. Rudi van der Bijl will always be remembered. In Boston there are Peter Brooke and Dean LeBaron. Then also from Washington is Charles van der

Mandle, a personal friend who moved back to The Hague. As my CDC activities were more recent, I have more good friends there—Bill Mc-Dougall, Michael Phair, Donald Peck, Robert Binyon, William Knight and Dudley Fishburn. Long gone are Michael Caine, Alan Walters and Ken Berrill. In South America there are Pancho Ravecca in Uruguay and Roberto Bornhausen in Brazil. In Asia, there is still Sukri Kaewcharoen in Bangkok and Toti Que in the Philippines.

Finally, the most important thing any of us do in life is bringing up our children and preparing them for their futures. Some people have had a real impact on the world for good (Mother Teresa) or evil (Hitler). But mostly the great events and the great discoveries were not the result of one person's efforts. Grooming the next generation is important as they are the ones that will contribute to the next round of events and discoveries. I'm reminded of a great book, *How the Scots Invented the Modern World*.

Well, I've rambled on into my 60th year in finance, as I write about it now in 2011, my 20th in retirement, after a fashion. So, children and grandchildren, I shall stop now.

Post Script

"Fading away" reminds me of my formative years, which had an obvious bearing on my journey through life so far … home and school, Cambridge University and my time in the Royal Navy, then the Royal Canadian Navy and Toronto University. That is, from 1926, when I was born in Hamilton, Ontario, to 1952. When I was a kid my family moved often between Canada and England—I had crossed the Atlantic 14 times by ship by age 14. That was exciting. But the most interesting times during that period were the World War II years. As we lived in Dorking, 25 miles south of London, I saw the Battle of Britain being fought overhead and later, in 1940, at a distance, I saw London being blitzed. I will never forget seeing the London docks burning during the first night of the bombing after the Germans gave up daytime raids. Also, watching—and hearing—the "flying bombs" go by in 1944 and '45 are still vivid memories. Luckily for the Gill family, the closest bomb to hit near our house was about a quarter of a mile away. I actually saw the Heinkel 111 drop them (two of them) and watched them fall.

I was lucky to get a ROTC-type naval scholarship to Cambridge for a year in 1944. What I remember most was rowing in my college "eight" and my first flight in a fighting aircraft—a U.S. Air Force B-17 on a test flight. My time in the navy was great. Training to be an "Observer" (a Navigator) in Trinidad in 1945 and then cruising in Canadian navy aircraft carriers to exotic ports such as Havana and Lisbon was fun. Flying from carriers was a lot less dangerous than most people think. The University of Toronto was just hard work and very little play—except for occasional weekends in New York and summers back flying with the navy. The RCN was very good to me: it provided me with the best summer job I could want.

PART IV

POST SCRIPT–
THE FORMATIVE YEARS

Bertram Thomas Gill (my father) in his early twenties, taken in Durban, South Africa, about 1919.

CHAPTER VIII

Home and School: 1926-1944

I t is said one's early childhood has an influence on one's professional life. I'm not sure that mine would be of interest to anyone, even my immediate family. However, son Chris and our daughters want to hear it all, so I shall start with my earliest memories, for whatever they are worth.

What we do in life is a function of our upbringing, education, our will, or lack of it, and luck. My parents gave me a sound basic education including, most importantly, teaching me the difference between right and wrong and the merits of diligence. My father was a businessman, which made that type of life natural for me, despite his rather checkered career. He emigrated from South Africa to England in 1922 to marry my mother, who he had met while in hospital in England. He had served in the South African army in German South West Africa and then in France from 1914 to 1918, in a light artillery regiment. The most important lesson he taught me was from that period. It was: "Feed your horse before you feed yourself. If your horse dies, you die." He had crossed the Kalahari Desert on a horse he called "John Gilpin" in 1914, in the first campaign against the Germans. So he knew of what he spoke.

My father eventually became an officer of a middle-sized London Stock Exchange-listed company affiliated with U.S. Steel. From what I recall of my younger years, we had a reasonably affluent life style. Rather

471

IFIED COPY OF AN ENTRY OF MARRIAGE

y fee for this certificate is 3s. 9d.
rch is necessary to find the entry,
is payable in addition.

Given at the GENERAL REGISTER OF
SOMERSET HOUSE

Application Number P.6.S. 52.

Registration District _Tonbridge_

L. Marriage solemnized at *the Parish Church*
e *Parish* of *St Thomas, Southborough* in the *County of Kent*

(1) When married	(2) Name and surname	(3) Age	(4) Condition	Rank or profession	(6) Residence at the time of marriage	(7) Father's name and surname	Rank o
June Sixth 1921	Bertram Thomas Gill	24	Bachelor	Accountant	All Saints South Lambeth	Albert Gill	Hote
	Lydia Louisa Davis	21	Spinster	—	St Thomas Southborough	Benjamin Davis	Coal

ied in the *Parish Church* according to the *Rites and Ceremonies* of the *Established Church after Banns*

marriage { Bertram Thomas Gill } in the { Netta Hackett F.W. Hackett | William Hubert
solemnized { Lydia Louisa Davis } presence { Leslie T. Gridlay Benjamin Davis Jun.
een us, of us,

TIFIED to be a true copy of an entry in the certified copy of a Register of Marriges in the District above mentioned.
n at the GENERAL REGISTER OFFICE, SOMERSET HOUSE, LONDON, under the Seal of the said Office, the 21st day of January 1966.

772907

This certificate is issued in pursuance of section 65 of the Marriage Act, 1949. Subsection (3) of that section provides that any certified copy of an entry purporting to be sealed or stamped with the seal of the General Register Office shall be received as evidence of the marriage to which it relates without any further or other proof of the entry, and no certified copy purporting to have been given in the said Office shall be of any force or effect unless it is sealed or stamped as aforesaid.
CAUTION—Any person who (1) falsifies any of the particulars on this certificate, or (2) uses falsified certificate as true, knowing it to be false, is liable to prosecution.

Marriage certificate of my parents, Bertram Thomas Gill and Lydia Louisa Davis, in Southborough, County of Kent, England, 6 June 1921.

like a military family, we moved frequently back and forth between Canada and England. By age 14, I had crossed the Atlantic 14 times. That was by ship in those days. I was born in Hamilton, Ontario on 6 July 1926. When I was about seven, when we were living in a little town 30 miles from London called Southborough in Kent, my father decided to establish his own company in Canada, in Hamilton. Some seven years later, in 1938, he decided to start another one in England. So we moved again. As World War II started a year later, this turned out to have been bad timing. I was conscious of the gradual decline of his fortunes. In 1941, the family Chrysler Airflow, a large and exotic car for its day— that he brought with us from Hamilton—was exchanged for the equivalent of a Volkswagen. The only luxury left was a television set—one of

472

the first. Unfortunately, because television transmissions could be used by German aircraft as homing beacons, the service stopped when the war started. I suppose I learned from my father's business record that one could fail just as easily as succeed.

Our frequent moves between Canada and England made me used to finding new friends and getting used to different environments. What follows on that early period will be a series of snapshots of incidents that somehow stayed in my mind. My first memory was when I was a toddler—I was still crawling rather than walking. We were in a garden and I was sitting on the ground. Suddenly, this huge animal came up to me. I was terrified. Later, mother told me it was a dog that just licked me in the usual friendly dog way. I thought of that experience a lot over the years. Perhaps it was a dream.

The next was when I was about four. I was about to attend a private kindergarten in Tunbridge Wells, to where we had just moved. Tunbridge Wells was a small country town in Kent about 40 miles (an hour by train) southeast of London. It was also about the same distance to Hastings on the south coast, where my mother's family lived. My parents had taken me to Paris during the summer before I started kindergarten. On the first day we were all asked by the headmistress, who was the wife of the local vicar, what we had done over the holiday. My turn arrived: "We went to Paris." What was the most interesting thing you did? "Going up the Eiffel Tower." What did you think of it? "It smelled of beer." Naturally, mother asked me how the first day had gone, so I told her all of this. She was mortified. What would the Vicar think of parents who somehow let their infant learn not only what beer was, but also what it smelled like? But all was forgiven. To the best of my knowledge, my parents were not ostracized.

Then there was the embarrassing incident at a cocktail party my parents gave. As a happy five-year-old, I remember prancing around the sitting guests. Wandering behind a sofa, I focused on one of my uncles. I thought: what nice hair he had, all neatly combed—usually I was in trouble over my unruly hair. What fun, I thought. I will just give it a little tug. To my consternation, it all came off in my hand. You can imagine the rest. My misplaced interest was probably helped by the fact that I had also played another little game at this party—taking sips out of the glasses left by the adults. Did I have my first martini then? Besides these incidents etched into memory, I have many pleasant memories of my childhood at that house in Tunbridge Wells. It had a large garden, with lots of trees and a large brick wall on the side against the road. I had two favorite games. One was lying on top of the wall and dropping (not throwing) stones onto the heads of passers by. I thought I was very clever. They could not see me, as the wall must have been about ten feet high. Eventually, though, there were complaints from neighbors. They knew there was a little monster in the family and they heard me giggling after the drops. That ended that game. The other was very harmless. I would get my mother to watch me climb a tree. Then I would scamper out along a branch to nearby trees and come down from one that was two or three away and hide. Mother was supposed to wait patiently until I came down from the first tree. Visiting my mother's family in Hastings on the south coast was a joy. Playing on the seashore was my favorite activity. It was a stony beach with lots of rocks and little ponds that sometimes had fish caught in them as the tide went out. There was also the usual pier with children's circus-like amusement stalls where my parents would take me to play the games and gobble assorted "sweets," as candies were called.

We moved back to Hamilton in 1932, when I was about six, in the middle of the Depression. Hamilton was then a small city, known as the Pittsburgh of Canada, as it had our two main steel plants. It was very different from Tunbridge Wells. To me it was huge, noisy and dirty. Our first house there was quite small, compared to the one in England, and on a very barren urban street. The second was larger and on a much better street, reflecting, I guess, improvement in my father's new business. The big event was the birth of my sister Judy (christened Angela Louise, but called Judy for reasons that escape me). That was 5 May 1933.

I went to a local primary school, but have little recollection of what I did until the last year. Towards the end of that year we were taken to the secondary school where we would be going next. I was amazed at the sight of this huge, elegant building, with large pillars at the front. It looked to me like a palace. The sophisticated, well-dressed young ladies walking about also impressed me. I couldn't believe they were students. I was thrilled by the prospect of going to this beautiful place. But we went back to England that summer. What I remember from that school period was that I suffered severely from asthma. During the winter I would be bedridden for about a week every month. I would wake up at night unable to breathe and crying. My parents spent many hours holding me through those nights. They were wonderful. I must have been taken to every specialist within a hundred miles. The thought was that I was allergic to something, so I was given every imaginable test and shot, but nothing was found. I just continued to suffer—as did my poor parents—until I simply grew out of it when I was about 14.

I must have had some friends at school in Hamilton, but the only one I remember was Bud Jackson, who came back into my life in 1946, when I visited Hamilton while on leave from the navy. But I do remember getting into trouble a few times with friends from school. Both involved starting fires. The first was a great experiment building a matchbox house in the cellar of our house. Setting it on fire seemed a good idea at the time. I deserved the severe punishment I received. The second time was in a field on the Niagara Escarpment behind our house. A harmless little bonfire became quite a big fire in the dry grass. Fortunately, the wind was towards the escarpment so it burnt itself out quickly. That time, I was really scared and guilty, but I wasn't caught. That was the end of my experience playing with fire for some time, except for trying my first cigarette. I didn't like it and only tried a cigarette again once— when I was 18. The cigarette escapade I always associate with a near bad experience playing another game. We kids used to play a war game with slingshots. Just after trying smoking we started one and I very nearly lost an eye. I remember vividly seeing this little stone coming at me. I could see it clearly and was mesmerized by it. I only lost sight of it when it hit me exactly between the eyes. I still have a small scar.

My father took me to my first baseball game in the local sports stadium. We had the ritual hotdog and coke. But what I remember most was losing my father in the crowd coming out after the game. It was only for a few minutes, but I was very scared. I lost all interest in going to games. I think my father was just as glad as he didn't seem very interested in spectator sports either. I think I only attended one other game in my life—a football game at the University of Toronto in my first year there. It was a matter of duty. But I did go to watch my father play tennis in those days. He was an active member of the local tennis club. That was boring to me too, but I didn't have much choice.

An event that remains clearly in my mind was the big demonstration by the labor unions supporting the unemployed. As a steel town, Hamilton had more than its share in a period when unemployment was very severe everywhere. There was no unemployment insurance in those days. But there were some forms of community organizations to help. One example was seen in groups of unemployed coming around the residential areas less affected on a designated day and filing up to the back doors asking for an apple, which we were all organized to provide. Individually, they thanked Mother politely and tipped their hats—they all dressed in suits and wore hats. There was no unpleasantness let alone violence. But I remember my father telling us that there was a lot of animosity between the different ethnic groups—the more recent immigrants were resented for taking the jobs of "real' Canadians" by offering to work for less. Being recent immigrants ourselves he said he was resented. Signs outside some of the company employment offices read: "Dogs and Englishmen need not apply."

Most summers we rented a house on Burlington Beach. Hamilton is on a bay off the western end of Lake Ontario and "The Beach" was the thin strip of land separating the lake from the bay. It was much more fun than the city in the summer but nothing is, or was, perfect. Lovely hot sunny days, but swimming was difficult because Lake Ontario's water was always freezing cold. It is a very deep lake, even close to shore, and the summer sun was never hot enough for long enough to heat it. What we did was float on water mattresses and take occasional ten-second freezing plunges. The end result was lots of sunburn. One summer we rented a house in an inland resort area, perhaps 40 miles from Hamilton. (As nowadays, fathers went to work most days and it was mothers and the kids who had most of the holiday.) The big difference for me was that I had my first experience with golf at the resort's nine-hole course.

My first drive was memorable. The tee was on one side of a small ravine and the fairway continued on the other side. The gap looked at the time like a mile, but it was probably only 200 feet. Somehow, my aim was perfect and my ball landed on the other side in the center of the course. It was downhill the rest of the day and for the rest of my short golfing career. As I discovered much later when I joined the navy, I had an eyesight problem. It was called "poor convergence." It meant I was poor at judging changing distances—as when balls approached or when trying to land an aircraft. The only other entertainment was radio, the odd movie, and the weekend drives. Actually, the Hamilton area—the area between Toronto to the east and Niagara to the south around the corner of the lake and the hilly area of the Niagara Escarpment—was quite pretty. The weekend drives, looking back, were a bit of a cultural thing. There were not many cars and not many roads. We would drive around the Hamilton Bay area—clockwise one time and counter-clockwise the next. This must have had some strange effect on me. For many years afterwards I had a recurring dream about these drives. Our car would crash off Burlington Bridge. Somehow, I would fall out as it fell and I would see my parents still in it and try to get back to them. I always woke up before we hit the water.

In those days, kids—even pre-teens—were obsessed with kid radio programs. I forget what they were, probably cowboys and Indians and cops and robbers (of a more gentle kind than now), but we couldn't miss a second. I was permitted, eventually, to have a then hi-tech device—earphones—so my parents weren't disturbed. But they did draw the line at listening during meals. I thought they were really cruel.

The trip back to England in 1938 was really the first time I remembered much about ocean crossings, although it was my fourteenth—something I was proud of—14 Atlantic crossing by ship by age 14 was a world record as far as I knew. While some of the trips were business for my father and some holidays, we all seemed to go. The only conscious memory until that last one was of coming into New York harbor the first time: quite a sight even in the 1930s. The ships we traveled in were either the fast new ones that took five days or the smaller ones that took ten days. That last trip was in one of the latter—a sister ship to the

Athenia, one of the first passenger ships torpedoed, with a large loss of life, at the beginning of WWII—I think it was called "Letitia." They were Cunard Line ships of about ten thousand tons as compared to the "Queens" which were 30,000 tons and up. It was a very stormy trip and Mother and Judy and I were seriously seasick. Most of my time was spent in bed wishing for an early death. But there was a wonderfully sympathetic Irish steward who brought me plain white bread—no butter or mayonnaise—chicken sandwiches. He said I had to eat and that was the only food I was likely to keep down. He was right about that—most of the time. One day, my father persuaded me to join him in the dining room for a meal. I agreed, but it was a big mistake. Fortunately, there were not many people there, but I only got past the first few tables before the sight and smell of food got the better of me. Much to my embarrassment, I threw up on someone's table as I was trying to flee the room.

One problem for a youngster moving back and forth between Canada and England frequently was that one picked up the accent pretty quickly. Between age two and 14 or so, we had lived three times in England and three times in Canada before the last trip back to England. While starting out speaking "Canadian," I learned to speak with an English accent, picked up a Canadian accent, then an English one again, followed by another Canadian one before going back to England in 1938. That gave me many experiences of having otherwise well meaning friends of my parents and schoolmates asking me to talk in my funny accent or teasing me about it. I hated it. The back and forth, though, probably explains why I still have a "mid Atlantic" accent even after over 60 years living in Canada and the U.S.

As my father was attempting to start his new business in London, my parents picked Dorking, a pretty little town 20-odd miles south, as a convenient place to live. After finding a house, their next big decision was schools for Judy and me. There was a search for private schools near Dorking—boarding, the U.K. thing, was too expensive. There was one for Judy quite near our house, but not for me. Judy was entitled because her life in England during and after the war was not as much fun as mine—and later I escaped to the navy and Canada. The only bad part of the house was the garden and its very large lawn. During the summer my Saturday task was to mow it—with the old fashioned push machine. It took the whole day and turned me off lawns for many years. (Remember our house in Georgetown: small garden and no grass.)

Otherwise those pre-war days were very pleasant for me. Several of my mother's sisters lived nearby, as did several other family friends. We had trips to the "Continent" and, of course, London. One of my aunts lived there in a fine apartment building that was all the rage at the time. It was called Dolphin Square and it was right on the Thames and near Parliament. (To "fast forward," in the 1980s an IFC colleague from Iraq told me that he knew it quite well: his father had bought the whole building with its 300 or 400 apartments several years previously.) In any event, as a well brought up 14-year-old, I was once given the treat of staying there with Auntie Nell. I followed my mother's instructions one day and invited her to tea. I had been given careful instructions as to how to go about this; where to take her; how to get there; what to order; and how to pay the bill. It went slightly wrong at the beginning. We arrived—by taxi—at the destination. I asked for the bill and, after working out the tip, paid. The taxi driver looked at it and returned my "six pence" tip with a grin and said: "Young man, I think you need this more than I do." Unfortunately, Mother had not thought to say the minimum tip was "half a crown" (five times six pence) and still only about a dollar in today's money. Oh well, I realized eventually that the whole matter—except the minimum tip—had been carefully scripted in advance by mother and Auntie Nell.

I went to Dorking County School, something similar to a U.S. high school but, in the local pecking order, slightly more prestigious than a regular high school but not as good as a preparatory school. That was where my interest in finance started. My mathematics master had a great approach to teaching otherwise indifferent students. He taught us 14- and 15-year-old students math by having each of us build a stock portfolio using the London Stock Exchange quotes and data from the daily papers. The idea was to see who did best over the school year, starting with a hypothetical 100,000 pounds each. We learned multiplication, division and percentages by calculating price-earnings ratios and dividend yields. In the process, we also learned that stock prices fluctuated

479

for reasons not always related to earnings trends; that different industries had different value characteristics; and, thus, that diversification was a good idea. It was a fascinating game and I loved it. I continued to read the financial pages whenever I could after that year, even if I did not have the money to do anything about it.

In a very different way, my chemistry master also had an influence on my life—fortunately a brief one. He mentioned casually one day while making some other point that it was curious that an explosive like gunpowder could be made from materials still easily purchased in stores, despite the war. I set out the next Saturday to see if he was right. He was. So the next obvious step was to see if combining the three ingredients in the proportions he mentioned actually did produce gunpowder. The trick, of course, was to test it. This I did by stuffing some in a pipe and inserting the pipe into the side of an anti-tank ditch in the fields behind our house. This was 1942 and the invasion threat was long past, so the trenches were abandoned. Out of reach of prying eyes, I lit my fuse and ran. My homemade bomb was a spectacular success! There was a very loud bang and a very large hole in the side of the trench. Unfortunately, the noise brought a policeman to the scene. He thought, naturally, that I was the perpetrator of the crime and I certainly looked guilty as I tried to explain that I had just come to see what had happened. He searched me and found nothing. I was very relieved and very lucky. Had he done it more thoroughly, he would have found my remaining supply in a bag in one of my pockets. While I probably could have proved I was not a saboteur, damaging "His Majesty's" defense lines would have been frowned on to say the least. On the other hand, he was an old man by my standards then—probably about 40. Too old to be in the forces but probably old enough to know I was just an irresponsible teenager.

As I was a poor student, the incentive to take math seriously was a great advantage. It was the only subject in which I excelled and, probably, what got me through my matriculation exams. There were seven subjects, of which we had to pass at least five. I knew I would fail physics and chemistry; they were just beyond me. The "three Rs," and history and geography, I thought I could manage. But my morale was not helped by a visit at home by the Head Master to my parents one evening. He told them he was very concerned I would fail. Probably galvanized by his visit, I just scraped through. It was years before I realized I had a reading problem; Chris and Melissa both inherited it.

I remember much less about school than I remember about the war. Because of Dorking's location we had a grandstand view of preparations for war; the Battle of Britain; the "Blitz" on London and preparations for "D-Day." There were many scenes I will never forget. The first was helping my father build an "Anderson Shelter"—a standard prefabricated air raid shelter. We dug a huge (to me, then) hole, put in the corrugated iron sides and roof, and equipped it with bunks, blankets and food. We didn't use it much after the first few air raid alarms. During the digging process I played a very nasty trick on my father. I saw a large flock of birds in the distance. I knew they were birds but they looked a bit like planes. So I cried out "German bombers" and pointed. Dad fell for it. Afterwards he made it painfully clear that it was not funny.

Dunkirk made the seriousness of war sink into my young and irresponsible 14-year-old head. After the remnants of the Allied armies escaped from France—some 300,000 of them—we saw them. The railway line from the South Coast ran past our school. We saw train after train full of soldiers every day for weeks. It was a sad sight. But we had no idea of the risks we all faced of a German invasion when our army had left all its equipment in France. We school kids sometimes went to railway crossings to wave and throw candies to them. Many threw us their caps! These we collected for a time. But they went out of favor when more exotic things started falling from the skies.

It seemed that the Battle of Britain was being fought over Dorking. We teenagers harvested spent bullets, anti-aircraft shell fragments and bits of aircraft wreckage. The last battle, on 15 September 1940, was unforgettable. Of the many memories that remain were seeing two German airmen parachuting. The first I saw floated past our garden about 100 yards up. It was amazing; he floated over a mile before he finally came down. He must have been wounded or dead because, rather than hanging vertically from his parachute, he was horizontal, with his arms and legs dangling and quite still. I could even see a medal dangling from

481

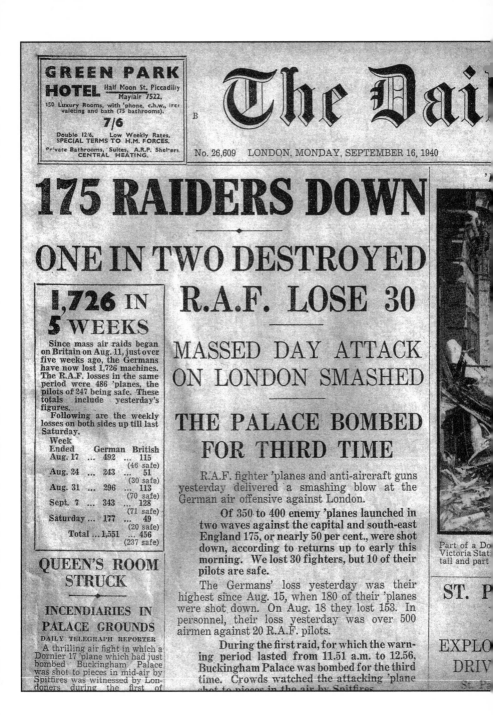

B

The Dail

No. 26,609   LONDON, MONDAY, SEPTEMBER 16, 1940

175 RAIDERS DOWN

ONE IN TWO DESTROYED

1,726 IN 5 WEEKS

Since mass air raids began on Britain on Aug. 11, just over five weeks ago, the Germans have now lost 1,726 machines. The R.A.F. losses in the same period were 486 'planes, the pilots of 247 being safe. These totals include yesterday's figures.

Following are the weekly losses on both sides up till last Saturday.

Week Ended	German	British
Aug. 17 ...	492 ...	115 (46 safe)
Aug. 24 ...	243 ...	51 (30 safe)
Aug. 31 ...	296 ...	113 (70 safe)
Sept. 7 ...	343 ...	128 (71 safe)
Saturday ...	177 ...	49 (20 safe)
Total ...1,551 ...		456 (237 safe)

QUEEN'S ROOM STRUCK

INCENDIARIES IN PALACE GROUNDS

DAILY TELEGRAPH REPORTER

A thrilling air fight in which a Dornier 17 'plane which had just bombed Buckingham Palace was shot to pieces in mid-air by Spitfires was witnessed by Londoners during the first of

R.A.F. LOSE 30

MASSED DAY ATTACK ON LONDON SMASHED

THE PALACE BOMBED FOR THIRD TIME

R.A.F. fighter 'planes and anti-aircraft guns yesterday delivered a smashing blow at the German air offensive against London.

Of 350 to 400 enemy 'planes launched in two waves against the capital and south-east England 175, or nearly 50 per cent., were shot down, according to returns up to early this morning. We lost 30 fighters, but 10 of their pilots are safe.

The Germans' loss yesterday was their highest since Aug. 15, when 180 of their 'planes were shot down. On Aug. 18 they lost 153. In personnel, their loss yesterday was over 500 airmen against 20 R.A.F. pilots.

During the first raid, for which the warning period lasted from 11.51 a.m. to 12.56, Buckingham Palace was bombed for the third time. Crowds watched the attacking 'plane shot to pieces in the air by Spitfires.

Part of a Do
Victoria Stati
tail and part

ST. P

EXPLO DRIV

St P

London's The Daily Mail, 16 September 1940 … "175 Raiders Down" was good for morale. (We later learned that the actual number downed was much lower.)

his neck. I thought it was an Iron Cross but who knows. He was in uniform rather than a flying suit. He was in sight for several minutes and he was the first "enemy" I had seen, and I was a 14-year-old and already determined to become a pilot. The second one was a bit gruesome. A German Heinkel 111 (twin-engine bomber) was caught in anti-aircraft fire on the way back from London. One of the defense batteries was a few miles from home, towards London. It had obviously badly damaged the plane as it was low and streaming smoke from one engine. About a mile away, with the plane flying towards us, the crew started bailing out. I could see quite clearly the last man coming out of the hatch just as another shell burst very close. The parachute opened, but all that was attached was a torso. Again, it floated almost overhead before coming to earth a mile or so away. One I did not see, because I was at school, was a pilot who landed in the farm fields about half a mile from home. Apparently, three local farm hands went after him with their pitchforks. He was saved by a couple of members of the Home Guard (local military units of men too old for regular service but young enough to support the regular army in fighting invaders) who were tracking his descent. Apparently they had a struggle to get him free to keep as a live prisoner. I learned this from my father, who happened to be one of the Home Guards participating in the rescue.

The arrival of the first refugee school children from London when the Blitz started was, in a way, exciting. They were from the East End and had pronounced "Cockney" accents. I don't think I had ever heard this before. We had four of these young girls billeted in our house for a while. I didn't know what to make of them. They were quite wild in a harmless way.

Another visitor to our house was more memorable. Just after the Battle of Britain, when the invasion scare was at its height, a friend of the family from Hamilton came for tea. He was a Canadian Army Brigadier General and he brought not only three of his staff officers, but also his security detail. I will never forget the excitement of seeing all of this "brass" sitting in our garden, with a detail of about 20 soldiers with Tommy guns standing guard around the house. I felt very important in the reflected glory.

Home and School

As soon as I was old enough—15—I joined the Air Training Corps (a reserve unit for kids waiting to join the RAF), became a "Firewatcher" (looking out for incendiary bombs) as part of the Civil Defense organization and a messenger for the Home Guard. All this kept me busy and out of trouble. Also, writing our matriculation exams (age 15 or 16 was the usual age for taking the exam in those days) in an air raid shelter gives the measure of how seriously the adults took the war risks. As I never actually saw anyone get hurt—except at a distance—and as no one in my family or anyone we even knew were killed or even seriously wounded during the war, it was mainly only a game for me. I was too young and callow to think much about people dying. That I might have been hurt or that we might have lost the war never occurred to me. It was fun taking part in air-raid drills and playing my small part when the air-raid sirens sounded. But there were never any incendiary bombs dropped when I was on duty. I had only two personal experiences with bombs. Everyone knew that if you heard it whistle on the way down, you were quite safe, but if it made a roaring noise you were at risk. I only heard the roaring once—when I was in bed one night with a bad cold. In the second that I heard the roar and recognized it, my first reaction was to get under the bed. But I was too sick to care so I just put my pillow over my face. The windows rattled when it exploded, but it was about a quarter of a mile away. It only got one house and no one was killed. We were all very lucky. Sadly, one of the few bomb fatalities in Dorking was a woman who had come down from London for a few days to get a rest from the Blitz. My last memory of bombings was during the period when single planes were attacking. We, the family, had just returned from shopping and I was unloading the car. Suddenly, out of the low clouds, coming from the north, a plane swept directly towards me. I thought I recognized the head-on silhouette as that of a Bristol Blenheim, one of our fighter/bombers. Then I thought: "No it has external bomb racks. It must be an He 111." In the split second gazing at it—it could not have been more then a quarter of a mile off—I saw the bombs detach. I rushed into the house shouting "bombs coming" or something like that. My father's reaction was "ridiculous, you couldn't see anything in this weather." He probably remembered my last alarm when we were building the air raid shelter. I said: "No, they are coming right towards us," and rushed out the back door into the garden. Again, we were lucky. The plane had veered to the left. I saw the two bombs quite clearly as they were coming down about a quarter of a mile to the east. The explosion was quite vivid but I thought rather small for what looked to me to be quite big bombs—not that I had seen any fall before.

However, Mother had a close call. She and Judy were walking in the country one day and, for no clear reason, a German fighter strafed the road they were on. Mother had her left foot nicked. This was during the winter of 1943/44 when there were lots of sneak attacks during the day by single German aircraft. I was safely off at Cambridge then. They didn't tell me about this until years later. I was strafed once but didn't know it at the time. I was at the local cinema one Saturday afternoon when a Dornier 17 decided that Dorking High Street looked like a good target and shot it up. In the cinema, we only heard loud banging noises on the roof. No one paid any attention. We only found out when we left after the show. Lots of bullets fired but hardly any damage and no one hit. But Uncle Leslie, Mother's sister Nell's husband, had a bit of bad luck. As many Englishmen did in those days, he stopped at a pub for a drink on the way home from work one evening. He picked the wrong one as it received a single bomb while he was there. But he was lucky; he only lost a finger.

In retrospect, we in Dorking were all very lucky. Not a single fatality amongst the local population while only 20 to 25 miles away there were of thousands in London and its suburbs. I still remember the first night the Germans gave up attacking the airfields and started bombing London. The sky to the north was one huge red glow—enhanced by the low cloud. It was the dockyard area burning. While there were many bigger raids after that, there was never one where the fires and the weather combined to light up the sky so much and for so long. The night of 10-11 May 1941, was the most devastating, but not for Dorking. (Read The Longest Night by Gavin Mortimer for a very moving account of it.)

Returning to the teenager game aspect, an important—and fun—part was trying to reach and scavenge equipment from downed German aircraft. (We were patriotic—we did not do it with crashed British planes.)

At the peak of the period, my collection included a radio from a German Messerschmitt Bf 109. One vivid memory was trying to reach a bomber I had seen shot down the night before. It was in a wooded area. We crept through to what I thought was the site. Crawling out from some bushes, I found myself staring at the sharp end of a bayonet, just inches from my face. I had found it, but the Army had got there first. Also, playing war games with the Home Guard was fun. At the time (late 1940 and early 1941) the Germans were expected to invade. Dorking was just on the wrong side of the third defense line.

I remember the Dorking Home Guard drilling with anything from swords and shotguns to serious weapons. My father, as an old soldier, was an early recruit. To begin, he had nothing; then a World War I rifle. A year later, when the scare was over and the real army was fully equipped again, he had quite an armory at home—a rifle, a Sten gun (a small machine gun), and a pistol. He kept all of these in the umbrella stand in the hall. The pistol was not his first, and there is a story about that. When he had no weapons other than the old shotgun, I came across a boy at school who boasted of having a revolver. I offered to swap my ME 109 radio for it. The deal was done and proudly I gave it to my father. The end of this story came when two policemen came to the house to ask how I had got it. It turned out it had been stolen. I had just assumed it was something from a German pilot. It was very, very embarrassing for my father, who should have known better, and terrifying for me. I do not seem to remember the details of this incident as well as I do the others—other than that they confiscated the gun.

My two years as an Air Cadet were great. Besides ground school—aircraft recognition, navigation, and rudimentary aircraft mechanics—we went on camps. One was to play soldiers, doing infantry training. Another one was to an air base where we were actually allowed one flight each. I was thrilled handling the controls of a Tiger Moth, the smallest and oldest single-engine biplane trainer in those days. The best experience was a one-year effort to build our own glider—a lot of hard but interesting work. But it ended badly. We had finally got it finished and air worthy—certified by our instructor. So we started our flying training. There were about ten of us. Naturally, seniority was the rule for who got behind the controls first, and I was in the middle. These were single-seaters so there was no "dual" instruction. The first step was being towed with all but the rudder locked. This was so you could learn how to keep the nose straight and the wings level. The second step was to be allowed to use all the controls but kept to such a low speed that the first take-offs and landings were only almost simultaneous small bumps. I got as far as qualifying on the first step. It was absolutely exhilarating and I could not wait my turn for steps two and three—actually flying the thing. I was barely 16 and the only thing I had driven until then was a bicycle. My seniors were all into step two, and I think one had actually qualified for step three. Sensibly our leaders did not want to risk anyone crashing the only glider we had until everyone had at least got through step two. Then tragedy struck. Unusual for southern England, there was a tremendous storm one night. The next day we found our hangar and our glider had, literally, been blown away. Both were totally destroyed.

The only time I ever felt nervous during that period was when seeing the "flying bombs"—the German V-1s—approaching. They were quite small—perhaps 15 feet long with a shorter wing span—and powered by a small but very noisy jet engine. Dorking was on the shortest land route from France to London and we saw a lot of them. The scary thing was waiting to hear the engines stop and the relief one felt when it had not happened before they came almost overhead. It was strange in a way that, even from dead ahead, you could still see the light of the exhaust flame. In a town with car traffic, you could still hear them approaching from some distance. I can still see in my mind's eye the red dots of the jet exhaust in the sky that I saw from my parent's bedroom window at night. Our house was in a valley and their room faced south so the V-1s would be aimed through the valley on their way to London. Some would hit the hills on either side; some would drop before they passed over; but most did pass over. As they approached, they seemed almost at eye level. The noise of the engines sometimes made the windows rattle as they passed, but it was reassuring to hear them. We were only in danger when the red dot disappeared and the engine noise stopped before it reached us.

Home and School

After finally managing to graduate from school in the summer of 1942 with my London University matriculation certificate, I had a year and a half to pass before I was old enough to join the navy. We graduated quite young in those days—I was just 16 and had finished my exams while still 15. But I had to wait for my seventeenth birthday before I could sign up. I had decided on the navy rather than the RAF because I liked my creature comforts. In the Air Force, you could end-up sleeping in tents and eating cold food. The Navy offered warm bunks and hot food. I had concluded that my perfect life would be to be a fighter pilot and die a hero's death when I was an old man of 30. It did not register with me then that, by volunteering for the Navy at 17, I avoided being called-up (English term for drafted) for the Army at 17-and-a-half. That would have had me fully trained as an infantryman just in time for D-Day. "Signing up" was quite an experience. After the usual form-filling and medical exams, I found my eyesight was not up to Pilot standard but acceptable for Observers (the Royal Navy's name for the back-seat man who did the navigation and electronics stuff—what the U.S. Navy calls a Radio Intercept Officer). This was a big disappointment but better than nothing. My problem was called "poor convergence"—I could not judge changing distances. This was an obvious problem when trying to land a plane, especially on an aircraft carrier. At least, though, it explained why I was so hopeless at sports involving hitting balls. The good news was that I found I qualified for the navy's equivalent of the ROTC program: a year—actually about eight months—at a university. I jumped at this because it meant I could start a few months earlier than otherwise. The final hurdle was the interview. This meant a trip to the Admiralty in London and facing a board of four senior officers, one of whom was a woman. I thought they must have been very senior because they seemed so old. Probably they were Captains and Commanders in their 30s and early 40s. Minutes afterwards I could not remember anything other than they seemed quite kindly. Somehow I was accepted and received a very formal certificate saying I was now Naval Airman Second Class Gill and to await posting to whichever university accepted me. I was amazed when I was notified later that I had got my first choice: Cambridge. For a non-" public school" boy who had only barely scraped through matriculation exams this was a miracle.

Having nothing else to do, I spent the waiting time at a temporary job working for an engineering company with offices near Dorking called Henley Wire and Cable. I was a trainee draughtsman, making blueprints for such complicated devices as hinges. It was interesting, though. My bosses took me to various sites in the south of England where they were building the things for which we were designing our gadgets. They were a pleasant group of people: mostly old, very few young like me, or female. Most of the 18- to 40-year-old males were off at war. One day we became rather close emotionally. It was just after the airborne attacks on three bridges in Holland—remember the film, A Bridge Too Far? Quite a few of the young men from Dorking were paratroopers, including one who had worked at Henley's and who was engaged to one of the girls. Not much work was done that day as we sat round a radio waiting for news. We learned later that the fiancé was one of the early "KIAs"—killed in action. I did not know it until after the war, but Henley's was one of the contractors building the cross-Channel fuel pipeline for the invasion of Europe. Notwithstanding it was a very temporary job I did take it seriously, even attending night courses at an engineering school. But it did not take long to see that engineering was not the career path for me: I was quite hopeless. The theoretical stuff was interesting—learning mechanical and electric engineering principles. It was the practical workshop tasks that were beyond me. The first simple task was filing a rough block of iron to make it a perfect cube with all sides the same length and even to one-hundredth of an inch. I never succeeded.

To attend these classes, I had to take the train to Guilford, some 15 miles from Dorking. There was a fair amount of "action" to watch while going back and forth, but mainly anti-aircraft fire and the occasional bomb in the distance. One night, though, I saw a bomber crash in flames quite close to the track. But there was one very sad experience. One evening when I arrived, there was a big crowd on the school football field. Curious as always, I joined them. What we were looking at were two clear three-to-six inch dents in the ice-hard ground—outlines of bodies. On one, I saw quite clearly the outline of his watch, which he must have been wearing outside his flying suit. They were only about 100 feet apart. Apparently two Mustangs—P-51s, the number one U.S. fighter at the time—had collided a few hours before. They were flying too low for the pilots' parachutes to open. We were all struck by the tragedy. It was the first time I had seen any of ours killed, even if I didn't actually see the bodies.

Notwithstanding the exciting things that happened during my wartime school days in Dorking, life also had its routine side. I remember, just before the last summer holiday of peace, my parents gave me the choice of riding lessons or golf. I don't remember why, but I chose golf. I should have known better after my golf experience when we lived in Hamilton. The local golf club was just a 15-minute bicycle ride away. I played a lot, mainly by myself. Occasionally, though, older men who were also alone asked me to join them. Being English, there was not much talking as we were strangers in the main. My last drive was my worst—and the last of my golfing career. I was playing with one of my contemporary friends. He was standing to my right and slightly behind, watching my drive. I hit the ball, didn't see it, but heard this "thump" beside me. I looked to my right and there he was flat on his back, unconscious. I had sliced the ball and hit him on the side of his head. It was a shot that would have been impossible to replicate—fast and over 90 degrees from the intended direction. It was several minutes before he came to. I was terrified, thinking I might have killed him. He hadn't the slightest idea what had hit him. A month later, the golf course was plowed-up and replaced by wheat fields and a few anti-aircraft gun emplacements.

That first year of the war, one of the great treats after school was having tea in one of the two local restaurants. Food was severely rationed but it wasn't until the war ended that I noticed it as a problem. We were never hungry, but such things as oranges and bananas just disappeared. I recall there was even a boys' club in Dorking. I suppose the idea even then was to keep the teenagers off the streets and out of trouble—an odd thought considering most of us boys were in one of the cadet corps and doing ARP (Air Raid Precautions) or Home Guard duties. But the club had such things as billiard tables and a series of lectures. One lecture

that had quite an impact on me was by a man who talked about the importance of reading serious books as a way to prepare for the outer world of work. While my mind was much more on joining up and flying, I read several of the current affairs books and biographies he recommended. It gave me the glimmer of an idea that I might end up doing something more constructive in my life after the war.

Another interest I had was English rugby. I was forced to play football (as soccer is called in the U.K.) and cricket at school, but I was a total failure: I just could not coordinate my eyes with my hands or feet. On the football team, I was told to be goalkeeper as that was the spot where I could cause the least damage, they thought. Nevertheless in a match with another school team, I scored an "own goal." This should have been impossible as the ball was just rolling slowly towards me in the middle of the goal area and there were no other players nearby. All I had to do was line myself up carefully and kick it straight ahead. I lined up all right, and I kicked it straight. It went straight, but straight up, over my head, and into the goal. Rugby was easier. Brute force was more important than precision. And I was big then—not only tall, but large. I had become the fat boy at school, having grown more sideways than upwards for a few years and was, at this time (just after school), beginning to grow taller rather than wider. In any event, during the last winter at home I played on the Dorking town team and really enjoyed it. Of course, my acceptance on the team had a lot to do with the fact that all the men who would normally have been on it were in the services. My lasting memory was the game we played against a neighboring town in a fog. Fogs in those days were serious fogs. From the middle of the field, not only could we not see the goal posts, we couldn't see the sides of the field.

One other thing we teenagers did was take the train to London to see the bombings. Not very clever, but no one seemed to notice as lots of people were going daily to London to work. But we didn't tell our parents. The train trips remind me of another very English wartime experience—the occasional combination of the blackout because of night air raids and the typical English winter fog. The latter was caused by the large amounts of coal and wood fires in peoples' houses. The combina-

491

tion of fog and smog had to be seen to be believed. I recall many times walking home from the railway station after my trips to Guilford when one literally could not see a foot ahead. On one street, I recall keeping my hand out to touch a wall on the inside so to avoid walking off the curb on the other. It was amazing: once wood and coal fires were banned in the 1950s, how those problems disappeared—an early example of improving the environment. In the meantime, the coal fire in our house was very important in those cold wartime winters. I can remember many an evening when we huddled around the fire—so close that our faces were uncomfortably hot, but our backs were still cold.

It was in late 1943 that I left home for Cambridge and the Navy. From Dorking to Cambridge was about a two-hour train ride via London. But I was going to another world. Except for short visits, I was never to live at home again. I often wonder what happened to my two main friends of those days—Robin Latcham and Tony deCourcy. We were in the same class in school. Robin also went into the Navy and became a Telegraphist Air Gunner, a "TAG." He married early and immigrated to Canada after the war. I saw Robin once in Toronto many years later, but we had grown apart by then. Tony became an architect. I recall we also only got together once after the war. It was at his invitation. We took the train to London to go to a concert at the Royal Albert Hall. I lost touch with both of them by 1947.

It is interesting that, while I received four "ribbons" for my naval service, the only times I saw any shooting was when I was a schoolboy.

CHAPTER IX

University of Cambridge and the Royal Navy: 1944–1946

When I volunteered for naval aviation, I had not thought especially of the advantages of the ROTC-type program the Royal Navy offered me. I had not thought about a university education at all in my enthusiasm to join up. Only after I had started at Cambridge did I begin to realize that being accepted into the Observer training program made it more likely that I would become a commissioned officer. In those days, unlike pilots and navigators in the U.S. military services, Royal Air Force pilots and navigators and Royal Navy pilots were not automatically commissioned. That was the British class system at work. It seems amazing now, but in those days in the U.K. there were many RAF Sergeant pilots flying Spitfires and captaining heavy bombers and the Royal Navy had Petty Officer pilots. It turned out that Observers were always commissioned: in the RN's wisdom, the Observer was the captain of the aircraft. It was the Observer who did the work of finding the enemy fleet and radioing back position, course and speed.

I had picked Cambridge over Oxford as my first choice because, having visited both towns with my parents years before the war, I remembered that Cambridge was the more attractive. It was a university with a town around it in a beautiful rural setting. Oxford was an industrial

*Cambridge, Pembroke College with a U.S. Army serviceman
in the foreground (1944). This is where I spent my year with the Royal Navy's
equivalent to the U.S. ROTC.*

city with a university in one corner. Both "campuses," if you can call them that, are very attractive: collections of ancient, often turreted, buildings surrounded by elegant gardens and lawns; narrow lanes and a river winding through. Of course, I knew nothing about educational standards or what the teaching process was. All I understood was that Oxford and Cambridge were superior to the "red brick" universities: that is, those newer universities in the big cities. Of course, Scotland was different: St. Andrews was also a real university.

The first thing I discovered from my acceptance letter was I had been accepted by a college, Pembroke College. I had never heard of it—or any of the other colleges for that matter. The University was—and remains—more of an administrative body. The teaching process was very different from what I was to experience later at the University of Toronto. The "Oxbridge" system centered on eight or so students for each Don who could be considered as similar to Lecturers or Tutors at U of T. The Dons were members of the quite independent colleges. As I recall it, the Professors were members of the university faculties. Only recently did I understand fully the uniqueness of the system when I read a book called The Dons: Mentors, Eccentrics and Geniuses. Besides giving the history of many of the better known Dons over the centuries, it explained how close a Labor government in England was to destroying the system in the 1960s. Apparently, in the interests of social equality, the Labor Party wanted to cut the funding to force Oxford and Cambridge to adopt the more European and American systems of state universities where the emphasis was on lectures and exams, with 500 or more students per teacher. That was what I was to experience later at the University of Toronto.

Settling in at Pembroke College was another unique experience. As a newcomer, I was placed in "rooms" outside the college. I shared a small one-bedroom apartment with another ROTC member: a young man from Cornwall with a very strong Cornish accent. He was even less adaptable to these new conditions than I. He lasted only a month. It was sad and strange. One day I came back to our room and found he had gone, without a word of explanation from anyone. After an initial introduction to the system, mainly by the staff, and meeting our respective

495

Dons, we were left to find our way. I recall my first social meeting was with the other members of the naval class. All, except the Cornishman and me, were public school boys. The conversation centered on mutual friends at their schools. We were ignored but not excluded. We just had nothing to say. Eventually, as naval training continued, and as we got involved in sports (rowing in my case) I became more or less accepted. Probably mainly because I was a Canadian and my accent was not too bad. In those days, more than now, accent was a mark of social class and just as important as to which school you went. After the first month, I felt quite comfortable and completely accepted. Actually, I did not find any of this particularly strange although later, reading the popular press on attitudes in class-conscious England, I wondered how it happened. My conclusion was that the English class system was not as rigid as claimed even in those days. To be accepted you just had to be reasonably intelligent (not too intelligent) and have reasonable manners. And, probably more important, not have an obvious chip on your shoulder.

While there, I "read"—and this was a good term for it as there was not much teaching—politics, history and economics: known as PHE. There were a few lectures. Mainly, it was writing papers for my Don, Wilfred Knox. He was a truly wonderful person. He was quite old then (well, maybe sixty), a Canon in the Church of England (historically, all Dons had been clerics), and a tremendously sympathetic teacher. I remember some four years later at Toronto, reading over some of my papers that he had corrected. They were truly awful: bad spelling, bad grammar, and not very clever. But his corrections were factual and kindly. I recalled the many times in his rooms for tea, when he administered to my academic needs, how gentle and understanding he was—to the point where I did not really realize what an under-educated callow fellow I was. For many years we exchanged two or three letters a year. He always seemed truly interested in what I was doing at the time. Only much later did I discover that he was a very well-known figure from a well-known family in English academia. He had three equally well-known brothers. One was a Monsignor in the Catholic Church, one had been editor of Punch, the British humor magazine with a reputation similar to that of The New Yorker, and one was a famous mathematician and civil servant. I will always have very fond memories of Wilfred Knox as my first mentor. How extremely fortunate I was.

Pembroke College, founded in 1347, was a distinguished old college —second in age only to Peterhouse. It was more renowned for sports than intellect, but it had many famous graduates over the years. Its older building included a chapel designed by Sir Christopher Wren and a dining hall that was equally grand. In my second term I graduated to rooms in college. They were impressive. I had more space for myself, then, than I had for a number of years after: a hallway, a living room, a kitchenette and a bedroom. Unfortunately, in keeping with the older Victorian building standards (my hall was modern compared to the 14th and 15th century wings in which others lived), the toilet was down the hall and the baths were in a different building. This latter was not much fun on cold rainy mornings. Another fascinating feature of domestic life in college was the "Scouts' or "Gips," the college servants that cleaned the rooms, lit the fires and made the beds for their "young gentlemen." Each four of us shared one. The other memorable staff group was the "Proctors" who were akin to military police. They patrolled the streets to make sure we students were properly attired in gowns, conducting ourselves as gentlemen and were in college by curfew. They were always polite, always firm and always wearing black bowler hats. I forget the exact time but the entrance—through the "Porters' Lodge"—was locked at night. If you happened to be out after curfew, the way in was through the old coal chute.

One way or another, I suppose largely through Wilfred Knox's introductions, we met and mingled a bit with several of the Fellows: older men in their 20s or 30s who were either unfit for military service or were doing other war work. There was a lot of scientific research and intelligence work going on at Cambridge. I recall traveling back from a rowing regatta in London with one of the scientists. While I only realized it much later, he hinted to me about German rocket developments. Six months or so later, we heard of the first "V-2" rockets striking London. Just as well the walls of that train compartment did not have ears or we both would have been in serious trouble with military intelligence. The most distinguished person I met at Cambridge was Professor Trevelyan.

Besides being Britain's leading historian, he was Dean of Trinity College at the time. But it was just some seminar he was leading that Wilfred Knox said I should attend. I did not realize I had a privileged invitation.

Thanks to the system, what I did mostly at Cambridge was row. I won a position in Pembroke College's "Second May Boat (War)," as number 7. These races were actually held in June. College "May Boats" were the entrants in the May Week races on the River Cam, which runs through Cambridge and from which the town got its name. "War" was added to the title because the colleges wanted to make it clear in the records that the crews, being there in wartime, were not up to the usually expected standard. As the river was too narrow for races to involve winning by passing other boats, moving ahead was achieved by bumping the stern of the boat ahead: hence the races were called "The Bumps." Each college had several Eights and the races were divided into four divisions, so there were four separate races each day for two days. Before the war, Pembroke fielded six May Boats, but by 1944 accidents to the boats had reduced the number to four. My boat was in the second division. Our wartime crew's performance got the boat back to the third division. In the first race, number six "caught a crab," as was the term for a bad oar stroke that could catapult the oarsman out of the boat. It was a big one—he ended up right in my lap, which stopped me as well as number eight behind me from pulling our weight on our oars. Except for participating in a weekend rowing regatta on the Thames (the course the Oxford-Cambridge races used), that was the end of my career as an oarsman in an eight. I did, however, do a lot of sculling on my own. Once I caught a remarkable crab. I was lifted right out of the boat and surfaced just in time to see my boat forging along under its own momentum without me. Finally, it slowed enough to capsize graciously. Sculls, as you know, have a high center of gravity, making them hard to climb in and out without tipping over. Once in, if you keep the ends of the oars balanced on the surface, they are quite stable. When rowing, they are like bicycles. The more speed, the more stable. But if you stop moving and take the oars out of the water, you have to be a trapeze artist to avoid going over.

My other sporting activity was sailing. I joined the Cambridge University Cruising Club. It had a fine clubhouse on the river downstream from the town and a fleet of about six 14-foot dinghies. As the river was only about 100 feet wide I gained considerable tacking skills.

Our Naval training was all of one day a week. Only on those days did we wear uniform. Unlike the U.S. Navy, where aviation cadets wore officers' uniforms, we wore ordinary seamen's "rig," including bellbottom trousers—and were treated as such. The only difference was a white band around our caps identifying us as officer candidates. Our drills and lectures were at Downing College. The lectures were mainly "seamanship" and naval history. The bad part was the physical training. Running was never my thing in those years. We were supposed to do six-minute miles as a qualification exam. I never made it. The worst was the five-mile run. I remember once the route ended with fording the river. Such a mass of us hit it that I think I was just swept across, never touching the bottom but certainly not swimming.

Those of us who were fledgling aviators were all fascinated by the U.S. air bases near Cambridge. We saw the fighters and bombers every day. Most days, we also saw the crews when they were on leave in town. I'm still embarrassed when I think of the times we enthusiasts accosted crew members in restaurants and even at the local tea dances, pestering them with questions about flying. They were invariably polite, but their eyes and thoughts were on the girls. How dumb we were.

One day, in what turned out to be a more productive way of learning about the U.S. Air Force, or Army Air Corp as it was then, two of us put on our uniforms and cycled to the nearest base. It must have been Bassingbourn. We went to the gate and told the guards we were going to be naval flyers and just wanted to come in and look around. He called an officer in public relations who, to our surprise, said "sure thing, do you guys want to take a ride?" You can imagine how excited we were. We were taken over to a crew area, introduced to a crew that was about to take their plane up for a test flight after some battle damage had been repaired. We were briefed; kitted-up and away we went. I was amazed; they were all so casual. The next morning they would be off on another mission. The crew chief (I guess that was what he was) showed us around the plane and let me operate the tail turret—move it, not fire the guns. Afterwards, the PR officer took us to the mess for a meal. Another amazing experience: a huge serving of roast beef and vegetables—and jam—followed by ice cream. We could not understand why there was jam with the beef, but we weren't complaining. The serving was at least a week's meat rations for us.

I tried to repay, if indirectly, the U.S. personnel the rest of my time at Cambridge. I had joined the English-Speaking Union—a large public service organization dedicated to improving relationships amongst the English-speaking peoples of the world. They had a branch in Cambridge to help U.S. and British Commonwealth (Empire then) service members. I went first to be a beneficiary. I was soon persuaded to be a tour guide showing servicemen the colleges. After my first harrowing experience, I loved doing it. That first time I was conscious of not knowing much about the other colleges. At the end of that tour, an American colonel from my group came up to thank me. He asked what I was doing there and how I enjoyed it. His parting comment was that he had enjoyed his three years there as an undergraduate before the war. Not a word about my obvious ignorance; he was a perfect gentleman.

My most moving experience was, again, to do with the war. We did not see much of it there, just the occasional German V-1 flying bomb that had gone astray. But I shall never forget the air armada flying off to France the night before D-Day—6 June 1944. Cambridge was a rallying point for both the bombers and the airborne troop carriers. In the early evening we saw and heard the DC-3s heading south with the paratroops. Later, we could hear the bombers. The roar was ear shattering all night. Sleep was impossible even if one was not moved by the obvious knowledge that what we were seeing and hearing was the prelude to the big battle.

I was sorry to leave Cambridge. It was a tremendous experience for me and I enjoyed every minute of every day. I think August was our last month. After a week's leave at home, the next move was back into uniform and off to HMS St. Vincent, the naval aviators' "boot camp" across the harbor from Portsmouth, the main naval base on the South Coast. St. Vincent was a "stone frigate;" that is, a land base rather than a ship. But all Royal Navy establishments are called ships as in "His Majesty's

Ship St. Vincent." (Now, with Queen Elizabeth, it would be "Her majesty's Ship.") You "came aboard" when you arrived and "went ashore" when you left. While "in"—never "on"—the ship, everything you did and said, and everywhere you went was "in a ship."

My first day as a full-time sailor started badly. About 20 of us from several universities were waiting in London to catch the designated train to Portsmouth. I was tall by English standards and that must have explained why they all thought I was the obvious leader type. So they all followed me blindly when we arrived at Portsmouth Harbor Station. The instructions were to turn right after getting off the train and get on the ferry that would be straight ahead which would take us to the town of Gosport across the harbor. There we would get a bus to "Vincent." Our arrival time was tied to the bus and ferry schedules meeting the train. "My" troop followed me onto the ferry, which cast off immediately. Gazing at the harbor, I was terrified to see our ferry was heading not across the harbor but straight out to sea. To France? Impossible: it was still enemy territory. But to where? We ended up an hour later at the Isle of Wight. What to do? Stay on the ferry for the return trip and find the right ferry, which I did, still followed by a somewhat disillusioned troop. Finally, we showed up at the front gate of HMS St. Vincent after three hours adrift—AWOL. We were greeted by a ferocious looking chief petty officer. From being a brilliant leader of men, I was convinced I was about to start my naval career as a convict in the "Brig," the RN term for jail. Fortunately, he must have seen worse, or I must have looked so pathetic that he hadn't the heart to charge me. All was forgiven. But it took me some time before my 20 companions forgave me.

Our six weeks at "Vincent" were quite an experience. All men (no women then) of the then "British Empire" who wanted to go into naval aviation had to join the Royal Navy as none of the other navies had a "Fleet Air Arm" or "Air Branch" as it was called as well. Australia, New Zealand, South Africa and Canada all had their own navies and air forces, but all were too small to have such specialist branches of their navies. That was not surprising, but it is long forgotten even by Canadians that Canada had some 1,000 ships in its navy and about the same number of aircraft in its air force in 1944. The end result was that the

2,000 of us who were at "Vincent" at any one time were from all over the world. Not just the four countries mentioned above, but also from such places as India, Hong Kong, the then Rhodesia and the West Indies. It was a real melting pot. The "Brits," who were in the majority, tended to look down on the "colonials," as we were called. This was a bit of a shock to some of the rest of us who had come straight from their homelands for the first time. They thought they would get some appreciation from the Brits for volunteering to help out.

The 2,000 of us were jammed into barracks rooms of about 50 men each. There were a few wash basins (cold water only) and toilets for each room. Showers were in another building about two minutes away at a fast run. The average class size was also about 50. They were called "courses" as we were divided up by category—Pilots, Observers and TAGs (Telegraphist Air Gunners)—each with a course number. I forget what my course number was, but it was significant because even-numbered courses did their flying training in Scotland and odd-numbered ones did it in Trinidad. Mine was an odd number. A winter in Scotland would not have been pleasant.

Our days started with a pre-breakfast five-mile run. There was then about 30 minutes to wash, change, have breakfast and get on parade. But the logistics were such that it was almost impossible to do all three in the time given unless you were amongst the first four back to get first crack at the four showers. This meant either not showering or not having breakfast. We became a smelly crowd. But we all discovered quickly that there were two other choices: to get onto the course boxing team or the water polo team. There were about 25 of us competing for the seven (I think it was seven) positions on our water polo team. I had never played before but I could swim better than most. The weeding-out process lasted three days. I survived despite my eyesight problem. The great advantage was the swim also served as a shower, so we could have breakfast. Anyway, I also hated running in those days. Much to my surprise, I turned out to be quite good at water polo and ended up playing on the St. Vincent team competing with other "ships'" teams during the last week of my time there.

The next event was morning "divisions" when all some 2,000 of us were lined up in platoons, companies, regiments, etc., in the best army style. We learned all the usual marching and drilling things. We were also taught how to be in charge of the units and give orders. The final ordeal each of us had to go through was to be brigade commander and run the whole show. Thinking back to that experience, I wonder what happened to my voice. I had no trouble then making the whole 2,000 hear me and carry out my orders in a proper military fashion. My relatives and friends tell me I murmur and mumble and am hardly hearable from a few feet away now. I know they are right, but what happened to my parade ground bark? Old age, maybe.

On the subject of drilling, a lasting memory of those days was of Chief Petty Officer Wilmott who was the chief drill instructor and disciplinarian. He was a very small man with a voice like a foghorn and binoculars for eyes. He had this wonderful ability to see the one man in the parade of 2,000 who did not have his cap on exactly "square" or was committing the sin of not looking directly ahead. I can still hear that voice saying: "B Company, third platoon, second rank, third man…" We were all terrified of him. On hearing "B," the other companies relaxed (mentally, no movement). Then finally "third man" and the rest stifled sighs of relief. The victim's punishment was not too bad, a little extra running, but it was the humiliation that hurt.

Boot camp training is probably more or less the same in every service in every country. In our case it was theory and practice: basic seamanship, weapons training, and building pride in the service. On the latter, I remember the day we spent rowing a "whaler"—a navy rowboat that had been a standard RN boat for centuries. It was quite unique in design, with two oars on the port side and three on the starboard (or was it the other way around?). What was the logic of that out-of-balance propulsion system? No one remembered. To continue the story, guided by a Petty Officer Boatswain, we five oarsmen battled the tide and the wind for about three hours to get around the harbor the long way to the side of HMS Victory—Nelson's flagship—which is still there to this day after over 200 years. As a rest, we were given a short history of Nelson and Victory. The final comment was on the mark. He said: "Well, that's a lot to live up to. If you don't make it here, you can always go to the

Army and join one of those Guards' regiments." They didn't call the Royal Navy the "senior service" for nothing.

One remarkable thing about our boot camp experience was that the training period for the whole 2,000 of us was extended by two weeks. The reason was that HM King George VI had decided to pay an inspection visit to the Portsmouth naval base. He was, of course, an ex naval officer and had served in World War I. We fledgling flyboys were honored by being selected to be members of his "Royal Guard of Honor." That meant starting by selecting a couple hundred of the tallest and smartest looking characters and drilling the life out of us for an extra hour a day for six weeks in advance. After the first two weeks, the two hundred were reduced to the final 99, plus a few spares, which was the ultimate number that comprised such a guard. There was one embarrassing incident, at least for me. We were organized in threes by height. The front row of three consisted of three Canadians. Geoffrey Payzant, from Halifax, who was slated for pilot training, and with whom I kept in touch for many years. I was next. The third, in the last row was "Dutch" van Steenburg. Obviously, we became pretty smart at doing the marching, presenting arms and all the rest. However, at the dress rehearsal the day before the big event, we went through our performance in front of all the Admirals in the Portsmouth Command. Here, I have to step back a bit and say that, amongst the many privations we suffered, as the lowest of the low in the naval hierarchy in wartime, was a shortage of toilet paper. So, it was routine when a new supply appeared that we all grabbed us much as we could for emergency use. The place we kept it—seamen's uniforms did not have much pocket space—was stuffed in our caps. The final part of the "drill"—after we had gone through the command "Royal Salute! Present Arms!" and then come back to the position of attention—was the order "Off Caps!" This meant that, with a very precise flourish, our right arms went up, our right hands grasped the side of our caps and, with one sharp swing, brought our caps down and held them over our hearts. It went perfectly except for one thing. From my cap came a flutter of little pieces of toilet paper that floated slowly to the ground in front of the Admirals. Unfortunately, I was right in front of them. I remember the horror in my heart as I realized what

504

With other fledgling flyboys, I was honored to be selected as a member of His Majesty's Royal Guard of Honor for the inspection visit by HM King George VI to the Portsmouth naval base in 1944. I am, literally, front and center in this photograph, within moments of inspection. In those days Royal Navy trainee flyers were ranked as ordinary seamen and did not become officers until they won their "wings." Consequently, we were wearing ordinary seamen's uniforms. This was unlike the U.S. Navy, which dressed its trainees as officer cadets.

was happening. I was staring straight ahead. I could not help but see the eyes of the Admiral only a few feet in front of me. He stared dead ahead. To my relief for the moment, the whole thing was ignored. We completed whatever it was we had to do and marched off. When we were dismissed by our Gunnery CPO, I assumed I was to be relieved on the spot and sent to the brig to await formal punishment. But, to my

505

everlasting relief, the whole matter was ignored. They all understood. "Guns" just said afterwards that we had better keep our personal reserves in our bunks the next day. The final show went off without a hitch. Again, being amongst the tallest we three Canadians still had center position for the inspection and led the guard. So we saw the King at quite close hand. He didn't say a word during the inspection, but he did look each of us in the eye. I remember he looked very, very tired, but I had never seen a king before. (The photo of this is still in my den.)

Those of us who survived St. Vincent—about 30 of the 50-odd that started our course—went on to the next phase of training. That was at Royal Naval Air Station Eastleigh, near Southport, which was north of Portsmouth. There, we specialized for the first time. We spent a month learning radio and radar theory, how to operate and repair the sets and sending and receiving Morse code. I don't remember much about the work, except we had to read and send Morse at 30 words a minute. Now, about 65 years later and with no practice since about 1947, I can still "work" Morse, but only at about ten words per minute. It is like riding a bicycle. Once you know how, you never forget. But times change and just a couple of years ago, Morse code as an "official" means of communication between ships and aircraft was finally and formally dropped. I seem to recall we used it in my reserve squadron in Toronto until I retired from flying in 1955. But most communication even then was "voice." The problem was, in those days, voice only worked on line-of-sight. As naval aircraft normally operated at no more than 3,000 feet, we had to depend on Morse when we were over 50 miles or so from "base."

The good thing about Eastleigh was the work was fun because it was more learning and less drilling. We only "fell in" (the term for lining up in columns of three for "divisions") once a day. But we had been well trained and treated it as a game. Thirty seconds before we were supposed to be on parade, the parade ground was deserted except for the Gunnery CPO and the duty officer in charge of the morning inspection. Thirty seconds later, all 200-odd of us were formed up in perfect order. The bad thing was that we were there in February during one of England's coldest winters in many years. One of our chores was washing

down the floors of our barracks and the workrooms every morning. It was more scraping than cleaning because when we poured our cold water (the only hot water we saw was in our tea) on the cold floors, it froze immediately. So, we had ice rinks for a while. But the time went quickly. Our next stop, after a week's leave, was an embarkation center near Dunfermline in Scotland. I don't remember a thing about the leave, but I do remember the night train from London to Edinburgh. It was standing room only. I slept in a luggage rack—those things above the seats in English train compartments. Actually, I didn't sleep much as the base of the rack was tilted at about a 30 degree angle towards the wall. Good for preventing luggage from falling out, but very uncomfortable for the human body. But it was a lot better than standing or lying on the floor and being stepped on.

The camp was interesting: 100-man barracks with several thousands of us in total. The camp was heavily guarded by Shore Patrols—the naval equivalent of Military Police—and entirely surrounded by a ten-foot barbed wire fence. All of this was designed not to keep the enemy out, but to keep us in. About 25 of those left on our course headed for Trinidad, and 100 or so pilots headed for Canada and the U.S. for their flying training. The rest were seamen going off to join ships, not all of them full of enthusiasm. The only human element of this that I remember was the fellow who had, secretly, got married on his leave. He was just 18 and, in getting married, had broken naval law. We had a lot of group loyalty by then and none of us was going to turn him in. But he was a sad case by the time we left two weeks later. We had no warning. We were just told to pack our bags—one big kit bag and a hammock—one morning and were marched out through the gate and through town to the railway station. It was the only time we saw the town of Dunfermline, a grim looking place. But we passed the local library that had an inscription indicating it had been donated by Andrew Carnegie, a local boy who had done well in the U.S. It made quite an impression. Only much later did I learn that he had donated hundreds of similar libraries around the U.K. and other countries.

After an hour on the train we ended at Glasgow docks where we boarded, of all ships, the Queen Mary—the largest and fastest Atlantic liner then. I had never sailed in her, but my father had. He took much delight later in telling me the space in which I had slept with several hundred others had been the first class lounge where he had spent much time in happier days. I was just as glad not to have known it then. They had put in rows of steel bunks ten deep. I think I was on about the sixth level. Getting in and out was quite a job. The ladder part was easy, but one tended to bang into others trying to sleep while on the way up or down. But at least we were above the water line and the air was relatively fresh. There were only two meals a day but the food was better than the Royal Navy fare we had had till then and there was much more of it. This was because the U.S. Army ran the ship. It was only the working crew that was British. The rest, including the gun crews, were all U.S. Army. Most of the passengers were U.S. wounded going home. It was the first most of us had seen of the dark side of war since the bombings —and that for me had been exciting, not bloody. It certainly sobered us up to see so many men missing arms and legs—and those were the lucky ones not in hospital wards. But this was March 1945, just after some of the hardest fighting in Europe.

I remembered my first cigarette as a 13-year-old when we saw the ship's Post Exchange. We could buy as much in the way of candies, soft drinks and cigarettes as we liked. In England, I think the candy ration was about four ounces a week then, so it was quite something. Cigarettes were rationed also. For the five-day trip we could "only" buy one carton each—for $2.00, less than the price of a package in England at the time, if you could get any. Even as a non-smoker, I couldn't turn down this bargain. I smoked one cigarette and quickly concluded I still didn't like them. So I gave the rest away. Soon we found that we naval types were not to be just passengers.

We were all assigned shipboard duties. As only could happen in the navy, we young trainees, who had never before seen a gun bigger than a .303 caliber rifle let alone a machine gun, were assigned to the 40-millimeter multi-barreled anti-aircraft guns. The other naval passengers— the seasoned crew of a cruiser returning to their ship after it had been repaired in Norfolk—were all assigned to the galley as cooks' helpers. But they didn't object as they could eat whatever and whenever they

508

wanted. We stood the usual duty watches—four hours on and eight hours off. My gun was on the starboard side just below the bridge. This was the first time I had experienced a steady wind of some 50 knots (about 65 mph) as the ship was steaming 30 knots into a 20-knot wind. Speed was of the essence. The fast liners did not travel in convoys and had no escorts after the first 100 miles out of port. The theory was, at 30 knots, they could outrun anything the Germans had. The only risk was a U-boat that just happened to have got itself positioned ahead of our line of course well in advance. Still, it would have been a hard shot. The U.S. Army gun crew I served with had been on the ship for two years and traveled many times to Europe and back, as well as to Australia and North Africa. The only sighting of the enemy they had was when a U-boat surfaced right beside the "Queen." It turned out that it had been sunk well before but because of the remaining buoyancy had settled just below the surface. The water pressure of 80,000 tons at 30 knots close by was enough to raise it temporarily. But, apparently, it all happened so fast that no one did a thing but watch it disappear below the surface again as the "Queen" left it astern. At least, that is what they told us. The fun part was the daily shooting practice. I had the easy job of just carrying the shells from the ready use locker and handing them to the loaders. My reputation was established when I dropped one. You have never seen so many people, literally, "hit the deck" so quickly. I just stood there and watched and then picked it up. No one said a word about it. You can imagine how humiliated I was—and how grateful to the Army guys for being so forgiving. I could have got some of them killed—along with myself. That was my first experience in the navy of nearly doing myself serious damage. There was one other, but that was later.

Arriving in New York to await the next posting was quite an experience. It was the first time I had seen the skyline since I was a child. And there was no blackout. The Queen docked at Pier 92, which was the old Cunard pier on the Hudson. We were marched off the ship into the interior of the pier. The first floor was for loading and unloading passengers and freight. I don't remember what the second floor used to be, but when we were there it was a gigantic barracks for Royal Naval personnel in transit. They packed some 1,000 of us in, relative to the Queen Mary's accommodations, quite spacious bunks—only two levels. Again, by our standards, there was lots of excellent food, but nothing to do and nowhere to go. There were two groups: the ships' crews who were moved out pretty quickly; then the fledgling aviators, who were there much longer—three weeks in the case of my course. This might sound great: young 18-year-olds from cold and rationed England suddenly in the middle of one of the world's great cities, with lots of food. But the officer in charge had other ideas. Looking back, he, his number two and their four petty officers must have been under some obscure form of punishment. Before or since, I have never come across six such unpleasant people. They devoted their days to drilling us and putting us through hours of physical training. Time off to see the sights? Hardly any—I think it was about two hours an evening for three evenings and Sunday afternoon each week. Then, the slightest excuse for disciplining us resulted in extra "duty" and leave canceled. I was lucky but unlucky. We were there Easter weekend and I was given two days' leave. Thanks to the USO (the United Service Organization, a still famous volunteer group that looked after servicemen, and that still exists) I was to spend the weekend with a family in their house in one of the suburbs. Unfortunately, that Friday morning, I was caught by one of those petty officers still climbing out of my bunk when the bugle stopped. I guess it was a matter of about five seconds, but he happened to be beside my bunk. So I was caught, found guilty and had my weekend leave canceled. I recall only one fun outing during those three weeks. That was a USO dance that a friend of my parents who lived in New York arranged for me to attend. It was in the ballroom of the Sherry-Netherland Hotel, on the corner of Fifth Avenue and 59th Street. New Yorkers could not have been more kind to us. In a way, I repaid that hospitality by using that hotel as my place to stay in New York whenever I visited on business in later years. I was a loyal guest there from about 1955 until about 1980. I stopped only when the World Bank, in its wisdom, decided we staff could not stay at five-star hotels.

After two weeks of being harassed by our officers, we were getting close to the breaking point. But there was not much we could do. However we did stumble on a form of military civil disobedience that was hard to punish more than we were already being punished. Whenever we were paraded with the entire group we would manage always to be out of line and out of step. Actually, especially those of us who had been in the King's Royal Guard of Honor, we were pretty good at parade work. But looking like an undisciplined rabble made our officers look bad. We suspected the senior officers knew what was going on. Finally, we plus another 150 seamen who were joining their cruiser in Norfolk were ordered to pack up and get going. We were marched across New York to Penn Station and put on a train to the U.S. Naval Base at Norfolk. It is strange to think back to that trip. While I had no idea of the route at the time, it must have been along the old track down the Eastern Shore and through Easton. I remembered the tunnel and the long bridge just before we arrived at Norfolk the first time we drove there from Easton in the 1990s. After the friendly treatment shown by the few civilians we had the chance to meet in New York, Norfolk was another world. We were marched from the station through the city to the base. No one actually threw rotten eggs at us, but we received a lot of verbal abuse from people in the streets. I had heard a lot of swear words after three months in the navy, but nothing like the words hurled at us that day. We couldn't understand it. Eventually, we found that some of the British ships' crews on shore leave in Norfolk had been pretty badly behaved. But it was still quite a shock. We thought we were on the same side. On the other hand, I remembered also that the good citizens of Dorking got very tired of the "occupying armies" by 1944—two years by the Canadian army followed by two years by the U.S. Army. The expression at the time was "over fed, over paid, over sexed and over here." Not very nice to young lonely kids who were there to protect them.

The base at Norfolk was another kind of shock. It was so big there were regular bus routes around it. It made the RN base at Portsmouth look tiny by comparison. When we got to the base we were put on buses —the crew to their ship, my course to a dining hall. A "chow hall" in U.S. Navy jargon. It also turned out that that was our barracks for the night. I slept on a table. We were just there for a few days and, fortunately, we were left alone, more or less. We spent the time touring the

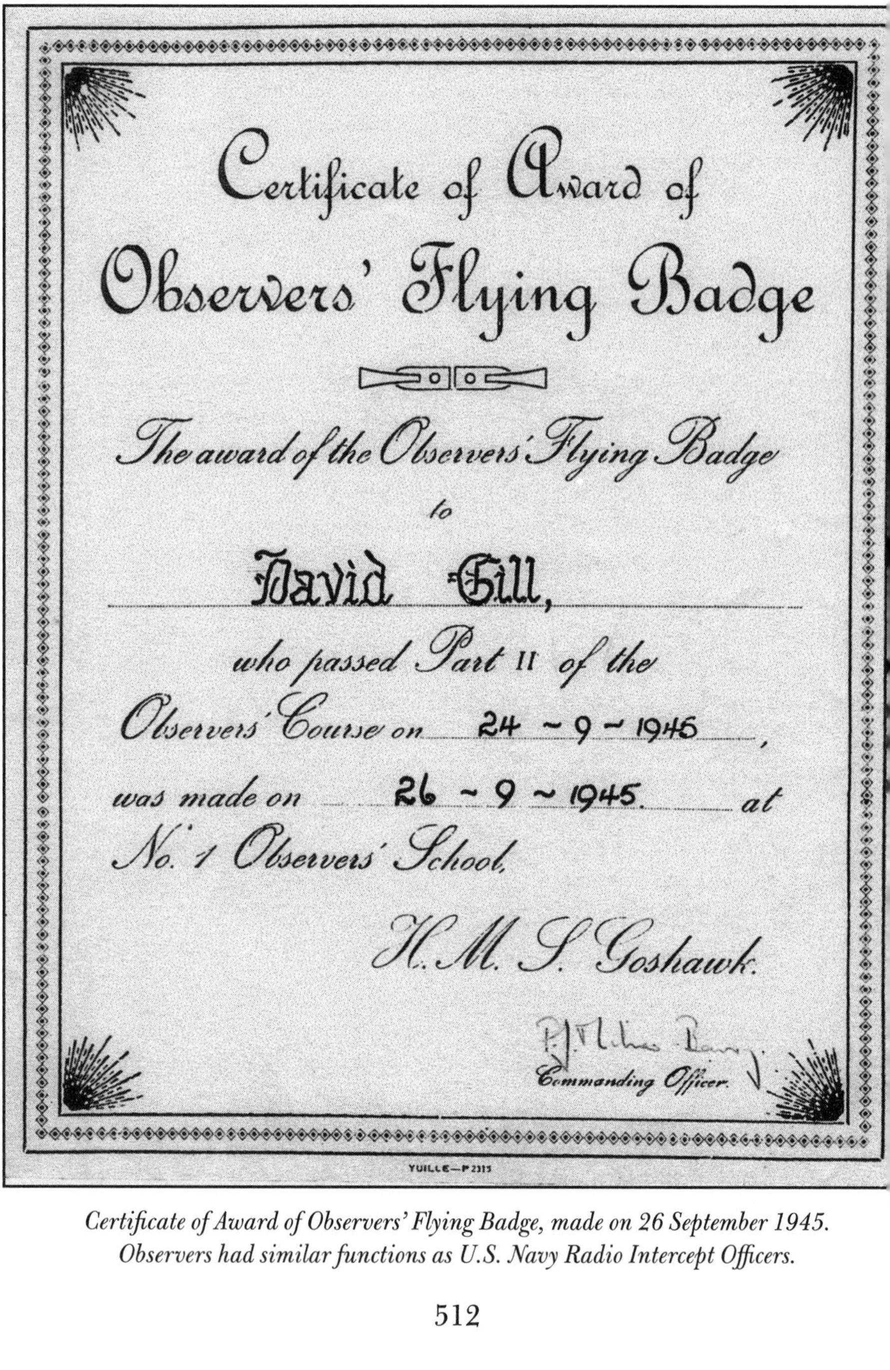

Certificate of Award of

Observers' Flying Badge

The award of the Observers' Flying Badge

to

David Gill,

who passed Part II *of the*

Observers' Course on 24 ~ 9 ~ 1945 ,

was made on 26 ~ 9 ~ 1945 *at*

No. 1 Observers' School,

H. M. S. Goshawk.

Commanding Officer.

YUILLE—P 2315

Certificate of Award of Observers' Flying Badge, made on 26 September 1945. Observers had similar functions as U.S. Navy Radio Intercept Officers.

base. At the docks there were several destroyers, cruisers and battleships, plus an aircraft carrier—the first we had seen close up since joining the navy. It is interesting to see how ship designations have changed. A "Frigate" in WWII was a 1,000-ton anti submarine ship. Nowadays frigates in the U.S. Navy are at least five times the size and are general purpose fighting machines. Equally interesting to us was the air station on the base. The first time we saw naval warplanes—and there seemed to be thousands of them—we were awestruck.

Finally, we were told yet again to pack and were bused down to the docks and put on a small passenger ship. It could have been only a few thousand tons. The passengers included our 25-odd trainee Observers, 50 or so RN sailors and several hundred U.S. sailors. We were relatively lucky in our accommodations in that the ones going farthest were housed in what had been the first-class cabins on the boat deck. Those getting off first were in the hold. The first stop was Guantanamo Bay— "Gitmo," as the Americans called it—the U.S. Naval Base in Cuba. The food was not as good as on the "Queen" so, given the chance to sneak ashore at Gitmo, most of us went AWOL for an hour or so. The main targets were the warehouses where we helped ourselves to cans of fruit —a wonderful luxury for us. I guess it was technically stealing so we would have been guilty of two crimes had we been caught.

All in all, though, it was almost a holiday cruise. While technically we were still in U-boat waters, and ships were still being sunk at the rate of several a week between Norfolk and South America, the crew seemed relaxed about gun drills and we "Limeys"—one of the more friendly terms the Americans in Norfolk used (as compared to "limey bastard" or worse)—had no duties. So it being April and we were soon in the Gulf Stream it was warm and sunny. Most of us broke out our shorts, took off our shirts and sunbathed. Unfortunately, no one bothered to tell us this was dangerous for people like us who rarely saw any sun. So we had a lot of seriously bad sunburn cases. I was one. I will always remember the beautiful sunsets. A gigantic yellow globe disappearing into a blue sea that gradually turned purple speckled with gold. Another memory that will always be with me was the time the Captain broadcast the news that President Roosevelt had died—12 April 1945. It was fol-

513

lowed by complete silence. There was no ceremony or memorial service, but the ship was very quiet for several days. It was a truly moving experience that even we foreigners aboard felt deeply. Finally, we pulled into Port of Spain harbor in Trinidad. Besides it being our second tropical island to see, what struck us was the number of sharks and stingrays we could see as we approached. The thought of flying over those waters did not seem so appealing.

Trinidad was, and is, a truly fascinating island, especially for 18- to 19-year-old boys coming from Britain. Besides the predominantly black part of the population, there were large minorities of Indians and Chinese—all brought there a hundred years before as slaves or indentured workers for the sugar cane fields. It was paradise then, with sandy beaches, tropical forests, mountains, and lush vegetation. Even the capital city, Port of Spain, was attractive with its white stone colonial style buildings; clean tree-lined streets and its remarkable parks. We started with a bus trip to Royal Naval Air Station Piarco. It was also the only commercial airfield on the island, about ten miles from Port of Spain. The most imposing building there was the Pan American Airlines guesthouse. Then, Trinidad was the staging base for Pan Am flights from New York and Miami to Caracas, Rio and Buenos Aires. The passengers spent the night at the guesthouse and had dinner and breakfast there. Consequently, it had an excellent dining room and staff. Those were the days when Pan Am was a truly great airline. Whenever we could we would crawl through the wire fence separating the commercial field from the naval field to have dinner at the guest house. The Pan Am people knew we were AWOL, but they looked after us and gave as the best dinners in all of Trinidad. The food the RN provided was awful and the local restaurants in Port of Spain, the few times we were allowed leave, were almost as bad.

Our Observer course was there for about six months—from late April until late September. There were about 30 of us again. The 25-odd that had survived so far plus a half dozen other Brits who had been either TAGs, who had seen active service and had been marked for promotion, or other naval airmen like us who had failed flying training as pilots but were considered bright enough to be Observers. We also had three mysterious Netherlanders who just showed up one day in their naval uniforms. We guessed they had escaped from Holland earlier on after fighting in the resistance. In any event they were all older man—probably in their twenties—and decidedly bigger than most of us. They kept rather to themselves. There were about five other courses going through the training at the same time. A new crowd arrived every month or so and the graduating course departed. Each course was housed in its own barracks hut. By past standards, the accommodation was pretty good: quite reasonable bunks (no layers), our own footlockers and a quite large bathroom and heads (toilets) area with lots of showers. There was only cold water but there was nothing wrong with that in the tropics. There were even several small swimming pools, as well as the usual soccer fields and other sports facilities. Our days started with reveille at 4.00 AM, a half-hour of physical training and then a "hot" breakfast. The hot breakfast was stipulated in the regulations as a requirement before flying. This must have started in Britain and related to operational flying. In any event our hot breakfast consisted of a corned beef sandwich (cold) and a brown liquid (warm) that tasted like a cross between tea, coffee and cocoa. The sandwich was spiced with dead ants cooked into the bread: just one of the joys of RN food. Oddly, though, even after eating them almost every day for six months, I still like corned beef sandwiches, although I pass on the ants.

Our training started at 5.30 with, on alternate days, either preparing and briefing for a 6.30 takeoff for flying training, followed by, at about 10.00, two hours of lectures—or the other way around. After lunch at noon, the rest of the day was ours for homework and fun. For most, fun was swimming, tennis and football, notwithstanding the heat. In the best naval tradition, starting with the three-watch system, we were allowed "ashore" (naval terms were always used) in the afternoons. A very early morning start was typical tropical routine for civilian life too. In the absence of air conditioning, it was simply too hot and humid to work in the afternoon. So, the standard civilian eight hour day started at 6.00 AM and finished around 2.00 PM.

I still have my old aviator's Log Book that records all of my flights. The RN used an RAF log book with the complicated title, "Royal Air

The Grumman Goose seaplane was the first military plane in which I flew along with six other trainee-Observers—it was 30 April 1945—during my flight training with the Royal Navy. Some years later, in 1970, I would again cross paths with the Goose at Out Island Airways in the Bahamas, where the Goose was a mainstay of OIA's small fleet. I was then at Schroders New York, and we became involved in re-structuring the airline. Ultimately, Schroders and I, personally, both made a "private equity" investment in the company. This photo was taken in Trinidad in 1945.

Force Flying Log Book for Navigators Air Bombers Air Gunners Flight Engineers." Consequently, I know my first training flight as a member of "Rodney Course" at "No. 1 Observers' School" (No. 2 was the one in Scotland) was on 30 April 1945 in a Grumman Goose. This was a twin-engine amphibian passenger plane with normally two pilots and twelve passenger seats. (A few of these are still flying, as I will get to later.) The pilot was Sub Lieutenant Williams (no co-pilot). We took off at 10.50 AM and, as my "Remarks" column indicates, it was a "familiarization flight: flew over several departure points." It lasted all of one hour and ten minutes. I remember every minute of it. It was my first real military training flight (my earlier rides in a Tiger Moth as an Air Cadet and in the B-17 didn't count). There were about ten of us trainees in the back, equipped with maps and intercom, plus an instructor. We just flew around the island, with the instructor pointing out the prominent departure points and landfalls and their positions relative to the airfield. It didn't take long, as the island was about 90 miles by 60 miles. The exciting part was when the pilot called on the intercom and said: "Would anyone like to come up and take over the controls …?" I didn't wait for the rest of what he said. I just dashed up, beating a few others into the co-pilot's seat. The pilot just said: "Stay on this course; the next landmark is that point dead ahead. I'm going to the head." Before I had a chance to react, he was out of his seat and into the main cabin. Fortunately, I knew enough to realize that, if I didn't touch any of the controls, the plane would probably just continue on its way even without the automatic pilot, which it did not have. To my immense relief, that is exactly what happened. I just sat there with my hands poised over the wheel and my feet off the rudder bars for what seemed hours, but was probably only a couple of minutes, until he came back. I said nothing. He said thanks. I went back to my seat. What I found out later was that the rest of his message was "…who has had some pilot training." I was just too keen for my own good.

For the next few months all our training flights were in Stinson Reliants, single-engine high-winged three-seaters. They were just small planes built for amateur pilots. We used them for our radio and navigational training. Usually, they would be one-and-a-half to two-hour flights on a triangular route from Trinidad to Barbados and back by way of Grenada, or the other way around. The idea was to go through the Morse communications procedures and plot our courses to get us back to where we were supposed to make a landfall. At first, we were routed so we could actually sight one of the other two islands, so we couldn't go too far wrong. Later, we were routed out of sight of land. It doesn't sound too complicated now but, in those days, with a plane that cruised at about 90 knots and winds varying from 20 to 30 knots, in two hours you could miss your return point by up to 60 miles and thus the whole of Trinidad by 30 miles. At our normal flying altitude of 1,500 to 2,000 feet, it meant you would not see the island even on a clear day until you were within 20 miles. We did not have any navigational aids so our navigation was all "dead reckoning"—you plotted your courses and speeds, and allowed for wind velocity, which gave you your actual track over the water. This you plotted on your chart. The track calculations were easy. The skill was in estimating wind speed and direction. As you could not rely on estimates from your base, and there was no radio communication (radio silence in wartime), one had to learn the maneuver to do this. It involved dropping a marker in the sea (a smoke bomb by day, a flare by night) and doing a perfect six-minute route away from it and back. With zero wind, you would be dead overhead at the end of the six minutes. So, with the aid of a stopwatch and a bearing compass, we could calculate how far away we were from the "datum" and, thus, the wind speed and direction, at least for that spot at that time. Six minutes was a significant time period—a tenth of an hour which made calculation easy. So, if we were 2.2 miles due south of the datum after six minutes, we knew the wind speed was 22 knots and the direction due north, or 000 degrees. We figured the distance by taking two compass bearings and plotting where they crossed. But this is getting too complicated. Our pilots and we spent a lot of time practicing that operation. At sea, in aircraft with no radar and radio silence, getting the wind right could be the difference between life and death flying from an aircraft carrier, especially in bad weather or at night.

Working the radio was more complicated and less fun. The Morse code part was easy, but there were a large number of coded signals and procedures to learn, and radios in those days consisted of vacuum tubes and had to be tuned by hand. It was easy to lose touch with your base. The only excitement I remember of this part was the occasion my bored pilot chose to "buzz" Bridgetown harbor in Barbados, flying inverted at about 50 feet. He picked the exact time I had to send a position report —and getting out the right message at the exactly right time was what we were learning to do. Working the key upside down was not so easy. On the other hand, I certainly sympathized with our pilots. While being in Trinidad was better than a lot of places, most of them had volunteered with the idea of being at least torpedo-bomber pilots flying with the fleet. So ending up flying planes designed for amateur pilots, chauffeuring green Observers on endless two-hour triangular trips could not have been very rewarding. The only excitement they ever had was when something went seriously wrong. For example, once we were coming back from one of those trips through a rather severe storm. We were supposed to be at 1,500 feet. We almost hit the coast, literally. My wind velocity calculation was obviously off as we got to the coast several minutes ahead of schedule: 1,500 feet of cliff—that should have been several miles away—suddenly appeared what seemed only feet ahead. Fortunately, my pilot had his eyes open and pulled into a steep climb, missing it by not much. It was all over before I even saw the coast. It was not a good day for me, but I was learning.

After four months, we graduated to flying in Fairey Barracudas. At the time, they were the most modern of the Navy's torpedo bombers, though very ungainly looking things. High-winged monoplanes, but with a wonderful view for the Observer, whose cockpit was under the wing with bulbous canopies on both sides so one could see straight down as well as dead ahead and astern. They were far better for Observers to do their jobs than any other aircraft in which I flew. All the others (except the Reliant) had the Observer perched above the wings, so there was very little visibility. Still we wondered how the things ever flew, let alone landed on carriers, because the undercarriage legs retracted into the wings and thus must have been 15 feet long compared to the three or four feet of most other single-engine aircraft. These we used for our radar training, tactical maneuvers and night flying. The main sport was doing night-time torpedo- or dive-bombing attacks, navigating by radar, on target ships. My greatest exploit was a night dive-bombing run where we blasted off with flares as we pulled-out at 50 feet over the target ship. The only problem was: I had picked up the wrong ship on my radar (I was about five miles out from our target ship). So I made this perfect attack on a Venezuelan passenger liner. It was about 10.00 PM and it must have scared the lives out of the crew and the passengers. Fortunately, the Venezuelans never reported us. On the other hand, they had their fun too. If you strayed too close to that part of their coast where they had a naval base, they used to use our planes for target practice. I was better at navigation by then so it never happened to me.

As to target practice, air gunnery was our next training task. I don't know why they trained us to shoot the back-seat machine guns because the only naval aircraft that had back-seat guns had TAGs to operate them. But it was exciting learning how to use the old WWI-version Lewis guns. We did this in another type of operational torpedo bomber, the Fairey Albacore, a single-engine biplane that was a modernized version of the old Swordfish, the RN's standard torpedo bomber through 1944. The big difference was that the Albacore had an enclosed cockpit whereas the Swordfish cockpits were all open. We fired at targets towed by other aircraft and at stationary targets in the sea. I remember being very disappointed at the results of my first towed target attack. I thought I had done very well as I could see, I thought, my incendiaries going right into the target. Unfortunately, the evidence, once I was shown the target on our return, showed less than the acceptable number of holes. But that wasn't as bad as another time when, in my enthusiasm at keeping on a moving target, I very nearly shot-off our own rudder. I stopped firing just as I saw the incendiaries getting what seemed like inches from it. In more modern versions of the Albacore—and most other aircraft with hand-operated guns not in turrets—they put up guard stops to prevent that kind of mistake. One of the instructions we received before we started firing at sea surface targets was to watch out for small fishing boats. They were supposed to keep out of our target area but …. The word was: if we hit any by mistake, make sure you killed the crew. If the wounded got ashore, there was a great fuss; but the locals didn't seem to mind if they lost a few. There was nothing in writing about that. Fortunately, I never saw a fishing boat in the firing area.

All in all, our flying training was a lot of fun. My only problem was my bad writing, which carried over into very untidy chart work. In fact, I was called in by my instructor and given a serious warning. I was under probation for a while. Had I not managed to improve, I would have been failed, which would have had serious consequences—that is, remaining a Naval Airman and put to work doing menial jobs, such as peeling potatoes. The ground instruction was also interesting. Especially the fleet tactics work. The RN in those days considered the Observer the "captain" of the aircraft. As the Fleet Air Arm's official marching anthem Wings over the Navy went: "… we are the eyes of the fleet, the navy's cavalry…." That was because the Observer was the spotter who told the admirals what the enemy was up to. He was supposed to understand fleet maneuvers and tactics. The pilot was just the driver. By 1945, that didn't go down so well with the pilots. The U.S. Navy was doing quite well without Observers or navigators despite the fact that their WWII missions were much longer than ours—three to five hours. I could understand that. By 1945 Observers were only really useful in anti-submarine work. Still, it was very interesting learning tactics and then playing fleet exercises where the game was you had to judge, or guess, what the enemy fleet's next move would be.

The only unpleasant aspect of our life at RNAS Piarco was the poor food and poor sanitation. The end result was that most of us suffered from various skin diseases—including ringworm. One funny side of this was my fight with a family of cockroaches that had taken up residence in my footlocker. After several efforts to soap them out, spray them out, and burn them out, I finally gave up. We came to terms. They stuck to one corner of one shelf and I had the rest.

I was one of the lucky ones on our course to be befriended by a number of the local civilians. So, during my leave periods I had an enjoyable time. It was mainly because my best friend on the course, Paul Lewin, an Englishman who had been at the Oxford ROTC, had family friends there. The first family I met myself, whose name I cannot recall, lived in Port of Spain. Paul's friends' father was general manager of the railway.

He and his wife introduced us to Commander Lavington, a retired RN type, who ran the oil fields. He and his family lived in San Fernando, at the southeast end of the island. Over the six months, Paul and I spent many wonderful weekends with these two couples, their families and friends. Some would be just for the day at one of the beaches near Port of Spain. There were also wonderful weekends with the Lavingtons in the south. San Fernando was my first experience of a company town. It was also where I learned to enjoy rum and ginger ale and rum punches. There must have been several thousand employees plus families there. The Lavingtons' home was a small beach resort. It took some time to get used to the life style. I shall always remember how gracious the Lavingtons were. As a retired senior naval officer, he could have been expected, when entertaining the troops in his home, to limit his hospitality to the officers, of which there were many in Trinidad. But no: Paul and I seemed to be his favorites. Getting to San Fernando was also rather an experience: a bus from Piarco to Port of Spain, then the train for the 60 miles to San Fernando. We were picked up there by car. The train took several hours, not because there were many towns to stop at—there was only one—but it stopped more where the locals wanted to get on or off, or the crew wanted to chat with someone by the track. We learned a lot about the local social scene from these friends. The clubs and restaurants were not segregated as one might have expected in a British colony in the 1940s. That said, it was pretty clear what the class system was. At the top were the English, then the French, then other whites from the island, then the Chinese then the Indians, then the rest, who were the descendants of the African slaves. At the bottom of the heap were the non-commissioned soldiers, sailors and airmen from wherever they came and regardless of race.

I was especially fortunate in having met a really local family. I think it started with meeting their third daughter at the local "NAFI"—I forget what the acronym stands for but it was the British equivalent of the U.S.O. She was one of the organizers. Her father was black, and well known as a local labor union leader. Her mother was Scottish. There were four daughters. The oldest two were blondes like their mother. The third, my friend, was a brunette who looked very Latin American, and the youngest was as dark skinned as her father. They were a wonderful, loving family, and they made me quite at home. I would not have been so welcoming had I been the Father. Both the older daughters had married British naval officers, who had both been killed—one in action and one who was on an Observer course. Unfortunately, he was on the wrong transport ship back to England. It was believed to have been torpedoed, because it was never heard from after it departed. So, we were a dangerous group for young girls to meet. Still, they could not have been friendlier to me and I spent many pleasant evenings in their home.

We had two other weekends that I shall not forget. One was a very quiet one organized by the "NAFI" in a monastery in the mountains west of Port of Spain. It was quiet, the food was excellent—we young fellows thought a lot about the food—and it was interesting. There we were, in a lovely old wooden building, high in the hills, with a view of the sea, with the coast of Venezuela visible when the clouds cleared. The monastery was quite high up, often above cloud level. I remember sitting on the veranda one evening looking at the Venezuelan coast, listening to Latin music—which sounded quite exotic to us young Brits. It seemed another world.

The other weekend was bittersweet. The navy had always given each Course a long weekend in Tobago—the "and Tobago" part of the now Republic of Trinidad and Tobago—half-way through. We were to fly over the 20-odd miles from the north coast to that truly paradise island in several of our larger planes to get about 50 of us—two Courses and some instructors—there. One of the planes, doing the usual daredevil low-flying thing, crashed into the sea. Five were killed and two survived, but badly injured. In the best stiff upper lip tradition, the rest of us had a great weekend at a wonderful resort hotel. The food was memorable. I remember the wonderful vegetables and fruit—something the navy didn't seem to have at Piarco. We drank a great deal. As best I remember it, it was great fun. Only when we got back and visited the one member of our Course on the plane that crashed, who was one of the survivors, did we sober up.

I think the two most important days for us in Trinidad were the days after "VE Day" and "VJ Day," the days the war ended in Europe and

Asia. Carnival is a celebration associated mainly with Rio and, perhaps, with New Orleans. But the V Day celebrations in Port of Spain were quite something. They started with military parades, so we young sailors had to march through Port of Spain at the head of the typical carnival-type procession. That was a pain for us. But the fun afterwards made it all worthwhile. VJ Day happened to occur three days after my Log Book recorded my last training flight. Looking at my Log Book now, it states that CPO Donegaul took me up in Barracuda B.38 at 2030 on 12 September for an exercise described as "SQ. RWN." I have no idea what that meant but, under "Remarks," I wrote "D.C.O.," which meant "duty carried out." I must have passed the final flying exam. I remember also the written exams, mainly because they were in the afternoon. It was so hot and humid our papers were drenched in sweat. I could not help thinking of the probation warning I had been given a month before and wondering whether my bad writing would do me in. But, somehow, I survived that too.

The last days in Trinidad are a bit of a haze. First was VJ Day. Then our "Wings" ceremony when the Commanding Officer formally gave us our Observer "badge," as it was called. That was followed by the rather disappointing news that we had been promoted to Petty Officer Observers rather than being commissioned officers. The reason was we were to be shipped back with a large group of personnel who were going home as the base was closing down. Consequently, there would have been too many officers for the ship to accommodate. So, we boarded HMS Campania, an auxiliary aircraft carrier turned into a troop ship, without wardroom (officers' mess) privileges. This meant no rum punches—not even the daily tot of neat rum all navy crewmen received at 11:30 that was a Royal Navy tradition—for the ten days of the trip. We were just passengers on a troop ship. The send-off though was rather special because the Lavingtons came. They knew, obviously, many of the officers leaving so it must have been an emotional time for them too. But they had the ship's captain seek out Paul and me down in the bowls of the ship where the newly minted Petty Officers were quartered so we could say a final good-bye.

Off we went—ten days at sea before arriving at Portsmouth again. I must confess that, while it was a pleasant cruise, free of any duties, it was very annoying to know that some of the luckier ones who were commissioned were enjoying the Royal Navy's "booze" before, during and after lunch and dinner. On our arrival in Portsmouth, we were billeted in an old army camp. It had cement bunks. This was the only time any of us used our navy hammocks that we had been lugging around for a year. The bunks were so uncomfortable that we all slung our hammocks and slept in them. It was the first and last time. But they were quite comfortable. I should have used mine more often, thinking back to sleeping in railway-car luggage racks and on tables. The sad thing about that last day as a non-commissioned officer was seeing one of our comrades who had failed the last exams. He was on duty as a guard at the main gate as we left. He saluted us smartly and smiled wanly. His name was Lokie Baird—a Scotsman and a fine fellow. But, for whatever reason he failed, the consequence was he was going to spend the next two years as an Ordinary Seaman under the "last in, last out rules" that applied to all servicemen at the end of the war.

We were told we would be receiving formal notification of our commissions immediately and that our first duty was to buy uniforms. That was an easy process because the principal naval tailor, Gieves Limited, in London would know exactly what was needed and we didn't have to worry about the costs as Gieves never pressed for payment. So, now, after having been a Naval Airman Second Class, a Naval Airman First Class, a Leading Naval Airman (equivalent to Corporal), an Acting Petty Officer Observer (Sergeant), I was now a Midshipman. My official title was Acting Temporary Midshipman (A), Royal Navy Volunteer Reserve. The "A" stood for Air Branch. The rank of Midshipman was equal to Ensign in the U.S. Navy. The only difference was that it was a function of age. As soon as I turned 19, I would become a Sub Lieutenant—Acting Temporary, of course—equal to a Lt. J.G. The joke was, as brand new reserve officers, we weren't sure whether the "Acting" referred to our Gentlemen status and the "Temporary" to our rank, or vice versa.

Gieves had an interesting history and tradition. There were other shops that could supply naval officers with uniforms, but it never occurred to any of us to seek out another shop. It was said that, for at least

David Gill earned his "wings"—the Observers' Flying Badge—September 1945.

the last 50 years, new recipients of commissions heard about it first in a letter from Gieves advising of their services. Later, one would receive a telegram (the usual means of official naval communication in those days) from the Admiralty. A good example of how deep was the tradition was a cartoon that appeared in Punch (a British humor weekly) the week after the D-Day landings. The background was an empty Normandy beach. The foreground was the formal morning suit-attired, bowler-hatted man from Gieves, standing in the sand, looking out to sea, with a large sign reading: "Gieves Limited. Orders received here." In any event, I reported dutifully at Gieves, which was at No. 1 Savile Row, the street where all of London's best tailors were located. My vital statistics were taken—sizes, that is; they already knew my rank, serial number and address. I was told to report for a first fitting in a week. Nothing was "off the rack" in Gieves. After my second fitting three weeks later I was fully equipped: two "No.5s"—the regular uniform—two white equivalents and two battledress working uniforms, two caps, two berets for my battledress, six white shirts with detachable collars and two black ties. All of the uniforms were adorned with my rank and wings. I was told the bill would be sent later. As to "No.5s," the RN had a system for numbering everything, including uniforms. As I recall it, No.1s were black "Mess Dress" (the naval version of "tails"), No.2s were the white tropical equivalent. No.3s were black "Mess Undress" (dinner jacket), and so on down to No.16s, which I think were khaki shorts and shirts. At one stage, later when in the Reserves in Toronto, I had the whole lot. But I never owned a sword. Until the war started, even reserve officers were required to have one for ceremonial occasions.

My next orders were to proceed to Royal Naval College, Greenwich, which was on the river just five miles from the center of London. Besides being the original training base for career officers, the Observatory there was where "Greenwich Mean Time" started. This was to take what was known as the "Knife and Fork" course." Officially it was a four-week officer indoctrination course; mainly; it was to make sure that we could actually behave like officers and gentlemen. But also we had lectures on naval history and strategy. Greenwich was a great setting for both aspects of the course: truly historic landmark buildings, including a Wren chapel and a dining room called the "Grand Hall" with 20-foot-high stained glass windows, and room for at least 60 at the table. We even had single "cabins" as sleeping quarters, even if we had to share bathrooms.

Our days started at a respectable 0700 with a WREN (Women's Royal Naval Service) orderly waking us up with tea. After breakfast (no "PT"—physical training), we had lectures until lunch, followed by more lectures until dinner. This is where we learned the serious stuff. Each dinner was formal. Including the senior instructors, there were about 60 of us at the great table, with silverware for six courses, linen napkins, and a steward behind every two chairs. I don't seem to recall wine, but there was port at the end for the toast to the King. It was quite evident that we were a mixed crowd. At the first dinner, nearly everyone figured out that the utensils beside the plates had to be used starting from the outside and working inward with each course. One got used to the stewards serving from our left and retrieving from the right. Only one poor devil, that first night, made a major error. He thought the finger bowl was for drinking. No one had much sympathy for him because he had always been the number one smart aleck of the course. Presumably he had concluded that he didn't have to do what most of us did when in doubt: look around to see what the senior officers were doing. The grueling part of the dinner was the tradition that the junior officer present, after the toast to the King, had to make the "thank you" speech. One of the rules for speaking was one could not talk about politics, religion, business, or women. That limited the subject matter, but the frightening part was just having to get up and make a speech in front of the whole gathering. You were supposed to be entertaining for about ten minutes. We each took turns, but it certainly took one's appetite away when it was your turn.

A pleasant part of our period at Greenwich was that, most evenings, we could go into London. I learned a lot about the West End of London during those weeks—and later that year while on leave at home. My connection to the English-Speaking Union helped immensely. Their headquarters were on Charles Street, which was just off Berkeley Square, the center of Mayfair. As they had rooms for members, I used to stay there. It was the best and cheapest hotel in London. It also had dances and other functions for servicemen from the English-speaking countries, so it was an opportunity to meet sweet young things in a very proper way. Midshipmen in those days earned half a guinea a day. What was a guinea? A guinea was 21 shillings—or one more shilling than a pound. What was the point of guineas? I really don't remember too well but I think it was a class thing. The upper classes—and naval officers were (temporarily) in that category—did not use such mundane things as pounds. In any event 10/6—which was the shorthand for half a guinea—was half the pay a Sergeant or a Petty Officer made and they did not have to pay for their uniforms or meals, as did we. On the other hand, the regulated price for a three-course meal at the four-star Lansdowne Restaurant on Berkeley Square was 10/6, so I could take a lady friend there occasionally and still feel I was maintaining appropriate standards. At the other extreme were much less expensive eateries in Soho. The problem was, when one ordered chicken, it was likely to be rabbit in disguise. If you ordered rabbit, the odds were you were being served cat. Sounds rather disgusting, but that was London and rationing. In any event, I lead a rather pleasant life then, even without much money. In today's dollars, 10/6 would be worth about $25. It was just as well young officers were supposed to spend most of their time at sea, where food, or most of it, and board were paid for. And, while you paid for your drinks, they were duty-free. So, at the time, the rum in the rum-and-ginger ale would cost less than the ginger ale.

The downside of this period was how cold, wet, dull and bleak Britain was, especially in the winter. We had won the war, but rationing was worse than it had been when I had left a year before. And it was a cold winter—very different from warm sunny Trinidad. That was when I first decided to go back to my Canadian roots. The Royal Canadian Navy had announced that they were seeking volunteers to transfer to its new "Air Branch." The deal was a two-year "hitch," which happened to be the time left for me to serve in the RN anyway. The differences were, in the RCN, we would be flying from an aircraft carrier and based in Halifax, Nova Scotia, with the opportunity for me to get to know Canada again and enjoy, in the meantime, good food and better living

529

conditions. Also, it did not escape my attention that the pay was over three times what the RN was providing.

The good news was I had to wait only a month before my transfer to the Royal Canadian Navy Reserve came through.

1920	Giles, J. L.	Magdalene	Normandy Mead, Woodside, Lymington
1944-5	Gill, D. A.	Caius*	24, Barrow Avenue, Carshalton, Surrey
1943-4	Gill, D. B.	Pembroke	Lyncroft, Chichester Road, Dorking
1930	Gillson, F.	King's	Broad Gardens, Porchester, Fareham
1932-3	Gilmore, J. A.	Caius	Univ. of Cape Town, Rosebank, Cape Town
1934-5	Girling, Harold, B.Chir.†	Emmanuel	Bridge House, Stratford-on-Avon
1933-4	Gladstone, G. C.	Clare	c/o Nat. Prov. Bank, 208-9, Piccadilly, W.1
1936-7	Gloag, Lt. K. B., R.N.	Magdalene	Roseville, Old Wortley Road, Kimberworth, Rotherham
1941-2	Glover, G. L., R.N.V.R.†	Jesus	2, Victoria Road, Trowbridge
1942-3	Glover, W. J.	Pembroke	Long Hayes, Abbotswood, Guildford
1931	Gold, H. P.	Jesus	Sandiway, Cheshire
1936-7	Goodbody, G. U.†	Peterhouse	Invergarry, Inverness-shire
1943-4	Goodman, D. W. V.	Peterhouse	White Hill Wood, Flamstead, Herts.
1941-2	Gordon, Lt. A. G., R.E.†	Jesus	The Beaches, Wetherall, Carlisle
1936-7	Gostling, J. V. T.	Jesus	c/o Barclays Bank, Chesterton Rd., Cambridge
1944-5	Goulder, Brian	St. Cath.'s*	6, Acre House Avenue, Lindley, Huddersfield
1945-6	Grant, D. W. M.	Trinity*	Weston, Crowborough Hill, Jarvis Brook, Sussex
1933-4	Grant, J. A.†	Trinity	c/o Glyn Mills & Co. (Holts Branch), Whitehall, W.1
1942-3	Grant, T. M.	Downing	Chasma Tang, Ashley Rd., New Milton, Hants.
1942-3	Grant, V. P.	Trinity	The Croft, Worlingham, Surrey
† Life Member	* In Residence	§ Port Officer	‡ Y.R.A. Representative

Cambridge University Cruising Club 1945-1946 ... Gill, D. B., Pembroke. "Cruising" was sai
14-foot dinghies in the river Cam that runs through Cambridge—hence the name of the latter

530

CAMBRIDGE UNIVERSITY CRUISING CLUB

(Founded May 20th, 1893)

Rules and List of Members

1945-46

CAMBRIDGE:

FOISTER AND JAGG, ST. ANDREW'S HILL

CHAPTER X

Royal Canadian Navy and University of Toronto: 1946–1952

After almost a year away I had mixed feelings on returning to England. Postwar England was depressing and the prospects for young ex servicemen looked dismal. It was a very cold winter and the food rationing made me feel that conditions in Trinidad had not been so bad after all. Consequently, returning to Canada seemed a good idea, albeit I really did not remember much about Canada. I suppose my final decision was influenced a lot by being assured of my continuing flying. In fact, on the way back from Trinidad, we used to talk about the possibilities of finding some other war for which we could sign on and use our new skills. Flying in military aircraft would be more fun than civilian work.

Returning to Canada also led to my thinking about university after my remaining two years in the navy. This would be paid for by the Canadian government's equivalent of the U.S. GI Bill. Staying in England would mean probably not finishing university because it was not until the 1960s that university degrees were important for business careers. Rather, what was important for getting the first job and then promotion in London was the right school and the right connections, which I did not have. In that sense, I made the right choice. What I did not know then was that, had I stayed in the RN, I would have had the same "GI Bill" equivalent rights that I had as a Canadian ex serviceman. But the excitement of the war and flying distracted me in those early years. I didn't do much career planning.

As it was, I spent two years active with the RCN, three years at Toronto University full time, then—from 1950 to 1952—more or less half-time at university and half-time with the navy. My Korean War was spent in European waters on a NATO "flag waving" cruise. So the two navies kept me out of harm's way during both wars.

It was in early January 1946 that I received my official transfer to the Royal Canadian Navy (Reserve). My orders were to report to RNAS Burscough, which was near Southport, on the west coast of England. I was to join 825 Squadron, the RCN's first active service squadron. Tradition was very important to the RN, as well as to the RCN. So we were pleased that the RN gave us "825 Squadron" to man. It had a record of which to be proud.

Joining the squadron as a Midshipman was rather like my first few weeks at Pembroke College. I didn't know a soul and I had no idea how to behave (except at meals, thanks to the "knife and fork" course) or what was expected of me. What was worse, everyone else was senior in rank—I was the only Midshipman—and they all seemed much older. For the first few days, at meals in the Wardroom (the dining room in naval parlance) and drinks in the Wardroom's Ante Room (the bar), I was afraid to say a word to anyone. And no one spoke to me. But once we started flying and I had watched our pilots all looking pretty foolish at first as they had never flown Fireflies (the aircraft with which we were equipped) before, the ice was broken. One hilarious incident was when one of our pilots, on his first attempt to taxi a Firefly, ran it into a hangar wall. Luckily also I was promoted in February from the rank of Acting Temporary Midshipman to Acting Temporary Sub Lieutenant (Lieutenant J.G. in the USN) but I was still the youngest, most junior officer on the Squadron. In the RN, midshipmen ("Middies") became "Subbies" at age nineteen. If you were over 19 when you first got your commission, you started as a Subby. In fact all promotions up to and including Lt. Commander were based on years in rank. Two years as a Subby and you became a full blown Lieutenant. After eight years in that rank you became a Lt. Commander. As I was to discover later, my promotion was, so to speak, a promotion put in place by the RN, not the RCN. The final result of that minor bureaucratic "snafu" was quite amusing, but more about that later.

The 825 Squadron was an Anti-Submarine Warfare (ASW) squadron, equipped with Fairey Fireflies. The Firefly was a two-seat single-engine carrier plane designed for several duties. It was a night fighter with four fixed 20-millimeter cannons firing forward, the same armament as Spitfires. Unfortunately, with a maximum speed of only about 200 knots, it lacked that key fighter requirement. It was also a dive-bomber because it could carry bombs and rockets on external racks. Finally, because it had radar and could carry depth charges, it was also an ASW aircraft. From the Observer's point of view, it wasn't the best at the latter, our real job, because visibility from the back seat was poor and the range—a little less than two hours without external fuel tanks—was insufficient for the job. Another minor problem was that if we had the external tanks, we couldn't carry depth charges. As was evident, this aircraft, like many RN aircraft of the day, was able to do many things, but it was good at none. The exception for ASW work was the Fairey Barracuda that I had flown in Trinidad

One of the good things about the Mother-Daughter arrangement between the Royal Navy and the RCN was that we could take over RN squadron names and therefore their traditions. 825 Squadron had been around since the 1920s. It was said that, in its ASW role in the 1930s, it was the first to sink a German U-boat—during the Spanish civil war. During WWII it defended Malta convoys in the Mediterranean and Russian convoys in the Arctic. Sadly, its best-known action ended in the deaths of 35 of the 36 aircrew members. This was when the squadron was equipped with Fairey Swordfish—three-seat biplanes that doubled as torpedo bombers as well as ASW aircraft—that carried out a torpedo attack on several German warships (including the infamous "pocket battleship" Bismarck) running through the English Channel in 1943. Because of a communications foul-up, the RAF fighter cover never materialized, so all 12 Swordfish were shot down as they made their run in. This was before they could even drop their torpedoes. The Commanding Officer, Lt. Commander Edmond Knight, received a posthumous Victoria Cross—Britain's highest award for valor. Another aspect of the tragedy was that the Germans' run from Brest, France was so unexpected that the only aircraft available for any kind of bombing attack in the English Channel was this single squadron. 825 Squadron was in the process of being re-formed with new personnel after a six-month spell on a carrier in the Mediterranean. As a result, this was the first mission against the enemy for the majority of the crews. It was said that all the Observers had just completed their training and that this was the first flight as crewmembers in the Squadron for most of them. The Swordfish, with a top speed of about 90 knots, flying a straight attack course at low level, were sitting ducks for the massed guns of a battleship, a heavy cruiser and their escorts.

One of the pre-World War II problems of the Royal Navy's Air Branch was that, because the seagoing "brass" of the navy really didn't have much confidence in the merits of naval aviation, it was small. Consequently, it did not have much "clout" when it came to resources to design and build the special types of aircraft needed for carrier operations. This was why, right through 1943, the ancient Swordfish, first built in the 1920s, was still the backbone of RN air power. By comparison, both the U.S. and the Japanese navies had very large air branches and excellent aircraft. Still, the RN's Air Branch had proved itself in battle. In fact, one attack by the plodding old Swordfish, known as the Battle of Taranto, against the main Italian fleet at anchor in its major base, caused so much damage that the Italian navy never recovered. Four battleships and several cruisers were put out of action. It is widely believed that the tactics used at Taranto were the model for the Japanese attack on Pearl Harbor. Also, it was Swordfish from HMS Ark Royal that crippled finally the German pocket battleship Bismarck in the North Atlantic. Looking back, it was amazing that those old biplanes with open cockpits were still flying into battle. Old sailors still recount fondly the story of the Swordfish that, trying to land on its carrier, couldn't catch-up even at full throttle. The carrier was doing its usual 30 knots, but the

Fairey "Swordfish" (DC3 in the background) in which we did our gunnery train-
ing. A great old aircraft. At the Battle of Taranto in November 1940, they sank
three Italian battleships in the harbor. The Swordfish was a serious fighting ma-
chine and the first in which I flew and actually fired a machine gun—though
only at a target during training. It also was key to winning two major sea battles
in WWII, well before my time.

wind was gusting to 60 knots. The poor old Swordfish could hardly make 90 knots flat out. We all felt very proud to be members of such a distinguished unit, albeit it was obvious that we were not going to be adding to its illustrious record.

Our sister squadron at Burscough was 803 Squadron, equipped with Seafires, the naval version of the Spitfire. Our two squadrons made up the RCN's first and only "Carrier Air Group." Between us, we had about 35 aircraft, the full complement for our first aircraft carrier, HMCS Warrior. Warrior was a light fleet carrier of 18,000 tons that we were to join and return to Halifax in that spring. Also forming up in Halifax at the same time were two other squadrons—826 as our sister ASW squadron, and 801, the other fighter squadron, which would be called the "Support Air Group." So with the 70-odd aircraft of the two air groups and about 30 assorted training and communications aircraft, the RCN's air

A "Firefly" after a bad carrier landing.

branch consisted of about 100 aircraft, 200 aircrew, 500 maintenance men and one aircraft carrier. It was a very small club. Most of the pilots were ex Royal Canadian Air Force pilots who had just finished their training. There were also about a dozen experienced RN pilots who had signed on to train us and because they wanted to stay in the navy. Of the 50 or so Observers, only about ten were Canadians and the rest were ex RN. At Burscough, our first job was to get to know each other and to get to know our new aircraft.

It was both fun and frightening for us Observers to watch our Pilots learn to fly the Fireflys. Except for the ex RN types, they had, till then, only flown in advanced trainers with 300 horsepower engines. So, moving to these machines with 1,500 horses was quite something. As Fireflys had separate cockpits for the pilot and the observer, the pilots had to learn by doing. There was no room for an instructor—unless he sat in the observer's cockpit. But as that had no flying controls and no forward visibility it was pointless. The first thing we noticed was that they all had trouble even taxiing the aircraft—they would go off the taxi strip to the right, straighten out, and then go off to the left. But, eventually, they all qualified without badly breaking any of the planes and we Observers then had to start going with them to learn our jobs with new radio and radar equipment. From my Log Book, I see my first flight with 825 was on 28 January 1946, in Firefly 414 with Lt. Watson piloting. I don't remember him at all. My comments stated it was a formation flight. It was not until 4 February that I flew with Sub Lieutenant Charles Bourque RCN(R). Charlie and I had the dubious distinction of being the first Canadian "crew" that the RCN had. Charlie was from Toronto, but was a true French Canadian in spirit, and was ex RCAF. As with me, he just wanted to continue flying. But he wanted to make it his career, while I was already planning to go to University of Toronto. We became good friends and didn't lose touch for a long time. Sadly, he died in 1988.

In our month at Burscough, and the next six weeks at RNAS Lee-on-Solent—the naval air station near Portsmouth—we Observers did very little flying as the main squadron task was to train the pilots. Besides, the weather was bad. Looking at my Log Book, I see I had all of 19 flights in the ten-week period. Finally, at the end of March, we boarded Warrior for the trip to Halifax and the air base at the airfield near Dartmouth across the river—aka RCAF (and later HMCS and RNCAS) Station Shearwater—that we shared with the Air Force and which was also the commercial airport for Halifax. As our pilots still were not checked out for carrier landings, the aircraft were hoisted on board the Warrior with the rest of the squadron stores. It is amazing how much equipment a squadron had. I found out about this because, as the most junior officer, I became squadron stores officer, which meant I was to supervise the move and make certain that everything was stored in the right place in the ship. Fortunately, there were several experienced squadron supply Petty Officers to do the real work and keep me out of trouble.

20-year-old "me" on a Firefly at Royal Canadian Naval Air Station
"Shearwater" near Halifax, Nova Scotia, 1946.

In that sense, the navy was like the army. It's the Petty Officers who actually take charge and get the job done. This was brought home to me when I first started learning the ship handling jobs that being a naval officer entailed. The RN's and the RCN's doctrine on the issue was that even an Air Branch officer was firstly a sailor and only secondly an aviator, albeit during the war there was not time to teach us "acting temporary" officers two sets of skills. I started learning to be a sailor a little later when we started taking-up duties as "second officer of the watch" —the trainee to the "OOW" who was in charge of the ship when the Captain was not on the "bridge," or "compass platform." On the way to Halifax we stopped off in Bermuda for a few days for an official visit —"flag waving" we called it. I happened to be the second OOW as we arrived and it was my duty to be in charge of dropping the anchor, on orders from the OOW. I was sent down to the bow where the anchor equipment was and told the CPO "Boatswain's Mate" to "carry on, Chief." That was the sum total of what I did. I understood even less. It is a foolish officer who gets in the way of an experienced Chief Petty Officer.

The cruise to Halifax was just that for us: a pleasure cruise. We couldn't fly because the pilots were not qualified for deck landings. There were not many ship's duties as there were 50 aviator officers to be second OOW, which meant about two four-hour watches each on the three-week voyage. The weather was not too bad for March, so I wasn't bothered by seasickness, which had been a serious problem for me on my Atlantic crossing in 1938. So we just had lectures from our instructor officers and got to learn a little about our ship. We also had time to learn about each other. I got to know our three senior squadron officers a bit. "Tatts" Tattersall, a career Royal Navy officer was our Commanding Officer, and a perfect gentleman. He never talked about what he had done during the war, but he had flown all five years of it. It was much the same for Tom Bartlett, our Senior Pilot, and Tony Sweeting, our Senior Observer. All I ever knew was that Tom had last flown operationally in an ASW squadron on convoys to Russia. Those were the worst duties of the war. The ship casualties were very heavy—from both U-boats and German shore-based aircraft. The water temperature in the Arctic was such that there were hardly any survivors from ships that sunk or aircraft that went down. Apparently, you lasted at the most five minutes in the water.

Canada's wartime recruitment policy was rather unique and the cause of a bit of a scandal after the European war ended. The policy was that, although there was conscription, it only applied to home service. Only volunteers were sent overseas. When the war in Europe ended, a fairly large contingent of Canadian ships—our two cruisers and a dozen or so destroyers—were to join the USN and RN fleets in the Pacific. Half way across the Pacific, it was concluded that, as so many men were opting to leave the navy as they had volunteered only for the war in Europe, they had to call for volunteers. To the great embarrassment of the admirals, over half voted to go home. As there were not enough crew replacements available to replace them, the Canadian fleet simply pulled out of the Pacific war. Perhaps the feeling of the sailors was roused by what had become common knowledge in Canada about the manpower situation in the Canadian army in Europe in late 1944. The politicians wanted to have a Canadian "Army" (that is a military unit of at least two divisions) so they did not have to be part of a British or American command. The trouble was there were never enough volunteers to replace the heavy casualties in France and Germany. Consequently, all the units were under-strength, making casualties even worse. This, quite naturally, caused a great deal of resentment amongst the fighting soldiers and serious political problems at home as both the soldiers and the public blamed ambitious Generals and callous politicians. The only thing Canada had to show for it was our own landing beach—Juno Beach—at Normandy and heavy casualties. I remember how touched our kids were when we took them to Normandy in 1984 and they saw the Canadian cemeteries. What struck all of us was that each cross registered the age of the victim—there were so many eighteen- and nineteen-year-olds. Now back to my story.

We arrived in Halifax in the beginning of May. It is an historic city for Canada as one of the oldest shipping centers and a principal naval base since the 17th century. It suffered two major crises related to the RCN. The first in WWI was when an ammunition ship blew up in the harbor, killing literally thousands of people, mainly civilians. The second was right after "VE Day." There was a major riot amongst the sailors ashore who went on a rampage and destroyed a large part of the town. This was a result of five years of resentment coming to a head. As the RCN's job was to protect convoys, the fleet's time was almost entirely 10 to 14 days going over to Europe, one or two days in port somewhere in Britain for refueling and re supplying, then 10 to 14 days at sea on the way back. The trouble was, unlike in British ports, the sailors lucky enough to get a few hours off duty to go ashore could not go to the local "pub" for a few—or a lot of—beers to let off steam. Halifax was a "dry" city. All they could do was, if the government beer stores happened to be open, buy a case there and drink it in the street. The civilians in Halifax had never been known as being particularly friendly to sailors at the best of times. This "public drunkenness" made matters worse. So when the war ended, large numbers of sailors on leave let off steam. The result could have been predicted. At least that was what the court martial decided during the trial of the Admiral-in-command at Halifax. He was dismissed from the Service. But most of us felt he was just the scapegoat.

Other than that, Halifax was, as far as I was concerned, a very pleasant place, especially during the summer. I was very fortunate in that my old friend from boot camp, Geoffrey Payzant, was still living there with his parents. So he took me under his wing. Geoffrey had been one of those whose pilot training in the U.S. was cut short before he got his "wings" because of the end of Lend Lease when the war ended. Lend Lease was the program started by President Roosevelt to finance the transfer of war materials to Britain before the U.S. came into the war. It also financed the training of RAF and RN pilots who were sent to the U.S. for flying training. So, being a Canadian, Geoffrey was demobilized right away. He was already enrolled at Dalhousie University in Halifax and studying the philosophy of music. He introduced me to his family and friends and, thus, I was accepted into the local community. We had a great deal of fun together. Much to my delight, as his family belonged to the local yacht club—the Royal Nova Scotia Yacht Squadron—I got in some serious sailing with Geoffrey and his friends.

In that first summer in Halifax, we were based at "Shearwater." There, the flying became more interesting. First, our pilots did their deck landing trials. Then the squadron flew out to join Warrior. I shall never forget that first flight with Charlie to make my first back-seat landing on the ship. It was Charlie's seventh. What was slightly terrifying for me was my first sight of the ship from about ten miles away while we were at about 2,000 feet. It looked too small. In any event, my Log Book entry recorded that this first deck landing took place on 17 July 1946 at about 1035. It was eleven days after my 20th birthday. Charlie made a good landing, catching the number three wire. But, from the back seat the experience, especially the first time, is quite something. In those days a carrier landing in a propeller driven aircraft, was unlike the standard "straight in" landing you experience in a jet aircraft nowadays or in a commercial aircraft landing on an airfield. Rather, once in the landing "circuit," approaching the ship head on, you fly at about 100 feet altitude parallel to the ship about 300 feet off the port (left) side, then make a steep 180-degree port-turn to arrive just over the stern. At that point the pilot levels out and cuts the engine, all the while guided by the "batsman," the ex pilot whose job it is to tell the pilot he is flying at the right speed at the right altitude and when to "cut." The theory is, when timed correctly, the plane sinks slowly to the deck and the "hook" caches the third of the ten wires stretched across the deck. It's OK if you catch any wire really: the trick is not to miss them all and run into the wire barrier after the tenth, as that breaks the plane. What was hair-raising for Observers in Fireflys was that when the pilot cuts the engine, all you can see is water. So, you have that sinking feeling until the plane actually hits the deck as it is not till then that you know he has made it. Obviously though, the odds of missing the ship are practically nil and bad landings were rare. To my knowledge, no aircrew have ever been killed or injured because of a bad landing on any of the RCN's carriers over the 15 or so years that the RCN had carriers. In any event, my first landing was quite a thrill and I was very pleased to be on the ship.

A typically bureaucratic event occurred around then. The RCN's personnel people finally noticed they had accepted my RN promotion to "Subby" despite my being in the RCN by then. They wanted to drop me back to Midshipman because RCN regulations said the minimum age for promotion was 19-1/2 while the RN's age was still 19. Fortunately, by the time they got around to this I was twenty so they couldn't demote me. But they could cut back my "seniority in rank" by the requisite six months. However, as could only happen in the services, when this was being done, the responsible clerk in Naval Headquarters got it backwards. Instead of subtracting six months from my seniority, he added six months. This resulted, exactly nine years later, in my becoming the RCN's youngest Lt. Commander. Because of that mistake that was never noticed, I had put in only seven years instead of the required eight as a Subby.

That September, the Air Group was given a month's leave. I decided to go back to Hamilton and have a look at Toronto University, just some 40 miles away. I stayed with my friend from elementary school days, "Bud" Jackson. His family was absolutely wonderful to me. They housed and fed me for three weeks while Bud and I wandered around doing what 20-somethings do. Bud had been in the Army for awhile but, being younger than I, didn't get much beyond boot camp. In Toronto I visited the Dean of Residence at University College and was accepted on the spot. He was another ex serviceman—an infantry major in Europe—but he had done his post-graduate work before the war. Claude Bissell was his name. Later, he became President of the university. The memorable part of that leave was going to New York with Charlie Bourque. I don't remember a great deal of what we did except hanging out in a very congenial bar on the Upper East Side called the Madison Lounge. It had a great piano player. We also went back to the Sherry-Netherland, just for old times' sake for me. The real memory, though, was of the night we left. We had a midnight train to Halifax. I don't remember where we were staying, but we checked out, wearing our uniforms for the trip and took the bus that, we were told, was the one to Penn Station. It must have been close to 2330, which was late for New York then. We were the only people on the bus. After a while, I noticed we were going past Central Park and realized suddenly that we were going uptown instead of downtown. In a panic, we rushed up to the driver, asking when we would get to the station. He said the obvious, that this was the bus from the station, and he was heading for Harlem. We explained our train was leaving and we couldn't miss it. So what should we do? With a big grin he said he had been in the service and he would get us there. He just turned the bus around and delivered us to the station with 15 minutes to spare.

Now that our pilots were proficient, we started serious ASW training. The then method of detecting submerged submarines was using gadgets called "sonobuoys." Sonobuoys sent out radar pulses that, if they hit a solid object, would sound a "ping" and bounce back to the sonobuoy receiver. The time it took gave the distance. The trick was to drop an accurate pattern of four buoys about two miles apart as a "box" around the target area. If you dropped them accurately, marked their positions on your plotting board, and then gauged from your receiver the correct time and distance of each "ping" and plotted that accurately, you had located the submarine. From then on, it was just a matter of repeating the exercise to follow the submarine's course and speed. Eventually, we would drop our practice depth charges, or bombs or fire-off our rockets. That is, we did from the back seat of our planes exactly what you have seen many times in movies about anti-submarine warfare, where the sonobuoy operator on a ship or another submarine does the same thing. The difference was that, in the ASW ship, the sonobuoy equipment was bigger and more accurate, so with just one transmitter/receiver you could get a pretty accurate direction and distance. Also, the operator did not have to do his own plotting, since the ship's navigator did that. For a couple of months, we flew around the Atlantic off Halifax practicing this, plus navigation and radar exercises for us and gunnery and dive-bombing exercises for the pilots.

By then we had our first real navigational aid—a radio beacon receiver that could be tuned to Dartmouth or Warrior. The transmitters emitted different Morse letters in 15-degree arcs. So, if one knew the sequence of the letter—for example if you knew from your beacon code book that "A" (dot dash) was followed clockwise by "D" (dash dot dot)—if you lost the A and picked up the D, to get back to base, all you had to do was turn to starboard (right). And keep within the 15-degree arc that gave you D. Conversely if "E" (dot) in the code book was counter-clockwise to "M" (dash dash) and after hearing M you lost it and picked up E, you knew you had to turn to port to get back. Further, the volume grew louder as you approached so you had an additional check. While the codes were changed daily, it was obvious that these beacons could not be used by ships during wartime as it was not too hard to figure out which way to turn to home-in on a ship if you were the attacker.

That was all very simple in theory but, tragically, we lost several aircraft over my ten years of flying because the crew got it wrong. I remember once being in the operations room of our carrier when that happened. We were off the Nova Scotian coast and, as was often the case, there was thick fog. This one aircraft was at the extreme edge of the ship's radar range and heading away when he should have been returning. Our last radio message confirmed he could hear the beacon clearly but not our radio transmissions warning them that they were "flying a reciprocal"—the term used when you read your compass backwards. In those days, it was not a digital read-out, but a bearing compass, so it often happened with inexperienced crews that, instead of steering "090," they took the reciprocal "270." This crew must have made the same mistake with the beacon signals. The worst part was they could not have been more than a few miles from the coast, had they seen or been able to pick it up on radar. Their transmissions gradually faded away. From 150 miles off, there was nothing immediate we could do. They must have run out of fuel and come down in the sea. But in the search operations that followed, not a trace was found. It was a sobering lesson for all of us and a real tragedy for the two in the plane and their families. It was hard to explain to the next of kin such a wasteful loss of life due to carelessness. That kind of accident was labeled "human error" in the records.

Charlie and I got along very well as friends and as a crew, except for one problem. Charlie, and most of the other pilots for that matter, did not like the idea that the Observer was the "captain" of the aircraft. I could understand that. The pilot flew the machine and, as the U.S. Navy had shown, could probably do their own navigating well enough. And they were the ones that fired the cannons and the rockets, and did the dive-bombing. The only things they didn't do—and could not do from the front seat—was work the radar and ASW equipment and aim the depth charges. The same applied with the Americans. They actually had two in the back, but both were petty officers and they certainly were not "captain." But we got over this and I made my compromise, having little choice. That was to let him do the "cockpit checks." In theory, and it applies to all military and civilian aircraft to this day, the second person, be he copilot, observer or whatever, would read off each item on the checklist before take-off and landing and the pilot was supposed to acknowledge and confirm each step as completed. Charlie refused to do this. His position was simple. I did not know how to fly and he was not, repeat not, going to listen to me telling him what to do regardless of the rules. This worked fine until our last landing aboard Warrior when we were returning to Halifax from Victoria, the RCN's West Coast base. More about that later.

I had my quirks too, which were just as dangerous as his, but not in a life-threatening way. As much as I loved flying and being in the navy, I had still not got over the harassing treatment we received from our officers on Pier 92. I was still a bit rebellious about what I saw as unnecessary strictness. Warrior had as senior officers a Captain, a Commander (the "XO") and a "First Lieutenant"—the man who really ran the crew. To me, they seemed reasonable types as RCN "Fish Heads" as we "flyboys" called the real sailors. The Air Department, as it was called, had a "Commander Flying," who was the CAG Commander, and a "Commander O" (for Observer), who was in charge of air operations and all the Observers. Both were regular RN (not Reservists) and both were a little pompous. Commander O was also rather condescending to us "colonials" who were not even real flyers, let alone sailors. So I tried to get even, in a very juvenile way. In his hearing, I would say to someone else nearby that I was going "upstairs" (instead of "up top") or "downstairs" (instead of "below") or to the bar (instead of to the "Ante Room"). He never said anything but I suspect that had I aspirations for a regular commission in the navy, he would have made certain that I was turned down. On the other hand, he had served as an Observer for five war years, so I guess he was entitled to a slightly superior attitude. On the positive side, when I was learning to drive a jeep I had a stupid accident, which he saw and also ignored—I backed into the side of a hangar. Thinking about bars in Her Majesty's Canadian ships, it is interesting to think that, in those days, no one thought anything of having a drink before lunch before flying. Now there is a strict "eight hour no drink before flying" rule.

In October 1946, we left Halifax for a cruise to spend the winter based at Victoria on the west coast. Ostensibly, this was to show the Westerners that we had an aircraft carrier. This naturally raised the point of having only one when we were a two-ocean country (three, if you counted the Arctic) with, supposedly, a two-ocean navy. It took a good two weeks to sail from Halifax to Victoria via the Panama Canal, as it was some 7,000 miles. It was a question of budgets and priorities. In September 1945, the RCN had over 1,000 ships, including two cruisers, two carriers (we provided only the ships' crews, while the RN provided all the Air Branch personnel) and some 25 destroyers. The "small ships" during the war and in the late 1940s were mainly ASW ships, ranging from 200-ton Fairmile coastal motor torpedo boats, to 1,000 ton frigates, which were the mainstay of the convoy escorts. By 1950, we had perhaps only about 100 ships, including the two cruisers, one carrier and twelve destroyers. So, instead of having operational fleets on both coasts, the so-called "capital ships"—the cruisers and the carrier—moved back and forth.

It was a great six-month cruise. My Log Book shows we visited Kingston Jamaica, Panama, Acapulco and San Diego on the way to Victoria. The flying part was pretty routine for Charlie and me. We had only two incidents. The first was on a dive-bombing run. Charlie got a bit carried away, despite it being his twentieth or so run, and was late in pulling out. Dive-bombing runs were always scary as far as I was concerned. We seemed to start out upside-down and then go straight down until I was sure we were going straight in. We had lots of "Gs" (the multiple of the momentum of your weight when changing direction quickly)—so I tended to black-out and not actually see how close we were to the surface. On this occasion, as I got myself together and looked out, I saw a jagged hole in our port wing, about ten feet from my cockpit. We had been so low that the bomb blast resulted in a large splinter hitting us. Fortunately, it missed the wing fuel tank—about 20 feet on the other side—and me. Equally fortunate, it didn't sever any of the control wires. Charlie did not get high marks for that run, notwithstanding he hit the target.

The second incident occurred the week before we were to arrive at Victoria. We had a complete hydraulic failure, resulting in our having to do a wheels-up landing, also without our flaps. This meant for a very high-speed approach. Charlie made a perfect landing, picking up number three wire dead center. As with all carrier landings, the wire stops the plane in about 50 feet and in about ten seconds. The emergency crew was right on-station and up on the wings trying to pull us out within seconds while the fire crew was spraying the aircraft. Fortunately, it did not burn and was, in fact, hardly damaged except for the propeller and the radar dome, which was on a rack under the fuselage. The only difficulty we had was actually getting out. These big guys dressed in their fire-protective clothing were all over us as we (separately, obviously) were trying to open our harnesses. Their big gloves made it impossible for them to do it, but they didn't seem to understand that it would have been easier for us if they had just kept their hands away. But it was comforting to know they knew their jobs. Had circumstances been different, they could have saved our lives.

All of this was saved for posterity because we had on board photographers and reporters from most newspapers in Canada. They had joined the ship in San Diego for the trip to Victoria—fun for them and good public relations for the navy. The end result was that "NAN"—the letters for our Firefly number 566—was on the front page of every newspaper in the country the next day, along with pictures of Charlie and me struggling with our rescuers. In my Log Book it is recorded as happening on 6 December 1946. Looking at it, I notice that Charlie was a "Subby" that day. But on December 15, when the Log Book states we flew from Warrior to RCAF Station Patricia Bay, he was a full Lieutenant —equivalent to a captain in the army. Not promoted because of his good piloting, but just because he had passed the two-year point as a Subby.

The only other thing I remember about the naval aspects of that first cruise was the fun of watching the planes land when we were not flying ourselves. As both our pilots and the fighter pilots of 803 Squadron had little experience actually flying from a carrier, they were not yet fully competent. Consequently, we had a few accidents. Fortunately, no one was injured but we did break a lot of aircraft. I have two vivid memories of accidents that should have caused fatalities. The first was with one of our Fireflies. It caught a wire, but was swinging to port and went off the deck into the catwalk—the passageway around the deck—and just below where the deck crews were stationed and where the ship's armament was. I happened to be on the spot with my camera. It seemed to be coming straight at me, but I clicked away until it came to rest, minus its port wing which was ripped off at it went over. I was just about 30 feet away and I was drenched with what I thought at first was fuel. Fortunately, it turned out to be hydraulic fluid or it would have caught fire. No one was hurt, but I must have been shaken up more than I thought. I found out when I had my film developed that, instead of a great series of a crash, I had one big blur. I was so excited I had forgotten to click the film forward.

The second accident involved a Seafire that had missed the wires and opened up to full throttle to go around again. Unfortunately, the pilot was a little late, as his hook caught the barrier—the heavy wire fence half-way down the deck that can be raised if a plane misses the landing wires to prevent it from crashing into the planes parked forward. It was an amazing sight! The plane continued to rise with its engine screaming under full power, the barrier stretched forward and starting to rise, pulled by the Seafire. For a moment it was hard to tell which would win. But, gradually, the plane slowed, still pointed up at about a 45-degree angle, and then literally seemed to stop and just hang there. Finally gravity and the strength of the barrier won, and the plane came crashing straight down onto the deck, but still with a slight nose-up attitude (tilt). The undercarriage collapsed, then the wings flopped down, the propeller splintered and the engine continued screaming away at full power for seconds before the pilot switched it off. Under the circumstances, that took a lot of presence of mind, but it prevented a fire because the whole structure of the aircraft just collapsed. Everyone who saw it stood there in stunned silence, except for the trusty crash crew that was right on it. I guess that was the on-the-job training that got them to Charlie and me so quickly a few weeks later.

As always, "liberty" in our ports of call was great fun. Jamaica was a wonderful place in those days. I recall there was a very elegant hotel called Myrtle Beach right on Kingston harbor. The officers' liberty boats used to deposit us at the end of their dock. At the shore end of the dock was a bar and a swimming pool, and all the delights expected of a first-class tropical resort hotel. Shortly after arrival in a new port, it was always routine for the captain and the ship's officers to have a reception on board for the local dignitaries. They would respond in kind, so we were well entertained. Our "fish head" captain got a bit carried away with how well we had all been treated. So, he decided to put on an air show for the locals the day of our departure. There were two things wrong with his plan as far as we were concerned. First, it was to start at 0700 Sunday morning, and it was obvious that our local friends, like us, had drunk far too much and gone to bed far too late the night—or early morning—before to be interested in getting up to see the show. The second thing was the show itself. He thought it would give the locals a thrill to see the air group take off from the ship while it was still at anchor in Kingston Harbor. Fortunately, Commander O had decided wisely that there was no need for his young fellows to participate in what was just going to be some formation flying over the city. But we all, dutifully, got up to cheer our pilots on. Take-off was scheduled for 0630. All the pilots were back aboard by 0600, so, so far so good. Our Catholic Padre made it by 0615, which made everyone feel better. The problem was, as expected, there was no wind. So, there they were, all of our 25-odd serviceable aircraft lined up to take off under very dangerous conditions: not so much the hangovers, but no wind across the deck, as opposed to the minimum safe wind speed of 20 knots along with the ship's speed. It was terrifying to watch each aircraft as it passed over the bow and dropped out of sight for what seemed minutes. But each staggered up somehow. The ship proceeded to sea; the CAG did its salute to the locals, and the aircraft landed back on deck. Unbelievably, not a single bent plane.

Panama was a bit of a let down. We all visited a few nightclubs and saw the sights, but there didn't seem many dignitaries for us to entertain either in Panama City or Balboa at the other end of the Canal. No one much entertained us, except the local bar girls. I guess there were just too many sailors passing through Panama for anyone to pay any attention. As to the eight-hour trip through the Canal, the first half-hour was interesting as we were towed through the first lock and could see the odd alligator looking for a free lunch. After that, I repaired to 825's Ready Room for poker. About twelve of us spent the entire remaining seven hours playing. We did the same thing on the way back when we were returning to Halifax.

Acapulco was especially interesting then as it was the Saint-Tropez of Mexico. It was tropical like Jamaica, but sophisticated and Spanish. There, our reception was great and, again, we were well looked after by the locals. As with our visit to Jamaica, we were there before tourists spoiled it. Of course, there were several impressive resort hotels, but it was mainly a resort for the Mexicans. A remarkable coincidence was meeting two very attractive blonde sisters who were Mexican of English extraction. Less than two years later, my first roommate at my Toronto University residence was a Mexican and these girls were his cousins. I remember Acapulco Bay's spectacular views, its relatively untouched forested mountains surrounding it and the miles of almost empty sandy beaches. What I remember most was my "walking on water" experience. I was swimming from one of the beaches by myself and decided I would strike out for the island on the inside of the reef. Acapulco Bay is almost enclosed by a large reef, with an island to one side. It was about a mile to the island and it seemed a good idea at the time. I had been told that no sharks came inside the reef—and that seemed to be proven by the number of other people swimming around and surfboarding. I got to the island, walked around for a few minutes and headed back. With only about a hundred yards to go, I noticed there was hardly anyone else swimming and those who were surfboarding were headed ashore at high speed. Looking farther out I saw five shark fins circling half way between where I was and the island beach I had just left. It would not have been much of an exaggeration to say I ran on water then. The other Acapulco event had to do with the law being laid down by Commander O that we had to be back aboard ship by the last liberty boat at midnight. One night one of our Observers missed it. In a slightly inebriated state, he "borrowed" a local fisherman's canoe and started to paddle out to the ship anchored in the bay. He must have fallen asleep. The next morning, a trawler came alongside and handed over the inert body of this fellow. They had found him just after dawn, past the reef, still fast asleep, with the canoe almost full of water. He was lucky to be alive. His legs, which must have been in the water for several hours, were almost frozen solid. I know; I felt them.

Next came San Diego. What was notable to us all was passing the USNAS North Island, the main naval air bases on the Pacific coast. It was right on the harbor, not two hundred yards from our route to our dock. There must have been at least a thousand naval aircraft lined up in clear sight. And there we were, with 20 then-serviceable aircraft left —half the RCN's operational air power. But the RCN, in the form of HMCS Uganda, the cruiser that was accompanying us, put on a splendid show that must have impressed those who saw it. Warrior had moved into its space at a dock in a measured way and was tying up. Then came Uganda into the next slip. It must have been doing at least five knots as it nosed in. Somehow, the Captain—only he could have been driving—brought it to a full stop within a foot of where it was to tie up. It was an awesome sight. Had anything gone wrong, 10,000 tons of steel could have ended up half way across the street at the end of the dock. I remember nothing about our few days there except that I went to the Zoo, which is quite famous. Then we were off again for the last lap to Victoria.

On Vancouver Island, Victoria is the capital of British Columbia and a very beautiful city. The locals tended to be more English than the English, in both accent and attitudes. In fact, the local "railway hotel" (the railways built palace-like hotels every 500 miles or so on their routes across Canada so passengers could break their journeys) served tea in the best English style. Appropriately, it was called The Empress. While I have visited most of those wonderful old hotels at one time or another, this was, and probably still is, the only one where you could close your eyes and open them again and imagine you were in England. However,

Victoria is small and we were based 20 miles out of town so we didn't spend much time there. Back in those days, not so many people had cars and certainly not young naval officers. As with RNAS Dartmouth, RCAF Station Patricia Bay was on an airfield shared with the commercial airport. The RCAF had a few transport aircraft there and not much else but the Officers' Mess, which was excellent. I remember fondly that they always had plates of sandwiches available after dinner for a pre-bedtime snack. A very civilized idea much appreciated by us young, always hungry, fellows. As we had arrived just before Christmas, there were holidays. Those of us who lived in the western part of the country went home. The rest of us—about a dozen—went to a ski resort in the northern part of the island. I was the only novice skier.

That was quite an experience: almost all day in a bus to get there. Then, with eight days to go, we found it was "dry." No one had warned us of this or told us to bring our own supplies. The skiing was quite a challenge for me. I had done it a bit in Hamilton when I was ten or twelve, but only on small slopes. Here, the first task was to get to the top of the hill, which was above the tree line. It took almost all day, as we had to walk it on our skis with special traction devices attached. I remember thinking, as we trudged up narrow trails through the trees, that getting down might be harder than getting up. Then as we passed above the tree line, we had to surmount what seemed to be a ten-foot sheer cliff. I asked our guide how we got down this. He just said there was another way. Foolishly, I believed him. Finally, we arrived at the little log cabin that signified we were at the top and it was time to prepare for the descent. All my so-called friends just launched off. I went very slowly. At the cliff, I found the "other way" was to take off the skis and more or less roll down. Stopping was the hard part. While the others were long gone by the time I arrived, I found out later that they just took it as a jump. It was after dark when I finally got back to the lodge. Fortunately, the last mile was relatively flat and I could see the lights so I could find my way. The others all thought it was very funny. I spent the rest of the time there reading.

Our flying activities were much the same, except we were exercising with our Pacific Fleet. What was especially pleasant was the scenery.

Victoria Island, the Strait of Juan de Fuca between it and the mainland of Canada to the east and the U.S. to the south, and the view of Mount Baker were all spectacularly beautiful. The combination of mountains, forests, and hundreds of small islands were wonderful to behold. The only problem was that it was winter and the weather was treacherous. Many a time, we found our way back to base by following a Trans Canada Airlines ("TCA," now called Air Canada) passenger plane coming in to land at Patricia Bay. They all seemed to start their approaches ten miles out, with wheels and flaps down. So it was easy to follow them. With the mountains and the weather, neither our radar nor the base's beacon worked very well.

We had our first squadron casualties there because of the weather. "Tatts" Tattersall was going on leave to join his wife who he had not seen for several months. TCA had stopped flying for the day so "Crash" Peaver, one of our ex RCAF pilots, volunteered to ferry Tatts over to Vancouver. They took off, transferred from Pat Bay control to Vancouver control for the 100-mile flight, and that was the last we heard or saw of them. We searched for two days: 2-3 February. When I think of it, it was remarkable that, while we lost many aircrew due to accidents from the three squadrons in which I served over ten years, none was due to carrier operations. We might have been careless, reckless or plain stupid, but our pilots kept their acts together doing what others thought was the most dangerous kind of flying. I remember we Observers, probably carried away by the old doctrine that we were in command, used to say the pilots had their brains in their feet. Wherever they had them—and they must have been in both places—I have no complaints. Thinking of fatalities, I think our figure was about ten percent killed annually. In some cases it was poor maintenance—my next close call, experienced with Pop Fotheringham, was the result of a mechanic failing to tighten a locking bolt on the rudder trim tab. In others it was poor navigation by the Observer. In others it was pilot error—how else can you explain mid-air collisions? In fact the only fatality while landing on one of our carriers, which happened several years after I retired from flying, was because the starboard wing of a plane folded on its own just as the pilot was coming in to land. He ejected—but straight into the side of the ship.

So his death had nothing to do with it being a carrier landing.

On 17 February, we flew back to Warrior for the return to Halifax. Lt. "Pop" Fotheringham had taken over as Commanding Officer of 825 —the first RCN officer to have a squadron command. A truly miserable way to gain a promotion, but "Pop" was a fine pilot and a great guy. He was called "Pop" because he was in his 30s. He had been a career "fish head" in the RCN and had transferred to the air branch towards the end of the war. Our flying activities were just to repeat the same old things. One of the luckiest things of my life happened on that cruise. On 6 March, 200 or so miles off the coast of Mexico, Charlie and I were strapped in, waiting to be launched-off on that damn catapult for a high level fighter intercept training mission. This would be a long—two-hour —flight for us at 10,000 feet. Charlie came up on our intercom and said he didn't feel well. We talked about it and agreed he should call Ops and warn them. While I was still strapped in, Charlie was told to get out. In the end, they had to carry him out. (It turned out that he had acute appendicitis and was operated on two hours later.) Out came Pop to take over. Eventually, we were blasted off and went on our intercept mission. Up at 10,000 feet, the plane went into a sudden left-hand turn and started spiraling down. Pop said he had on full right rudder, and still could not get us out of the turn. Following the rules, I sent out a "Mayday" distress call to alert the ship. Pop and I talked about it for a few minutes, thankful that we were at 10,000 feet rather than our usual 2,000. He suggested bailing out. That did not appeal to me because Observers had been warned that bailing out of the back seat of a Firefly usually cost you, literally, an arm or a leg as you hit the tail of the plane. So, I pointed out that we were a long way from help and there were sharks down there. We discussed other options. Pop tried dropping the flaps and the undercarriage. That worked. We could now fly more or less straight, but we had a 30 degree list to port. Not comfortable. And Pop said he still had to have on full right rudder. Anyhow, he lined us up on what I thought was the right course to get back to the ship—which was a lot closer than land. Thanks to Pop we made it back and per-suaded them to let us try landing on board rather than ditching along-side. Pop did a magnificent job of getting the port wing—and port wheel

—up just in time to catch the number three wire. When we stopped, the emergency crew came out to help. It was just as well because, after an hour of having all his strength in his right leg keeping us under control, it was completely paralyzed. It took several days before he could walk properly again. I hate to think what might have happened had Charlie's pain held off for another few minutes and he had been in that position. Regardless of what might have happened to me, he would not have survived three or four hours in the water.

Our first port of call was San Pedro, the Port of Los Angeles and local home of the U.S. Navy. We all visited Los Angeles, but I cannot say I was impressed. It was just another town, bigger than San Diego, but not much different. I think, as always anywhere, it is the people you know or meet that make the difference. The old navy reception worked its usual magic. I remember meeting several well-known Hollywood celebrities, including Peter Lawford. He spent a lot of time talking to me that he could have spent with more interesting people. But we were not there that long before it was off to another poker-playing session to get us through the Panama Canal. As to flying, it was more of the same.

Our next port of call was Havana. In early 1947 that was quite a city. Again, the reception and reciprocation from the local community was wonderful. We had a great time ashore. I remember the Copacabana, the great Havana nightclub. I also remember a great party at the home of an expatriate Canadian in the hills behind Havana. In retrospect, I suspect he was into something illegal. It was a fun few days.

From Cuba we went to Bermuda for night deck landing trials for our pilots. This started 18 April. For me, though, it was a tedious time. I had already applied for entry to the University of Toronto, University College, for first year "Commerce," the appropriate course for those interested in business and finance. I confess here that my early interest in finance had faded a bit in favor of just flying. But the frustrations of the navy bureaucracy brought it back. To be clear, it wasn't the flying part, it was the tedious job of learning to be a "fish head" and having to stand those interminable jobs as "Officer of the Watch" in harbor. Being Second OOW at sea was interesting because things were happening. In harbor, even promoted to "OOW," being alongside a dock or at anchor, nothing much happened. But I did have a few rather traumatic experiences in those junior Fish Head roles in charge of the ship. The first was when I was called to witness the results of two young aircraft mechanics who thought de-icing fluid was a good substitute for booze. It was mainly alcohol, but it was very dangerous. One was unconscious for over a day. The other was less fortunate. He was blinded—I think permanently. My job was to be the initial charging officer for what was later a court martial.

But I found around that time that bureaucracy was not limited to the navy. The University of Toronto decided that, despite my London University matriculation and my two terms at Cambridge, I did not meet the lofty standards of "U of T." Therefore, if I wanted to start first year as an ex serviceman and graduate with honors in a four-year course after three years, I had to take an extra mathematics course. This I could do by a correspondence course. That's what I did during the eleven days our pilots were doing their night deck landing trials at the then U.S. Army air field in Bermuda—Kindley Field—which was also the local commercial airport. Why it was still U.S. Army after the U.S. Air Force had been formed, I had no idea. In any event, we lived in what had been aircraft packing cases as our officers' "cabins," but the food, as always in U.S. bases, was good. During the day, I would go down to the local beach to work on my correspondence course. As I had always been strong in mathematics, it was easy but time consuming. So I did not really enjoy the pleasures of Bermuda that time. Still, better to be studying on a Bermudian beach in the spring than doing it in Scotland in the winter.

We did a bit of night flying from Kindley, but not much. Unlike a lot of pilots who claim to prefer flying at night, I would rather be able to see land or sea. Finally, we put to sea to let our pilots do the real thing. That was a disaster. Twelve 825 squadron pilots took off from Kindley. After the first eight to land on the ship broke their planes, Commander Air gave up and sent the rest back. Fortunately, none were serious accidents. But there was no point to wiping out the entire squadron in one night. My main Kindley Field experience when we were flying from Warrior was getting there. One of the other pilots, Stew Soward, and I were doing one of our training exercises when we had yet another hydraulic failure. This time Warrior decided we should go to Kindley, which was only about 100 miles away. There were other aircraft coming back and they did not want to risk fouling the deck with a crashed aircraft. That was a sensible decision. The problem for us was that no one was expecting us at Kindley and we were running short of fuel. When I finally picked up Bermuda on radar, Stew made a "Mayday" call. The cryptic answer he received from the Kindley control tower was to "wait." A few minutes later, he tried again and got another "wait." Stew, with only a few minutes of fuel left, was in no mood for this. He just radioed back and said he was making a straight-in landing on the first runway he saw. The response was silence. So we landed. After touching down on our belly it seemed to take forever to stop. Smoke was pouring in through the floor. The screaming, scraping noise was deafening. Finally we stopped in a cloud of smoke. Unlike my similar landing on Warrior, we had no trouble getting out of our cockpits, as there was no one about to help or hinder us. In fact, we stood around for about ten minutes before a lone fire truck appeared. It turned out that, as no aircraft were expected during that period, the duty controller had wandered off (for a siesta) and left a corporal in charge with instructions to call him if anything happened. That is exactly what the corporal did. The problem was the duty controller was not answering his phone. After that experience, I concluded I would rather crash land on a ship than an airfield any day.

One could say I was a little "accident prone" in Bermuda. During our last night anchored in Hamilton Bay, I was shipwrecked. A group of us were in the last liberty boat back to the ship during a sudden thunderstorm. In the pitch dark, half way back, there was a jarring crunch and we came to a stop. We assumed we had hit a rock and the boat, which was carrying about 50 of us, was going to sink. My first reaction was to move my wallet from my jacket to my pants. We would be swimming soon and shoes and jackets would be a hindrance. The first to rush out of the cabin wearing a life preserver was our Anglican chaplain. This broke the tension a bit—the boat was surging badly but it wasn't yet sinking. We all laughed and asked him how it was he was the only one with a life preserver. He claimed he was just bringing it up for the most in need. The fact was, the rest of us hadn't thought of life preservers. But this story had a happy ending, more or less. The rock had only taken off the propeller. So the boatswain just called for another boat to tow us back to port. We ended up sleeping in the lounge of the Royal Bermuda Yacht Club. It was a luxurious place but too crowded that night.

We headed back to Halifax at the end of April. There were the usual training missions on the way. A little form attached to my Log Book states that, as of 15/5/47, I was "above average"—six for navigation, five for radio and radar, and six for airmanship. (Five doesn't sound above average, but it was navy scoring: one to eight. It was signed by Peter Grady as Senior O and V.G. Grieve as Commander (Operations) for Warrior. I don't remember when Peter came aboard, or when Grieve became Commander "Ops" or when the title was changed. But, it was good to know that, after flying for about 17 months with 825, I must have been accepted as reasonably competent. That does not mean that what follows about Charlie meant anything different, but this is what happened. We were on what we thought would be our last training mission before arriving. Charlie had got engaged to a beautiful and charming girl just before we had departed six months earlier, so he was looking forward to getting back. He received the "cut" signal from the landing control officer and made his usual good landing. The deck crew unhooked the wire and waved us forward to the parking area. Charlie opened the throttle to taxi forward. Instead of a roar as the engine kicked in, there was a grunt as it stopped. After a two-second pause, the order came from Commander Ops to push us forward, and six large men did just that. We were stunned. If we had been a second later in our landing approach we would either have landed in the sea, or hit the stern of the ship. What had happened was that Charlie had forgotten to switch to the main fuel tank, which was part of the cockpit check on landing. Our wing tanks had about 20 minutes' fuel each and the main about 90 minutes', so the drill was to use up the wing tanks first and then go to main. The cockpit landing check was, amongst other things, to make sure you were on the main tank. Charlie and I were ordered to the compass platform to explain to the Captain and Commander Ops what had happened. Actually, by the time we got there, they knew. So it was just a matter of meting out punishment. I was lucky. Everyone knew of Charlie's quirks, so I escaped blame—not that I was proud of it. Charlie's punishment, however, was seven days as Squadron duty officer, starting the first day we docked. Well, at least he could invite his fiancée, Pat, on board for dinners. Considering what happens nowadays, that was a pretty light punishment. On the other hand, back then, there was nothing wrong with drinking and driving, or drinking and flying.

On 14 May 1947, we (Lt. Commander Jim Hunter, another RCN "fish head" who had taken up flying after the war, and I) flew back to Dartmouth as the squadron moved ashore the day Warrior docked in Halifax. This was my last flight with 825 Squadron. It was sad to leave, but I was leaving active service anyway, and Warrior and 825 were leaving for another cruise in three months—two months before I would become a civilian and a student again. So I was posted to 826 Squadron and remained at Shearwater.

My memories of the RCN in those last months were: first, I was given a free ride back to England in Warrior to see my parents; second, I was sent on a flight to Toronto; third, an international "incident;" and, finally, my "mustering out" medical exam.

The trip home was another adventure. Warrior was being used as a form of troop ship to transport a couple of thousand Boy Scouts for a Jamboree in Britain. A great idea, but the weather did not cooperate. It was even worse than my Atlantic crossing in 1938. In Warrior in bad weather on our cruises, I was never actually sick to the extent of vomiting. Usually flying saved me. I was never airsick, so once we were off the ship I was fine. On this trip there were no aircraft, just Boy Scouts all over the place. The passageway decks were awash with vomit. I have never felt so much like giving up and dying. As an indication of the severity of the weather, we actually "shipped it green" over the compass platform a number of times. "Shipping it green" means whole waves washing over, not just spray. And the compass platform was 60 feet above the deck. I survived and, fortunately, was able to fly back to Halifax commercially.

By happy coincidence—or were my naval friends just being considerate in my last month of service—my last task was to navigate a Firefly to the de Havilland plant in Toronto that had the Canadian service contract for Fairey Aviation, the manufacturer of the Firefly. Consulting my Log Book, I see that Lt. Williamson (I don't remember him at all) and I flew on 8 August to Montreal and on to Toronto. What was especially pleasant about this was meeting the Fairey representative there. Ken Hay-Roe was another ex RCAF pilot. He had been in the RCAF Reserve before the war and thus spent the full five years in the U.K., France and Germany, flying army cooperation aircraft (a liaison aircraft). The result was that, besides making sure our plane was properly refitted, he looked after us too. Ken and I became good friends.

The "incident" was the unexpected arrival of an unmarked B-17 that had obviously once belonged to the U.S. Air Force. It was fully equipped with guns and was crewed by a group of ten serious looking guys who seemed to live in the plane for the week it was with us. We were all interested and tried to befriend and talk to them, but they didn't want to mix. It really wasn't until it just took off one day that we found out what had happened. It was a surplus bomber that had, like many hundreds, been sold as war surplus. The buyer was obviously an Israeli sympathizer as he turned it over to this group of ex USAF B-17 crewmen who happened all to be Jewish. The Canadian government went through the motions of impounding the aircraft because what they were intending to do was illegal, supposedly. That said, our seniors at Dartmouth just turned the proverbial "blind eye" one day and, somehow, they just fueled and took off for Israel. I suppose there was some mild wrist-slapping but, mainly, we were cheering them on. It wasn't that we were taking sides politically; it was just that we admired them for going off to war.

The medical exam was just a routine mustering thing, as I was a healthy young man of 21 by then. But I remember vividly the last thing the last doctor said: "Young man, you are going to have to watch your weight." I asked why. Being a typical navy medical man, he ignored my question and turned to the next patient.

According to my Log Book, I was attached to 743 Squadron, of the

18th Carrier Air Group for my last two months at RCNAS Dartmouth. My last page of my Log Book for that period was signed (verified as accurate) by F.W. Bradley, LCDR (P), RCN as Commanding Officer, 18 CAG, and R.A. Monks, LCDR (P), RCN as training Officer, 18 CAG. The names had changed, the squadron number had changed and even the rank acronyms had changed. I don't remember any of them. I had started out as an Acting Temporary Midshipman (A), RNVR and ended up, then, as a Lt. (O), RCN (R). During my two years as a trainee Observer and then as a "real" Observer, I had logged 252 hours day-flying and 25 hours night-flying. This came to about 280 flights and 65 deck landings and 12 catapult or rocket-assisted take-offs from carriers. Not much flying time compared to what I am told young naval aviators experience nowadays, but probably a lot more fun. At least, looking back, I enjoyed it all immensely. At the time however, I was glad to be out of it. I did not like the discipline and, towards the end, the long periods of inactivity, which was another way of describing the many hours spent as Squadron duty officer when we were ashore or as Officer of the Watch when we were in Warrior but not at sea.

It was a bit of a traumatic experience moving to Toronto. Fortunately, I was well received by University College as a result of my earlier meeting with the Dean of Residence. I was placed in what was then the favored men's residence, "73 St. George Street." That was its address, right on the University College campus. It was an old, three-floor Victorian house. There were some 20 of us there, two to each of the ten bedrooms. We had a "janitor" who cleaned and made our beds. Meals were in the college cafeteria. Compared to Pembroke College it was all very austere. I had picked University College sight unseen as, from my limited research, I had found all the other colleges were church affiliated—Trinity was Anglican, St. Michael's was Catholic, Victoria College was United Church and so on. These were all men's colleges—there were also separate women's colleges for the three main churches. University College was both co-educational (but not the dormitories) and non-denominational, which fit my agnostic tendencies at the time. De facto, it was also the Jewish College. While Toronto University was not considered the best university in Canada—number one then was McGill in Montreal—it was in Toronto. For anyone interested in a business or financial career in Canada, Toronto was the place to be—and that was why I had picked it.

The site of the university campus was, and is, quite beautiful. In the center of the city, it is separated from the Provincial Parliament buildings —Toronto is the Capital of Ontario—by an attractive park. Also close is the Royal Ontario Museum and Bloor Street, Toronto's best upscale shopping and dining area. Straddling Avenue Road, it was Toronto's "Fifth Avenue." That said, most of those good things are better now than they were in 1947. In those days Toronto was a "provincial" city in the worst sense. There were few restaurants deserving of the name and the cultural life really was the Museum, the Art Gallery and one theatre group. As to nightlife, there was none. Not until 1949 did the city fathers allow the licensing of the first "cocktail lounge." I went to the opening night—at least open for the public. I never went again. Prior to that there were "beer parlors"—one room for men and one for women —where only beer was served. There was no mixing of the boys and girls in those days, at least not in drinking establishments. That said, "Toronto the good" or "Hog town," as jealous types from other cities used to call it, had been even less interesting in the past. It was said that, in the 1920s and 1930s, on Sundays there was no public transportation and the only place you could buy a meal was in a hotel, if you were staying there.

The better nightspots, in fact, were the officers' messes of the various military reserve units. Toronto was a true British garrison (colonial) town. As I recall it, there were at least four reserve army regiments with their own quarters, two RCAF reserve squadrons, assorted specialist units, such as an army engineering unit and, of course, a naval reserve base—HMCS York, a stone frigate on the shores of Lake Ontario. One of my first actions on getting to Toronto was to apply to join the active." Unfortunately, there was a surfeit of reserve officers and York had no interest whatsoever in Flyboys. So my reserve navy fun did not start until later. That was good in that it helped enforce my studying regimen.

I made a few friends at 73 St. George Street. Hugh Shaw was the best. An Englishman, ex RAFVR who had had his pilot training ended by the end of Lend Lease as had Geoffrey Payzant. He had done something which I had never realized as possible. That is, he got a U.K. ex service-man's grant to attend university in Canada. I was rather jealous because his monthly "pocket money" allowance (our grateful governments both paid full fees and board) was about $50 whereas mine was $30, which was a fair amount of money in those days. Hugh and I had a good time together. Through my English-Speaking Union ("ESU") membership, we went to New York for weekends about once a month. Oddly, in those days the airfare was quite cheap. We met through the ESU a delightful Swiss family. What their connection to the ESU was remained a mystery. The patriarch was a well-known portrait painter around the turn of the century. Amongst many stories, he told us of a session painting President McKinley the day the USS Maine was sunk in Havana harbor—15 February 1898—a causal factor starting the Spanish-American War. During the war, they had been living in Switzerland; his wife's family owned a resort hotel near the German border. By remarkable coincidence, several years later I met an ex RCAF pilot who had been shot down and escaped into Switzerland. It was the Benziger family that took him in and kept him at their hotel until he moved on—small world. In any event, Hugh and I would please the Benzigers by going to Mass with them and their two delightful grand-daughters at St. Patrick's Cathedral on the Sundays we were there. Afterwards there was always a sumptuous lunch at their apartment on Central Park South.

Our first Christmas in Toronto was not such fun, though. Hugh and I were the only two to stay in the residence. It was far too expensive to go home to visit our respective parents for a week. I remember the miserable Christmas Eve; sitting huddled in our overcoats because the heat was off. Dean Bissell came over to say hello and had a sherry with us. I remember making a point of showing him a can of orange juice or something that was frozen solid. It made no impression whatsoever. We had a much better Christmas the next year. Thanks to the ESU, we were invited to a lovely farmhouse in Pennsylvania Dutch Country that was the country retreat of a New York family. Also there as guests were three members of the Oxford University debating society. It was a wonderful four days. But Hugh and I both felt like illiterate peasants when talking with those three Oxford Union debaters.

Another friend was George MacDonald. George had been a POW for four years as a "guest" of the Japanese. He had been in that unfortunate Canadian army battalion that had arrived in Hong Kong, then a Crown colony, a few days before its 1941 surrender to the Japanese. He was a complete physical wreck still, after two years in hospital. His experience in the final year in Tokyo was fascinating. His group of prisoners was put to work on the docks; he assumed this was intended to discourage the U.S. bombing. Finally, near the end, their treatment became much better when the Japanese began to realize they were losing. Not only was the food marginally better, they were given better protection during the air raids than the locals got. For example, during major fire raids, the army guards pushed civilians out of the canals to make room for the prisoners. Few remember now but those air raids resulted in tens of thousands of civilian deaths and the destruction of tens of square miles of the main cities due mainly to fire bombing. The most interesting incident he told was about being with a group of Japanese dockworkers. They noticed the Japanese had stopped working and were all just staring at one of their mates cutting off the end of a steel beam with an acetylene torch some four floors up. He and the other prisoners wondered why. Then they noticed the worker was sitting on the wrong side. The thing was, his fellow workers didn't bother to tell him; they just waited to see what he would do. Apparently, he just kept cutting away until the end broke off. He fell and was killed—so much for the value of life and comradeship in Japan. As he said, their treatment of prisoners was not surprising when you considered such things.

As I was intending to make my career in finance, I enrolled in a course called "Commerce and Finance." Today, it is probably called Business Administration. It was a four-year honors course but, as an ex serviceman, I could graduate in three years. This was nothing to do with having been to Cambridge. It was only because, besides being a serviceman, I had passed the remedial mathematics course. What became very evident was that the teaching system was much more learning by memorizing than was the Cambridge system. The term for the latter was Socratic, I think. It was probably a better technical education, but there was little if any give-or-take between students and professors. One of my least happy memories was attending a lecture by Harold Innes, Canada's foremost economic historian of the day: a great intellect, but an awful teacher. One of his books, Empire and Communications, is still a classic. His thesis was that empires that lasted over time were based on communications cast in stone (literally) whereas empires that became physically large were dependent on fast and broad communications systems (radio in his day)—hence the difference between the Roman Empire and the Third Reich. That day, Innes was lecturing to his usual class of about 500. He mumbled and his sentences did not always make sense, even if you could hear them. We were all trying to take notes. At one point, I asked my neighbor—I thought very unobtrusively—what he had just said. Somehow, Innes saw me lean over and thought I was being obstructive. In a very firm voice, for a change, I was summarily dismissed from the class. It reminded me of CPO Wilmott at boot camp.

My first-year studies included accounting, statistics and calculus, plus some economic history. Except for the history, I found it boring and difficult, and very different from Cambridge. Much to my surprise I did very well that year, although the last few weeks were traumatic. I came down with chicken pox and was confined to the infirmary. I assumed I would not be better in time to take the exams and, were I to take them in my weakened state, I was sure to fail. I did recover and I did take them with everyone else. My first word of the results was when a friend called me and said I was third. I thought he meant I had third-class honors, which sounded reasonable. But what he meant was that I was third in the class of 600. Not only that but I scored 100% on the calculus exam. To this day, I have no idea what calculus is about. But I did memorize the formulae and so could repeat them. I was amazed. Notwithstanding this, I determined to switch to Political Science and Economics, which seemed a more serious academic course. I had become a bit of an idealist and decided that university was for improving the mind and should not be treated as just a trade school. The university year started in early September and ended in mid-April. Historically, for schools and universities, this had to do with the harsh winters and the short harvesting season. Kids were expected to go back to the farm and help with the harvest—or into the forests to cut trees—during the summer holidays.

This was unlike the U.K. system, where students were not expected to work and there were, consequently, three relatively long breaks each year. The Canadian system meant very short Christmas and Easter (spring break in the U.S.) holidays to compensate for the long summer working period. We were a frontier society still.

I had a better idea for the summer. I went back to active service for four months. I had the fun of flying and, as a Lieutenant with flying pay, got much better paid than was possible in any other job I could have found. So it was back to RCNAS Dartmouth, where I joined 18 Carrier Air Group. Looking at my Log Book, it seems we spent most of the summer doing routine training exercises from Dartmouth. There was one exception that summer. It was to do with a "flying saucer" scare. There was much in the press about such sightings at the time, but not anything about what we saw and did. On the base's radar, there were several "contacts" some hundred miles out to sea, approaching the coast at some 600 knots—solid contacts that were not in dispute by any of the radar people. At that time, there were not many jet fighters around that could travel at that speed, and certainly none off the coast of Nova Scotia. Consequently, the powers that be wanted some proof or contact with whatever it was. We—18 CAG—had two aircraft waiting at the end of the runway constantly for about a week, waiting for the next contact. These were the fighters rather than 826 Squadron's Fireflys. Still, their maximum speed was only about 400 knots so it was hard to see what could have been accomplished. As it turned out, whatever it or they were, they moved on to other parts of the world before our fighters were in place.

Other than that excitement, I have few recollections of anything else that summer. That is, except that I was rash enough to write a treatise on the state of the RCN's air branch. I detailed all of the problems as I saw them, including lack of sufficient aviation fuel for effective training, lack of spare parts for the aircraft and lack of adequate tools for the mechanics. It was not a literary masterpiece by any means, but it got to high levels in Naval Headquarters (called CNHQ). But nothing much was done about it. I was not even punished as a whistle-blower. My Log Book shows that my last flight was another ferry trip to Toronto and back. That was just in time to say goodbye to my last 825 Squadron commander, Pop Fotheringham. He had switched to Seafires and was rejoining Warrior. I remember standing beside him as he strapped himself into his Seafire. He looked far too big to fit into the cockpit. Seafires were built for the average-sized Englishman, who was several inches shorter than his Canadian or American counterparts. And Pop was big even by our standards.

So, it was back to "school" for the second year. Except for the Christmas in the U.S. already mentioned, the year was not memorable. But at least my new courses were much more interesting, which was a blessing. Canadian economic history was becoming a very fascinating subject. One piece of incidental information I acquired was the reason the British were better at keeping Indian tribes fighting on their side during the 19th century wars than were the French. It seemed the Indians preferred the rum the British army provided to the brandy they got from the French. So, a side advantage of the "triangle trade" the British had with the West Indies—from whence the rum—was defeating the French attempts to colonize Canada. Also, I got to know a few more of the residents of 73 St. George Street and some of the students who lived in Toronto. Of the former, John Bull (his real name) became a good chum. He was a continuing Commerce student and in 1951 went on to be one of the first Canadians to go to Stanford Business School. Sadly, John died four years ago. All of the students who came from Toronto lived at home, making it hard for out-of-towners to get to know them. I don't remember how I met the Hill family—Harris and Jane and their parents. Harris was an ex RCAF pilot, but too young to go off to war, so we had that in common, which must have had something to do with it. Jane was his younger sister but, because of Harris' service time, they ended up both in the same year as I studying political science and economics. I remember lots of fun times with them and their friends, and staying sometimes in the Hill family home in Rosedale. Harris became a schoolteacher and Jane married one of our classmates and settled down as a good full-time "mum." Another friend was Ian Townley, another Torontonian. I often went to dinner at his house, which was a pleasant change from the university cafeteria. Sadly, Ian died at 45 from a heart attack. He was the first of my non-navy friends to go.

A real blessing was that Geoffrey Payzant came to Toronto to do graduate work. By then, he had married Mary Lou, his college sweetheart. She was—and is—a great girl. I was very impressed with her in Halifax. She was the only 19- or 20-year-old that I met there (or anywhere for that matter) with a real full-length fur coat. They set-up house near the university and we had many a pleasant evening together. Amongst their many musical friends—Geoffrey's thesis was on some esoteric subset of the philosophy of music—was Glenn Gould, who went on to be a famous pianist. In later years, his audience thought he was quite eccentric because he always wore an overcoat, scarf and gloves when giving a formal recital. Actually, he was no less eccentric when he was in his twenties. Geoffrey and Glenn have also died.

The only rather unfortunate experience I had that year was an optional "pass" course I had to take. Fortunately, the marks did not count in one's final results. I took "Military Studies," thinking it would be easy. It was the only course in which I got a "D." I think the ex army officer who taught it didn't think I took his course sufficiently seriously. He was quite right.

Then came the spring and the start of another summer holiday flying. Happily, I went back to 826 Squadron, 18 CAG, then aboard the RCN's new carrier, HMCS "Magnificent," "Maggie"—as she was called affectionately—was of the same class as Warrior, but with better equipment. We were supposed to be spending the next three months exercising in the North Atlantic with the U.S. Navy.

My Log Book shows my first flight that summer was on 3 June. In fact my only two flights from Maggie were that day. The next day, a Friday, the Captain decided to anchor in a bay off a well-known summer resort. Rumor had it that he had a girlfriend there. It was a large bay, ending at a small fishing port. We entered around 1900 (7.00 PM) on a lovely warm spring evening. We were at harbor stations and the portholes were open. I was in the Ante Room having my usual pre-dinner drink, standing at the bar. Suddenly, there was a loud thud and then a wild vibrating feeling—as if in a car without tires running over railway ties at speed. I grabbed the bar with one hand and my glass with the other. Looking out of the porthole, I saw a 4.7" gun barrel flash past followed by the superstructure of one of our escort destroyers. The noise and the ship stopped. We had hit a rock. After a moment of silence, the "action stations" alarm sounded. My station was the Squadron ready room. We were ordered on deck and to help move our aircraft to the stern of the flight deck. They were parked forward—roughly over the gash in the bottom—so getting as much weight shifted aft was essential. While this was going on, our escorts took our lines and started pulling us astern. I think it took only about 30 minutes from 1937 (7.37 PM) the time my Log Book records "Maggie aground," to the time we were freed. That part reflected remarkably good seamanship. What caused it was not. It turned out that several mistakes were made. First, we should have stayed at sea. Second, we entered a bay in which no ship of Maggie's size had been before, moving at 15 knots when a much slower speed would have been prudent. Finally, our charts were not up-to-date. We had hit a submerged pinnacle of rock that made a gash almost 150 feet long in our belly at high tide. The rock was not on the charts we had, but was on the new ones that had arrived at the dockyard the day Maggie put to sea. That there was no way he could have known about the new chart was the only excuse the Captain had. He was tried at a court martial and found guilty. His only punishment was that his only other commands after that were "stone frigates." He and we were very lucky. For several reasons it could have been much worse. First, he had just given the "execute" order to our escorts, which were in line astern behind us, to move to line abreast. That was why I saw the gun barrel close up. Had they not already started their turns, odds were that they would all have plowed into us. Second, the gash in our belly, while long, was shallow rather than deep, so we didn't take much water immediately. Third, getting the weight moved aft and the destroyers pulling within about 30 minutes got us off before the tide started receding. Had they not been that quick, "Maggie" would have broken her back sitting pinned on the rock. And no one was hurt, notwithstanding one of the towing cables snapped and whipped into the ship. It would have cut through anyone in its way.

That was the end of that cruise. We limped back to Halifax with a 15-degree list to port. The aircraft were lifted off by crane and carted over to Dartmouth. The rest of the month was spent doing our usual training from Dartmouth. Then a great thing happened. Some very clever people in CNHQ arranged for us to spend the rest of the summer at U.S. Naval Air Station Quonset Point in Rhode Island. My trusty Log Book shows that, on 8 July, all 30-odd of 18 CAG's Fireflys and Seafires took off for Quonset Point. I remember that, once in radio range of the Quonset "Tower," we called up for approach instructions but could not understand a word they said in reply. It was almost as if "American" was a foreign language. We finally sorted it all out and landed. Quonset reminded me of USNAS North Island at San Diego: what seemed like thousands of planes on this gigantic airfield. Here were we, at the time half of Canada's naval air power. 18 CAG was lost in a small corner of this gigantic base. If a visitor did not know where to look, he would never have been able to find us. But it was a great experience to be there. My first flight was in a USN P2V "Neptune," a twin-engine ASW aircraft with a crew of six. That was on 14 July. My job, such as it was, was to see how they did what we did. The short answer was they had a much more modern aircraft with better equipment and six people to operate it. Also, as it was much larger, it could patrol for much longer. I flew a lot in the P2Vs and the average time was about four hours 15 minutes compared to our usual one hour ten. I have fond memories of those flights and the occasional "nights ashore" with the pilots. One of them drove a Cadillac. I was awed by this as by comparison we Canadians were poorly paid and could barely afford any kind of car.

As to our routine flying, 826 Squadron spent the four months doing more of the same training we would have done from Maggie. The difference was doing it in a larger arena with the U.S. Navy, which was a fascinating experience. Also, we spent a week aboard USS "Saipan," a so-called "jeep" carrier that, at 14,000 tons, was even smaller than ours. The task was deck-landing trials for our pilots. For us Observers, it was just a holiday cruise, with a bit of watch-keeping thrown in. But keeping us at sea in a "dry" ship would keep us out of trouble. (There are several stories as to why the U.S. Navy does not allow booze. The main one was the Prohibition period started it. Another had to do with a ship's officers becoming so drunk in harbor that they couldn't put to sea.) In retrospect, looking at the page in my Log Book where my Squadron and the CAG commanding officers "signed off" on my training period, I can't help but have a warm feeling about them and that period. Also in my Log Book is a letter with the heading "United States Atlantic Fleet Air Force," dated 19 September 1949, giving me a 3.7 (out of 4.0) grade average for my training in "Operation of Airborne Electronics Equipment."

To expand on warm feelings about that summer at Quonset Point, it was also a wonderful holiday experience. Narragansett Bay at that time was a delightful resort area and the local citizenry, like Americans everywhere, were very friendly and hospitable. I also became a temporary member of the local beach club, which was great fun. Also, there was a fine summer theatre nearby—Matunuck by the Sea—which is still going strong. I went there at least once a week. As our days started at about 6.00 AM and finished at about 3.00 PM, except when we were night flying, it was almost as good as being a guest at a four-star resort hotel. Quonset was only about 30 miles across the Bay from Newport so I also saw how the seriously rich lived. At least, for a 23-year-old Canadian who had not seen much of the luxuries of life, that's what it seemed like. Well, all good things come to an end so, in mid-September, it was back to Toronto for what I assumed was my last year.

It is hard for me to recall anything of significance that happened that final year as an undergraduate. What does stand out, unfortunately, was how I finally messed up a pretty good academic record. During final exams, before the very last one, I had every reason to graduate with first class honors. The last exam was, somehow, timed ten days after the penultimate one. Our professor had said that we would all get As or Bs. So I didn't think I had to study that much. Besides it was only history of philosophy, which was pretty easy. He gave me a C, which swung the balance from a "First" to a "Second" as the end result of three years' studying. But it was my own fault. On a more humorous note, my family and fiends will be impressed to hear how I wrote my exams. I used a portable typewriter. It did not take much explaining to my various professors that giving me this dispensation would be good for them as well. They had all experienced my poor handwriting.

During this period there was the usual job hunting/recruiting going on. I accepted a job as a financial analyst with Sun Life Assurance Company in Montreal, Canada's largest insurance company. This was exactly what I wanted, as it was one of the best entry routes to finance in Canada. Previously, I had thought of going to the Sloan School at MIT —somehow, I felt a Harvard MBA was a bit too commercial even then, but I don't remember how I rationalized becoming a financial analyst as less so. Unfortunately—or maybe fortunately—while MIT accepted me, they would not give me a scholarship, so I declined. I could have got the Canadian government to finance it, but I did not think of that at the time. I was quite happy with the prospect of starting off a new life in September—after one more summer having fun being a flyboy.

On 30 May 1950, I had my first flight of the year with 825 Squadron back at Dartmouth. That summer, the Korean War started. I remember all of my civilian friends felt very uncertain about the future. We navy types were very excited. Almost the entire Canadian Navy went off to the war. The exceptions were "Maggie" and her three escort destroyers.

We found our war duty was to be part of NATO's Atlantic Fleet. What that turned out to be was a three-month "flag waving" cruise to most of the NATO ports in Europe. I was supposed to have reported to Sun Life in mid-September. I asked for permission to start 1 December, a few days after we were due back. They said September or they would take someone else. I didn't see how I could back out at the beginning of a war, even if we were going in the other direction—so much for Sun Life's and my different views of patriotism. I went flag-waving and Sun Life hired the next in line. Curiously, many years later, I found that someone I did business with at Sun was that person. He ended up many years later as CEO and chairman of Sun Life.

That cruise took us from Halifax first to Londonderry the RN base in Northern Ireland, then, in turn, to Glasgow, Oslo, Gothenburg, Copenhagen, Rotterdam, Cherbourg, Portsmouth, Lisbon, Gibraltar, Bermuda and back to Halifax. It was quite a trip. We did a fair amount of flying, even if the Admirals did have the idea initially of leaving the CAG behind so they would have more room for large receptions. Fortunately, the NATO types had better ideas and we were actually able to "project" a little power, as the current expression goes. This was mainly training exercises with the Royal Navy around Ireland and Scotland, chasing their submarines. After that it was mainly receptions and dinners in all the above-named cities. We were royally entertained, met a lot of interesting people and saw some wonderful sights. This was the first time any of us had seen continental Europe since we were kids, if we had been there at all.

While Maggie was in harbor at Londonderry and Glasgow, the CAG was based at air stations ashore. Londonderry was not an exciting town, but I had two rather interesting experiences. One was a night in a pub with some of the guys. Standing at the bar, I got into conversation with an older Irish couple. When it came out I was from Toronto, they asked if I had ever met their daughter's fiancée. Amazingly, I had: he was my roommate. The other was a result of running into another Irishman at another pub. He volunteered to take a few of us on a drive across the border into County Donegal. Besides "tea" at yet another pub—which had the biggest and best ham sandwiches I had ever had—he took us to a friend's house to deliver something. I suspect he was in the smuggling business: three naval officers in uniform were good cover for him. The day we were to join the ship for the run to Glasgow, our aircraft had an electrical problem, so we had to leave the next day to fly directly to RNAS Lossiemouth. It was a miserably foggy, cloudy day and, halfway there, all of our electronics gave up. That was where our "dead reckoning" navigational training paid off. While I think we passed right through the commercial approach paths for Glasgow Airport (almost a capital offense these days), we finally came down out of the clouds at about 500 feet with the airfield in sight half a mile away. I was very relieved, as it had been two years since I had last been entirely without electronic aids and out of sight of any landmarks for over an hour.

Gothenburg was the next port of call. I don't remember much about it except we were given a fine lunch at the local brewery. (Now, through Lena, who was from Gothenburg, I know it quite well.) Sailing from Gothenburg to Copenhagen, we were warned that there were still mines about. In the middle of the night, there was a very loud clang against the hull right below the cabin in which 12 of us junior officers were bunked. You have never seen so many wake-up and get on deck so quickly. We thought it was a mine, but it turned out to be a buoy. Apparently, the officer of the watch wanted to make sure he was approaching the right one. At least he was on the correct side of it. At a reception on the ship in Copenhagen, one of our pilots befriended someone from the Soviet Embassy—we invited representatives from all of the embassies, including those of a potential enemy. His family were Ukrainian immigrants to Canada, so he grew up speaking Russian. Apparently, he boasted a bit about how well our side was doing in Korea—almost up to the Yalu River that day. The Russian said we were in for a surprise soon. Two days later, the Chinese joined in and our side was routed for a time.

The next stop was Rotterdam. It had been rebuilt by 1950—after being pretty well flattened by the German air force in 1940. The Dutch were very hospitable: Canadians were especially welcome, as it was the Canadian army that liberated Holland in 1945. I spent a very fun weekend with the family of a Dutch naval captain. I remembered the 50-kilometer bicycle ride with his daughter vividly for several weeks, as I had trouble standing up. One has to go through this experience of peddling a bicycle for half a day after not having been on one for years to understand what it does to your leg muscles. I also remember the wild evening after a reception at one of the Dutch naval bases. It ended at about midnight when the three of us remaining were taken aboard one of their submarines for a "nightcap." The captain was woken so we could get into their wardroom—otherwise his cabin—for the event. We drank Dutch gin and ate pickled shark meat. The taste stayed with me for several days. That was the last time I tried Dutch gin and shark meat.

While at Cherbourg for a week, the CAG flew ashore to a French naval airfield. We were impressed with the rather casual attitude of the mechanics. I watched one working on an engine, between sips from his bottle of wine. One day I joined some of our pilots at a local restaurant for lunch. This was my first experience with champagne cocktails. I was impressed by how sophisticated they were. More fun was that some of us got a flight on a French transport plane to Paris for an evening. It was taking our admiral and some senior types there for some important function, but there was room for a few of us junior types who were clever enough to find and seize the opportunity. I remember my seat was actually the floor. No safety belts. My only recollection of that evening was that we ended up at a nightclub in Montmartre where we thought we had been invited as guests of some grateful Frenchmen. No such luck.

The most beautiful sight of the whole trip was entering Lisbon harbor at sunrise. I can still remember the sun reflecting off the white and pastel colored houses on the hills. The most memorable event there was a lunch put on by the Portuguese navy. As was usual there, it went on until late afternoon. After who knows how many cocktails before lunch, glasses of wine with lunch and brandies after lunch, I happened to be the junior officer next to the more senior types. My neighbor to my right was Portuguese. I heard our Commander Air to his right saying it was getting late and he was being flown to Oporto for a naval reception there. The response from our Portuguese friend was something like: "Don't worry, you won't miss the flight, I'm your pilot."

Gibraltar was different again. It was a real garrison town and very British. What was striking was that the airfield—a narrow strip with the sea at both ends—was separated from Spain by nothing but a strip of barbed wire. On our side was a line of RAF and RN aircraft. On their side was a row of machine-gun emplacements. I suppose it was a matter of both sides making statements. I gather nothing has changed. The citizens of Gibraltar voted to remain "British" much to the annoyance of the Spanish who have been demanding for some 200 years that it should be returned to their sovereignty. Our last stop on the way home was Bermuda. It was even more British than Gibraltar and is still one of my favorite small island holiday destinations, just ahead of Mauritius. We arrived back at Halifax at the end of November. By then, I had concluded that, having been away for six months and lost my only job opportunity, I had better get back to Toronto University. In September, I had applied to, and been accepted for late arrival by Toronto's Graduate School of Political Science and Economics. That seemed the best way to get back to the "real world." It helped that the ever-grateful Canadian government would pay for it—a very generous reward for my participation in the Korean War. It was slightly embarrassing in a way, especially as my service at the end of WWII was also about as far away from the fighting fronts as one could get.

As the Korean War was still on, Canada had mobilized to some extent. The RCN established several reserve ASW squadrons across the country. Consequently, when I returned in December, I was welcomed also at HMCS York, which had spurned me three years previously. As the reserve squadrons did not start operating for another year, I was drafted to be a part-time recruiting officer.

At York I met a lot of friendly souls, some of whom remain good friends still. Bill McDougall and Cavan Atkinson became my closest friends. Both were in the University Naval Training Division (UNTD), the RCN's ROTC. Bill, whose family had lived in Toronto for many generations, was slightly younger than I and was in his final year at Trinity College. More about Bill later. Cavan was six years older and had been in the RCAF from 1942 until 1946 in the U.K. and India. He had first tried to join up as a pilot in 1940 when he was 18, but failed the eyesight test so badly that he was not accepted even in a non-flying job. Two years later casualties had taken their toll and the standards were lowered to the point where he was finally let in as a clerk. When I met him he was studying law at St. Michael's College and had joined the UNTD for officer training. Sadly, Cavan died three years ago. Another two were Hugh Franks and Peter Newman. Hugh, like Bill, was at Trinity and in the UNTD. Hugh's father was a very engaging man and one of Canada's most distinguished scientists. He invented the "G-suit"— the anti-blackout suit—that fighter pilots and astronauts still use. Peter was also UNTD. Peter and his family were refugees from Czechoslovakia. I remember his father telling me that, had it not been for 12-year-old Peter who found their means of escape on his own, the family would not have made the last boat to leave Cherbourg before the Germans arrived in 1940. Hugh and Peter both became my assistants in the recruiting business. Peter went on into navy PR, as he was starting out as a journalist in civilian life. He is now one of Canada's most acclaimed writers of biographies and Canadian history. Hugh went into the investment management business in Toronto.

We have pleasant memories of staying with Hugh and Amelia over Christmas one year at their family farm near Collingwood in Northern Ontario. It must have been a hard winter. One morning we found the heavy snow of the night before meant we couldn't force the doors open and had to get out by climbing through a window.

I settled down in a small one-room apartment near the university, signed up for three courses and one thesis rather than six courses. That was a mistake. Over the year and a half, I received an "A" for each of the three courses but never finished the thesis. That is, I finished all the research and the second draft, but never finalized it. This is one of my best kept secrets. As I, somehow, fared fairly well in life without it, I kept it from Chris, Sarah and Melissa because it always worried me that, had they known, they might have followed my bad example.

As to what I did during that period, most of my time was with the navy. As I was relatively senior by then, both Bill and Peter became my assistants when they graduated that first May and got their commissions. As a local recruiter, my job was to speak at high schools and service clubs about the glory and fun of being in the navy (for the first group) and its importance to Canada (to the second group). So it was more general public relations than signing people up. I will never forget my first engagement. It was a lunch meeting of the Rotary Club of Oshawa, a middle-sized town 30 miles east of Toronto, famous as the locale of the main General Motors plant in Canada. I wrote what I felt was a very impressive piece—and it probably wasn't too bad as I did not get any negative comments from either my navy bosses or the audience. My problem was I hated the idea of standing up before a large audience and speaking. What was the final shock was to find, half way through lunch, that it was to be broadcast "live" on the local radio station. I survived, but I don't know how. To this day, after how many hundred such talks, I still hate doing it. I think the only difference is that, for the last several years, I have realized that half of any audience isn't listening and the other half won't remember the event a day later. So, what does it matter? Of course, my family and friends always say there is another half of the audience that couldn't hear a word because of my habitual mumbling. Over the period I visited practically every town in Ontario with a population of over a couple of thousand.

The usual procedure was to spend two days in each. Bill or Peter did the advance work of setting up my schedule of meetings, but I went alone. I would visit the Mayor, the two head churchmen (Catholics and Anglicans comprised over 90% of the population), the Chief of Police, the principal of the high school, and the president of the service club at which I would be speaking. That would be the first day. The next morning would be the school assembly and the service club for lunch. If the town had a reserve army regiment—and most with a population of over 10,000 did—I would usually be invited for drinks in the Mess and often taken to dinner. It is surprising how the military tradition continued in small-town Canada. It was rewarding to me how friendly and open people were. With some 5,000 Canadian army troops fighting in Korea along with some air force aircraft and navy ships, I could have quite understood a coolness on the part of parents—and most of the community leaders I was seeing were parents—but that was never the case. It is often said that one difference between Canada and the U.S. is that Canadians accept authority much more readily than do Americans. I think it is true—not because we are more docile but more because Canada was built by immigrants most of whom were looking for opportunities. So, we were more "in it together" in spirit whilst America was built more by immigrants fleeing persecution or resisting English rule. That's probably an over simplification and, certainly, my French Canadian friends would have a different view. One special memory was of the Catholic priest in a town in northeast Ontario close to the Quebec border. I suppose because he was sympathetic to my problems as a recruiter he told me about the problems of keeping his "flock" loyal to the church. He had a large "pie chart" on the wall behind his desk. The slices showed numbers and percentages of Catholics, Anglicans and "others."

I had bought my first car, a second-hand "Morris Minor," to take me on these expeditions when they were relatively close to Toronto. That was not a good car. I cannot remember how many times it broke down. So, on longer trips—100 miles or more—I took the train. One forgets how big Ontario is. Probably 90% of the population in those days lived along the ribbon from Windsor at the western end of Lake Erie to Kingston just beyond the eastern end of Lake Ontario—300 miles long and about 50 miles deep. The other 10% lived north and east towards Ottawa. From Toronto it's 900 miles to the border of Manitoba. My farthest trip was to Timmins, the nickel mining town 300 miles northeast. I still remember that the miners seemed all to have cars that were bigger than their houses, a contrast in a way to the towns approaching the Quebec border. The communities there were very much French-Canadian. Most had very large cathedrals dominating a cluster of very small houses. Looking back, those towns in the hinterland of Ontario were very much "third world." But then Canada had half its present population and a very low standard of living in the countryside.

My only memory of my economics courses was the one on the "theory of linear competition." Put simply, it can be explained as follows. If a market is equally distributed along a straight line, two competitors offering identical products at the same price will both station themselves at the center. The theory is each will get 100% of the customers on "their" side of the line and have a fighting chance of getting some from the other's territory. What could be more simple and obvious? Not only would it apply to economics, but also to anything else where there was competition. That's why most politicians gravitate towards the center of public opinion. My thesis was on competition in the airline industry. My argument, coincidentally, was that those airlines that limited their fleets to one type of aircraft for long-haul and one type for short-haul did best. To sum up the end of my academic period then, I simply put off the final editing of the thesis. There was no time pressure and there was much else more interesting to do. There were two final deciding factors. First, out of the blue, I was offered an interesting job. Second, our Toronto reserve squadron—VC 920—finally began to form up. But both events were not until 1952.

After university closed for the summer holidays in 1951, I went on a great summer expedition with Bill McDougall. Bill had been active for several years with the ISS—International Students' Society. As a Canadian delegate, he had been all over the world for its meetings. He asked me to be another Canadian delegate at a meeting in Oslo as he was, by then, a high level functionary. We traveled from New York to Hamburg in a converted troop ship. The cargo was 600 students of whom 590 were U.S. College girls. It was an interesting trip. After a week at the conference, we went to Stockholm and to Helsinki. The father of the

Norwegian family I had met in Oslo the year before had said that Finland was the most interesting country in Scandinavia so missing it would be foolish. He had served as a doctor with the Finnish army during their fight against the Russian in 1940 and had great admiration for the Finns. I was grateful to him for insisting we went there and for arranging an introduction to his Finnish friends.

We traveled to Stockholm by train and then to Helsinki by boat. The Helsinki friend, a wonderful woman who was then head of the Finnish Red Cross, but who had been a doctor with the army during the war, met us at the dock. She and her husband took us all over Helsinki. We saw the great statue to their first liberator from the Russians, Field Marshall Mannerheim, and to the grave of Sibelius. Mannerheim's was an interesting story. He had been an officer in the Imperial Russian army when the Finns revolted against the Russians and started their war of independence. He went to his commanding officer and said, as a native born Finn, he felt it was his duty to fight for Finland. Consequently, he wished to resign his commission in the Russian army. Permission was granted. Amazing: I can't imagine that kind of thing happening in our new world. We also spent an evening on their yacht in Helsinki harbor. That was the first time I had ever been in a sailboat with a cabin. The most interesting part was meeting his Finnish army buddy, whose wounded leg he had amputated, and who became a friend thereafter. I cannot remember his name, but he, his wife and his daughter plus her husband—Pikki and Hans Rydmann—met us at the Tempera station. Hans and Pikki were there because they spoke English. It was funny because we were introduced as friends of the parent's friends. But Bill and I were in our early twenties while Hans and Pikki were in their forties, with young teenage daughters. Our peg-legged host was about 70. The week we spent with them was absolutely wonderful. They were terrific hosts. Remember that Finland had just escaped being a Soviet vassal state and, forced to pay massive reparations to the Soviets, Finland was still impoverished in those days.

Hans and his father-in-law told us of the "Winter War" when they held back the Russians alone. Then, four more years of war on the German side when the Russians tried it again. They both—along with almost all Finnish males between 16 and 70—went into the forests to fight the Russians in 1939 and did not come out until 1945. "Peg-Leg" as I shall call him, used to wave his cane and shout "kill Russkies" with a big grin and show us the mementos he had taken from his victims. They were a rather wealthy family, controlling a major forestry company, of which Hans was the CEO, so we lacked nothing while there. In fact, we had too much of everything, especially liquor. I remember the day started with Peg-Leg banging our door at about 6.00 shouting "sauna, sauna." Minutes later we were sweltering. Minutes after that we were diving into the lake and disappearing in a cloud of steam—it was October in Northern Finland. Then we retired to his cabin by the lake and drank beer while he took trout out of his fish pond and fried them for breakfast. Never has breakfast been so good. One dinner they gave for us was great as always but a bit of an ordeal. Scandinavians in those days were very formal. The ladies could only sip their wine or schnapps when a gentleman raised his glass to toast her—"Skal!" Then the lady could return the toast. There were a lot of toasts that evening. I learned halfway through the dinner that the oldest foreign guest was expected at the end of dinner to "Skal!" to the hostess and make a short speech of thanks. I realized that I, at 25, was the oldest foreign guest. That was where my RN "knife and fork" school training helped.

The most interesting experience was visiting a factory that was building locomotives for the Russians as part of their reparations. The agreement included not allowing anyone not essential to the work to be allowed in the plant. We were warned to keep our mouths closed as there were Soviet agents supervising the work. I have no idea how they got us in or out, or how they explained what we were doing there. But Hans served on their board so he was well accepted. That visit made me admire the Finns more than any nationality I had met. I still think it is absolutely amazing how they—a tiny country—stood up to the Soviets.

After that, needing a trip home and, for whatever reason, still being needed by the navy, I went by train from Helsinki to Naples to join "Maggie" and the 881 Squadron, 30 CAG. Maggie was there for NATO exercises with the Italian Navy. Thirty hours in a third-class compartment was not fun. But I confess to a break in London while I picked up my large metal trunk with my naval uniforms. I cannot remember how I was so far-sighted as to be able to arrange a ride back in Maggie but it was nearly a calamity. Crossing the border from Switzerland to Italy, Customs took the case out of the baggage compartment to examine it. Purely by chance, just before the train was to move on, I went back to check that it was back aboard. It wasn't. After much shouting I found it and got it loaded. I cannot imagine what would have happened if I had tried to join Maggie without my uniforms. As it was, I joined the ship the day before we proceeded to sea for our exercises. I started flying for the first time in Grumman Avengers (the famous WWII U.S. Navy torpedo bombers that the RCN used to replace the Fireflys) with Lt. Freddie Rice as my pilot and with Petty Officer Cando as my Observers' Mate. It appeared the RCN had great confidence in my abilities—or the pilots had their own views as to the relevance of the people in the back seats.

There had been major changes to the RCN in 1951. First, after continuing bad experiences depending on U.K. suppliers for spare parts for our Fireflys and Sea Furies—the fighter squadrons had obtained the latest RN aircraft the previous year—we switched to U.S. Navy aircraft. Second, the navy as a whole finally rebelled against the "younger brother" attitude towards us displayed by many RN officers. Most Canadian ships in WWII were built in Canada of U.K. design. Now, that is in 1950, we had designed and built our first class of destroyers, the St. Laurent Class—12 ships of 2,000 tons. They were quite revolutionary for the time. The Americans called them "Cadillacs." It was an apt term, especially as older classes of destroyers were known, affectionately, as "tin cans."" It certainly gave us confidence that we did not need a "big brother," especially one that could not keep us supplied.

One of the many results was "825 Squadron" became "VS 881," the "VS" standing for naval ASW squadron. ("VF" stood for fighter squadron, etc.) The new aircraft we received, which I flew in that summer, were actually quite old. The RCN bought some 50 "TBMs"—Grumman Avengers, built by General Motors—hence the "M" rather than the "G" for TBGs, Avengers actually built by Grumman, the designers. In any event, I first saw these aircraft as they arrived with the torpedo bomber configuration of the cockpits. We changed that to suit

585

ASW needs. Whether it was because the Avengers had had, originally, a crew of three, or because the RCN had decided independently that what two of us had been doing for several years now needed three (Parkinson's law?) is not important. In any event the Admirals decided there should be a third crew member called an "Observer's Mate"—a rank straight out of the RN's play book which was strange considering the other changes. The Observer's Mate was to be the radioman—the RN's old Telegraphist Air Gunner, but without a gun. I suppose it made our jobs as Observers easier because I don't recall that the aircraft had any additional electronic gadgets. That said, the Avenger was a much bigger, and thus more comfortable, aircraft to fly in and do our job.

It was a great cruise. We spent many a day anchored off interesting Mediterranean towns, going ashore and seeing the sights. It was my first visit to the Riviera and I thought it was absolutely beautiful. While still in Naples, I also went to Rome for a reception hosted by the Canadian Embassy. That was not a new experience as I had been to many similar ones the year before. But Rome was different. What I did not do while in Naples was go to Capri, which even then had the reputation as one of the most beautiful parts of Italy. That would have meant getting up at about 5.00 AM one morning. I didn't have the strength. I still haven't been to Capri.

My Log Book showed that my first flight with Freddie Rice and PO Cando was on 4 October. We had left Naples and were heading for Gibraltar, at that time flying off St. Raphael, searching for the "enemy." Freddie was a very friendly, laid back ex RCAF pilot, a bit overweight, with a habit of always carrying in the bomb bay a case of Coke. He drank that with scotch. After this cruise, back at Dartmouth, the medical officer warned him to get his weight down. He thought it meant giving up scotch and coke. No, the doctor said, scotch is OK; it's the coke that has to go. Sadly, Freddie was killed in a mid-air collision a few months later.

Besides the fun part, from the naval point of view, I had two interesting experiences. One was as officer of the watch—OOW—at anchor in Naples Bay. I was supervising the arrival of an Italian Admiral. This meant special attention to the ladder from the boarding point and making sure the guard of honor was properly squared away and bugles, etc. ready. I was to give the orders, salute, and turn him over to the Commander to take him to our admiral. I had never done that kind of thing before. Consequently, I was pretty tense. Just before the arrival, I received an emergency message: "OOW to the Starboard side aft! Fire in the scow alongside." The word "fire" implies serious trouble on an aircraft carrier loaded with aviation fuel. Panic! What to do! Fortunately, there was a good Officer of the Day on duty. He called immediately and said he would handle the fire and I would look after the ceremonies. I was much relieved, but it turned out that I had the harder job, as the fire was a false alarm. The second involved one of our exercises. We were to seek the enemy fleet. I found it and did the reporting back. At the debriefing after our return, I stated that the enemy was where we were told to expect it but, on our return, Maggie was 60 miles out of position. This caused consternation amongst the ship's Navigator and his two assistants. I guess I had, unknowingly, displayed the usual flyboy arrogance and they had felt the usual fish head insecurity, so they thought I was right. Only some time later did they figure out from my chart that I was wrong. By that time, all were too ashamed to admit or claim anything.

On the return to Halifax, though, the fish heads got even. While in Gibraltar I had gone to the sick bay with a minor irritant. The "Surgeon" as all naval doctors are called, said I should have a minor operation. He said this was a great time to do it as we were going to be at sea for ten days with no flying and I might just as well get it over with before returning to Toronto. Now I know only the most naive teenager would ever let a naval doctor practice on you. The inevitable happened. I ended up at the veterans' hospital in Toronto to have the operation repeated. Murphy's Law took over, and I suffered from some kind of penicillin reaction. The day I got out after the second operation, I went to stay at Bill McDougall's grandfather's house with Bill. Getting out of bed the next morning, my legs just collapsed. I spent a further few months in hospital. Bill's grandfather—Joe McDougall, or "Colonel" to his friends—was a great fellow. He had commanded an infantry regiment in World War I. He had a successful business career and had just retired as CEO of a major manufacturing company. He seemed to enjoy chatting with Bill and me about our naval experiences. Afterwards, Bill said he had never realized the old boy could be such fun. In fact he told us some quite risqué stories, which quite shocked Bill. Not the stories themselves but that his otherwise very proper and severe grandfather told them. I rarely remember stories, but one of his stays with me. It was a WWI story about a cavalry regiment that was just converting to tanks. The scene was the Officers' Mess. The Colonel was exclaiming that it was impossible to get his horse into one of those machines. His adjutant explained that, sadly, the horses had to go. He then asked what they were going to do about the regimental motto which, in Latin, was "love and gallop." For a while, no one had an answer. Finally a junior officer said: "It's easy, sir, we just modernize it to 'screw and bolt'."

For the first months of 1952, Bill and I did our recruiting thing. That Spring I received my job offer from Nesbitt, Thomson, and that summer Bill went off to Europe and then to Oxford. And so started a new life.

July 26th, 1948.

Mr. D.B. Gill,
Chichester Road,
Dorking, Surrey, England.

Dear Mr. Gill:

On behalf of the Council and
Staff of University College I wish to congratu-
late you most heartily on your standing in first
class honours in the honour course of Commerce
and Finance. The ranking which you have won is
indicative both of your industry and of your
ability in the field of your studies. Your
achievement also adds to the pride and satisfaction of the College in which you are enrolled.
We trust that you may continue to foster a deep
interest in the subjects to which you have so
successfully devoted yourself.

With warmest regards and all best wishes,
I am,

Yours sincerely,

[signature]

Principal.

Congratulatory letter from University College, Toronto, 26 July 1948,
where I spent three years earning a BA degree.

Index

A

Index

Index

Index

596

Index

Index

Index